ISBN 978-0-265-18345-8
PIBN 10178513

This book is a reproduction of an important historical work. Forgotten Books uses
state-of-the-art technology to digitally reconstruct the work, preserving the original format
whilst repairing imperfections present in the aged copy. In rare cases, an imperfection in
the original, such as a blemish or missing page, may be replicated in our edition. We do,
however, repair the vast majority of imperfections successfully; any imperfections that
remain are intentionally left to preserve the state of such historical works.

A

PRACTICAL COMMENTARY

UPON THE

FIRST EPISTLE OF ST. PETER;

AND OTHER

EXPOSITORY WORKS:

BY THE MOST REVEREND FATHER IN GOD,

ROBERT LEIGHTON, D.D.,

ARCHBISHOP OF GLASGOW.

———

TO WHICH IS PREFIXED,

A LIFE OF THE AUTHOR,

BY

THE REV. JOHN NORMAN PEARSON, A. M.,

OF TRINITY COLLEGE, CAMBRIDGE, AND CHAPLAIN TO THE
MOST NOBLE THE MARQUESS OF WELLESLEY.

———

Οὕτω θεῶν καὶ ἀνθρώπων θείων καὶ εὐδαιμόνων βίος, ἀπαλλαγὴ τῶν ἄλλων τῶν τῇδε, βίος
ἀνήδονος τῶν τῇδε, φυγὴ μόνου πρὸς μόνον.—PLOTINI ENNEAD. 6. L. 9. c. xi.

A NEW EDITION,—IN TWO VOLUMES.

VOLUME II.

LONDON:

JAMES DUNCAN, 37, PATERNOSTER-ROW;

HATCHARD AND SON, SEELEY AND SONS, AND J. NISBET, LONDON;
PARKER, OXFORD, J. AND J. J. DEIGHTON, CAMBRIDGE;
AND BELL AND BRADFUTE, EDINBURGH.

———

MDCCCXXX.

LONDON :
Printed by WILLIAM CLOWES,
Stamford-street.

CONTENTS OF THE SECOND VOLUME.

A

PRACTICAL COMMENTARY

UPON THE

FIRST EPISTLE GENERAL

OF

ST. PETER.

CHAPTER II. VERSE 21—23.

Ver. 21. For even hereunto were ye called; because Christ also suffered for us, leaving us an example, that ye should follow his steps;

Ver. 22. Who did not sin, neither was guile found in his mouth;

Ver. 23. Who when he was reviled, reviled not again ; when he suffered, he threatened not; but committed himself to him that judgeth righ-teously.

THE rules that God hath set men to live by, are universally just, and there is a universal obligation upon all men to obey them ; but as they are particularly addressed to His own peo-ple in his word, *they*, out of question, are particularly bound to yield obedience, and have many peculiar persuasives to it, not extending to others, which are therefore usually represented to them, and pressed upon them in the holy Scriptures. Thus the preface of the Law runs to Israel : Besides that *I am Jeho-vah*, and have supreme power to give men laws, it is added, *I am thy God*, especially thy deliverer from slavery and bondage, and so have a peculiar right to thy obedience. (Deut. vii. 6.) Thus, the Apostle here urgeth this point in hand, of inoffen-siveness and patience, particularly in Christian servants, but so as it fits every Christian in his station, *For hereunto*, says he, *ye are called.* Whatsoever others do, though they think it too straight a rule, yet you are tied to it by your own calling and profession as you are Christians; and this is evidently the highest and clearest reason that can be, and of greatest power with a Christian, namely, the example of Jesus Christ himself: *For Christ also suffered for us,* &c.

So it is all but one entire argument, *viz.,* that they ought thus to behave themselves, because it is the very thing they are called to, as their conformity to Jesus Christ, whose they profess to be, yea, with whom, as Christians, they profess themselves to be one.

Hereunto were ye called.] This, in the general, is a thing that ought to be ever before our eye, to consider the nature and end of our calling, and to endeavour in all things to act suitably to it; to think in every occurrence, What doth the calling of a Christian require of me in this? But the truth is, the most do not mind this. We profess ourselves to be Christians, and never think what kind of behaviour this obliges us to, and what manner of persons it becomes us to be *in all holy conversation,* but *walk disorderly,* out of our rank, *inordinately.* You that are profane, were you called by the Gospel to serve the world and your lusts? Were you called to swearing and rioting and voluptuousness? Hear you not the Apostle testifying the contrary in express terms, that *God hath not called us to uncleanness, but unto holiness?* (1 Thes. iv. 7.) You that are of proud, contentious spirits, do you act suitably to this holy calling? No, for *we are called to peace,* says the same Apostle. (1 Cor. vii. 15.) But we study not this holy calling, and therefore we walk so incongruously, so unlike the Gospel; *we lie and do not the truth,* as St. John speaks (1 John i. 6); our actions belie us.

The particular things that Christians are here said to be called to, are, *suffering,* as their lot, and *patience,* as their duty, even under the most unjust and undeserved sufferings.

And both these are as large as the sphere of this calling. Not only servants and others of a mean condition, who, lying low, are the more subject to rigours and injuries, but generally, all who are called to godliness, are likewise called to sufferings. (2 Tim. iii. 12.) All that will follow Christ, must do it in his livery; they must take up their cross. This is a very harsh and unpleasing article of the Gospel to a carnal mind, but the Scriptures conceal it not. Men are not led blindfold into sufferings, and drawn into a bidden snare by the Gospel's invitations; they are told it very often, that they may not pretend a surprisal, nor have any just plea for starting back again. So our Saviour tells his disciples why he was so express and plain with them in this, *These things have I told you, that ye be not offended* (John xvi. 1); as if he had said, I have shewed you the ruggedness of your way, that you may not stumble at it, taking it to be a smooth, plain one. But then, where this is spoken of, it is usually allayed with the mention of those comforts that accompany these sufferings, or of that glory which follows them. The doctrine of the Apostles, which was so verified in their own persons, was this, *That we must through much tribulation enter into the kingdom of God* (Acts xiv. 22). An unpleasant way indeed, if you look no further, but a *kingdom* at the end of it, and that *the kingdom of God*, will tranfuse pleasure into the most painful step in it all. It seems a sad condition that falls to the share of godly men in this world, to be eminent in sorrows and troubles. *Many are the afflictions of the righteous* (Psal. xxxiv. 19): but that which follows, weighs them abundantly down in consolation, that the Lord Himself is engaged in their afflictions, both for their deliverance out of them in due time, and, in the mean time, for their support and preservation under them: *The Lord delivers them out of them all,* and till He does that, *He keepeth all their bones.* This was literally verified in the natural body of Christ, as St. John observes, (John xix. 36,) and it holds spiritually true in his mystical body. The Lord supports the spirits of believers in their troubles, with such solid consolations as are the pillars and strength of their souls, as the bones are of the body, which the Hebrew word for them imports. So *He keepeth all his bones;* and

the desperate condition of wicked men is opposed to this, (verse
21,) to illustrate it, *Evil shall slay the wicked.*

Thus, (John xvi. 33,) they are forewarned in the close, what
to expect at the world's hands, as they were divers times before
in that same sermon ; but it is a sweet testament, take it altogether : *Ye shall have tribulation in the world, but peace in
Me.* And seeing He hath jointly bequeathed these two to his
followers, were it not great folly to renounce such a bargain,
and to let go that peace for fear of this trouble ? The trouble
is but *in the world,* but the *peace* is *in Him,* who weighs down
thousands of worlds.

So, then, they do exceedingly mistake and misreckon who
would reconcile Christ and the world, who would have the
Church of Christ, or, at least, themselves for their own shares,
enjoy both kinds of peace together ; would willingly have peace
in Christ, but are very loth to part with the world's peace.
They would be Christians, but they are very ill satisfied when
they hear of any thing but ease and prosperity in that estate,
and willingly forget the tenor of the Gospel in this ; and so,
when times of trouble and sufferings come, their minds are as
new and uncouth to it, as if they had not been told of it beforehand. They like better St. Peter's carnal advice to Christ, to
avoid suffering, (Matt. xvi. 22,) than his Apostolic doctrine to
Christians, teaching them, that as Christ *suffered,* so they
likewise *are called to suffering.* Men are ready to think as
Peter did, that Christ should favour himself more in his own
body, his Church, than to expose it to so much suffering ; and
most would be of Rome's mind in this, at least in affection,
that the badge of the Church should be pomp and prosperity,
and not the cross : the true cross and afflictions are too heavy
and painful.

But *God's thoughts are not as ours :* those whom He calls to
a kingdom, He calls to sufferings as the way to it. He will
have the heirs of heaven know that they are not at home on
earth, and that *this is not their rest.* He will not have them,
with the abused world, fancy a happiness here, and, as St.

Augustine says, *Beatam vitam quærere in regione mortis*—seek a happy life in the region of death. The reproaches and wrongs that encounter them shall elevate their minds often to that land of peace and rest, *where righteousness dwells*. (2 Pet. iii. 13.) The hard taskmaster shall make them weary of Egypt, which, otherwise, possibly, they would comply too well with; shall dispose them for deliverance, and make it welcome, which, it may be, they might but coldly desire, if they were better used.

He knows what He does, who secretly serves His own good purposes by men's evil ones, and by the *plowers that make long furrows* on the back of his Church, (Psal. cxxix. 3,) makes it a fruitful field to Himself. Therefore it is great folly, and unadvisedness, to take up a prejudice against His way, to think it might be better as we would model it, and to complain of the order of things, whereas we should complain of disordered minds: but we had rather have all altered and changed for us, the very course of Providence, than seek the change of our own perverse hearts. But the right temper of a Christian is, to run always cross to the corrupt stream of the world and human iniquity, and to be willingly carried along with the stream of Divine Providence, and not at all to stir a hand, no, nor a thought, to row against that mighty current; and not only is he carried with it upon necessity, because there is no steering against it, but cheerfully and voluntarily; not because he must, but because he would.

And this is the other thing to which Christians are jointly called; as to suffering, so to *calmness of mind* and *patience in suffering*, although their suffering be most unjust; yea this is truly a part of that duty they are called to, to maintain that integrity and inoffensiveness of life that may make their sufferings at men's hands always unjust. The entire duty here is innocence and patience; doing willingly no wrong to others, and yet cheerfully suffering wrong when done to themselves. If either of the two be wanting, their suffering does not credit their profession, but dishonours it. If they be patient under deserved suffering, their guiltiness darkens their patience: and if their sufferings be undeserved, yea and the cause of them honourable, yet impatience under them stains both their sufferings and their cause, and seems in part to justify the very injustice that is used against them; but when innocence and patience meet together in suffering, their sufferings are in their perfect lustre. These are they who honour religion, and shame the enemies of it. It was the concurrence of these two that was the very triumph of the martyrs in times of persecution, that tormented their tormentors, and made them *more than conquerors* even in sufferings.

Now that we are called both to suffering and to this manner of suffering, the Apostle puts out of question, by the supreme example of our Lord Jesus Christ; for the sum of our calling is, *to follow Him.* Now in both these, in suffering, and in suffering innocently and patiently, the whole history of the Gospel testifies how complete a pattern He is. And the Apostle gives us here a summary, yet a very clear account of it.

The words have in them these two things, I. The perfection of this example. II. Our obligation to follow it.

I. The example he sets off to the full, 1. In regard of the greatness of our Saviour's sufferings. 2. In regard of His spotlessness and patience in suffering.

The first, we have in that word, *He suffered;* and afterwards, at ver. 24, we have His crucifixion and His stripes expressly specified.

Now this is reason enough, and carries it beyond all other reason, why Christians are called to a suffering life, seeing the Lord and Author of that calling suffered himself so much. *The Captain,* or Leader, *of our salvation,* as the Apostle speaks, was *consecrated by suffering,* Heb. ii. 10: that was the way by which *He entered into the holy place,* where He is now *our everlasting High-Priest, making intercession for us.* If He be our Leader to salvation, must not we follow Him in the way He leads, whatsoever it is? If it be (as we see it is) by the way of sufferings, we must either follow on in that way, or fall short of salvation; for there is no other leader, nor any other

way than that which He opened ; so that there is not only a
congruity in it, that His followers be conformed to Him in
suffering, but a necessity, if they will follow Him on till they
attain to glory.   And the consideration of both these cannot
but argue a Christian into a resolution for this *via regia*, this
royal way of suffering that leads to glory, through which their
King and Lord himself went to His glory.   It could hardly be
believed, at first, that this was *His* way, and we can as hardly
yet believe that it must be ours.   *O fools, and slow of heart to
believe! Ought not Christ to have suffered these things, and
so to enter into His glory?* (Luke xxiv. 25, 26.)

Would you be at glory, and will you not follow your Leader
in the only way to it?   Must there be another way cut out for
you by yourself?   O absurd!   *Shall the servant be greater
than his master?* (John xiii. 6.)   Are not you fairly dealt with?
If you have a mind to Christ, you shall have full as much of
the world's good will as He had : *if it hate you*, He bids you
remember *how it hated Him*. (John xv. 18.)

But though there were a way to do otherwise, would you not,
if the love of Christ possessed your hearts, rather choose to
share with Him in His lot, and would you not find delight in
the very trouble of it ?   Is not this conformity to Jesus the
great ambition of all his true-hearted followers?   *We carry
about in the body the dying of the Lord Jesus*, says the great
Apostle (2 Cor. iv. 10).   Besides the unspeakable advantage to
come, which goes linked with this, that, *if we suffer with Him,
we shall reign with Him*, (2 Tim. ii. 12,) there is a glory, even
in this present resemblance, that we are conformed to the image
of the Son of God in sufferings.   Why should we desire to
leave Him?   Are you not one with Him?   Can you choose
but have the same common friends and enemies?   Would you
willingly, if it might be, could you find in your heart to be
friends with that world which hated your Lord and Master?
Would you have nothing but kindness and ease, where He had
nothing but enmity and trouble?   Or would you not rather,
when you think aright of it, refuse and disdain to be so unlike

Him? As that good Duke said, when they would have crowned him King of Jerusalem, *No,* said he, *by no means; I will not wear a crown of gold where Jesus was crowned with thorns.*

2. His spotlessness, and patience in suffering, are both of them set here before us; the one ver. 22, the other ver. 23.

Whosoever thou art who makest such a noise about the injustice of what thou sufferest, and thinkest to justify thy impatience by thine innocence, let me ask thee, Art thou more just and innocent than He who is here set before thee? Or art thou able to come near him in this point? *Who did no sin, neither was guile found in his mouth.* This is to signify perfect holiness, according to that declaration, (James iii. 2,) *If any man offend not in word, the same is a perfect man.* Man is a little world, a world of wickedness; and that little part of him, *the tongue,* is termed by St. James *a world of iniquity.* But all Christ's words, as well as His actions, and all His thoughts, flowed from a pure spring that had not any thing defiled in it; and therefore no temptation, either from men or Satan, could seize on Him. Other men may seem clear as long as they are unstirred, but move and trouble them, and the mud arises; but he was nothing but holiness, a pure fountain, all purity to the bottom; and therefore stir and trouble Him as they would, He was still alike clear. *The prince of this world cometh, and hath nothing in me.* (John xiv. 39.)

This is the main ground of our confidence in Him, that He is *a holy, harmless, undefiled High-priest;* and *such a one became us,* says the Apostle, who are so sinful. (Heb. vii. 26.) The more sinful we are, the more need that our High-Priest should be sinless; and being so, we may build upon His perfection, as standing in our stead, yea, we are invested with Him and His righteousness.

Again, *there was no guile found in His mouth.* This serves to convince us concerning all the promises that He hath made, that they are nothing but truth. Hath he said, *Him that cometh to me I will in no wise cast out!* (John vi. 37.) Then you need not fear, how unworthy and vile soever you may be;

do but come to Him, and you have His word that he will not shut the door against you. And as He hath promised access, so he hath further promised ease and souls' rest to those that come. (Matt. xi. 30.) Then be confident to find that in Him too, for there was never a false or guileful word found in His mouth.

But to consider it only in the present action, this speaks Him the most innocent sufferer that ever was, not only judicially just in His cause, but entirely just in His person, altogether righteous; and yet, condemned to death, and an opprobrious death of malefactors, and set betwixt two, as chief of the three! *I am*, says he, *the rose of Sharon, and the lily of the valley;* and the Spouse saith of Him, *My well-beloved is white and ruddy* (Cant. ii. 1; v. 10): thus, indeed, He was in His death, ruddy in his bloodshed, and white in his innocence, and withal in his meekness and patience; the other thing wherein He is here so exemplary.

Who, when he was reviled, reviled not again.] This spotless Lamb of God was a Lamb both in guiltlessness and silence; and the Prophet Isaiah expresses the resemblance, in that *He was brought as a lamb to the slaughter.* (Isa. liii. 7.) He suffered not only an unjust sentence of death, but withal unjust revilings, *the contradictions of sinners.* No one ever did so little deserve revilings; no one ever could have said so much in his own just defence, and to the just reproach of his enemies; and yet, in both, He preferred silence. No one could ever threaten so heavy things as He could against his enemies, and have made good all he threatened, and yet, no such thing was heard from Him. The heavens and the earth, as it were, spoke their resentment of His death who made them; but He was silent; or what He spoke makes this still good, how far he was from revilings and threatenings. As spices pounded, or precious ointment poured out, give their smell most, thus *His name was an ointment* then *poured forth,* together with his blood, (Cant. i. 3,) and, filling heaven and earth with its sweet perfume, was a savour of rest and peace in both, appeasing the wrath of God, and so quieting the consciences of men. And even in this particular was it then most fragrant, in that all the torments of the cross and all the revilings of the multitude racked him as it were for some answer, yet could draw no other from Him than this, *Father, forgive them, for they know not what they do.*

But for those to whom this mercy belonged not, the Apostle tells us what He did ; instead of revilings and threatenings, *He committeth all to Him who judgeth righteously.* And this is the true method of Christian patience, that which quiets the mind, and keeps it from the boiling, tumultuous thoughts of revenge, to turn the whole matter into God's hand, to resign it over to Him, to prosecute when and as He thinks good. Not as the most, who had rather, if they had power, do for themselves, and be their own avengers ; and because they have not power, do offer up such bitter curses and prayers for revenge unto God, as are most hateful to Him, and are far from this calm and holy way of committing matters to His judgment. The common way of referring things to God, is indeed impious and dishonourable to Him, being really no other than calling Him to be a servant and executioner to our passion. We ordinarily mistake His justice, and judge of it according to our own precipitant and distempered minds. If wicked men be not crossed in their designs, and their wickedness evidently crushed, just when we would have it, we are ready to give up the matter as desperate, or at least to abate of those confident and reverential thoughts of Divine justice which we owe Him. Howsoever things go, this ought to be fixed in our hearts, that *He who sitteth in heaven* judgeth righteously, and executes that His righteous judgment in the fittest season. We poor worms, whose whole life is but a *hand-breadth* in itself, and is *as nothing* unto God, think a few months or years a great matter ; but to him who *inhabiteth eternity, a thousand years are but as one day,* as our Apostle teaches us, in his second Epistle, ch. iii. ver. 8.

Our Saviour, in that time of his humiliation and suffering,

committed himself and his cause (for that is best expressed, in that nothing is expressed but *He committed*) *to Him who judgeth righteously*, and the issue shall be, that *all his enemies shall become his footstool,* and He himself shall judge them. But that which is given us here to learn from his carriage toward them in his suffering, is, that quietness and moderation of mind, even under unjust sufferings, make us like Him : not to reply to reproach with reproach, as our custom is, to give one ill word for another, or two for one, to be sure not to be behind. Men take a pride in this, and think it ridiculous simplicity so to suffer, and this makes strifes and contention so much abound; but it is a great mistake. You think it greatness of spirit to bear nothing, to put up with no wrong, whereas indeed it is great weakness and baseness. It is true greatness of spirit, to despise the most of those things which set you usually on fire one against another ; especially, being done after a Christian manner, it were a part of the spirit of Christ in you : and is there any spirit greater than that, think you ? Oh ! that there were less of the spirit of the Dragon, and more of the spirit of the Dove amongst us.

II. Our obligation to follow the example of Christ, besides being enforced by its own excellency, is intimated in these two things contained in the words : 1. The design of His behaviour for this use, to be as an example to us. 2. Our interest in Him, and those His sufferings, wherein He so carried himself.

1. That His behaviour was intended for an example, *Leaving us an example, &c.* He left His footsteps as a copy (as the word in the original ὑπογραμμὸν imports) to be followed by us ; every step of His is a letter of this copy ; and particularly in this point of suffering, He wrote us a pure and perfect copy of obedience, in clear and great letters, in His own blood.

His whole life is our rule : not, indeed, His miraculous works, His footsteps walking on the sea, and such like, they are not for our following ; but His obedience, holiness, meekness, and humility are our copy, which we should continually study. The shorter and more effectual way, they say, of teaching, is by example; but above all, this matchless Example is the happiest way of teaching. *He that follows me,* says our Lord, *shall not walk in darkness.* (John viii. 12.)

He that aims high, shoots the higher for it, though he shoot not so high as he aims. This is what ennobles the spirit of a Christian, the propounding of this our high pattern, the example of Jesus Christ.

The imitation of men in worthless things is low and servile; the imitation of their virtues is commendable, but if we aim no higher, it is both imperfect and unsafe. The Apostle St. Paul will have no imitation, but with regard to this Supreme Pattern: *Be ye followers of me, as I am of Christ.* (1 Cor. xi. 1.) One Christian may take the example of Christ as exhibited in many things, in another, but still he must examine all by the original primitive copy, the footsteps of Christ himself, following nothing, but as it is conformable to that, and looking chiefly on Him, both as the most perfect and most effectual example. (See Heb. xii. 2.) There is *a cloud of witnesses* and examples, but look above them all, to Him who is as high above them, as the sun is above the clouds. As in the Covenant of Grace the way is better, a living way indeed, so there is this advantage also, that we are not left to our own skill for following it, but taught by the Spirit. In the delivery of the Law, God shewed his glory and greatness by the manner of giving it, but the Law was written only in dead tables. But Christ, the living law, teaches, by obeying it, how to obey it; and this, too, is the advantage of the Gospel, that the Law is twice written over unto believers, first, in the example of Christ, and then, inwardly in their hearts by his Spirit. There is, together with that copy of all grace in Him, a spirit derived from Him, enabling believers to follow Him in their measure. They may not only see Him *as the only begotten Son of God, full of grace and truth,* as it is, John i. 14, but, as there it follows, *they receive of his fulness, grace for grace.* The love of Christ makes the soul delight to converse with Him; and converse and love together, make it learn His behaviour: as men that live much together, especially if they do much affect one another, will insensibly contract one another's habits and cus--toms.

The other thing obliging us is, 2dly, Our interest in Him and His sufferings; *He suffered for us.* And to this the Apostle returns, ver. 24. Observe only from the tie of these two, that if we neglect His example set before us, we cannot enjoy any right assurance of His suffering for us; but if we do seriously endeavour to follow Him, then we may expect to obtain life through His death, and those steps of His wherein we walk, will bring us ere long to be *where He is.*

Ver. 24. Who his own self bare our sins in his own body on the tree, that we, being dead to sin, should live unto righteousness; by whose stripes ye were healed.

THAT which is deepest in the heart, is generally most in the mouth; that which abounds within, runs over most by the tongue or pen. When men light upon the speaking of that subject which possesses their affection, they can hardly be taken off, or drawn from it again. Thus the Apostles in their writings, when they make mention any way of Christ suffering for us, love to dwell on it, as that which they take most delight to speak of; such delicacy, such sweetness is in it to a spiritual taste, that they like to keep it in their mouth, and are never out of their theme, when they insist on Jesus Christ, though they have but named Him by occasion of some other doctrine; for He is the great subject of all they have to say.

Thus here, the Apostle had spoken of Christ in the foregoing words very fitly to his present subject, setting Him before Christian servants, and all suffering Christians, as their complete example, both in point of much suffering, and of perfect innocence and patience in suffering; and he had expressed their obligation to study and follow that Example; yet he cannot leave it so, but having said that all those His sufferings, wherein He was so exemplary, were for us, as a chief consideration for which we should study to be like Him, he returns to that again, and enlarges upon it in words partly the same, partly very near those of that Evangelist among the Prophets, Isaiah, (ch. liii. verse 4.

And it suits very well with his main scope, to press this point, as giving both very much strength and sweetness to the exhortation ; for surely it is most reasonable that we willingly conform to Him in suffering, who had never been an example of suffering, nor subject at all to sufferings, nor in any degree capable of them, but for us ; and it is most comfortable in *these light sufferings of this present moment*, to consider that He hath freed us from the sufferings of eternity, by suffering Himself in our stead in the fulness of time.

That Jesus Christ is, in doing and in suffering, our supreme and matchless example, and that He came to do so, is a truth ; but that He is nothing further, and came for no other end, is, you see, a high point of falsehood. For how should man be enabled to learn and follow that example of obedience, unless there were more than an example in Christ ? and what would become of that great reckoning of disobedience that man stands guilty of ? No, these are notions far too narrow. He came to *bear our sins in his own body on the tree*, and, for this purpose, had a body fitted for him and given him to bear this burden, to do this as the will of his Father, to stand for us instead of all offerings and sacrifices ; and *by that will*, says the Apostle, *we are sanctified, through the offering of the body of Jesus Christ, once for all.* (Heb. x. 9.)

This was His business, not only to rectify sinful man by His example, but to redeem him by His blood. *He was a Teacher come from God:* as a Prophet, He teaches us the way of life, and as the best and greatest of prophets, is perfectly like His doctrine ; and His actions (which in all teachers is the liveliest part of doctrine), His carriage in life and death, is our great pattern and instruction. But what is said of his Forerunner, is more eminently true of Christ: He is *a Prophet, and more than a Prophet*,—a Priest satisfying justice for us, and a King

THE FIRST EPISTLE OF PETER.

conquering sin and death for us ; an example indeed, but more than an example,—our *sacrifice,* and *our life,* our *all in all.* It is our duty to *walk as He walked,* to make Him the pattern of our steps (1 John ii. 6) ; but our comfort and salvation lie in this, that *He is the propitiation for our sins* (v. 2). So in the first chapter of that Epistle, (v. 7,) *We are to walk in the light, as He is in the light;* but, for all our walking, we have need of that which follows, that bears the great weight,— *The blood of Jesus Christ cleanseth us from all sin.* And so still, that glory which He possesseth in His own person, is the pledge of ours : He is there for *us, He lives to make inter- cession for us,* says the Apostle (Heb. vii. 25) ; and, *I go to prepare a place for you,* says our Lord himself. (John xiv. 2.)

We have in the words these two great points, and in the same order as the words lie : I. The Nature and Quality of the sufferings of Jesus Christ ; and, II. The End of them.

I. In this expression of the Nature and Quality of the suffer- ings of Christ, we are to consider, 1. The Commutation of the persons, *He himself—for us.* 2. The Work undertaken and performed, *He bare our sins in His own body on the tree.*

1. The act or sentence of the Law against the breach of it standing in force, and Divine justice expecting satisfaction, Death was the necessary and inseparable consequent of Sin. If you say, the supreme Majesty of God, being accountable to none, might have forgiven all without satisfaction, we are not to contest that, nor foolishly to offer to sound the bottomless depth of His absolute prerogative. Christ implies in his prayer, (Matt. xxvi. 39,) that it was *impossible* that he could escape *that cup;* but the impossibility is resolved into his Father's will, as the cause of it. But this we may clearly see, following the track of the holy Scriptures, (our only safe way,) that this way wherein our salvation is contrived is most excellent, and suitable to the greatness and goodness of God ; so full of wonders of wisdom and love, that the Angels, as our Apostle tells us before, cannot forbear looking on it, and admiring it : for all their exact knowledge, yet they still find it infinitely

beyond their knowledge, still in astonishment and admiration of what they see, and still in search, looking in to see more; those cherubim still having their .eyes fixed on this Mercy-Seat.

Justice might indeed have seized on rebellious Man, and laid the pronounced punishment on him. Mercy might have freely acquitted him, and pardoned all. But can we name any place where Mercy and Justice, as relating to condemned man, could have met and shined jointly in full aspect, save only in Jesus Christ?—in whom, indeed, *Mercy and Truth met, and Righteousness and Peace kissed each other* (Psal. lxxxv. 10); yea, in whose person the Parties concerned, that were at so great a distance, met so near, as nearer cannot be imagined.

And not only was this the sole way for the consistency of these two, Justice and Mercy, but take each of them severally, and they could not have been manifested in so full lustre in any other way. God's just hatred of sin did, out of doubt, appear more in punishing His only begotten Son for it, than if the whole race of mankind had suffered for it eternally. Again, it raises the notion of mercy to the highest, that sin is not only forgiven us, but for this end God's own co-eternal Son is given to us, and for us. Consider what He is, and what we are; He the *Son of His love,* and we, enemies. Therefore it is emphatically expressed in the words, *God so loved the world* (John iii. 16): that Love amounts to this much, that is, was so great as *to give His Son;* but how great that love is cannot be uttered. *In this,* says the Apostle, (Rom. v. 8,) *God commendeth His love to us,* sets it off to the highest, gives us the richest and strongest evidence of it.

The foundation of this plan, this appearing of Christ for us, and undergoing and answering all in our stead, lies in the decree of God, where it was plotted and contrived, in the whole way of it, from eternity; and the Father and the Son being one, and their Thoughts and will one, They were perfectly agreed on it; and those likewise for whom it should hold, were agreed upon, and their names written down, according to which they are said to be *given unto Christ to redeem.* And just according to that model, did all the work proceed, and was accomplished in all points, perfectly answering to the pattern of it in the mind of God. As it was preconcluded there, that the Son should undertake the business, this matchless piece of service for His Father, and that, by His interposing, men should be reconciled and saved; so, that He might be altogether a fit person for the work, it was resolved, that as He was already fit for it by the almightiness of His Deity and Godhead, and the acceptableness of His person to the Father, as the Son of God, so he should be further fitted by wonderfully uniting weakness to Almightiness, the frailty of man to the power of God. Because suffering for man was a main point of the work, therefore, as His being the Son of God made Him acceptable to God, so His being the Son of man made Him suitable to man, in whose business He had engaged himself, and suitable to the business itself to be performed. And not only was there in Him, by his human nature, a conformity to man, (for that might have been accomplished by a new created body,) but a consanguinity with man, by a body framed of the same piece,—this Redeemer, a Kinsman, (as the Hebrew word *goel* is,)—only purified for His use, as was needful, and framed, after a peculiar manner, in the womb of a virgin, as it is expressed, Heb. x. 5, *Thou hast fitted a body for me,*—having no sin itself, because ordained to have so much of our sins: as it is here, *He bare our sins in His own body.*

And this looks back to the primitive transaction and purpose. *Lo! I come to do thy will,* says the Son. (Psal. xl. 7.) *Behold my servant whom I have chosen,* says the Father, (Isa. xliii. 10,) this master-piece of My works; no one in heaven or earth is fit to serve me, but my own Son. And as He came into the world according to that decree and will, so He goes out of it again in that way. *The Son of Man goeth as is determined,* (Luke xxii. 22:) it was wickedly and maliciously done by men against Him, but it was *determined* (which is what he there speaks of) wisely and graciously by His Father, with His own

consent. As in those two-faced pictures, look upon the crucifying of Christ one way, as complotted by a treacherous disciple
and malicious priests and rulers, and nothing more deformed
and hateful than the authors of it; but view it again, as determined in God's counsel, for the restoring of lost mankind,
and it is full of unspeakable beauty and sweetness,—infinite
wisdom and love in every trait of it.

Thus also, as to the persons for whom Christ engaged to
suffer, their coming unto Him looks back to that first donation
of the Father, as flowing from that: *All that the Father giveth
me shall come unto me.* (John vi. 37.)

Now this being God's great design, it is that which He
would have men eye and consider more than all the rest of His
works; and yet it is least of all considered by the most! The
other Covenant, made with the first Adam, was but to make
way, and, if we may so speak, to make work for this. For He
knew that it would not hold; therefore, as this New Covenant
became needful by the breach of the other, so the failing of
that other sets off and commends the firmness of this. The
former was made with a man in his best condition, and yet he
kept it not: even then, he proved vanity, as it is, Psal. xxxix.
5, *Verily, every man, in his best estate, is altogether vanity.*
So that the second, that it might be stronger, is made with A
Man indeed, to supply the place of the former, but he is *God-
Man*, to be surer than the former, and therefore it holds. And
this is the difference, as the Apostle expresses it, that the first
Adam, in that Covenant, was laid as a foundation, and, though
we say not that the Church, in its true notion, was built on
him, yet the estate of the whole race of mankind, the materials
which the Church is built of, lay on him for that time; and it
failed. But upon this rock, the second Adam, is the Church
so firmly built, that *the gates of hell cannot prevail against
her. The first man, Adam, was made a living soul; the last
Adam was made a quickening* (or life-giving) *spirit.* (1 Cor.
xv. 45.) The First had life, but he transferred it not, yea, he
kept it not for himself, but drew in and transferred death; but

the Second, by death, conveys life to all that are reckoned his seed: *He bare their sins.*

2. As to the work itself. He bare them *on the tree.* In that outside of His suffering, the visible kind of death inflicted on Him, in that it was hanging on the tree of the cross, there was an analogy with the end and main work; and it was ordered by the Lord with regard unto that end, being a death declared *accursed by the Law,* as the Apostle St. Paul observes, (Gal. iii. 13,) and so declaring Him who was *God blessed for ever,* to have been *made a curse* (that is, accounted as accursed) for us, that we might be blessed in Him, *in whom,* according to the promise, *all the nations of the earth are blessed.*

But that wherein lay the strength and main stress of His sufferings, was this invisible weight, which none could see who gazed on Him, but which He felt more than all the rest; *He bare our sins.* In this there are three things. 1. The weight of sin. 2. The transferring of it upon Christ. 3. His bearing of it.

1. He bare sin as a heavy burden; so the word *bearing* imports in general, (ἀνήνεγκεν,) and those two words particularly used by the prophet, Isa. liii. 4, to which these allude, (סבל נשא,) imply the *bearing of some great mass* or *load.* And such sin is; for it hath the wrath of an offended God hanging at it, indissolubly tied to it, of which, who can bear the least? And therefore the least sin, being the procuring cause of it, will press a man down for ever, that he shall not be able to rise. *Who can stand before Thee when once Thou art angry?* says the Psalmist, Psal. lxxvi. 7. And the Prophet, Jer. iii. 12, *Return, backsliding Israel, and I will not cause my wrath to fall upon thee—to fall* as a great weight: or as a millstone, and crush the soul.

But senseless we go light under the burden of sin, and feel it not, we complain not of it, and are therefore truly said to be *dead in it;* otherwise it could not but press us, and press out complaints. *O! wretched man that I am! who*

shall deliver me?   A profane, secure sinner thinks it nothing
to break the holy Law of God, to please his flesh, or the
world ; he counts sin a light matter, *makes a mock* of it, as
Solomon says, Prov. xiv. 9.   But a stirring conscience is of
another mind : *Mine iniquities are gone over my head ; as a
heavy burden, they are too heavy for me.* (Psal. xxxviii. 4.)

Sin is such a burden as makes the very frame of heaven
and earth, which is not guilty of it, yea the whole creation, to
crack and groan, (it is the Apostle's doctrine, Rom. viii. 22,)
and yet the impenitent heart, whose guiltiness it is, continues
unmoved, groaneth not; for your accustomed groaning is no
such matter.

Yea, to consider it in connexion with the present subject,
where we may best read what it is, Sin was a heavy load to
Jesus Christ.   In Psal. xl. 12, the Psalmist, speaking in the
person of Christ, complains heavily, *Innumerable evils have
compassed me about : Mine iniquities* (not His, as done by
Him, but yet His, by His undertaking to pay for them) *have
taken hold of me, so that I am not able to look up ; they are
more than the hairs of my head, therefore my heart faileth
me.*   And surely, that which pressed *Him* so sore who upholds Heaven and earth, no other in Heaven or on earth could
have sustained and surmounted, but would have sunk and
perished under it.   Was it, think you, the pain of that common
outside of his death, though very painful, that drew such a word
from him, *My God, my God, why hast thou forsaken me?*
Or was it the fear of that beforehand, that pressed a *sweat of
blood* from him? No, it was this burden of sin, the first of
which was committed in the garden of Eden, that then began
to be laid upon Him and fastened upon his shoulders in the
garden of Gethsemane, ten thousand times heavier than the
cross which he was caused to bear.   That might be for a while
turned over to another, but this could not.   This was the cup
he trembled at more than at that gall and vinegar to be afterwards offered to him by his crucifiers, or any part of his external sufferings : it was the bitter cup of wrath due to sin,

which his Father put into his hand, and caused him to drink, the very same thing that is here called the *bearing our sins in his body*.

And consider, that the very smallest sins contributed to make up this load, and made it so much the heavier; and therefore, though sins be comparatively smaller and greater, yet learn thence to account no sin in itself small, which offends the great God, and which lay heavy upon your great Redeemer, in the day of His sufferings.

At His apprehension, besides the soldiers, that invisible crowd of the sins he was to suffer for came about him, for it was these that laid strongest hold on him; he could easily have shaken off all the rest, as appears Matt. xxvi. 33, but our sins laid the arrest on him, being accounted His, as it is in that forecited place, Psal. xl. 12, *Mine iniquities*. Now, amongst these were even those sins we call small; they were of the number that took him, and they were amongst those instruments of his bloodshed. If the greater were as the spear that pierced his side, the less were as the nails that pierced his hands and his feet, and the very least as the thorns that were set on his precious head. And the multitude of them made up what was wanting in their magnitude; though they were small, they were many.

2. They were transferred upon Him by virtue of that covenant we spoke of. They became His debt, and He responsible for all they came to. Seeing you have accepted of this business according to My will, (may we conceive the Father saying to his Son,) you must go through with it; you are engaged in it, but it is no other than what you understood perfectly before; you knew what it would cost you, and yet, out of joint love with Me to those I named to be saved by you, you were as willing as I to the whole undertaking. Now therefore the time is come, that I must lay upon you the sins of all those persons, and you must bear them; the sins of all those believers who lived before, and all who are to come after, to the end of the world. *The Lord laid on Him the iniquity*

of us all, says the Prophet, Isa. liii. 6, took] it off from us
and charged it on him, made it *to meet on Him,* or *to fall in
together,* as the word in the original imports.   The sins of all,·
in all ages, before and after, who were to be saved, all their
guiltiness met together on His back upon the Cross.   Whosoever of all that number had least sin, yet had no small
burden to cast on Him : and to give accession to the whole
weight, *every man hath had his own way of wandering,* as
the Prophet there expresseth it, and He paid for all ; all fell
on Him.   And as in testimony of his meekness and patience,
so in this respect likewise was He so silent in His sufferings,
that though His enemies dealt most unjustly with Him, yet
He stood as convicted before the justice-seat of His Father,
under the imputed guilt of all our sins, and so eyeing Him,
and accounting His business to be chiefly with Him, he did
patiently bear the due punishment of all our sins at His Father's
hand, according to that of the Psalmist, *I was dumb, I opened
not my mouth because Thou didst it.* (Psal. xxxix. 9.)   Therefore the Prophet immediately subjoins the description of his
silent carriage, to that which he had spoken of, the confluence
of our iniquities upon Him : *As a sheep before her shearers
is dumb, so He openeth not His mouth.* (Isa. liii. 7.)

And if our sins were thus accounted His, then, in the same
way, and for that very reason, His sufferings and satisfaction
must of necessity be accounted ours.   As He said for his disciples to the men who came to take him, *If it be me ye seek,
then let these go free;* so He said for all believers, to his
Father, His wrath then seizing on him, If on me Thou wilt
lay hold, then let these go free.   And thus the agreement was :
*He was made sin for us who knew no sin, that we might be
made the righteousness of God in Him.* (2 Cor. v. *ult.*)

So then, there is a union betwixt believers and Jesus Christ,
by which this interchange is made ; He being charged with
their sins, and they clothed with his satisfaction and righteousness.   This union is founded, 1st, in God's decree of Election,
running to this effect, that they should live in Christ, and so,

choosing the Head and the whole mystical Body as one, and reckoning their debt as his, in His own purpose, that He might receive satisfaction, and they salvation, in their Head, Christ. The execution of that purpose and union, began in Christ's incarnation, it being for them, though the nature he assumed is theirs in common with other men. It is said, (Heb. ii. 16,) *He took not on Him the nature of Angels, but the seed of Abraham*, the company of believers : He became man for their sakes, because they are men. That he is of the same nature with unbelieving men who perish, is but by accident, as it were ; there is no good to them in that, but the great evil of deeper condemnation, if they hear of Him, and believe not ; but He was made man to be like, yea, to be one with, the Elect, *and He is not ashamed to call them brethren;* as the Apostle there says, (Heb. ii. 11). 2dly, This union is also founded in the actual intention of the Son so made man ; He presenting himself to the Father in all He did and suffered, *as for them*, having them, and them only, in His eye and thoughts, in all. *For their sakes do I sanctify myself.* (John xvii. 1, 9.) Again, 3dly, This union is applied and performed in them, when they are converted and ingrafted into Jesus Christ by faith ; and this doth actually discharge them of their own sins, and entitle them to His righteousness, and so justify them in the sight of God. 4thly, The consummation of this union, is in glory, which is the result and fruit of all the former. As it began in Heaven, it is completed there ; but betwixt these two in Heaven, the intervention of those other two degrees of it on earth was necessary, being intended in the first, as tending to the attainment of the last. These four steps of it are all distinctly expressed in our Lord's own prayer. (John xvii.) 1st, God's purpose that the Son should give *eternal life to those whom He hath given Him*, (ver. 2). 2dly, The Son's undertaking and accomplishing their redemption, in ver. 4, *I have finished the work which Thou gavest me to do.* 3dly, The application of this union, and its performance in them, by their *faith*, their *believing*, and *keeping*

His word, ver. 6, 8, and in several of the subsequent verses
And then lastly, the consummation of this union, (ver. 24,) *I
will that they whom Thou hast given me, be with me where I
am.* There meet the first donation, and the last.

Now, to obtain this life for them, Christ died *in their stead.*
He appeared as the High Priest, being perfectly and truly what
the name was on their plate of gold, *Holiness to the Lord,*
Exod. xxviii. 36, and so *bearing their iniquity,* as it is there
added of Aaron, ver. 38. But because the High Priest was not
the Redeemer, but only prefigured him, he did not himself
suffer for the people's sin, but turned it over upon the beasts
which he sacrificed, signifying that translation of sin, by laying
his hand upon the head of the beast. But Jesus Christ is both
the great high-priest and the great sacrifice in one; and this
seems to be here implied in these words, *Himself bare our sins
in His own body,* which the Priest under the Law did not.
So, Isa. liii. 10, and Heb. ix. 12, *He made His soul an offering
for sin.* He offered up himself, his *whole self.* In the history
of the Gospel, it is said, that *His soul was heavy,* and chiefly
suffered; but it is the bearing sin in *His body,* and offering it,
that is oftenest mentioned as the visible part of the sacrifice,
and as His way of offering it, not excluding the other. Thus,
(Rom. xii. 1,) we are exhorted to give *our bodies,* in opposition
to the bodies of beasts, and they are therefore called *a living
sacrifice,* which they are not without the soul. So, Christ's
bearing it *in His body,* imports the bearing of it in his soul too.

3. His *bearing* of our sins, hints that He was active and
willing in his suffering for us; it was not a constrained offering.
He laid down his life, as He himself tells us, (John x. 18); and
this expression here, *He bare,* implies, He took willingly off,
lifted from us that burden, to bear it Himself. It was counted
an ill sign amongst the heathens, when the beasts went unwillingly to be sacrificed, and drew back, and a good omen when
they went willingly. But never was sacrifice so willing as our
Great Sacrifice; and we may be assured He hath appeased his
Father's wrath, and wrought atonement for us. Isaac was in

this a type of Christ; we hear of no reluctance; he submitted quietly to be bound when he was to be offered up. There are two words used in Isaiah, ch. liii., v. 4, the one signifying *bearing*, the other, *taking away*. This *bearing* includes, also, that *taking away of the sins of the world,* spoken of by St. John, ch. i., v. 29, which answers to both ; and so He, the Great Antitype, answers to both the goats, the sin-offering and the scape-goat. (Levit. xvi.) He did bear our sins on his cross, and from thence did bear them away to his grave, and there they are buried ; and they whose sins He did so bear, and take away, and bury, shall hear no more of them as theirs to bear. Is he not, then, worthy to be beheld, in that notion under which John, in the fore-mentioned text, viewed Him, and designates Him ?—*Behold the Lamb of God, which beareth and taketh away the sins of the world!*

You, then, who are gazing on vanity, be persuaded to turn your eyes this way, and behold this lasting wonder, this Lord of Life dying ! But the most, alas ! want a due eye for this Object. It is the eye of faith alone that looks aright on Him, and is daily discovering new worlds of excellency and delight in this crucified Saviour ; that can view Him daily, as hanging on the Cross, without the childish, gaudy help of a crucifix, and grow in the knowledge of that Love which passeth know-ledge, and rejoice itself in frequent thinking and speaking of Him, instead of those idle and vain thoughts at the best, and empty discourses, wherein the most delight, and wear out the day. What is all knowledge but painted folly in comparison of this ? Hadst thou Solomon's faculty to discourse of all plants, and hadst not the right knowledge of this *root of Jesse ;* wert thou singular in the knowledge of the stars and of the course of the heavens, and couldst walk through the spheres with a *Jacob's staff,* but ignorant of this *star of Jacob ;* if thou knewest the histories of all time, and the life and death of all the most famous princes, and could rehearse them all, but dost not spiritually know and apply to thyself the death of Jesus as thy life ; thou art still a wretched fool, and all thy knowledge with thee shall quickly perish. On the other side, if thy capacity or breeding hath denied thee the knowledge of all these things wherein men glory so much, yet, do but learn *Christ crucified*, and what wouldst thou have more? That shall make thee happy for ever. *For this is life eternal, to know thee the only true God, and Jesus Christ whom thou hast sent.* (John xvii. 3.)

Here St. Paul takes up his rest, *I determined to know nothing but Jesus Christ and him crucified.* (1 Cor. ii. 2.) As if he had said, Whatsoever I knew besides, I resolved to be as if I knew nothing besides this, the only knowledge wherein I will rejoice myself, and which I will labour to impart to others. I have tried and compared the rest, and find them all unworthy of their room beside this, and my whole soul too little for this. I have passed this judgment and sentence on all. I have adjudged myself to deny all other knowledge, and confined myself within this circle, and I am not straitened. No, there is room enough in it; it is larger than heaven and earth, *Christ and Him* crucified; the most despised and ignominious part of knowledge, yet the sweetest and most comfortable part of all: the root whence all our hopes of life, and all our spiritual joys do spring.

But the greatest part of mankind hear this subject as a story. Some are a little moved with the present sound of it, but they draw it not home into their hearts, to make it theirs, and to find salvation in it, but still cleave to sin, and love sin better than Him who suffered for it.

But you whose hearts the Lord hath deeply humbled under a sense of sin, come to this depth of consolation, and try it, that you may have experience of the sweetness and riches of it. Study this point thoroughly, and you will find it answer all, and quiet your consciences. Apply this *bearing of sin* by the Lord Jesus for you, for it is published and made known to you for this purpose. This is the genuine and true use of it, as of the *brazen serpent*, not that the people might emptily gaze on the fabric of it, but that those that looked on it might be cured.

When all that can be said, is said against you, " It is true,'' may you say, " but it is all satisfied for; He on whom I rest, made it His, and did bear it for me." The person of Christ is of more worth than all men, yea, than all the creatures; and therefore, his life was a full ransom for the greatest offender.

And as for outward troubles and sufferings, which were the occasion of this doctrine in this place, they are all made exceeding light by the removal of this great pressure. Let the Lord lay on me what He will, seeing He hath taken off my sin, and laid that on His own Son in my stead. I may suffer many things, but He hath borne that for me, which alone was able to make me miserable.

And you that have this persuasion, how will your hearts be taken up with his love, *who has so loved you as to give himself for you;* who interposed Himself to bear off from you the stroke of everlasting death, and encountered all the wrath due to us, and went through with that great work, by reason of his unspeakable love! Let Him never go forth from my heart, who for my sake refused to go down from the cross.

II. The End of these Sufferings. *That we being dead to sin, should live unto righteousness.*] The Lord doth nothing in vain; He hath not made the least of his works to no purpose; *in wisdom hath He made them all,* says the Psalmist. And this is true, not only in regard of their excellent frame and order, but of their end, which is a chief point of wisdom. So then, in order to the right knowledge of this great work put into the hands of Jesus Christ, it is of special concern to understand what is its End.

Now this is the thing which Divine wisdom and love aimed at in that great undertaking, and therefore it will be our truest wisdom, and the truest evidence of our reflex love, to intend the same thing, that in this *the same mind may be in us, that was in Christ Jesus* in his suffering for us; for this very end it is expressed, *That we being dead to sin, should live to righteousness.*

In this there are three things to be considered: 1st, What

this death and life is ; 2dly, The designing of it in the sufferings and death of Jesus Christ; 3dly, The effecting of it by
them.

1st, What this death and life is. Whatsoever it is, surely
it is no small change that bears the name of the great and last
natural change that we are subject to, a *death*, and then another kind of life succeeding to it.

In this the greatest part of mankind are mistaken, that they
take any slight alteration in themselves for true conversion. A
world of people are deluded with superficial moral changes in
their life, some rectifying of their outward actions and course
of life, and somewhat too in the temper and habit of their mind.
Far from reaching the bottom of nature's wickedness, and
laying the axe to the root of the tree, it is such a work as men
can make a shift with by themselves. But the renovation which
the Spirit of God worketh, is like Himself: it is so deep and
total a work, that it is justly called by the name of the most
substantial works and productions; *a new birth*, and more
than that, *a new creation*, and here, *a death* and a kind of *life*
following it.

This *death to sin* supposes a former *living in it*, and to it;
and while a man does so, he is said indeed to be *dead in sin*,
and yet withal, this is true, that he lives in sin, as the Apostle,
speaking of widows, joins the expressions, 1 Tim. v. 6, *She
that liveth in pleasure is dead while she liveth.* So, Eph. ii.
1, *Dead in trespasses and sins*, and he adds, *wherein ye
walked*, which imports a life, such an one as it is ; and more
expressly, (ver. 3,) *We had our conversation in the lusts of our
flesh.* Now, thus to live in sin, is termed being dead in it,
because, in that condition, man is indeed dead in respect of that
Divine life of the soul, that happy being which it should have
in union with God, for which it was made, and without which
it had better not be at all. For that life, as it is different from
its natural being, and a kind of life above it, so it is contrary
to that corrupt being and life it hath in sin ; and therefore, to
live in sin, is to be dead in it, being a deprivement of that

Divine being, that life of the soul in God, in comparison whereof not only the base life it hath in sin, but the very natural life it hath in the body, and which the body hath by it, is not worthy of the name of life. You see the body, when the thread of its union with the soul is cut, becomes not only straightway a motionless lump, but within a little time, a putrefied, noisome carcass; and thus the soul by sin cut off from God who is its life, as is the soul that of the body, hath not only no moving faculty in good, but becomes full of rottenness and vileness : as the word is, (Psalm xiv. 2,) *They are gone aside and become filthy.* The soul, by turning away from God, turns filthy ; yet, as a man thus spiritually dead, lives naturally, so, because he acts and spends that natural life in the ways of sin, he is said to *live in sin.* Yea, there is somewhat more in that expression than the mere passing of his life in that way ; for instead of that happy life his soul should have in God, he pleases himself in the miserable life of sin, that which is his death, as if it were the proper life of his soul : *living in it* imports that natural propension he hath to sin, and the continual delight he takes in it, as in his element, and living to it, as if that were the very end of his being. In that estate, neither his body nor his mind stirreth without sin. Setting aside his manifest breaches of the Law, those actions that are evidently and totally sinful, his natural actions, his eating and drinking, his religious actions, his praying, and hearing, and preaching, are sin at the bottom. And generally, his heart is no other than a forge of sin. *Every imagination*, every fiction of things framed there, *is only evil continually ;* (Gen. vi. 5 ;) every day, and all the day long, it is his very trade and life.

Now, in opposition to this life of sin, this living in it and to it, a Christian is said to *die to sin*, to be cut off or separated from it. In our miserable natural state, there is as close a union betwixt us and sin, as betwixt our souls and bodies: it lives in us, and we in it, and the longer we live in that condition, the more the union grows, and the harder it is to dissolve it ; and it is as old as the union of soul and body, begun with it, so that nothing but the death here spoken of can part them. And this death, in this relative sense, is mutual: in the work of conversion, sin dies, and the soul dies to sin, and these two are really one and the same thing. The Spirit of God kills both at one blow, sin in the soul, and the soul to sin ; as the Apostle says of himself and the world, Gal. vi. 14, each is crucified to the other.

And there are in it chiefly these two things, which make the difference, [1.] The solidity, and [2.] The universality of this change, here represented under the notion of Death.

Many things may lie in a man's way betwixt him and the acting of divers sins which possibly he affects most. Some restraints, either outward or inward, may be upon him, the authority of others, the fear of shame or punishment, or the check of an enlightened conscience ; and though by reason of these, he commit not the sin he would, yet he *lives in it*, be-cause he *loves* it, because he would commit it: as we say, the soul lives not so much where it animates, as where it loves. And generally, that metaphorical kind of life, by which man is said to live in any thing, hath its principal seat in the affec‑tion : that is the immediate link of the union in such a life ; and the untying and death consists chiefly in the disengagement of the heart, the breaking off the affection from it. *Ye that love the Lord,* says the Psalmist, *hate evil.* (Psal. xcvii. 10.) An unrenewed mind may have some temporary dislikes even of its beloved sins in cold blood, but it returns to like them within a while. A man may not only have times of cessation from his wonted way of sinning, but, by reason of the society wherein he is, and the withdrawing of occasions to sin, and divers other causes, his very desire after it may seem to himself to be abated, and yet he may be not dead to sin, but only asleep to it ; and therefore, when a temptation, backed with opportunity and other inducing circumstances, comes and jogs him, he awakes, and arises, and follows it.

A man may for a while distaste some meat which he loves, (possibly upon a surfeit,) but he quickly regains his liking of it.

Every quarrel with sin, every fit of dislike to it, is not that hatred which is implied in dying to sin. Upon the lively representation of the deformity of his sin to his mind, certainly a natural man may fall out with it; but this is but as the little jars of husband and wife, which are far from dissolving the marriage: it is not a fixed hatred, such as amongst the Jews inferred a divorce—*If thou hate her, put her away ;* that is to die to it; as by a legal divorce the husband and wife are civilly dead one to another in regard of the tie and use of marriage.

Again, some men's education, and custom, and moral principles, may free them from the grossest kind of sins, yea, a man's temper may be averse from them, but they are alive to their own kind of sins, such as possibly are not so deformed in the common account, covetousness, or pride, or hardness of heart, and either a hatred or a disdain of the ways of holiness, which are too strict for them, and exceed their size. Besides, for the good of human society, and for the interest of his own church and people, God restrains many natural men from the height of wickedness, and gives them moral virtues. There be very many, and very common sins, which more refined natures, it may be, are scarcely tempted to ; but as in their diet, and apparel, and other things in their natural life, they have the same kind of being with other persons, though they are more neat and elegant, so in this living to sin, they live the same life with other ungodly men, though with a little more delicacy.

They consider not that the devils are not in themselves subject to, nor capable of, many of those sins that are accounted grossest amongst men, and yet are greater rebels and enemies to God than men are.

But to be *dead to sin* goes deeper, and extends further than all this; it involves a most inward alienation of heart from sin, and most universal from all sin, an antipathy to the most beloved sin. Not only doth the believer forbear sin, but he hates it—*I hate vain thoughts* (Psal. cxix. 113) ; and not only doth he hate some sins, but all—*I hate every false way* (ver. 128). A stroke at the heart does it, which is the certainest and quickest

death of any wound.   For in this dying to sin, the whole man
of necessity dies to it : the mind dies to the device and study of
sin, that vein of invention becomes dead ; the hand dies to the
acting of it ; the ear, to the delightful hearing of things profane and sinful ; the tongue, to the world's dialect of oaths, and
rotten speaking, and calumny, and evil-speaking, which is the
commonest effect of the tongue's life in sin,—the very natural
heat of sin exerts and vents itself most that way ; the eye becomes dead to that intemperate look that Solomon speaks of,
when he cautions us against *eying the wine when it is red,
and well coloured in the cup* (Prov. xxiii. 31): it is not taken
with looking on the glittering skin of that *serpent* till it *bite* and
sting, as there he adds.   It becomes also dead to that unchaste
look which kindles fire in the heart, to which Job blindfolded
and deadened his eyes, by an express compact and agreement
with them : *I have made a covenant with mine eyes.*   (Job.
xxxi. 1.)

The eye of a godly man is not fixed on the false sparkling of
the world's pomp, honour, and wealth ; it is dead to them,
being quite dazzled with a greater beauty.   The grass looks
fine in the morning, when it is set with those liquid pearls, the
drops of dew that shine upon it ; but if you can look but a
little while on the body of the sun, and then look down again,
the eye is as it were dead ; it sees not that faint shining on
the earth that it thought so gay before : and as the eye is
blinded, and dies to it, so, within a few hours, that gaiety quite
evanishes and dies itself.

Men think it strange that the Godly are not fond of their
diet, that their appetite is not stirred with desire of their delights and dainties ; they know not that such as be Christians
indeed, are dead to those things, and the best dishes that are
set before a dead man give him not a stomach.   The godly
man's *throat is cut to those meats*, as Solomon advises in another subject, Prov. xxiii. 2.   But why may not you be a
little more sociable, to follow the fashion of the world, and take
a share with your neighbours, may some say, without so pre-

cisely and narrowly examining every thing? It is true, says the Christian, that the time was when I advised as little with conscience as others, but sought myself, and pleaded myself, as they do, and looked no further; but that was when *I was alive to those ways;* but now, truly *I am dead to them:* and can you look for activity and conversation from a dead man? The pleasures of sin wherein I lived are still the same, but I am not the same. Are you such a sneak and a fool, says the natural man, as to bear affronts, and swallow them, and say nothing? Can you suffer to be so abused by such and such a wrong? Indeed, says the Christian again, I could once have resented an injury as you or another would, and had somewhat of what you call high-heartedness, when I was alive after your fashion; but now, that humour is not only something cooled, but it is killed in me; it is cold dead, as ye say; and a Greater Spirit, I think, than my own hath taught me another lesson, hath made me both deaf and dumb that way, and hath given me a new vent, and another language, and another Party to speak to on such occasions. *They that seek my hurt,* says David, *speak mischievous things, and imagine deceits all the day long.* What doth he in this case? *But I, as a deaf man, heard not, and I was as a dumb man that openeth not his mouth.* And why? *For in thee, O Lord, do I hope.* (Psal. xxxviii. 12—15.) And for this deadness that you despise, I have seen Him who died for me, *who, when he was reviled, reviled not again.*

This is the true character of a Christian: he is *dead to sin.* But, alas! where is this Christian to be found? And yet, thus is every one who truly partakes of Christ; he is dead to sin really. Hypocrites have an historical kind of death like this, as players in tragedies. Those players have loose bags of blood that receive the wound: so the hypocrite in some externals, and it may be, in that which is as near him as any outward thing, his purse, may suffer some bloodshed of that for Christ. But this death to sin is not a swooning fit, that one may recover out of again: the Apostle (Rom. vi. 4) adds, that the believer *is buried with Christ.*

But this is an unpleasant subject, to talk thus of death and burial. The very name of death, in the softest sense it can have, makes a sour melancholy discourse. It is so indeed, if you take it alone, if there were not, for the life that is lost, a far better one immediately following; but so it is here; *living unto righteousness* succeeds *dying to sin.*

That which makes natural death so affrightful, the *King of terrors,* as Job calls it, (ch. xviii. 14,) is mainly this faint belief and assurance of the resurrection and glory to come; and without some lively apprehension of this, all men's moral resolutions and discourses are too weak cordials against this fear. They may set a good face on it, and speak big, and so cover the fear they cannot cure ; but certainly, they are a little ridiculous, who would persuade men to be content to die, by reasoning from the necessity and unavoidableness of it, which, taken alone, rather may beget a desperate discontent, than a quiet compliance. The very weakness of that argument is, that it is too strong, *durum telum.* That of company is fantastic: it may please the imagination, but satisfies not the judgment. Nor are the miseries of life, though an argument somewhat more proper, a full persuasive to meet death without reluctance: the oldest, the most decrepit, and most diseased persons, yet naturally fall not out with life, but could have a mind to it still ; and the very truth is this, the worst cottage any one dwells in, he is loth to go out of, till he knows of a better. And the reason why that which is so hideous to others, was so sweet to martyrs, (Heb. xi. 35,) and other godly men who have heartily embraced death, and welcomed it though in very terrible shapes, was, because they had firm assurance of immortality beyond it. The ugly Death's head, when the light of glory shines through the holes of it, is comely and lovely. To look upon Death as Eternity's birth-day, is that which makes it not only tolerable, but amiable. *Hic dies pos-*

tremus, æterni natalis est, is the word I admire more than any
other that ever dropt from a heathen.

Thus here, the strongest inducement to this Death, is the
true notion and contemplation of this Life unto which it transfers us. It is most necessary to represent this, for a natural
man hath as great an aversion every whit from this figurative
death, this *dying to sin,* as from natural death ; and there is
the more necessity of persuading him to this, because his consent is necessary to it. No man diés this death to sin, unwillingly, although no man is naturally willing to it. Much of
this death consists in a man's consenting thus to die ; and this
is not only a lawful, but a laudable, yea, a necessary self-
murder. *Mortify, therefore, your members which are upon
the earth,* says the Apostle, Col. iii. 5. Now no sinner would
be content to *die to sin,* if that were all ; but if it be passing
to a more excellent *life,* then he gaineth, and it were a folly
not to seek this death. It was a strange power of Plato's discourse of the soul's immortality, that moved a young man,
upon reading it, to throw himself into the sea, that he might
leap through it to that immortality ; but truly, were this life
of God, this *life to righteousness,* and the excellency and delight of it known, it would gain many minds to this death
whereby we step into it.

But there is a necessity of a new being as the principle of
new action and motion. The Apostle says, *While ye served
sin, ye were free from righteousness* (Rom. vi. 20) ; so it is,
while ye were alive to sin, ye were dead to righteousness. But
there is a new breath of life from Heaven, breathed on the
soul. Then lives the soul indeed, when it is one with God,
and sees *light in His light,* (Psal. xxxii. 9,)—hath a spiritual
knowledge of Him, and therefore sovereignly loves Him, and
delights in His will. And this is indeed *to live unto righteousness,* which, in a comprehensive sense, takes in all the
framé of a Christian life ; and all the duties of it towards God
and towards men.

By this new nature, the very natural motion of the soul so taken, is obedience to God ; and walking in the paths of righteousness, it can no more live in the habit and ways of sin, than a man can live under water. Sin is not the Christian's element ; it is as much too gross for his renewed soul, as the water is for his body : he may fall into it, but he cannot breathe in it ; cannot take delight, and continue to live in it. *But his delight is in the law of the Lord.* (Psal. i. 2.) That is the walk which his soul refreshes itself in ; he loves it entirely, and loves it most, where it most crosses the remainders of corruption that are within him. He bends the strength of his soul to please God ; aims wholly at that ; it takes up his thoughts early and late. He hath no other purpose in his being and living, than only to honour his Lord. This is, *to live to righteousness.* He doth not make a by-work of it, a study for his spare hours : no, it is his main business, his all. *In His law doth he meditate day and night.* This life, like the natural one, is seated in the heart, and from thence diffuses itself to the whole man ; he *loves* righteousness, and *receiveth the truth* (as the Apostle speaks) *in the love of it.* A natural man may do many things which, as to their shell and outside, are righteous ; but he lives not to righteousness, because his heart is not possessed and ruled by the love of it. But this life makes the godly man delight to walk uprightly and to speak of righteousness; his language and ways carry the resemblance of his heart. I know it is easiest to act that part of religion which is in the tongue, but the Christian, nevertheless, ought not to be spiritually dumb. Because some birds are taught to speak, men do not for that give it over, and leave off to speak. *The mouth of the righteous speaketh wisdom, and his tongue talketh of judgment.* And his feet strive to keep pace with his tongue, which gives evidence of its unfeignedness : *None of his steps shall slide,* or, he shall not stagger in his steps. But that which is betwixt these, is the common spring of both : *The law of God is in his heart ;* (see Psal.

xxxvii. 30, 31;) and from thence, as Solomon says, *are the issues of his life.* (Prov. iv. 3.) That law in his heart, is the principle of *this living to righteousness.*

2. The second thing here, is, that it was the design of the sufferings and death of Christ, to produce in us this death and life : *He bare sin*, and died for it, that we might die to it.

Out of some conviction of the consequence of sin, many have a confused desire to be justified, to have sin pardoned, who look no further : they think not on the importance and neces-sity of Sanctification, the nature whereof is expressed by this *dying to sin*, and *living to righteousness.*

But here we see that Sanctification is necessary as inseparably connected with Justification, not only as its companion, but as its end, which, in some sort, raises it above the other. We see that it was the thing which God eyed and intended, in taking away the guiltiness of sin, that we might be renewed and sancti-fied. If we compare them in point of time, looking backward, holiness was always necessary unto happiness, but satisfying for sin and the pardon of it, were made necessary by sin: or, if we look forward, the estate we are appointed to, and for which we are delivered from wrath, is an estate of perfect holiness. When we reflect upon that great work of redemption, we see it aimed at there, *Redeemed to be holy.* (Eph. v. 25, 26; Tit. ii. 14.) And if we go yet higher, to the very spring, the decree of election, with regard to that it is said, (Eph. i. 14,) *Chosen before, that we should be holy.* And the end shall suit the design : *Nothing shall enter into the new Jerusalem, that is defiled*, or unholy ; nothing but perfect purity is there ; not a spot of sinful pollution, not a *wrinkle* of the old man. For this end was that great work undertaken by the Son of God, that he might frame out of polluted mankind a new and holy generation to his Father, who might compass His throne in the life of glory, and give Him pure praises, and behold His face in that eternity. Now, for this end it was needful, according to the all-wise purpose of the Father, that the guiltiness of sin and sentence of death should be once removed ; and thus, the burden of that lay upon Christ's shoulders on the cross. That done, it is further necessary, that souls so delivered be likewise purified and renewed, for they are designed for perfection of holiness in the end, and it must begin here.

Yet it is not possible to persuade men of this, that Christ had this in his eye and purpose when he was lifted up upon the cross, and looked upon the whole company of those his Father had given him to save, that he would redeem them to be a number of holy persons. We would be redeemed; who is there that would not? But Christ would have his redeemed ones holy; and they who are not true to this His end, but cross and oppose Him in it, may hear of Redemption long and often, but little to their comfort.. Are you resolved still to abuse and delude yourselves? Well, whether you will believe it or not, this is once more told you : there is unspeakable comfort in the death of Christ, but it belongs only to those who *are dead to sin, and alive to righteousness.* This circle shuts out the impenitent world ; there it closes, and cannot be broken through; but all who are penitent, are by their effectual calling lifted into it, translated from that accursed condition wherein they were. So then, if you will live in your sins, you may ; but then, resolve withal to bear them yourselves, for Christ, in his bearing of sin, meant the benefit of none but such as in due time are thus dead, and thus alive, with Him.

3. But then, in the third place, Christ's sufferings and death effect all this. [1.] As the exemplary cause, the lively contemplation of Christ crucified, is the most powerful of all thoughts to separate the heart and sin. But [2.] besides this example, working as a moral cause, Christ is the effective natural cause of this death and life; for he is one with the believer, and there is a real influence of his death and life into their souls. This mysterious union of Christ and the believer, is that whereon both their justification and sanctification, the whole frame of their salvation and happiness, depends. And in this particular view the Apostle still insists on it, speaking of Christ and believers as one in his death and resurrection, *cruci-*

fied with him, dead with him, buried with him, and risen with him. (Rom. vi. 4, &c.) Being arisen, he applies his death to those he died for, and by it kills the life of sin in them, and so is avenged on it for its being the cause of his death : according to that expression of the Psalmist, *Raise me up that I may requite them.* (Psal. xli. 10.) Christ infuses, and then actuates and stirs up that faith and love in them, by which they are united to him; and these work powerfully in producing this.

[3.] Faith looks so steadfastly on its suffering Saviour, that as they say, *Intellectus fit illud quod intelligit,* the mind becomes that which it contemplates. It makes the soul like him, assimilates and *conforms it to his death,* as the Apostle speaks, Phil. iii. 10. That which Papists fabulously say of some of their saints, that they received the impression of the wounds of Christ in their body, is true, in a spiritual sense, of the soul of every one that is indeed a saint and a believer : it takes the very print of his death, by beholding him, and *dies to sin ;* and then takes that of his rising again, and *lives to righteousness.* As it applies it to *justify,* so, to *mortify,* drawing virtue from it. Thus said one, " Christ aimed at this in all those sufferings which, with so much love, he went through ; and shall I disappoint him, and not serve his end ?"

[4.] That other powerful grace of Love joins in this work with Faith ; for love desires nothing more than likeness and conformity : though it be a painful resemblance, so much the better and fitter to testify love. Therefore it will have the soul die with Him who died for it, and the very same kind of death : *I am crucified with Christ,* says the great Apostle (Gal. ii. 20.) The love of Christ in the soul, takes the very nails that fastened him to the cross, and crucifies the soul to the world, and to sin. *Love is strong as death,* particularly in this. The strongest and liveliest body, when death seizes it, must yield, and that become motionless, which was so vigorous before : thus the soul that is most active and unwearied in sin, when this love seizes it, is killed to sin; and as death separates a man from his dearest friends, and society, this love breaks all its ties and friendship with sin.   Generally, as Plato hath it, love takes away one's living in one's self, and transfers it into the party loved ; but the divine love of Christ doth it in the truest and highest manner.

By whose stripes ye were healed.]   The misery of fallen man, and the mercy of his deliverance, are both of them such a depth, that no one expression, yea, no variety of expressions added one to another, can fathom them.   Here we have divers very significant ones.   1. The guiltiness of sin as an intolerable burden, pressing the soul and sinking it, and that transferred and laid on a stronger back : *He bare.*   Then, 2. The same wretchedness, under the notion of a strange disease, by all other means incurable, *healed by His stripes.*   And 3. It is again represented by the forlorn condition of a sheep wandering, and our salvation to be found only in the love and wisdom of our great Shepherd.   And all these are borrowed from that sweet and clear prophecy in the fifty-third chapter of Isaiah.

The polluted nature of man is no other than a bundle of desperate diseases : he is spiritually dead, as the Scriptures often teach.   Now this contradicts not, nor at all lessens the matter ; but only because this misery, justly called *death,* exists in a subject animated with a natural life, therefore, so considered, it may bear the name and sense of sickness, or wounds : and therefore it is gross misprision,—they are as much out in their argument as in their conclusion, who would extract out of these expressions any evidence that there are remains of spiritual life, or good, in our corrupted nature.   But they are not worthy the contest, though vain heads think to argue themselves into life, and are seeking that life, by logic, in miserable nature, which they should seek, by faith, in Jesus Christ, namely, in these *His stripes,* by which *we are healed.*

It were a large task to name our spiritual maladies ; how much more severally to unfold their natures ! Such a multitude of corrupt false principles in the mind, which, as gangrenes, do spread themselves through the soul, and defile the whole man ; that total gross blindness and unbelief in spiritual

THE FIRST EPISTLE OF PETER.

things, and that stone of the heart, hardness and impenitency; lethargies of senselessness and security; and then, (for there be such complications of spiritual diseases in us, as in naturals are altogether impossible,) such burning fevers of inordinate affections and desires, of lust, and malice, and envy, such racking and tormenting cares of covetousness, and *feeding on earth and ashes,* (as the Prophet speaks in another case, Isa. xliv. 20,) according to the depraved appetite that accompanies some diseases; such tumours of pride and self-conceit, that break forth, as filthy botches, in men's words, and carriage one with another! In a word, what a wonderful disorder must needs be in the natural soul, by the frequent interchanges and fight of contrary passions within it! And, besides all these, how many deadly wounds do we receive from without, by the temptations of Satan and the world! We entertain them, and by weapons with which they furnish us, we willingly wound ourselves; as the Apostle says of them *who will be rich,* they *fall into divers snares and noisome lusts, and pierce themselves through with many sorrows.* (1 Tim. vi. 9, 10.)

Did we see it, no infirmary or hospital was ever so full of loathsome and miserable spectacles, as, in a spiritual sense, our wretched nature is in any one of us apart: how much more when multitudes of us are met together! But our evils are hid from us, and we perish miserably in a dream of happiness! This makes up and completes our wretchedness, that we feel it not with our other diseases; and this makes it worse still. This was the Church's disease, Rev. iii. 17: *Thou sayest, I am rich, and knowest not that thou art poor,* &c. We are usually full of complaints of trifling griefs which are of small moment, and think not on, nor feel our dangerous maladies: as he who shewed a physician his sore finger, but the physician told him he had more need to think on the cure of a dangerous imposthume within him, which he perceived by looking at him, though himself did not feel it.

In dangerous maladies or wounds, there be these evils: a tendency to death, and with that, the apprehension of the terror and fear of it, and the present distemper of the body. So there are in sin, 1. The guiltiness of sin binding over the soul to death, the most frightful eternal death; 2. The terror of conscience in the apprehension of that death, or the wrath that is the consequence and end of sin ; 3. The raging and prevailing power of sin, which is the ill habitude and distemper of the soul.   But these *Stripes*, and that blood which issued from them, are a sound cure.   Applied unto the soul, they take away the guiltiness of sin, and death deserved, and free us from our engagement to those everlasting scourgings and lashes of the wrath of God ; and they are likewise the only cure of those present terrors and pangs of conscience, arising from the sense of that wrath and sentence of death upon the soul.   Our iniquities which met on Him, laid open to the rod that back which in itself was free.   Those hands which never wrought iniquity, and those feet which never declined from the way of righteousness, yet, for our works and wanderings, were pierced; and that tongue dropped with vinegar and gall on the cross, which never spoke a guileful nor sinful word.   The blood of those Stripes is that balm issuing from that Tree of Life so pierced, which can alone give ease to the conscience, and heal the wounds of it : they deliver from the power of sin, working by their influence a loathing of sin, which was the cause of them ; they cleanse out the vicious humours of our corrupt nature, by opening that issue of repentance: *They shall look on Him and mourn over Him whom they have pierced.* (Zech. xii. 10.)

Now, to the end it may thus cure, it must be applied : it is the only receipt, but in order to heal, it must be received. The most sovereign medicines cure not in any other manner, and therefore, still their first letter is, R, *Recipe*, take such a thing.

This is amongst the wonders of that great work that the sovereign Lord of all, who binds and looses at His pleasure the influences of heaven, and the power and workings of all the creatures, would himself in our flesh be thus bound, the only Son bound as a slave, and scourged as a malefactor ! And his willing obedience made this an acceptable and expiating sacrifice, amongst the rest of his sufferings : *He gave his back to the smiters.* (Isa. l. 6.)

Now, it cannot be, that any one who is thus healed, reflecting upon this cure, can again take any constant delight in sin. It is impossible so far to forget both the grief it bred themselves, and that which it cost their Lord, as to make a new agreement with it, to live in the pleasure of it.

His stripes.] Turn your thoughts, every one of you, to consider this; you that are not healed, that you may be healed ; and you that are, apply it still to perfect the cure in that part wherein it is gradual and not complete ; and for the ease you have found, bless and love Him who endured so much uneasiness to that end.   There is a sweet mixture of sorrow and joy in contemplating these Stripes ; sorrow, surely, by sympathy, that they were *His* stripes, and joy, that they were our healing. Christians are too little mindful and sensible of this, and it may be, are somewhat guilty of that with which Ephraim is charged, Hos. xi. 3, *They knew not that I healed them.*

Ver. 25.   For ye were as sheep going astray, but are now returned to the Shepherd and Bishop of your souls.

In these few words, we have a brief and yet clear representation of the wretchedness of our natural condition, and of our happiness in Christ.   The resemblance is borrowed from the same place in the prophet Isaiah, (Chap. liii. ver. 6.)

Not to press the comparison, or as it is too usual with commentators, to strain it beyond the purpose, in reference to our lost estate, this is all, or the main circumstance wherein the resemblance with sheep holds,—our *wandering*, as forlorn and exposed to destruction, like a sheep that has strayed and wandered from the fold.   So taken, it imports, indeed, the loss of a better condition, the loss of the safety and happiness of the soul, of that good which is proper to it, as the suitable good of the brute creature here named, is, safe and good pasture.

That we may know there is no one exempt in nature from the guiltiness and misery of this wandering, the Prophet is express as to the universality of it. *All we have gone astray.* And though the Apostle here applies it in particular to his brethren, yet it falls not amiss to any others, *Ye were as sheep going astray.* Yea, the Prophet there, to the collective universal, adds a distributive, *Every man to his own way*, or a man to his way. They agree in this, that they all wander, though they differ in their several ways. There is an inbred proneness to stray in them all, more than in sheep, which are creatures naturally wandering, for each man hath his own way.

And this is our folly, that we flatter ourselves by comparison, and every one is pleased with himself because he is free from some wanderings of others; not considering that he is a wanderer too, though in another way; he hath his way, as those he looks on have theirs. And as men agree in wandering, though they differ in their way, so those ways agree in this, that they lead unto misery, and shall end in that. Think you there is no way to Hell, but the way to open profaneness? Yes, surely, many a way that seems smooth and *clean in a man's own eyes*, and yet will end in condemnation. Truth is but one, Error endless and interminable. As we say of natural life and death, so may we say in respect of spiritual, the way to life is one, but there are many out of it. *Lethi mille aditus.* Each one hath not opportunity nor ability for every sin, or every degree of sin, but each sins after his own mode and power. (Isa. xl. 20.)

Thy tongue, it may be, wanders not in the common path-road of oaths and curses, yet it wanders in secret calumnies, in detraction and defaming of others, though so conveyed as it scarcely appears; or if thou speak them not, yet thou art pleased to hear them. It wanders in trifling away the precious hours of irrecoverable time, with vain unprofitable babblings in thy converse; or if thou art much alone, or in company much silent, yet is not thy foolish mind still hunting vanity, following this self-pleasing design or the other, and seldom, and very slightly, if at all, conversant with God and the things of heaven, which, although they alone have the truest and the highest pleasure in them, yet to thy carnal mind are tasteless and unsavoury? There is scarcely any thing so light and childish, that thou wilt not more willingly and liberally bestow thy retired thoughts on, than upon those excellent, incomparable delights. Oh! the foolish heart of man! When it may seem deep and serious, how often is it at Domitian's exercise in his study, *catching flies!*

Men account little of the wandering of their hearts, and yet truly, that is most of all to be considered ; for *from thence are the issues of life* (Prov. iv. 23). It is the heart that hath forgotten God, and is roving after vanity : this causes all the errors of men's words and actions. A wandering heart makes wandering eyes, feet, and tongue it is the leading wanderer, that misleads all the rest. And as we are here called *straying sheep,* so within the heart itself of each of us, there is, as it were, a whole wandering flock, a multitude of fictions, (Gen. viii. 21,) ungodly devices. The word that signifies the evil of the thought in Hebrew, here רע from רוע is taken from that which signifies feeding of a flock, and it likewise signifies wandering ; and so these meet in our thoughts, they are a great flock and a wandering flock. This is the natural freedom of our thoughts ; they are free to wander from God and Heaven, and to carry us to perdition. And we are ¡guilty of many pollutions this way, which we never acted. Men are less sensible of heart-wickedness, if it break not forth ; but the heart is far more active in sin than any of the senses, or the whole body. The motion of spirits is far swifter than that of bodies. The mind can make a greater progress in any of these wanderings in one hour, than the body is able to follow in many days.

When the body is tied to attendance in the exercises wherein we are employed, yet know you not—(it is so much the worse if you do not know, and feel it, and bewail it)—know you not, I say, that the heart can take its liberty, and leave you nothing but a carcass ? This the unrenewed heart doth continually. *They come and sit before me as my people, but their heart is*

after their covetousness.   (Ezek. xxxiii. 31.)   It hath another
way to go, another God to wait on.

But are now returned.]   Whatsoever are the several ways
of our straying, all our wandering originates in the aversion of
the heart from God, whence of necessity follows a continual
unsettledness and disquiet.   The mind, *as a wave of the sea,
tossed to and fro with the wind,* tumbles from one sin and
vanity to another, and finds no rest; or, as a sick person tosses
from one side to another, and from one part of his bed to another, and perhaps changes his bed, in hope of ease, but still
it is further off, thus is the soul in all its wanderings.   But
shift and change as it will, no rest shall it find until it come to
this *returning* (Jer. ii. 36) :   *Why gaddest thou about so much
to change thy way ?   Thou shalt be ashamed of Egypt as thou
wast of Assyria.*   Nothing but sorrow and shame, till you
change all those ways for this one.   *Return, O Israel, says the
Lord, if thou wilt return, return unto Me.*   It is not changing
one of your own ways for another, that will profit you; but
in returning to Me is your salvation.

Seeing we find in our own experience, besides the woful end
of our wanderings, the present perplexity and disquiet of them,
why are we not persuaded to this, to give up with them all ?
Return unto thy rest, O my soul, says David: (Psalm. cxvi. 7 :)
this were our wisdom.

But is not that God in whom we expect rest, incensed against
us for our wandering ?   and is He not, being offended, *a con-
suming fire ?*   True; but this is the way to find acceptance and
peace, and satisfying comforts in returning : come first to this
Shepherd of souls, Jesus Christ, and by Him, come unto the
Father.   *No man comes unto the Father,* says he, *but by me.*
This is *via regia,* the high and right way of returning unto
God.   John x. 11 :   *I am the good shepherd;* and ver. 9, *I
am the door: by Me if any man enter in, he shall be saved.*
But if he miss this Door, he shall miss salvation too.   *Ye are
returned,* says the Apostle, *unto the Shepherd and Bishop of
your souls.*

There be three things necessary to restore us to our happiness, whence we have departed in our wanderings: 1. To take away the guiltiness of those former wanderings; 2. To reduce us into the way again; 3. To keep and lead us in it.

Now all these are performable only by this great Shepherd. 1. He did satisfy for the offence of our wanderings, and so remove our guiltiness. He himself, the Shepherd, became a sacrifice for His flock, a sheep or spotless lamb. So Isaiah liii. 6: *We like sheep have gone astray;* and immediately after the mention of our straying, it is added, *The Lord laid,* or, *made meet on him the iniquity of us all,* of all our strayings; and ver. 7, *He is brought as a lamb to the slaughter.* He who is our Shepherd, the same is the Lamb for sacrifice. So our Apostle, (ch. i.) *We are redeemed, not by silver and gold, but by the precious blood of Christ, as of a lamb without blemish and without spot.* So John x. 11: *He is the good Shepherd that lays down his life for his sheep.* Men think not on this: many of them who have some thoughts of returning and amendment, think not that there is a satisfaction due for past wanderings; and therefore they pass by Christ, and consider not the necessity of returning to Him, and by Him to the Father.

2. He brings them back into the way of life: *Ye are returned.* But think not it is by their own knowledge and skill that they discover their error, and find out the right path, or that by their own strength they return into it. No, if we would contest grammaticisms, the word here is passive: *ye are returned,* reduced, or caused to return. But this truth hangs not on so weak notions as are often used, either for or against it. In that prophecy, Ezek. xxxiv. 16, God says, *I will seek and bring again,* &c. And (Psalm xxiii. 3) David says, *He restoreth* or *returneth my soul.* And that this is the work of this Shepherd, the Lord Jesus, God-man, is clearly and frequently taught in the Gospel. He came for this very end: it was His errand and business in the world, *to seek and to save that which was lost.* And thus it is represented in the parable: (Luke xv. 4, 5:) he *goes after that which is lost, until he find it,* and then, having

found it, doth not only shew it the way, and say to it, Return, and so leave it to come after, but *he lays it on his shoulder*, and brings it home; and notwithstanding all his pains, instead of complaining against it for wandering, he rejoices in that he hath found and recovered it: *he lays it on his shoulder rejoicing.* And in this there is as much of the resemblance as in any other thing. Lost man can no more return unsought, than a sheep that wandereth, which is observed of all creatures to have least of that skill. Men may have some confused thoughts of returning, but to know the way and to come, unless they be sought out, they are unable. This is David's suit, though acquainted with the fold, *I have gone astray like a lost sheep: Lord, seek thy servant.* (Psalm cxix. *ult.*) This did our great and good Shepherd, through those difficult ways He was to pass for finding us, wherein He not only hazarded, but really laid down his life; and those shoulders which did bear the iniquity of our wanderings, by expiation, upon the same doth He bear and bring us back from it by effectual conversion.

3. He keeps and leads us on in that way into which he hath restored us. He leaves us not again to try our own skill, whether we can walk to heaven alone, being set into the path of it, but He still conducts us in it by his own hand, and that is the cause of our persisting in it, and attaining the blessed end of it. *He restoreth my soul*, says the Psalmist (Psalm xxiii. 2); and that is not all: he adds, *He leadeth me in the paths of righteousness for His name's sake.* Those paths are the *green pastures* meant, and the *still waters* that he speaks of. And thus we may judge whether we are of his flock. Are we *led in the paths of righteousness?* Do we delight ourselves in Him, and in his ways? Are they the proper refreshment of our souls? Do we find *His word sweet unto our taste?* Are we taken with the *green pastures* in it, and the crystal streams of consolations that glide through it? Can we discern *His voice*, and does it draw our hearts, so that we follow it? (John x. 27.)

The Shepherd and Bishop.] It was the style of Kings, to

be called Shepherds; and is the dignity of the Ministers of the Gospel, to have both these names. But this great Shepherd and Bishop is peculiarly worthy of these names, as supreme: He alone is the universal Shepherd and Bishop, and none but an antichrist, who makes himself as Christ, killing and destroying the flock, will assume this title which belongs only to the Lord, the great Owner of His flock. He himself is their great Shepherd and Bishop. All shepherds and bishops who are truly such, have their function and place from Him; they hold of Him, and follow His rule and example, in their inspection of the flock. It were the happiness of kingdoms, if magistrates and kings would set Him, His love, and meekness, and equity, before their eyes in their government. And all those who are properly His bishops, are under especial obligations to study this pattern, to warm their affections to the flock, and to excite a tender care of their salvation, by looking on this *Arch-bishop* and *Arch-shepherd*, (as our Apostle calls Him,) and in their measure, to follow his footsteps, spending their life and strength in seeking the good of His sheep, considering that they are subordinately shepherds of souls, that is, in dispensing spiritual things; so far the title is communicable.

The Lord Jesus is supremely and singularly such: they under Him are shepherds of souls, because their diligence concerns the soul, which excludes not the body in spiritual respects, as it is capable of things spiritual and eternal, by its union with the soul. But Christ is sovereign Shepherd of souls above all, and singular, in that He not only teaches them the doctrine of salvation, but purchased salvation for them, and inasmuch as He reaches the soul powerfully, which ministers by their own power cannot do. He lays hold on it, and restores, and leads it, and causes it to walk in His ways. In this sense it agrees to Him alone, as supreme, in the incommunicable sense.

And from His guidance, power, and love, flows all the comfort of his flock. When they consider their own folly and weakness, this alone gives them confidence, that His hand guides them ; and they believe in His strength, far surpassing that of the roaring lion. (John x. 28—30.) His wisdom, in knowing their particular state and their weakness, and His tender love in pitying them, and applying himself to it. Other shepherds, even faithful ones, may mistake them, and not know the way of leading them in some particulars, and they may be sometimes wanting in that tender affection that they owe ; or, if they have that, yet they are not able to bear them up, and support them powerfully : but this Shepherd is perfeet in all these respects. (Isa. xl. 11.) The young and weak Christians, or the elder at weak times, when they are big and heavy with some inward exercise of mind, which shall bring forth advantage and peace to them afterwards, them He *leads gently*, and uses them with the tenderness that their weakness requires.

And, in the general, He provides for His flock, and heals them when they are any way hurt, and washes them, and makes them fruitful ; so that they are as that flock described, Cant. iv. 2 ; they are comely, but their Shepherd much more so : *Formosi pecoris custos, formosior ipse.* They are given Him in the Father's purpose and choice, and so, those that return, are, even while they wander, *sheep* in some other sense than the rest which perish. They are, in the secret love of Election, of Christ's sheepfold, though not as yet actually brought into it. But when His time comes, wheresoever they wander, and how far off soever, even those who have strayed most, yet He restores them, and rejoices Heaven with their return, and leads them till He bring them to partake of the joy that is there. That is the end of the way wherein He guides them. (John x. 27, 28.) *They hear my voice and follow me.* And they shall never repent of having done so. To follow Him, is to follow life, for *He is the life.* He is in that glory which we desire ; and where would we be, if not where He is, who, at his departure from the world, said, *Where I am, there they shall be also ?* To this happy meeting and heavenly abode, may God, of His infinite mercy, bring us, through *Jesus Christ our Lord!* Amen.

CHAPTER III.

Ver. 1. Likewise, ye wives, be in subjection to your own husbands : that if any one obey not the word, they also, without the word, may be won by the conversation of the wives.

THE *tabernacle of the sun* (Psal. xix. 4) is set high in the Heavens; but it is so, that it may have influence below upon the earth. And the *word of God*, which is spoken of there immediately after, as being in many ways like it, holds resemblance in this particular: it is a sublime heavenly light, and yet descends, in its use, to the lives of men, in the variety of their stations, to warm and to enlighten, to regulate their affections and actions in whatsoever course of life they are called to. By a perfect revolution or circuit, as there it is said of the sun, it visits all ranks and estates; *its going forth is from the end of Heaven, and its circuit unto the ends of it, and there is nothing hid from the 'heat of it;* it disdains not to teach the very servants in their low condition and employments, how to behave themselves, and sets before them no meaner example than that of Jesus Christ, which is the highest of all examples. So here, the Apostle proceeds to give rules adapted to that relation which is the main one in families, that of *Husbands* and *Wives*. As for the order, it is indifferent; yet, possibly, he begins here at the duties of wives, because his former rules were given to inferiors, to subjects and servants; and the duty he commends particularly here to them, is, *subjection: Likewise, ye wives, be in subjection,* &c.

After men have said all they can, and much, it may be, to little purpose, in running the parallel between these two estates of life, marriage and celibacy, the result will be found, I conceive, all things being truly estimated, very little odds, even in

natural respects, in the things themselves, saving only as the
particular condition of persons, and the hand of Divine Providence, turn the balance the one way or the other.   The writing of satires against either, or panegyrics on the one in prejudice of the other, is but a caprice of men's minds, according to
their own humour ; but in respect of religion, the Apostle,
having scanned the subject to the full, leaves it indifferent,
only requiring in those who are so engaged, hearts as disengaged as may be, *that they that marry be as if they married
not*, &c. (1 Cor. vii. 29, 31.)   Within a while, it will be all
one ; as he adds that grave reason, *For the fashion* [σχῆμα]
of this world passeth—it is but a pageant, a shew of an hour
long [παράγει] *goes by*, and is no more seen.   Thus, the great
pomps and solemnities of marriages of kings and princes in
former times, where are they ?   Oh ! how unseemly is it to
have an immortal soul drowned in the esteem and affection
of any thing that perishes, and to be cold and indifferent in
seeking after a good that will last as long as itself !   Aspire to
that good which is the only match for the soul, that close
union with God which cannot be dissolved, which He calls an
everlasting marriage (Hos. ii. 19) ;   that will make you happy,
either with the other, or without it.   All the happiness of the
most excellent persons, and the very top of all affection and
prosperity meeting in human marriages, are but a dark and
weak representation of the solid joy which is in that mysterious
Divine union of the spirit of man with the *Father of Spirits*,
from whom it issues.   But this by the way.

   The common spring of all mutual duties, on both sides, must
be supposed to be *love ;* that peculiar conjugal love which
makes them one, will infuse such sweetness into the authority
of the Husband and the obedience of the Wife, as will make
their lives harmonious, like the sound of a well-tuned instrument ; whereas without that, having such a universal conjuncture of interest in all their affairs, they cannot escape frequent
contests and discords, which is a sound more unpleasant than
the jarring of untuned strings to an exact ear.   And this

should be considered in the choice, that it be not, as it is too often, (which causeth so many domestic ills,) contracted only as a bargain of outward advantages, but as an union of hearts. And where this is not, and there is something wanting in this point of affection, there, if the parties, or either of them, have any saving knowledge of God, and access to Him in prayer, they will be earnest suitors for His help in this, that His hand may set right what no other can ; that He who is love itself, may infuse that mutual love into their hearts now, which they should have sought sooner. And certainly, they who sensibly want this, and yet seek it not of Him, what wonder is it, though they find much bitterness and discontent ? Yea, where they agree, if it be only in natural affection, their observance of the duties required, is not by far either so comfortable and pleasing, or so sure and lasting, as when it ariseth from a religious and Christian love in both, which will cover many failings, and take things by the best side.

Love is the prime duty in both, the basis of all ; but because the particular character of it, as proper to the Wife, is conjugal obedience and subjection, therefore that is usually specified ; as Eph. v. 12, *Wives, submit yourselves unto your own husbands, as unto the Lord ;* so here. Now if it be such obedience as ought to arise from a special kind of love, then, the Wife would remember this, that it must not be constrained, uncheerful obedience : and the Husband would remember, that he ought not to require base and servi e obedience ; for both these are contrary to that love, whereof this obedience must carry the true tincture and relish, as flowing from it ; there all will hold right, where love commands, and love obeys.

This subjection, as all other, is qualified thus, that it be *in the Lord.* His authority is primitive, and binds first, and all others have their patents and privileges from Him ; therefore He is supremely and absolutely to be observed in all. If the Husband would draw the Wife to an irreligious course of life, he is not to be followed in this, but in all things indifferent this obedience must hold; which yet forbids not a modest advice and representation to the Husband, of that which is more convenient, but that done, a submissive yielding to the Husband's will is the suiting of this rule. Yea, possibly the Husband may not only imprudently but unlawfully will that which, if not in its own nature a thing unlawful, the Wife by reason of his will may obey lawfully, yea, could not lawfully disobey.

Now, though this subjection was a fundamental law of pure nature, and came from that Hand which made all things in perfect order, yet sin, which hath imbittered all human things with a curse, hath disrelished this subjection, and made it taste somewhat of a punishment, (Gen. iii. 16,) and that as a suitable punishment of the woman's abuse of the power she had with the man, to the drawing of him to disobedience against God.

The bitterness in this subjection arises from the corruption of nature in both: in the Wife a perverse desire rather to command, or at least a repining discontent at the obligation to obey; and this is increased by the disorder, and imprudence, and harshness of Husbands in the use of their authority.

But in a Christian, the conscience of Divine appointment will carry it, and weigh down all difficulties; for the Wife considers her station, that she is set in it, [ὑποτασσόμεναι,] it is the rank the Lord's hand hath placed her in, and therefore she will not break it: from respect and love to Him, she can digest much frowardness in a husband, and make that her patient subjection a sacrifice to God: Lord, I offer this to thee, and for thy sake I humbly bear it.

The worth and love of a husband may cause that respect, where this rule moves not; but the Christian Wife who hath love to God, though her husband be not so comely, nor so wise, nor any way so amiable, as many others, yet because he is her *own husband*, and because of the Lord's command in the general, and His providence in the particular disposal of His own, therefore she loves and obeys.

That if any obey not the word.] This supposes a particular

câse, and applies the rule to it, taking it for granted that a
believing wife will cheerfully observe and respect a believing
husband, but if he is an unbeliever, yet that unties not this
engagement; yea, there is something in this case which presses
it and binds it the more, a singular good which probably may
follow upon obeying such. By *that good conversation*, they
may be gained, who believe not the word: not that they could
be fully converted without the word; but having a prejudice
against the word, that may be removed by the carriage of a
believing wife, and they may be somewhat mollified, and prepared, and induced to hearken to religion, and take it into consideration.

This gives not Christians a warrant to draw on themselves
this task, and make themselves this work, by choosing to be
joined to an unbeliever, either a profane or merely an unconverted husband or wife; but teacheth them, being so matched,
what should be their great desire, and their suitable carriage in
order to the attainment of it. And in the primitive Christian
times, this fell out often: by the gospel preached, the husband
might be converted from gross infidelity, Judaism, or Paganism,
and not the wife; or the wife, (which is the supposition here,)
and not the husband; and then came in the use of this consideration.

And this is the freedom of Divine Grace to pick and choose
where It will, *one of a family, or two of a tribe,* as the
Prophet hath it, Jer. iii. 14; and according to our Saviour's
word, *two in one bed, the one taken and the other left;*
(Luke xvii. 34;) some selected ones in a congregation, or in
a house, a child, possibly, or servant, or wife, while It leaves
the rest. The Apostle seems to imply particularly, that there
were many instances of this, wives being converts, and their
husbands unbelieving. We can determine nothing as to their
conjecture, who think that there will be more of that sex,
here called the *weaker vessels*, than of the other, who shall be
vessels of honour, which God seasons with grace here, and hereafter will fill with glory; but this is clear, that many of them are

converted, while many men, and divers of them very wise and learned men, having the same or far greater means and opportunities, do perish in unbelief. This, I say, evidences the liberty and the power of the Spirit of God, that *wind that bloweth where it listeth ;* and withal it suits with that word of the Apostle, that the Lord this way abases those things that men account so much of, *and hath chosen the weak things of the world to confound the mighty.* (1 Cor. i. 26.) Nor doth the pliableness and tenderness of their affections (though Grace, once wrought, may make good use of that) make their conversion easier, but the harder rather, for through nature's corruption, they would by that be led to yield more to evil than to good ; but the efficacy of Grace appears much in establishing their hearts in the love of God, and in making them, when once possessed with that, to be inflexible and invincible by the temptations of the world, and the strength and sleights of Satan.

That which is here said of *their conversation,* holds of the Husband in the like case, and of friends and kindred, and generally, of all Christians, in reference to them with whom they converse; that their spotless, holy carriage as Christians, and, in their particular stations, as Christian husbands, or wives, or friends, is a very likely and hopeful means of converting others who believe not. Men who are prejudiced, observe actions a great deal more than words. In those first times especially, the blameless carriage of Christians did much to the increasing of their number.

Strive, ye wives, and others, to adorn and commend the religion you profess to others, especially those nearest you, who are averse. Give no just cause of scandal and prejudice against religion. Beware not only of gross failings and ways of sin, but of such imprudences as may expose you and your profession. Study both a holy and a wise carriage, and pray much for it. *If any of you lack wisdom, let him ask of God that giveth to all men liberally, and upbraideth not, and it shall be given him.* (Jam. i. 5.)

But if wives and other private Christians be thus obliged, how much more the ministers of the word! Oh! that we could remember our deep obligations to holiness of life! It has been rightly said, *Either teach none, or let your life teach too.* *Cohelleth, anima concionatrix,* the *preaching soul,* must the preacher be, (Eccl. i. 1,) the word of life springing from inward affection, and then, *vita concionatrix,* the *preaching life.* The Sunday's sermon lasts but an hour or two, but holiness of life is a continued sermon all the week long.

They also without the word may be won.] The conversion of a soul is an inestimable gain; it is a high trading and design to go about it. Oh! the precious soul, but how undervalued by most! Will we believe Him who knew well the price of it, for He paid it, that the whole visible world is not worth one so , the gaining of it all cannot countervail that loss? (Matt. xvi. 26.) This, wives, and husbands, and parents, and friends, if themselves converted, would consider seriously, and apply themselves to pray much that their unconverted relations, in nature dead, may be enlivened, and that they may receive them from death; and they would esteem nothing, rest in no natural content or gain without that, at least, without using incessant diligence in seeking it, and their utmost skill and pains. But above all, this is the peculiar task of ministers, as the Apostle often repeats it of himself, that *unto the Jews* he *became as a Jew,* that he might *gain the Jews,* &c. (1 Cor. ix.) All gains on earth are base in comparison with this. *Me malè amando, me perdidi; et te solum quærendo et purè amando, me et te pariter inveni:* By loving self amiss, myself I lost; by seeking Thee, and singly, sincerely loving Thee, at once myself and Thee I found. (Thomas à Kempis.) A soul converted is *gained* to itself, *gained* to the pastor, or friend, or wife, or husband, who sought it, and *gained* to Jesus Christ; added to His treasury, who thought not His own precious blood too dear to lay out for this gain.

Ver. 2.   While they behold your chaste conversation coupled with fear.

As all graces are connected in their own nature, so it is altogether necessary that they be found in connexion for the end
here propounded, the conversion of those who are strangers to
religion, and possessed with false notions of it, and prejudices
against it.   It is not the regularity of some particular actions,
nor the observance of some duties, that will serve ; but it is an
even uniform frame of life that the Apostle here teaches Christian wives, particularly in reference to this end, the gaining, or
conversion of unbelieving husbands.   And this we have both
in that word, *their conversation*, which signifies the whole
course and tract of their lives, and in the particular specifying
of the several duties proper to that relation and state of life.
1. Subjection. 2. Chastity. 3. Fear. 4. Modesty in outward
ornaments.   5. The inward ornaments of meekness and quietness of spirit.

The combination of these things makes up such a wife, and
the exercise of them throughout her life makes up such a conversation, as adorns and commends the religion she professes,
and is a fit, and may be a successful means of converting the
husband who as yet professes it not.

Chaste conversation.]   It is the proper character of a Christian, to study purity in all things, as the word (ἁγνὴν) in its
extent signifies.   Let the world turn that to a reproach, call
them as you will, this is sure, that none have less fancy and
presumption of *purity*, than those who have most desire of it.
But the particular pureness here intended, is, as it is rendered,
that of *chastity*, as the word is often taken ; it being a grace
that peculiarly deserves that name, as the sins contrary to it
are usually and deservedly called *uncleanness*.   It is the pure
whiteness of the soul to be chaste, to abhor and disdain the
swinish puddle of lust, than which there is nothing that doth
more debase the excellent soul ; nothing that more evidently
draws it down below itself, and makes it truly brutish.   The
three kinds of chastity—virginal, conjugal, and vidual, are all

of them acceptable to God, and suitable to the profession of a Christian; therefore, in general only, whatsoever be our condition in life, let us in that way conform to it, and follow the Apostle's rule, *possessing* these our earthen *vessels*, our bodies, in *holiness* and *honour;* (by which is there expressed this same chastity;) and this we shall do, if we rightly remember our calling as Christians, in what sort of life soever; as there he tells us, *God hath not called us to uncleanness, but unto holiness.* (1 Thes. iv. 7.)

With fear.] Either a reverential respect to their husbands, or, the fear of God; whence flows best both that and all other observance, whether of conjugal or any other Christian duties. Be not presumptuous, as some, because you aie chaste, but so contemper your conversation with a religious fear of God, that you dare not take liberty to offend Him in any other thing, and, according to His institution, with a reverential fear of your husbands, shunning to offend them. But possibly, this fear doth particularly relate to the other duty with which it was joined, *Chaste conversation with fear;* fearing the least stain of chastity, or the very least appearance of any thing not suiting with it. It is a delicate, timorous grace, afraid of the least air, or shadow of any thing that hath but a resemblance of wronging it, in carriage, or speech, or apparel, as follows in the 3d and 4th verses.

Ver. 3.   Whose adorning, let it not be that outward adorning of plaiting the hair, and of wearing of gold, or of putting on of apparel;

Ver. 4. But let it be the hidden man of the heart, in that which is not corruptible, even the ornament of a meek and quiet spirit, which is in the sight of God of great price.

THAT nothing may be wanting to the qualifying of a Christian wife, she is taught how to dress herself: supposing a general desire, but especially in that sex, of ornament and comeliness: the sex which began first our engagement to the necessity of clothing, having still a peculiar propensity to be curious in that, to improve the necessity to an advantage.

The direction here given corrects the misplacing of this diligence, and addresses it right : *Let it not be of the outward man, in plaiting*, &c.

Our perverse, crooked hearts turn all we use into disorder. Those two necessities of our life, *food* and *raiment*, how few know the right measure and bounds of them ! Unless poverty be our carver, and cut us short, who, almost, is there that is not bent to something excessive ! Far more are beholden to the lowliness of their estate, than to the lowliness of their mind, for sobriety in these things ; and yet, some will not be so bounded neither, but will profusely lavish out upon trifles, to the sensible prejudice of their estate.

It is not my purpose, nor do I think it very needful, to debate many particulars of apparel and ornament of the body, their lawfulness or unlawfulness : only,

First, It is out of doubt, that though clothing was first drawn on by necessity, yet all regard of comeliness and ornament in apparel is not unlawful ; nor doth the Apostle's expression here, rightly considered, fasten that upon the adorning he here speaks of. He doth no more universally condemn the use of gold for ornament, than he doth any other comely raiment, which here he means by that general word of *putting on of apparel;* for his [*not*] is comparative,—*not this adorning, but the ornament of a meek spirit,* that rather, and as being much more comely and precious ; as that known expression, *I will have mercy, and not sacrifice.*

Secondly, According to the different place and quality of persons, there may be a difference in this : thus, the robes of judges and princes are not only for personal ornament, but because there is in them, especially to vulgar eyes, which seldom look deeper than the outside of things, there is, I say, in that apparel a representation of authority or majesty, which befits their place ; and besides this, other persons who are not in public place, men, or women, (who are here particularly directed,) yet may have in this some mark of their rank ; and in persons otherwise little distant, some allowance may be made for the habits and breeding of some beyond others, or the quality of their society, and those with whom they converse.

Thirdly, It is not impossible that there may be in some an affected pride in the meanness of apparel, and in others, under either neat or rich attire, a very humble unaffected mind; using it upon some of the aforementioned engagements, or such like, and yet the heart not at all upon it. *Magnus qui fictilibus utitur tanquam argento, nec ille minor qui argento tanquam fictilibus*, says Seneca : Great is he who enjoys his earthenware as if it were plate, and not less great is the man to whom all his plate is no more than earthenware.

Fourthly, It is as sure as any of these, that real excess and vanity in apparel will creep in, and will always willingly convey itself under the cloak of some of these honest and lawful considerations. This is a prime piece of our heart's deceit, not only to hold out fair pretences to others, but to put the trick upon ourselves, to make ourselves believe we are right and single-minded in those things wherein we are directly serving our lusts and feeding our own vanity.

Fifthly, To a sincere and humble Christian, very little either dispute or discourse concerning this will be needful. A tender conscience, and a heart purified from vanity and weaned from the world, will be sure to regulate this, and all other things of this nature, after the safest manner, and will be wary, 1. Of lightness and fantastic garb in apparel, which is the very bush or sign hanging out, that tells a vain mind lodges within; and 2. Of excessive costliness, which both argues and feeds the pride of the heart, and defrauds, if not others of their dues, yet the poor of thy charity, which, in God's sight, is a due debt too. Far more comfort shalt thou have on thy death-bed, to remember that such a time, instead of putting lace on my own clothes, I helped a naked back to clothing, I abated somewhat of my former superfluities, to supply the poor's necessities—far sweeter will this be, than to remember, that I could needlessly cast away many pounds to serve my pride, rather than give a penny to relieve the poor.

As conscientious Christians will not exceed in the thing itself, so, in as far as they use lawful ornament and comeliness, they will do it without bestowing much either of diligence or delight on the business.

To have the mind taken and pleased with such things, is so foolish and childish a thing, that if most might not find it in themselves, they would wonder at it in many others, of years and common sense. *Non bis pueri, sed semper:* Not twice children, but always. And yet truly, it is a disease that few escape. It is strange upon how poor things men and women will be vain, and think themselves somebody; not only upon some comeliness in their face or feature, which though poor, is yet a part of themselves, but of things merely without them; that they are well lodged, or well mounted, or well apparelled, either richly, or well in fashion. Light empty minds are, like bladders, blown up with any thing. And they who perceive not this in themselves, are the most drowned in it; but such as have found it out, and abhor their own follies, are still hunting and following these in themselves, to beat them out of their hearts, and to shame them from such fopperies. The soul fallen from God, hath lost its true worth and beauty; and therefore it basely descends to these mean things, to serve and dress the body, and take share with it of its unworthy borrowed ornaments, while it hath lost and forgotten God, and seeks not after Him, knows not that He alone is the beauty and ornament of the soul, (Jer. ii. 32,) His spirit, and the graces of it, its rich attire, as is here particularly specified in one excellent grace, and it holds true in the rest.

The Apostle doth indeed expressly, on purpose, check and forbid vanity and excess in apparel, and excessive delight in lawful decorum, but his prime end is to recommend this other ornament of the soul, *The hidden man of the heart.*

It is the thing the best philosophy aimed at, as some of their wisest men do express it, to reduce men, as much as may be, from their body to their soul; but this is the thing that true religion alone doth effectually and thoroughly, calling them off from the pampering and feeding of a morsel for the worms, to the nourishing of that immortal being infused into it, and directing them to the proper nourishment of souls, the *Bread that came down from Heaven.* (John vi. 27.)

So here, the Apostle pulls off from Christian women their vain outside ornaments; but is not this a wrong, to spoil all their dressing and fineness? No, he doth this, only to send them to a better wardrobe: there is much profit in the change.

All the gold and other riches of the temple prefigured the excellent graces of Christians: of Christ indeed first, as having all fulness in Himself, and as furnishing it to them, but secondarily, of Christians, as the living temples of God. So, Psalm xlv. 13, the Church is *all glorious,* but it is *within.* And the embroidery, the variety of graces, the lively colours of other graces, shine best on the dark ground of humility. Christ delights to give much ornament to his Church, commends what she hath, and adds more. *Thy neck is comely with chains: we will make thee borders of gold.* (Cant. i. 10, 11.)

The particular grace the Apostle recommends, is particularly suitable to his subject in hand, the conjugal duty of wives; nothing so much adorning their whole carriage, as this *meekness* and *quietness of spirit.* But it is, withal, the comeliness of every Christian, in every estate. It is not a woman's garment or ornament, improper for men. There is somewhat (as I may say) of a particular cut or fashion of it for wives towards their husbands, and in their domestic affairs; but men, all men ought to wear of the same stuff, yea, if I may so speak, of the same piece, for it is in all one and the same spirit, and fits the stoutest and greatest commanders. Moses was a great general, and yet not less great in this virtue, *the meekest man on earth.*

Nothing is more uncomely in a wife than an uncomposed, turbulent spirit, that is put out of frame with every trifle, and inventive of false causes of disquietness and fretting to itself. And so in a husband, and in all, an unquiet, passionate mind lays itself naked, and discovers its own deformity to all. The greatest part of things that vex us, do so not from their own nature or weight, but from the unsettledness of our minds. *Multa nos offendunt quæ non lædunt:* Many things offend us which do not hurt us. How comely is it to see a composed, firm mind and carriage, that is not lightly moved!

I urge not a stoical stupidity, but that in things which deserve sharp reproof, the mind keep in its own station and seat still, not shaken out of itself, as the most are; that the tongue utter not unseemly, rash words, nor the hand act any thing that discovers the mind hath lost its command for the time. But truly, the most know so ill how to use just anger upon just cause, that it is easier, and the safer extreme, not to be angry, but still calm and serene, as the upper region; not as the place of continual tempest and storms, as the most are. Let it pass for a kind of sheepishness to be meek; it is a likeness to Him who *was as a sheep before the shearers, not opening his mouth;* it is a portion of *His* spirit.

The Apostle commends his exchange of ornaments, by two things. 1. This is incorruptible, and therefore fits an incorruptible soul. Your varieties of jewels and rich apparel are perishing things; you shall one day see a heap made of all, and that all on a flame. And in reference to yourselves, they perish sooner. When death strips you of your nearest garment, your flesh, all the others, which were but loose upper garments above it, must off too: it gets indeed a covering to the grave, but the soul is left stark naked, if no other clothing be provided for it, for the body was but borrowed; then it is made bare of all. But spiritual ornaments, and this of humility, and meekness amongst them, remain and are incorruptible; they neither wear out, nor go out of fashion, but are still the better for the wearing, and shall last eternity, and shine there in full lustre.

And, 2, Because the opinion of others is much regarded in matter of apparel, and it is mostly in respect to this that we use ornament in it, he tells us of the account in which this is held: men think it poor and mean, nothing more exposed to contempt than the *spirit of meekness,* it is mere folly with men,—that is no matter; this overweighs all their disesteem, *It is with God*

of great price; and things are indeed as He values them, and
no otherwise. Though it be not the country fashion, yet it is
the fashion at Court, yea it is the King's own fashion, Matt.
xi. 29, *Learn of me, for I am meek and lowly of heart.* Some,
who are court-bred, will send for the masters of fashions; though
they live not in the Court, and though the peasants think them
strange dresses, yet they regard not that, but use them as finest
and best. Care not what the world say; you are not to stay
long with them. Desire to have both fashions and stuffs from
Court, from Heaven, this *spirit of meekness,* and it shall be
sent you. It is never right in any thing with us, till we attain
to this, to tread on the opinion of men, and eye nothing but
God's approbation.

Ver. 5. For after this manner, in the old time, the holy women also,
who trusted in God, adorned themselves.

Ver. 6. Even as Sarah obeyed Abraham, calling him Lord; whose
daughters ye are as long as ye do well, and are not afraid with any
amazement.

THE Apostle enforces his doctrine by example, the most com-
pendious way of teaching. Hence, the right way to use the
Scriptures, is, to regulate our manners by them; as by their
precepts, so by their examples.. And for this end it is that a
great part of the Bible is historical. There is not in the Saints
a transmigration of souls, but there is, so to speak, a oneness
of soul, they being in all ages partakers of the self-same spirit.
Hence, pious and obedient wives are here called the *daughters
of Sarah.* Such women are here designated as, 1. Holy;
2. Believing; 3. Firm and resolute; *not afraid with any
amazement.* Though by nature they are fearful, yet they are
rendered of undaunted spirits, by a holy, clean, and pure conscience. Believing wives, who fear God, are not terrified;
their minds are established in a due obedience to God, and
also towards their husbands.

Ver. 7. Likewise, ye husbands, dwell with them, according to knowledge, giving honour unto the wife, as unto the weaker vessel, and as being heirs together of the grace of life; that your prayers be not hindered.

YOUR wives are subject to you, but you likewise are subject to this word, by which all ought, in all stations, to be directed, and by which, however, all shall one day be judged. And are you *alike* subject as they [ὁμοίως]: parents as children, masters as servants, and kings as their subjects; all hold of a Superior, and it is high treason against the majesty of God, for any, in any place of command, to dream of an unbounded absolute authority, in opposition to Him.

A spirit of prudence, or *knowledge*, particularly suitable and relating to this subject, is required as the light and rule by which the Husband's whole economy and carriage is to be guided. It is required that he endeavour after that civil prudence for the ordering of his affairs, which tends to the good of his family : but chiefly a pious, religious prudence, for regulating his mind and carriage as a Christian husband ; that he study the rule of Scripture in this particular, which many do not, neither advising with it what they should do, nor laying it, by reflection, upon their past actions, examining by it what they have done. Now, this is the great fault in all praetical things: most know something of them, but inadvertency and inconsideration, our not ordering our ways by that light, is the thing that spoils all.

Knowledge is required in the Wife, but more eminently in *the Husband*, as the head, the proper seat of knowledge. It is possible, that the Wife may sometimes have the advantage of knowledge, either natural wit and judgment, or a great measure of understanding of spiritual things: but this still holds, that the Husband is bound to improve the measure both of natural and of spiritual gifts that he hath, or can attain to, and to apply them usefully to the ordering of his conjugal carriage ; and that he understand himself obliged somewhat the more, in the very notion of a husband, both to seek after and to use that prudence which is peculiarly required for his due deportment. And a Christian wife, who is more largely en-dowed, yet will shew all due respect to the measure of wisdom, though it be less, which is bestowed upon her husband.

Dwell with them.] This indeed implies and supposes their abiding with their wives, so far as their calling and lawful affairs permit ; but I conceive, that what it expressly means, is, all the conversation and duties of that estate ; that they so behave themselves in dwelling with them, as becomes *men of knowledge,* wise and prudent husbands ; which returns them usually the gain of the full reverence and respect due to them, of which they rob and divest themselves, who are either of a foolish or trifling carriage, or of too austere and rigid a conver-sation.

Giving honour unto the Wife.] This, I conceive, is not, as some take it, convenient maintenance, though that is a requisite duty too, and may be taken in under this word : but it seems to be, chiefly, a due conjugal esteem of them, and respect to them, the Husband not vilifying and despising them, which will be apt to grieve and exasperate them ; not disclosing the weaknesses of the wife to others, nor observing them too narrowly himself, but hiding them both from others, and his own eyes by love ; not seeing them further than love itself requires, that is, to the wise rectifying of them by mild advices and admonitions that flow from love. And to this the reasons indeed suit well. It seems at first a little incongruous, *Honour* because *weaker,* but not when we consider the kind of honour ; not of reve-rence as superior, for that is their part, but of esteem and re-spect, without which, indeed, love cannot consist, for we cannot love that which we do not in some good measure esteem. And care should be taken that they be not contemned and slighted, even because they are weaker ; for, of all injuries, contempt is one of the most smarting and sensible, especially to weak per-sons, who feel most exactly the least touches of this. *Omne infirmum naturâ querulum ; Every weak being is naturally peevish ;* whereas greater spirits are a little harder against opi-

nion, and more indifferent for it. Some wives may, indeed, be
of a stronger mind and judgment than their husbands, yet these
rules respect the general condition of the sexes, and speak of
the females as ordinarily weaker.

Again, Love, which is ever to be supposed one article, and
the main one, (for nothing indeed can be right where that supposition proves false,) love, I say, supposed, this reason is very
enforcing, that the weaker the vessels be, the more tenderly
they should be used; and the more a prudent passing by of
frailties is needful, there love will study it, and bestow it the
more. Yea, this tie, you know, makes two one; and that
which is a part of ourselves, the more it needs in that respect,
the *more comeliness we put upon it,* as the Apostle St. Paul
tells us, 1 Cor. xii. 23. And this further may be considered,
that there is a mutual need of this *honouring,* which consists in
not despising and in covering of frailties, as is even implied in
this, that the Woman is not called simply weak, but the *weaker,*
and the Husband, who is generally, by nature's advantage, or
should be the stronger, yet is weak too; for both are vessels
of earth, and therefore frail; both polluted with sin, and
therefore subject to a multitude of sinful follies and frailties.
But as the particular frailty of their nature pleads on behalf of
women for that *honour,* so, the other reason added, is taken,
not from their particular disadvantage, but from their common privilege and advantage of grace as Christians, that the
Christian Husband and Wife are equally *co-heirs* of the same
grace of life.

As being heirs together of the grace of life.] This is that
which most strongly binds all these duties on the hearts of
Husbands and Wives, and most strongly indeed binds their
hearts together, and makes them one. If each be reconciled
unto God in Christ, and so an heir of life, and one with God,
then are they truly one in God with each other; and that
is the surest and sweetest union that can be. Natural love
hath risen very high in some husbands and wives; but the
highest of it falls very far short of that which holds in God

Hearts concentring in Him, are most and excellently one.
That love which is cemented by youth and beauty, when these
moulder and decay, as soon they do, fades too. That is
somewhat purer, and so more lasting, which holds in a natural or moral harmony of minds; yet these likewise may alter
and change by some great accident. But the most refined,
most spiritual, and most indissoluble, is that which is knit with
the highest and purest Spirit. And the ignorance or disregard
of this, is the great cause of so much bitterness, or so little
true sweetness, in the life of most married persons; because
God is left out, because they meet not as one in Him.

Heirs together.] Loth will they be to despise one another,
who are both bought with the precious blood of one Redeemer,
and loth to grieve one another. Being in Him brought into
peace with God, they will entertain true peace betwixt themselves, and not suffer any thing to disturb it. They have
hopes to meet, one day, where is nothing but perfect concord
and peace; they will therefore live as heirs of that life here,
and make their present estate as like to Heaven as they can,
and so, a pledge and evidence of their title to that inheritance
of peace which is there laid up for them. And they will not
fail to put one another often in mind of those hopes and that
inheritance, and mutually to advance and further each other
towards it. Where this is not the case, it is to little purpose
to speak of other rules. Where neither party aspires to
this heirship, live they otherwise as they will, there is one
common inheritance abiding them, one inheritance of everlasting flames; and, as they do increase the sin and guiltiness
of one another by their irreligious conversation, so that which
some of them do wickedly here, upon no great cause, they shall
have full cause for doing there; cause to curse the time of their
coming together, and that shall be a piece of their exercise
for ever. But happy those persons, in any society of marriage or friendship, who converse together as those that shall
live eternally together in glory. This indeed is the sum of all
duties.

Life.] A sweet word, but sweetest of all in this sense! That life above, is indeed alone worthy the name, and this we have here, in comparison, let it not be called life, but a continual dying, an incessant journey towards the grave. If you reckon years, it is but a short moment to him that attains the fullest old age; but reckon miseries and sorrows, it is long to him that dies young. Oh! that this only blessed life were more known, and then it would be more desired.

Grace.] This is the tenor of this heirship, Free Grace: this *life* is a free gift. (Rom. vi. *ult.*) No life so spotless, either in marriage or virginity, as to lay claim to this life upon other terms. If we consider but a little what it is, and what we are, this will be quickly out of question with us; and we shall be most gladly content to hold it thus, by deed of gift, and shall admire and extol that Grace which bestows it.

That your prayers be not hindered.] He supposes in Christians the necessary and frequent use of this; takes it for granted, that the heirs of life cannot live without prayer. This is the proper breathing and language of these heirs, none of whom are dumb; they can all speak. These heirs, if they be alone, they pray alone; if heirs together, and living together, they pray together. Can the husband and wife have that love, wisdom, and meekness, which may make their life happy, and that blessing which may make their affairs successful, while they neglect God, the only giver of these and all good things? You think these needless motives, but you cannot think how it would sweeten your converse if it were used: it is prayer that sanctifies, seasons, and blesses all. And it is not enough that they pray when with the family, but even husband and wife together by themselves, and also with their children; that they, especially the mother, as being most with them in their childhood, when they begin to be capable, may draw them apart, and offer them to God, often praying with them, and instructing them in their youth; for they are pliable while young, as glass is when hot, but after, will sooner break than bend.

But, above all, Prayer is necessary as they are heirs of Heaven, often sending up their desires thither. You that are not much in prayer, appear as if you look for no more than what you have here. If you had an inheritance and treasure above, would not your hearts delight to be there? Thus, the heart of a Christian is in the constant frame of it, but after a special manner Prayer raises the soul above the world, and sets it in Heaven; it is its near access unto God, and dealing with Him, specially about those affairs which concern that inheritance. Now in this lies a great part of the comfort a Christian can have here; and the Apostle knew this, that he would gain any thing at their hands, which he pressed by this argument, that otherwise they would be *hindered in their prayers*. He knew that they who are acquainted with prayer, find such unspeakable sweetness in it, that they will rather do any thing than be prejudiced in that.

Now the breach of conjugal love, the jars and contentions of husband and wife, do, out of doubt, so leaven and imbitter their spirits, that they are exceeding unfit for prayer, which is the sweet harmony of the soul in God's ears; and when the soul is so far out of tune as those distempers make it, He cannot but perceive it, whose ear is the most exact of all, for He made and tuned the ear, and is the fountain of harmony. It cuts the sinews and strength of prayer, makes breaches and gaps, as wounds at which the spirits fly out, as the cutting of a vein, by which, as they speak, it bleeds to death. When the soul is calm and composed, it may behold the face of God shining on it. And those who pray together should not only have hearts in tune within themselves in their own frame, but tuned together; especially husband and wife, who are one, they should have hearts consorted and sweetly tuned to each other for prayer. So the word is, (ἐὰν συμφωνήσωσιν,) Matt xviii. 19.

And it is true, in the general, that all unwary walking in Christians wrongs their communion with Heaven, and casts a damp upon their prayers, so as to clog the wings of it. These

two mutually help one another, *prayer* and *holy conversation:*
the more exactly we walk, the more fit are we for prayer; and
the more we pray, the more are we enabled to walk exactly;
and it is a happy life to find the correspondence of these two,
calling on the Lord, and *departing from iniquity.* (1 Tim. ii.
19.)   Therefore, that you may pray much, live holily; and,
that you may live holily, be much in prayer.   Surely such are
the heirs of glory, and this is their way to it.

Ver. 8. Finally, be ye all of one mind, having compassion one of another;
love as brethren, be pitiful, be courteous.

HERE the particular rules the Apostle gives to several relations,
fall in again to the main current of his general exhortation,
which concerns us all as Christians.   The return of his discourse to this universality, is expressed in that *Finally,* and the
universality of these duties in *All.*   It is neither possible nor
convenient to descend to every particular; but there is supposed
in a Christian an ingenuous and prudent spirit, to adapt those
general rules to his particular actions and conversation; squaring by them beforehand, and examining by them after.   And
yet therein the most fail.   Men hear these as general discourses,
and let them pass so; they apply them not, or, if they do, it is
readily to some other person.   But they are addressed to all,
that each one may regulate himself by them; and so these
divine truths are like a well-drawn picture, which looks particularly upon every one amongst the great multitude that look
upon it.   And this one verse hath a cluster of five Christian
graces or virtues.   That which is in the middle, as the stalk
or root of the rest, *Love* and the others growing out of it, two
on each side, *Unanimity* and *Sympathy* on the one, and *Pity*
and *Courtesy* on the other.   But we shall take them as they lie.

Of one mind.] This doth not only mean union in judgment,
but it extends likewise to affection and action; especially in so
far as they relate to, and depend upon, the other.   And so, I
conceive, it comprehends, in its full latitude, a harmony and

agreement of minds, and affections, and carriage in Christians, as making up one body, and a serious study of preserving and increasing that agreement in all things, but especially in spiritual things, in which their communion doth primely consist. And because, in this, the consent of their judgments in matters of religion is a prime point, therefore we will consider that a little more particularly.

And *First*, What it is not.

1. It is not a careless indifferency concerning those things. Not to be troubled about them at all, nor to make any judgment concerning them, this is not a loving agreement, arising from oneness of spirit, but a dead stupidity, arguing a total spiritlessness. As the agreement of a number of dead bodies together, which indeed do not strive and contest, that is, they move not at all, because they live not; so, that concord in things of religion, which is a not considering them, nor acting of the mind about them, is the fruit and sign either of gross ignorance, or of irreligion. They who are wholly ignorant of spiritual things, are content you determine and impose upon them what you will; as in the dark there is no difference nor choice of colours, they are all one. But, 2. Which is worse, in some this peaceableness about religion arises from an universal unbelief and disaffection; and that sometimes comes of the much search and knowledge of debates and controversies in religion. Men having so many disputes about religion in their heads, and no life of religion in their hearts, fall into a conceit that all is but juggling, and that the easiest way is, to believe nothing; and these agree with any, or rather with none. Sometimes it is from a profane supercilious disdain of all these things; and many there be among these of Gallio's temper, who *care for none of these things*, and who account all questions in religion, as he did, but matter of words and names. And by this all religions may agree together. But that were not a natural union produced by the active heat of the spirit, but a confusion rather, arising from the want of it; not a knitting together, but a freezing together, as cold congregates all bodies,

how heterogeneous soever, sticks, stones, and water ; but heat
makes first a separation of different things, and then unites
those that are of the same nature.

And to one or other of these two is reducible much of the
common quietness of people's minds about religion. All that
implicit Romish agreement which they boast of, what is it, but
a brutish ignorance of spiritual things, authorised and recommended for that very purpose? And amongst the learned of
them, there are as many idle differences and disputes as amongst
any. It is an easy way, indeed, to agree, if all will put out
their eyes and follow the blind guiding of their judge of controversies. This is that πάνσοφον φάρμακον, their great device
for peace, to let the Pope determine all. If all will resolve to
be cozened by him, he will agree them all. As if the consciences
of men should only find peace by being led by the nose at one
man's pleasure ! A way the Apostle Paul clearly renounces :
*Not for that we have dominion over your faith, but are helpers
of your joy ; for by faith ye stand.* (2 Cor. i. 24.)

And though we have escaped this, yet much of our common
union of minds, I fear, proceeds from no other than the aforementioned causes, want of knowledge, and want of affection to
religion. You that boast you live conformably to the appointments of the Church, and that no one hears of your noise, we
may thank the ignorance of your minds for that kind of quietness. But the unanimity here required is another thing ; and
before I unfold it, I shall premise this, That although it be
very difficult, and it may be impossible, to determine what
things are alone fundamental in religion, under the notion of
difference, intended by that word, yet it is undoubted that
there be some truths more absolutely necessary, and therefore
accordingly more clearly revealed than some others ; there are
μέγαλα τοῦ νόμου, *great things of the Law*, and so of the
Gospel. And though no part of Divine truth, once fully
cleared, ought to be slighted, yet there are things that may be
true, and still are but of less importance, and of less evidence
than others ; and this difference is wisely to be considered by

Christians, for the interest of this agreement of minds here re-commended. And concerning it we may safely conclude,

1. That Christians ought to have a clear and unanimous belief of the mysteries and principles of faith, to agree in those without controversy. 2. They ought to be diligent in the re-search of truth in all things that concern faith and religion; and withal to use all due means for the fullest consent and agreement in them all, that possibly can be attained. 3. Perfect and universal consent in all, after all industry bestowed on it, for any thing we know, is not here attainable, neither betwixt all churches, nor all persons in one and the same church; and therefore, though church-meetings and synods, as the fittest and most effectual way to this unity, should endeavour to bring the church to the fullest agreement that may be, yet they should beware lest the straining it too high in all things rather break it, and an overdiligence in appointing uniformities remove them further from it. Leaving a latitude and indif-ferency in things capable of it, is often a stronger preserver of peace and unity. But this by the way. We will rather give some few rules that may be of use to every particular Christian, toward this common Christian good of Unity of Mind.

1st, Beware of two extremes, which often cause divisions, *captivity to custom*, on the one hand, and *affectation of novelty*, on the other.

2dly, Labour for a staid mind, that will not be tossed with every *wind of doctrine*, or appearance of reason, as some who, like vanes, are easily blown to any side with mistakes of the Scriptures, either arising in their own minds, or suggested by others.

3dly, In unclear and doubtful things, be not pertinacious, as the weakest minds are readiest to be upon seeming reason, which, when tried, will possibly fall to nothing; yet they are most assured, and cannot suffer a different thought in any from their own. There is naturally this *Popeness* in every man's mind, and most, I say, in the shallowest; a kind of fancied *infallibility* in themselves, which makes then *contentious*, (con.

trary to the Apostle's rule, Phil. ii. 3, *Let nothing be done through strife or vain glory,*) and as earnest upon differing in the smallest punctilio, as in a high article of faith. Stronger spirits are usually more patient of contradiction, and less violent, especially in doubtful things; and they who see farthest, are least peremptory in their determinations. The Apostle, in his second Epistle to Timothy, hath a word, *the spirit of a sound mind :* it is a good, sound constitution of mind, not to feel every blast, either of seeming reason to be taken with it, or of cross opinion to be offended at it.

4thly, Join that which is there, *the spirit of love,* in this particular : not at all abating affection for every light difference. And this the most are a little to blame in ; whereas the abundance of that should rather fill up the gap of these petty disagreements, that they do not appear, nor be at all sensibly to be found. No more disaffection ought to follow this, than the difference of our faces and complexions, or feature of body, which cannot be found in any two alike in all things.

And these things would be of easier persuasion, if we considered, 1. How supple and flexible a thing human reason is, and therefore not lightly to be trusted to, especially in Divine things; for *here, we know but in part.* (1 Cor. xiii. 9.) 2. The small importance of some things that have bred much noise and dissension in the world, as the Apostle speaks of the tongue, *How little a spark, how great a fire will it kindle ;* (James iii. 5.) And a great many of those debates, which cost men so much pains and time, are as far from clear decision as when they began, and are possibly of so little moment that, if they were ended, their profit would not quit the cost. 3. Consider the strength of Christian charity, which, if it dwelt much in our hearts, would preserve this union of mind amidst very many different thoughts, such as they may be, and would teach us that excellent lesson the Apostle gives to this purpose, (Phil. iii. 15.) *Let us therefore, as many as be perfect, be thus minded : and if in any thing ye be otherwise minded, God shall reveal even this unto you. Nevertheless, whereto we have already attained, let us walk by the same rule, let us mind the same thing.* Let us follow our Lord unanimously, in what He hath clearly manifested to us, and given us with one consent to embrace; as the spheres, notwithstanding each one hath its particular motion, yet all are wheeled about together with the first.

And this leads us to consider the further extent of this word, to agree in heart and in conversation, walking by the rule of those undoubted truths we have received. And in this I shall recommend these two things to you:

1. In the defence of the Truth, as the Lord shall call us, let us be of one mind, and all as one man. Satan acts by that maxim, and all his followers have it, *Divide and conquer;* and therefore let us hold that counter-maxim, *Union invincible.*

2. In the practice of that Truth agree as one. Let your conversation be uniform, by being squared to that one rule, and in all spiritual exercises join as one; be *of one heart and mind.* Would not our public worship, think you, prove much more both comfortable and profitable, if our hearts met in it as one, so that we would say of our hearing the word, as he, (Acts x. 33,) *We are all here present before God, to hear all things that are commanded of God?*—if our prayers ascended up as one pillar of incense to the Throne of grace; if they besieged it as an army, *stipato agmine Deum obsidentes,* as Tertullian speaks, all surrounding it together to obtain favour for ourselves and the Church? This is much with God, the *consent of hearts* petitioning. *Fama est junctas fortius ire preces:* It is believed that united prayers ascend with greater efficacy. So says our Saviour, (Matt. xviii. 20,) *Where two or three are gathered*—not their bodies within the same walls only, for so they are but so many carcasses, tumbled together, and the promise of His being amongst us is not made to that, *for He is the God of the living and not of the dead;* (Matt. xxii. 32;) it is the spirit of darkness that abides amongst the tombs and graves; but—*gathered in my name,* one in that one holy name, written upon their hearts, and uniting them, and

so thence expressed in their joint services and invocations. So
He says there of them who *agree upon any thing they shall
ask,* (συμφωνήσουσιν,) if all their hearts present and hold it up
together, if they make one cry or song of it, that harmony of
their hearts shall be sweet in the Lord's ears, and shall draw a
gracious answer out of His hand : *if ye agree,* your joint petitions shall be as it were an arrest or decree that shall stand in
Heaven: *it shall be done for them of my Father which is in
Heaven.* But alas! where is our agreement? The greater
number of hearts say nothing, and others speak with such
wavering and such a jarring harsh noise, being out of tune,
earthly, too low set, that they spoil all, and disappoint the
answers. Were the censer filled with those united prayers
heavenwards, it would be filled with fire earthwards against
the enemies of the Church.

And in your private society, seek unanimously your own
and each other's spiritual good; not only agreeing in your
affairs and civil converse, but having *one heart and mind* as
Christians. To eat and drink together, if you do no more, is
such society as beasts may have : to do these in the excess, to
eat and drink intemperately together, is a society worse than
that of beasts, and below them. To discourse together of civil
business, is to converse as men; but the peculiar converse of
Christians in that notion, as born again to immortality, an
unfading inheritance above, is to further one another towards
that, to put one another in mind of Heaven and Heavenly
things. And it is strange that men who profess to be Christians,
when they meet, either fill one another's ears with lies and profane speeches, or with vanities and trifles, or, at the best, with
the affairs of the earth, and not a word of those things that
should most possess the heart, and where the mind should be
most set, but are ready to reproach and taunt any such thing
in others. What! are you ashamed of Christ and religion?
Why do you profess it then? Is there such a thing, think ye,
as the *communing of saints?* If not, why say you believe it?
It is a truth, think of it as you will. The public ministry will

profit little any where, where a people, or some part of them, are not thus one, and do not live together as of one mind, and use diligently all due means of edifying one another in their holy faith. How much of the primitive Christian's praise and profit is involved in the word, *They were together* [ὁμοθυμαδὸν] *with one accord, with one mind;* and so they grew; *the Lord added to the church.* (Acts ii. 1, 44, 47.)

Consider, 1. How the wicked are one in their ungodly designs and practices. *The scales of Leviathan,* as Luther expresses it, are *linked together;* shall not the Lord's followers be one in him? They unite to undermine the peace of the Church; shall not the godly join their prayers to countermine them?

2. There is in the hearts of all the saints one spirit; how then can they be but one? Since they have the same purpose and journey, and tend to the same home, why should they not walk together in that way? When they shall arrive there, they shall be fully one, and of one mind, not a jar nor difference, all their harps perfectly in tune to that one new song.

Having compassion.] This testifies, that it is not a bare speculative agreement of opinions that is the badge of Christian unity; for this may accidentally be, where there is no further union; but that they are themselves one, and have one life, in that they feel how it is one with another. There is a living sympathy amongst them, as making up one body, animated with one spirit; for that is the reason why the members of the body have that mutual feeling, even the most remote and distant, and the most excellent with the meanest. This the Apostle urges at large, Rom. xii. 4, and 1 Cor. xii. 14—17.

And this lively sense is in every living member of the body of Christ towards the whole, and towards each other particular part. This makes a Christian rejoice in the welfare and good of another, as if it were his own, and feel their griefs and distresses, as if himself were really a sharer in them; for the word comprehends all feeling together, feeling of joy as well as grief. (Heb. xiii. 3; 1 Cor. xii. 26.) And always, where

there is most of grace and of the Spirit of Jesus Christ, there
is most of this sympathy. The Apostle St. Paul, as he was
eminent in all grace, had a large portion of this. (2 Cor. xi. 29.)
And if this ought to be in reference to their outward condition,
much more in spiritual things there should be rejoicing at the
increases and flourishing of grace in others. That base envy
which dwells in the hearts of rotten hypocrites, who would
have all engrossed to themselves, argues that they move not
further than the compass of *self;* that the pure love of God,
and the sincere love of their brethren flowing from it, are not
in them. But when the heart can unfeignedly rejoice in the
Lord's bounty to others, and the lustre of grace in others, far
outshining their own, truly it is an evidence that what grace
such a one hath is upright and good, and that the law of love
is engraven on his heart. And where that is, there will be
likewise, on the other side, a compassionate, tender sense of the
infirmities and frailties of their brethren ; whereas some account it a sign of much advancement and spiritual proficiency,
to be able to sit in judgment upon the qualifications and
actions of others, and to lavish out severe censures round about
them : to sentence one weak and of poor abilities, and another
proud and lofty, and a third covetous, *&c.;* and thus to go on
in a censor-like magisterial strain. But it were truly an evidence of more grace, not to get upon the bench to judge them,
but to sit down rather and mourn for them, when they are
manifestly and really faulty, and as for their ordinary infirmities, to consider and bear them. These are the characters we
find in the Scriptures, of stronger Christians. (Rom. xv. 1,
Gal. vi. 1.) This holy and humble sympathy argues indeed a
strong Christian. *Nil tam spiritualem virum indicat, quàm
peccati alieni tractatio : Nothing truly shews a spiritual
man so much, as the dealing with another man's sin.* Far
will he be from the ordinary way of insulting and trampling
upon the weak, or using rigour and bitterness, even against
some gross falls of a Christian : but will rather vent his compassion in tears, than his passion in fiery railings ; will bewail

the frailty of man, and our dangerous condition in this life, amidst so many snares and temptations, and such strong and subtle enemies.

2dly, As this sympathy works towards particular Christians in their several conditions, so, by the same reason, it acts, and that more eminently, towards the Church, and the public affairs that concern its good. And this, we find, hath breathed forth from the hearts of the saints in former times, in so many pathetical complaints and prayers for Zion. Thus David, in his saddest times, when he might seem most dispensable to forget other things, and be wholly taken up with lamenting his own fall, yet, even there, he leaves not out the Church: Psal li. 17, *In Thy good pleasure, do good to Zion.* And though his heart was broken all to pieces, yet the very pieces cry no less for the building of Jerusalem's wall, than for the binding up and healing of itself. And in that cxxii. Psalm, which seems to be the expression of his joy on being exalted to the throne and sitting peaceably on it, yet he still thus prays for *the peace of Jerusalem.* And the penman of the cxxxvii. Psalm, makes it an execrable oversight to forget Jerusalem, or to remember it coldly or secondarily: no less will serve him than to *prefer it to his chief joy.* Whatsoever else is *top* or *head of his joy,* (as the word is,) Jerusalem's welfare shall be its crown, shall be set above it. And the prophet, whoever it was, that wrote that cii. Psalm, and in it poured out that prayer from *an afflicted soul,* comforts himself in this, that Zion shall be favoured. *My days are like a shadow that declineth, and I am withered like grass,* but it matters not what becomes of me; let me languish and wither away, provided Zion flourish; though I feel nothing but pains and troubles, *yet Thou wilt arise and shew mercy to Zion :* I am content; that satisfies me.

But where is now this spirit of high sympathy with the Church? Surely, if there were any remains of it in us, it is now a fit time to exert it. If we be not altogether dead, surely we shall be stirred with the voice of those late strokes of God's hand, and be driven to more humble and earnest prayer by it. When will men change their poor, base grumblings about their private concerns, Oh! what shall I do? &c., into strong cries for the Church of God, and the public deliverance of all these kingdoms from the raging sword? But vile selfishness undoes us, the most looking no further. If themselves and theirs might be secured, how many would regard little what became of the rest! As one said, *When I am dead let the world be fired.* But the Christian mind is of a larger sphere, looks not only upon more than itself in present, but even to after times and ages, and can rejoice in the good to come, when itself shall not be here to partake of it: it is more dilated, and liker unto God, and to our Head, Jesus Christ. *The Lord,* says the Prophet, (Isa. lxiii. 9,) *in all his people's affliction, was afflicted himself.* And Jesus Christ accounts the sufferings of His body, the Church, His own; *Saul, Saul, why persecutest thou me?* (Acts ix. 4.) The heel was trod upon on earth, and the Head crieth from Heaven, as sensible of it. And this in all our evils, especially our spiritual griefs, is a high point of comfort to us, that our Lord Jesus is not insensible of them. This emboldens us to complain ourselves, and to put in our petitions for help to the throne of Grace through His hand, knowing that when He presents them, He will speak his own sense of our condition, and move for us as it were for Himself, as we have it sweetly expressed, Heb. iv. 15, 16. Now, as it is our comfort, so it is our pattern.

Love as brethren.] Hence springs this feeling we speak of: love is the cause of union, and union the cause of sympathy, and of that unanimity mentioned before. They who have the same spirit uniting and animating them, cannot but have the same mind and the same feelings. And this spirit is derived from that Head, Christ, in whom Christians *live, and move, and have their being,* their new and excellent being, and so, living in Him, they love Him, and are one in Him: they are *brethren,* as here the word is; their fraternity holds in Him. He is the head of it, *the first-born among many brethren.*

(Rom. viii. 29.) Men are brethren in two natural respects,—their bodies are of the same earth, and their souls breathed from the same God ; but this third fraternity, which is founded in Christ, is far more excellent and more firm than the other two ; for being one in Him, they have there taken in the other two, inasmuch as in Him is our whole nature: He is the *man Christ Jesus.* But to the advantage, and it is an infinite one, of being one in Him, we are united to the Divine nature in Him, *who is God blessed for ever;* (Rom. ix. 5;) and this is the highest, certainly, and the strongest union that can be imagined. Now this is *a great mystery* indeed, as the Apostle says, Eph. v. 32, speaking of this same point, the union of Christ and his Church, whence their union and communion one with another, who make up that body, the Church, is derived. In Christ, every believer *is born of God,* is His son ; and so, they are not only brethren, one with another, who are so born, but Christ himself owns them as his brethren ; *Both he who sanctifies, and they who are sanctified, are all of one, for which cause he is not ashamed to call them brethren.* (Heb. ii. 11.)

Sin broke all to pieces, man from God, and men from one another. Christ's work in the world was, *union.* To make up these breaches He came down, and began the union which was his work, in the wonderful union made in his person that was to work it, making God and man one. And as the nature of man was reconciled, so, by what He performed, the persons of men are united to God. Faith makes them one with Christ, and He makes them one with the Father, and hence results this oneness amongst themselves: concentring and meeting in Jesus Christ, and in the Father through Him, they are made one together. And that this was His great work, we may read in His prayer, John xvii., where it is the burden and main strain, the great request He so reiterates, *That they may be one, as we are one,* (ver. 11.) A high comparison, such as man durst not name, but after Him who so warrants us ! And again, ver. 21, *That they all may be one, as Thou,*

Father, art in me, and I in thee, that they also may be one in us.

So that certainly, where this exists, it is the ground-work of another kind of friendship and love than the world is acquainted with, or is able to judge of, and hath more worth in one drachm of it, than all the quintessence of civil or natural affection can amount to. The friendships of the world, the best of them, are but tied with chains of glass; but this fraternal love of Christians is a golden chain, both more precious and more strong and lasting; the others are worthless and brittle.

The Christian owes and pays a general charity and good-will to all; but peculiar and intimate friendship he cannot have, except with such as come within the compass of this fraternal love, which, after a special manner, flows from God, and returns to Him, and abides in Him, and shall remain unto eternity.

Where this love is and abounds, it will banish far away all those dissensions and bitternesses, and those frivolous mistakings which are so frequent among most persons. It will teach men wisely and gently to admonish one another, where it is needful; but further than that, it will pass by many offences and failings, it will *cover a multitude of sins,* and will very much sweeten society, making it truly profitable; therefore the Psalmist calls it both *good and pleasant, that brethren dwell together in unity :* it perfumes all, as the precious ointment upon the head of Aaron. (Psalm cxxxiii. 2, 3.)

But many who are called Christians are not indeed of this brotherhood, and, therefore, no wonder they know not what this love means, but are either of restless, unquiet spirits, *biting and devouring one another,* as, the Apostle speaks, or, at the best, only civilly smooth and peaceable in their carriage, rather scorners than partakers of this spiritual love and fraternity. These are strangers to Christ, not brought into acquaintance and union with Him, and therefore void of the life of grace, and the fruits of it, whereof this is a chief one. Oh how few amongst multitudes that throng in as we do here together, are indeed partakers of the *glorious liberty of the sons of God,* or ambitious of that high and happy estate!

As for you that know these things, and have a portion in them, who have your *communion with the Father and his Son Jesus Christ,* (1 John i. 3,) I beseech you, adorn your holy profession, and testify yourselves the disciples and the brethren of Jesus Christ by this mutual love. Seek to understand better what it is, and to know it more practically. Consider that source of love, that *love which the Father hath bestowed upon us,* in this, *that we should be called the sons of God,* (1 John iii. 1,) and so be brethren, and thence draw more of this sweet stream of love. *God is love,* says the same Apostle; therefore, surely, where there is most of God, there is most of this divine grace, this holy love. Look upon and study much that infinite love of God and his Son Jesus Christ towards us. *He gave his only begotten Son;* the Son *gave Himself:* He sweetened his bitter cup with his transcendent love, and this He hath recommended to us, that *Even as He loved us, so should we love one another.* (John xv. 12.) We know we cannot reach this highest pattern; that is not meant; but the more we look on it, the higher we shall reach in this love, and shall learn some measure of such love on earth as is in Heaven, and that which so begins here, shall there be perfected.

Be pitiful, be courteous.] The roots of plants are hidden under ground, so that themselves are not seen, but they appear in their branches, and flowers, and fruits, which argue there is a root and life in them; thus, the graces of the Spirit planted in the soul, though themselves invisible, yet discover their being and life in the tract of a Christian's life, his words, and actions, and the frame of his carriage. Thus faith shews that *it lives,* as the Apostle St. James teacheth at large. (Jam. ii. 14, *&c.*) And thus Love is a grace of so active a nature, that it is still working, and yet never weary. *Your labour of love,* says the Apostle, Heb. vi. 10: it labours, but delight makes the hardest labour sweet and easy. And so proper is action to it, that all action is null without it. (1 Cor. xiii. 1—3.) Yea, it knits faith and action together; it is the link that unites them. *Faith worketh*, but it is, as the Apostle teaches us, *by love*. (Gal. v. 6.) So then, where this root is, these fruits will spring from it, and discover it, *Pity* and *Courtesy*.

These are of a larger extent in their full sphere than the preceding graces; for, from a general love due to all, they act towards all, to men, or humanity, in the general; and this not from a bare natural tenderness, which softer complexions may have, nor from a prudent moral consideration of their own possible falling under the like or greater calamities, but out of obedience to God, who requires this mercifulness in all His children, and cannot own them for His, unless in this they resemble Him. And it is indeed an evidence of a truly Christian mind, to have much of this pity to the miseries of all, being rightly principled, and acting after a pious and Christian manner towards the sick and poor, of what condition soever; yea, pitying most the spiritual misery of ungodly men, their hardness of heart and unbelief, and earnestly wishing their conversion; not repining at the long-suffering of God, as if thou wouldst have the bridge cut because thou art over, as St. Augustine speaks, but longing rather to see that *long-suffering and goodness of God lead them to repentance* (Rom. ii. 4); being grieved to see men ruining themselves, and diligently working their own destruction, *going in any way of wickedness*, (as Solomon speaks of one particularly,) *as an ox to the slaughter or a fool to the correction of the stocks.* (Prov. vii. 22.) Certainly, the ungodly man is an object of the highest pity.

But there is a special debt of this pity to those whom we love as brethren in our Lord Jesus: they are most closely linked to us by a peculiar fraternal love. Their sufferings and calamities will move the bowels that have Christian affection within them. Nor is it an empty, helpless pity, but carries with it the real communication of our help to our utmost power. [εὔσπλαγχνοι.] Not only bowels that are moved themselves with pity, but that move the hand to succour; for by this word, the natural affection of parents, and of the more tender parent, the mother, is expressed, who do not idly behold and bemoan their children being sick or distressed, but provide all possible help; their bowels are not only stirred, but dilated and enlarged towards them.

And if our feeling bowels and helping hand are due to all, and particularly to the godly, and we ought to pay this debt in outward distresses, how much more in their soul afflictions!— the rather because these are most heavy in themselves, and least understood, and therefore least regarded ; yea, sometimes rendered yet heavier by natural friends, possibly by their bitter scoffs and taunts, or by their slighting, or, at best, by their misapplying of proper helps and remedies, which, as unfit medicines, do rather exasperate the disease ; therefore they that do understand and can be sensible of that kind of wound, ought so much the more to be tender and pitiful towards it, and to deal mercifully and gently with it. It may be, very weak things sometimes trouble a weak Christian ; but there is in the spirit of the godly, a humble condescension learned from Christ, who *broke not the bruised reed, nor quenched the smoking flax.*

The least difficulties and scruples in a tender conscience should not be roughly encountered; they are as a knot in a silken thread, and require a gentle and wary hand to loose them.

Now, this tenderness of bowels and inclination to pity all, especially Christians, and them especially in their peculiar pressures is not a weakness, as some kind of spirits take it to be; this, even naturally, is a generous pity in the greatest spirits. Christian pity is not womanish, yea, it is more than manly, it is Divine. There is of natural pity most in the best and most ingenuous natures, but where it is spiritual, it is a prime lineament of the image of God; and the more absolute and disengaged it is, in regard of those towards whom it acts, the more it is like unto God; looking upon misery as a sufficient incentive of pity and mercy, without the ingredient of any other consideration. It is merely a vulgar piece of goodness, to be helpful and bountiful to friends, or to such as are within appearance of requital ; it is a trading kind of commerce, that ; but pity and bounty, which need no inducements but the meeting of a fit object to work on, where it can expect nothing, save only the privilege of doing good, (which in itself is so sweet,) is God-like indeed.   He is rich in bounty without any necessity, yea, or possibility of return from us ; for we have neither any thing to confer upon Him, nor hath he need of receiving any thing, who is the Spring of goodness and of being.

And that we may the better understand Him in this, He is pleased to express this His merciful nature in our notion and language, by *bowels of mercy and pity*, (Isa. liv. 7, 8,) and the *stirring* and *sounding* of them, (Hos. xi. 8,) *by the pity of a father*, (Psal. ciii. 13,) and by that *of a mother;* (Isa. xlix. 15 ;) as if nothing could be tender and significant enough to express His compassions.   Hence, our redemption ; (Isa. lxiii. 9 ;) hence, all our hopes of happiness.   The gracious Lord saw his poor creatures undone by sin, and no power in heaven or on earth able to rescue them, but His own alone ; therefore his pity was moved, and His hand answers his heart.   *His own arm brought salvation ;* He sent *the deliverer out of Zion to turn away iniquity from Jacob.* (Rom. xi. 26.)   And in all exigencies of His children, He is overcome with their complaints, and cannot hold out against their moanings.   He may, as Joseph, seem strange for a while, but cannot act that strangeness long.   His heart moves and sounds to theirs, gives the echo to their griefs and groans ; as they say of two strings that are perfect unisons, touch the one, the other also sounds. *Surely I have heard Ephraim bemoaning himself . . . . . Is Ephraim my dear son ?* (Jer. xxxi. 18.)   Oh ! the unspeakable privilege to have Him for our Father, who is *the Father of mercies and compassions*, and those not barren, fruitless pityings, for He is withal *the God of all consolations.*   Do not think that He can shut out a bleeding soul that comes to Him, or refuse to take, and to bind up, and heal, a broken heart that offers itself to Him, puts itself into his hand, and entreats his help.   Doth he

require pity of us, and doth he give it to us, and is it not infinitely more in Himself? All that is in angels and men, is
but an insensible drop to that Ocean.

Let us then consider, that we are obliged both to pity, especially towards our Christian brethren, and to use all means for
their help within our reach; to have bowels stirred with the
report of such bloodsheds and cruelties as come to our ears,
and to bestir ourselves according to our places and power for
them. But surely all are to move this one way for their help,
to run to the *Throne of Grace*. If your bowels sound for your
brethren, let them sound that way for them, to represent their
estate to Him who is highest, both in pity and in power, for
He expects to be remembranced by us: He put that office
upon His people, to be His recorders for Zion, and they are
traitors to it, who neglect the discharge of that trust.

Courteous.] The former relates to the afflictions of others,
this to our whole carriage with them in any condition. And
yet there is a particular regard to be paid to it in communicating good, in supplying their wants, or comforting them that
are distressed; that it be not done, or rather, I may say, undone in doing, with such supercilious roughness, venting itself
either in looks or words, or any way, as sours it, and destroys
the very being of a benefit, and turns it rather into an injury.
And generally, the whole conversation of men is made unpleasant by cynical harshness and disdain.

This Courteousness which the Apostle recommends, is contrary to that evil, not only in the surface and outward behaviour; no, religion doth not prescribe, nor is satisfied with such
courtesy as goes no deeper than words and gestures, which
sometimes is most contrary to that singleness which religion
owns. These are the upper garments of malice; saluting him
aloud in the morning, whom they are undermining all the day.
Or sometimes, though more innocent, yet it may be troublesome, merely by the vain affectation and excess of it. Even
this becomes not a wise man, much less a Christian. An over-
study or acting of that, is a token of emptiness, and is below a

solid mind. Though Christians know such things, and could outdo the studiers of it, yet they (as it indeed deserves) do despise it. Nor is it that graver and wiser way of external plausible deportment, that answers fully this word : it is the outer-half indeed, but the thing is [φιλοφροσύνη] a radical sweetness in the temper of the mind, that spreads itself into a man's words and actions ; and this not merely natural, a gentle, kind disposition, (which is indeed a natural advantage that some have,) but this is spiritual, a new nature descended from heaven, and so, in its original and kind, far excelling the other ; it supplies it where it is not in nature, and doth not only increase it where it is, but elevates it above itself, renews it, and sets a more excellent stamp upon it. Religion is in this mistaken sometimes, in that men think it imprints an unkindly roughness and austerity upon the mind and carriage. It doth indeed bar and banish all vanity and lightness, and all compliance and easy partaking with sin. Religion strains, and quite breaks that point of false and injurious courtesy, to suffer thy brother's soul to run the hazard of perishing, and to share in his guiltiness, by not admonishing him after that seasonable, and prudent, and gentle manner (for that indeed should be studied) which becomes thee as a Christian, and that particular respective manner which becomes thy station. These things rightly qualifying it, it doth no wrong to good manners and the courtesy here enjoined, but is truly a part of it, by due admonitions and reproofs to seek to reclaim a sinner ; for it were the worst unkindness not to do it. *Thou shalt not hate thy brother, thou shalt in any wise rebuke thy brother, and not suffer sin upon him.* (Levit. xix. 17).

But that which is true lovingness of heart and carriage, religion doth not only in no way prejudice, but, you see, requires it in the rule, and where it is wrought in the heart, works and causes it there ; fetches out that crookedness and harshness which are otherwise invincible in some humours: *Emollit mores, nec sinit esse feros; Makes the wolf dwell with the lamb.* This, Christians should study, and belie the prejudices

which the world take up against the power of Godliness ; they
should study to be inwardly so minded, and of such outward
behaviour, as becomes that Spirit of Grace which dwells in
them, endeavouring to gain *those that are without,* by their
kind, obliging conversation.

In some copies, it is [ταπεινόφρονες] *Humble ;* and indeed, as
this is excellent in itself, and a chief characteristic of a Christian, it agrees well with all those mentioned, and carries along
with it this inward and real, not acted, courteousness.   Not to
insist on it now, it gains at all hands with God and with men ;
receives much grace from God, and kills envy, and commands
respect and good-will from men.

Those showers of grace that slide off from the lofty mountains, rest on the valleys, and make them fruitful.   *He giveth
grace to the lowly,* loves to bestow it where there is most room
to receive it, and most return of ingenuous and entire praises
upon the receipt, and such is the humble heart.   And truly, as
much humility gains much grace, so it grows by it.

It is one of the world's reproaches against those who go be-
yond their size in religion, that they are proud and self-conceited.
Christians, beware there be nothing in you justifying this.
Surely they who have most true grace are least guilty of this.
Common knowledge and gifts may *puff up,* but grace does not.

He whom the Lord loads most with his richest gifts, stoops
lowest, as pressed down with the weight of them.   *Ille est qui
superbire nescit, cui Deus ostendit misericordiam suam :* The
free love of God humbles that heart most to which it is most
manifested.

And towards men, humility graces all grace and all gifts ; it
glorifies God, and teaches others so to do.   It is *conservatrix
virtutum,* the *preserver of graces.*   Sometimes it seems to
wrong them by hiding them ; but indeed it is their safety.
Hezekiah by a vain shewing of his jewels and treasures, forfeited
them all: *Prodendo perdidit.*

Ver. 9. Not rendering evil for evil, or railing for railing; but contrari-
wise, blessing; Knowing that ye are thereunto called, that ye should
inherit a blessing.

OPPOSITION helps grace both to more strength and more lustre.
When Christian charity is not encountered by the world's ma-
lignance, it hath an easier task; but assaulted and overcoming,
it shines the brighter, and rises the higher; and thus it is when
it *renders not evil for evil.*

To repay good with evil is, amongst men, the top of iniquity;
yet this is our universal guiltiness towards God, He multiplying
mercies, and we vying with multiplied sins: as the Lord complains of Israel, *As they were increased, so they sinned.* The
lowest step of mutual good amongst men, is, not to be bent to
provoke others with injuries, and, being unoffended, to offend
none. But this, not to repay offences, nor *render evil for evil,*
is a Christian's rule; and yet, further, to return *good* for *evil,*
and *blessing* for *cursing,* is not only counselled, (as some vainly
distinguish,) but commanded. (Matt. v. 44.)

It is true, the most have no ambition for this degree of goodness; they aspire no further than to do or say no evil unpro-
voked, and think themselves sufficiently just and equitable, if
they keep within that; but this is lame, is only half the rule.
Thou thinkest injury obliges thee, or, if not so, yet excuses
thee, to revenge, or at least disobliges thee, unties thy engagement of wishing and doing good. But these are all gross
practical errors. For,

1st. The second injury done by way of revenge, differs from
the first that provoked it, little or nothing, but only in point
of time; and certainly, no one man's sin can procure privilege
to another to sin in that or the like kind. If another hath
broken the bonds of his allegiance and obedience to God, and
of charity to thee, yet thou art not the less tied by the same
bonds still.

2dly. By revenge of injuries thou usurpest upon God's prerogative, who is *The Avenger,* as the Apostle teaches, Rom.

xii. 19. This doth not forbid either the Magistrate's sword for just punishment of offenders, or the Soldier's sword in a just war; but such revenges as, without authority, or a lawful call, the pride and perverseness of men do multiply one against another; in which is involved a presumptuous contempt of God and His supreme authority, or at, least, the unbelief and neglect of it.

3dly. It cannot be genuine upright goodness that hath its d ependenceupon the goodness of others who are about us: as they say of the vain-glorious man, his virtue lieth in the beholder's eye. If thy meekness and charity be such as lieth in the good and mild carriage of others towards thee in their hands and tongues, thou art not owner of it intrinsically. Such quiet and calm, if none provoke thee, is but an accidental, uncertain cessation of thy turbulent spirit unstirred; but move it, and it exerts itself according to its nature, sending up that mud which lay at the bottom: whereas true grace doth then most manifest what it is, when those things which are most contrary, surround and assault it; it cannot correspond and hold game with injuries and railings; it hath no faculty for that, for *answering evil with evil*. A tongue inured to graciousness, and mild speeches, and blessings, and a heart stored so within, can vent no other, try it and stir it as you will. A Christian acts and speaks, not according to what others are towards him, but according to what he is through the grace and Spirit of God in him; as they say, *Quicquid recipitur, recipitur ad modum recipientis:* The same things are differently received, and work differently, according to the nature and way of that which receives them. A little spark blows up one of a sulphureous temper, and *many coals*, greater injuries and reproaches, are quenched and lose their force, being thrown at another of a *cool spirit*, as the original expression is, Prov. xvii. 27.

They who have malice, and bitterness, and cursings within, though these sleep, it may be, yet, awake them with the like, and the provision comes forth *out of the abundance of the heart:* give them an ill word, and they have another, or two for one, in readiness for you. So, where the soul is furnished with spiritual blessings, their blessings come forth, even in answer to reproaches, and indignities. *The mouth of the wise is a tree of life,* says Solomon; (Prov. x. 11;) it can bear no other fruit, but according to its kind, and the nature of the root. An honest, spiritual heart, pluck at it who will, they can pull no other fruit than such fruit. Love and meekness lodge there, and therefore, whosoever knocks, these make the answer.

Let the world account it a despicable simplicity, seek you still more of that dove-like spirit, the spirit of meekness and blessing. It is a poor glory to vie in railings, to contest in that faculty, or in any kind of vindictive returns of evil: the most abject creatures have abundance of that great spirit, as foolish poor-spirited persons account it; but *it is the glory of man to pass by a transgression,* (Prov. xix. 11,) it is the noblest victory. And as we mentioned, the Highest Example, God, is our pattern in love and compassions: we are well warranted to endeavour to be like Him in this. Men esteem much more highly some other virtues which make more shew, and trample upon these, love, and compassion, and meekness. But though these violets grow low, and are of a dark colour, yet they are of a very sweet and diffusive smell, odoriferous graces; and the Lord propounds Himself our example in them, Matt. v. 44—48. To *love them that hate you, and bless them that curse you,* is to be truly *the children of your Father,* your Father *which is in Heaven.* It is a kind of perfection: v. 48. *Be ye therefore perfect, even as your Father which is in Heaven is perfect. He maketh His sun to rise on the evil and on the good.* Be you like it: howsoever men behave themselves, keep you your course, and let your benign influence, as you can, do good to all. And Jesus Christ sets in himself these things before us, *learn of me,* not to heal the sick, or raise the dead, but *learn, for I am meek and lowly in heart.* (Matt. xi. 29.) And if you be his followers, this is your way, as the Apostle here addeth, *Hereunto are you called;* and this is the end of it, agreeably to the way, *that you may inherit a blessing.*

[Εἰδότες, ὅτι] *Knowing that.*] Understanding aright the nature of your holy calling, and then, considering it wisely, and conforming to it.

Those who have nothing beyond an external calling and profession of Christianity, are wholly blind in this point, and do not think what this imports, *A Christian.* Could they be drawn to this, it were much, it were indeed all, to know to what they are called, and to answer to it, to walk like it. But as one calls a certain sort of lawyers, *indoctum docto-rum genus,* we may call the most *an unchristian kind of Christians.*

' Yea, even those who are really partakers of this spiritual and effectual call, yet are often very defective in this; in view-ing their rule, and laying it to their life, their hearts, and words, and actions, and squaring by it; in often asking them-selves, Suits this my calling? Is this like a Christian? It is a main point in any civil station, for a man to have a carriage suitable and convenient to his station and condition, that his actions become him : *Caput artis est decere quod facias.* But how many incongruities and solecisms do we commit, forget-ting ourselves, who we are, and what we are called to; to what as our duty, and to what as our portion and inheritance. And these indeed agree together; we are *called* to an *unde-filed, a holy inheritance,* and therefore *called* likewise to be *holy* in our way to it ; for that contains all. We are *called* to a better estate at home, and *called* to be fitted for it while we are here; *called* to an *inheritance of light,* and therefore *called* to *walk* as *children of light;* and so here, *called* to *blessing* as our inheritance, and to *blessing* as our duty ; for this [εἰς τοῦτο, *Thereunto*] relates to both, looks back to the one, and forward to the other, the way, and the end, both *blessing.*

The fulness of this inheritance is reserved till we come to that land where it lieth; there it abideth us; but the earnests of that fulness of blessing are bestowed on us here: *spiritual blessings in heavenly places in Christ*, (Eph. i. 3,) they descend from those heavenly places upon the heart, that precious name of our Lord Jesus poured on our hearts. If we be indeed interested in him, (as we pretend,) and have peace with God through our Lord Jesus Christ, we are put in possession of that blessing of forgiveness of sin, and on terms of love and amity with the Father, being reconciled by the blood of His Son, and then blessed with the anointing of the Spirit, the graces infused from Heaven. Now, all these do so cure the bitter, accursed distempers of the natural heart, and so perfume it, that it cannot well breathe any thing but sweetness and blessing towards others: being itself thus blessed of the Lord, it echoes blessing both to God and men, echoes to His blessing of it; and its words and whole carriage are *as the smell of a field that the Lord hath blessed,* as old Isaac said of his son's garments. (Gen. xxvii. 27.) The Lord having spoken pardon to a soul, and instead of the curse due to sin, blessed it with a title to glory, it easily and readily speaks pardon, and not only pardon, but blessing also, even to those that outrage it most, and deserve worst of it; reflecting still on that, Oh! what deserved I at my Lord's hands! When so many talents are forgiven me, shall I stick at forgiving a few pence!

And then, *called to inherit a blessing;* every believer *an heir of blessing!* And not only are the spiritual blessings he hath received, but even his largeness of blessing others is a pledge to him, an evidence of that heirship; as those who are prone to cursing, though provoked, yet may look upon that as a sad mark, that they are heirs of a curse: Psal. cix. 17, *As he loved cursing, so let it come unto him.* Shall not they who delight in cursing have enough of it, when they shall hear that doleful word, *Go ye cursed,* &c.? And on the other side, as for the sons of blessing, who spared it not to any, the blessing they are heirs to, is blessedness itself, and they are to be entered into it by that joyful speech, *Come, ye blessed of my Father.*

Men can but bless one another in good wishes, and can bless the Lord only in praises and applauding his blessedness; but the Lord's blessing is, really *making blessed;* an operative word, which brings the thing with it.

Inherit a blessing.] Not called to be exempted from troubles and injuries here, and to be extolled and favoured by the world, but, on the contrary, rather to suffer the utmost of their malice, and to be the mark of their arrows, of wrongs, and scoffs, and reproaches. But it matters not; this weighs down all, *you are called to inherit a blessing*, which all their cursings and hatred cannot deprive you of. For as this inheriting of blessing enforces the duty of blessing others, upon a Christian, so it encourages him to go through the hardest contrary measure he receives from the world. If the world should bless you, and applaud you never so loudly, yet their blessings cannot be called an inheritance; they fly away, and die out in the air, have no substance at all, much less that endurance that may make them an inheritance. *Qui thesaurum tuum alieno in ore constituis, ignoras quod arca ista non clauditur?* You who trust your treasure to another man's keeping, are you aware that you are leaving it in an open chest? And more generally, is there any thing here that deserves to be so called? The surest inheritances are not more than for term of life to any one man: their abiding is for others who succeed, but he removes. *Si hæc sunt vestra, tollite ea vobiscum:* (S. BERNARD:) If these things are yours, take them away with you. And when a man is to remove from all he hath possessed and rejoiced in here, then, *fool* indeed, if nothing be provided for the longer (O! how much longer) abode he must make elsewhere! Will he not then bewail his madness, that he was hunting a shadow all his lifetime? And may be, he is turned out of all his quiet possessions and easy dwelling before that; (and in these times we may the more

readily think of this ;) but at the utmost at night, when he
should be for most rest, when that sad night comes after this
day of fairest prosperity, the unbelieving, unrepenting sinner
lies down in sorrow, in a woeful bed.   Then must he, whether
he will or no, enter on the possession of this inheritance of
everlasting burnings.   He hath an inheritance indeed, but he
had better want it, and himself too be turned to nothing.   Do
you believe there are treasures which neither thief breaks into,
nor is there any inward moth to corrupt them, an inheritance
which, though the whole world be turned upside down, is in
no hazard of a touch of damage, *a kingdom,* that not only
cannot fall, but *cannot be shaken?*   (Heb. xii. 28.)   *Oh ! be
wise, and consider your latter end,* and whatsoever you do,
look after this blessed inheritance.   Seek to have the right to
it in Jesus Christ, and the evidences and seals of it from His
Spirit ; and if it be so with you, your hearts will be upon it,
and your lives will be conformed to it.

Ver. 10.   For he that will love life, and see good days, let him refrain his
tongue from evil, and his lips that they speak no guile.

THE rich bounty of God diffuses itself throughout the world
upon all ; yet there is a select number who have peculiar
blessings of his *right hand,* which the rest of the world share
not in ; and even as to common blessings, they are differenced
by a peculiar title to them, and sweetness in them : their blessings are blessings indeed, and entirely so, outside and inside,
and more so within than they appear without : *the Lord* himself
is their portion, and *they are his.*   This is their blessedness,
which in a low estate they can challenge, and so outvie all the
painted prosperity of the world.   Some kind of blessings do
abundantly run over upon others ; but *the cup of blessings*
belongs unto the godly by a new right from heaven, graciously
conferred upon them.   Others are sent away *with gifts,* (as
some apply that passage, Gen. xxv. 5, 6,) but the inheritance
is Isaac's.   They are called to be *the sons of God,* and are
hke him, as his children, in goodness and blessings.   The

inheritance of blessing is theirs alone:—*Called*, says the Apostle, *to inherit a blessing*. And all the promises in the great charter of both testaments run in that appropriating style, entailed to them, as the only heirs. Thus this fitly is translated from the one testament to the other, by the Apostle, for his present purpose—*He that will love*, &c. (See Psalm xxxiv. 13, 14.)

Consider, 1. The qualification required. 2. The blessing annexed and ascertained to it; the scope being to recommend a rule so exact, and for that purpose to propound a good so important and desirable, as a sufficient attractive to study and conform to that rule.

The rule is all of it one straight line, running through the whole tract of a godly man's life; yet you see clearly that it is not cut asunder indeed, but only marked into four, whereof the two latter parcels are somewhat longer, more generally reaching a man's ways, the two former particularly regulating the tongue.

In the ten words of the Law which God delivered in so singular a manner both by word and writ from his own mouth and hand, there be two, which if not wholly, yet most especially and most expressly concern the tongue, as a very considerable, though a small part of man; and of these four words, here two are bestowed on it.

The Apostle, St. James, is large in this, teaching the great concernment of this point. *It is a little member*, (says he, chap. iii. ver. 5,) *but boasteth great things*, needs a strong bridle; and the bridling of it makes much for the ruling the whole course of a man's life, as the Apostle there applies the resemblance; yea, he gives the skill of this as the very character of perfection. And if we consider it, it must indeed be of very great consequence how we use the tongue, it being the main outlet of the thoughts of the heart, and the mean of society amongst men in all affairs civil and spiritual; by which men give birth to the conceptions of their own minds, and seek to beget the like in the minds of others. The bit that is here made for men's mouths, hath these two halves that make it up: 1. To refrain from open evil speaking. 2. From double and guileful speaking.

From evil.] This is a large field, the evil of the tongue; but I give it too narrow a name: we have good warrant to give it a much larger—A whole universe, *a world of iniquity*, (Jam. iii. 6,) a vast bulk of evils, and great variety of them, as of countries on the earth, or creatures in the world ; and multitudes of such are venomous and full of deadly poison, and not a few, monsters, new productions of wickedness, *semper aliquid novi*, as they say of Africa.

There be in the daily discourses of the greatest part of men, many things that belong to this *world of evil*, and yet pass unsuspected, so that we do not think them to be within its compass ; not using due diligence and exactness in our discoveries of the several parts of it, although it is all within ourselves, yea within a small part of ourselves, our tongues.

It were too quick a fancy to think to travel over this world of iniquity, the whole circuit of it, in an hour, yea, or so much as to aim exactly at all the parts that can be taken of it in the smallest map : but some of the chief we would particularly take notice of in the several four parts of it; for it will without constraint hold resemblance in that division, with the other, the habitable world.

I. *Profane* speech, that which is grossly and manifestly wicked; and in that part lie, 1. Impious speeches, which directly reflect upon the glory and name of God; blasphemies, and oaths, and cursings, of which there is so great, so lamentable abundance amongst us, the whole land overspread and defiled with it, the common noise that meets a man in streets and houses, and almost in all places where he comes ; and to these, join what are not uncommon amongst us neither, scoffs and mocking at religion, the power and strictness of it, not only by the grosser sort, but by pretenders to some kind of goodness ; for they who have attained to a self-pleasing pitch of civility or formal religion, have usually that point of presumption with it, that they make their own size the model and rule to examine all by.. What is below it, they condemn indeed as profane; but what is beyond it, they account needless and affected preciseness: and, therefore, are as ready as others to let fly invectives or bitter taunts against it, which are the keen and poisoned shafts of the tongue, and a persecution that shall be called to a strict account. 2. Impure or filthy speaking, which either pollutes or offends the hearers, and is the noisome breath of a rotten polluted heart.

II. Consider next, as another grand part of the tongue, *Uncharitable* speeches, tending to the defaming and disgrace of others; and these are likewise of two sorts, 1. Open railing and reproaches; 2. Secret slander and detraction. The former is unjust and cruel, but it is somewhat the less dangerous, because open. It is a fight in plain field; but truly it is no piece of a Christian's warfare to encounter it in the same kind. The sons of peace are not for these tongue-combats; they are often, no doubt, set upon so, but they have another abler way of overcoming it than by the use of the same weapon; for they break and blunt the point of ill-reproaches by meekness, and triumph over cursings with more abundant blessing, as is enjoined in the former words, which are seconded with these out of Psalm xxxiv. 13, 14. But they that enter the lists in this kind, and are provided one for another with enraged minds, are usually not unprovided of weapons, but lay hold on any thing that comes next;—*Furor arma ministrat;*—as your drunkards in their quarrels, in their cups and pots, if they have any other great reproach, they lay about them with that, as their sword; but if they want that, true or untrue, pertinent or impertinent, all is one, they cast out any revilings that come next to hand. But there is not only wickedness, but something of baseness in this kind of conflicts, that makes them more abound amongst the baser sort, and not so frequent with such as are but of a more civil breeding and quality than the vulgar.

But the other kind—detraction, is more universal amongst all sorts, as being a far easier way of mischief in this kind, and of better conveyance. Railings cry out the matter openly, but detraction works all by surprises and stratagem, and mines under ground, and therefore is much more pernicious. The former are as the *arrows that fly by day*, but this, *as the pestilence that walketh in darkness*, (as these two are mentioned together in Psalm xci. 5, 6,) it spreads and infects secretly and insensibly, is not felt but in the effects of it; and it works either by calumnies altogether forged and untrue, of which malice is inventive, or by the advantage of real faults, of which it is very discerning, and these are stretched and aggravated to the utmost. It is not expressible how deep a wound a tongue sharpened to this work will give, with a very little word and little noise,—*as a razor*, as it is called in Psal. lii. 2, which with a small touch cuts very deep,—taking things by the worst handle, whereas charity will try about all ways for a good acceptation and sense of things, and takes all by the best. This pest is still killing some almost in all companies; it *casteth down many wounded*, as it is said of the strange woman, Prov. vii. 26. And they convey it under fair prefacing of commendation; so giving them poison in wine, both that it may pass the better, and penetrate the more. This is a great sin, one which the Lord ranks with the first, when he sets them in order against a man: (Psal. l. 20:) *Thou sittest and speakest against thy brother.*

III. *Vain fruitless* speeches are an evil of the tongue, not only those they call *harmless lies*, which some poor people take a pleasure in, and trade much in, light buffooneries and foolish jestings, but the greatest part of those discourses which men account the *blameless* entertainments one of another, come within the compass of this evil; frothy, unsavoury stuff, tending to no purpose nor good at all; *effectless words*, ἀργὸν, as our Saviour speaks, Matt. xii. 36, of which we must *render account in the day of judgment*, for that very reason.

They are in this *world of evil*, in the tongue ; if no other way ill, yet ill they are, as the Arabian deserts and barren sands, because they are fruitless.

IV. *Doubleness and guile :* so great a part, that it is here particularly named a part, though the evil of it is less known and discerned ; and so there is in it, as I may say, much *terra incognita ;* yet it is of a very large compass, as large, we may confidently say, as all the other three together. What of men's speech is not manifestly evil in any of the other kinds, is the most of it naught this way : speech good to appearance, plausible and fair, but not upright ; not silver, but *silver dross*, as Solomon calls it ; burning lips, &c. (Prov. xxvi. 23.) Each almost, some way or other, speaking falsehood and deceit to his neighbour ; and daring to act thus falsely with God in his services, and our protestations of obedience to him ; religious speeches abused by some in hypocrisy, as holy vestments, for a mask or disguise ; doing nothing but *compassing him about with lies*, as he complains of Ephraim, Hos. xi. 12 ; deceiving indeed ourselves, while we think to deceive Him who cannot be deceived, and *will not be mocked*. (Psal. xvii. 1 ; Gal. vi. 7.) He saw through the disguises and hypocrisy of his own people, when they came to inquire at him, and yet still entertained their heart-idols, as he tells the prophet, Ezek. xiv. 3.

The sins of each of us, would we enter into a strict account of ourselves, would be found to arise to a great sum in this kind ; and they that do put themselves upon the work of self-trial, find, no doubt, abundant matter of deepest humbling, though they had no more, even in the sin of their lips, and are by it often astonished at the Lord's patience, considering his holiness ; as Isaiah cried out : (ch. vi. ver. 5 :) having seen the Lord in a glorious vision, this in particular falls upon his thoughts concerning himself and the people—*polluted lips : Woe is me*, &c. And indeed it is a thing the godly mind cannot be satisfied with, to make mention of the Lord, till their lips be *touched with a coal from* the heavenly fire of *the altar ;* and they especially that are called to be the Lord's

messengers, will say as St. Bernard, " Had the prophet need
" of a coal to unpollute his lips, then do ministers require
" *totum globum igneum*, a whole globe of fire." Go through
the land, and see if the sins of this kind will not take up
much of the bill against us, which the Lord seems now to
have taken into his hands and to be reading, and about to
take order with it, because we will not. Would we set ourselves to read it, he would let it fall. Is it not because of
oaths that *the land mourns*, or I am sure hath now high cause
to mourn ? Mockings at *the power of godliness* fly thick in
most congregations and societies. And what is there to be
found almost but mutual detractions and supplantings of the
good name of another, *tongues taught to speak lies*, (Jer. ix.
4, 5,) and that frame, or sew and *weave together deceits*, as it
is in Psal. l. 19 ? And even the godly, as they may be
subject to other sins, so may they be under some degree of
this ; and too many are very much subject, by reason of their
unwatchfulness and not staying themselves in this point,
though not to profane, yet to vain, and it may be to detractive
speeches ; sometimes possibly not with malicious intention, but
out of an inadvertence of this evil, readier to stick on the
failings of men, and it may be of other Christians, than to
consider, and commend, and follow what is laudable in them ;
and it may be, in their best discourses, not endeavouring to
have hearts purified, as becomes them, from all guile and self-
ends. Oh ! it is a thing needs much diligent study, and is
worth it all, to be thoroughly sincere and unfeigned in all,
and particularly in these things. Our Saviour's innocence is
expressed so, *In his mouth was found no guile.* (Chap. ii.
of this Epist. v. 22.)

But to add something for remedy of these evils in some
part discovered ; for to vanquish this world of evils is a great
conquest.

1. It must be done at the heart ; otherwise it will be but a
mountebank cure, a false imagined conquest. The weights
and wheels are *there*, and the clock strikes according to their

motion. Even he that speaks contrary to what is within him, guilefully contrary to his inward conviction and knowledge, yet speaks conformably to what is within him in the temper and frame of his heart, which is double, *a heart and a heart*, as the Psalmist hath it. (Psal. xii. 2.) A guileful heart makes guileful tongue and lips. It is the work-house, where is the forge of deceits and slanders, and other evil speakings; and the tongue is only the outer shop where they are vended, and the lips the door of it; so then such ware as is made within, such and no other can be set out. From evil thoughts, evil speakings; from a profane heart, profane words; and from a malicious heart, bitter or calumnious words; and from a deceitful heart, guileful words, well varnished, but lined with rottenness. And so in the general, *from the abundance of the heart the mouth speaketh*, as our Saviour teaches, Matt. xii. 34. That which the heart is full of, runs over by the tongue: if the heart be full of God, the tongue will delight to speak of him; much of heavenly things within will sweetly breathe forth something of their smell by the mouth; and if nothing but earth is there, all that man's discourse will have an earthly smell; and if nothing but wind, vanity, and folly, the speech will be airy, and vain, and purposeless. *The mouth of the righteous speaketh wisdom:—the law of his God is in his heart.* (Psal. xxxvii. 30, 31.) *Thy law*, says David, (Psal. xl. 8,) *is within my heart*, or as the Hebrew phrase is, *in the midst of my bowels;* and that, as from the centre, sends forth the lines and rays of suitable words, and *I will not, cannot refrain*, as there it is added, (verse 9,) *I have preached righteousness: lo, I have not refrained my lips.* So no more can the evil heart *refrain the tongue from evil*, as here is directed. *The tongue of the righteous*, says Solomon, *is as fine silver, but the heart of the wicked is little worth.* (Prov. x. 20.) It makes the antithesis *in the root;* his *heart* is little worth, and therefore his *tongue* has no silver in it; he may be *worth thousands*, (as we speak,) that is, indeed, in his chests or lands, and yet himself, his heart, and all the thoughts of it, not worth a penny.

If thou art inured to oaths or cursing, in any kind or fashion of it, taking the great *name of God* any ways *in vain,* do not favour thyself in it as a small offence : to excuse it by custom, is to wash thyself with ink : and to plead that thou art long practised in that sin, is to accuse thyself deeper. If thou wouldst indeed be delivered from it, think not that a slight dislike of it (when reproved) will do; but seek for a due knowledge of the majesty of God, and thence a deep reverence of him in thy heart ; and that will certainly cure that habituated evil of thy tongue; will quite alter that bias which the custom thou speakest of hath given it ; will cast it in a new mould, and teach it a new language ; will turn thy regardless abuse of that name, by vain oaths and asseverations, into a holy frequent use of it in prayers and praises. Thou wilt not then dare dishonour that blessed name, which saints and angels bless and adore ; but wilt set in with them to bless it.

None that know the weight of that name will dally with it, and *lightly lift it up ;* (as that word translated *taking in vain,* in the third commandment, signifies ;) they that do continue to *lift it up in vain,* as it were, to sport themselves with it, will find the weight of it falling back upon them, and crushing them to pieces.

In like manner a purified heart will unteach the tongue all filthy impure speeches, and will give it a holy strain; and the spirit of charity and humility will banish that mischievous humour, which sets so deep in the most, of reproaching and disgracing others in any kind either openly or secretly. For it is wicked self-love and pride of heart, whence these do spring, searching and disclosing the failings of others, on which love will rather cast a mantle to hide them.

It is an argument of a candid ingenuous mind, to delight in the good name and commendation of others ; to pass by their defects, and take notice of their virtues ; and to speak and hear of those willingly, and not endure either to speak or hear of the other; for in this indeed you may be little less guilty than the evil speaker, in taking pleasure in it, though you speak it not. And this is a piece of men's natural perverseness, to drink in tales and calumnies * ; and he that doth this, will readily, from the delight he hath in hearing, slide insensibly into the humour of evil speaking. It is strange how most persons dispense with themselves in this point, and that in scarcely any societies shall we find a hatred of this ill, but rather some tokens of taking pleasure in it ; and until a Christian sets himself to an inward watchfulness over his heart, not suffering in it any thought that is uncharitable, or vain self-esteem, upon the sight of others' frailties, he will still be subject to somewhat of this, in the tongue or ear at least. So, then, as for the evil of guile in the tongue, a sincere heart, *truth in the inward parts,* powerfully redresses it ; therefore it is expressed, Psal. xv. 2, *That speaketh the truth from his heart ;* thence it flows. Seek much after this, to speak nothing with God, nor men, but what is the sense of a single unfeigned heart. O sweet truth ! excellent but rare sincerity ! he that *loves that truth within,* alone can work it there ; seek it of him.

2dly. Be choice in your society, *Sit not with vain persons,* (Psal. xxvi. 4,) whose tongues have nothing else to utter, but impurity, or malice, or folly. Men readily learn the dialect and tone of the people amongst whom they live. If you sit down in the chair of scorners, if you take a seat with them, you shall quickly take a share of their diet with them, and sitting amongst them, take your turn, in time, of speaking with them in their own language. But frequent the company of grave and godly persons, in whose hearts and lips piety, and love, and wisdom are set, and it is the way to learn their language.

3dly. Use a little of the bridle in the quantity of speech †.

* Obtrectatio et livor primis auribus accipiuntur.
† Χωρὶς τὸ τ' εἰπεῖν πολλὰ καὶ τὰ καίρια. ÆSCHYL.

Incline a little rather to sparing than lavishing, for *in many words there wants not sin.* That flux of the tongue, that prating and babbling disease, is very common; and hence so many impertinencies, yea, so many of those worse ills in their discourses, whispering about, and inquiring, and censuring this and that. A childish delight! and yet most men carry it with them all along to speak of persons and things not concerning us*. And this draws men to speak many things which agree not with the rules of wisdom, and charity, and sincerity. *He that refraineth his lips is wise,* saith Solomon: (Prov. x. 19:) a vessel without a cover cannot escape uncleanness. Much might be avoided by a little refraining of this; much of the infection and sin that are occasioned by the many babblings that are usual. And were it no worse, is it not a sufficient evil, that they waste away that time, precious time, which cannot be recovered, which the most just or most thankful man in the world cannot restore? He that spares speech, *favors his tongue* indeed, as the Latin phrase is, [*favere linguæ;*] not he that looses the reins and lets it run. He that refrains his lips may ponder and pre-examine what he utters, whether it be profitable or reasonable or no; and so the tongue of the just is as *fined silver;* (Prov. x. 20;) it is refined in the wise forethought and pondering of the heart: according to the saying, *Bis ad limam priusquam semel ad linguam. Twice to the file ere once to the tongue.* Even to utter knowledge and wise things profusely, holds not of wisdom, and a little usually makes most noise; as the Hebrew proverb is, *Stater in lagena bis bis clamat. A penny in an earthen pot keeps a great sound and tinkling.* Certainly it is the way to have much inward peace, to be wary in this point. Men think to have solace by much free unbounded discourse with others, and when they have done, they find it otherwise, and sometimes contrary. He is wise that hath learned to speak little with others, and much with himself and

* Οὐδὶν οὕτως ἡδὺ τοῖς ἀνθρώποις ὡς τὸ λαλεῖν τὰ ἀλλότρια. 2 Orat. 1.

with God. How much might be gained for our souls, if we would make a right use of this silence! So David, dumb to men, found his tongue to God. (Psal. xxxviii. 13, 15.) A spiritually minded man is quickly weary of other discourse, but of that which he loves, and wherewith his affection is possessed and taken up: *Grave æstimant quicquid illud non sonat quod intus amant.* And by experience, a Christian will find it, when the Lord is pleased to shew him most favour in prayer or other spiritual exercise, how unsavoury it makes other discourses after it; as they who have tasted something singularly sweet, think other things that are less sweet altogether tasteless and unpleasant.

4thly. In the use of the tongue, when thou dost speak, divert it from evil and guile, by a habit of, and delight in, profitable and gracious discourse. Thus St. Paul makes the opposition, Eph. iv. 29. Let there be no *rotten communication,* (σαπρὸς λόγος,) and yet he urges not total silence neither, but enjoins such speech *as may edify and administer grace to the hearers.*

Now in this we should consider, to the end such discourses may be more fruitful, both what is the true end of them, and the right means suiting it. They are not only, nor principally, for the learning of some new things, or the canvassing of debated questions, but their chief good is the warming of the heart; stirring up in it love to God, and remembrance of our present and after estate, our mortality and immortality; and extolling the ways of holiness, and the promises and comforts of the Gospel, and the excellency of Jesus Christ; and in these sometimes one particular, sometimes another, as our particular condition requires, or any occasion makes them pertinent. Therefore, in these discourses, seek not so much either to vent thy knowledge, or to increase it, as to know more spiritually and effectually what thou dost know. And in this way those mean despised truths, that every one thinks he is sufficiently seen in, will have a new sweetness and use in them, which thou didst not so well perceive before, (for these flowers cannot be sucked dry,) and in this humble sincere way thou shalt *grow in grace and in knowledge* too.

There is no sweeter entertainment than for travellers to be remembering their country, their blessed home, and the happiness abiding them there, and to be refreshing and encouraging one another in the hopes of it; strengthening their hearts against all the hard encounters and difficulties in the way; often overlooking this moment, and helping each other to higher apprehensions of that vision of God which we expect.

And are not such discourses much more worthy the choosing, than the base trash we usually fill one another's ears withal? Were our tongues given us to exchange folly and sin? or were they not framed for the glorifying of God, and therefore are called *our glory?* Some take the expression for the soul; but they must be one in this work, and then, indeed, are both our tongues and our souls truly our glory, when they are busied in exalting His, and are turned together to that. *That my glory may sing praise to thee and not be silent.* (Psal. xxx. 12.) Instead of calumnies, and lies, and vanities, the carrion which flies, base minds, feed on, to delight in Divine things and extolling of God, is for a *man to eat Angel's food.* An excellent task for the tongue is that which David chooseth: (Psal. xxxv. 28:) *And my tongue shall speak of thy righteousness, and of thy praise all the day long.* Were the day ten days long, no vacant room for any unholy, or offensive, or feigned speech! And they lose not, who love to speak praise to Him, for He loves to speak peace to them; and instead of the world's vain tongue-liberty, to have such intercourse and discourse is no sad melancholy life, as the world mistakes it.

Ver. 11. Let him eschew evil, and do good; let him seek peace, and ensue it.

THIS is a full and complete rule; but it is our miserable folly to mistake so far, as to embrace evil under the notion of good; and not only contrary to the nature of the thing, but contrary to our own experience, still to be pursuing that which is still flying further off from us, catching at a vanishing shadow of delight, with nothing to fasten upon but real guiltiness and misery. Childish minds! we have been so often gulled, and yet never grow wiser, still bewitched and deluded with dreams: *a deceived heart* (a mocked or deluded heart) *hath turned him aside.* (Isa. xliv. 20.) When we think that we are surest, have that hand that holds fastest, our right hand, upon some good, and that now surely we are sped,—even then it proves *a lie in our right hand,* slips through as a handful of air and proves nothing, promises fair, but doth but mock us; (as the same word is used by Jacob, Gen. xxxi. 7, expressing the unfaithfulness of his uncle who changed his ways so often;) yet still we foolishly and madly trust it! When it makes so gross a lie, that we might easily, if we took it to the light, see through it, being a lie so often discovered, and of known falsehood, yet some new dream or disguise makes it pass with us again, and we go round in that mill, having our eyes put out like Samson, and still we are where we were, engaged in perpetual fruitless toil. Strange! that the base deceitful lusts of sin should still keep their credit with us! but *the beast hath a false prophet* at his side, (Rev. xix. 20,) to commend him and set him off with new inventions, and *causes us to err by his lies,* as it is said of the false prophets, Jer. xxiii. 32. But evil it is still; not only void of all good, but the very deformity and debasement of the soul; defacing in it the Divine image of its Maker, and impressing on it the vile image of Satan. And then, further, it is attended with shame and sorrow: even at the very best, *it is a sowing of the wind,*—there is no solid good in it,— and withal a *reaping of the whirlwind,* vexations and horrors. (Hos. viii. 7.) They that know it under a sense of this afterview, as attended with the wrath of an offended God,—ask them what they think of it; whether they would not, in those thoughts, choose any trouble or pain though ever so great, rather than willingly to adventure on the ways of sin.

Obedience is that good, that beauty and comeliness of the

soul, that conformity with the holy will of God, that hath peace and sweetness in it ; the hardest exercise of it is truly delightful even at present, and hereafter it shall fully be so. Would we but learn to consider it thus, to know sin to be the greatest evil, and the holy will of God the highest good, it would be easy to persuade and prevail with men to comply with this advice, to *eschew* the one, and *do* the other.

These do not only reach the actions, but require an intrinsical aversion of the heart from sin, and a propension to holiness and the love of it.

Eschew.] The very motion and bias of the soul must be turned from sin, and carried towards God. And this is principally to be considered by us, and inquired after within us,— *an abhorrence of that which is evil,* as the Scripture speaks, Rom. xii. 9 : not a simple forbearing, but hating and loathing it, and this springing from the love of God. *Ye that love the Lord, hate evil,* says the Psalmist, xcvii. 10. You will do so, cannot choose but do so ; and so may you know that love to him to be upright and true.

And where this love is, the avoidance of sin, and walking in holiness, or *doing good*, will be, 1. More constant, not wavering with the variation of outward circumstances, of occasion, or society, or secrecy, but going on in its natural course ; as the sun is as far from the earth, and goes as fast, under a cloud, as when it is in our sight, and goes cheerfully, because from a natural principle it *rejoiceth as a strong man to run*, (Psal. xix. 5,) such is the obedience of a renewed mind. And, 2. More universal, as proceeding from an abhorrence of all sin ; as natural antipathies are against the whole kind of any thing. 3. More exact, keeping afar off from the very appearances of sin, and from all the inducements and steps towards it. And this is the true way of *eschewing* it.

Not a little time of constrained forbearance during a night, or the day of participating of the communion, or a little time before, and some few days after such services ; for thus, with the most, sin is not dispossessed and cast out, but retires inward and lurks in the heart. Being beset with those ordinances, it knows they last but awhile, and therefore it gets into its strength, and keeps close there, till they be out of sight and disappear again, and be a good way off, so that it thinks itself out of their danger, a good many days having passed, and then it comes forth and returns to exert itself with liberty, yea, it may be, with more vigour, as it were to regain the time it hath been forced to lose and lie idle in.

They again miss of the right manner of this eschewing, who think themselves, possibly, some body in it, in that they do avoid the gross sins wherein the vulgar sort of sinners wallow, or do eschew such evils as they have little or no inclination of nature to. But where the heart stands against sin, as a breach of God's law and an offence against his majesty, as Joseph, *Shall I do this evil, and sin against God?* (Gen. xxxix. 9,) there, it will carry a man against all kind of sin, the most refined and the most beloved sin, wherein the truth of this aversion is most tried and approved. As they who have a strong natural dislike of some kind of meat, dress it as you will, and mingle it with what they love best, yet will not willingly eat of it; and if they be surprised and deceived some way to swallow some of it, yet they will discover it afterwards, and be restless till they have vomited it up again; thus is it with the heart which hath that inward contrariety to sin wrought in it by a new nature,—it will consent to no reconcilement with it, nor with any kind of it; as in those deadly feuds which were against whole families and names without exception. The renewed soul will *have no fellowship with the unfruitful works of darkness,* as the Apostle speaks, Eph. v. 11. For *what agreement is there betwixt light and darkness?* (2 Cor. vi. 14.) And this hatred of sin works most against sin in a man's self; as in things we abhor, our reluctance rises most when they are nearest us. A godly man hates sin in others, as hateful wheresoever it is found; but because it is nearest him in himself, he hates it most there. They who by their nature and breeding are somewhat delicate, like not to see any thing uncleanly any

where, but least of all in their own house, and upon their own
clothes or skin.   This makes the godly man, indeed, flee
not only the society of evil men, but from himself; he goes
out of his old self; and till this be done, a man does not indeed flee sin, but carries it still with him as an evil companion, or an evil guide rather, that misleads him still from
the paths of life.   And there is much, first in the true discovery, and then in the thorough disunion of the heart from
that sin which is most of all a man's self, that from which he can
with the greatest difficulty escape, *that besets him the most,*
(εὐπερίστατος, Heb. xii. 1,) and lieth in his way on all hands,
hath him at every turn: to disengage one's self and get free
from that, to eschew that evil, is difficult indeed.   And the
task in this is the harder, if this evil be, as oftentimes it may
be, not some gross sin, but one more subtle, less seen, and
therefore not so easily avoided; but for this an impartial
search must be used: if it be amongst those things that seem
most necessary, and that cannot be dispensed with, an idol hid
amongst the stuff, yet thence must it be drawn forth and cast
out.

The right eschewing of evil involves a wary avoidance of
all occasions and beginnings of it.   *Flee from sin* (says the
wise man) *as from a serpent.* (Eccles. ii. 2.) We are not to be
tampering with it, and coming near it, and thinking to charm
it; " for (as one says) who will not laugh at the charmer that
' is bitten by a serpent?"   He that thinks he hath power and
skill to handle it without danger, let him observe Solomon's
advice concerning the strange woman: he says not only, *Go
not into her house,* but, *Remove thy way far from her, and
come not near the door of her house.* (Prov. v. 8.) So teaches
he wisely for the avoiding of that other sin near to it, *Look
not on the wine when it is red in the cup.* (Prov. xxiii. 31.)
They that are bold and adventurous are often wounded: thus,
he that removeth stones shall be hurt thereby. (Eccles. x. 9.) If
we know our own weakness and the strength of sin, we shall
fear to expose ourselves to hazards, and be willing even to

abridge ourselves of some things lawful when they prove dangerous ; for he that will do always all he lawfully may, shall often do something that lawfully he may not.

Thus for the other, [*Do good,*] the main thing is, to be inwardly principled for it ; to have a heart stamped with the love of God and his commandments ; to do all for conscience of his will, and love to him, and desire of his glory. A good action, even the best kind of actions, in an evil hand, and from an evil unsanctified heart, passes amongst evils. *Delight in the Lord* and in his ways. David's, *Oh ! how love I thy law,* (Psal. cxix. 17,) tells that he esteems it above the richest and pleasantest things on earth, but how much he esteems and loves it he cannot express.

And upon this will follow (as observed in regard to eschewing evil) a constant tract and course of obedience, moving directly contrary to the stream of wickedness about a man, and also against the bent of his own corrupt heart within him ; a serious desire and endeavour to do all the good that is within our calling and reach, but especially that particular good of our calling, that which *is in our hand,* and is peculiarly required of us. For in this some deceive themselves ; they look upon such a condition as they imagine were fit for them, or such as is in their eye when they look upon others, and they think if they were such persons, and had such a place, and such power and opportunities, they would do great matters ; and in the mean time they neglect that good to which they are called, and which they have in some measure power and place to do. This is the roving sickly humour of our minds, and speaks their weakness ; as sick persons would still change their bed, or posture, or place of abode, thinking to be better. But a staid mind applies itself to the duties of *its own station,* and seeks to glorify him who set it there, reverencing his wisdom in disposing of it so. And there is certainty of a blessed approbation of this conduct. Be thy station never so low, it is not the high condition, but much fidelity, secures it : *Thou hast been faithful in little.* (Luke xix. 17.) We must care not only to answer occasions when they call, but to catch at them, and seek them out; yea, to frame occasions of doing good, whether in the Lord's immediate service, delighting in that, private and public, or in doing good to men, in assisting one with our means, another with *our admonitions, another* with counsel or comfort as we can; labouring not only *to have something* of that good which is most contrary to our nature, but even *to be eminent in that,* setting Christian resolution, and both the example and strength of our Lord against all oppositions, and difficulties, and discouragements: *Looking unto Jesus, the autho*r *and finisher of our faith.* (Heb. xii. 2.)

We see, then, our Rule, and it is the rule of peace and happiness; what hinders but we apply our hearts to it? This is our work, and setting aside the advantage that follows, consider the thing in itself: 1. The opposition of sin and obedience, under the name of *evil* and *good;* 2. The composition of our rule in these expressions, *Eschew* and *Do.* Consider it thus— *evil* and *good,* and it will persuade us to *eschew* and *do.*

And if you are persuaded to it, then, 1. Desire light from above, to discover to you what is evil and offensive to God in any kind, and what pleaseth him, what is his will; (for that is the rule and reason of good in our actions, *that ye may prove what is the good, and holy, and acceptable will of God,* Rom. xii. 2;) and to discover in yourselves what is most adverse and repugnant to that will. 2. Seek a renewed mind to hate that evil, even such as is the closest and most connatural to you, and to love that good, even that which is most contrary. 3. Seek strength and skill, that by Another Spirit than your own, you may *avoid evil and do good,* and resist the incursions and solicitings of evil, the artifices and violences of Satan, who is both a *serpent* and a *lion;* and seek for power against your own inward corruption, and the fallacies of your own heart. And thus you shall be able for *every good work,* and be kept in such a measure as suits your present estate, *blameless in spirit, soul, and body, to the coming of Jesus Christ.* (1 Thess. v. 23.)

"Oh!" but says the humble Christian, "I am often entan-
"gled and plunged in soul-evils, and often frustrated in my

" thoughts against these evils, and in my aims at the good,
" which is my task and duty."

And was not this Paul's condition? May you not complain
in his language? And happy will you be if you do so with
some measure of his feeling; happy in crying out of *wretchedness!* Was not this his malady? *When I would do good, evil
is present with me!* (Rom. vii. 21.) But know at once, that
though thy duty is this, *to eschew evil and do good*, yet thy
salvation is more surely founded than on thine own good. That
perfection which answers to justice and the Law, is not required
of thee. Thou art to *walk not after the flesh, but after the
Spirit;* but in so walking, whether in a low or a high measure,
still thy comfort lieth in this, that *there is no condemnation to
them that are in Christ Jesus*, as the Apostle begins the next
chapter, Rom. viii., after his sad complaints. Again, consider
his thoughts in the close of the viith. chapter, on perceiving the
work of God in himself, and distinguishing that from the corrupt
motions of nature, and so finding at once matter of heavy complaint, and yet of cheerful exultation: *O! wretched man that
I am;* and yet with the same breath, *Thanks to God, through
Christ Jesus our Lord.*

So, then, mourn with him, and yet rejoice with him, and go
on with courage as he did, still *fighting the good fight of
faith*. When thou fallest in the mire, be ashamed and humbled, yet return and wash in *the fountain opened*, and return
and beg new strength *to walk more surely*. Learn to trust
thyself less, and God more, and up and be doing against thy
enemies, how tall and mighty soever be the sons of Anak. *Be
of good courage*, and the Lord shall be with thee, and *shall
strengthen thy heart*, and establish thy goings.

Do not lie down to rest upon lazy conclusions, that it is well
enough with thee, because thou art out of the common puddle
of profaneness; but look further, to *cleanse thyself from all
filthiness of flesh and spirit, perfecting holiness in the fear of
God*. (2 Cor. vii. 1.) Do not think thy little is enough, or that
thou hast reason to despair of attaining more, but press, *press*

hard toward the mark and prize of thy high calling. (Phil. iii. 14.) Do not think all is lost, because thou art at present foiled. *Novit se sæpe vicisse post sanguinem,* says Seneca: The experienced soldier knows that he hath often won the day after a fall, or a wound received; and be assured, that after the short combats of a moment follows an eternity of triumph.

Let him seek peace, and ensue it.] Omitting the many acceptations of the word *Peace,* here particularly external peace with men, I conceive, is meant; and this is to be sought, and not only to be sought when it is willingly found, but we are to pursue and follow it when it seems to fly away; but yet, so to pursue it, as never to step out of the way of holiness and righteousness after it, and to forsake this rule that goes before it, of *eschewing evil and doing good.* Yea, mainly in so doing is peace to be sought and pursued, and it is most readily to be found and overtaken in that way; for *the fruit of righteousness is peace.* (James iii. 18.)

1st, Consider that an unpeaceable, turbulent disposition is the badge of a wicked mind; *as the raging sea, still casting up mire and dirt.* (Isai. lvii. 20.) But this love of peace, and in all good ways seeking and pursuing it, is the true character *of the children of God,* who is *the God of peace.* True, the ungodly (to prevent their own just challenge, as Ahab) call the friends of true religion, disturbers, and the *troublers of Israel;* (1 Kings xviii. 17;) and this will still be their impudence: but certainly, they *that love the welfare of Jerusalem, do seek, and pray for,* and work for *peace* all they can, as a chief blessing, and the fruitful womb of multitudes of blessings.

2dly, Consider, then, that to be deprived of peace is a heavy judgment, and calls for our prayers and tears to pursue it and entreat its return; calls us to seek it from His hand who is the sovereign dispenser of peace and war, to seek to *be at peace with him, and thereby good, all good, shall come unto us,* (Job xxii. 21,) and particularly this great good of outward peace in due time; and the very judgment of war shall in the event be turned into a blessing. We may pursue it amongst men, and not overtake it; we may use all good means, and fall short; but pursue it up as far as the throne of grace, seek it by prayer, and that will overtake it, will be sure to find it in God's hand, *who stilleth the waves of the sea, and the tumults of the people. If he give quietness, who then can disturb?* (Psal. lxv. 7; Job xxxiv. 29.)

He that will love life.] This is the attractive,—*Life. Long life and days of good,* is the thing men most desire; for if they be evil days, then so much the worse that they be long, and the shortest of such seem too long; and if short, being good, this cuts off the enjoyment of that good: but these two complete the good, and suit it to men's wishes,—length and prosperity of life.

It is here supposed that all would be happy, that all desire it, being carried to that by nature, to seek their own good: but he that *will love it,* that means here, that will wisely love it, that will take the way to it, and be true to his desire, *must refrain his tongue from evil, and his lips that they speak no guile; he must eschew evil and do good, seek peace, and ensue it.* You desire to see good days, and yet hinder them by sinful provocations; you desire good clear days, and yet cloud them by your guiltiness.

Thus, many desire good here, yea, and confusedly desire the good of the life to come, because they hear it is life, and long life, and that good is to be found in it, yea, nothing but good: but in this is our folly, we will not love it wisely. The face of our desire is towards it, but in our course we are rowing from it, down into the dead sea. You would all have better times, peace and plenty, and freedom from the molestation and expense of our present condition: why will you not be persuaded to seek it in the true way of it?

But how is this? Do not the righteous often pass their days indistress and sorrow, so as to have *few and evil days,* as Jacob speaks, Gen. xlix. 7? Yet is there a truth in this promise, annexing outward good things to godliness, *as having the promises of this life and that which is to come.* (1 Tim. iv. 8.)

And it is so accomplished to them, when the Lord sees it convenient and conducive to their highest good: but that he most
aims at, and they themselves do most desire; and therefore, if
the abatement of outward good, either as to the length or sweetness of this life, serve his main end and theirs better, they are
agreed upon this gainful commutation of good for infinitely
better.

The life of a godly man, though short in comparison of the
utmost of nature's course, yet may be long in value, in respect
of his activity and attainment to much spiritual good. He may
be said to live much in a little time; whereas they that wear
out their days in folly and sin, *diu vivunt, sed parum, i. e.*
they live long, but little; or, as the same writer again speaks,
non diu vixit, diu fuit, i. e., he lived not long, but existed
long. And the good of the godly man's days, though unseen
good, surpasses all the world's mirth and prosperity, which
makes a noise, but is hollow within, as the *crackling of thorns,*
a great sound, but little heat, and quickly done. As St. Augustine says of Abraham, he had *dies bonos in Deo, licet malos
in seculo,* good days in God, though evil days in his generation; a believer can make up an ill day with a good God, and
enjoying him, he hath solid peace. But then that which is
abiding, that length of days, and that dwelling in the house of
God in that length of days, is what *eye hath not seen, nor ear
heard,* &c. (1 Cor. ii. 9.) They are, indeed, *good days,* or
rather one everlasting day, which has *no need of the sun nor of
the moon,* but immediately flows from the first and increased
Light, *the Father of Lights;* His glory shines in it, *and the
Lamb is the light thereof.*

Ver. 12. For the eyes of the Lord are over the righteous, and his ears
are open unto their prayers; but the face of the Lord is against them
that do evil.

THE wisest knowledge of things is, to know them in their causes;
but there is no knowledge of causes so happy and useful, as
clearly to know and firmly to believe the universal dependence

of all things upon the First and Highest Cause, the Cause of causes, the spring of being and goodness, the wise and just Ruler of the world.

This the Psalmist, Psalm xxxiv. 15, 16, as here with him the Apostle, gives as the true reason of that truth they have averred in the former words, the connexion of holiness and happiness. If life, and peace, and all good be in God's hand to bestow when it pleaseth him, then surely the way to it is an obedient and regular walking in observance of his will; and the way of sin is the way to ruin: *For the eyes of the Lord are upon the righteous, &c., and his face is against them that do evil.*

In the words there is a double opposition; of persons, and of their portion.

1*st*, Of persons, The *righteous* and *evil-doers.* These two words are often used in the Scriptures, and particularly in the book of Psalms, to express the godly and the wicked ; and so this righteousness is not absolute perfection or sinlessness, nor is the opposed evil every act of sin or breach of God's law : but the righteous be they that are students of obedience and holiness, that desire to walk as in the sight of God, and to *walk with God,* as Enoch did ; that are glad when they can any way serve him, and grieved when they offend him ; that feel and bewail their unrighteousness, and are earnestly breathing and advancing forward ; have a sincere and unfeigned love to all the commandments of God, and diligently endeavour to observe them; that vehemently hate what most pleases their corrupt nature, and love the command that crosses it most; this is an imperfect kind of perfection. (See Phil. iii. 12, 15.)

On the other side, evil-doers are they that commit sin *with greediness;* that walk in it, make it their way ; that live in sin as their element, *taking pleasure in unrighteousness,* as the Apostle speaks, 2 Thess. xi. 12; their great faculty, their great delight lies in sin; they are skilful and cheerful evil-doers. Not any one man in all kinds of sins ; that is impossible ; there is a concatenation of sin, and one disposes and induces to another ; but yet one ungodly man is commonly more versed in and delighted with some one kind of sin, another with some other. He forbears none because it is evil and hateful to God, but as he cannot travel over the whole globe of wickedness, and go the full circuit, he walks up and down in his accustomed way of sin. No one mechanic is good at all trades, nor is any man expert in all arts ; but he is an evil-doer that follows the particular trade of the sin he hath chosen, is active and diligent in that, and finds it sweet. In a word, this opposition lieth mainly in the bent of the affection, or in the way it is set. The godly man hates the evil he possibly by temptation hath been drawn to do, and loves the good he is frustrated of, and, having intended, hath not attained to do. The sinner, who hath his denomination from sin as his course, hates the good which he is sometimes forced to do, and loves that sin which many times he does not, either wanting occasion and means, so that he cannot do it, or through the check of an enlightened conscience, possibly dares not do ; and though so bound up from the act, as a dog in a chain, yet the habit, the natural inclination and desire in him, is still the same, the strength of his affection is carried to sin. So in the weakest godly man, there is that predominant sincerity and desire of holy walking, according to which he is called a righteous person ; the Lord is pleased to give him that name, and account him so, being upright in heart, though often failing. There is a righteousness of a higher strain, upon which his salvation hangs ; that is not in him, but upon him ; he is clothed with it ; but this other kind, which consists of sincerity and of true and hearty, though imperfect, obedience, is the righteousness here meant, and opposed to evil-doing.

2dly, Their opposite condition, or portion, is expressed in the highest notion of it, that wherein the very being of happiness and misery lieth, the favour and anger of God. As their natures differ most by the habit of their affection towards God, as their main distinguishing character, so the difference of their estate consists in the point of his affection towards them, expressed here in our language, by the divers aspects of his countenance ; because our love or hatred usually looks out and shews itself that way.

Now for the other word expressing His favour to the righteous, by *the openness of his ear*,—the opposition in the other needed not be expressed ; for either the wicked pray not, or if they do, it is indeed no prayer, the Lord doth not account or receive it as such ; and if his face be set against them, certainly his ear is shut against them too, and so shut, that it openeth not to their loudest prayer. *Though they cry in mine ears with a loud voice, yet will I not hear them,* says the Lord. (Ezek. viii. 18.)

And before we pass to the particulars of their condition, as here we have them described, this we would consider a little, and apply it to our present business,—Who are the persons whom the Lord thus regards, and to whose prayer he opens his ear.

This we pretend to be seeking after, that the Lord would look favourably upon us, and hearken to our suits, for ourselves, and this land, and the whole Church of God within these kingdoms. Indeed *the fervent prayer of a faithful man availeth much* [πολὺ ἰσχύει] ; it is of great strength, a mighty thing, that can bind and loose the influences of heaven ; (as there is instanced, James v. 16 ;) and if the prayer of a righteous man, be it but of one righteous man, how much more the combined cries of many of them together ! And that we judge not the righteousness there and here mentioned to be a thing above human estate, Elias, says the Apostle, *was a man,* and *a man subject to like passions as we are,* and yet such a righteous person as the Lord had an eye and gave ear to in so great a matter. But where are those righteous fasters and prayers in great congregations ? How few, if any, are to be found, who are such but in the lowest sense and measure, real lovers and inquirers after holiness ! What are our meetings here, but assemblies of evil-doers, rebellious children, ignorant and profane persons, or dead formal professors; and so, the more of us, the worse, incensing the Lord the more; and the multitude of prayers, though we could and would continue many days, all to no purpose from such as we. *Though ye make many prayers, when ye multiply prayer, I will not hear: and when ye spread forth your hands, I will hide mine eyes from you.* (Isa. i. 11.) Your hands are so filthy, that if you would follow me to lay hold of me with them, you drive me further off; as one with foul hands following a person that is neat, to catch hold of him; and *if you spread them out before me,* my eyes are pure, you will make me turn away; I cannot endure to look upon them, *I will hide mine eyes from you.* And fasting, added with prayer, will not do it, nor make it pass. *When they fast I will not hear their cry.* (Jer. xiv. 12.)

It is the sin of his people that provokes Him, instead of looking favourably upon them, to have *his eyes upon them for evil and not for good,* as He threatens, Amos ix. 4.; and therefore, without putting away of that, prayer is lost breath, doth no good.

They that still retain their sins, and will not hearken to his voice, how can they expect but that justly threatened retaliation, Prov. i. 26, 28, and that the Lord, in holy scorn, in the day of their distress, should send them for help and comfort to those things which they have made their gods, and preferred before him in their trouble? *They will say, arise and save us; but where are the gods that thou hast made thee? Let them arise, if they can save thee in the time of thy trouble.* (Jer. ii. 28.)

And not only do open and gross impieties thus disappoint our prayers, but the lodging of any sin in our affection. *If I regard iniquity in my heart,* says the Psalmist, (Psal. lxvi. 18,) *the Lord will not hear my voice.* The word is, *If I see iniquity;* if mine eye look pleasantly upon it, His will not look so upon me, nor shall I find his ear so ready and open. He says not, If I do sin, but, *If I regard it in my heart.* The heart's entertaining and embracing a sin, though it be a smaller

sin, is more than the simple falling into sin. And as the ungodly do for this reason lose all their prayers, a godly man
may suffer this way, in some degree, upon some degree of
guiltiness. The heart being seduced, it may be, and entangled
for a time by some sinful lust, Christians are sure to find a
stop in their prayers, that they neither go nor come so quickly
and so comfortably as before. . Any sinful humour, as rheums
do our voice, binds up the voice of prayer, makes it not so
clear and shrill as it was wont; and the accusing guilt of it as-
cending, shuts up the Lord's ear, that he doth not so readily
hear and answer as before. And thus that sweet correspondence is interrupted, which all the delights of the world cannot
compensate. If, then, you would have easy and sweet accesses
to God in prayer,

1. Seek a holy heart; entertain a constant care and study
of holiness; admit no parley with sin; do not so much as
hearken to it, if you would be readily heard.

2. Seek a broken heart; the Lord is ever at hand to that,
as it is in Psal. xxxiv., whence the Apostle cites the words now
under our consideration, *He is nigh to them that are of a contrite
spirit* (v. 18, &c.); it is an excellent way to prevail. The breaking of the heart multiplies petitioners; every piece of it hath a
voice, and a very strong and very moving voice, that enters his
ear, and stirs the bowels and compassions of the Lord towards it.

3. Seek an humble heart. That may present its suit always;
the court is constantly there, even within it; the Great King
loves to make his abode and residence in it. (Isa. lvii. 15.)
This is the thing that the Lord so delights in and requires;
he will not fail to accept of it; it is his choice, (Mic. vi. 7, 8,)
Wherewith shall I come before the Lord? &c. *He hath shewed
thee, O man, what is good; and what doth the Lord require
of thee, but to do justly, and love mercy?* There is this
righteousness, and that as a great part making it up, *to walk
humbly with thy God;* in the original, *humble to walk with
thy God;* he cannot agree with a proud heart; he hates, resists
it; and *two cannot walk together unless they be agreed,* as

the prophet speaks, Amos iii. 3.   The humble heart only is company for God, hath liberty to walk and converse with Him. *He gives grace to the humble;* he bows his ear, if thou lift not up thy neck: proud beggars he turns away with disdain, and the humblest suitors always speed best with him.   *The righteous,* not such in their own eyes, but in His, through his gracious dignation and acceptance.   And is there not reason to come humbly before Him,—base worms, to the most holy and most high God?

The eyes of the Lord.]   We see, 1. That both are *in his sight,* the righteous and the wicked; all of them, and all their ways.   His eye is on the one, and his face on the other, as the word is; but so on these as to be against them.   It is therefore rendered as denoting his eye of knowledge and observance, marking them and their actions, which is equally upon both. *There is no darkness nor shadow of death where the workers of iniquity may hide themselves.*   (Job. xxxiv. 22.)   Foolishly and wretchedly done, to do that, or think that, which we would hide from the Lord, and then to think that we can hide it!   The prophet speaks woe to such: *Woe to them that dig deep to hide their counsel from the Lord, and their works are in the dark, and they say, Who seeth us, and who knoweth us?*   (Isa. xxix. 15.)   And this is the grand principle of all wickedness, (not, it may be, expressly stated, but secretly lying in the soul,) an habitual forgetting of God and his eye, not considering that he beholds us.   *Ye that forget God,* says the Psalmist (l. 22); thence all impiety proceeds; and, on the other side, *the remembrance* of his eye is a radical point of piety and holiness, in which the cxxxixth Psalm is large and excellent.

But, 2. As the Lord doth thus equally see both, so as that his eye and countenance imports his mind concerning them and towards them, the manner of his beholding them is different, yea, contrary.   And from the other,—the beholding them in common—knowing their ways—arises this different beholding, which (as usually words of sense signify also the affection,

verba sensus connotant affectus) is the approving and dis-
liking, the loving and hating them, and their ways: so He
peculiarly *knows the righteous* and their *ways*, (Psal. i. 6,) and
knows not, never knew, the workers of iniquity; even those
that by their profession would plead most acquaintance, and
familiar converse, *eating and drinking in his presence*, and
yet, *I know you not whence you are.* (Luke xiii. 26.) It is
not a breaking off from former acquaintance ; no, He doth not
that ; He disavows none that ever were truly acquainted with
him. So the other evangelist hath it, Matt. vii. 29, of · those
that thought to have been in no small account, *I never knew
you, depart from me;* and the convincing reason lies in that,
Ye workers of iniquity : none of his favourites and friends
are such.

Thus here, His eye, His gracious eye for good, is on the
righteous; and His face, His angry looks, His just wrath
against evil-doers.

In the xith Psalm we have this expressed much after the
same way. First, what we spoke of God's knowing and beholding in common the righteous and wicked, and their ways,
is represented by his *sitting on high*, where he may mark, and
see clearly throughout all places and all hearts. *His throne is
in Heaven, his eyes behold, his eye-lids try the children of
men.* (Ver. 4.) He sits in Heaven, not as in a chair of rest,
regardless of human things, but on *a throne* for governing
and judging; though with as little uneasiness and disturbance,
as if there were nothing to be done that way. *His eyes behold*,
not in a fruitless contemplation or knowledge, but *His eye-lids
try*, which signifies an intent inspection, such as men usually
make with a kind of motion of their eye-lids. Then upon this
is added the different portion of the righteous and wicked, in
his beholding them and dealing with them: *The Lord trieth
the righteous*, ver. 5, approves what is good in them, and by
trial and affliction doth purge out what is evil; and in both
these there is love; *but the wicked, and him that loveth violence, His soul hateth;* and therefore, as here, *His face is*

against them. His soul and face are all one, but these things are expressed after our manner. He looks upon them with indignation; and thence come the storms in the next verse, *Snares rained down,* ver. 6; the wariest foot cannot avoid such snares, they come down upon them from above: *Fire and brimstone and burning tempest;* (alluding to *Sodom's* judgment, as an emblem of the punishment of all the wicked;) *this is the portion of their cup.* There is a cup for them; but His children drink not with them. *They* have another cup; *the Lord* himself *is the portion of their cup.* (Psal. xvi. 5.) As the xith Psalm closes, *The righteous Lord loveth righteousness: his countenance doth behold the upright:* that is another beholding than the former, a gracious, loving beholding; as here, *His eyes are upon the righteous.*

Now the persuasion of this truth is the main establishment of a godly mind, amidst all the present confusions that appear in things; and it is so here intended, as well as in the Psalm I have mentioned, and throughout the Scriptures.

To look upon the present flourishing and prosperity of evil-doers, and on the distresses and sorrows of the godly, is a dark obscure matter in itself; but the way to be cleared and comforted, is to look above them to the Lord. *They looked unto him and were lightened;* (Psal. xxxiv. 5.) That answers all doubts, to believe this undoubted providence and justice, the eye of God that sees all, yea, rules all these things. And in the midst of all the painted happiness of wicked men, this is enough to make them miserable, *The Lord's face is against them;* and they shall surely find it so. He hath wrath and judgment in store, and *will bring it forth to light,* will execute it in due time; he is preparing for them that cup spoken of, and they shall drink it. So in the saddest condition of his church and a believing soul, to know this, that the Lord's eye is even then upon them, and that he is upon thoughts of peace and love to them, is that which settles and composes the mind. Thus, in that Psalm before cited, it was such difficulties that did drive David's thoughts to that for satisfaction: *If the foundations be destroyed, what can the righteous do?* (Psal. xi. 2.) In the time of such great shakings and confusions, the righteous man can do nothing to it, but the righteous Lord can do enough; He can do all, *The righteous Lord that loveth righteousness.* While all seems to go upside down, *He is on his throne,* He is *trying and judging,* and will appear to be judge. This is the thing that faithful souls should learn to look to, and not lose view and firm belief of, and should desire the Lord himself to raise their minds to it, when they are ready to sink. Natural strength and resolution will not serve the turn; floods may come that will arise above that; something above a man's own spirit must support him; therefore say with David, (Psal. lxi. 2,) *When my spirit is overwhelmed, lead me to the rock that is higher than I.* They think sometimes it is so hard with them, that He regards not; but he assures them to the contrary, *I have graven thee upon the palms of mine hands,* (Isa. xlix. 16.) I cannot look upon my own hands, but I must remember thee: *And thy walls are continually before me.* This is what the spouse seeks for, *Set me as a seal upon thine arm.* (Cant. viii. 6.)

Now a little more particularly to consider the expressions, and their scope here; how is that made good which the former words teach, that they who walk in the ways of wickedness can expect no good, but are certainly miserable? Thus: *the face of the Lord is against them.* Prosper they may in their affairs and estates, may have riches, and posterity, and friends, and the world caressing them and smiling on them on all hands; but there is that one thing that damps all, *the face of the Lord is against them.* This they feel not indeed for the time; it is an invisible ill, out of sight and out of mind with them; but there is a time of the appearing of *this face of the Lord against them, the revelation of his righteous judgment,* as the Apostle speaks, Rom. ii. 5. Sometimes they have precursory days of it here; there is, however, one great prefixed day, *a day of darkness* to them indeed, wherein they shall know what this is, that now sounds so light, *to have the face of the Lord against them.* A look of it is more terrible than all present miseries combined together; what then shall the eternity of it be? *to be punished* (as the Apostle speaks) *with everlasting destruction from the presence of the Lord, and the glory of his power!* (2 Thess. i. 9.)

Are we not then impertinent foolish creatures, who are so thoughtful how our poor business here succeed with us, and how we are accounted of in the world, and how the faces of men are towards us, and scarcely ever enter into a secret serious enquiry how the countenance of God is to us, whether favourably shining on us, or still angrily *set against us,* as it is against all impenitent sinners?

The face of the soul being towards God, turned away from the world and sin, argues for it, that His face is not against it, but that he hath graciously looked upon it, and by a look of love hath drawn it towards himself; for we act not first in that. *Non amatur Deus nisi de Deo:* There is no love of God but what comes from God. It is He that prevents us, and by the beams of his love kindles love in our hearts. Now the soul that is thus set towards him, it may be, doth not constantly see here his face shining full and clear upon it, but often clouded; nay, it may be, such a soul hath not yet at all seen it sensibly; yet this it may conclude, "Seeing *my desires are towards him,* "and my chief desire is the sweet *light of his countenance,* "though as yet I find not his face shining on me, yet I am "persuaded it is not *set against me* to destroy me." Misbelief, when the soul is much under its influence and distempered by it, may suggest this sometimes too; but yet still there is some spark of hope that it is otherwise, that the eye of the Lord's pity is even in that estate upon us, and will in time manifest itself to be so.

To the other question, What assurance have the godly for that *seeing of good,* these blessings you speak of? This is the answer: *The eyes of the Lord are upon them, and his ears open to their prayer.* If you think him wise enough to know what is good for them, and rich enough to afford it, they are sure of one thing, He loves them; they have **His** good will; His heart is towards them, and therefore His eye and His ear. Can they then want any good? If *many days* and outward good things be indeed good for them, they cannot miss of these. He hath given them already much better things than these, and hath yet far better in store for them; and what way soever the world go with them, this itself is happiness enough, that they are in His love, *whose loving kindness is better than life*. (Psal. lxiii. 3.) Sweet days have they that live in it. What better days would courtiers wish, than to be still in the eye and favour of 'the king, to be certain of his good will towards them, and to know of access and of a gracious acceptance of all their suits? Now thus it is with all the servants of the Great King, without prejudice one to another; He is ready to receive their requests, and able and willing to do them all good. Happy estate of a believer! He must not account himself poor and destitute in any condition, for he hath favour at court; he hath the King's eye and his ear; *the eyes of the Lord are upon him, and His ears open to his prayers*.

The eyes of the Lord are upon the righteous.] This hath in it, 1. His love, the propension of his heart towards them. The eye is the servant of the affection; it naturally turns that way most, where the heart is. Therefore thus the Lord is pleased to speak of his love to his own. He views still all the world, but he looks upon them with a peculiar delight; his eye is still on them, as it were, turned towards them from all the rest of the world. Though he doth not always let them see these his looks, (for it is not said, they always are in sight of it; no, not here;) yet still, his eye is indeed upon them, attracted by the beauty of grace in them, his own work indeed, the beauty that he himself hath put upon them. And so as to the other, his ear too; he is willing to do for them what they ask; he loves even to hear them speak; finds a sweetness in the voice of their prayers, that makes his ear not only *open to their prayers*, but desirous of them as sweet music. Thus he speaks of both, Cant. ii. 14: *My dove, let me see thy countenance, let me hear thy voice, for sweet is thy voice, and thy countenance is comely.*

2. The phrase expresses his good providence and readiness to do them good ; to supply their wants, and order their affairs for them ; to answer their desires, and thus to let them find the fruits of that love which so leads his eye and ear towards them. *His eye is upon them ;* he is devising and thinking what to do for them ; it is the thing he thinks on most. His eyes are upon all, but they are busied, as he is pleased to express it, *they run to and fro through the earth, to show himself strong in behalf of them whose heart is perfect towards him,* &c. (2 Chron. xvi. 9.) So Deut. xi. 12 : *His eyes are all the year on the land.* No wonder, then, he answers their suits in what is good for them, when it is still in his thoughts before. *He prevents them with the blessings of his goodness,* (Psal. xxi. 3 :) they cannot be so mindful of themselves, as he is of them.

This is an unspeakable comfort, when a poor believer is in great perplexity of any kind in his outward or spiritual condition. "Well, I see no way ; I am blind in this, but there " are *eyes upon me,* that see well what is best. The Lord is " minding me, and bringing about all to my advantage. *I am " poor and needy indeed, but the Lord thinketh on me.*" (Psal. xl. 17.) That turns the balance. Would not a man, though he had nothing, think himself happy, if some great prince was busily thinking how to advance and enrich him? Much more if a number of kings were upon this thought, and devising together. Yet *these thoughts might perish,* as the Psalmist speaks, Psal. cxlvi. 4. How much more solid happiness is it, to have Him, whose power is greatest, and whose thoughts fail not, eyeing thee, and devising thy good, and asking us, as it were, *What shall be done to the man whom the king will honour?*

And his ears are open unto their prayer.] What suits thou hast, thou mayest speak freely : he will not refuse thee any thing that is for thy good.

"O ! but I am not *righteous,* and all this is for the righteous,

" only." Yet thou wouldst be such a one. Wouldst thou indeed? then in part thou art: (as he who modestly and wisely changed the name of *wise-men* into *philosophers,* lovers of wisdom,) art thou not righteous? yet (φιλοδίκαιος) a *lover of righteousness* thou art ; then thou art one of the righteous. If still thine own unrighteousness be in thine eye, it may and should be so, to humble thee ; but if it should scare thee from coming unto God, and offering thy suits with this persuasion, that *his ear is open,* should it make thee think that his favourable eye is not toward thee, yet there is mercy ; creep in under the robe of his Son. Thou art sure *he* is *Jesus Christ the righteous,* and that the Father's eye is on him with delight, and then it shall be so on thee, being in him. Put thy petitions into his hand, who is the great Master of Requests; thou canst not doubt that he hath access, and that he hath that ear open to him, which thou thinkest shut to thee.

The exercise of prayer being so important, and bearing so great a part in the life and comfort of a Christian, it deserves to be very seriously considered. We will therefore subjoin some few considerations concerning it.

Prayer may be considered in a threefold notion. 1. As a duty we owe to God. As it is from Him we expect and receive all, it is a very reasonable homage and acknowledgment, thus to testify the dependence of our being and life on him, and the dependence of our souls upon him, for being, and life, and all good ; that we be daily suitors before his throne, and go to him for all. 2. As it constitutes the dignity and the delight of a spiritual mind, to have so near access unto God, and such liberty to speak to him. 3. As a proper and sure means, by Divine appointment and promise, of obtaining at the hands of God those good things that are needful and convenient for us. And although some believers of lower knowledge do not (it may be) so distinctly know, and others not so particularly consider, all these in it, yet there is a latent notion of them all in the heart of every godly person, which stirs them and puts them on to the constant use of prayer, and to a love of it.

And as they are in these respects inclined and bent to the exercise of prayer, the Lord's ear is in like manner inclined to hear their prayer in these respects. 1. He takes it well at their hands, that they do offer it up as due worship to him that they desire thus as they can to serve him. He accepts of those offerings graciously, passes by the imperfections in them, and hath regard to their sincere intention and desire. 2. It pleases him well that they delight in prayer, as converse with him; that they love to be much with him, and to speak to him often, and still aspire, by this way, to more acquaintance with him; that they are ambitious of this. 3. He willingly hears their prayers as the expressions of their necessities and desires; being both rich and bountiful, he loves to have blessings drawn out of his hands that way; as full breasts delight to be drawn. The Lord's treasure is always full, and therefore he is always communicative. In the first respect, prayer is acceptable to the Lord *as incense and sacrifice*, as David desires, Psal. cxli. 12: the Lord receives it as Divine worship done to him. In the second respect, prayer is as the visits and sweet entertainment and discourse of friends together, and so is pleasing to the Lord, as the free opening of the mind, the *pouring out of the heart to him*, as it is called, Psal. lxii. 8; and David, in Psal. v. 1, calls it *his words* and *his meditation ;* the word for that signifies *discourse* or *conference.* And, in the third sense, the Lord receives prayer as the suits of petitioners who are in favour with him, and whom he readily accords to. And this the word for *supplication* in the original, and the word here rendered *prayer,* and that rendered *cry* in the Psalm, do mean; and in that sense, the Lord's open ear and hearkening hath in it his readiness to answer, as one that doth hear, and to answer graciously and really, as hearing favourably.

I shall now add some directions : I. For prayer, that it may be accepted and answered. II. For observing the answers of it.

I. For prayer. 1. The qualification of the heart that offers it. 2. The way of offering it.

1. As to the qualification of the heart, it must be in some measure, 1*st,* a holy heart, according to that word here, *the righteous.* There must be *no regarding iniquity,* no entertaining of friendship with any sin, but a permanent love and desire of holiness. Thus, indeed, a man prays within himself, as in a sanctified place, whither the Lord's ear inclines, as of old to the Temple. He needs not run superstitiously to a church, &c. *Intra te ora, sed vide priùs an sis templum Dei:* Pray inwardly, but first see whether thou art thyself a temple of God. The sanctified man's body is the *temple of the Holy Ghost,* as the Apostle speaks, 1 Cor. vi. 19; and his soul is the priest in it that offers sacrifice: both holy to the Lord, consecrated to him. 2*dly,* It must be a believing heart, for there is no praying without this. Faith is the very life of prayer, whence spring hope and comfort with it, to uphold the soul, and keep it steady under storms with the promises; and as Aaron and Hur to Moses, keeping it from fainting, strengthening the hands when they would begin to fail. Such is the force of that word, Psal. x. 17; for the *preparing of the heart,* which God gives as an assurance and pledge of his *inclining his ear to hear,* signifies the *establishing of the heart;* that, indeed, is a main point of its preparedness, and due disposition for prayer. Now this is done by faith, without which, the soul, as the Apostle St. James speaks, is a rolling unquiet thing, *as a wave of the sea,* of itself unstable as the waters, and then *driven with the wind and tossed* to and fro with every temptation. See and feel thine own unworthiness as much as thou canst, for thou art never bidden to believe in thyself; no, but that is countermanded as faith's great enemy. But what hath thy unworthiness to say against free promises of grace, which are the basis of thy faith? So then believe, that you may pray: this is David's advice, (Ps. lxii. 8,) *Trust in him at all times, ye people,* and then, *pour out your hearts before him.* Confide in him as a most faithful and powerful friend, and then you will open your hearts to him.

2. For the way of offering up prayer. It is a great art, a

main point of the secret of religion, to be skilled in it, and of great concern for the comfort and success of it. Much is here to be considered, but for the present take these advices briefly. [1.] Offer not to speak to him without the heart in some measure seasoned and prepossessed with the sense of his greatness and holiness. And there is much in this; considering wisely to whom we speak, *the King, the Lord of glory,* and setting the soul before him, in his presence; and then reflecting on ourselves, and seeing what we are, how wretched, and base, and filthy, and unworthy of such access to so great a Majesty. The want of this *preparing of the heart* to speak in the Lord's ear, by the consideration of God and ourselves, is that which fills the exercise of prayer with much guiltiness; makes the heart careless, and slight, and irreverent, and so displeases the Lord, and disappoints ourselves of that comfort in prayer, and those answers of it, of which, otherwise, we should have more experience. We rush in before him with any thing, provided we can tumble out a few words; and do not weigh these things, and compose our hearts with serious thoughts and conceptions of God. The soul that studies and endeavours this most, hath much to do to attain to any right apprehensions of him; (for *how little know we of him!*) yet should we, at least, set ourselves before him as the purest and greatest Spirit; a being infinitely more excellent than our minds or any creature can conceive. This would fill the soul with awe and reverence, and ballast it, so as to make it go more even through the exercise; to consider *the Lord,* as that prophet saw him, *sitting on his throne, and all the hosts of heaven standing by him,* on his right hand and on his left, (1 Kings xxii. 19,) and thyself a defiled sinner coming before him, *velut è palude suâ vilis ranuncula,* as a vile frog creeping out of some pool, as St. Bernard expresses it: how would this fill thee with holy fear! Oh! his greatness and our baseness; and Oh! the distance! This is Solomon's advice: *Be not rash with thy mouth, and let not thy heart be hasty to utter any thing before God, for God is in heaven and thou upon earth, therefore let thy words be few.* (Eccl. v. 2.) This would keep us from our ordinary babblings, that heart nonsense, which, though the words be sense, yet, through the inattention of the heart, are but as impertinent confused dreams in the Lord's ear; as there it follows, ver. 3.

[2.] When thou addressest thyself to prayer, desire and depend upon the assistance and inspiration of the Holy Spirit of God; without which thou art not able truly to pray. It is a supernatural work, and therefore the principle of it must be supernatural. He that hath nothing of the Spirit of God, cannot pray at all: he may howl as a beast in his necessity or distress, or may speak words of prayer, as some birds learn the language of men; but pray he cannot. And they that have that Spirit ought to seek the movings and actual workings of it in them in prayer, as the particular *help of their infirmities,* teaching both what to ask, (a thing which of ourselves we know not,) and then enabling them to ask, breathing forth their desires in such sighs and groans as are the breath, not simply of their own, but of God's Spirit.

[3.] As these two precautions are to be taken before prayer, so, in the exercise of it, you should learn to keep a watchful eye over your own hearts throughout, for every step of the way, that they start not out. And in order to this, strive to keep up a continual remembrance of that presence of God, which, in the entry of the work, is to be set before the eye of the soul. And our endeavour ought to be to fix it upon that view, that it turn not aside nor downwards, but from beginning to end keep sight of Him, who sees and marks whether we do so or no. They that are most inspective and watchful in this, will still be faulty in it; but certainly, the less watchful, the more faulty. And this we ought to do, to be aspiring daily to more stability of mind in prayer, and to be driving out somewhat of that roving and wandering, which is so universal an evil, and certainly so grievous, not to those who have it most, but who observe and discover it most and endeavour most against it. A strange thing! that the mind, even the renewed mind, should be so ready, not only at other times, but in the exercise of prayer, wherein we peculiarly come so near to God, yet even then to slip out and leave him, and follow some poor vanity or other instead of him! Surely the godly man, when he thinks on this, is exceedingly ashamed of himself, cannot tell what to think of it. *God his exceeding joy*, whom, in his right thoughts, he esteems so much above the world and all things in it, yet to use him thus!—when he is speaking to him, to break off from that, and hold discourse, or change a word with some base thought that steps in, and whispers to him; or, at the best, not to be stedfastly minding the Lord to whom he speaks, and possessed with the regard of His presence, and of his business and errand with Him.

This is no small piece of our misery here: these wanderings are evidence to us, that we are not at home. But though we should be humbled for this, and still be labouring against it, yet should we not be so discouraged, as to be driven from the work. Satan would desire no better than that; it were to help him to his wish. And sometimes a Christian may be driven to think, " What shall I still do thus, abusing my Lord's name, " and the privilege he hath given me? I had better leave off." No, not so by any means. Strive against the miserable evil that is within thee, but cast not away thy happiness. Be doing still. It is a froward childish humour, when any thing agrees not to our mind, to throw all away. Thou mayest come off, as Jacob, with *halting* from thy *wrestlings*, and yet obtain *the blessing* for which thou wrestlest.

[4.] Those graces which are the due qualities of the heart, disposing it for prayer in the exercise of it, should be excited and acted, as holiness, the love of it, the desire of increase and growth of it: so the humbling and melting of the heart, and chiefly faith, which is mainly set on work in prayer, draw forth the sweetnesses and virtues of the promises, teaching us to desire earnestly their performance to the soul, and to believe that they shall be performed; to have before our eyes His goodness and faithfulness who hath promised, and to rest upon that. And for success in prayer, exercising faith in it, it is altogether necessary to interpose the Mediator, and to look through him, and to speak and petition by him, who warns us of this, that there is no other way to speed: *No man cometh to the Father but by me.* (John xiv. 6.) As the Jews when they prayed, looked toward the temple, where was the mercy-seat, and the peculiar presence of God [*Schechinah*], thus ought we in all our praying to look on Christ, who is our *propitiatory*, and *in whom the fulness of the Godhead dwells bodily.* (Col. ii. 9.) The forgetting of this may be the cause of our many disappointments.

[5.] Fervency; not to seek coldly: that presages refusal. There must be fire in the sacrifice, otherwise it ascends not. There is no sacrifice without incense, and no incense without fire. Our remiss, dead hearts are not likely to do much for the Church of God, nor for ourselves. Where are those strong cries that should pierce the heavens? *His ear is open to their cry.* He hears the faintest, coldest prayer, but not with that delight and propenseness to grant it; his ear is not on it, as the word there is, Psal. lv. 17; he takes no pleasure in hearing it; but cries, heart-cries, oh! these take his ear, and move his bowels; for these are the voice, the cries of his own children. A strange word of encouragement to importunity is that, *Give him no rest,* (Isa. lxii. 7,) suffer him not to be quiet till *he make Jerusalem a praise in the earth.* A few such suitors in these times were worth thousands such as we are. Our prayers stick in our breasts, scarcely come forth; much less do they go up and ascend with that piercing force that would open up the way for deliverances to come down.

But in this there must be some difference between temporal and spiritual things. That prayer which is in the right strain, cannot be too fervent in any thing; but the desire of the thing in temporals may be too earnest. A feverish distempered heat diseases the soul; therefore, in these things, a holy indifferency concerning the particular may, and should, be joined with the fervency of prayer. But in spiritual things, there is no danger in vehemency of desire. *Covet* these, *hunger and thirst* for them, be incessantly ardent in their suit; yet even in these, in some particulars, (as with respect to the degree and measure of grace, and some peculiar furtherances,) they should be presented so with earnestness, as that withal it be with a reverence and resignation of it to the wisdom and love of our Father.

II. For the other point, the answer of our prayers, which is implied in this *openness of the ear*, it is a thing very needful to be considered and attended to. If we think that prayer is indeed a thing that God takes notice of, and hath regard to in his dealings with his children, it is certainly a point of duty and wisdom in them, to observe how he takes notice of it, and bends his ear to it, and puts his hand to help, and so answers it. This both furnishes matter of praise, and stirs up the heart to render it. Therefore in the Psalms, the *hearing of prayer* is so often observed and recorded, and made a part of the song of praise. And withal it endears both God and prayer unto the soul, as we have both together, Psal. cxvi. 1: *I love the Lord because he hath heard my voice and my supplications.* The transposition in the original is pathetical, *I love, because the Lord hath heard my voice.* I am in love, and particularly this causes it; I have found so much kindness in the Lord, I cannot but love. *He hath heard my voice.* And then it wins his esteem and affection to prayer. Seeing I find this virtue in it, we shall never part again; *I will call upon him as long as I live.* Seeing prayer draweth help and favours from heaven, I shall not be to seek for a way in any want or strait that can befal me.

In this there is need of direction; but too many rules may as much confuse a matter as too few, and do many times perplex the mind and multiply doubts; as many laws do multiply pleading. Briefly then,

1. Slothful minds do often neglect the answers of God, even when they are most legible in the grant of the very thing itself that was desired. It may be through a total inadvertence in this kind, through never thinking on things as answers of our requests; or possibly, a continual eager pursuit of more, turns away the mind from considering what it hath upon request

obtained; we are still so bent upon what further we would have, that we never think what is already done for us, which is one of the most ordinary causes of ingratitude.

2. But though it be not in the same thing that we desire, that our prayers are answered, yet, when the Lord changes our petitions in his answers, it is always for the better. He regards (according to that known word of St. Augustine, *Si non ad voluntatem, ad utilitatem*) our *well* more than our *will*. We beg deliverance; we are not unanswered, if he give patience and support. Be it under a spiritual trial or temptation, *My grace is sufficient for thee.* And where the Lord doth thus, it is certainly better for the time, than the other would be. Observe here, *His ears are open to the righteous,* but *his eyes are on them too.* They have not so his ear as to induce him blindly to give them what they ask, whether it be fit or no; but *his eye is on them,* to see and consider their estate, and to know better than themselves what is best, and accordingly to answer. This is no prejudice, but a great privilege, and the happiness of his children, that they have a Father who knows what is fit for them, and *withholds no good* from them. And this commutation and exchange of our requests a Christian observing, may usually find out the particular answer of his prayers; and if sometimes he doth not, then his best way is not to subtilize and amuse himself much in that, but rather to keep on in the exercise, knowing (as the Apostle speaks in another case) this for certain, *that their labours shall not be in vain in the Lord,* (1 Cor. xv. *ult. ;*) and as the prophet hath it, (Isa. xlv. 19,) *He hath not said unto the house of Jacob, seek ye me in vain.*

3. Only this we should always remember, not to set bounds and limits to the Lord in point of time, not to set him a day, that thou wilt attend so long and no longer. How patiently will some men bestow long attendance on others, where they expect some very poor good or courtesy at their hands! Yet we are very brisk and hasty with Him who never delays us but for our good, to ripen those mercies for us which we, as foolish

children, would pluck while they are green and have neither
that sweetness and goodness in them which they shall have in
his time.   All his works are done in their season.   Were there
nothing to check our impatiences, but his greatness, and the
greatness of those things we ask for, and our own unworthiness,
these considerations might curb them, and persuade us how
reasonable it is that we should wait.   He is a King well worth
waiting on ; and there is in the very waiting on Him an honour
and a happiness far above us.   And the things we seek are
great, forgiveness of sins, evidence of sonship and heirship ;
heirship of a kingdom ; and we condemned rebels, born heirs
of the bottomless pit !   And shall such as we be in such haste
with such a Lord in so great requests !   But further, the
attendance which this reason enforces, is sweetened by the consideration of his wisdom and love, that he hath foreseen and
chosen the very hour for each mercy fit for us, and will not
delay it a moment.   Never any yet repented their waiting, but
found it fully recompensed with the opportune answer in such
a time as they were then forced to confess was the only best.
I waited patiently, says the Psalmist, *in waiting I waited*,
but it was all well bestowed, *He inclined to me and heard my
cry, brought me up*, &c. (Psal. xl. 1.)   And then he afterwards
falls into admiration of the Lord's method, his *wonderful workings and thoughts to us-ward.*   " While I was waiting and
" saw nothing, thy *thoughts were towards* and for me, and thou
" didst then *work* when thy goodness was most remarkable and
" *wonderful.*"

When thou art in great affliction, outward or inward, thou
thinkest (it may be) He regards thee not.   Yea, but He doth.
Thou art his gold, he knows the time of refining thee, and of
then taking thee out of the furnace ; he is versed and skilful in
that work.   Thou sayest, " I have cried long for power against
" sin, and for some evidence of pardon, and find no answer to
" either ;" yet, leave him not.   He never yet cast away any
that sought him, and stayed by him, and resolved, whatsoever
came of it, to lie at his footstool, and to wait, were it all their

lifetime, for a good word or a good look from him. And they choose well who make that their great desire and expectation; for one of his good words or looks will make them happy for ever; and as He is truth itself, they are sure not to miss of it. *Blessed are all they that wait for him.* And thou that sayest thou canst not find pardon of sin, and power against it; yet consider whence are those desires of both, which thou once didst not care for. Why dost thou hate that sin which thou didst love, and art troubled and burdened with the guilt of it, under which thou wentest so easily, and which thou didst not feel before? Are not these something of his own work? Yes, surely. And know He will not leave it unfinished, nor *forsake the work of his hands.* (Psal. cxxxviii. 8.) *His eye may be on thee* though thou seest Him not, *and his ear open to thy cry,* though for the present He speaks not to thee as thou desirest. It is not said, that His children always see and hear him sensibly; but yet, when they do not, He is beholding them and hearing them graciously, and will show himself to them, and answer them seasonably.

David says, (Psal. xxii. 2,) *I cry in the day-time, and thou hearest not, and in the night season, and am not silent;* yet will he not entertain hard thoughts of God, nor conclude against him; on the contrary, he acknowledges, *Thou art holy,* (ver. 3,) where, by *holiness,* is meant his faithfulness (I conceive) to his own; as it follows, *Thou that inhabitest the praises of Israel,* to wit, for the favours he hath showed his people, as ver. 4, *Our fathers trusted in thee.*

Let the Lord's open ear persuade us to make much use of it. *Clavis diei et sera noctis:* The key of day and the lock of night. Be much in this sweet and fruitful exercise of prayer, together and apart, under the sense of these three considerations mentioned above; the duty, the dignity, and the utility of prayer.

1. The *duty:* It is due to the Lord to be worshipped and acknowledged thus, as the fountain of good. How will men crouch and bow one to another upon small requests; and shall

He only be neglected by the most, from whom *all* have *life and breath and all things!* (as the Apostle speaks in his sermon, Acts xvii. 25.) And then,

2. Consider the *dignity* of this, to be admitted into so near converse with the highest majesty. Were there nothing to follow, no answer at all, Prayer pays itself in the excellency of its nature, and the sweetness that the soul finds in it. Poor wretched man, to be admitted into heaven while he is on earth, and there to come and speak his mind freely to the Lord of heaven and earth, as his friend, as his Father! to empty all his complaints into his bosom; when wearied with the follies and miseries of the world, to refresh his soul in his God. Where there is any thing of his love, this is a privilege of the highest sweetness; for they who love, find much delight n discoursing together, and count all hours short, and think the day runs too fast that is so spent; and they who are much in this exercise, the Lord doth impart *his secrets* much to them. See Psal. xxv. 14.

3. Consider again, it is the most profitable exercise; no lost time, as profane hearts judge it, but only time gained. All blessings attend this work. It is the richest traffic in the world, for it trades with heaven, and brings home what is most precious there. And as holiness disposes to prayer, so prayer befriends holiness, increases it much. Nothing so refines and purifies the soul, as frequent prayer. If the often conversing with wise men doth so teach and advance the soul in wisdom, how much more then will converse with God! This makes the soul despise the things of the world, and in a manner makes it Divine; winds up the soul from the earth, acquainting it with delights that are infinitely sweeter.

The natural heart is full-stuffed with prejudices against the way of holiness, which dissuade and detain it; and therefore the holy Scriptures most fitly dwell much on this point, asserting the true advantage of it to the soul, and removing those mistakes which it has in respect of that way.

Thus here, and to press it the more home, ver. 10, &c., the

Apostle, having used the Psalmist's words, now follows it forth in his own, and extends what was said concerning the particular way of meekness and love, &c., in the general doctrine, to all the paths of *righteousness*.

The main conclusion is, that happiness is the certain consequent and fruit of holiness; all good, even outward good, so far as it holds good, and is not inconsistent with a higher good. If we did believe this more, we should feel it more, and so, upon feeling and experiment, believe it more strongly. All the heavy judgments we feel or fear, are they not the fruit of our own ways of profaneness, and pride, and malice, and abounding ungodliness? All cry out of hard times, evil days; and yet, who is taking the right way to better them? Yea, who is not still helping to make them worse? Are we not ourselves the greatest enemies of our own peace? Who looks either rightly backward, reflecting on his former ways, or rightly forward, to direct better his way that is before him? Who either says, *What have I done?* (as Jer. viii. 6.) or, *What ought I to do?* (Acts xvi. 30.) And indeed, the one of these depends on the other. *Consilium futurum ex præterito venit* (SENECA): "Future determination springs from the past." *I considered my ways*, says David, turned them over and over, (as the word is,) *and then I turned my feet unto thy testimonies.* (Psal. cxix. 59.)

Are there any, for all the judgments fallen on us, or that threaten us, returning apace with regret and hatred of sin, hastening unto God, and *mourning and weeping as they go*, bedewing each step with their tears? Yea, where is that newness of life that the word has called for so long, and that now the word and the rod together are so loudly calling for? Who is more *refraining his tongue from evil, and his lips from guile;* changing oaths, and lies, and calumnies, into a new language, into prayers, and reverend speaking of God, and joining a suitable consonant carriage? Who is *eschewing evil and doing good*, labouring to be fertile in holiness, *to bring forth much fruit to God?* This were the way *to see good days* indeed; this is the way to the longest life, the only long life and *length of days*, one eternal day : as St. Augustine comments on those words, *One day in thy courts is better than a thousand* (Psal. lxxxiv. 10.) *Millia dierum desiderant homines, et multum volunt hic vivere; contemnant millia dierum, desiderent unum, qui non habet ortum et occasum, cui non cedit hesternus, quem non urget crastinus.* " Men desire thousands of days, and wish to live long here : rather let them despise thousands of days, and desire that one which hath neither dawn nor darkening, to which no yesterday gives place, which yields to no to-morrow."

The reason added is above all exception, it is supreme : *The eyes of the Lord*, &c. If He who made times and seasons, and commands and forms them as he will, **if He** can give *good days*, or make men happy, then the only sure way to it must be the way of His obedience ; to be in the constant favour of the great King, and still in His gracious thoughts ; to have **His** eye and His ear. If this will serve the turn, (and if this do it not, I pray you, what will ?) then the righteous man is the only happy man, *For the eyes of the Lord are upon him*, &c. Surer happy days may be expected hence, than theirs who draw them from the aspect of the stars ; the eyes of the Father of lights benignly beholding them, the *trine aspect* of the blessed Trinity. The love He carries to them, draws His eye still towards them ; there is no forgetting of them, nor slipping of the fit season to do them good : His mind, I may say, runs on that. He sees how it is with them, and receives their suits gladly, rejoicing to put favours upon them. He is their assured friend, yea, He is their Father : what then can they want ? Surely they cannot miss of any good that His love and power can help them to.

But His face is against them that do evil.] So our happiness and misery are in *His face*, His looks. Nothing so comfortable as His favourable face, nothing so terrible again as His face—*His anger*, as the Hebrew word is often taken, that signifies *His face*. And yet, how many sleep sound under this misery ! But believe it, it is a dead and a deadly sleep ; **the**

Lord standing in terms of enmity with thee, and yet thy soul *at ease!* Pitiful, accursed ease ! I regard not the differences of your outward estate ; that is not a thing worth the speaking of. If thou be poor and base, and in the world's eye but a wretch, and withal under the hatred of God, as being an impenitent, hardened sinner, those other things are nothing ; this is the top, yea, the total sum of thy misery. Or be thou beautiful, or rich, or noble, or witty, or all these together, or what thou wilt, yet is *the face of the Lord against thee?* Think as thou wilt, thy estate *(splendida miseria)* is not to be envied, but lamented—I cannot say, much good do it thee ; with all thy enjoyments, for it is certain they can do thee no good ; and if thou dost not believe this now, the day is at hand wherein thou shalt be forced to believe it, finding it then irrevocably true. If you will, you may still follow *the things of the world, walk after the lusts of your own hearts,* neglect God, and please yourselves ; but, as Solomon's word is of judgment, (Eccl. ix. 9,) *Remember that the face of the Lord is against thee,* and in that judgment He shall unveil it, and let thee see it against thee. Oh, the most terrible of all sights !

The godly often do not see the Lord's favourable looks, while he is eyeing them ; and the wicked usually do not see nor perceive, neither will believe that *His face is against them ;* but, besides that the day of full discovery is coming, the Lord doth sometimes let both the one and the other know somewhat how He stands affected towards them. In peculiar deliverances and mercies He tells His own that He forgets them not, but both sees and hears them when they think He does neither, after that loving and gracious manner which they desire, and which is here meant ; and sometimes He lets forth glances of His bright countenance, darts in a beam upon their souls that is more worth than many worlds. And on the other side, He is pleased sometimes to make it known that His face is against the wicked, either by remarkable outward judgments, which to them are the vent of His just enmity against them, or to some He speaks it more home in horrors and affrights of conscience, which to them are earnests and pledges of their full misery, that *inheritance of woe* reserved, as the joys and comforts of believers are, of their *inheritance of glory.*

Therefore, if you have any belief of these things, be persuaded, be entreated to forsake the way of ungodliness. Do not flatter yourselves and dream of escaping, when you hear of outward judgments on your neighbours and brethren, but tremble and be humbled. Remember our Saviour's words, *Think ye that those on whom the tower of Siloam fell, were greater sinners than others? I tell you nay, but, except ye repent, ye shall all likewise perish.* (Luke xiii. 4, 5.) This seeming harsh word, He who was wisdom and sweetness itself uttered, and even in it spoke like a Saviour: he speaks of perishing, that they might not perish, and presses repentance by the heavy doom of impenitence.

When you hear of this, there is none of you would willingly choose it, that the Lord's face should be against you, although upon very high offers made to you of other things. You think, I know, that the very sound of it is somewhat fearful, and on the other side, have possibly some confused notion of His favour as a thing desirable ; and yet do not bestir yourselves, to avoid the one and inquire after the other : which is certainly by reason of your unbelief. For if you think of the love of God, as His word speaks of it, and as you will say you do, whence is it, I pray you, that there is no trifle in this world that will not take more deeply with you, and which you follow not with more earnestness, than this great business of reconciliation with God, in order to your finding His face not against you, but graciously towards you, *His eyes upon you, and his ears open to your prayer?*

Your blessedness is not, no , believe it, it is not where most of you seek it, in things below you. How can that be ? It must be a higher good to make you happy. While you labour and sweat for it in any thing under the sun, your pains run all to waste ; you seek a happy life in the region of death. Here,

here it is alone, in the love and favour of God, in having His countenance and friendship, and free access and converse; and this is nowhere to be found, but in the ways of holiness.

Ver. 13.   And who is he that will harm you, if you be followers of that which is good?

THIS the Apostle adds, as a further reason of the safety and happiness of that way he points out, a reason drawn from its own nature.   There is something even intrinsical in a meek, and upright, and holy carriage, that is apt, in part, to free a man from many evils and mischiefs which the ungodly are exposed to, and do readily draw upon themselves.   Your spotless and harmless deportment will much bind up the hands even of your enemies, and sometimes, possibly, somewhat allay and cool the malice of their hearts, that they cannot so rage against you as otherwise they might.   It will be somewhat strange and monstrous to range against the innocent.   *Who is he that will harm you?*   Here are two things, I. The carriage. II. The advantage of it.

I.   Their carriage is expressed: *followers of that which is good*.   The Greek word is, *imitators*.

There is an imitation of men that is impious and wicked, which consists in taking the copy of their sins.   Again, there is an imitation which though not so grossly evil, yet is poor and servile, being in mean things, yea, sometimes descending to imitate the very imperfections of others, as fancying some comeliness in them; as some of Basil's scholars, who imitated his slow speaking, which he had a little in the extreme, and could not help.   But this is always laudable, and worthy of the best minds, to be *imitators of that which is good*, wheresoever they find it; for that stays not in any man's person, as the ultimate pattern, but rises to the highest grace, being man's nearest likeness to God, His image and resemblance, (and so, following the example of the saints in holiness, we look higher than them, and consider them as receivers, but God as the first owner and dispenser of grace,) bearing His stamp and superscription, and belonging peculiarly to Him, in what hand soever it be found, as carrying the mark of no other owner than Him.

The word of God contains our copy in its perfection, and very legible and clear; and so, the imitation of good, in the complete rule of it, is the regulating of our ways by the word. But even there we find, besides general rules, the particular tracks of life of divers eminent holy persons, and those on purpose set before us, that we may know holiness not to be an idle, imaginary thing, but that men have really been holy, though not altogether sinless, yet holy and spiritual in some good measure; have shined as lights amidst a perverse generation, as greater stars in a dark night, and were yet *men*, as St. James says of Elias, like us in nature (ὁμοιοπαθεῖς) and in the frailty of it: *subject to like passions as we are.* (James v. 17.) Why may we not then aspire to be holy as they were, and attain to it?—although we should fall short of the degree, yet not stopping at a small measure, but running further, *pressing still forward toward the mark;* following them in the way they went, though at a distance; not reaching them, and yet walking, yea, running after them as fast as we can; not judging of holiness by our own sloth and natural averseness, taking it for a singularity fit only for rare, extraordinary persons, such as prophets and apostles were, or as the Church of Rome fancies those to be, to whom it vouchsafes a room in the roll of saints. Do you not know that holiness is the only *via regia*, this *following of good*, the path wherein all the children of God must walk, one following after another, each striving to equal; and, if they could, to outstrip even those they look on as most advanced in it? This is, amongst many others, a misconceit in the Romish Church, that they seem to make holiness a kind of impropriate good, which the common sort can have little share in, almost all piety being shut up within cloister-walls, as its only fit dwelling; but it hath not liked their lodging, it seems; it has flown over the walls away from them, for there is little of it even there to be found. Their opinion, however, places it there, as having little to do abroad in the world; whereas, the truth is, that all Christians have this for their common task, though some are under more peculiar obligations to study this one copy. Look on the rule of holiness, and be followers of it, and followers or imitators one of another, so far as their carriage agrees with that primitive copy, as written after it. *Be ye followers of me,* μιμηται, says the Apostle, even to the meanest Christians amongst those he wrote to, but thus, *as I am of Christ.* (1 Cor. xi. 1.)

Is it thus with us? Are we zealous and emulous followers of that which is good, exciting each other by our example to a holy and Christian conversation, *provoking one another* (so the Apostle's word is) *to love and to good works?* (Heb. x. 24.) Or, are not the most mutual corrupters of each other, and of the places and societies where they live; some leading, and others following, in their ungodliness; not regarding the course of those who are most desirous to walk holily, or, if at all, doing it with a corrupt and evil eye, not in order to study and follow what is good in them, their way of holiness, but to espy any the least wrong step, to take exact notice of any imperfection or malignant slander, and by this, either to reproach religion, or to hearten or harden themselves in their irreligion and ungodliness, seeking warrant for their own willing licentiousness in the unwilling failings of God's children? And, in their converse with such as themselves, they are following their profane way, and flattering and blessing one another in it. "What need we be so precise?" And, "If I should not do as others, they would laugh at me, I should pass for a fool." Well, thou wilt be a fool of the most wretched kind, rather than be accounted one by such as are fools, and know not at all wherein true wisdom consists.

Thus the most are carried with the stream of this wicked world, their own inward corruption easily agreeing and suiting with it; every man, as a drop, falling into a torrent, and easily made one, and running along with it into that dead sea where it empties itself.

But those whom the Lord hath a purpose to sever and save, He carries in a course contrary even to that violent stream. And these are the students of holiness, *the followers of good*, who bend their endeavours thus, and look on all sides diligently, on what may animate and advance them; on the example of the saints in former times, and on the good they espy in those who live together with them; and above all, studying that perfect rule in the Scriptures, and that highest and first Pattern there so often set before them, even the Author of that rule, the Lord himself, *to be holy as He is holy, to be bountiful and merciful as their heavenly Father*, and in all labouring to be, as the Apostle exhorts, *followers of God as dear children.* (Eph. v. 1, 2.) [Τέλος ἀνθρώπου ὁμοίωσις Θεῷ, says Pythagoras.] Children who are beloved of their father, and do love and reverence him, will be ambitious to be like him, and particularly aim at the following of any virtues or excellency in him. Now, thus it is most reasonable that it should be in the children of God, their Father being the highest and best of all excellency and perfection.

But this excellent pattern is drawn down nearer their view, in the Son, Jesus Christ; where we have that Highest Example made low, and yet losing nothing of its perfection, so that we may study God in man, and read all our lesson, without any blot, even in our own nature. And this is truly the only way to be the best proficients in this following and imitating of all good. In Him we may learn all, even those lessons which men most despise, God teaching them by acting them, and calling us to follow: *Learn of me, for I am meek and lowly in heart.* (Matt. xi. 29.) But this is too large a subject. Would you advance in all grace? Study Christ much, and you shall find not only the pattern in Him, but strength and skill from Him, to follow it.

II. The advantage; *Who is he that will harm you?*

The very name of it says so much; it is *a good*, worthy the following for itself. But there is this further to enforce it, that, besides higher benefit, it oftentimes cuts off the occasions of present evils and disturbances, which otherwise are incident to men. *Who is he that will harm you?* Men, evil men, will often be overcome by our blameless and harmless behaviour.

    1. In the life of a godly man, taken together in the whole body and frame of it, there is a grave beauty or comeliness, which oftentimes forces some kind of reverence and respect to it, even in ungodly minds.

    2. Though a natural man cannot love them spiritually, as graces of the Spirit of God, (for so only the partakers of them are lovers of them,) yet he may have, and usually hath, a natural liking and esteem of some kind of virtues which are in a Christian, and are not, in their right nature, to be found in any other, though a moralist may have somewhat like them ; *meekness*, and *patience*, and *charity*, and *fidelity*, &c.

    3. These, and other such like graces, do make a Christian life so inoffensive and calm, that, except where the matter of their God or religion is made the crime, malice itself can scarcely tell where to fasten its teeth or lay hold ; it hath nothing to pull by, though it would, yea, oftentimes, for want of work or occasions, it will fall asleep for awhile. Whereas ungodliness and iniquity, sometimes by breaking out into notorious crimes, draws out the sword of civil justice, and where it rises not so high, yet it involves men in frequent contentions and quarrels. (Prov. xxiii. 29.) How often are the lusts and pride, and covetousness of men, paid with dangers, and troubles, and vexation, which, besides what is abiding them hereafter, do even in this present life spring out of them ! These, the godly pass free of by their just, and mild, and humble carriage. *Whence so many jars and strifes* among the greatest part, but from their unchristian hearts and lives, *from their lusts that war in their members*, as St. James says, their self-love and unmortified passions? One will abate nothing of his will, nor the other of his. Thus, where pride and passion meet on both sides, it cannot be but a fire will be kindled ; when hard flints strike together, the sparks will fly about : but a soft, mild spirit is a great

preserver of its own peace, kills the power of contest; as wool-packs, or such like soft matter, must deaden the force of bullets. *A soft answer turns away wrath,* says Solomon, Prov. xv. 1, beats it off, *breaks the bone,* as he says, the very strength of it, as the bones are of the body.

And thus we find it, those who think themselves high-spirited, and will bear least, as they speak, are often, even by that, forced to bow most, or to burst under it; while humility and meekness escape many a burden, and . many a blow, always keeping peace within, and often without too.

Reflection 1. If this were duly considered, might it not do somewhat to induce your minds to love the way of religion, for that it would so much abate the turbulency and unquietness that abound in the lives of men, a great part whereof, the most do procure by the earthliness and distemper of their own carnal minds, and the disorder in their ways that arises thence ?

Reflection 2. You whose hearts are set towards God, and your feet entered into His ways, I hope will find no reason for a change, but many reasons to commend and endear those ways to you every day more than the last, and, amongst the rest, even this, that in them you escape many even present mischiefs which you see the ways of the world are full of. And, if you will be careful to ply your rule and study your copy better, you shall find it more so. The more you *follow that which is good,* the more shall you avoid a number of outward evils, which are ordinarily drawn upon men by their own enormities and passions. Keep as close as you can to the genuine, even track of a Christian walk, and labour r a prudent and meek behaviour, adorning your holy profession, and this shall adorn you, and sometimes gain *those that are without,* yea, even your enemies shall be constrained to approve it.

It is well known how much the spotless lives and patient sufferings of the primitive Christians did sometimes work upon their beholders, yea, on their persecutors, and persuaded some who would not share with them in their religion, yet to speak-

and write on their behalf. Seeing, then, that reason and experience do jointly aver it, that the lives of men conversant together have generally a great influence one upon another, (for example is an animated or living rule, and is both the shortest and most powerful way of teaching,)—

[1.] Whosoever of you are in an exemplary or leading place in relation to others, be it many or few, be ye, first, *followers of God.* Set before you the rule of holiness, and withal, the best and highest examples of those who have walked according to it, and then you will be leading in it those who are under you, and they being bent to follow you, in so doing will *follow that which is good.* Lead and draw them on, by admonishing, and counselling, and exhorting ; but especially, by walking. Pastors, be [τύποι] *ensamples* to the flock, or *models*, as our Apostle hath it, (1 Pet. v. 3,) that they may be stamped aright, taking the impression of your lives. Sound doctrine alone will not serve. Though the water you give your flocks be pure, yet if you lay spotted rods before them, it will bring forth spotted lives in them. Either teach not at all, or teach by the rhetoric of your lives*. Elders, be such in grave and pious carriage, whatsoever be your years ; for young men may be so, and, possibly, gray hairs may have nothing under them but gaddishness and folly many years old, habituated and inveterate ungodliness. Parents and Masters, let your children and servants read in your lives the life and power of godliness, the Practice of Piety not lying in your windows or corners of your houses, and confined within the clasp of the book, bearing that or any such like title, but shining in your lives.

[2.] You that are easily receptive of the impression of example, beware of the stamp of unholiness, and of a carnal, formal course of profession, whereof the examples are most abounding ; but though they be fewer who bear the lively image of God impressed on their hearts and expressed in their

---

* Ἡ μὴ διδάσκειν, ἢ διδάσκειν τῷ τρόπῳ.

actions, yet, study these, and be followers of them, as they are of
Christ. I know you will espy much irregular and unsanctified
carriage in us who are set up for the ministry, and if you look
round, you will find the world lying in wickedness; yet, if
there be any who have any sparks of Divine light in them,
converse with those, and follow them.

[3.] And, generally, this I say to all, (for none are so complete but they may espy some imitable and emulable good,
even in meaner Christians,) acquaint yourselves with the word,
the rule of holiness; and then, with an eye to that, look on
one another, and be zealous of progress in the ways of holiness. Choose to converse with such as may excite you and
advance you, both by their advice and example. Let not a
corrupt generation in which you live, be the worse by you, nor
you the worse by it. As far as you necessarily engage in some
conversation with those who are unholy, let them not pull you
into the mire, but, if you can, help them out. And let not
any custom of sin prevailing about you, by being familiarly
seen, gain upon you, so as to think it fashionable and comely,
yea, or so as not to think it deformed and hateful. Know, that
you must row against the stream of wickedness in the world,
unless you would be carried with it to the dead sea, or lake of
perdition. Take that grave counsel given Rom. xii. 2: *Be
not conformed to this world, but be ye transformed by the
renewing of your mind;* that is, the daily advancement in
renovation, purifying and refining every day.

Now, in this way you shall have sweet inward peace and joy,
as well as some outward advantage, in that men, except they
are monstrously cruel and malicious, will not so readily *harm
you;* it will abate much of their rage. But, however, if you
do not escape suffering by your holy carriage, yea, *if you
suffer* even for it, yet in that *are ye happy* (as the Apostle
immediately adds),—

Ver. 14. But and if ye suffer for righteousness sake, happy are ye; and be not afraid of their terror, neither be troubled.

In this verse are two things: First, Even in the most blameless way of a Christian, his suffering is supposed. Secondly, His happiness, even in suffering, is asserted.

I. Suffering is supposed, notwithstanding righteousness, yea, *for righteousness;* and that, not as a rare unusual accident, but as the frequent lot of Christians; as Luther calls Persecution, *malus genius Evangelii, The evil genius of the Gospel.* And we, being forewarned of this, as not only the possible, but the frequent lot of the saints, ought not to hearken to the false prophecies of our own self-love, which divines what it would gladly have, and easily persuades us to believe it. Think not that any prudence will lead you by all oppositions and malice of an ungodly world. Many winter blasts will meet you in the most inoffensive way of religion, if you keep straight to it. Suffering and war with the world, is a part of the godly man's portion here, which seems hard, but take it altogether, it is sweet: none in their wits will refuse that legacy entire, *In the world ye shall have trouble, but in me ye shall have peace.* (John xvi. *ult.*)

Look about you, and see if there be any estate of man, or course of life, exempted from troubles. The greatest are usually subject to greatest vexations; as the largest bodies have the largest shadows attending them. We need not tell nobles and rich men, that contentment doth not dwell in great palaces and titles, nor in full coffers; they feel it, that they are not free of much anguish and molestation, and that a proportionable train of cares, as constantly as of servants, follows great place and wealth. Riches and trouble, or noise, are signified by the same Hebrew word. Compare Job xxxvi. 19, with xxx. 24. And kings find that their crowns, which are set so richly with diamonds without, are lined with thorns within. And if we speak of men who are *servants to unrighteousness,* besides what is to come, are they not often forced to suffer, amongst the service of their lusts, the distempers that attend unhealthy intemperance, the poverty that dogs luxury at the heels, and the fit punishment of voluptuous persons in painful diseases which either quickly cut the thread of life, or make their aged bones full of the sins of their youth? (Job xx. 11.) Take what way you will, there is no place or condition so fenced and guarded, but public calamities, or personal griefs, find a way to reach us.

Seeing, then, we must suffer, whatever course we take, this kind of suffering, *to suffer for righteousness,* is far the best. What Julius Cæsar said ill of doing ill, *Si violandum est jus, regnandi causâ violandum,* we may well say of suffering ill: If it must be, it is best to be for a kingdom. And these are the terms on which Christians are called to suffer for righteousness; *If we will reign with Christ,* certain it is *we must suffer with Him ;* and, *if we do suffer with Him,* it is as certain *we shall reign with Him.* (2 Tim. ii. 12.) And therefore such sufferers are *happy.*

But I shall prosecute this suffering for righteousness, only with relation to the Apostle's present reasoning. His conclusion he establishes, 1. From the favour and protection of God; 2. From the nature of the thing itself. Now, we would consider the consistence of this supposition with those reasons.

1st. From the favour or protection of God. *The eyes of the Lord* being *on the righteous* for their good, and *His ear open to their prayer,* how is it that, notwithstanding all this favour and inspection, they are so much exposed to suffering, and even for the regard and affection they bear towards Him, *suffering for righteousness?* These seem not to agree well; yet they do.

It is not said that His eye is so on them, as that He will never see them afflicted, nor have them suffer any thing; no, but this is their great privilege and comfort in suffering, that His gracious eye is then upon them, and sees their trouble, and His ear towards them, not so as to grant them an exemption, (for that they will not seek for,) but seasonable deliverance, and, in the mean while, strong support, as is evident in that xxxivth

Psalm. If His eye be always on them, He sees them suffer often, for *their afflictions are many*, (ver. 19,) and if His ear be to them, He hears many sighs and cries pressed out by sufferings. And they are content; this is enough, yea, better than not to suffer; they suffer, and often directly for Him, but He sees it all, takes perfect notice of it, therefore it is not lost. And they are forced to cry, but none of their cries escape His ear. He hears, and He manifests that He sees and hears, for *He delivers them;* and till He does, He keeps them from being crushed under the weight of the suffering: *He keeps all his bones, not one of them is broken.* (Verse 20.) He sees, yea, appoints and provides these conflicts for his choicest servants. He sets His champions to encounter the malice of Satan and the World, for His sake, to give proof of the truth and the strength of their love to Him for whom they suffer, and to overcome even in suffering.

He is sure of His designed advantages out of the sufferings of His Church and of his saints for His name. He loses nothing, and they lose nothing; but their enemies, when they rage most, and prevail most, are ever the greatest losers. His own glory grows, the graces of his people grow, yea, their very number grows, and that sometimes most by their greatest sufferings. This was evident in the first ages of the Christian Church. Where were the glory of so much invincible love and patience, if they had not been so put to it?

2dly. For the other argument, that the said *following of good* would preserve from *harm*, it speaks truly the nature of the thing, what it is apt to do, and what, in some measure, it often doth; but considering the nature of the World, *its enmity against God,* and religion, that strong poison in the serpent's seed, it is not strange that it often proves otherwise; that notwithstanding the righteous carriage of Christians, yea, even *because* of it, they suffer much. It is a resolved case, *All that will live godly must suffer persecution.* (2 Tim. iii. 12.) It meets a Christian in his entrance to the way of the Kingdom, and goes along all the way. No sooner canst thou

begin to seek the way to Heaven, but the World will seek how
to vex and molest thee, and make that way grievous ; if no other
way, by scoffs and taunts, intended as bitter blasts to destroy
the tender blossom or bud of religion, or, as Herod, to kill
Christ newly born. You shall no sooner begin to enquire after
God, but, twenty to one, they will begin to enquire whether
thou art gone mad. But if thou knowest *who it is whom thou
hast trusted,* and whom thou lovest, this is a small matter.
What though it were deeper and sharper sufferings, yet still,
if you suffer for righteousness, happy are you.

Which is the IId. thing that was proposed, and more particularly imports, 1. That a Christian under the heaviest load
of sufferings for righteousness, is yet still *happy,* notwithstanding those sufferings. 2. That he is happier even by those
sufferings. And,

1. All the sufferings and distresses of this world are not
able to destroy the happiness of a Christian, nor to diminish it ;
yea, they cannot at all touch it ; it is out of their reach. If it
were built on worldly enjoyments, then, worldly privations and
sufferings might shake it, yea, might undo it : when those rotten
props fail, that which rests on them must fall. He that hath
set his heart on his riches, a few hours can make him miserable.
He that lives on popular applause, it is almost in any body's
power to rob him of his happiness; a little slight or disgrace
undoes him. Or whatsoever the soul fixes on of these moving,
unfixed things, pluck them from it, and it must cry after them,
Ye have taken away my gods. But the believer's happiness
is safe, out of the reach of shot. He may be impoverished, and
imprisoned, and tortured, and killed, but this one thing is out
of hazard—he cannot be miserable ; still, in the midst of all
these, he subsists a happy man. If all friends be shut out, yet
the visits of the Comforter may be frequent, bringing him glad
tidings from Heaven, and communing with him of the love of
Christ, and solacing him in that. It was a great word for a
heathen to say of his false accusers, *Kill me they may, but they
cannot hurt me.* How much more confidently may the Christian

say so! Banishment he fears not, for his country is above; nor death, for that sends him home into that country.

The believing soul, having hold of Jesus Christ, can easily despise the best and the worst of the world, and defy all that is in it; can share with the Apostle in that defiance which he gives, *I am persuaded that neither death nor life shall separate me from the love of God which is in Christ Jesus our Lord:* Rom. viii. ult. Yea, what though the frame of the world were a dissolving, and falling to pieces! This happiness holds, and is not stirred by it; for it is built upon that Rock of eternity, that stirs not, nor changes at all.

Our main work, truly, if you will believe it, is this; to provide this immovable happiness, which amidst all changes, and losses, and sufferings, may hold firm. You *may be free, choose it rather*—not to stand to the courtesy of any thing about you, nor of any man, whether enemy or friend, for the tenure of your happiness. Lay it higher and surer, and if you be wise, provide such a peace as will remain untouched in the hottest flame, such a light as will shine in the deepest dungeon, and such a life as is safe even in death itself, that life which is *hid with Christ in God.* (Col. iii. 3.)

But if in other sufferings, even the worst and saddest, the believer is still a happy man, then, more especially in those that are the best kind, sufferings for righteousness. Not only do they not detract from his happiness, but,

2. They concur and give accession to it; he is happy even so by suffering. As will appear from the following considerations.

[1.] It is the happiness of a Christian, until he attain perfection, to be advancing towards it: to be daily refining from sin, and growing richer and stronger in the graces that make up a Christian, a new creature; to attain a higher degree of patience and meekness, and humility; to have the heart more weaned from the earth and fixed on heaven. Now, as other afflictions of the saints do help them in these, their sufferings for righteousness, the unrighteous and injurious dealings of

the world with them, have a particular fitness for this purpose. Those trials that come immediately from God's own
hand, seem to bind to a patient and humble compliance, with
more authority, and (I may say) necessity; there is no plea,
no place for so much as a word, unless it be directly and expressly against the Lord's own dealing; but unjust suffering
at the hands of men requires that respect unto God, (without
whose hand they cannot move,) that for His sake, and for reverence and love to him, a Christian can go through those with
that mild evenness of spirit which overcomes even in suffering.

And there is nothing outward more fit to persuade a man to
give up with the world and its friendship, than to feel much of
its enmity and malice, and that directly venting itself against
religion, making that the very quarrel, which is of all things
dearest to a Christian, and in the highest esteem with him.

If the world should caress them, and smile on them, they
might be ready to forget their home, or at least to abate in the
frequent thoughts and fervent desires of it, and to turn into
some familiarity with the world, and favourable thoughts of it,
so as to let out somewhat of their hearts after it; and thus,
Grace would grow faint by the diversion and calling forth of
the spirits; as in summer, in the hottest and fairest weather,
it is with the body.

It is an observation confirmed by the experience of all ages,
that when the Church flourished most in outward peace and
wealth, it abated most of its spiritual lustre, which is its genuine and true beauty, *opibus major, virtutibus minor;* and
when it seemed most miserable by persecutions and sufferings,
it was most happy in sincerity, and zeal, and vigour of grace.
When the moon shines brightest towards the earth, it is dark
heaven-wards; and, on the contrary, when it appears not, it is
nearest the sun, and clear towards heaven.

[2.] Persecuted Christians are happy in acting and evi-
dencing, by those sufferings for God, their love to Him. Love
delights in difficulties, and grows in them. The more a Christian suffers for Christ, the more he loves Him, and accounts

·Him the dearer; and the more he loves him, still the more can he suffer for Him.

[3.] They are happy, as in testifying love to Christ and glorifying Him, so in their conformity with Him, which is love's ambition. Love affects likeness and harmony at any rate. A believer would readily take it as an affront, that the World should be kind to him, that was so harsh and cruel to his beloved Lord and Master. Canst thou expect, or wouldst thou wish, smooth language from that World which reviled thy Jesus, which called him Beelzebub? Couldst thou own and accept friendship at its hands, which buffeted Him, and shed His blood? Or art thou not, rather, most willing to share with Him, and of St. Paul's mind, *an ambassador in chains;* [Πρεσβεύω ἐν ἁλύσει;] *God forbid that I should glory in any thing save in the cross of Christ, whereby the world is crucified unto me, and I unto the world.* (Gal. vi. 14.)

[4.] Suffering Christians are happy in the rich supplies of spiritual comfort and joy, which in those times of suffering are usual; so that as *their sufferings for Christ do abound, their consolations in him abound much more,* as the Apostle testifies, 2 Cor. i. 5. God is speaking most peace to the soul, when the world speaks most war and enmity against it; and this compensates abundantly. When the Christian lays the greatest sufferings men can inflict, in the one balance, and the least glances of God's countenance in the other, he says, it is worth all the enduring of those, to enjoy this: he says with David, (Psal. cix. 28,) *Let them curse, but bless Thou:* let them frown, but smile Thou. And thus God usually doth; he refreshes such as are prisoners for Him, with visits which they would gladly buy again with the hardest restraints and debarring of nearest friends. The World cannot but misjudge the state of suffering Christians; it sees, as St. Bernard speaks, their crosses, but not their anointings: *vident cruces nostras, unctiones non vident.* Was not Stephen, think you, in a happy posture even in his enemies' hands? Was he afraid of ᵗthe showers of stones coming about his ears, who saw the heavens opened, and Jesus standing on the Father's right hand, so little troubled with their stoning of him, that, as the text hath it, in the midst of them *he fell asleep?*   (Acts vii. 60.)

[5.] If those sufferings be so small, that they are weighed down even by present comforts, and so the Christian be happy in them in that regard, how much more doth the *weight of glory* that follows surpass these sufferings ! They *are not worthy to come in comparison,* they are as nothing to that *glory that shall be revealed,* in the Apostle's arithmetic, Rom. viii. 18, [λογίζομαι,] when I have cast up the sum of the sufferings of this present time, this instant *now,* [τὸ νῦν,] they amount to just nothing in respect of that glory.   Now, these sufferings are happy, because they are the way to this happiness, and pledges of it, and, if any thing can do, they raise the very degree of it.   However, it is an *exceeding excellent weight of glory.* The Hebrew word which signifies *glory,* signifies *weight.* Earthly glories are all *too light,* τὸ ἐλαφρὸν, except in the weight of the cares and sorrows that attend them; but that hath the weight of complete blessedness. Speak not of all the sufferings, nor of all the prosperities of this poor life, nor of any thing in it, as worthy of a thought, when *that glory* is named; yea, let not this life be called *life,* when we mention that other life, which our Lord, by his death, hath purchased for us.

Be not afraid of their terror.]   No time nor place in the world is so favourable to religion, that it is not still needful to arm a Christian mind against the outward oppositions and discouragements he shall meet with in his way to Heaven. This is the Apostle's scope here ; and he doth it, 1*st,* by an Assertion, 2*dly,* by an Exhortation : The Assertion, that, in *suffering for righteousness,* they *are happy ;* the Exhortation, agreeably to the Assertion, that *they fear not.* Why should they fear any thing, who are assured of happiness, yea, whc are the more happy by reason of those very things that seem most to be feared ?

The words are in part borrowed from the Prophet Isaiah.

who relates them as the Lord's words to him and other godly persons with him in that time, countermanding in them that carnal distrustful fear, which drove a profane king and people to seek help rather any where than in God, who was their strength: *Fear not their fear, nor be afraid; but sanctify the Lord of Hosts himself, and let Him be your fear, and let Him be your dread.* (Isaiah viii. 12, 13.) This the Apostle extends as a universal rule for Christians in the midst of their greatest troubles and dangers.

The things opposed here, are, a perplexing, troubling *fear of sufferings,* as the soul's distemper, and a *sanctifying of God in the heart,* as the sovereign cure of it, and the true principle of a healthful, sound constitution of mind.

Natural fear, though not evil in itself, yet, in the natural man, is constantly irregular and disordered in the actings of it, still missing its due object, or measure, or both; either running in a wrong channel, or over-running the banks. As there are no pure elements to be found here in this lower part of the world, but only in the philosopher's books, (who define them as pure, but they find them so nowhere,) thus we may speak of our natural passions, as not sinful in their nature, yet in us who are naturally sinful, yea, full of sin, they cannot escape the mixture and alloy of it.

Sin hath put the soul into universal disorder, so that it neither loves nor hates what it ought, nor as it ought; hath neither right joy, nor sorrow, nor hope, nor fear. A very small matter stirs and troubles it; and as waters that are stirred, (so the word ταραχθῆτε signifies,) having dregs in the bottom, become muddy and impure, thus the soul, by carnal fear, is confused, and there is neither quiet nor clearness in it. A *troubled sea,* as it *cannot rest,* so, in its restlessness, it *casts up mire,* as the prophet speaks, Isa. lvii. 20. Thus it is with the unrenewed heart of man: the least blasts that arise, disturb it and make it restless, and its own impurity makes it cast up mire. Yea, it is never right with the natural man: either he is asleep in carnal confidence, or, being shaken out of that, he is hurried and tumbled to and fro with carnal fears; he is either in a lethargy, or in a fever, or trembling ague. When troubles are at a distance, he is ready to fold his hands, and take his ease as long as it may be; and then, being surprised when they come rushing on him, his sluggish ease is paid with a surcharge of perplexing and affrighting fears. And is not this the condition of the most?

Now, because these evils are not fully cured in the Believer, but he is subject to carnal security, (as David, *I said in my prosperity, I shall never be moved,*) and he is filled with undue fears and doubts in the apprehensions or feeling of trouble, (as the Psalmist likewise complaining, confesses the dejection and disquietness of his soul, and again, that he had almost lost his standing, *My feet had well nigh slipped,*) therefore, it is very needful to caution them often with such words sa these, *Fear not their fear, neither be ye troubled.* You may take it objectively, *their fear:* Be not afraid of the world's malice, or any thing it can effect. Or it may be taken subjectively, as the Prophet means: Do not you fear after the manner of the world; be not distrustfully troubled with any affliction that can befal you. Surely it is pertinent in either sense, or in both together; *Fear not what they can do, nor fear as they do.*

If we look on the condition of men, ourselves and others, are not the minds of the greatest part continually tossed, and their lives worn out betwixt vain hopes and fears[*], providing incessantly new matter of disquiet to themselves?

Contemplative men have always taken notice of this grand malady in our nature, and have attempted in many ways the cure of it, have bestowed much pains in seeking out prescriptions and rules for the attainment of a settled tranquillity of spirit, free from the fears and troubles that perplex us; but they have proved but mountebanks, who give big words enough, and do little or nothing, *all physicians of no value,*

---

[*] Hæc inter dubii vivimus et morimur.

or of nothing, good for nothing, as Job speaks. (Job xiii. 4.)
Some things they have said well concerning the outward causes
of the inward evil, and of the inefficacy of inferior outward
things to help it; but they have not descended to the bottom
and inward cause of this our wretched unquiet condition;
much less have they ascended to the true and only remedy of
it. In this, Divine light is needful, and here we have it in the
following verse.

Ver. 15. But sanctify the Lord God in your hearts; and be ready always
to give an answer to every man that asketh you, a reason of the hope
that is in you, with meekness and fear.

IMPLYING the cause of all our fears and troubles to be this,
our ignorance and disregard of God; and the due knowledge
and acknowledgment of Him, to be the only establishment
and strength of the mind.

In the words we may consider these three things: 1. This
Respect of God, as it is here expressed, *Sanctify the Lord
God;* 2. The Seat of it, *In your hearts;* 3. The Fruit of
it, the power that this sanctifying of God in the heart hath,
to rid that heart of those fears and troubles to which it is here
opposed as their proper remedy.

Sanctify the Lord God.] He is holy, most holy, the Fountain
of holiness. It is He, He alone, who powerfully sanctifies us,
and then, and not till then, we sanctify Him. When He hath
made us holy, we know and confess Him to be holy, we worship and serve our holy God, we glorify Him with our whole
souls and all our affections. We sanctify Him by acknowledging His greatness and power, and goodness, and, (which is
here more particularly intended,) we do this by a holy fear of
Him, and faith in Him. These within us confess His greatness, and power, and goodness: as the Prophet is express,
Sanctify Him, and let Him be your fear and your dread
(Isa. viii. 13); and then he adds, If thus you sanctify Him, you
shall further sanctify Him, *He shall be your sanctuary:* you
shall account Him so, in believing in Him, and shall find Him

so, in his protecting you ; you shall repose on Him for safety. And these particularly cure the heart of undue fears.

In your hearts.] We are to be sanctified in our words and actions, but primarily in our hearts, as the root and principle of the rest. He *sanctifies* His own *throughout*, makes their language and their lives holy, but first, and most of all, their hearts. And, as He chiefly sanctifies the heart, it chiefly sanctifies Him ; acknowledges and worships Him often when the tongue and body do not, and possibly cannot well join with it ; it fears, and loves, and trusts in Him, which properly the outward man cannot do, though it does follow and is acted on by these affections, and so shares in them according to its capacity.

Beware of an external, superficial sanctifying of God, for He accepts it not ; He will interpret that a profaning of Him and His name. *Be not deceived, God is not mocked.* (Gal. vi. 7.) He looks, through all visages and appearances, in upon the heart ; sees how it entertains Him, and stands affected to Him ; whether it be possessed with reverence and love, more than either thy tongue or carriage can express. And if it be not so, all thy seeming worship is but injury, and thy speaking of Him is but babbling, be thy discourse never so excellent ; yea, the more thou hast seemed to sanctify God, while thy heart hath not been chief in the business, thou shalt not, by such service, have the less, but the more fear and trouble in the day of trouble, when it comes upon thee. No estate is so far off from true consolation, and so full of horrors, as that of the rotten-hearted hypocrite ; his rotten heart is sooner shaken to pieces than any other. If you would have heart-peace in God, you must have this heart-sanctifying of Him. It is the heart that is vexed and troubled with fears, the disease is there ; and if the prescribed remedy reach not thither, it will do no good. But let your hearts sanctify Him, and then He shall fortify and establish your hearts.

This sanctifying of God in the heart composes the heart, and frees it from fears.

First, In general, the turning of the heart to consider and regard God, takes it off from those vain, empty, windy things, that are the usual causes and matter of its fears. It feeds on wind, and therefore the bowels are tormented within. The heart is subject to disturbance, because it lets out itself to such things, and lets in such things into itself, as are ever in motion, and full of instability and restlessness; and so it cannot be at quiet, till God come in and cast out these, and keep the heart within, that it wander out no more to them.

Secondly, Fear and Faith in the Believer more particularly work in this,—

1. That Fear, as greatest, overtops and nullifies all lesser fears: the heart possessed with this fear, hath no room for the other. It resolves the heart, in point of duty, what it should and must do, that it must not offend God by any means, lays that down as indisputable, and so eases it of doubtings and debates in that kind—whether shall I comply with the world, and abate somewhat of the sincerity and exact way of religion to please men, or to escape persecution or reproaches: no, it is unquestionably best, and only necessary, *to obey Him rather than men*, to retain His favour, be it with displeasing the most respected and considerable persons we know; yea, rather to choose the universal and highest displeasure of all the world for ever, than His smallest discountenance for a moment. It counts that the only indispensable necessity, to cleave unto God, and obey Him. If I pray, I shall be accused, might Daniel think, but yet, pray I must, come on it what will. So, if I worship God in my prayer, they will mock me, I shall pass for a fool; no matter for that, it must be done: I must call on God, and strive to walk with Him. This sets the mind at ease, not to be halting betwixt two opinions, but resolved what to do. *We are not careful*, said they, *to answer thee, O King—our God can deliver us*, but if not, this we have put out of deliberation, *we will not worship the image.* (Dan. iii. 16.) As one said, *Non oportet vivere, sed oportet navigare*, so we may say, It is not necessary to have the favour of the world, nor to have

riches, nor to live, but it is necessary to hold fast the truth, and to walk holily, to sanctify the name of our Lord, and honour Him, whether in life or death.

2. Faith in God clears the mind, and dispels carnal fears. It is the most sure help: *What time I am afraid*, says David, *I will trust in thee.* (Psalm lvi. 3.) It resolves the mind concerning the event, and scatters the multitude of perplexing thoughts which arise about that: What shall become of this and that? What if such an enemy prevail? What if the place of our abode grow dangerous, and we be not provided, as others are, for a removal? No matter, says Faith, though all fail, I know of one thing that will not; I have a refuge which all the strength of nature and art cannot break in upon or demolish, *a high defence, my Rock in whom I trust.* (Psalm lxii. 5, 6.) The firm belief of, and resting on His power, and wisdom, and love, gives a clear satisfying answer to all doubts and fears. It suffers us not to stand to jangle with each trifling, grumbling objection, but carries all before it, makes day in the soul, and so chases away those fears that vex us only in the dark, as affrightful fancies do. This is indeed *to sanctify God*, and to give Him his own glory, to *rest on Him*. And it is a fruitful homage which is thus done to Him, returning us so much peace and victory over fears and troubles, in the persuasion that nothing *can separate from His love;* that only we feared, and so the things that cannot reach that can be easily despised.

Seek to have the Lord in your hearts, and sanctify Him there. He shall make them strong, and carry them through all dangers. *Though I walk*, says David, *through the valley of the shadow of death, I will fear no ill, for thou art with me.* (Psalm xxiii. So, xxvii. 1.) What is it that makes the Church so firm and stout: *Though the sea roar, and the mountains be cast into the midst of the sea, yet we will not fear?* It is this: *God is in the midst of her; she shall not be moved.* (Psalm xlvi. 2, 5.) No wonder; He is immovable, and therefore doth establish all where He resides. If the world be in the middle of the heart, it will be often shaken, for all there is continual motion and change; but God in it, keeps it stable. Labour, therefore, to get God into your hearts, residing in the midst of them, and then, in the midst of all conditions, they shall not move.

Our condition is universally exposed to fears and troubles, and no man is so stupid but he studies and projects for some fence against them, some bulwark to break the incursion of evils, and so to bring his mind to some ease, ridding it of the fear of them. Thus the most vulgar spirits do in their way; for even the brutes, from whom such do not much differ in their actings, and course of life too, are instructed by nature to provide themselves and their young ones with shelters, the birds their nests, and the beasts their holes and dens. Thus, men gape and pant after gain with a confused, ill-examined fancy of quiet and safety in it, if once they might reach such a day, as to say with the rich fool in the gospel, *Soul, take thine ease, thou hast much goods laid up for many years;* though warned by his short ease, and by many watch-words, yea, by daily experience, that days may come, yea, one day will, when fear and trouble shall rush in, and break over the highest tower of riches, that there is a day, called the *day of wrath,* wherein they *profit not at all.* (Prov. xi. 4.) Thus, men seek safety in the greatness, or multitude, or supposed faithfulness of friends; they seek by any means to be strongly underset this way, to have many, and powerful, and trust-worthy friends. But wiser men, perceiving the unsafety and vanity of these and all external things, have cast about for some higher course. They see a necessity of withdrawing a man from externals, which do nothing but mock and deceive those most who trust most to them; but they cannot tell whither to direct him. The best of them bring him *into himself,* and think to quiet him so, but the truth is, he finds as little to support him there; there is nothing truly strong enough within him, to hold out against the many sorrows and fears which still from without do assault him. So then, though it is well done, to call off a man from outward things, as moving sands, that he build not on them, yet this is not enough; for his own spirit is as unsettled a piece as is in all the world, and must have some higher strength than its own, to fortify and fix it. This is the way that is here taught, *Fear not their fear, but sanctify the Lord your God in your hearts;* and if you can attain this latter, the former will follow of itself.

In the general, then, God taking the place formerly possessed by things full of motion and unquietness, makes firm and establishes the heart. More particularly,

On the one hand, the fear of God turns other fears out of doors; there is no room for them where this great fear is; and though greater than they all, yet it disturbs not as they do, yea, it brings as great quiet as they brought trouble. It is an ease to have but one thing for the heart to deal withal, for many times the multitude of carnal fears is more troublesome than their weight, as flies that vex most by their number.

Again, this fear is not a terrible apprehension of God as an enemy, but a sweet composed reverence of God as our King, yea, as our Father; as very great, but no less good than great; so highly esteeming His favour, as fearing most of all things to offend Him in any kind; especially if the soul should either have been formerly, on the one hand, under the lash of His apprehended displeasure, or, on the other side, have had some sensible tastes of his love, and have been entertained in His *banqueting house,* where *His banner over it was love.* Cant. ii. 4.

His children fear Him for His goodness; are afraid to lose sight of that, or to deprive themselves of any of its influences; desire to live in His favour, and then for other things they are not very thoughtful.

On the other hand, Faith carries the soul above all doubts, assures it that if sufferings, or sickness, or death come, nothing can separate it from Him. This suffices; yea, what though He may hide His face for a time, though that is the hardest of all, yet there is no separation. Faith sets the soul in God, and where is safety, if it be not there? It rests on those persuasions it hath concerning Him, and that interest it hath in Him. Faith believes that He sits and rules the affairs of the world, with an all-seeing eye and an all-moving hand. The greatest affairs surcharge Him not, and the very smallest escape him not. He orders the march of all armies, and the events of battles, and yet, thou and thy particular condition slip not out of His view. The very *hairs of thy head are numbered;* are not then all thy steps, and the hazards of them, known to Him, and all thy desires before Him? Doth He not *number thy wanderings,* every weary step thou art driven to, and *put thy tears in His bottle?* (Psalm lvii. 8.) Thou mayest assure thyself, that however thy matters seem to go, all is contrived to subserve thy good, especially thy chief and highest good. There is a regular motion in them, though the wheels do seem to run cross. *All these things are against me,* said old Jacob, and yet they were all for him.

In all estates, I know of no heart's ease, but to believe; to sanctify and honour thy God, in resting on His word. If thou art persuaded of His love, surely that will carry thee above all distrustful fears. If thou art not clear in that point, yet depend and resolve to stay by Him, yea, to stay on Him, till He shew himself unto thee. Thou hast some fear of Him; thou canst not deny it without gross injury to him and thyself; thou wouldst willingly walk in all well-pleasing unto Him: well then, *who is among you that feareth the Lord, though he see no present light, yet let him trust in the name of the Lord, and stay upon his God.* (Isa. l. 10.) Press this upon thy soul, for there is not such another charm for all its fears and disquiet; therefore repeat it still with David, sing this still, till it be stilled, and chide thy distrustful heart into believing: *Why art thou cast down, O my soul? why art thou disquieted within me? Hope in God, for I shall yet praise Him.* (Psalm xlii. 5.) Though I am all out of tune for the present, never a right string in my soul, yet He will put forth His hand, and redress all, and I *shall yet once again praise,* and therefore, even now, I will hope.

It is true, some may say, God is a safe shelter and refuge, but He is holy, and holy men may find admittance and protection, but can so vile a sinner as I look to be protected and taken in under His safeguard? Go try. *Knock* at His door, *and* (take it not on our word, but on His own) *it shall be opened to thee;* that once done, thou shalt have a happy life of it in the worst times. Faith hath this privilege, never to be ashamed; it takes sanctuary in God, and sits and sings. *under the shadow of his wings,* as David speaks. (Psalm lxiii. 7.)

Whence the unsettledness of men's minds in trouble, or when it is near, but because they are far off from God? The heart is shaken as the leaves of the tree with the wind, there is no stability of spirit; God is not sanctified in it, and no wonder, for He is not known. Strange this ignorance of God, and of the precious promises of His word! The most, living and dying strangers to Him! When trouble comes, they have not Him *as a known refuge,* but have to begin to seek after Him, and to inquire the way to Him; they cannot go to Him as acquainted, and engaged by His own covenant with them. Others have some empty knowledge, and can discourse of scripture, and sermons, and spiritual comforts, while yet they have none of that fear and trust which quiet the soul: they have notions of God in their heads, but God is not sanctified in their hearts.

If you will be advised, this is the way to have a high and strong spirit indeed, and to be above troubles and fears: seek for a more lively and divine knowledge of God than most as yet have, and rest not till you bring Him into your hearts, and then you shall rest indeed in Him.

Sanctify Him by fearing Him. *Let Him be your fear and your dread,* not only as to outward, gross offences; fear an oath, fear to profane the Lord's holy day, but fear also all irregular earthly desires; fear the distempered affecting of any thing, the entertaining of any thing in the secret of your hearts, that may give distaste to your Beloved. Take heed, respect the Great Person you have in your company, who lodges within you, the Holy Spirit. *Grieve Him not;* it will turn to your own grief if you do, for all your comfort is in His hand, and flows from Him. If you be but in heart dallying with sin, it will unfit you for suffering outward troubles, and make your spirit low and base in the day of trial; yea, it will fill you with inward trouble, and disturb that peace which, I am sure, you who know it esteem more than all the peace and flourishing of this world. Outward troubles do not molest or stir inward peace, but an unholy, unsanctified affection doth. All the winds without, cause not an earthquake, but that within its own bowels doth. Christians are much their own enemies in unwary walking; hereby they deprive themselves of those comforts they might have in God, and so are often almost as perplexed and full of fears, upon small occasions, as worldlings are.

Sanctify Him by believing. Study the main question, your *reconcilement* with Him; labour to bring that to some point, and then, in all other occurrences, Faith will uphold you, by enabling you to rely on God as now yours. For these three things make up the soul's peace : 1st, To have right apprehensions of God, looking on Him in Christ, and according to that covenant that holds in him. And, 2dly, a particular apprehension, that is, laying hold on Him in that covenant as gracious and merciful, as satisfied and appeased in Christ, smelling in his sacrifice, (which was himself,) a savour of rest, and setting Himself before me, that I may rely on Him in that notion. 3dly, A persuasion, that by so relying on Him, my soul is as one, yea, is one with Him. Yet, while this is wanting, as to a believer it may be, the other is our duty, to sanctify the Lord in believing the word of grace, and believing on Him, reposing on His word. And this, even severed from the other, doth deliver in a good measure, from distracting fears and troubles, and sets the soul at safety.

Whence is it, that in times of persecution or trouble, men are troubled within, and racked with fears, but because, instead of depending upon God, their hearts are glued to such things as are in hazard by those troubles without, their estates, or their ease, or their lives? The soul destitute of God esteems so highly these things, that it cannot but exceedingly feel when they are in danger, and fear their loss most, gaping after some imagined good, Oh! if I had but this, I were well ;—but then,

such or such a thing may step in and break all my projects.
And this troubles the poor spirit of the man who hath no higher
designs than such as, are so easily blasted, and still, as any
thing in man lifts up his soul to *vanity*, it must needs fall down
again into *vexation*.   There is a word or two in the Hebrew
for *idols*, that signify withal *troubles**, and *terrors†.   And so
it is certainly : all our idols prove so to us ; they fill us with
nothing but anguish and troubles, with unprofitable cares and
fears, that are good for nothing, but to be fit punishments of
that folly out of which they arise.   The ardent love or self-
willed desire of prosperity, or wealth, or credit in the world,
carries with it, as inseparably tied to it, a bundle of fears and
inward troubles.   *They that will be rich*, says the Apostle,
fall into a snare, and many noisome and hurtful lusts, and,
as he adds in the next verse, *they pierce themselves through
with many sorrows*. (1 Tim. vi. 9.)   He who hath set his heart
upon an estate, or a commodious dwelling and lands, or upon a
healthful and long life, cannot but be in continued alarms, renewing his fears concerning them.   Especially in troublous
times, the least rumour of any thing that threateneth to deprive
him of those advantages strikes him to the heart, because his
heart is in them.   I am well seated, thinks he, and I am of a
sound, strong constitution, and may have many a good day.
Oh ! but besides the arrows of pestilence that are flying round
about, the sword of a cruel enemy is not far off.   This will
affright and trouble a heart void of God.   But if thou wouldst
readily answer and dispel all these, and such like fears, *sanctify
the Lord God in thy heart*.   The soul that eyes God, renounces
these things, looks on them at a great distance, as things far
from the heart, and which therefore cannot easily trouble it,
but it looks on God as within the heart, *sanctifies Him in it*,
and rests on Him.

The word of God cures the many foolish hopes and fears that

*[*Tigirim*,] Isa. xlv. 16. from [*Tszus*,] arctavit, hostiliter egit.
†[*Miphletzeth*,] 1 Kings xv. 13, from [*Phalatz*,] contremiscere, et
[*Emim*,] Job xv. 25, from [*Aim*,] formidabilis, terrificus.

we are naturally subject to, by representing to us hopes and fears of a far higher nature, which swallow up and drown the other, as inundations and land-floods do the little ditches in those meadows that they overflow. *Fear not*, says our Saviour, *him that can kill the body*—What then? Fear must have some work—He adds, *But fear Him who can kill both soul and body.* Thus, in the passage cited here, *Fear not their fear, but sanctify the Lord, and let Him be your fear and your dread.* And so, as for the hopes of the world, care not though you lose them for God; there is a *hope in you* (as it follows here) that is far above them.

Be ready always to give an answer.] The real Christian is *all for Christ*, hath given up all right of himself to his Lord and Master, to be all His, to do and suffer for Him, and, therefore, he surely will not fail in this which is least, to speak for Him upon all occasions. If he sanctify Him in his heart, the tongue will follow, *and be ready* [πρὸς ἀπολογίαν] *to give an answer*, a defence or apology. Of this, here are four things to be noted.

1st, The need of it, *Men will ask an account.*

2dly, The matter or subject of it, *The hope in you.*

3dly, The manner, *With meekness and fear.*

4thly, The faculty for it, *Be ready.*

1. The need of a defence or apology. Religion is always the thing in the world that hath the greatest calumnies and prejudices cast upon it; and this engages those who love it to endeavour to clear and disburthen it of them. This they do chiefly by the course of their lives. The saints, by their blameless actions and patient sufferings, do write most real and convincing *Apologies;* yet, sometimes, it is expedient, yea, necessary, to add verbal defences, and to vindicate, not so much themselves, as their Lord and His truth, as suffering in the reproaches cast upon them. Did they rest in their own persons, a regardless contempt of them were usually the fittest answer; *Spreta vilescerent.* But where the holy profession of Christians is likely to receive either the main or the indirect blow, and a

word of defence may do any thing to ward it off, there we ought not to spare to do it.

Christian prudence goes a great way in the regulating of this; for holy things are not to be cast to dogs. Some are not capable of receiving rational answers, especially in Divine things; they were not only lost upon them, but religion dis- honoured by the contest. But we are to answer every one that *inquires a reason*, or an account; which supposes something receptive of it. We ought to judge ourselves engaged to give it, be it an enemy, if he will hear; if it gain him not, it may in part convince and cool him; much more, should it be one who ingenuously inquires for satisfaction, and possibly inclines to receive the truth, but is prejudiced against it by false misre- presentations of it: for Satan and the profane world are very inventive of such shapes and colours as may make truth most odious, drawing monstrous misconsequences out of it, and belying the practices of Christians, making their assemblies horrible and vile by false imputations; and thus are they often necessitated to declare the true tenor, both of their belief and their lives, in confessions of faith, and remonstrances of their carriage and custom.

The very name of Christians, in the primitive times, was made hateful by the foulest aspersions of strange wickednesses committed in their meetings; and these passed credibly through with all who were not particularly acquainted with them. Thus it also was with the Waldenses; and so both were forced to publish Apologies. And, as here enjoined, every one is bound, seasonably, to clear himself, and his brethren, and religion: *Be ye always ready.* It is not always to be done to every one, but, being ready to do it, we must consider when, and to whom, and how far. But,

2. All that they are to give account of, is comprised here under this, *The hope that is in you.* Faith is the root of all graces, of all obedience and holiness; and Hope is so near in nature to it, that the one is commonly named for the other: for the things that *Faith* apprehends and lays hold on as present,

in the truth of Divine promises, *Hope* looks out for as to come in their certain performance. To believe a promise to be true before it be performed, is no other than to believe that it shall be performed; and Hope expects that.

Many rich and excellent things do the saints receive, even in their mean, despised condition here; but their *hope* is rather mentioned as the subject they may speak and give account of with most advantage, both because all they receive, at present, is but as nothing compared to what they hope for, and because, such as it is, it cannot be made known at all to a natural man, being so clouded with their afflictions and sorrows. These he sees, but their graces and comforts he cannot see; and, therefore, the very ground of higher hopes, of somewhat to come, though he knows not what it is, speaks more satisfaction. To hear of another life, and a happiness hoped for, any man will confess it says something, and deserves to be considered.

So, then, the whole sum of religion goes under this word, *the hope that is in you,* for two reasons : first, for that it doth indeed all resolve and terminate into things to come, and secondly, as it leads and carries on the soul towards them by all the graces in it, and all the exercise of them, and through all services and sufferings ; aiming at this, as its main scope, to keep that life to come in the believer's eye, till he get it in his hand; to sustain the hope of it, and bring him to possess it. Therefore the Apostle calls Faith *the substance of things hoped for,* that which makes them be before they be, gives a solidity and substance to them. The name of *hope,* in other things, scarcely suits with such a meaning, but sounds a kind of uncertainty, and is somewhat airy ; for all other hopes but this it is a very true word of Seneca's, *Spes est nomen boni incerti : Hope is the name of an uncertain good.* But the Gospel, being entertained by Faith, furnishes a Hope that hath substance and reality in it; and all its truths do concentrate into this, to give such a hope. There was in St. Paul's word, besides the fitness for his stratagem at that time, a truth suitable to this, where he designates his whole cause for which he was called in question, by the name of his *Hope of the resurrection.* (Acts xxiii. 6.)

And, indeed, this Hope carries its own apology in it, both for itself and for religion. What can more pertinently answer all exceptions against the way of godliness than this, to represent what hopes the saints have who walk in that way? If you ask, Whither tends all this your preciseness and singularity? Why cannot you live as your neighbours and the rest of the world about you? Truly, the reason is this: we have somewhat further to look to than our present condition, and far more considerable than any thing here; we have a hope of blessedness after time, a hope to dwell in the presence of God, where our Lord Christ is gone before us ; and we know that *as many as have this hope must purify themselves even as He is pure.* (1 John iii. 3.) The City we tend to is holy, and *no unclean thing shall enter into it.* (Rev. xxi. 17.) The hopes we have cannot subsist in the way of the ungodly world ; they cannot breathe in that air, but are choked and stifled with it ; and therefore we must take another way, unless we will forego our hopes, and ruin ourselves for company. But all that bustle of godliness you make is (say you) but ostentation and hypocrisy. That may be your judgment, but, if it were so, we had but a poor bargain. Such persons *have their reward;* that which they desire *to be seen of men* is given them, and they can look for no more ; but we should be loth to have it so with us: That which our eye is upon is to come ; our hopes are the thing which upholds us. We know that we shall appear before the Judge of hearts, where shews and formalities will not pass, and we are persuaded that *the hope of the hypocrite shall perish:* (Job viii. 13 :) no man shall be so much disappointed and ashamed as he. But the *Hope* that we have *maketh not ashamed.* (Rom. v. 5.) And while we consider that, so far are we from the regarding of men's eyes, that, were it not we are bound to profess our hope, and avow religion, and to walk conformably to it, even before men, we would be content to pass through altogether unseen ; and we desire to pass as if it were. so, as regardless either of the approbation, or of the reproaches and mistakes of men, as if it were no such thing, for it is indeed nothing.

Yea, the hopes we have make all things sweet. Therefore do we go through disgraces and sufferings with patience, yea; with joy, because of that Hope of glory and joy laid up for us. A Christian can *take joyfully the spoiling of his goods, know-. ing that he hath in heaven a better and an enduring substance.* (Heb. x. 34.)

The Hope.] All the estate of a believer lieth in hope, and it is a royal estate. As for outward things, the children of God have what He thinks fit to serve them, but those are not their portion, and therefore He gives often more of the world to those who shall have no more hereafter ; but all their flourish and lustre is but a base advantage, as a lackey's gaudy clothes, which usually make more shew than his who is heir of the estate. How often, under a mean outward condition, and very. despicable every way, goes an heir of glory, *born of God*, and so royal ; born to a *crown that fadeth not*, an estate of hopes, but so rich and so certain hopes, that the least thought of them surpasses all the world's possessions ! Men think of somewhat for the present, *a bird in hand*, as you say, the best of it : but the odds is in this, that when all present things shall be past and swept away, as if they had not been, then shall these Hopers be in eternal possession ; *they* only shall have all for ever, who seemed to have little or nothing here.

Oh ! how much happier, to be the meanest expectant of the glory to come, than the sole possessor of all this world. These expectants are often kept short in earthly things, and, had they the greatest abundance of them, yet they cannot rest in that. Even so all the spiritual blessings that they do possess here are nothing to *the hope that is in them*, but as an earnest-penny to their great inheritance, which, indeed, confirms their hope, and assures unto them that full estate ; and therefore, be it never so small, they may look on it with joy, not so much regarding it simply in itself, as in relation to that which it seals and ascertains the soul of. Be it never so small, yet it is a pledge of the great glory and happiness which we desire to share in.

It is the grand comfort of a Christian, to look often beyond all that he can possess or attain here ; and as to answer others, when he is put to it concerning his Hope, so to *answer himself* concerning all his present griefs and wants : I have a poor traveller's lot here, little friendship and many straits, but yet I may go cheerfully homewards, for thither I shall come, and there I have riches and honour enough, a palace and a crown abiding me.   Here, nothing but *depth calling unto depth*, one calamity and trouble, as waves, following another : but I have a hope of that *rest that remaineth for the people of God.* I feel the infirmities of a mortal state, but my hopes of immortality content me under them.   I find strong and cruel assaults of temptations breaking in upon me, but, for all that, I have the assured hope of a full victory, and then, of everlasting peace. *I find a law in my members* rebelling against *the law of my mind,* which is the worst of all evils, so much strength of corruption within me ; yet there is withal a hope within me of deliverance, and I look over all to that ; *I lift up my head, because the day of my redemption draws nigh.* This I dare avow and proclaim to all, and am not ashamed *to answer* concerning this blessed Hope.

3. But for the Manner of this, it is to be done with *meekness and fear ;* meekness towards men, and reverential fear towards God.

With meekness.] A Christian is not, therefore, to be blustering and flying out into invectives, because he hath the better of it, against any man that questions him touching this Hope ; as some think themselves certainly authorized to rough speech, because they plead for truth, and are on its side.   On the contrary, so much the rather study meekness, for the glory and advantage of the truth. It needs not the service of passion ; yea, nothing so disserves it, as passion when set to serve it. The *Spirit of truth* is withal the *Spirit of meekness.* The Dove that rested on that great champion of truth, who is The Truth itself, is from Him derived to the lovers of truth, and they ought to seek the participation of it. Imprudence makes some kind of Christians lose much of their labour, in speaking for religion, and drive those further off, whom they would draw into it.

And fear.] Divine things are never to be spoken of in a light, perfunctory way, but with a reverent, grave temper of spirit ; and, for this reason, some choice is to be made both of time and persons. The confidence that attends this hope makes the believer not fear men, to whom he answers, but still he fears his God, for whom he answers, and whose interest is chief in those things he speaks of. The soul that hath the deepest sense of spiritual things, and the truest knowledge of God, is most afraid to miscarry in speaking of Him, most tender and wary how to acquit itself when engaged to speak of and for God.

4. We have the faculty for this apology, *Be ready.* In this are implied knowledge, and affection, and courage. As for knowledge, it is not required of every Christian to be able to prosecute subtilties, and encounter the sophistry of adversaries, especially in obscure points ; but all are bound to know so much, as to be able to aver that hope that is in them, the main doctrine of grace and salvation, wherein the most of men are lamentably ignorant. Affection sets all on work ; whatever faculty the mind hath, it will not suffer it to be useless, and it hardens it against hazards in defence of the truth.

But the only way so to know and love the truth, and to have courage to avow it, is, to have the Lord *sanctified in the heart.* Men may dispute stoutly against Popery and errors, and yet be strangers to God and this hope. But surely it is the liveliest defence, and that which alone returns comfort within, when it arises from the peculiar interest of the soul in God, and in those truths and that hope which are questioned : it is then like pleading for the nearest friend, and for a man's own rights and inheritance. This will animate and give edge to it, when you apologize, not for a hope you have heard or read of barely, but for a hope *within you;* not merely a hope in believers in general, but in *you,* by a particular sense of that hope within.

But, although you should find it not so strong in you, as to your particular interest, yet are you seeking after it, and desiring it mainly? Is it your chief design to attain unto it? Then forbear not, if you have occasion, to speak for it, and commend it to others, and to maintain the sweetness and certainty of it.

And, to the end you may be the more established in it, and so the stronger to answer for it, not only against men, but against that great adversary who seeks so much to infringe and overbear it, know the right foundation of it; build it never on yourselves, or any thing in yourselves. The work of grace may evidence to you the truth of your hope, but the ground it fastens on is Jesus Christ, in whom all our rights and evidences hold good ; his death assuring us of freedom from condemnation, and his life and possession of glory being the foundation of our hope. (Heb. vi. 19.) If you would have it immoveable, rest it there ; lay all this hope on him, and, when assaulted, fetch all your answers for it from him, for it is *Christ in you* that is your *hope of glory.* (Col. i. 27.)

Ver. 16. Having a good conscience, that whereas they speak evil of you, as of evil doers, they may be ashamed that falsely accuse your good conversation in Christ.

THE *prosperity of fools is their destruction,* says Solomon. (Prov. i. 32.) But none of God's children die of this disease— of too much ease. He knows well how to breed them, and fit them for a kingdom. He keeps them in exercise, but yet so as they are not surcharged. He not only directs them how to overcome, but enables and supports them in all their conflicts, and gives them victory. One main thing, tending to their support and victory, is what is here required in the saints, and is withal wrought and maintained in them by the Spirit of God, *Having a good conscience,* &c.

I. We have here Two Parties opposed in contest—the evil tongues of the ungodly, and the good conscience and conversation of the Christian : *they speak evil of you, and falsely accuse you,* but do you have *a good conscience.*

II. The Success of their Contest : the good conscience prevails, and the evil-speakers are ashamed.

I. The Parties engaged : *They speak evil.*] This is a general evil in the corrupt nature of man, though in some it rises to a greater height than in others. Are not tables and chambers, and almost all societies and meetings full of it ? And even those who have some dislikings of it, are too easily carried away with the stream, and, for company's sake, take a share, if not by lending their word, yet lending their ear, and willingly hearing the detractions of others : unless it be of their friends, or such as they have interest in, they insensibly slide into some forced complacency, and easily receive the impression of calumnies and defamings. But the most are more active in this evil, can cast in their penny to make up the shot; have their taunt or criticism upon somebody in readiness, to make up the feast, such as most companies entertain one another withal, but it is a vile diet. Satan's name, as the Syriac calls him, is, *an Eater of calumnies.* This tongue-evil hath its root in the heart, in a perverse constitution there, in pride and self-love. An overweening esteem that men naturally have of themselves, mounts them into the Censor's chair, gives them a fancied authority of judging others, and self-love, a desire to be esteemed; and, for that end, they spare not to depress others, and load them with disgraces and injurious censures, seeking upon their ruins to raise themselves: as Sallust speaks, *Ex alieni nominis jacturá gradum sibi faciunt ad gloriam.*

But this bent of the unrenewed heart and tongue to evil-speaking, works and vents in the world most against those who walk most contrary to the course of the world : against such, this furnace of the tongue, *kindled from hell*, as St. James tells us, is made seven times hotter than ordinary. As for sincere Christians, they say, A company of hypocrites, who so godly? but yet, they are false, and malicious, and proud, &c. No kind of carriage in them shall escape, but there shall be some device to wrest and misname it. If they be cheerful in society, that shall be accounted more liberty than suits with their profession ; if of a graver or sad temper, that shall pass for sullen severity. Thus perversely were John the Baptist and Christ censured by the Jews. (Matt. xi. 18, 19.) If they be diligent and wary in their affairs, then, in the World's construction, they are as covetous and worldly as any ; if careless and remiss in them, then silly, witless creatures, good for nothing. Still something stands cross.

The enemies of religion have not any where so quick an eye, as in observing the ways of such *as seek after God: my re-markers,* David calls them, Psal. lvi. 6—they who scan my ways, as the word implies,—will not let the least step pass un-examined. If nothing be found faulty, then their invention works, either forging complete falsehoods, or disguising some-thing that lies open to mistake. Or, if they can catch hold on any real failing, there is no end of their triumph and insulta-tions. 1. They aggravate and raise it to the highest. 2. While they will not admit to be themselves judged of by their con-stant walk, they scruple not to judge of the condition of a Christian by any one particular action wherein he doth, or seems at least to, miscarry. 3. They rest not there, but make one failing of one Christian the reproach of all : Take up your devotees, there is never a one of them better. 4. Nor rest they there, but make the personal failings of those who profess it, the disgrace of religion itself. Now, all these are very crooked rules, and such as use them are guilty of gross injustice. For,

1. There is a great difference between a thing taken favour-ably, and the same action misconstrued. And,

2. A great difference betwixt one particular act, and a man's estate or inward frame, which they either consider not, or wil-lingly or maliciously neglect.

3. How large is the difference that there is betwixt one and

another in the measure of grace, as well as of prudence, either in their natural disposition, or in grace, or possibly in both ! Some who are honest in the matter of religion, yet, being very weak, may miscarry in such things as other Christians come seldom near the hazard of. And though some should wholly forsake the way of godliness, wherein they seemed to walk, yet why should that reflect upon such as are real and stedfast in it? *They went out from us,* says the Apostle, *but were not of us.* (1 John ii. 19.) *Offences* of this kind *must* be, but the *wo* rests on him by *whom they come,* not on other Christians. And if it spread further than the party offending, the wo is to the profane world, that take offence at religion because of him: as our Saviour hath expressed it, *Wo to the world because of offences;* (Matt. xviii. 7;) they shall stumble and fall, and break their necks upon these stumbling blocks or scandals. Thou who art profane, and seest the failing of a minister or Christian, and art hardened by it, this is a judgment to thee, that thou meetest with such a block in thy way. *Wo to the world!* It is a judgment on a place, when God permits religion, in the persons of some, to be scandalous.

4. Religion itself remains still the same : whatsoever be the failings and blots of one or more who profess it, it is itself pure and spotless. If it teach not holiness, and meekness, and humility, and all good, purely, then except against it. But if it be *a straight golden reed* by which the Temple is measured, (Rev. xxi. 15,) then let it have its own esteem, both of straightness and preciousness, whatsoever unevenness be found in those who profess to receive it.

Suspect and search yourselves, even in general, for this evil of evil-speaking. Consider that we are to give [λογον λογῶν] *an account of words;* and if of idle [ἄργον ῥῆμα] workless words, how much more of lying or biting words!—*De verbo mendaci aut mordaci,* as St. Bernard has it. Learn more humility and self-censure. Blunt that fire-edge upon your own hard and disordered hearts, that others may meet with nothing but charity and lenity at your hands.

But particularly beware of this, in more or less, in earnest. or in jest, to reproach religion, or those who profess it. Know how particularly the glorious name of GOD is interested in. that; and they who dare be affronting Him, what shall they say? How shall they stand, when He calls them to account? If you have not attained to it, yet do not bark against it, but the rather esteem highly of religion. Love it, and the very appearance of it, wherever you find it. Give it respect and your good word at least; and, from an external approba-. tion, Oh! that you would aspire to inward acquaintance with it, and then no more were needful to be said in this: it would commend itself to you sufficiently. But, in the mean time, be ashamed, be afraid of that professed enmity against God that is amongst you, a malignant, hateful spirit against those who desire to walk holily, whetting your tongues against them.

Consider, what do you mean? This religion which we all profess, is it the way to heaven, or is it not? Do you believe this word or not? If you do not, what do you here! If you do, then you must believe too, that those who walk closest by this rule are surest in that way; those who dare not share in your oaths, and excessive cups, and profane conversation. What can you say? It is not possible to open your mouth against them, without renouncing this word and faith: there-. fore, either declare you are no Christians, and that Christ is not yours, or, in His name, I enjoin you, that you dare no more speak an ill word of Christianity, and the power of re-. ligion, and those who seek after it. There are not many higher signs of a reprobate mind, than to have a bitter, viru-lent spirit against the children of God. Seek that tie of affec-tion and fraternity, on which the beloved Apostle, St. John, lays such stress, when he says, *Hereby we know that we are translated from death to life, because we love the brethren.* (1 John iii. 14.)

But because those hissings are the natural voice of the Ser-pent's seed, expect them, you that have a mind to follow

Christ, and take this guard against them that you are here directed to take: *Having a good conscience.*

It is a fruitless verbal debate, whether Conscience be a faculty or habit, or not. As in other things, so in this, which most of all requires more solid and useful consideration, the vain mind of man feedeth on the wind, loves to be busy to no purpose, *magno conatu magnas nugas.* How much better is it to have this supernatural goodness of conscience, than to dispute about the nature of it; to find it duly teaching and admonishing, reproving and comforting, rather than to define it most exactly! *Malo sentire compunctionem, quàm scire ejus definitionem.*

When all is examined, Conscience will be found to be no other than the *mind of man, under the notion of a particular reference to himself and his own actions.* And there is a twofold goodness of the Conscience, *purity* and *tranquillity;* and this latter flows from the former, so that the former is the thing we ought primarily to study, and the latter will follow of itself. For a time, indeed, the conscience that is in a good measure pure, may be unpeaceable, but still it is the apprehension and sense of present or former impurity, that makes it so; for, without the consideration of guiltiness, there is nothing that can trouble it: it cannot apprehend the wrath of God, but with relation unto sin.

The goodness of conscience here recommended, is, *the integrity and holiness of the whole inward man in a Christian.* So, the ingredients of it are, 1. A due light or knowledge of our rule: that, like the lamps in the Temple, must be still burning within, as filthiness is always the companion of darkness. Therefore, if you would have a good conscience, you must by all means have so much light, so much knowledge of the will of God, as may regulate you, and shew your way, may teach you how to do, and speak, and think, as in His presence.

2. A constant regard and using of this light, applying it to all things; not sleeping, but working by it; still seeking a

nearer conformity with the known will of our God; daily re-
dressing and ordering the affections by it; not sparing to knock
off whatsoever we find irregular within, that our hearts may be
polished and brought to a right frame by that rule. And this
is the daily inward work of the Christian, his great business,
to purify himself, as the Lord is pure. (1 John iii. 3.)

And, 3. For the advancing of this work, there is needful a
frequent search of our hearts and of our actions, not only to
consider what we are to do, but what we have done. These
reflex inquiries, as they are a main part of the Conscience's
proper work, are a chief means of making and keeping the
Conscience good; first, by acquainting the soul with its own
state, with the motions and inclinations that are most natural
to it; secondly, by stirring it up to work out, and purge away
by repentance, the pollution it hath contracted by any outward
act or inward motion of sin; and, thirdly, this search both excites and enables the Conscience to be more watchful; teaches
how to avoid and prevent the like errors for the time to come.
As natural wise men labour to gain thus much out of their former oversights in their affairs, to be the wiser and warier by
them, and lay up that as bought wit, which they have paid
dear for, and therefore are careful to make their best advantage
of it; so God makes the consideration of their falls preserva-
tives to his children from falling again, makes a medicine of
this poison.

Thus, that the conscience may be good, it must be enlightened, and it must be watchful, both advising before, and after
censuring, according to that light.

The greater part of mankind little regard this: they walk by
guess, having perhaps ignorant consciences, and the blind, you
say, swallow many a fly. Yea, how many consciences are without sense, *as seared with an hot iron;* (1 Tim. iv. 2;) so stupified, that they feel nothing! Others rest satisfied with a civil
righteousness, an imagined goodness of conscience, because they
are free from gross crimes. Others, who know the rule of
Christianity, yet study not a conscientious respect to it in all

things: they cast some transient looks upon the rule and their own hearts, it may be, but sit not down to compare them, make it not their business, have time for any thing but that, *Non vacant bonæ menti.* They do not, with St. Paul, exercise themselves in this, *to have a conscience void of offence towards God and men.* (Acts xxiv. 16.) Those were his *Ascetics,* [ἀσκῶ] ; he exhausted himself in striving against what might defile the conscience ; or, as the word signifies, *elaborately wrought and dressed* his conscience, [ἀσκήσασα χιτῶνα, HOM.] Think you, while other things cannot be done without diligence and intention, that this is a work to be done at random ? No, it is the most exact and curious of all works, to have the conscience right, and keep it so; as watches, or other such neat pieces of workmanship, except they be daily wound up and skilfully handled, will quickly go wrong. Yea, besides daily inspection, conscience should, like those, at sometimes be taken to pieces, and more accurately cleansed, for the best kept will gather soil and dust. Sometimes a Christian should set himself to a more solemn examination of his own heart, beyond his daily search ; and all little enough to have so precious a good as this, *a good conscience.* They who are most diligent and vigilant, find nothing to abate as superfluous, but still need of more. The heart is to be *kept with all diligence,* or above all keeping. (Prov. iv. 23.) Corruption within is ready to grow and gain upon it, if it be never so little neglected, and from without, to invade it, and get in. We breathe in a corrupt, infected air, and have need daily to *antidóte* the heart against it.

You that are studying to be excellent in this art of a good conscience, go on, seek daily progress in it. The study of conscience is a more sweet, profitable study than that of all science, wherein is much vexation, and, for the most part, little or no fruit. Read this book diligently, and correct your *errata* by that other book, the word of God. Labour to have it pure and right. Other books and works are [περιεργὰ] *curious,* and [παρεργὰ,] *by-works,* they shall not appear, but this is one of the books that shall be opened in that great day, *according to which we must be judged.* (Rev. xx. 12.)

On this follows a good conversation, as inseparably connected with a good conscience. Grace is of a lively, active nature, and doth act like itself. Holiness in the heart will be holiness in the life too ; not some good actions, but a good conversation an uniform, even tract of life, the whole revolution of it regular. The inequality of some Christians' ways doth breed much discredit to religion, and discomfort to themselves.

But observe here, 1. The order of these two. 2. The principle of both.

1. The order. First, the Conscience good, and then, the Conversation. *Make the tree good and the fruit will be good,* says our Saviour: (Matt. xii. 33:) so, here, a good conscience is the root of a good conversation. Most men begin at the wrong end of this work. They would reform the outward man first : that will do no good, it will be but dead work.

Do not rest upon external reformations, they will not hold ; there is no abiding, nor any advantage, in such a work. You think, when reproved, Oh! I will mend and set about the redress of some outward things. But this is as good as to do nothing. The *mind and conscience being defiled,* as the Apostle speaks, Tit. i. 15, doth defile all the rest : it is a mire in the spring ; although the pipes are cleansed, they will grow quickly foul again. If Christians, in their progress in grace, would eye this most, that the conscience be growing purer, the heart more spiritual, the affections more regular and heavenly, their outward carriage would be holier ; whereas, the outward work of performing duties, and being much exercised in religion, may, by the neglect of this, be labour in vain, and amend nothing soundly. To set the outward actions right, though with an honest intention, and not so to regard and find out the inward disorder of the heart, whence that in the actions flows, is but to be still putting the index of a clock right with your finger, while it is foul, or out of order within, which is a con-

tinual business, and does no good. Oh ! but a purified conscience, a soul renewed and refined in its temper and affections,
will make things go right without, in all the duties and acts of
our callings.

2. The principle of good in both, is Christ: *Your good conversation in Christ.* The conversation is not good, unless in
Him ; so neither is the conscience.

[1.] *In Him,* as to our persons: we must be in Him, and
then the conscience and conversation will be good in Him.
The conscience that is morally good, having some kind of vir-
tuous habits, yet being out of Christ, is nothing but pollution
in the sight of God. It must be washed in His blood, ere it
can be clean ; all our pains will not cleanse it, floods of tears
will not do it; it is blood, and that blood alone that hath the
virtue of *purging the conscience from dead works.* (Heb.
ix. 14.)

[2.] *In Him,* as the perfect pattern of holiness; the heart
and life must be conformed to Him, and so made truly good.

[3.] *In Him,* as the Source of Grace, whence it is first derived, and always fed, and maintained, and made active : a
Spirit goes forth from Him that cleanseth our spirits, and so
makes our conversation clean and holy.

If thou wouldst have thy conscience and heart purified and
pacified, and have thy life certified, go to Christ for all, make
use of Him ; as of His blood to wash off thy guiltiness, so of
His Spirit to purify and sanctify thee. If thou wouldst have
thy heart reserved for God, pure as His temple ; if thou
wouldst have thy lusts cast out which pollute thee, and findest
no power to do it ; go to Him, desire Him to scourge out that
filthy rabble, that abuse His house and make it a den of thieves.
Seek this, as the only way to have thy soul and thy ways
righted, to *be in Christ,* and then *walk in Him.* Let thy
conversation be in Christ. Study Him, and follow Him : look
on His way, on His graces, His obedience, and humility, and
meekness, till, by looking on them, they make the very idea of
thee new, as the painter doth of a face he would draw to the

life. So behold His glory, that thou mayest be *transformed from glory to glory*. But as it is there added, this must be *by the Spirit of the Lord:* 2 Cor. iii. 18. Do not, therefore, look on Him simply, as an example without thee, but as life within thee. Having *received Him*, walk not only like Him, but *in Him*, as the Apostle St. Paul speaks, Col. ii. 6. And as the word is here, *have your conversation* not only according to Christ, but *in Christ*. *Draw from His fulness grace for grace*. (John i. 16.)

II. The other thing in the words, is, the advantage of this good conscience and conversation. 1. There is even an external success attends it, in respect of the malicious, ungodly world : *They shall be ashamed that falsely accuse you*. Thus often it is even most evident to men ; the victory of innocency, silent innocency, most strongly confuting all calumny, making the ungodly, false accusers hide their heads. Thus, without stirring, the integrity of a Christian conquers ; as a rock, unremoved, breaks the waters that are dashing against it. And this is not only a lawful but a laudable way of revenge, shaming calumny out of it, and punishing evil-speakers by well-doing ; shewing really how false their accusers were. This is the most powerful apology and refutation ; as the sophister who would prove there was no motion, was best answered by the philosopher's rising up and walking. And without this good conscience and conversation, we cut ourselves short of other apologies for religion, whatsoever we say for it. One unchristian action will disgrace it more than we can repair by the largest and best-framed speeches on its behalf.

Let those, therefore, who have given their names to Christ, honour Him, and their holy profession, most this way. Speak for Him as occasion requires ;—why should we not, provided it be *with meekness and fear*, as our Apostle hath taught ?—but let this be the main defence of religion : live suitably to it, and commend it so. Thus all should do who are called Christians ; they should adorn that holy profession with holy conversation. But the most are nothing better than spots and blots, some wal-

lowing in the mire, and provoking one another to all uncleanness. Oh ! the unchristian life of Christians ! an evil to be
much lamented, more than all the troubles we sustain ! But
these, indeed, do thus deny Christ, and declare that they ar
not His. So many as have any reality of Christ in you, be so
much the more holy, the more wicked the rest are. Strive to
make it up, and to honour that name which they disgrace. And
if they will reproach you, because ye walk not with them, and
cast the mire of false reproaches on you, take no notice, but g
on your way ; it will dry, and easily rub off. Be not troubled
with misjudgings ; shame them out of it by your blameless and
holy carriage, for that will do most to put lies out of countenance. However, if they continue impudent, the day is at
hand, wherein all the enemies of Christ shall be *all clothed over
and covered with shame*, and they who have kept a good conscience, and walked in Christ, *shall lift up their faces with joy*.

2. There is an intrinsical good in this goodness of conscience, that sweetens all sufferings : as it follows,

Ver. 17. For it is better, if the will of God be so, that ye suffer for well-
doing, than for evil-doing.

THERE is a necessity of suffering in any way wherein ye can
walk ; if ye choose the way of wickedness, you shall not, by
doing so, escape suffering ; and that supposed, this is by far
the better, to suffer *in well-doing*, and *for* it, than to suffer
either *for doing evil*, or simply to suffer *in that way*, (as the
words run,) κακοποιοῦντας πάσχειν, *to suffer doing evil*.

The way of the ungodly is not exempt from suffering, even
at present. Setting aside the judgment and wrath to come,
they often suffer from the hands of men, whether justly or unjustly, and often from the immediate hand of God, who is always just, both in this and the other, causing the sinner *to eat
of the fruit of his own ways*. (Prov. i. 30.) When profane
ungodly men offer violences and wrongs one to another, in this
God is just against both, in that wherein they themselves
O 2

are both unjust: they are both rebellious against Him, and so, though they intend not to take up His quarrel, He means it Himself, and sets them to lash one another. The wicked profess their combined enmity against the children of God, yet they are not always at peace amongst themselves : they often revile and defame each other, and so it is kept up on both sides. Whereas, the godly cannot hold them game in that, being like their Lord, *who, when he was reviled, reviled not again.* Besides, although the ungodly flourish at some times, yet they have their days of suffering, are subject to the common miseries of the life of man, and the common calamities of evil times ; the sword and the pestilence, and such like public judgments. Now, in what kind soever it be that they suffer, they are at a great disadvantage, compared with the godly, in their sufferings.

Here impure consciences may lie sleeping, while men are at ease themselves ; but when any great trouble comes and shakes them, then, suddenly, the conscience begins to awake and bustle, and proves more grievous to them, than all that comes on them from without. When they remember their despising of the ways of God, their neglecting of Him and holy things, whence they are convinced how comfort might be reaped in these days of distress, this cuts and galls them most, looking back at their licentious, profane ways ; each of them strikes to the heart. As the Apostle calls sin *the sting of death,* so is it of all sufferings, and the sting that strikes deepest into the very soul : no stripes are like those that are secretly given by an accusing conscience. *Surdo verbere cedit.* Juv.

A sad condition it is, to have from thence the greatest anguish whence the greatest comfort should be expected ; to have thickest darkness, whence they should look for the clearest light. Men who have evil consciences, love not to be with them, are not much with themselves : as St. Augustine compares them to such as have shrewd wives, they love not to be much at home. But yet, outward distress sets a man inward, as foul weather drives him home, and there, where he should find comfort, he is met with such accusations as are *like a continual dropping*, as Solomon speaks of a contentious woman. (Prov. xix. 3.) It is a most wretched state, to live under sufferings or afflictions of any kind, and be a stranger to God; for a man to have God and his conscience against him, that should be his solace in times of distress; being knocked off from the comforts of the world, whereon he rested, and having no provision of spiritual comfort within, nor expectation from above.

But the children of God, in their sufferings, especially in such as are encountered for God, can retire within themselves, and rejoice in the testimony of a good conscience, yea, in the possession of Christ dwelling within them. All the trouble that befals them, is but as the rattling of hail upon the tiles of the house, to a man who is sitting within a warm room at a rich banquet; and such is a good conscience, a feast, yea, *a continual feast.* The Believer looks on his Christ, and in Him reads his deliverance from condemnation, and that is a strong comfort, a cordial that keeps him from fainting in the greatest distresses. When the conscience gives this testimony, that sin is forgiven, it raises the soul above outward sufferings. Tell the Christian of loss of goods, or liberty, or friends, or life, he answers all with this: Christ is mine, and my sin is pardoned; that is enough for me. What would I not have suffered, to have been delivered from the wrath of God, if any suffering of mine in this world could have done that? Now that is done to my hand, all other sufferings are light; they are *light,* and *but for a moment.* One thought of eternity drowns the whole time of the world's duration, which is but as one instant, or twinkling of an eye, betwixt eternity before, and eternity after; how much less is any short life, (and a small part of that is spent in sufferings,) yea, what is it, though it were all sufferings without interruption, which yet it is not! When I look forward to the crown, all vanishes, and I think it *less than nothing.* Now, these things the good conscience speaks to the Christian in his sufferings; therefore, certainly, his choice is best, who provides it for his companion against evil and troublous times. If moral integrity went so far, (as truly it did in some men who had much of it.) that they scorned all hard encounters, and esteemed this a sufficient bulwark, a strength impregnable, *Hic murus aheneus esto, nil conscire sibi,* how much more the Christian's good conscience, which alone is truly such !

As the Christian may thus look inward, and rejoice in tribulation, so there is another look, *upward,* that is here likewise mentioned, that allays very much all the sufferings of the saints: *If the will of God be so.*

The Christian mind hath still one eye to this, looking above the hand of men, and all inferior causes, in suffering, whether for the name of God, or otherwise; he looks on the sovereign will of God, and sweetly complies with that in all. Neither is there any thing that doth more powerfully compose and quiet the mind than this; it makes it invincibly firm and, content, when it hath attained this self-resignation to the *will of God,* so as to agree to that in every thing. This is the very thing wherein tranquillity of spirit lies: it is no riddle, nor hard to be understood, yet few attain it. And, I pray you, what is gained by our reluctances and repinings, but pain to ourselves? God *doth what He will,* whether we consent or not. Our disagreeing doth not prevent His purposes, but our own peace: if we will not be led, we are drawn. We must suffer, if He will; but if we will what He wills, even in suffering, that makes it sweet and easy ; when our mind goes along with His, and we willingly move with that stream of providence, which will carry us with it, even though we row against it; in which case we still have nothing but toil and weariness for our pains. -

But this hard argument of Necessity is needless to the child of God, who, persuaded of the wisdom and love of his Father, knows that to be truly best for Him that His hand bestows. Sufferings are unpleasant to the flesh, and it will grumble; but the voice of the Spirit of God, in His children, is that of that good king, Isa. xxxix. 8: *Good is the word of the Lord.* Let him do with me as seemeth good in His eyes. My foolish heart would think these things I suffer might be abated, but my wise and heavenly Father thinks otherwise. He hath His design of honour to Himself, and good to me in these, which I would be loth to cross if I might. I might do God more service by those temporal advantages, but doth not He know best what is fit? Cannot he advance His grace more by the want of these things I desire, than I could do myself by having them? Cannot He make me a gainer by sickness and poverty, and disgraces, and loss of friends and children, by making up all in Himself, and teaching me more of His all-sufficiency? Yea, even concerning the affairs of my soul, I am to give up all to His good pleasure. Though I desire the light of his countenance above all things in this world, yet, if He see fit to hide it sometimes, if that be His will, let me not murmur. There is nothing lost by this obedient temper; yea, what way soever He deals with us, there is much more advantage in it. No soul shall enjoy so much in all estates, as that which hath divested and renounced itself, and hath no will but God's.

Ver. 18. For Christ also hath once suffered for sins, the just for the unjust, (that he might bring us to God,) being put to death in the flesh, but quickened by the Spirit.

THE whole life of a Christian is a steady aiming at conformity with Christ; so that in any thing, whether doing or suffering, there can be no argument so apposite and persuasive as His example, and no exercise of obedience, either active or passive, so difficult, but the view and contemplation of that example will powerfully sweeten it. The Apostle doth not decline the frequent use of it. Here we have it thus: *For Christ also suffered.*

Though the doctrine of Christian suffering is the occasion of his speaking of Christ's suffering, yet he insists on it beyond the simple necessity of that argument, for its own excellency and for further usefulness. So we shall consider the double capacity. I. As an encouragement and engagement for Christians to suffer. II. As the great point of their faith, whereon all

their hopes and happiness depend, being the means of their restoration to God.

I. The due consideration of Christ's sufferings doth much
temper all the sufferings of Christians, especially such as are
directly for Christ.

It is some known ease to the mind, in any distress, to look
upon examples of the like, or greater distress, in present or
former times. *Ferre quam sortem patiuntur omnes.* It diverts
the eye from continual poring on our own suffering; and, when
we return to view it again, it lessens it, abates of the imagined
bulk and greatness of it. Thus public, thus spiritual troubles
are lightened; and particularly the sufferings and temptations
of the godly, by the consideration of this as their common lot,
their highway, not new in the person of any: *No temptation
has befallen you, but what is common to men.* (1 Cor. x. 13.)
If we trace the lives of the most eminent saints, shall we not
find every notable step that is recorded, marked with a new
cross, one trouble following on another, *velut unda pellitur
undá*, as the waves do, in an incessant succession? Is not this
manifest in the life of Abraham, and of Jacob, and the rest of
God's worthies, in the Scriptures? And doth not this make it
an unreasonable, absurd thought, to dream of an exemption?
Would any one have a new untrodden way cut out for him,
free of thorns, and strewed with flowers all along? Does he
expect to meet with no contradictions, nor hard measure from
the world, or imagine that there may be such a dexterity necessary, as to keep its good will, and the friendship of God too?
This will not be; and it is a universal conclusion, *All that will
live godly in Christ Jesus, must suffer persecution.* (2 Tim.
iii. 12.) This is the path to the kingdom, that which all the
sons of God, the heirs of it, have gone in, even Christ; according to that well known word, One son without sin, but not one
without suffering: *Christ also suffered.*

The example and company of the saints in suffering is very
considerable, but that of Christ is more so than any other, yea,
than all the rest together. Therefore the Apostle, having re-

presented the former at large, ends in this, as the top of all, Heb. xii. 1, 2: *There is a race set before us*, it is to be run, and *run with patience*, and *without fainting:* now, he tells us of a *cloud of witnesses*, a cloud made up of instances of believers suffering before us, and the heat of the day wherein we run is somewhat cooled even by that cloud compassing us; but the main strength of our comfort here, lies in *looking to Jesus*, in the eyeing of His sufferings and their issue. The considering and contemplating of Him will be the strongest cordial, will keep you from *wearying* and *fainting* in the way, as it is verse 3.

The singular power of this instance, lies in many particulars considerable in it. To specify some chief things briefly in the steps of the present words: Consider, 1. The Greatness of the Example.

[1.] The greatness of the person, *Christ*, which is marked out to us by the manner of expression, [καὶ Χριστὸς,] *Christ also;* besides and beyond all others, *even Christ himself.*

There can be no higher example. Not only are the sons of adoption sufferers, but the *begotten*, the *only begotten Son*, the Eternal Heir of glory, in whom all the rest have their title, their sonship and heirship, derived from, and dependent on His; not only all the saints, but the King of saints. Who now shall repine at suffering? Shall the wretched sons of men refuse to suffer, after the suffering of the spotless, glorious Son of God? As St. Bernard speaks of pride, *Ubi se humiliavit Majestas, vermiculus infletur et intumescat*—After Majesty, Highest Majesty, to teach us humility, hath so humbled Himself, how wicked and impudent a thing will it be for a worm to swell, to be high conceited! Since thus our Lord hath taught us by suffering in his own person, and hath dignified sufferings so, we should certainly rather be ambitious than afraid of them.

[2.] The greatness and the continuance of His sufferings. That which the Apostle speaks here of, *His once suffering*, hath its truth; taking in all, *He suffered once;* His whole life was one continued line of suffering, from the manger to the

cross. All that lay betwixt was suitable; His estate and
entertainment throughout his whole life, agreed well with so
mean a beginning, and so reproachful an end, of it. Forced
upon a flight, while he could not go, and living till he appeared
in public, in a very mean despised condition, as the carpenter's
son ; and, afterwards, his best works paid with envy and revilings, called a *wine-bibber*, and a *caster out of devils by the
prince of devils;* his life often laid in wait and sought for. Art
thou mean in thy birth and life, despised, misjudged, and reviled, on all hands? Look how it was with Him, who had
more right than thou hast to better entertainment in the world.
Thou wilt not deny it was his own; *it was made by Him, and
He was in it, and it knew Him not.* Are thy friends harsh
to thee? *He came unto his own, and His own received him
not.* Hast thou a mean cottage, or art thou drawn from it and
hast no dwelling, and art thou every way poor and ill-aecom-
modated? He was as poor as thou canst be, *and had not
where to lay his head,* worse provided than the *birds* and
foxes! But then, consider to what a height His sufferings rose
in the end, that most remarkable part of them here meant by
his *once suffering for sins.* If thou shouldst be cut off by a
violent death, or in the prime of thy years, mayst thou not look
upon Him as going before thee in both these? And in so ignominious a way! Scourged, buffeted, and spit on, He endured
all, *He gave his back to the smiters,* and then, as the same
prophet hath it, *He was numbered amongst the transgressors:*
Isa liii. *ult.* When they had used him with all that shame,
they hanged him betwixt two thieves, and they that passed by
wagged their heads, and darted taunts at Him, as at a mark
fixed to the cross: *they scoffed and said, He saved others,
himself he cannot save. He endured the cross, and despised
the shame,* says the Apostle, Heb. xii. 2.

Thus we see the outside of His sufferings. But the Christian
is subject to grievous temptations and sad desertions, which are
heavier by far than the sufferings which indeed the Apostle
speaks of here. Yet even in these, this same argument of his

holds. For our Saviour is not acquainted with, nor ignorant of, either of those, though still *without sin*. If any of *that* had been in any of His sufferings, it had not furthered, but undone all our comfort in Him. But *tempted* He was; He suffered that way too, and the temptations were terrible, as you know. And was there not some strong conflict when he fell down and prayed in the garden, and *sweat drops of blood?* Was there not an awful eclipse, when he cried out on the cross, *My God, my God, why hast thou forsaken me?* So that, even in these, we may apply this comfort, and stay ourselves or our souls on Him, and go to Him as a compassionate High-priest. Heb. iv. 15. *For Christ also suffered.*

2. Consider the Fitness of the Example. As the same is every way great, yea, *greatest,* so it is fit, the *fittest* to take with a Christian, to set before him, as being so near a pattern, wherein he hath so much interest. As the argument is strong in itself, so, to the new man, the Christian man, it is particularly strongest; it binds him most, as it is not far fetched, but *exemplum domesticum,* a home pattern; as when you persuade men to virtue, by the example of those that they have a near relation to. They are *His servants,* and shall they, or would they, think to *be greater than their Master,* to be exempt from His lot in the world? They are *His soldiers,* and will they refuse to follow Him, and to endure with Him? *Suffer hardship,* says the Apostle to Timothy, *as a good soldier of Jesus Christ.* (2 Tim. ii. 3.) Will not a word from Him put a vigour in them to go after Him, whether upon any march or service, when he calls them friends, *Commilitones,* as they tell us was Julius Cæsar's word, which wrought so much on his trained bands? Yea, *He is not ashamed to call them Brethren,* (Heb. ii. 11,) and will they be ashamed to share with Him, and to be known by their suitable estate, to be His brethren?

3. Consider the Efficacy of the Example. There is, from these sufferings of Christ, such a result of safety and comfort to a Christian, as makes them a most effectual encouragement to suffering, which is this: if He *suffered once,* and that was

for sin, now that heavy, intolerable suffering for sin is once taken out of the Believer's way, it makes all other sufferings light, exceeding light, as nothing in his account. *He suffered once for sin,* so that to them who lay hold on Him this holds sure, that sin is never to be suffered for in the way of strict justice again, as not by Him, so, not by them who are in Him ; for *He suffered for sins once,* and it was for *their* sins, every poor believer's. So now, the soul, finding itself rid of that fear, goes cheerfully through all other hazards and sufferings.

Whereas the soul, perplexed about that question, finds no relief in all other enjoyments ; all propositions of lower comforts are unsavoury and troublesome to it. Tell it of peace and prosperity ; say, however the world go, you shall have ease and pleasure, and you shall be honoured and esteemed by all ; though you could make a man sure of these, yet if his conscience be working and stirred about the matter of his sin, and the wrath of God which is tied close to sin, he will wonder at your impertinency, in that you speak so far from the purpose. Say what you will of these, he still asks, What do you mean by this ? Those things answer not to me. Do you think that I can find comfort in them, so long as my sin is unpardoned, and there is a sentence of eternal death standing above my head ? I feel even an impress of somewhat of that hot indignation ; some flashes of it, flying and lighting upon the face of my soul, and how can I take pleasure in these things you speak of ? And though I should be senseless, and feel nothing of this all my life, yet, how soon shall I have done with it, and the delights that reach no further. And then to have *everlasting burnings,* an eternity of wrath to enter to ! How can I be satisfied with that estate :—All you offer a man in this posture, is as if you should set dainty fare, and bring music with it, before a man lying almost pressed to death under great weights, and should bid him eat and be merry, but lift not off his pressure : you do but mock the man and add to his misery. On the contrary, he that hath got but a

view of his Christ, and reads his own pardon in Christ's sufferings, can rejoice in this, in the midst of all other sufferings,
and look on death without apprehension, yea, with gladness,
for the *sting is out.* Christ hath made all pleasant to him by
this one thing, that *he suffered once for sins.* Christ hath perfumed the cross and the grave, and made all sweet. The pardoned man finds himself light, skips and leaps, and *through
Christ strengthening him,* he can encounter any trouble. If
you think to shut up his spirit within outward sufferings, he is
now, as Samson in his strength, able to carry away on his back
the gates with which you would enclose him. Yea, he can
submit patiently to the Lord's hand in any correction: Thou
hast forgiven my sin, therefore deal with me as thou wilt;
all is well.

Refl. 1. Let us learn to consider more deeply, and to esteem
more highly, Christ and His suffering, to silence our grumbling at our petty light crosses; for so they are, in comparison of His. Will not the great odds of His perfect innocency, and of the nature and measure of His sufferings; will
not the sense of the redemption of our souls from death by His
death; will none of these, nor all of them, argue us into more
thankfulness and love to Him, and patience in our trials?
Why will we then be called Christians? It is impossible to be
fretful and malcontent with the Lord's dealing with us in any
kind, till first we have forgotten how He dealt with His
dearest Son for our sakes. As St. Bernard speaks, *Enimvero
non sentiunt sua, qui illius vulnera intuentur:* They truly
feel not their own wounds who contemplate His. But these
things are not weighed by the most. We hear and speak of
them, but our hearts receive not the impressions of them;
therefore we repine against our Lord and Father, and drown a
hundred great blessings in any little trouble that befalls us.

Refl. 2. Seek surer interest in Christ and His suffering,
than the most either have attained, or are aspiring to; otherwise all that He suffered here will afford thee no ease or comfort in any kind of suffering. No, though thou suffer for a

good cause, even for His cause, still this will be an extraneous, foreign thing to thee, and to tell thee of His sufferings will work no otherwise with thee than some other common story. And as in the day of peace thou regardest it no more, so in the day of thy trouble thou shalt receive no more comfort from it. Other things, which you esteemed, shall have no comfort to speak to you: *though you pursue them with words*, (as Solomon says of the poor man's friends, Prov. xix. 7,) *yet they shall be wanting to you*. And then you will surely find how happy it were to have this to turn you to, that the Lord Jesus suffered for sins, and for your sins, and therefore hath made it a light and comfortable business to you, to undergo momentary, passing sufferings.

Days of trial will come ; do you not see they are on us already ? Be persuaded, therefore, to turn your eyes and desires more towards Christ. This is the thing we would still press: the support and happiness of your souls lie on it. But, you will not believe it. Oh, that you knew the comforts and sweetness of Christ! Oh, that one would speak, who knew more of them ! Were you once but entered into this knowledge of Him, and the virtue of His sufferings, you would account all your days but lost wherein you have not known Him ; and in all times, your hearts would find no refreshment like to the remembrance of His love.

Having somewhat considered these Sufferings, as the Apostle's argument for his present purpose, we come now,

II. To take a nearer view of the particulars by which he illustrates them, as the main point of our faith and comfort. Of them, here are two things to be remarked, their Cause and their Kind.

First, Their Cause; both their meretorious cause and their final cause; first, what in us procured these sufferings unto Christ, and secondly, what those His sufferings procured unto us. Our guiltiness brought suffering upon Him; and His suffering brings us unto God.

1*st*, For the meritorious cause, what in us brought sufferings on Christ. The evil of sin hath the evil of punishment inseparably connected with it. We are under a natural obligation of obedience unto God, and He justly urges it; so that where the *command* of His Law is broken, the *curse* of it presently followeth. And though it was simply in the power of the Supreme Lawgiver to have dispensed with the infliction, yet having in His wisdom purposed to be known a just God in that way, following forth the tenor of His Law, of necessity there must be a suffering for sin.

Thus, the angels who keep not their station, falling from it, fell into a dungeon, where they are, *under chains of darkness, reserved to the judgment of the great day.* (Jude 6) Man also fell under the sentence of death, but in this is the difference betwixt man and them: they were not one of them, as the parent or common root of the rest, but each one fell or stood for himself alone, so a part of them only perished; but Man fell altogether, so that not one of all the race could escape condemnation, unless some other way of satisfaction be found out. And here it is: *Christ suffered for sins, the just for the unjust. Father,* says he, *I have glorified thee on earth.* (John xvii. 3.) In this plot, indeed, do all the Divine attributes shine in their full lustre; infinite mercy, and immense justice, and power, and wisdom. Looking on Christ as ordained for that purpose, *I have found a ransom,* says the Father, one fit to redeem man, a kinsman, one of that very same stock, the Son of Man; one able to redeem man by satisfying Me, and fulfilling all I lay upon him; *My Son, my only begotten Son, in whom my soul delights.* And He is willing, undertakes all, says, *Lo, I come.* (Psal. xl. 7.) We are agreed upon the way of this redemption; yea, upon the persons to be redeemed. It is not a roving blind bargain, a price paid for we know not whom. Hear his own words; *Thou hast given the Son* (says the Son to the Father) *power over all flesh, that he should give eternal life to as many as Thou hast given him;* and *all mine are thine, and thine are mine, and I am glorified in them.* (John xvii. 2, 10.)

For the sins of these He suffered, standing in their room; and what he did and suffered according to the law of that Covenant was done and suffered by them. All the sins of all the elect were made up into a huge bundle, and bound upon His shoulders. So the prophet speaks in their name: *Surely He hath borne our griefs, and carried our sorrows:* and *The Lord laid* [*or made to meet*] *on Him the iniquity of us all.* (Isa. liii. 5.) He had spoken of many ways of sin, and said, *We have turned every one to his own way;* here he binds up all in the word *iniquity,* as all one sin, as if it were that one transgression of the first Adam, that brought on the curse of his seed, borne by the Second Adam, to take it away from all that are His seed, who are in Him as their Root.

He is the great High Priest appearing before God with the names of the Elect upon His shoulders, and in His heart bearing them and all their burdens, and offering for them, not any other sacrifice than *Himself;* charging all their sin on Himself, as the priest did the sins of the people on the head of the sacrifice. *He, by the Eternal Spirit,* says the Apostle, *offered up himself without spot unto God, spotless and sinless:* (Heb. ix. 14:) and so He alone is fit to take away our sin, being a satisfactory oblation for it. He suffered: in Him was our ransom, and thus it was paid. In the man, Christ, was the Deity, and so His blood was, as the Apostle calls it, *the blood of God;* (Acts xx. 28;) and he being pierced, it came forth, and was told down as the rich price of our redemption. *Not silver, nor gold, nor corruptible things,* as our Apostle hath it before, *but the precious blood of Christ, as of a lamb without blemish.*

Obs. 1. Shall any man offer to bear the name of a Christian, who pleases himself in the way of sin, and can delight and sport himself with it, when he considers this, that Christ suffered for sin? Do not think it, you who still account sin sweet, which He found so bitter, and account that light, which was so heavy to Him, and made His *soul heavy to the death.* You are yet far off from Him. If you were in Him, and

one with Him, there would be some harmony of your hearts
with His, and some sympathy with those sufferings, as endured
by your Lord, your Head, and for you. They who, with a
right view, see Him as pierced by their sins, that sight pierces
them, and makes them mourn, brings forth tears, beholding
the gushing forth of His blood. This makes the real Christian an avowed enemy to sin. Shall I ever be friends with
that, says he, which killed my Lord? No, but I will ever kill
it, and do it by applying His death. The true penitent is
sworn to be the death of sin: he may be surprised by it, but
there is no possibility of reconcilement betwixt them.

Thou that livest kindly and familiarly with sin, and either
openly declarest thyself for it, or hast a secret love for it,
where canst thou reap any comfort? Not from these sufferings.
To thee, continuing in that posture, it is all one as if Christ
had not suffered for sins; yea, it is worse than if no such thing
had been, that there is salvation, and terms of mercy offered
unto thee, and yet thou perishest; that there is *balm in
Gilead*, and yet thou art not healed. And if thou hast not comfort from Jesus crucified, I know not whence thou canst have
any that will hold out. Look about thee, tell me what thou
seest, either in thy possession or in thy hopes, that thou
esteemest most, and layest thy confidence on. Or, to deal
more liberally with thee, see what estate thou wouldst choose,
hadst thou thy wish; stretch thy fancy to devise an earthly
happiness. These times are full of unquietness; but give thee
a time of the calmest peace, not an air of trouble stirring; put
thee where thou wilt, far off from fear of sword and pestilence, and encompass thee with children, friends, and possessions, and honours, and comfort, and health to enjoy all these;
yet, one thing thou must admit in the midst of them all,
within a while thou must die, and having no real portion in
Christ, but only a deluding dream of it, thou sinkest through
that death into another death far more terrible. Of all thou
enjoyest, nothing goes along with thee but unpardoned sin,
and that delivers thee up to endless sorrow. *Oh that* you

were wise and *would consider your latter end!* Do not still gaze about you upon trifles, but yet be entreated to take notice of your Saviour, and receive him, that he ·may be yours. Fasten your belief and your love on Him. Give all your heart to Him, who stuck not to give Himself an offering for your sins.

Obs. 2. To you who have fled unto Him for refuge, if sensible of the Church's distress, be upheld with this thought, that He who suffered for it, will not suffer it to be undone. All the rage of enemies, yea, *the gates of hell shall not prevail against it.* He may, for a time, suffer the Church to be brought low for the sins of His people, and other wise reasons, but He will not utterly forsake it. Though· there is much chaff, yet He hath a precious number in these kingdoms, for whom He shed his blood : many God hath called, and many He has yet to call; He will not lose any of His flock which he bought so dear, (Acts xx. 28,) and for their sake He will, at one time or another, repair our breaches, and establish His throne in these kingdoms. For yourselves, what can affright you while this is in your eye ? Let others tremble at the apprehension of sword or pestilence ; but surely you have, for them and all other hazards, a most satisfying answer in this : My Christ hath suffered for sin : I am not to fear that; and *that* set aside, I know the worst is but death—I am wrong; truly, that is the best : to be *dissolved, and to be with Christ,* is [πολλῷ μᾶλλον κρεῖσσον] *much more better.* (Phil. i. 23.) *So, being justified by faith*, believers *have peace with God*, and *rejoice in hope of the glory of God, glorifying even in tribulations.* (Rom. v. 1—3.)

This were a happy estate indeed. But what shall they think who have no assurance, they who doubt that Christ is theirs, and that He suffered for their sins? I know no way but to believe on Him, and then you shall know that He is yours. From this arises the grand mistake of many : they would first know that Christ is theirs, and then would believe : which cannot be, because He becomes ours by believing. It is that which gives title and propriety to Him. He is set before sinners as a Saviour who hath suffered for sin, that they may look to him and be saved; that they may lay over their souls on him, and then, they may be assured he suffered for them.

Say, then, what is it that scares thee from Christ? This, thou seest, is a poor groundless exception, for He is set before thee as a Saviour to believe on, that so He may be thy Saviour. Why wilt thou not come unto Him? Why refusest thou to believe? Art thou a sinner? Art thou unjust? Then, He is fit for thy case: He suffered for sins, *the Just for the unjust.* Oh! but so many and so great sins! Yea, is that it? It is true indeed, and good reason thou hast to think so; but 1*st*, Consider whether they be excepted in the proclamation of Christ, the pardon that comes in His name: if not, if He make no exception, why wilt thou? 2*dly*, Consider if thou wilt call them greater than this sacrifice, *He suffered.* Take due notice of the greatness and worth, first, of His person, and then, of His sufferings, and thou wilt not dare to say thy sin goes above the value of his suffering, or that thou art too unjust for Him to justify thee. Be as unrighteous as thou canst be, art thou convinced of it? then, know that Jesus the just is more righteous than thy unrighteousness. And, after all is said that any sinner hath to say, they are yet, without exception, *blessed who trust in Him.* (Psalm ii. *ult.*)

2*dly.* We have the *final cause* of His sufferings, *That he might bring us to God.*] It is the chief point of wisdom, to proportion means to their end: therefore, the all-wise God, in putting His only Son to so hard a task, had a high end in this, and this was it, *That he might bring us unto God.* In this we have three things: 1*st*, The nature of this good,—nearness unto God. 2*dly*, Our deprivement of it, by our own sin; 3*dly*, Our restoration to it, by Christ's sufferings.

[1.] The nature of this good. God hath suited every creature he had made, with a convenient good to which it tends, and, in the obtainment of which it rests and is satisfied.

Natural bodies have all their own natural place, whither, if not hindered, they move incessantly till they be in it; and they declare, by resting there, that they are (as I may say) where they would be. Sensitive creatures are carried to seek a sensitive good, as agreeable to their rank in being, and, attaining that, aim no further. Now, in this is the excellency of Man, that he is made capable of a communion with his Maker, and, because capable of it, is unsatisfied without it : the soul, being cut out (so to speak) to that largeness, cannot be filled with less. Though he is fallen from his right to that good, and from all right desire of it, yet, not from a capacity of it, no, nor from a necessity of it, for the answering and filling of his capacity.

Though the heart once gone from God, turns continually further away from Him, and moves not towards Him, till it be renewed, yet, even in that wandering, it retains that natural relation to God, as its centre, that it hath no true rest elsewhere, nor can by any means find it. It is made for Him, and is therefore still restless till it meet with Him.

It is true, the natural man takes much pains to quiet his heart by other things, and digests many vexations with hopes of contentment in the end and accomplishment of some design he hath; but still the heart misgives. Many times he attains not the thing he seeks ; but if he do, yet he never attains the satisfaction he seeks and expects in it, but only learns from that to desire something further, and still hunts on after a fancy, drives his own shadow before him, and never overtakes it ; and if he did, yet it is but a shadow. And so, in running from God, besides the sad end, he carries an interwoven punishment with his sin, the natural disquiet and vexation of his spirit ; fluttering to and fro, and *finding no rest for the sole of his foot ;* the *waters* of inconstancy and vanity *covering the whole face of the earth.*

We study to debase our souls, and to make them content with less than they are made for ; yea, we strive to make them carnal, that they may be pleased with sensible things. And in this, men attain a brutish content for a time, forgetting their higher good. But certainly, we cannot think it sufficient, and that no more were to be desired beyond ease and plenty, and pleasures of sense; for then, a beast in good case, and a good pastu e, might contest with us in point of happiness, and carry it away—for that sensitive good he enjoys without sin, and without the vexation that is mixed with us in all.

These things are too gross and heavy. The soul, the immortal soul, descended from heaven, must either be more happy or remain miserable. The highest, the Increated Spirit, is the proper good, *the Father of Spirits*, that pure and full good which raises the soul above itself; whereas all other things draw it down below itself. So, then, it is never well with the soul, but when it is near unto God, yea, in its union with Him, married to Him: mismatching itself elsewhere, it hath never any thing but shame and sorrow. *All that forsake thee shall be ashamed,* says the Prophet, Jer. xvii. 13; and the Psalmist, *They that are far off from Thee shall perish.* (Psalm lxxiii. 27.) And this is indeed our natural miserable condition, and it is often expressed this way, by estrangedness and distance from God. See Eph. ii., where the Gentiles are spoken of as *far off* by their profession and nation, but both Jews and Gentiles are far off by their natural foundation, and both are brought near by the blood of the New Covenant.

[2.] And this is the second thing here implied, that we are *far off by reason of sin;* otherwise there were no need of Christ, especially in this way of suffering for sin, *to bring us unto God.* At the first, Sin, as the breach of God's command, broke off Man, and separated him from God, and ever since the soul remains naturally remote from God. 1. It lies under a sentence of exile, pronounced by the justice of God; condemned to banishment from God, who is the life and light of the soul, as the soul itself is of the body. 2. It is under a flat impossibility of returning by itself; and that in two respects: first, because of the guiltiness of sin standing betwixt, as an unpassable mountain or wall of separation; secondly, because of the dominion of sin keeping the soul captive, yea, still drawing it further off from God, increasing the distance and the enmity every day. Nor is there, either in heaven or under heaven, any way to remove this enmity, and make up this distance, and restore Man to the possession of God, but this one, By Christ, and by Him suffering for sins.

[3.] Our restoration to nearness to God is by Christ's sufferings. He endured the sentence pronounced against man, yea, even in this particular notion of it, as a sentence of exile from God: one main ingredient in His suffering, was, that sensible desertion by his Heavenly Father, of which He cried out, *My God, my God, why hast thou forsaken me!* And, by suffering the sentence pronounced, he took away the guiltiness of sin, He himself being *spotless* and *undefiled*. *For such an High Priest became us*, Heb. vii. 26: the more defiled we were, the more did we stand in need of an undefiled Priest and Sacrifice; and He was both. Therefore the Apostle here very fitly mentions this qualification of our Saviour, as necessary for restoring us unto God, *the Just for the unjust*. So taking on Himself, and taking away, the guilt of sin, setting his strong shoulder to remove that mountain, He made way or access for man unto God.

This the Apostle hath excellently expressed, Eph. ii. 16: *He hath reconciled us by His cross, having slain the enmity :* He killed the quarrel betwixt God and us, killed it by His death; brings the Parties together, and hath laid a sure foundation of agreement in His own sufferings; appeases His Father's wrath by them, and by the same appeases the sinner's conscience. All that God hath to say, in point of justice, is answered there; all that the poor humbled sinner hath to say is answered too. He hath offered up such an atonement as satisfies the Father, so that He is content that sinners should come in and be reconciled. And then, Christ gives notice of this to the soul, to remove all jealousies. It is full of fear: though it would, it dares not approach unto God, apprehending Him to be *a consuming fire*. They who have done the offence, are usually the hardest to reconcile, because they are still in doubt of their pardon. But Christ assures the soul of a full and hearty forgiveness, quenching the flaming wrath of God by His blood. No, says Christ, upon my warrant come in; you will now find my Father otherwise than you imagine: He hath declared Himself satisfied at my hands, and is willing to receive you, to be heartily and thoroughly friends; never to hear a word more, of the quarrel that was betwixt you; to grant a full oblivion. And if the soul bear back still through distrust, He takes it by the hand, and draws it forward, leads it unto His Father; (as the word προσαγωγη imports;) presents it to Him, and leaves not the matter till it be made a full and sure agreement.

But for this purpose, that the soul may be both able and willing to come unto God, the sufferings of Christ take away that other impediment. As they satisfy the sentence, and thereby remove the guiltiness of sin, so He hath by them purchased a deliverance from the tyrannous *power* of sin, which detains the soul from God, after all the way has been made for its return. And he hath a power of applying His sufferings to the soul's deliverance, in that kind too. He opens the prison doors to them who are led captive; and because the great chain is upon the heart willingly enthralled in sin, He, by His sovereign power, takes off that, frees the heart from the love of sin, and shews what a base, slavish condition it is in, by representing, in His effectual way, the goodness of God, His readiness to entertain a returning sinner, and the sweetness and happiness of communion with Him. Thus He powerfully persuades the heart to shake off all, and, without further delay, to return unto God, so as to be received into favour and friendship, and to walk in the way of friendship with God, to give up itself to His obedience, to disdain the vile service of sin, and live suitably to the dignity of fellowship and union with God.

And there is nothing but the power of Christ alone that is able to effect this, to persuade a sinner to return, to bring home a heart unto God. Common mercies of God, though they have a leading faculty to repentance, (Rom. ii. 4,) yet, the rebellious heart will not be led by them. The judgments of God, public or personal, though they ought to drive us to God, yet the heart, unchanged, runs the further from God. Do we not see it by ourselves and other sinners about us? They look not at all towards him who smites, much less do they return; or if any more serious thoughts of returning arise upon the surprise of an affliction, how soon vanish they, either the stroke abating, or the heart, by time, growing hard and senseless under it! Indeed, when it is renewed and brought in by Christ, then all other things have a sanctified influence, according to their quality, to stir up a Christian to seek after fuller communion, closer walk, and nearer access to God. But leave Christ out, I say, and all other means work not this way; neither the works nor the word of God sounding daily in his ear, *Return, return.* Let the noise of the rod speak it too, and both join together to make the cry the louder, *yet the wicked will do wickedly* (Dan. xii. 10.); will not hearken to the voice of God, will not *see the hand of God lifted up* (Isa. xxvi. 11); will not be persuaded to go in and seek peace and reconcilement with God, though declaring himself provoked to punish, and to behave Himself as an enemy against his own people. How many there are, who, in their own particular, have been very sharply lashed with divers scourges on their bodies, or their families, and yet are never a whit the nearer God for it all, their hearts as proud, and earthly, and vain, as ever! and let Him lay on ever so much, they will still be the same. Only a Divine virtue, going forth from Christ *lifted up*, *draws men* unto Him; and, being come unto Him, He brings them unto the Father.

Reflection 1. You who are still strangers to God, who declare yourselves to be so, by living as strangers far off from Him, do not still continue to abuse yourselves so grossly. Can you think any consolation yours that arises from the sufferings of Christ, while it is so evident they have not gained their end upon you, have not brought you to God? Truly,

most of you seem to think that our Lord Jesus suffered rather
to the end we might neglect God, and disobey Him securely,
than to restore us to Him. Hath He purchased you a liberty
to sin? Or is not deliverance from sin, which alone is true
liberty, the thing He aimed at, and agreed for, and laid down
His life for?

2. Why let we His blood still run in vain as to us? He
hath *by it opened up our way to God*, and yet we refuse to
make use of it! Oh! how few come in! Those who are
brought unto God, and received into friendship with Him,
entertain that friendship, they delight in His company, love to
be much with Him : is it so with us? By being so near, they
become like unto Him, know His will better every day, and
grow more conformable to it. But, alas! in the most, there
is nothing of this.

3. But even they who are brought unto God, may be faulty
in this, in part, not applying so sweet a privilege. They can
comply and be too friendly with the vain world, can pass
many days without a lively communion with God, not aspiring
to the increase of that, as the thing our Lord hath purchased
for us, and that wherein all our happiness and welfare lie, here
and hereafter. Your hearts are cleaving to folly ; you are not
delighting yourselves in the Lord, not refreshed with this nearness to Him, and union with Him; your thoughts are not
often on it, nor is it your study to walk conformably to it:
certainly it ought to be thus, and you should be persuaded to
endeavour that it may be thus with you.

4. Remember this for your comfort, that as you are brought
unto God by Jesus Christ, so you are kept in that union by
Him. It is a firmer knot than the first was ; there is no
power of hell can dissolve it. He suffered once to bring us
once unto God, never to depart again. As he suffered once
for all, so we are brought once for all. We may be sensibly nearer at one time than another, but yet we can never
be separate or cut off, being once knit by Christ, as the bond
of our union. *Neither principalities, nor powers,* (&c.) *shall*

be able to separate us from the love of God, because it holds *in Christ Jesus our Lord.* (Rom. viii. 37, 38.)

Secondly, as to the Kind of our Lord's Sufferings; *Being put to death in the flesh, but quickened by the Spirit.*] The true life of a Christian, is, to eye Christ in every step of his life, both as his rule, and as his strength; looking to Him as his pattern, both in doing and suffering, and drawing power from Him for going through both; for the look of Faith doth that, fetches life from Jesus to enable it for all, being without Him able for nothing. Therefore, the Apostle doth still set this before his brethren; and having mentioned Christ's suffering in general, the condition and end of it, he here specifies the particular kind of it, that which was the utmost point, *put to death in the flesh,* and then adds this issue out of it, *quickened by the Spirit.*

This is at once the strongest engagement, and the strongest encouragement. Was He, our Head, crowned with thorns, and shall the Body look for garlands? Are we redeemed from hell and condemnation by Him, and can any such refuse any service He calls them to? They who are *washed in the Lamb's blood, will follow Him whithersoever he goes;* (Rev. xiv. 4;) and, following him through, they shall find their journey's end overpay all the troubles and sufferings of the way. *These are they,* said the Elder who appeared in vision to John, *who came out of great tribulation:* tribulation, and great tribulation, yet, they came out of it, and gloriously too, arrayed in *long white robes!* The scarlet Strumpet (as follows in that book) dyed her garments red in the blood of the saints; but this is their happiness, that *their garments are washed white in the blood of the Lamb.* (Rev. vii. 14.)

Once take away sin, and all suffering is light. Now, that is done by this, *His once suffering for sin:* those who are in Him shall hear no more of that as condemning them, binding over to suffer that wrath which is due to sin. Now, this puts an invincible strength into the soul for enduring all other things, how hard soever.

Put to death.] This is the utmost point, and that which men are most startled at, *to die:* and a violent death, *put to death;* and yet He hath led in this way, who *is the Captain of our salvation. In the flesh.* Under this second phrase, His human nature, and His Divine nature and power, are distinguished. *Put to death in the flesh,* is a very fit expression, not only (as is usual) taking the flesh for the whole manhood, but because death is most properly spoken of that very person, or his flesh. The whole man suffers death, a dissolution, or taking to pieces, and the soul suffers a separation, or dislodging; but death, or the privation of life and sense, belongs particularly to the flesh or body. But the *Spirit,* here opposed to the *flesh* or body, is certainly of a higher nature and power than is the human soul, which cannot of itself return to re-inhabit and quicken the body.

Put to death.] His death was both voluntary and violent. That same power which restored His life could have kept it exempted from death; but the design was for death. He therefore took our flesh, to put it off thus, and to offer it up as a sacrifice, which, to be acceptable, must of necessity be free and voluntary; and, in that sense, He is said to have died even by that same Spirit, which here, in opposition to death, is said to quicken him. (See Heb. ix. 14.) *Through the Eternal Spirit He offered Himself without spot unto God.* They accounted it an ill-boding sign when the sacrifices came constrained to the altar, and drew back, and, on the contrary, were gladdened with the hopes of success, when they came cheerfully forward; but never sacrifice came so willingly all the way, and from the first step knew whither he was going. Yet because no other sacrifice would serve, He was most content to become one; *Sacrifices and burnt offerings Thou didst not desire: and then said I, Lo I come.* (Psal. xl. 6, 7.) He was not only a willing sacrifice, as Isaac, bound peaceably, and laid on the altar, but His own sacrificer. The beasts, if they came willingly, yet offered not themselves; but He *offered up himself;* and thus, not only by a willingness far above all those *sacrifices of bullocks and goats*, but *by the eternal Spirit*, He offered up Himself. Therefore He says, in this regard, *I lay down my life for my sheep;* it is not pulled from me, but I lay it down. And so it is often expressed by [ἀπέθανε] *he died;* and yet this suits with it, [θανατωθείς] *put to death.* Yea, it was also expedient to be thus, that His death should be violent, and so the more penal, to carry the more clear expression of a punishment, and such a violent death as had both ignomony and a curse tied to it, and this inflicted in a judicial way ; (though, as from the hands of men, most unjustly ;) that he should stand and be judged, and condemned to death as a guilty person, carrying in that person the persons of so many who should otherwise have fallen under condemnation, as indeed guilty. *He was numbered with transgressors*, (as the Prophet hath it,) *bearing the sins of many.* (Isa. liii. *ult.*)

Thus, then, there was in His death external violence joined with internal willingness. But what is there to be found but complications of wonders in our Lord Jesus? Oh! high inconceivable mystery of godliness! *God manifested in the flesh!* Nothing in this world so strange and sweet as that conjuncture, *God Man, humanitas Dei!* What a strong foundation of friendship and union betwixt the person of man and God, that their natures met in so close embraces in one Person! And then, look on, and see so poor and despised an outward condition through His life, yet having hid under it the majesty of God, *all the brightness of the Father's glory!* And this is the top of all, that He was *put to death in the flesh;* the Lord of life dying, the Lord of glory clothed with shame! But it quickly appeared what kind of person it was that died, by this, *He was put to death*, indeed, *in the flesh, but quickened by the Spirit.*

Quickened.] He was indeed too great a morsel for the Grave to digest. For all its vast craving mouth and devouring appetite, crying *Sheol, Give, give,* yet was it forced to give Him up again, as the fish to give up the Prophet Jonah, who, in that, was the figure of Christ. The chains of that prison are strong, but He was too strong a prisoner to be held by them; as our Apostle hath it in his sermon, (Acts ii. 24,) that it was *not possible that He should be kept by them.* They thought all was sure when they had rolled-to the stone, and sealed it; that then the Grave had indeed shut her mouth upon Him; it appeared a done business to them, and looked as if it were very complete in His enemies' eyes, and very desperate to His friends, His poor disciples and followers. Were they not near the point of giving over, when they said, *This is the third day,* &c., and, *We thought this had been He that should have delivered Israel?* (Luke xxiv. 21.) And yet he was then with them, who was indeed the *deliverer* and *salvation of Israel.* That rolling of the stone to the grave, was as if they had rolled it towards the East in the night, to stop the rising of the sun the next morning; much further above all their watches and their power was this *Sun of Righteousness* in His rising again. That body which was entombed was united to the spring of life, the divine Spirit of the Godhead that quickened.

Reflection 1. Thus the Church, which is likewise His Body, when it seems undone, when it is brought to the lowest posture and state, yet by virtue of that mystical union with Jesus Christ, (as his natural body, by personal union with his Deity,) shall be preserved from destruction, and shall be delivered and raised in due time. Yea, as He was nearest His exaltation in the lowest step of His humiliation, so is it with His Church: when things are brought to the most hopeless appearance, then shall light arise out of darkness. *Cum duplicantur lateres venit Moses.*

Therefore, as we ought to seek a more humble sense of Sion's distress, so we should also be solicitous not to let go this hope, that her mighty Lord will, in the end, be glorious in her deliverance, and that all her sufferings and low estate shall be as a dark ground to set off the lustre of her restoration, when the Lord shall visit her with salvation; as in the rising of Jesus

Christ, His almighty power and Deity were more manifested than if He had not died. And therefore we may say confidently with the Psalmist to his Lord, (Psal. lxxi. 20,) *Thou who hast shewed me great and sore troubles, shalt quicken me again, and shalt bring me up from the depths of the earth: Thou shalt increase my greatness, and comfort me on every side.* Yea, the Church comes more beautiful out of the deepest distress: let it be overwhelmed with waves, yet it sinks not, but rises up as only washed. And in this confidence we ought to rejoice, even in the midst of our sorrows, and though we live not to see them, yet even in beholding afar off, to be gladdened with the great things the Lord will do for His Church in the latter times. He will certainly *make bare His holy arm in the eyes of the nations,* and *all the ends of the earth shall see the salvation of our God.* (Isa. lii. 10.) His King whom He *hath set on His holy hill,* shall grow in His conquests and glory, and all that rise against Him *shall He break with a rod of iron.* (Psal. ii.) He was humbled once, but His glory shall be for ever. *As many were astonished at Him, His visage being marred more than any man,* they shall be as much astonished at His beauty and glory: *So shall He sprinkle many nations; the kings shall shut their mouths at Him.* (Isa. lii. 14, 15.) According as here we find that remarkable evidence of His Divine power in rising from the dead: *Put to death in the flesh but quickened by the Spirit.*

Refl. 2. Thus may a believing soul at the lowest, when, to its own sense, it is given over unto death, and swallowed up of it, as it were *in the belly of hell,* yet look up to this Divine power. He whose soul was not left there, will not leave thine there. Yea, when thou art most sunk in thy sad apprehensions, and far off to thy thinking, then is He nearest to raise and comfort thee; as sometimes it grows darkest immediately before day. Rest on His power and goodness, which never failed any who did so. *It is He* (as David says) *who lifts up the soul from the gates of death.* (Psal. ix. 13.)

Refl. 3. Would any of you be cured of that common disease, the fear of death ? Look this way,. and you shall find more than you seek ; you shall be taught, not only not to fear, but to love it. Consider, 1. His death : *He died.* By that, thou who receivest Him as thy life, mayest be sure of this, that thou art, by that, His death, freed from the second death. *Descendit huc vita nostra, et tulit mortem nostram, et occidit eam de abundantiâ vitæ suæ :* He who is our life, says Augustine, descended hither, and bore our death, killing it by the abounding of His life. And that is the great point. Let that have the name which was given to the other, *the most terrible of all terrible things ;* and, as the second death is removed, this death which thou art to pass through, is, I may say, beautified and sweetened ; the ugly visage of it becomes amiable, when ye look on it in Christ, and in his death : that puts such a pleasing comeliness upon it, that whereas others fly from it with affright, the Believer cannot choose but embrace it. He longs to lie down in that bed of rest, since his Lord lay in it, and hath warmed that cold bed, and purified it with His fragrant body. 2. But especially be looking forward to His return thence, *quickened by the Spirit ;* this being to those who are in Him the certain pledge, yea, the effectual cause, of that blessed resurrection which is in their hopes. There is that union betwixt them, that they shall rise by the communication, and virtue of his rising ; not simply by His power, for so the wicked to their grief shall be raised, but they by His life, as theirs. Therefore it is so often reiterated, John vi., where He speaks of Himself as the *living* and *life-giving Bread* to Believers, *1 will raise them up at the last day.* This comfort we have even for the house of clay we lay down ; and as for our more considerable part, our immortal souls, this His death and rising hath provided for them, at their dislodging, an entrance into that glory where He is. Now, if these things were lively apprehended and laid hold on, Christ made ours, and the first resurrection manifest in us, were we quickened by His Spirit to newness of life, certainly there would not be a more welcome and refreshing thought, nor a sweeter discourse to us than that of death. And no matter for the kind of it. Were it a violent death, so was His. Were it what we account most judgment-like amongst diseases, the plague; was not His death very painful? And was it not an accursed death? And by that curse endured by Him in His, is not the curse taken away to the Believer? Oh how welcome will that day be, that day of deliverance! To be out of this woful prison, I regard not at what door I go out, being at once freed from so many deaths, and let in to enjoy Him who is my life.

Ver. 19. By which also he went and preached unto the spirits in prison.

Ver. 20. Which sometime were disobedient, when once the long-suffering of God waited in the days of Noah, while the ark was a preparing, wherein few, that is, eight souls, were saved by water.

Ver. 21. The like figure whereunto, even baptism, doth also now save us, (not the putting away of the filth of the flesh, but the answer of a good conscience towards God,) by the resurrection of Jesus Christ.

THERE is nothing that so much concerns a Christian to know, as the excellency of Jesus Christ, His person and works; so that it is always pertinent to insist much on that subject. The Apostle, having spoken of this Spirit or Divine nature, and the power of it, as raising Him from the dead, takes occasion to speak of another work of that Spirit, to wit, the emission and publishing of his Divine doctrine; and that, not as a new thing following His death and rising, but as the same in substance with that which was, by the same Spirit, promulgated long before, even to the first inhabitants of the world. *Quickened by the Spirit*, that is, in our days, says the Apostle; but then, long before that, by the same Spirit, *He went and preached to the spirits in prison*.

This place is somewhat obscure in itself, but as it usually happens, made more so by the various fancies and contests of interpreters, aiming or pretending to clear it. These I like never to make a noise of. They who dream of the *descent of Christ's soul into hell*, think this place sounds somewhat that way; but, being examined, it proves no way suitable, nor can,

by the strongest wresting, be drawn to fit their purpose. For,
1. That it was to preach, He went thither, they are not willing
to avow ; though the end they assign is as groundless and imaginary as this is. 2. They would have His business to be with
the spirits of the faithful deceased before His coming ; but here
we see it is with the disobedient. And, 3. His Spirit here is
the same with the sense of the foregoing words, which mean
not His soul, but His eternal Deity. 4. Nor is it *the spirits
that were in prison*, as they read it, but *the spirits in prison*,
which, by the opposition of their former condition, *sometime*,
or *formerly disobedient*, doth clearly speak their present condition, as the just consequence and fruit of their disobedience.

Other misinterpretations I mention not, taking it as agreeable
to the whole strain of the Apostle's words *, that Jesus Christ
did, before His appearing in the flesh, speak by His Spirit in
His servants to those of the foregoing ages, yea, the most
ancient of them, declaring to them the way of life, though
rejected by the unbelief of the most part. This is inter-
jected in the mentioning of Christ's sufferings and exaltation
after them. And, after all, the Apostle returns to that again,
and to the exhortation which he strengthens by it ; but so as
that this discourse taken in, is pertinently adapted to the

* Thus I then thought, but do now apprehend another sense, as probable, if not more, even that so much rejected by most interpreters : the
mission of the Spirit, and preaching of the Gospel by it, after His resurrection, preaching to sinners, and converting them, according to the
prophecy which He first fulfilled in person, and, after, more amply, in His
apostles. That prophecy I mean, Isa. lx. 1. The Spirit came upon Him,
and it was sent from Him on His apostles, to preach to *spirits in prison ;
to preach liberty to those captives*, captive spirits, and therefore called *spirits in prison*, to illustrate the thing the more, by opposition to that spirit
of Christ, *the spirit of liberty*, setting them free. And this is to shew the
greater efficacy of Christ's preaching, than of Noah's ; though he was a
signal preacher of righteousness, yet only himself and his family, eight
persons, were saved by him ; but multitudes of all nations by the spirit
and preaching of Christ in the Gospel ; and that by the seal of baptism,
the resurrection of Christ being represented in the return from the water,
and our dying with Him, by immersion ; and that figure of Baptism is
like their Ark.

present subject. The Apostle's aim in it we may conceive to be this, (his main scope being to encourage his brethren in the faith of Christ, and the way of holiness, against all opposition and hardship,) so to instruct his brethren in Christ's perpetual influence into His Church in all ages, even before His Incarnation, as that they might, at the same time, see the great unbelief of the world, yea, their opposing of Divine truth, and the small number of those who receive it, and so not be discouraged by the fewness of their number, and the hatred of the world, finding that salvation in Jesus Christ, dead and risen again, which the rest miss of by their own wilful refusal. And this very point he insists on clearly in the following chapter, ver. 3, 4. And the very ways of ungodliness there specified, which believers renounce, were those that the world was guilty of in those days, and in which they were surprised by the Flood: *They ate and drank till the Flood came upon them.*

In the words of these three verses, we have three things : First, An assertion concerning the preaching of Christ, and the persons He preached to. Secondly, The designation and description of the time or age wherein that was, and the particular way of God's dealing with them. Thirdly, The adapting or applying of the example to Christians.—First, the Assertion concerning the preaching of Christ, and the persons He preached to, in these words, which I take together, *By the which Spirit he went and preached to the spirits in prison, which sometime were disobedient.*

In these words we have A Preacher and his Hearers. With regard to the Preacher, we shall find here, 1st. His ability. 2dly. His activity in the use of it.

1st. His ability is altogether singular and matchless, the very spring of all abilities, the Spirit of wisdom Himself, being the co-eternal Son of God. That Spirit He preached by, was the same as that by which He raised Himself from the dead; and without this Spirit, there is no preaching. Now he was, as our Apostle calls him, *a preacher of righteousness,* but it was by the power of this Spirit ; for in Him did this Spirit preach

The Son is the wisdom of the Father, His name is the Word; not only for that by Him *all things were created*, as John hath it, (John i. 4,) the Son being that power by which, as by the word of His mouth, all things were made; but He is *The Word*, likewise, *as revealing the Father*, declaring to us the counsel and will of God: therefore He is, by the same Evangelist, in the same place, called that *Light which illuminates the world*, (John i. 9,) without which, Man, called the lesser world, the intellectual world, were as the greater world without the sun. And all who bring aright the doctrine of saving wisdom, derive it necessarily from Him; all preachers draw from this sovereign Preacher, as the fountain of Divine light. As all the planets receive their light from the sun, and by that diffusing itself amongst them, it is not diminished in the sun, but only communicated to them, remaining still full and entire in it as its source; thus doth the Spirit flow from Christ, in a particular degree, unto those He sends forth in His name, and is in them that He preaches by the power and light of His eternal Spirit.

Hither, then, must all those come who would be rightly supplied and enabled for that work. It is impossible to speak duly of Him in any measure, but by His Spirit; there must be particular access, and a receiving of instructions from Him, and a transfusion of His Spirit into ours. Oh! were it thus with us, how sweet were it to speak of Him! To be much in prayer, much in dependence on Him, and drawing from Him, would do much more in this, than reading and studying, seeking after arts, and tongues, and common knowledge. These, indeed, are not to be despised nor neglected. *Utilis lectio, utilis eruditio, sed magis unctio necessaria, quippe quæ sola docet de omnibus*, says Bernard: *Reading is good, and learning good, but above all, anointing is necessary, that anointing that teacheth all things.* And you who are for your own interest, be earnest with this Lord, this Fountain of Spirit, to let forth more of it upon his messengers in these times. You would receive back the fruit of it, were ye busy this way ; you would find more life and refreshing sweetness in the word of life, how weak and worthless soever they were who brought it ; it should descend as sweet showers upon the valleys, and make them fruitful.

2d. We have the activity of Christ as a preacher. By this Spirit, it is said here, *He preached.* Not only did He so in the days of His abode on earth, but in all times, both before and after. He never left His Church altogether destitute of saving light, which He dispensed Himself, and conveyed by the hands of His servants; therefore it is said, *He preached,* that this may be no excuse for times after He is ascended into heaven, no, nor for times before He descended to the earth in human flesh. Though he preached not then, nor does now in His flesh, yet *by His Spirit* He then preached, and still doth; so that according to what was chief in Him, He was still present with His Church, and preaching in it, and is so to the end of the world, this His infinite Spirit being every where. Yet it is said here, by which *He went and preached,* signifying the remarkable clearness of His administration that way. As when He appears eminently in any work of His own, or in taking notice of our works, God is said to come down, (as in reference to those cities of Babel and Sodom, *Let us go down,* and, *I will go down and see;* Gen. xi. 5, 7; xviii. 21; so Exod. iii. 8, *I am come down to deliver Israel;*) thus here, so clearly did He admonish them by Noah, coming, as it were, Himself, on purpose to declare his mind to them. And this word, I conceive, is the rather used to shew what equality there is in this. He came indeed, visibly, and dwelt amongst men, when he became flesh; yet before that He visited them by His Spirit; He went by that, and preached. And so, in after-times, Himself being ascended, and not having come visibly in His flesh to all, but to the Jews only, yet, in the preaching of the Apostles to the Gentiles, as the great Apostle says of Him in that expression, Eph. ii. 17, *He came and preached to you which were afar off.* And this He continues to do in the ministry of His word ; and therefore, says He, *He that despiseth you despiseth me.* (Luke x. 16.)

Were this considered, it could not but procure far more respect to the word, and more acceptance of it. Would you think that, in His word, Christ speaks by His eternal Spirit, yea, that He comes and preaches, addresses Himself particularly to you in it; could you slight Him thus, and turn Him off with daily refusals, or delays at least ? Think, it is too long you have so unworthily used so great a Lord, who brings unto you so great salvation ; who came once in so wonderful a way to work that salvation for us in His flesh, and is still coming to offer it unto us by His Spirit; who does Himself preach to us, telling us what He undertook on our behalf, and how He hath performed all, and that now, nothing rests but that we receive Him, and believe on Him, and all is ours. But alas ! from the most the return is, what we have here, *disobedience !*

Which sometime were disobedient.] There are two things in these Hearers, by which they are characterized ; their present condition in the time the Apostle was speaking of them, *spirits in prison,* and their former disposition, when the Spirit of Christ was preaching to them, *sometime disobedient.* This latter went first in time, and was the cause of the other ; therefore, of it first.

1. *Sometime disobedient.*] If you look to their visible subordinate preacher, you find he was a holy man, and an able and diligent preacher of righteousness, both in his doctrine, and in the track of his life, which is the most powerful preaching; on both which accounts, it seems strange that he prevailed so little. But it appears much more so, if we look higher, even to this height at which the Apostle points, that almighty *Spirit of Christ* who preached to them. And yet, they were disobedient ! The word is [ἀπειθήσασι], *they were not persuaded ;* it signifies both unbelief and disobedience, and that very fitly, unbelief being in itself the grand disobe-

dience: it is the mind's not yielding to Divine truth, and so, the spring of all disobedience in affection and action. And this *root of bitterness*, this unbelief, is deeply fastened in our natural hearts; and without a change in them, a taking them to pieces, they cannot be good. It is as a tree firmly rooted, which cannot be plucked up without loosening the ground round about it. And this accursed root brings forth fruit unto death, because the word is not believed, neither the threats of the Law, nor the promises of the Gospel; therefore men cleave unto their sins, and speak peace unto themselves while they are under the curse.

It may seem very strange that the Gospel is so fruitless amongst us; yea, that neither word nor rod, both preaching aloud to us the doctrine of humiliation and repentance, persuades any man to return, or so much as to turn inward, and question himself, to say, What have I done? But thus it will be, till the Spirit be poured from on high, to open and soften hearts. This is to be desired, as much wanting in the ministry of the word; but were it there, that would not serve unless it were by a concurrent work within the heart meeting the word, and making the impressions of it there; for here we find the Spirit went and preached; and yet, the spirits of the hearers still remained unbelieving and disobedient. It is therefore a combined work of this Spirit in the preacher and the hearers, that makes it successful, otherwise it is but shouting in a dead man's ear; there must be *something within*, as one said in a like case.

2. *To the spirits in prison.*] That is now their posture; and because he speaks of them as in that posture, he calls them spirits; for it is their spirits that are in that prison. He likewise calls them spirits to whom the Spirit of Christ preached, because it is indeed that which the preaching of the word aims at; it hath to do with the spirits of men. It is not content to be at their ear with a sound, but works on their minds and spirits some way, either to believe and receive, or to be hardened and sealed up to judgment by it, which is for

rebels. If disobedience follow on the preaching of that word, *the prison* follows on that disobedience ; and that word, by which they would not be bound to obedience, binds them over to that prison, whence they shall never escape, nor be released for ever.

Take notice of it, and know that you are warned, you who will not receive salvation, offering, pressing itself upon you. You are every day in that way of disobedience, hastening to this perpetual imprisonment.

Consider, you now sit and hear this word ; so did those who are here spoken of : they had their time on earth, and much patience was used towards them. And though you are not to be swept away by a flood of waters, yet you are daily carried on by the flood of time and mortality. (Psal. xc. 5.) And how soon you shall be on the other side, and sent into eternity, you know not. I beseech you, be yet wise ; hearken to the offers yet made you ; for in His name I yet once again make a tender of Jesus Christ, and salvation in Him, to all that will let go their sins, to lay hold on Him. Oh ! do not destroy yourselves. You are in prison ; He proclaims unto you liberty. Christ is still following us Himself with treaties. *Clamans dictis, factis, morte, vitâ, descensu, ascensu, clamans ut redeamus ad eum :* (Augustine) Crying aloud by His words, by His deeds, by His death, by His life, by his coming down from heaven, by His ascension into it, crying to us to return to Him. Christ proclaims your liberty, and will you not aceept of it ? Think, though you are pleased with your present thraldom and prison, it reserves you (if you come not forth) to this other prison, that shall not please you : these chains of spiritual darkness in which you are, unless you be freed, will deliver you up to the *chains of everlasting darkness,* wherein these hopeless prisoners are *kept to the judgment of the great day.* But if you will receive Jesus Christ, presently upon that, life, and liberty, and blessedness, are made yours. *If the Son make you free, you shall be free indeed.* (John viii. 35.)

When once the long-suffering of God waited in the days of Noah.] There are two main continuing wonders in the world, the bounty of God, and the disloyalty of man; and the succession of times is nothing but new editions of these two. One grand example is here set before us, an œcumenical example as large as the whole world; on the part of God, much patience, and yet, on man's part, invincible disobedience. Here are two things in the instance. 1*st*. The Lord's general dealing with the world of the ungodly at that time. 2*dly*, His peculiar way with his own chosen, Noah and his family : He waited patiently for all the rest, but He effectually saved them.

Observe, first, The *time* designated thus, *In the days of Noah*. There were many great and powerful persons in those days, who overtopped Noah (no doubt) in outward respects ; as, in their stature, the proud giants. And they begot children, *mighty men of old, men of renown*, as the text hath it, Gen. vi. 3 ; and yet, as themselves perished in the flood, so their names are drowned. They had their big thoughts, certainly, that their houses and *their names* should *continue*, as the Psalmist speaks, (Psalm xlix. 11,) and yet they are sunk in perpetual oblivion ; while Noah's name, who walked in humble obedience, you see in these most precious records of God's own Book, still looks fresh, and smells sweet, and hath this honour, that the very age of the world is marked with this name, to be known by it: *In the days of Noah*. That which profane ambitious persons do idolatrously seek after, they are often remarkably disappointed of. They would have their names memorable and famous, yet they rot; they are either buried with them, or remembered with disgrace, rotting above ground, as carcasses uninterred, and so are the more noisome ; it being as little credit to them to be mentioned, as for Pilate that his name is in the Confession of Faith. But the name and remembrance of the righteous is still sweet and delightful; as the name of Abraham the father of the faithful, and those of Isaac and Jacob : their names are embalmed indeed, so that they cannot rot, embalmed with God's own name,

[*Eternal*] THAT name being wrapped about theirs, *the God of Abraham, Isaac, and Jacob.*

Thus is Noah here mentioned as preferred of God; and so, in the second Epistle, as *a preacher of righteousness,* and Heb. xi. among those worthies whose honour is, that *they believed.* This is only a name, a small thing, not to be mentioned in comparison of their other privileges, and especially of that venerable life and glory which they are heirs to; and indeed, it is a thing they regard very little; yet this we see, that even this advantage follows them, and flies from the vain and ungodly who haunt and pursue it.

The Lord's dealing with the wicked in those times, before he swept them away by the Deluge, is represented in these two particulars: 1. Long-suffering; and withal, 2. Clear warning.

1. Long-suffering—long forbearing to be angry, as the Hebrew word is in the proclamation of the Divine name, Exod. xxxiv. 6, which supposes a great provocation, and the continuance of it, and yet, patience continuing. And in this appears the goodness of God: considering how hateful sin is to Him, and how powerful He is to punish it, how easy were it, if it pleased Him, in one moment to cut off all the ungodly, high and low, throughout the whole world! Yet he bears, and forbears to punish! Oh! what a world of sin is every day committed in nations, in cities, and villages, yea, in families, which He doth not strike with present judgments, and not only forbears to punish, but multiplies his common mercies on them, *sun and rain and fruitful seasons.* (Acts xiv. 17.)

Yea, there is so much of this, that it falls under a gross misconstruction; yet He bears that too. *Because sentence against an evil-work is not speedily executed, therefore the heart of the sons of men is fully set in them to do evil.* (Eccles. viii. 11.) Because there is not so much as *a word* of it for the time, (so the word is,) this swells and fills the heart of man, and makes it *big to do evil.* And not only is the Lord's long-suffering mistaken by the ungodly, but even by His own, who should understand Him better, and know the true sense of his ways, yet sometimes they are misled in this point: beholding His forbearance of punishing the workers of iniquity, instead of magnifying his patience, they fall very near into questioning His justice and providence. See Psal. xiii., Jer. xii., Job xx., &c. Our narrow, hasty spirits, left to their own measures, take not in those larger views that would satisfy us in respect to the ways of God, and forget the immense largeness of His wise designs, His deep reach from one age to another, yea, from eternity to eternity. We consider not, 1. How easily he can right himself, in point of justice, when He will; that none can make escape from Him, how loose soever their guard seem, and how great liberty soever appears in their present condition. *Nemo decoquit huic creditori.* 2. That as He can most easily, so He will most seasonably, be known in executing judgment; and that His justice shall shine the brighter, by all that patience He hath used, by the sun of prosperity. 3. We think not how little that time is to Him, which seems long to us, to whom *a thousand years are as one day.* It seemed a long time of the Church's distress and their enemies' triumph, in those seventy years of the Babylonish captivity; and yet, in God's language, it is spoken of as *a moment, a small moment.* (Isa. liv. 7.) However, in the issue, the Lord always clears himself. He is indeed long-suffering and patient, but the impenitent abusers of His patience pay interest for all the time of that forbearance, in the weight of judgment when it comes upon them. But thus, we see, the Lord deals. Thus He dealt with the world in the beginning, *when all flesh had corrupted their way ; yet,* saith he, *their days shall be one hundred and twenty years.* (Gen. vi. 3.)

Let us learn to curb and cool our brisk humours towards even stubborn sinners. Be grieved at their sin, for that is your duty; but think it not strange, nor fret at it, that they continue to abuse the long-suffering of God, and yet that He continues ever abused by suffering them. Zeal is good, but as it springs from love, if it be right, so it is requited by love, and carries the impressions of it: of love to God, and so a complacency in His way, liking it because it is His; and of love to men, so as to be pleased with that waiting for them, in the possibility, at least, of their being reclaimed; knowing that, however, if they return not, yet the Lord will not lose His own at their hands. *Wilt thou,* said those two fiery disciples, *that we call for fire, as Elias?* Oh! but the spirit of the dove rested on Him who told them, *They knew not what spirit they were of.* (Luke ix. 55, *q. d.*) You speak of Elias, and you think you are of his spirit in this motion, but you mistake yourselves; this comes from another spirit than you imagine. Instead of looking for such sudden justice without you, look inward, and see whence that is: examine and correct that within you.

When you are tempted to take ill that goodness and patience of God to sinners, consider, 1. Can this be right, to differ from His mind in any thing? Is it not our only wisdom and ever safe rule, to think as He thinks, and will as He wills? And I pray you, does He not hate sin more than you do? Is not His interest in punishing it deeper than yours? And if you be zealous for His interest, as you pretend, then be so with Him, and in his way; for starting from that surely you are wrong. Consider, 2. Did He not wait for thee? What had become of thee, if long-suffering had not subserved his purpose of further mercy, of free pardon to thee? And why wilt thou not always allow that to which thou art so much obliged? Wouldst thou have the bridge cut, because thou art so over? Surely thou wilt not own so gross a thought. Therefore, esteem thy God still the more, as thou seest the more of his long-suffering to sinners; and learn for Him, and with Him, to bear and wait.

2. But this was not a dumb forbearance, such as may serve for a surprise, but continual teaching and warning were joined with it, as remarked before. We see, they wanted not preaching of the choicest kind. He, the *Son of God,* by His Eternal *Spirit, went and preached with them;* it was His truth in Noah's mouth. And with that, we have a continued real sermon,

expressed in this verse, *While the ark was preparing :* that spoke God's mind, and every knock (as the usual observation is) of the hammers and tools used in building, preached to them, threatening aloud designed judgment, and exhorting to prevent it. And therefore that word is added, ἐξεδέχετο, that the long-suffering of God *waited,* or expected ; expected a believing of His word, and a returning from their wickedness. But we see no such thing followed ; they took their own course still, and therefore the Lord took His. They had polluted the earth with their wickedness : now the Lord would have the cleansing by repentance ; that being denied, it must be another way, by a flood. And because they and their sins remained one, they would not part with them, therefore was one work made of both ; they and their sins, as inseparable, must be cleansed away together.

Thus impenitency, under much long-suffering, makes judgment full and complete. I appeal to you, hath not the Lord used much forbearance towards us ? Hath He not patiently spared us, and clearly warned us, and waited long for the fruit of all ? Hath any thing been wanting ? Have not temporal mercies been multiplied on us ? Have not the spiritual riches of the Gospel been opened up to us ?

And each of you, for yourselves, consider how it is with you after so much long-suffering of God, which none of you can deny He hath used towards you, and so many gracious invitations, with that patience. Have they gained your hearts, or do you still remain servants to sin, still strangers to Him, and formal worshippers ? I beseech you, think on it, what will be the issue of that course. Is it a light matter to you, *to die in your sins,* and to have *the wrath of God abiding on you?* to have refused Christ so often, and that after you have been so often requested to receive salvation ? After the Lord hath followed you with entreaties, hath called to you so often, *Why will ye die?* yet, wilfully to perish, and withal to have all these entreaties come in and accuse you, and make your burden heavier ? Would you willingly die in this estate ? If not, then think that yet He is waiting, if at length you will return. This one day more of His waiting you have, and of His speaking to you ; and some who were here with you the last day, are taken away since. *Oh, that we were wise, and would consider our latter end!* Though there were neither sword nor pestilence near you, you must die, and, for any thing you know, quickly. Why wear you out the day of grace and those precious seasons still, as uncertain of Christ, yea, as undiligent after him, as you were long ago? As you love your souls, be more serious in their business. This was the undoing of the sinners we are speaking of; they were all for present things. *They ate and drank, they married,* in a continued course, without ceasing, and without minding their after-estate. (Luke xvii. 27.) They were drowned in these things, and that drowned them in a flood. Noah did also eat and drink, but his main work was, during that time, the preparing of the ark. The necessities of this life the children of God are tied to, and forced to bestow some time and pains on them ; but the thing that takes up their hearts, that which the bent of their souls is set on, is, their interest in Jesus Christ : and all your wise designs are but a pleasing madness, till this be chief with you. Others have had as much of God's patience, and as fair opportunity, as you, whose souls and Christ had never met, and now know that they never shall. They had their time of worldly projects and enjoyment, as you now have, and followed them, as if they had been immortally to abide with them ; but they are passed away as a shadow, and we are posting after them, and within awhile shall lie down in the dust. Oh ! how happy they whose hearts are not here, trading with vanity and gathering vexation, but whose thoughts are on that blessed life above trouble ! Certainly, they who pass for fools in the world, are the only *children of wisdom,* they who have renounced their lusts and their own wills, have yielded up themselves to Jesus, taking Him for their King, and have their minds resting on Him as their salvation.

While the ark was a preparing.] Observe, The delay of

the Lord's determined judgment on the ungodly was indeed long-suffering towards them, but here was more in it to Noah and his family; the providing for their preservation, and, till that was completed for them, the rest were spared. Thus, the very forbearance which the ungodly do enjoy, is usually involved with the interest of the godly; some thing of that usually goes into it; and so it is in a great part for their sakes, that the rest are both spared and furnished with common mercies. The saints are usually the scorn and contempt of others, yet are they, by that love the Lord carries towards them, the very arches and pillars of states, and kingdoms, and families, where they are, yea, of the world, (*Semen sanctum statumen terræ,*) the frame whereof is continued mainly in regard to them. (Isa. vi. 13.) But they who are ungrateful to the great Maker and Upholder of it, and regardless of Him, what wonder if they take no notice of the advantage they receive by the concernment of His children in the world? Observe here,

I. The Work. II. The End of it. I. In the Work, the preparing of the Ark, observe, 1st, God's appointment; 2dly, Noah's obedience.

1*st*. It was God's appointment. His power was not tied to this, yet His wisdom chose it. He who steered the course of this Ark safely all that time, could have preserved those He designed it for without it; but thus it pleases the Lord, usually, to mix His most wonderful deliverances with some selected means; exercising in that way our obedience in their use, yet so as that the singular power of His hand in them, whereon faith rests, doth clearly appear, doing by them what, in a more natural way, they could not possibly effect.

2*dly*. For the obedience of Noah, if we should insist on the difficulties, both in this work and in the way of their preservation by it, it would look the clearer, and be found very remarkable. Considering the length of the work, the great pains in providing materials, especially considering the opposition that probably he met with in it from the profane about him, the mightier of them, or, at least, the hatred and continual scoffs of all sorts, it required principles of an invincible resolution to go through with it. What (would they say) means this old dotard to do? Whither this monstrous voyage? And inasmuch as it spoke, as no doubt he told them, their ruin and his safety, this would incense them so much the more. You look far before you, and what! shall we all perish, and you alone escape? But, through all, the sovereign command and gracious promise of his God carried him, regarding their scoffs and threats as little in making the Ark, as he did afterwards the noise of the waters about it, when he was sitting safe within it. This his obedience, having indeed so boisterous winds to encounter, had need of a well-fastened root, that it might stand and hold out against them all, and so it had. The Apostle St. Paul tells us what the root of it was: *By faith, being warned of God, he prepared an ark.* (Heb. xi. 7.) And there is no living and lasting obedience but what springs from that root. He believed what the Lord spake of His determined judgment on the ungodly world, and from the belief of that arose that holy fear which is expressly mentioned, (Heb. xi. 7,) as exciting him to this work; and he believed the word of promise, which the Lord spake concerning his preservation by the Ark: and the belief of these two carried him strongly on to the work, and through it, against all counter-blasts and opposition; overcame both his own doubtings and the mockings of the wicked, while he still looked to Him who was the master and contriver of the work.

Till we attain such a fixed view of our God, and such firm persuasion of His truth, and power, and goodness, it will never be right with us; there will be nothing but wavering and unsettledness in our spirits and in our ways. Every little discouragement from within or from without, that meets us, will be likely to turn us over. We shall not walk in an even course, but still be reeling and staggering, till Faith be set wholly upon its own basis, the proper foundation of it: not set betwixt two, upon one strong prop, and another that is rotten, partly on

God, and partly on creature helps and encouragements, or our own strength. Our only safe and happy way is, in humble obedience, in His own strength to follow His appointments, without standing and questioning the matter, and to resign the conduct of all to His wisdom and love ; to put the rudder of our life into his hand, to steer the course of it as seemeth Him good, resting quietly on His word of promise for our safety. Lord, whither thou wilt, and which way thou wilt, be Thou my guide, and it sufficeth.

This absolute following of God, and trusting Him with all, is marked as the true character of faith in Abraham ; his going after God away from his country, *not knowing,* nor asking, *whither he went,* secure in his guide. And so, in that other greater point of offering his son, he silenced all disputes about it, by that mighty conclusion of faith, *accounting that he was able to raise him from the dead.* (Heb. xi. 8, 19.) Thus it is said, v. 7, *By faith, Noah prepared the ark.* He did not argue and question, How shall this be done, and if it were, how shall I get all the kinds of beasts gathered together to put into it, and how shall it be ended when we are shut in ? No, but he believed firmly that it should be finished by him, and he be saved by it ; and he was not disappointed.

II. The End of this work was, the *saving of* Noah and his family from the general Deluge, wherein all the rest perished.

Here it will be fit to consider the point of the preservation of the godly in ordinary and common calamities, briefly in these positions.

1. It is certain that the children of God, as they are not exempted from the common, universal calamities and evils of this life, which befal the rest of men, so not from any particular kind of them. As it is *appointed* for them, with all others, *once to die,* so we find them not privileged from any kind of disease, or other way of death ; not from falling by sword, or by pestilence, or in a frenzy of a fever, or any kind of sudden death : yea, when these, or such like, are on a land by way of public judgment, the godly are not altogether exempted from

them, but may fall in them with others ; as we find Moses dying in the wilderness with those he brought out of Egypt. Now though it was for a particular failing in the wilderness, yet, it evinces that there is in this no infringement upon their privileges, nothing contrary to the love of God towards them, and His covenant with them.

2. The promises made to the godly, of preservation from common-judgments, have their truth, and are made good in many of them who are so preserved, though they do not hold absolutely and universally. For they are ever to be understood in subordination to their highest good; but when they are preserved, they ought to take it as a gracious accomplishment even of these promises to them, which the wicked, many of whom do likewise escape, have no right to, but are preserved for after-judgment.

3. It is certain, that the curse and sting is taken out of all those evils incident to the godly with others, in life and death, which makes the main difference, though to the eye of the world invisible. And it may be observed, that in those common judgments of sword, or pestilence, or other epidemic diseases, a great part of those who are cut off are of the wickedest, though the Lord may send of those arrows to some few of his own, to call them home.

The full and clear distinction of the godly and the wicked, being reserved for their after-estate in eternity, it needs not seem strange that in many things it appears not here. One thing, above all others, most grievous to the child of God, may take away the wonder of other things they suffer in common, that is, the remainders of sin in them while they are in the flesh : though there is a spirit in them above it, and contrary to it, which makes the difference, yet sometimes the too much likeness, especially in the prevailings of corruption, doth confuse the matter, not only to others' eyes, but to their own.

4. Though the great distinction and severing be reserved to that great and solemn day which shall clear all, yet the Lord is pleased, in part, more remarkably at sometimes to distinguish

His own from the ungodly, in the execution of temporal judgments, and to give these as preludes of that final and full
judgment. And this instance of Noah was one of the most
eminent in that kind, being the most general judgment that
ever befel the world, or that shall befal it to the last, and so
the liveliest figure of it ; this was by water, as the second shall
be by fire. It was most congruous that it should resemble it
in this, as the chief point; the saving of righteous Noah and
his family from it, prefiguring the eternal salvation of believers,
as our Apostle teacheth.

Wherein few, that is, eight persons, were saved by water.]
This great point of the fewness of those who are saved in the
other greater salvation, as in this, I shall not now prosecute :
only,

1. If so few, then, the inquiry into ourselves, whether we
be of these few, should be more diligent, and followed more
home, than it is as yet with the most of us. We are wary in
our trifles, and only in this easily deceived, yea, our own de-
ceivers in this great point. Is not this folly far beyond what
you usually say of some, *Penny wise and pound foolish ;* to
be wise for a moment, and fools for eternity ?

2. You who are indeed seeking the way of life, be not discouraged by your fewness. It hath always been so. You see
here how few of the whole world were saved. And is it not
better to be of the few in the Ark, than of the multitude in the
waters ? Let them fret, as ordinarily they do, to see so few
more diligent for Heaven ; as no doubt they did in the case
of Noah. And this is what galls them, that any should have
higher names and surer hopes this way : What ! are none but
such as you going to heaven ? Think you all of us damned ?
What can we say, but that there is a flood of wrath awaiting
many, and certainly, all that are out of the Ark, shall perish in it.

3. This is that main truth that I would leave with you :
look on Jesus Christ as the Ark, of whom this was a figure,
and believe it, out of Him there is nothing but certain destruction, a deluge of wrath, all the world over, on those who are

out of Christ. Oh! it is our life, our only safety, to be in Him. But these things are not believed. Men think they believe them, and do not. Were it believed, that we are under the sentence of eternal death in our natural state, and that there is no escape but by removing out of ourselves unto Christ, Oh, what thronging would there be to Him! Whereas, now, He invites and calls, and how few are persuaded to come to Him! Noah believed the Lord's word of judgment against the world, believed His promise made to him, and prepared an ark. Is it not a high sign of unbelief, that there being an ark of everlasting salvation ready prepared to our hand, we will not so much as come to it? Will you be persuaded certainly, that the Ark-door stands open? His offers are free; do but come, and try if He will turn you away. No, He will not: *Him that comes to me, I will in no ways cast out.* (John vi. 37.) And as there is such acceptance and sure preservation in Him, there is as sure perishing without Him, trust on what you will. Be you of a giant's stature, (as many of them were,) to help you to climb up (as they would surely do when the Flood came on) to the highest mountains and tallest trees, yet it shall overtake you. Make your best of your worldly advantages, or good parts, or civil righteousness, all shall prove poor shifts from the flood of wrath, which rises above all these, and drowns them. Only the Ark of our salvation is safe. Think how gladly they would have been within the Ark, when they found death without it; and now, it was too late! How would many who now despise Christ, wish to honour Him one day! Men, so long as they thought to be safe on the earth, would never betake them to the Ark, would think it a prison; and could men find salvation any where else, they would never come to Christ for it: this is, because they know Him not. But yet, be it necessity, let that drive thee in; and then, being in Him, thou shalt find reason to love Him for Himself, besides the salvation thou hast in Him.

You who have fled into Him for refuge, wrong Him not so far as to question your safety. What though the floods of thy former guiltiness rise high, thine Ark shall still be above them; and the higher they rise, the higher He shall rise, shall have the more glory in freely justifying and saving thee. Though thou find the remaining power of sin still within thee, yet it shall not sink thine ark. There was in this Ark, sin, yet they were saved from the Flood. If 'thou dost believe, that puts thee in Christ, and He will bring thee safe through, without splitting or sinking.

As thou art bound to account thyself safe in Him, so to admire that love which set thee there. Noah was a holy man; but whence were both his holiness and his preservation while the world perished, but because *he found favour* or *free grace,* as the word is, in the eyes of the Lord? And no doubt, he did much contemplate this, being secure within, when the cries of the rest drowning, were about him. Thus think thou: Seeing so few are saved in this blessed Ark wherein I am, in comparison of the multitudes that perish in the deluge, whence is this? Why was I chosen, and so many about me left, why, but because it pleased Him? But all is strait here. We have neither hearts nor time for ample thoughts of this love, till we be beyond time; then shall we admire and praise without ceasing, and without wearying.

As the Example the Apostle here makes use of, is great and remarkable, so, *Thirdly,* it is fit and suitable for the instruction of Christians, to whom he proceeds to adapt and apply it, in the particular resemblance of it to the rule of Christianity. *The like figure whereunto, even Baptism, doth also now save us.*

In these words we have, I. The end of Baptism; II. The proper virtue or efficacy of it for that End; and III. A resemblance in both these to Noah's preservation in the Flood.

I. The end of Baptism, to *save us.* This is the great common end of all the ordinances of God; that one high mark they all aim at. And the great and common mistake in regard to them, is, that they are not so understood and used. We come and sit awhile, and, if we can keep awake, give the word the hearing; but how few of us receive it as *the in-grafted word that is able to save our souls!* Were it thus taken, what sweetness would be found in it, which most who hear and read it are strangers to! How precious would those lines be, if we looked on them thus, and saw them meeting and concentring in salvation as their end! Thus, likewise, were the sacraments considered indeed as seals of this inherit-ance, annexed to the great charter of it, seals of salvation, this would powerfully beget a fit appetite for the Lord's Sup-per, when we are invited to it, and would beget a due esteem of Baptism; would teach you more frequent and fruitful thoughts of your own Baptism, and more pious considerations of it when you require it for your children. A natural eye looks upon bread, and wine, and water, and sees the outward difference of their use there, that they are set apart and differ-enced (as is evident by external circumstances) from their common use; but the main of the difference, wherein their excellency lies, it sees not, as the eye of faith above that espies salvation under them. And Oh, what a different thing are they to it, from what they are to a formal user of them! We should aspire to know the hidden rich things of God, that are wrapped up in His ordinances. We stick in the shell and surface of them, and seek no further; that makes them un-beautiful and unsavoury to us, and that use of them turns into an empty custom. Let us be more earnest with Him who hath appointed them, and made this their end, *to save us,* that He would clear up the eye of our souls, to see them thus under this relation, and to see how they are suited to this their end, and tend to it. And let us seriously seek salvation in them, from His own hand, and we shall find it.

Doth save us.] So that this salvation of Noah and his fa-mily from the Deluge, and all outward deliverances and salva-tions, are but dark shadows of this. Let them not be spoken of, these reprisals and prolongings of this present life, in com-parison of the deliverance of the soul from death, the second death; the stretching of a moment, compared to the concernment of eternity. How would any of you welcome a full and sure protection from common dangers, if such were to be had, that you should be ascertained of safety from sword and pestilence ; that whatever others suffered about you, you and your family should be free ! And those who have escaped a near danger of this kind, are apt to rest there, as if no more were to be feared ; whereas this common favour may be shewn to those who are afar off from God. And what though you be not only thus far safe, but, I say, if you were secured for the future, (which none of you absolutely are,) yet, when you are put out of danger of sword and plague, still, death remains, and sin and wrath may be remaining with it. And shall it not be all one, to die under these in a time of public peace and welfare, as if it were now ? Yea, it may be something more unhappy, by reason of the increase of the heap of sin and wrath, guiltiness being augmented by life prolonged ; and more grievous, to be pulled away from the world, in the midst of peaceable enjoyment, and to have everlasting darkness succeed to that short sun-shine of thy day of ease ; happiness of a short date, and misery for ever ! What availed it wicked Ham to outlive the Flood, to inherit a curse after it ; to be kept undrowned in the waters, to see himself and his posterity blasted with his father's curse? Think seriously, what will be the end of all thy temporary safety and preservation, if thou share not in this salvation, and find not thyself sealed and marked for it ? What will it avail, to flatter thyself with a dream of happiness, and *walk in the light* of a few *sparks* that will soon die out, and *then lie down in sorrow ?* (Isa. l. 11.) A sad bed that, which the most have to go to, after they have wearied themselves all the day, all their life, in a chace of vanity !

II. The next thing is, the power and virtue of this means for its end. That Baptism hath a power, is clear, in that it is so expressly said, *it doth save us:* what kind of power, is equally clear from the way it is here expressed ; not by a natural force of the element ; though adapted and sacramentally used, it only can wash away the filth of the body ; its physical efficacy or power reaches no further : but it is in the hand of the Spirit of God, as other sacraments are, and as the word itself is, to purify the conscience, and convey grace and salvation to the soul, by the reference it hath to, and union with, that which it represents. It saves *by the answer of a good conscience unto God,* and it affords that, *by the resurrection of Jesus from the dead.*

Thus, then, we have a true account of the power of this, and so, of other sacraments, and a discovery of the error of two extremes : (1.) Of those who ascribe too much to them, as if they wrought by a natural inherent virtue, and carried grace in them inseparably ; (2.) Of those who ascribe too little to them, making them only signs and badges of our profession. Signs they are, but more than signs merely representing ; they are means exhibiting, and seals confirming, grace to the faithful. But the working of faith, and the conveying of Christ into the soul to be received by faith, is not a thing put into them to do of themselves, but still in the Supreme Hand that appointed them : and He indeed both causes the souls of His own to receive these His seals with faith, and makes them effectual to confirm that faith which receives them so. They are then, in a word, neither empty signs to them who believe, nor effectual causes of grace to them who believe not.

The mistake, on both sides, arises from the want of duly considering the relative nature of these seals, and that kind of union that is betwixt them and the grace they represent, which is real, though not natural or physical, as they speak ; so that, though they do not save all who partake of them, yet they do really and effectually save believers, (for whose salvation they are means,) as the other external ordinances of God do. Though they have not that power which is peculiar to the Author of them, yet a power they have, such as befits their nature, and by reason of which they are truly said to sanctify and justify, and so to save, as the Apostle here avers of Baptism.

Now that which is intended for our help, our carnal minds
are ready to turn into a hinderance and disadvantage. The
Lord representing invisible things to the eye, and confirming
His promises even by visible seals, we are apt, from the gross-
ness of our unspiritual hearts, instead of stepping up by that
which is earthly, to the Divine spiritual things represented, to
stay in the outward element, and go no further. Therefore,
the Apostle, to lead us into the inside of this seal of Baptism,
is very clear in designating the effect and fruit of it : *Not* (says
he) the *putting away the filth of the flesh ;* (and water, if
you look no further, can do no more ;) there is an invisible
impurity upon our nature, chiefly on our invisible part, our
soul: this washing means the taking away of that, and where
it reaches its true effect, it doth so purify the conscience, and
makes it good, truly so, in the sight of God, who is the judge
of it.

Consider, 1. It is a pitiful thing to see the ignorance of the
most, professing Christianity, and partaking of the outward
seals of it, yet not knowing what they mean; not apprehending the spiritual dignity and virtue of them. Blind in
the *mysteries of the kingdom,* they are not so much as sensible of that blindness. And being ignorant of the nature of
these holy things, they cannot have a due esteem of them,
which arises out of the view of their inward worth and efficacy.
A confused fancy they have of some good in them, and this
rising to the other extreme, to a superstitious confidence in the
simple performance and participation of them, as if that carried some inseparable virtue with it, which none could miss of,
who are sprinkled with the waters of Baptism, and share in
the elements of bread and wine in the Lord's Supper.

And what is the utmost plea of the most for their title to
heaven, but that in these relative and external things they are
Christians; that they are baptized, hear the word, and are
admitted to the Lord's Table ?—Not considering how many
have gone through all these, who yet daily are going on in
the ways of death, never coming near Jesus Christ, *who is the*

way, and the truth, and the life, whom the word, and the seals of it, hold forth to believers. And they are washed in His blood, and quickened with His life, and made like Him, and co-heirs of glory with Him.

2. Even those who have some clearer notion of the nature and fruit of the seals of grace, yet are in a practical error, in that they look not with due diligence into themselves, inquiring after the efficiency of them in their hearts ; do not study the life of Christ, to know more what it is, and then, to search into themselves for the truth and the growth of that life within them. Is it not an unbecoming thing, for a Christian (when he is about to appear before the Lord at his Table, and so looks something more narrowly within) to find as little faith, as little Divine affection, a heart as unmortified to the world, as cold towards Christ, as before his last address to the same Table, after the intervening, possibly, of many months; in which time, had he been careful often to reflect inwards on his heart, and to look back upon that new sealing in his last participation, he might probably have been more conformable ? And, truly, as there is much guiltiness cleaves to us in this, so, generally, much more in reference to this other sacrament that is here the Apostle's subject, *Baptism,* which being but once administered, and that in infancy, is very seldom and slightly considered by many, even real Christians. And so we are at a loss in that profit and comfort, that increase of both holiness and faith, which the frequent recollecting of it, after a spiritual manner, would no doubt advance us to. And not only do we neglect to put ourselves upon the thoughts of it in private, but, in the frequent opportunities of such thoughts in public, we let it pass unregarded, are idle, inconsiderate, and so, truly guilty beholders. And the more frequently we have these opportunities, the less are we touched with them; they become common, and work not, and the slighting of them grows as common with us as the thing. Yea, when the engagement is more special and personal, when parents are to present their infants to this ordinance, (and then might, and certainly ought

to have a more particular and fixed eye upon it, and themselves
as being sealed with it, to ask within after the fruit and power
of it, and to stir up themselves anew to the actings of faith, and
to ambition after newness of life, and, with earnest prayer for
their children, to be suitors for themselves, for further evidence
of their interest in Christ,) yet possibly, many are not much
engaged in these things even at such times, but are more busied
to prepare their house for entertaining their friends, than to
prepare their hearts for offering up their infant unto God to be
sealed, and withal to make a new offer of their own hearts to
him, to have renewed on them the inward seal of the covenant
of grace, the outward seal whereof they did receive, as it is
now to be conferred upon their infant.

Did we often look upon the face of our souls, the beholding
of the many spots with which we have defiled them after our
washing, might work us to shame and grief, and would drive
us by renewed application to wash often in that blood which
that water figures, which alone can fetch out the stain of sin ;
and then, it would put us upon renewed purposes of purity, to
walk more carefully, to avoid the pollutions of the world we
walk in, and to purge out the pollutions of the hearts that we
carry about with us, which defile us more than all the world
besides.   It would work a holy disdain of sin, often to contemplate ourselves as washed in so precious a laver. Shall I, would
the Christian say, considering that I am now cleansed in the
precious blood of my Lord Jesus, run again into that puddle
out of which He so graciously took me, and made me clean ?
Let the swine wallow in it : He hath made me of his sheepfold.
He hath made me of that excellent order for which all are consecrated by that washing, who partake of it : *He hath washed
us in His blood, and made us kings and priests unto God the
Father.*   Am I of these, and shall I debase myself to the vile
pleasures of sin ?   No, I will think myself too good to serve
any sinful lusts: seeing that he hath looked on me, and taken
me up, and washed and dignified me, and that I am wholly
His, all my study and business shall.be, to honour and magnify Him.

The answer of a good conscience, &c.] The taking away of spiritual filthiness, as the true and saving effect of Baptism, the Apostle here expresses by that which is the further result and effect of it, *The answer of a good conscience unto God;* for it is the washing away of that filthiness which both makes the conscience good, and, in making it such, fits it to make answer unto God. A good conscience, in its full sense, is a pure conscience and a peaceable conscience; and it cannot, indeed, be peaceably good, unless it be purely good. And although, on the other side, it may want the present enjoyment of peace, being purified, yet certainly, in a purified conscience, there is a title and right to peace; it is radically there, even when it appears not; and, in due time, it shall appear, shall spring forth, bud, and flourish.

The purified and good condition of the whole soul may well, as here it doth, go under the name of the good conscience, it being so prime a faculty of it, and as the glass of the whole soul, wherein the estate of it is represented. Therefore, Heb. ix., the efficacy of the blood of Christ is expressed thus, that it *purifieth our consciences from dead works;* which expression is the same thing in effect with that here, *the answer of a good conscience unto God.*

The answer [ἐπερώτημα,] the asking or questioning of conscience, which comprises likewise its answer; for the word intends the whole correspondence of the conscience with God, and with itself as towards God, or in the sight of God. And indeed, God's questioning it, is by itself; it is His deputy in the soul. He makes it pose itself for him, and before him, concerning its own condition, and so, the answer it gives itself in that posture, He as it were sitting and hearing it in his presence, is an answer made unto Him. This questioning and answering, (if such a thing were at this time, as it was certainly soon after,) yet means not the questions and answers used in the baptism of persons who, being of years, professed their faith in answering the questions moved; it possibly alludes unto that; but it further, by way of resemblance, expresses the inward questioning and answering which is transacted within, betwixt the soul and itself, and the soul and God, and so is allusively called ἐπερώτημα, a questioning and answering, but it is distinctively specified, εἰς Θεόν: whereas the other was towards men, this is unto God.

A good conscience is a waking, speaking conscience, and the conscience that questions itself most, is of all sorts the best; that which is dumb, therefore, or asleep, and is not active and frequent in self-inquiries, is not a good conscience. The word is judicial, ἐπερώτημα, alluding to the *interrogation* used in Law for the trial and executing of processes. And this is the great business of conscience, to sit, and examine, and judge within; to *hold courts* in the soul. And it is of continual necessity that it be so: there can be no vacation of this judicature, without great damage to the estate of the soul: yea, not a day ought to pass without a session of conscience within; for daily disorders arise in the soul, which, if they pass on, will grow and gather more, and so breed more difficulty in their trial and redress. Yet men do easily turn from this work as hard and unpleasant, and make many a long vacation in the year, and protract it from one day to another. In the morning, they must go about their business, and at night, they are weary and sleepy, and all the day long one affair steps in after another; and in case of that failing, some trifling company or other; and so their days pass on, while the soul is overgrown with impurities and disorders.

You know what confusions, and disorders, and evils, will abound amongst a rude people, where there is no kind of court or judicature held. Thus is it with that unruly rabble, the lusts and passions of our souls, when there is no discipline nor judgment within, or where there is but a neglect and intermission of it for a short time. And the most part of souls are in the posture of ruin: their vile affections, as a headstrong, tumultuous multitude, that will not suffer a deputed judge to sit amongst them, cry down their consciences, and make a continual noise, that the voice of it may not be heard, and so force it to desist, and leave them to their own ways.

But you who take this course, know you are providing the severest judgment for yourselves by this disturbing of judgment, as when a people rise against an inferior judge, the prince or supreme magistrate who sent him, hearing of it, doth not fail to vindicate his honour and justice in their exemplary punishment.

Will you not answer unto conscience, but when it begins to speak, turn to business or company, that you may not hear it? Know, that it and you must answer unto God; and when He shall make inquiry, it must report, and report as the truth is, knowing that there is no hiding the matter from Him; Lord, there are, to my knowledge, a world of enormities within the circuit I had to judge, and I would have judged them, but was forcibly withstood and interrupted; and was not strong enough to resist the tumultuous power that rose against me; now the matter comes into Thine own hand to judge it Thyself. What shall the soul say in that day, when conscience shall make such an answer unto God, and it shall come under the severity of His justice for all? Whereas, if it had given way to the conscience to find out, and judge, and rectify matters, so that it could have answered concerning its procedure that way, God would accept this as the answer of a good conscience, and what conscience had done, he would not do over again: It hath judged; then, I acquit. *For if we would judge ourselves,* (says the Apostle,) *we should not be judged.* 1 Cor. xi. 31.

The questioning or inquiry of conscience, and so, its report or answer unto God, extends to all the affairs of the soul, all the affections and motions of it, and all the actions and carriage of the whole man. The open wickedness of the most, testifies against them, that though sprinkled with water in Baptism, yet they are strangers to the power and gracious efficacy of it. Not being *baptized with the Holy Ghost and with fire,* they have still their dross and filth remaining in them, and nothing else appearing in their ways; so that their consciences cannot so much as make a good answer for them unto men, much less unto God. What shall it answer for them, being judged, but that they are swearers, and cursers, and drunkards, or unclean? or that they are slanderers, delighting to pass their hours in descanting on the actions and ways of others, and looking through the miscoloured glass of their own malice and pride; that they are neglecters of God and holy things, lovers of themselves and their own pleasures, more than lovers of God? And have such as these impudence enough to call themselves Christians, and to pretend themselves to be such as are washed in the blood of Christ? Yes, they do this. But be ashamed and confounded in yourselves, you that remain in this condition. Yea, although thou art blameless in men's eyes, and possibly in thy own eyes too, yet thou mayest be *filthy* still in the sight of God. There is such *a generation,* a multitude of them, *that are pure in their own eyes, and yet are not washed from their filthiness;* (Prov. xxx. 12;) moral evil persons who are most satisfied with their own estate, or such as have further *a form of godliness,* but their lusts are not mortified by *the power of it,* secret pride and earthliness of mind, and vain glory, and carnal wisdom, being still entertained with pleasure within.

These are foul pollutions, filthy and hateful in the sight of God; so that where it is thus, that such guests are in peaceable possession of the heart, there the blood and Spirit of Christ are not yet come; neither can there be this answer of a good conscience unto God.

This *answer of a good conscience unto God,* as likewise its questioning, to enable itself for that answer, is touching two great points, which are of chief concern to the soul, its *justification,* and its *sanctification;* for Baptism is the seal of both, and purifies the conscience in both respects. *That* water is the figure both of the blood and the water, the justifying blood of Christ, and the pure water of the sanctifying Spirit of Christ: He takes away the condemning guiltiness of sin, by the one, and the polluting filthiness, by the other.

Now, the Conscience of a real Believer, inquiring within, upon right discovery will make this answer unto God: Lord, I have found that there is no standing before Thee, for the soul in itself is overwhelmed with a world of guiltiness: but I find a blood sprinkled upon it, that hath, I am sure, virtue enough to purge it all away, and to present it pure unto Thee; and I know that wheresoever Thou findest that blood sprinkled, Thine anger is quenched and appeased immediately upon the sight of it. Thine hand cannot smite where that blood is before Thine eye.—And this the Lord does agree to, and authorizes the Conscience, upon this account, to return back an answer of safety and peace to the soul.

So for the other point: Lord, I find a living work of holiness on this soul: though there is yet corruption there, yet it is as a continual grief and vexation, it is an implacable hatred, there is no peace betwixt them, but continual enmity and hostility; and if I cannot say much of the high degrees of grace, and faith in Christ, and love to him, and heavenliness of mind, yet, I may say, there is a beginning of these: at least, this I most confidently affirm, that there are real and earnest desires of the soul after these things. It would know and conform to Thy will, and be delivered from itself and its own will; and though it were to the highest displeasure of all the world, it would gladly walk in all well-pleasing unto Thee. Now, He who sees the truth of these things, knowing it to be thus, owns it as His own work, and engages Himself to advance it, and bring it to perfection. This is a taste of that intercourse which the purified conscience hath with God, as the saving fruit of Baptism.

And all this it doth, not of itself, but by virtue of *the resurrection of Jesus Christ,* which refers both to the remote effect, *salvation,* and to the nearer effect, as a means and pledge of that, *the purifying of the conscience.*

By this, His death, and the effusion of His blood in his sufferings, are not excluded, but are included in it, his resurrection being the evidence of that whole work of expiation, both completed and accepted: full payment being made by our Surety, and so, He set free, His freedom is the cause and the assurance of ours. Therefore the Apostle St. Paul expresses it so, that *He died for our sins, and rose for our righteousness;* and our Apostle shews us the worth of our *living hope* in this same resurrection, chap. i. ver. 3. *Blessed be the God and Father of our Lord Jesus Christ, who, according to His abundant mercy, hath begotten us again unto a lively hope, by the resurrection of Jesus Christ from the dead.*

Now, that Baptism doth apply and seal to the Believer his interest in the death and resurrection of Christ, the Apostle St. Paul teaches to the full, Rom. vi. 4: *We are buried with Him,* says he, *by baptism into his death, that like as Christ was raised up from the dead by the glory of the Father, even so we should also walk in newness of life.* The dipping into the waters representing our dying with Christ; and the return thence, our rising with Him.

The last thing is, the resemblance of Baptism, in these things, to the saving of Noah in the Flood. And it holds in that we spoke of last ; for he seemed to have rather entered into a grave, as dead, than into a safeguard of life, in going into the Ark ; yet, being buried there, he rose again, as it were, in his coming forth to begin a new world. The waters of the Flood drowned the ungodly, as a heap of filthiness washed them away, them and their sin together as one, being inseparable; and upon the same waters the Ark floating preserved Noah. Thus, the waters of Baptism are intended as a deluge to drown sin and to save the Believer, who by faith is separated both from the world and from his sin; so, it sinks, and he is saved.

And there is, further, another thing specified by the Apostle, wherein, though it be a little hard, yet he chiefly intends the parallel; the *fewness* of those that are saved by both. For though many are sprinkled with the elemental water of Baptism, yet, few, so as to attain by it the *answer of a good conscience towards God,* and to live by participation of the resurrection and life of Christ.

Thou that seest the world perishing in a deluge of wrath, and art now most thoughtful for this, how thou shalt escape it, fly into Christ as thy safety, and rest secure there. Thou shalt find life in His death, and that life further ascertained to thee in His rising again. So full and clear a title to life hast thou in these two, that thou canst challenge all adversaries upon this very ground, as unconquerable whilst thou standest on it, and mayest speak thy challenge in the Apostle's style, *It is God that justifieth, who shall condemn?* But how know you that He justifies? *It is Christ that died, yea, rather, that is risen, who sitteth at the right hand of God, who also maketh intercession for us.* Rom. viii. 33, 34. It alludes to that place, Isa. l. 8, where Christ speaks of himself, but in the name of all who adhere to him; *He is near that justifies me; who is he that will contend with me?* So that what Christ speaks there, the Apostle, with good reason, imparts to each believer as in Him. If no more is to be laid to Christ's charge, He being now acquitted, as is clear by His rising again; then, neither to thine, who art clothed with Him, and one with Him.

This is the grand answer of a good conscience; and, in point of justifying them before God, there can be no answer but this. What have any to say to thee? Thy debt is paid by Him who undertook it; and He is free. Answer all accusations with this, *Christ is risen.*

And then, for the mortifying of sin, and strengthening of thy graces, look daily on that death and resurrection. Study them, set thine eye upon them, till thy heart take on the impression of them by much spiritual and affectionate looking on them. *Beholding the glory of thy Lord* Christ, then, be *transformed into it.* (2 Cor. iii. 18.) It is not only a moral pattern or copy, but an effectual cause of thy sanctification, having real influence into thy soul. Dead with Him, and again alive with Him! Oh happiness and dignity unspeakable, to have this life known and cleared to your souls! If it were, how would it make you live above the world, and all the vain hopes and fears of this wretched life, and the fear of death itself! Yea, it would make that visage of death most lovely, which to the world is most affrightful.

It is the Apostle's maxim, that the *carnal mind is enmity against God;* and as it is universally true of every carnal mind, so of all the motions and thoughts of it. Even where it seems to agree with God, yet it is still contrary; if it acknowledge and conform to His ordinance, yet, even in so doing, it is on directly opposite terms to Him, particularly in this, that what He esteems most in them, the carnal mind makes least account of. He chiefly eyes and values the inside; the natural man dwells and rests in the shell and surface of them. God, according to His spiritual nature, looks most on the more spiritual part of His worship and worshippers; the carnal mind is in this, just like itself, altogether for the sensible external part, and unable to look beyond it. Therefore the Apostle here, having taken occasion to speak of Baptism in terms that contain a parallel and resemblance between it and the Flood, is express in correcting this mistake. It is not, says he, *the putting away of the filth of the flesh, but the answer of a good conscience.*

Were it possible to persuade you, I would recommend one thing to you: learn to look on the ordinances of God suitably to their nature, spiritually, and enquire after the spiritual effect and working of them upon your consciences. We would willingly have all religion reduced to externals; this is our natural choice; and we would pay all in this coin, as cheaper and easier by far, and would compound for the spiritual part, rather to add and give more external performance and ceremony. Hence the natural complacency in Popery, which is all for this service of the flesh, and body-services; and to those prescribed by God, will deal so liberally with Him, in that kind, as to add more, and frame new devices and rites, what you will in this kind, sprinklings, and washings, and anointings, and incense. But whither tends all this? Is it not a gross mistaking of God, to think Him thus pleased? Or, is it not a direct affront, knowing that He is not pleased with these, but desires another thing, to thrust that upon Him which He cares not for, and refuse Him what He calls for?—that single, humble heart-worship and walking with Him, that purity of spirit and conscience which only He prizes; no outward service being acceptable, but for these, as they tend to this end and do attain it. Give me, saith He, nothing, if you give not this. Oh! saith the carnal mind, any thing but this Thou shalt have; as many washings and offerings as Thou wilt, *thousands of rams, and ten thousand rivers of oil;* yea, rather than fail, *let the fruit of my body go for the sin of my soul.* (Mic. vi. 6.) Thus we: will the outward use of the word and sacraments do it? then, all shall be well. Baptized we are; and shall I hear much and communicate often, if I can reach it? Shall I be exact in point of family-worship? Shall I pray in secret? All this I do, or at least I now promise. Aye, but when all that is done, there is yet one thing may be wanting, and if it be so, all that amounts to nothing. Is thy conscience purified and made good by all these; or art thou seeking and aiming at this, by the use of all means? Then certainly thou shalt find life in them. But does thy heart still remain uncleansed from the old ways, not purified from the pollutions of the world? Do thy beloved sins still lodge with thee, and keep possession of thy heart? Then art thou still a stranger to Christ, and an enemy to God. The word and seals of life are dead to thee, and thou art still dead in the use of them all. Know you not, that many have made shipwreck upon the very rock of salvation? that many who were baptized as well as you, and as constant attendants on all the worship and ordinances of God as you, yet have remained without Christ, and died in their sins, and are now past recovery? Oh that you would be warned! There are still multitudes running headlong that same course, tending to destruction, through the midst of all the means of salvation; the saddest way of all to it, through word and sacraments, and all heavenly ordinances, to be walking hell-wards! Christians, and yet no Christians; baptized, and yet unbaptized! As the Prophet takes in the profane multitude of God's own people with the nations, Jer. ix. 26, *Egypt, and Judah, and Edom; all these nations are uncircumcised;* and the worst came last; *and all the house of Israel are uncircumcised in the heart:* thus, thus, the most of us are unbaptized in the heart. And as this is the way of personal destruction, so it is that, as the Prophet there declares, which brings upon the Church so many public judgments; and as the Apostle tells the Corinthians, (1 Eph. xi. 30,) that for the abuse of the Lord's Table, *many were sick, and many slept.* Certainly, our abuse of the holy things of God, and want of their proper spiritual fruits, are amongst the prime sins of this land, for which so many slain have fallen in the fields by the sword, and in the streets by pestilence ; and more are likely yet to fall, if we thus continue to provoke the Lord to his face. For it is the most avowed, direct affront, to profane His holy things ; and this we do while we answer not their proper end, and are not inwardly sanctified by them. We have no other word, nor other sacraments, to recommend to you, than those which you have used so long to no purpose ; only we would call you from the dead forms, to seek the living power of them, that you perish not.

You think the *renouncing of Baptism* a horrible word, and that we would speak so only of witches ; yet it is a common guiltiness that cleaves to all who renounce not the filthy lusts and the self-will of their own hearts. For Baptism carries in it a renouncing of these ; and so, the cleaving unto these is a renouncing of it. Oh ! we all were sealed for God in Baptism ; but who lives as if it was so ? How few have the impression of it on the conscience, and the expression of it in the walk and fruit of their life ! We do not, as clean-washed persons, abhor and fly all pollutions, *all fellowship with the unfruitful works of darkness.*

We have been a long time hearers of the Gospel, whereof Baptism is the seal, and most of us often at the Lord's Table. What hath all this done upon us ? Ask within : Are your hearts changed ? Is there a new creation there ? Where is that spiritual-mindedness ? Are your hearts dead to the world and sin, and alive to God, *your consciences purged from dead works ?*

What mean you ? Is not this the end of all the ordinances, to make all clean, and to renew and make good the conscience, to bring the soul and your Lord into a happy amity, and a good correspondence, that it may not only be on speaking terms, but often speak and converse with Him?—may have liberty both to demand and answer, as the original word implies? that it may speak the language of faith and humble obedience unto God, and that He may speak the language of peace to it, and both, the language of the Lord each to the other?

That conscience 'alone is good, which is much busied in this work, in demanding and answering; which speaks much with itself, and much with God. This is both the sign that it is good, and the means to make it better. That soul will doubtless be very wary in its walk, which takes daily account of itself, and renders up that account unto God. It will not live by guess, but naturally examine each step beforehand, because it is resolved to examine all after; will consider well what it should do, because it means to ask over again what it hath done, and not only to answer itself, but to make a faithful report of all unto God; to lay all before Him, continually upon trial made; to tell Him what is in any measure well done, as His own work, and bless Him for that; and tell Him, too, all the slips and miscarriages of the day, as our own; complaining of ourselves in His presence, and still entreating free pardon, and more wisdom to walk more holily and exactly, and gaining, even by our failings, more humility and more watchfulness.

If you would have your consciences answer well, they must inquire and question much beforehand. Whether is this I purpose and go about, agreeable to my Lord's will? Will it please Him? Ask that more, and regard that more, than this, which the most follow. Will it please or profit myself? Fits that my own humour? And examine not only the bulk and substance of thy ways and actions, but the manner of them, how thy heart is set. So think it not enough to go to church, or to pray, but *take heed how ye hear;* consider how pure He is, and how piercing His eye, whom thou servest.

Then, again, afterwards; think it not enough, I was praying, or hearing, or reading, it was a good work, what need I question it further? No, but be still reflecting and asking

how it was done: How have I heard, how have I prayed?
Was my heart humbled by the discoveries of sin, from the
word? Was it refreshed with the promises of grace? Did
it he level under the word, to receive the stamp of it? Was it
in prayer set and kept in a holy bent towards God? Did it
breathe forth real and earnest desires into His ear; or was it
remiss, and roving, and dead in the service? So, in my
society with others, in such and such company, what was spent
of my time, and how did I employ it? Did I seek to honour
my Lord, and to edify my brethren, by my carriage and
speeches; or did the time run out in trifling vain discourse?
When alone, what is the carriage and walk of my heart?
Where it hath most liberty to move in its own pace, is it delighted in converse with God? Are the thoughts of heavenly
things frequent and sweet to it; or does it run after the earth
and the delights of it, spinning out itself in impertinent vain
contrivances?

The neglect of such inquiries, is that which entertains and
increases the impurity of the soul, so that men are afraid to
look into themselves, and to look up to God. But oh! what
a foolish course is this, to shift off what cannot be avoided!
In the end, answer must be made to that All-seeing Judge
with whom we have to do, and to whom we owe our accompts.

And, truly, it should be seriously considered, what makes
this good conscience, which makes an acceptable answer unto
God. That appears by the opposition, *not the putting away
the filth of the flesh;* then, it *is* the putting away of *soul-filthi-
ness;* so it is the renewing and purifying of the conscience,
that makes it good, pure, and peaceable. In the purifying, it
may be troubled, which is but the stirring in cleansing of it,
and makes more quiet in the end, as physic, or the lancing of
a sore; and after it is in some measure cleansed, it may have
fits of trouble, which yet still add further purity and further
peace. So there is no hazard in that work; but all the misery
is, a dead security of the conscience while remaining filthy, and
yet unstirred; or, after some stirring or pricking, as a wound

THE FIRST EPISTLE OF PETER.

not thoroughly cured, skinned over, which will but breed more vexation in the end ; it will fester and grow more difficult to be cured, and if it be cured, it must be by deeper cutting and more pain, than if at first it had endured a thorough search.

O, my brethren ! take heed of sleeping unto death in carnal ease. Resolve to take no rest till you be in the element and place of soul-rest, where solid rest indeed is. Rest not till you be with Christ. Though all the world should offer their best, turn them by with disdain ; if they will not be turned by, throw them down, and go over them, and trample upon them. Say, you have no rest to give me, nor will I take any at your hands, nor from any creature. There is no rest for me till I be under His shadow, who endured so much trouble to purchase my rest, and whom having found, I may sit down quiet and satisfied ; and when the men of the world make boast of the highest content, I will outvie them all with this one word-*My beloved is mine, and I am His.*

The answer of a good conscience toward God.] The con, science of man is never rightly at peace in itself, till it be rightly persuaded of peace with God, which, while it remains filthy, it cannot be ; for He is holy, and iniquity cannot dwell with *Him.* What *communion betwixt light and darkness?* (2 Cor. vi. 14.) So then, the conscience must be cleansed, ere it can look upon God with assurance and peace. This cleansing is sacramentally performed by Baptism ; effectually, by the Spirit of Christ and the blood of Christ ; and He lives to impart both : therefore here is mentioned his resurrection from the dead, as that, by virtue whereof we are assured of this purifying and peace. Then can the conscience, in some measure with confidence, answer, Lord, though polluted by former sins, and by sin still dwelling in me, yet Thou seest that my desires are to be daily more like my Saviour ; I would have more love and zeal for Thee, more hatred of sin. It can answer with St. Peter, when he was posed, *Lovest Thou me?* Lord, I appeal to thine own eye, who seest my heart : *Lord, Thou knowest that I love Thee ;* at least I desire to love thee, and to desire

Thee ; and that is love.   Willingly would I do Thee more
suitable service, and honour Thy name more ; and I do sincerely desire more grace for this, that Thou mayest have more
glory ; and I entreat the light of Thy countenance for this end,
that, by seeing it, my heart may be more weaned from the
world, and knit unto Thyself.   Thus it answers touching its
inward frame and the work of holiness by the Spirit of holiness dwelling in it.   But, to answer Justice, touching the point
of guilt, it flies *to the Blood of sprinkling,* fetches all its
answer thence, turns over the matter upon it, and that Blood
answers for it ; for it doth speak, and *speak better things than
the blood of Abel;* (Heb. xii. 24;) speaks full payment of all
that can be exacted from the sinner ; and that is a sufficient
answer.

The conscience is then, in this point, at first made speechless,
driven to a nonplus in itself, hath from itself no answer to
make ; but then it turns about to Christ, and finds what to
say : Lord, there is indeed in me nothing but guiltiness ; I
have deserved death ; but I have fled into the City of refuge
which Thou hast appointed ; there I resolve to abide, to live
and die there.   If Justice pursue me, it shall find me there :
I take sanctuary in Jesus.   The arrest laid upon me, will light
upon Him, and He hath wherewithal to answer it.   He can
straightway declare He hath paid all, and can make it good.
He hath the acquittance to shew ; yea, His own liberty is a
real sign of it.   He was in prison, and is let free, which tells
that all is satisfied.   Therefore the answer here rises out of the
resurrection of Jesus Christ.

And in this very thing lies our peace, and our way, and all
our happiness.   Oh ! it is worth your time and pains, to try
your interest in this ; it is the only thing worthy your highest
diligence.   But the most are out of their wits, running like a
number of distracted persons, and still in a deal of business,
but to what end they know not.   You are unwilling to be deceived in those things which, at their best and surest, do but
deceive you when all is done ; but are content to be deceived

in that which is your great concernment. You are your own deeeivers in it; gladly gulled with shadows of. faith and repentance, false touches of sorrow, and false flashes of joy, and are not careful to have your souls really unbottomed from themselves, and built upon Christ; to have Him your treasure, your righteousness, your all, and to have Him your answer unto God your Father. But if you will yet be advised, let go all, to lay hold on Him : lay your souls on Him, and leave Him not. He is *a tried foundation-stone,* and *he that trusts on Him shall not be confounded.*

Ver. 22. Who is gone into Heaven, and is on the right hand of God; angels, and authorities, and powers, being made subject unto him.

THIS is added on purpose to shew us, further, what He is, how high and glorious a Saviour we have !

We have here four points or steps of the exaltation of Christ : 1. Resurrection from the dead ; 2. Ascension into Heaven; 3. Sitting at the right hand of God ; 4. In that posture, His royal authority over the angels. The particulars are clear in themselves. Of the sitting at the right hand of God you are not ignorant that it is a borrowed expression, drawn from Earth to Heaven, to bring down some notion of Heaven to us ; to signify to us in our language, suitably to our customs, the supreme dignity of Jesus Christ, God and Man, the Mediator of the new covenant, His matchless nearness unto His Father, and the sovereignty given Him over Heaven and Earth. And that of the subjection of angels, is but a more particular specifying of that His dignity and power, as enthroned at the Father's right hand, they being the most elevated and glorious creatures : so that His authority over all the world is implied in that subjection of the highest and noblest part of it. His victory and triumph over the angels of darkness, is an evidence of His invincible power and greatness, and matter of comfort to his saints ; but this, here, intends His supremacy over the glorious elect angels.

That there is amongst them priority, we find ; that there is a comely order in their differences, cannot be doubted; but to marshal their degrees and stations above, is a point, not only of vain, fruitless curiosity, but of presumptuous intrusion. Whether these are names of their different particular dignities, or only different names of their general excellency and power, as I think it cannot be certainly well determined, so, it imports us not to determine : only, this we know, and are particularly taught from this place, that whatsoever is their common dignity, both in names and differences, they are all subject to our glorious Head, Christ.

What confirmation they have in their estate by Him, (though piously asserted by divines,) is not so infallibly clear from the alleged scriptures, which may bear another sense. But this is certain, that He is their king, and they acknowledge Him to be so, and do incessantly admire and adore Him. They rejoice in His glory, and in the glory and happiness of mankind through Him. They yield Him most cheerful obedience, and serve Him readily in the good of His Church, and of each particular believer, as He deputes and employs them.

This is the thing here intended, having in it these two : His Dignity above them, and His Authority over them.

1. Such is His Dignity, that even that nature which he stooped below them to take on, He hath carried up and raised above them : the very earth, the flesh of man, being exalted in His person above all those heavenly spirits, who are of so excellent and pure a being in their nature, and from the beginning of the world, have been clothed with so transcendent glory. A parcel of clay is made so bright, and set so high, as to outshine those bright flaming spirits, those Stars of the morning, that flesh being united to the Fountain of Light, the blessed Deity in the person of the Son.

In coming to fetch and put on this garment, He made himself *lower than the angels ;* but carrying it with Him, at His return to His eternal throne, and sitting down with it there, it is raised high above them ; as the Apostle teaches excellently and amply: *To which of them, said He, Sit on my right hand?* Heb. i. 2.

This they look upon with perpetual wonder, but not with envy or repining. No, amongst all their eyes, no such eye is to be found. Yea, they rejoice in the infinite wisdom of God in this design, and His infinite love to poor lost mankind. It is wonderful, indeed, to see him filling the room of their fallen brethren, with new guests from earth, yea, with such as are born heirs of hell; but that not only sinful men should thus be raised to a participation of glory with them who are spotless, sinless spirits, but their flesh, in their Redeemer, should be dignified with a glory so far beyond them,—this is that mystery the angels are intent on looking and prying into, and cannot, nor ever shall, see the bottom of it, for it hath none.

2. Jesus Christ is not only exalted above the angels in absolute dignity, but in relative authority over them. He is made Captain over those heavenly bands; they are all under His command, for all services wherein it pleases Him to employ them; and the great employment He hath, is the attending on his Church, and on particular elect ones. *Are they not all ministering spirits, sent forth to minister to them that shall be heirs of salvation?* (Heb. i. *ult.*) They are the servants of Christ, and in Him, and at His appointment, the servants of every believer; and are many ways serviceable and useful for their good, which truly we do not duly consider. There is no danger of overvaluing them, and inclining to worship them upon this consideration; yea, if we take it right, it will rather take us off from that. The angel judged his argument strong enough to St. John against that, that he was but *his fellow servant.* (Rev. xix. 10.) But this is more, that they are servants to us, although not therefore inferior, it being an honorary service. Yet certainly they are inferior to our Head, and so to His mystical body, taken in that notion, as a part of Him.

Reflection 1. The height of this our Saviour's glory will appear the more, if we reflect on the descent from which he

ascended to it. Oh! how low did we bring down so high a
Majesty, into the pit wherein we had fallen, by climbing to be
higher than He had set us! It was high indeed, as we were
fallen so low, and yet He against whom our sin was committed,
came down to help us up again, and to take hold of us,—*took
us on;* so the word is [ἐπιλαμϐάνεται], Heb. ii. 16. He *took
not hold of the angels,*—let them go, hath left them to die for
ever—*but he took hold of the seed of Abraham,* and took on
Him indeed their flesh, dwelling amongst us, and in a mean
part. He *emptied himself,* ἐκένωσε (Phil. ii. 7), and became
of no repute. And further, after he descended to the earth,
and into our flesh, in it he became *obedient to death* upon the
cross, and descended into the grave. And by these steps, He
was walking towards that glory wherein He now is : *He abased
himself, wherefore,* says the Apostle, *God hath highly exalted
him :* Phil. ii. 8. So He says of Himself, *Ought not Christ
first to suffer these things, and so enter into his glory?*
(Luke xxiv. 26.) Now this, indeed, it is pertinent to consider.
The Apostle is here upon the point of Christ's suffering ; that
is his theme, and therefore he is so particular in the ascend-
ing of Christ to His glory. Who, of those that would come
thither, will refuse to follow Him in the way wherein He led,
He, [ἀρχηγός] *the Leader of our faith?* (Heb. xii. 2.) And
who, of those that follow Him, will not love and delight to
follow Him through any way, the lowest and darkest? It is
excellent and safe, and then, it ends you see where.

Refl. 2. Think not strange of the Lord's method with His
Church, in bringing her to so low and desperate a posture
many times. Can she be in a condition more seemingly desperate than was her Head,—not only in ignominious sufferings,
but dead and laid in the grave, and the stone rolled to it and
sealed, and all made sure? And yet He rose and ascended,
and now sits in glory, and shall sit *till all his enemies become
his footstool.* Do not fear for Him, that they shall overtop,
yea, or be able to reach Him who is exalted higher than the
heavens ; neither be afraid for His Church, which is His body,

and, if her Head be safe and alive, cannot but partake of safety and life with Him. Though she were, to sight, dead and laid in the grave, yet shall she arise thence, and be more glorious than before, (Isa. xxvi. 19,) and still the deeper her distress, shall rise the higher in the day of deliverance.

Thus, in His dealing with a soul, observe the Lord's method. Think it not strange that He brings a soul low, very low, which He means to comfort and exalt very high in grace and glory; that He leads it by hell-gates to heaven; that it be at that point, *My God, my God, why hast Thou forsaken me?* Was not the Head put to use that word, and so to speak it, as the head speaks for the body, seasoning it for His members, and sweetening that bitter cup by His own drinking of it? O! what a hard condition may a soul be brought unto, and put to think, *Can He love me, and intend mercy for me, who leaves me to this?* And yet, in all, the Lord is preparing it thus for comfort and blessedness.

Refl. 3. Turn your thoughts more frequently to this excellent subject, the glorious high estate of our *great High Priest.* The angels admire this mystery, and we slight it! They rejoice in it, and we, whom it certainly more nearly concerns, are not moved with it; we do not draw that comfort and instruction from it, which it would plentifully afford, if it were sought after. It would comfort us against all troubles and fears to reflect, Is He not on high, who hath undertaken for us? Doth any thing befall us, but it is past first in Heaven? And shall any thing pass there to our prejudice or damage? He sits there, and is upon the council of all, who hath loved us, and given Himself for us; yea, who, as He descended thence for us, did likewise ascend thither again for us. He hath made our inheritance which He purchased, there sure to us, taking possession for us, and in our name, since He is there, not only as the Son of God, but as our Surety, and as our Head. And so the Believer may think himself even already possessed of this right, inasmuch as his Christ is there. The saints are glorified already in their Head. *Ubi*

Caput meum regnat, ibi me regnare credo : Where he reigns, there I believe myself to reign, says Augustine. And consider in all thy straits and troubles, outward or inward, they are not hid from Him. He knows them and feels them; thy compassionate High Priest hath a gracious sense of thy frailties, and griefs, fears, and temptations, and will not suffer thee to be surcharged. He is still presenting thy estate to the Father, and using that interest and power which He hath in His affection, for thy good. And what wouldst thou more? Art thou one whose heart desires to rest upon Him, and cleave to Him? Thou art knit so to Him, that His resurrection and glory secure thee thine. His life and thine are not two, but one 'life, as that of the head and members; and if He could not be overcome of death, thou canst not neither. Oh! that sweet word, *Because I live, ye shall live also.* (John xiv. 19.)

Let thy thoughts and carriage be moulded in this contemplation rightly, ever to look on thy exalted Head. Consider His glory ; see not only thy nature raised in Him above the angels, but thy person interested by faith in that His glory ; and then, think thyself too good to serve any base lust. Look down on sin and the world with a holy disdain, being united to Him who is so exalted and so glorious. And let not thy mind creep here: engage not thy heart to any thing that time and this earth can afford. Oh! why are we so little where there is such a spring of delightful and high thoughts for us? *If ye be risen with Christ, seek those things which are above, where He sits.* (Col. iii. 1.) What mean you? Are ye such as will let go your interest in this once crucified, and now glorified, Jesus? If not, why are ye not more conformable to it? Why does it not possess your hearts more? Ought it not to be thus? Should not our hearts be where our treasure, where our blessed Head is? Oh! how unreasonable, how unfriendly is it, how much may we be ashamed to have room in our hearts for earnest thoughts, or desires, or delights, about any thing besides Him?

Were this deeply wrought upon the hearts of those that

have a right in it, would there be found in them any attachment to the poor things that are passing away? Would death be a terrible word? Yea, would it not be one of the sweetest, most rejoicing thoughts, to solace and ease the heart under all pressures, to look forward to that day of liberty? This infectious disease * may keep possession all the winter, and grow hot with the year again. Do not flatter yourselves, and think it is past; you have yet remembering strokes to keep it in your eye. But, however, shall we abide always here? Or is there any reason, when things are duly weighed, why we should desire it? Well, if you would be untied beforehand, and so feel your separation from this world less, this is the only way: Look up to Him who draws up all hearts that do indeed behold Him. Then, I say, thy heart shall be removed beforehand; and the rest is easy and sweet. When that is done, all is gained. And consider, how He desires the completion of our union with Him. Shall it be His request and earnest desire, and shall it not be ours too, *thaw here He is, there we may be also?* (John xvii. 24.) Let us expect it with patient submission, yet striving by desires and suits, and looking out for our release from this body of sin and death.

CHAPTER IV.

Ver. 1. Forasmuch then as Christ hath suffered for us in the flesh, arm yourselves likewise with the same mind; for he that hath suffered in the flesh hath ceased from sin.

THE main of a Christian's duty lies in these two things, patience in suffering, and avoidance of sin, ἀνέχου καὶ ἀπέχου, and they have a natural influence each upon the other. Although affliction simply doth not, yet affliction sweetly and humbly carried, doth purify and disengage the heart from sin, wean it

* This probably refers to the Pestilence in 1665. See the lecture on chap. iv. 6. "Though the Pestilence doth not affright you so," &c.

from the world and the common ways of it. And again, holy
and exact walking keeps the soul in a sound, healthful temper,
and so enables it to patient suffering, to bear things more
easily; as a strong body endures fatigue, heat, cold, and hardship, with ease, a small part whereof would surcharge a sickly
constitution. The consciousness of sin, and careless unholy
courses, do wonderfully weaken a soul, and distemper it, so
that it is not able to endure much ; every little thing disturbs
it. Therefore, the Apostle hath reason, both to insist so much
on these two points in this Epistle, and likewise to interweave
the one so often with the other, pressing jointly throughout,
the cheerful bearing of all kinds of afflictions, and the careful
forbearing all kinds of sin ; and out of the one discourse, he
slides into the other ; as here.

And as the things agree in their nature, so, in their great
pattern and principle, Jesus Christ: and the Apostle still
draws both from thence : that of patience, ch. iii. v. 18, that
of holiness, here : *Forasmuch, then, as Christ hath suffered
for us*, &c.

The chief study of a Christian, and the very thing that
makes him to be a Christian, is, conformity with Christ.
*Summa religionis imitari quem colis : This is the sum of reli-
gion*, (said that wise heathen, Pythagoras,) *to be like him
whom thou worshippest*. But this example being in itself too
sublime, is brought down to our view in Christ; the brightness of God is veiled, and veiled in our own flesh, that we may
be able to look on it. The inaccessible light of the Deity is
so attempered in the humanity of Christ, that we may read
our lesson by it in Him, and may direct our walk by it. And
that truly is our only way ; there is nothing but wandering and
perishing in all other ways, nothing but darkness and misery
out of Him ; but *He that follows me*, says He, *shall not walk
in darkness*. John viii. 12. And therefore is He set before
us in the Gospel, in so clear and lively colours, that we may
make this our whole endeavour, to be like Him.

Consider here: 1. The high engagement to this conformity; 2. The nature of it; 3. The actual improvement of it.

1. The engagement lies in this, that He suffered for us. Of this we have treated before. Only, in reference to this, had He come down, as some have mis-imagined it, only to set us this perfect way of obedience, and give us an example of it in our own nature, this had been very much : that the Son of God should descend to teach wretched man, and the great King descend into man, and dwell in a tabernacle of clay, to set up a school in it, for such ignorant, accursed creatures, and should, in his own person, act the hardest lessons, both in doing and suffering, to lead us in both. But the matter goes yet higher than this. Oh ! how much higher hath He suffered, not simply as our rule, but as our surety, and in our stead ! *He suffered for us in the flesh.* We are the more obliged to make His suffering our example, because it was to us more than an example ; it was our ransom.

This makes the conformity reasonable in a double respect. [1.] It is *due* that we follow Him, who led thus as the *Captain of our Salvation ;* that we follow Him in suffering, and in doing, seeing both were so for us. It is strange how some armies have addicted themselves to their Head, so as to be at his call night and day, in summer and winter, to refuse no travail or endurance of hardship for him, and all only to please him, and serve his inclination and ambition ; as Cæsar's trained bands, especially the veterans, it is a wonder what they endured in counter-marches, and in traversing from one country to another. But besides that our Lord and Leader is so great and excellent, and so well deserves following for his own worth, this lays upon us an obligation beyond all conceiving, that he first suffered for us, that he endured such hatred of men, and such wrath of God the Father, and went through death, so vile a death, to procure our life. What can be too bitter to endure, or too sweet to forsake, to follow Him ? Were this duly considered, should we cleave to our lusts, or to our ease ? Should we not be willing to go through fire and water, yea, through death itself, yea, were it possible, through many deaths, to follow him.

[2.] Consider, as this conformity is *due*, so it is made *easy* by that His suffering for us. Our burden, which pressed us to hell, being taken off, is not all that is left to suffer or to do, as nothing? Our chains which bound us over to eternal death, being knocked off, shall we not walk, shall we not run, in His ways? Oh! think what that burden and yoke was which he hath eased us of, how heavy, how unsufferable it was, and then we shall think, what He so truly says, that all he lays on is sweet; *His yoke easy, and His burden light.* Oh! the happy change, to be rescued from the vilest slavery, and called to conformity and fellowship with the Son of God!

2. The nature of this conformity, (to shew the nearness of it,) is expressed in the very same terms as in the Pattern: it is not a remote resemblance, but the same thing, even *suffering in the flesh.* But that we may understand rightly what suffering is here meant, it is plainly this, *ceasing from sin.* So that *suffering in the flesh,* here, is not simply the enduring of afflictions, which is a part of the Christian's conformity to his Head, Christ, (Rom. viii. 29,) but implies a more inward and spiritual suffering. It is the suffering and the dying of our corruption, the taking away of the life of sin by the death of Christ: that death of His sinless flesh works in the Believer the death of sinful flesh, that is, the corruption of his nature, which is so usually in Scripture called *flesh.* Sin makes man base, drowns him in flesh and the lusts of it, makes the very soul become gross and earthly, turns it, as it were, to flesh. So the Apostle calls the very mind that is unrenewed, *a carnal mind:* Rom. viii. 7.

And what doth the mind of a natural man hunt after and run out into, from one day and year to another? Is it not on the things of this base world, and *(corporis negotium)* the concernment of his flesh? What would he have, but be accommodated to eat, and drink, and dress, and live at ease? *He minds earthly things,* savours and relishes them, and cares for them.

Examine the most of your pains and time, and your strongest desires, and most serious thoughts, whether they go not this way, to raise yourselves and yours in your worldly condition. Yea, the highest projects of the greatest natural spirits are but earth still, in respect of things truly spiritual. All their state designs go not beyond this poor life that perishes in the flesh, and is daily perishing, even while we are busiest in upholding it and providing for it. Present things and this lodge of clay, this flesh and its interest, take up most of our time and pains; the most? yea, all, till that change be wrought which the Apostle speaks of, till Christ be put on: Rom. xiii. 14. *Put ye on the Lord Jesus Christ,* and then, the other will easily follow, which follows in the words, *Make no provision for the flesh, to fulfil the lusts thereof.* Once in Christ, and then your necessary general care for this natural life will be regulated and moderated by the Spirit. And as for all unlawful and enormous desires of the flesh, you shall be rid of providing for these. Instead of all provision for the life of the flesh in that sense, there is another guest, and another life, for you now to wait on and furnish for. In them who are in Christ, that flesh is dead; they are freed from its drudgery. *He that hath suffered in the flesh, hath rested from sin.*

Ceased from sin.] He is at rest from it, a godly death, as they who *die in the Lord* rest from their labours. (Rev. xiv. 13.) He that hath suffered in the flesh, and is dead to it, dies indeed in the Lord, rests from the base turmoil of sin; it is no longer his master. As our sin was the cause of Christ's death, His death is the death of sin in us; and that, not simply as he bore a moral pattern of it, but as the real working cause of it, it hath an effectual influence on the soul, kills it to sin. *I am crucified with Christ,* says St. Paul. (Gal. ii. 20.) Faith so looks on the death of Christ, that it takes the impression of it, sets it on the heart, kills it unto sin. Christ and the believer do not only become one in law, so that His death stands for theirs, but one in nature, so that His death for sin causes theirs to it. They are *baptized into his death.* (Rom. vi. 3.)

T 2

This suffering in the flesh being unto death, and such a death (*crucifying*), hath indeed pain in it ; but what then ? It must be so like His, and the Believer be like Him, in willingly enduring it. All the pain of His suffering in the flesh, His love to us digested and went through with ; so, all the pain to our nature in severing and pulling us from our beloved sins, and in our dying to them, if His love be planted in our hearts, that will sweeten it, and make us delight in it. Love desires nothing more than likeness, and shares willingly in all with the party loved ; and above all love, this Divine love is purest and highest, and works most strongly that way ; takes pleasure in that pain, and is a voluntary death, as Plato calls love. It is *strong as death*, says Solomon. (Cant. viii. 6.) As death makes the strongest body fall to the ground, so doth the love of Christ make the most active and lively sinner dead to his sin ; and as death severs a man from his dearest and most familiar friends, thus doth the love of Christ, and his death flowing from it, sever the heart from its most beloved sins.

I beseech you, seek to have your hearts set against sin, to hate it, to wound it, and be dying daily to it. Be not satisfied, unless ye feel an abatement of it, and a life within you. Disdain that base service, and being bought at so high a rate, think yourselves too good to be slaves to any base lust. You are called to a more excellent and more honourable service. And of this suffering in the flesh, we may safely say, what the Apostle speaks of the sufferings with and for Christ, Rom. viii. 17, that the partakers of these sufferings are co-heirs of glory with Christ : *If we suffer thus with Him, we shall also be glorified with Him ;* if we die with Him, we shall live with him for ever.

3. We have the actual improvement of this Conformity : *Arm yourselves with the same mind,* or *thoughts* of this mortification. Death, taken naturally, in its proper sense, being an entire privation of life, admits not of degrees ; but this figurative death, this mortification of the flesh in a Christian, is gradual. In so far as he is renewed, and is animated and acted

on by the Spirit of Christ, he is thoroughly mortified; (for this death, and that new life joined with it, and here added, *ver. 2*, go together, and grow together;) but because he is not totally renewed, and there is in him the remains of that corruption still, which is here called flesh, therefore it is his great task, to be gaining further upon it, and overcoming and mortifying it every day. And to this tend the frequent exhortations of this nature: *Mortify your members that are on the earth.* So, Rom. vi., *Likewise reckon yourselves dead to sin,* and *Let it not reign in your mortal bodies.* Thus here, *Arm yourselves with the same mind,* or with this very thought. Consider and apply that suffering of Christ in the flesh, to the end that you with Him suffering in the flesh, may cease from sin. Think that it ought to be thus, and seek that it may be thus, with you.

Arm yourselves.] There is still fighting, and sin will be molesting you ; though wounded to death, yet will it struggle for life, and seek to wound its enemy; it will assault the graces that are in you. Do not think, if it be once struck, and you have given it a stab near to the heart, by the *sword of the Spirit,* that therefore it will stir no more. No, so long as you live in the flesh, in these bowels there will be remainders of the life of this flesh, your natural corruption ; therefore ye must be armed against it. Sin will not give you rest, so long as there is a drop of blood in its veins, one spark of life in it ; and that will be so long as you have life here. This old man is stout, and will fight himself to death; and at the weakest it will rouse up itself, and exert its dying spirits, as men will do sometimes more eagerly than when they were not so weak, nor so near death.

This the children of God often find to their grief, that corruptions which they thought had been cold dead, stir and rise up again, and set upon them. A passion or lust, that after some great stroke, lay a long while as dead, stirred not, and therefore they thought to have heard no more of it, though it shall never recover fully again, to be lively as before, yet will revive in such a measure as to molest, and possibly to foil them yet again.   Therefore is it continually necessary that they live in arms, and put them not off to their dying day; till they put off the body, and be altogether free of the flesh. You may take the Lord's promise for victory in the end ; that shall not fail ; but do not promise yourself ease in the way, for that will not hold. If at some times you be undermost, give not all for lost : he hath often won the day, who hath been foiled and wounded in the fight.   But likewise take not all for won, so as to have no more conflict, when sometimes you have the better, as in particular battles.   Be not desperate when you lose, nor secure when you gain them : when it is worst with you, do not throw away your arms, nor lay them away when you are at best.

Now, the way to be armed is this, *the same mind :* How would my Lord, Christ, carry himself in this case? And what was *His* business in all places and companies ? Was is not to do the will, and advance the glory of his Father? If 1 be injured and reviled, consider how would He do in this ? Would He repay one injury with another, one reproach with another reproach ? No, *being reviled, he reviled not again.* Well, through His strength, this shall be my way too. Thus ought it to be with the Christian, framing all his ways, and words, and very thoughts, upon that model, *the mind of Christ,* and study-ing in all things to walk even as he walked ; studying it much, as the reason and rule of mortification, and drawing from it, as the real cause and spring of mortification.

The pious contemplation of His death will most powerfully kill the love of sin in the soul, and kindle an ardent hatred of it. The Believer, looking on his Jesus as crucified for him and *wounded for his transgressions,* and taking in deep thoughts of his spotless innocency, which deserved no such thing, and of his matchless love, which yet endured it all for him, will then naturally think, Shall I be a friend to that which was His deadly enemy ?   Shall sin be sweet to me, which was so bitter to Him, and that for my sake ?   Shall I ever lend it a good look, or entertain a favourable thought of that which shed my Lord's blood? Shall I live in that for which He died, and died to kill it in me? Oh! let it not be.

To the end it may not be, let such really apply *that* Death, to work this on the soul; (for this is always to be added, and is the main thing indeed;) by holding and fastening that Death close to the soul, effectually to kill the effects of sin in it; to stifle and crush them dead, by pressing that death on the heart; looking on it, not only as a most complete model, but as having a most effectual virtue for this effect; and desiring Him, entreating our Lord himself, who communicates Himself and the virtue of His death to the Believer, that He would powerfully cause it to flow in upon us, and let us feel the virtue of it.

It is, then, the only thriving and growing life, to be much in the lively contemplation and application of Jesus Christ; to be continually studying Him, and conversing with Him, and drawing from Him, *receiving of his fulness, grace for grace.* (John i. 16.) Wouldst thou have much power against sin, and much increase of holiness, let thine eye be much on Christ; set thine heart on Him; let it dwell in Him, and be still with Him. When sin is likely to prevail in any kind, go to Him, tell Him of the insurrection of His enemies, and thy inability to resist, and desire Him to suppress them, and to help thee against them, that they may gain nothing by their stirring, but some new wound. If thy heart begin to be taken with, and move towards sin, lay it before Him; the beams of His love shall eat out that fire of those sinful lusts. Wouldst thou have thy pride, and passions, and love of the world, and self-love, killed, go sue for the virtue of His death, and that shall do it. Seek His Spirit— the Spirit of meekness, and humility, and Divine love. Look on Him, and He shall draw thy heart heavenwards, and unite it to Himself, and make it like Himself. And is not that the thing thou desirest?

Ver 2. That he no longer should live the rest of his time in the flesh to the lusts of men, but to the will of God.

Ver. 3. For the time past of our life may suffice us to have wrought the will of the Gentiles, when we walked in lasciviousness, lusts, excess of wine, revellings, banquetings, and abominable idolatries.

THE chains of sin are so strong, and so fastened on our nature, that there is in us no power to break them off, till a mightier and stronger Spirit than our own come into us. The Spirit of Christ dropped into the soul, makes it able to *break through a troop, and leap over a wall,* as David speaks of himself, when furnished with the strength of his God. (Psal. xviii. 29.) Men's resolutions fall to nothing; and as a prisoner who attempts to escape, and does not, is bound faster, thus usually it is with men in their self-purposes of forsaking sin: they leave out Christ in the work, and so remain in their captivity, yea, it grows upon them. And while we press them to free them-selves, and shew not Christ to them, we put them upon an im-possibility. But a look to Him makes it feasible and easy. Faith in Him, and that love to Him which faith begets, break through and surmount all difficulties. It is the powerful love of Christ, that kills the love of sin, and kindles the love of holi-ness in the soul; makes it a willing sharer in His death, and so, a happy partaker of His life. For that always follows, and must of necessity, as here is added: *He that hath suffered in the flesh, hath ceased from sin,*—is crucified and dead to it; but he loses nothing; yea, it is his great gain, to lose that deadly life of the flesh for a new spiritual life, a life indeed *living unto God:* that is the end why he so dies that he may thus live—*That he no longer should live to the lusts of men,* and yet, live far better, *live to the will of God.* He that is one with Christ by believing, is one with Him throughout, in death and in life. As Christ rose from the dead, so he that is dead to sin with Him, through the power of His death, rises to that new life with Him, through the power of His resur-rection. And these two constitute our sanctification, which, whosoever do partake of Christ, and are found in Him, do certainly draw from Him. Thus are they joined, Rom. vi. 11: *Likewise reckon you yourselves dead indeed to sin, but alive to God,* and both, *through Christ Jesus our Lord.*

All they who do really come to Jesus Christ, as they come to Him as their Saviour to be clothed with Him, and made righteous by Him, so they come likewise to Him as their Sanctifier, to be made new and holy by Him, to die and live with Him, to *follow the Lamb wheresoever he goes,* through the hardest sufferings, and death itself. And this spiritual suffering and dying with Him, is the universal way of all his followers; they are all martyrs thus in the crucifying of sinful flesh, and so dying for Him, and with Him. And they may well go cheerfully through. Though it bear the unpleasant name of *death,* yet as the other death is, (which makes it so little terrible, yea, often to appear so very desirable to them,) so is this, the way to a far more excellent and happy life; so that they may pass through it gladly, both for the company and the end of it. It is with Christ they go into His death, as unto life in His life. Though a believer might be free from these terms, he would not. No, surely. Could he be content with that easy life of sin, instead of the Divine life of Christ? No, he will do thus, and *not accept of deliverance, that he may obtain* (as the Apostle speaks of the martyrs) *a better resurrection:* Heb. xi. 35. Think on it again, you to whom your sins are dear still, and this life sweet; you are yet far from Christ and His life.

The Apostle, with the intent to press this more home, expresses more at large the nature of the opposite estates and lives that he speaks of, and so, 1. Sets before his Christian brethren the dignity of that new life; and then, 2. By a particular reflection upon the former life, he presses the change. The former life he calls, a living *to the lusts of men;* this new spiritual life, a living *to the will of God.*

The lusts of men.] Such as are common to the corrupt nature of man; such as every man may find in himself, and perceive in others. The Apostle, in the third verse more particularly, for further clearness, specifies those kinds of men that were most notorious in these lusts, and those kinds of lusts that were most notorious in men. Writing to the dispersed Jews, he calls sinful lusts the *will of the Gentiles,* as having least control of contrary light in them ; (and yet, the Jews walked in the same, though they had the Law as a light and rule for avoiding of them ;) and implies, that these lusts were unbeseeming even their former condition as Jews, but much more unsuitable to them, as now Christians. Some of the grossest of these lusts he names, meaning all the rest, all the ways of sin, and so representing their vileness in the more lively manner. Not, as some take it, when they hear of such heinous sins, as if it were to lessen the evil of sins of a more civil nature by the comparison, or as if freedom from these were a blameless condition, and a change of it needless ; no, the Holy Ghost means it just contrary, that we may judge of all sin, and of our sinful nature, by our estimate of those sins that are most discernible and abominable. All sin, though not equal in degree, yet is of one nature, and originally springs from one root, arising from the same unholy nature of man, and contrary to the same holy nature and will of God.

So then, 1. Those who walk in these highways of impiety, and yet will have the name of *Christians,* they are the shame of Christians, and the professed enemies of Jesus Christ, and of all others the most hateful to Him : they seem to have taken on His name, for no other end than to shame and disgrace it. But He will vindicate himself, and the blot shall rest upon these impudent persons, who dare hold up their faces in the Church of God as parts of it, and are indeed nothing but the dishonour of it, spots and blots ; who dare profess to worship God as His people, and remain unclean, riotous, and profane persons. How suits thy sitting here before the Lord, and thy sitting with vile ungodly company on the ale-bench ? How agrees the word, sounds it well, There goes a drunken Christian, an unclean, a basely covetous, or earthly-minded, Christian ?

And the naming of the latter is not besides the text, but agreeable to the very words of it; for the Apostle warrants us to take it under the name of *idolatry*, and in that name he reckons it to be mortified by a Christian: Col. iii. 5: *Mortify therefore your members which are upon the earth, fornication, uncleanness, inordinate affection, evil concupiscence, and covetousness, which is* IDOLATRY.

2. But yet, men who are someway exempted from the blot of these foul impieties, may still remain slaves to sin, alive to it, and dead to God, living to the lusts of men, and not to the will of God, pleasing others and themselves, and displeasing Him. And the smoothest, best-bred, and most moralized natural man, is in this base thraldom; and he is the more miserable, in that he dreams of liberty in the midst of his chains, thinks himself clean by looking on those that wallow in gross profaneness; takes measure of himself by the most crooked lives of ungodly men about him, and so thinks himself very straight; but lays not the straight rule of the will of God to his ways and heart, which if he did, he would then discover much crookedness in his ways, and much more in his heart, that now he sees not, but takes it to be square and even.

Therefore I advise and desire you to look more narrowly to yourselves in this, and see whether you be not still living to your own lusts and wills instead of to God, seeking, in all your ways, to advance and please yourselves, and not Him. Is not the bent of your hearts set that way? Do not your whole desires and endeavours run in that channel, how you and yours may be somebody, and how you may have wherewithal to serve the flesh, and to be accounted of and respected amongst men? And if we trace it home, all a man's honouring and pleasing of others, tends to, and ends in, pleasing of himself: it resolves into that. And is it not so meant by him? He pleases men, either that he may gain by them, or be respected by them, or that something that is still pleasing to himself, may be the return of it. So, self is the grand idol, for which all other heart-idolatries are committed; and, indeed, in the unrenewed heart there is no scarcity of them. Oh! what multitudes, what heaps, if the wall were digged through, and the light of God going before us, and leading us in to see them! The natural motion and way of the natural heart, is no other than still seeking out new inventions, a forge of new gods, still either forming them to itself, or worshipping those it hath already framed; committing spiritual fornication from God, with the creature, and multiplying lovers every where, as it is tempted; as the Lord complains of His people, *upon every high hill, and under every green tree.* (Jer. ii. 20; iii. 6.)

You will not believe so much ill of yourselves, will not be convinced of this unpleasant but necessary truth; and this a part of our self-pleasing, that we please ourselves in this, that we will not see it, either in our callings and ordinary ways, or in our religious exercises. For even in these we naturally aim at nothing but ourselves; either our reputation, or, at best, our own safety and peace; either to stop the cry of conscience for the present, or to escape the wrath that is to come; but not in a spiritual regard of the will of God, and out of pure love to Himself for Himself: yet thus it should be, and that love, the divine fire in all our sacrifices. The carnal mind is in the dark, and sees not its vileness in living to itself, will not confess it to be so. But when God comes into the soul, He lets it see itself, and all its idols and idolatries, and forces it to abhor and loathe itself for all its abominations; and having discovered its filthiness to itself, then He purges and cleanses it for Himself, *from all its filthiness, and from all its idols,* (Ezek. xxxvi. 25,) according to His promise, and comes in and takes possession of it for Himself, enthrones Himself in the heart. And it is never right nor happy till that be done.

But to the will of God.] We readily take any little slight change for true conversion, but we may see here that we mistake it; it doth not barely knock off some obvious apparent enormities, but casts all in a new mould, alters the whole frame of the heart and life, kills a man, and makes him alive again. And this new life is contrary to the old: for the change is made with that intent, *that he live no longer to the lusts of men, but to the will of God.* He is now, indeed, *a new creature,* having a new judgment and new thoughts of things, and so, accordingly, new desires and affections, and answerably to these, new actions: *Old things are past away and dead, and all things are become new.* (2 Cor. v. 17.)

Political men have observed, that in states, if alterations must be, it is better to alter many things than a few. And physicians have the same remark for one's habit and custom for bodily health, upon the same ground; because things do so relate one to another, that except they be adapted and suited together in the change, it avails not; yea, it sometimes proves the worse in the whole, though a few things in particular seem to be bettered. Thus, half-reformations in a Christian turn to his prejudice: it is only best to be reformed throughout, and to give up with all idols; not to live one half to himself and the world, and, as it were, another half to God, for that is but falsely so, and, in reality, it cannot be. The only way is, to make a heap of all, to have all sacrificed together, and to live to no lust, but altogether and only to God. Thus it must be: there is no monster in the new creation, no half new creature, *either all, or not at all,* ὅλος ἢ μὴ ὅλως. We have to deal with the Maker and the Searcher of the heart in this turn, and He will have nothing unless He have the heart, and none of that neither, unless He have it all. If thou pass over into His kingdom, and become His subject, thou must have Him for thy only sovereign. *Omnisque potestus impatiens consortis:* Royalty can admit of no rivalry, and least of all, the highest and best of all. If Christ be thy king, then His laws and sceptre must rule all in thee: thou must now acknowledge no foreign power; that will be treason.

And if He be thy husband, thou must renounce all others. Wilt thou provoke Him to jealousy? Yea, beware how thou givest a thought or a look of thy affection any other way, for He will spy it, and will not endure it. The title of a husband is as strict and tender, as the other of a king.

It is only best to be thus: it is thy great advantage and happiness, to be thus entirely freed from so many tyrannous base lords, and to be now subject only to one, and He so great, and withal so gracious and sweet a king, *the Prince of Peace.* Thou wast hurried before, and racked with the very multitude of them. Thy lusts, so many cruel task-masters over thee, they gave thee no rest, and the work they set thee to was base and slavish, more than the burdens, and pots, and toiling in the clay of Egypt; thou wast held to work in, the earth, to pain, and to soil and foul thyself with their drudgery.

Now, thou hast but One to serve, and that is a great ease; and it is no slavery, but true honour, to serve so excellent a Lord, and in so high services; for He puts thee upon nothing but what is neat, and what is honourable. Thou art as *a vessel of honour* in His house, for his best employments. Now, thou art not in pain how to please this person and the other, nor needest thou vex thyself to gain men, to study their approbation and honour, nor to keep to thine own lusts and observe their will. Thou hast none but thy God to please in all; and if He be pleased, thou mayest disregard who be displeased. His will is not fickle and changing as men's are, and as thine own is. He hath told thee what He likes and desires, and He alters not; so that now thou knowest whom thou hast to do withal, and what to do, whom to please, and what will please Him, and this cannot but much settle thy mind, and put thee at ease. Thou mayest say heartily, as rejoicing in the change of so many for one, and of such for such a One, as the Church says, Isa. xxvi. 13, *O Lord our God, other lords beside Thee have had dominion over me, but now, by Thee only will I make mention of Thy name;* now, none but Thyself, not so much as the *name* of them any more, away with them: through Thy grace, Thou only shalt be my God. It cannot endure that any thing be named with Thee.

Now, 1. that it may be thus, that we may wholly live *to the will of God,* we must *know* His will, what it is. Persons grossly ignorant of God and of His will, cannot live to Him.

We cannot *have fellowship with Him, and walk in darkness;* for H E *is light.* (1 John i. 6, 7.) This takes off a great many amongst us, who have not so much as a common notion of the will of God. But besides, that knowledge which is a part, and (I may say) the first part, of the renewed image of God, is not a natural knowledge of spiritual things, merely, attained by human teaching or industry, but it is a beam of God's own, issuing from Himself, both enlightening and enlivening the whole soul: it gains the affection and stirs to action, and so, indeed, it acts, and increases by acting; for the more we walk according to what we know of the will of God, the more we shall be advanced to know more. This is the real *proving what is His good, and holy, and acceptable will.* (Rom. xii. 2.) So says Christ, *If any one will do the will of my Father, he shall know of the doctrine.* (John vii. 17.) Our lying off from the lively úse of known truth, keeps us low in the knowledge of God and communion with Him.

2. So then, upon that knowledge of God's will, where it is spiritual and from Himself, follows the suiting of the heart with it, the affections taking the stamp of it, and agreeing with it, *receiving the truth in the love of it,* so that the heart may be transformed into it; and now it is not driven to obedience violently, but sweetly moving to it, by love within the heart, framed to the love of God, and so of His will.

3. As Divine knowledge begets this affection, so this affection will bring forth action, real obedience. For these three are inseparably linked, and each dependent on, and the product of the others. The affection is not blind, but flowing from knowledge; nor the actual obedience constrained, but flowing from affection; and the affection is not idle, seeing it brings forth obedience; nor is the knowledge dead, seeing it begets affection.

Thus the renewed, the living Christian, is all for God, a sacrifice entirely offered up to God, and *a living sacrifice,* which lives to God. He takes no more notice of his own carnal will; hath renounced that to embrace the holy will of

God ; and therefore, though there is a contrary law and will in him, yet he does not acknowledge it, but only the law of Christ, as now established in him ; that law of love, by which he is sweetly and willingly led. Real obedience consults not now with flesh and blood, what will please them, but only inquires what will please his God, and knowing His mind, thus resolves to demur no more, nor to ask consent of any other ; that he will do, and it is reason enough to him: My Lord wills it, therefore, in His strength, I will do it ; for now I live to His will, it is my life to study and obey it.

Now, we know what is the true character of the redeemed of Christ, that they are freed from the service of themselves and of the world, yea, dead to it, and have no life but for God, as altogether His.

Let it, then, be our study and ambition, to attain this, and to grow in it ; to be daily further freed from all other ways and desires, and more wholly addicted to the will of our God ; displeased when we find any thing else stir or move within us but that, making that the spring of our motion in every work.

1. Because we know that His sovereign will is (and is most justly) the glory of His name, therefore we are not to rest till this be set up in our view, as our end in all things, and we are to account all our plausible doings as hateful, (as indeed they are,) which are not aimed at this end ; yea, endeavouring to have it as frequently and as expressly before us as we can, still keeping our eye on the mark ; throwing away, yea, undoing our own interest, not seeking ourselves in any thing, but Him in all.

2. As living to His will is in all things to be our end, so, in all the way to that end, it is to be the rule of every step. For we cannot attain His end but in his way ; nor can we attain it without a resignation of the way to His prescription, taking all our directions from Him, how we shall honour him in all. The soul that lives to Him, hath enough to make any thing not only warrantable but amiable in seeking His will ; and he not only does it, but delights to do it. This is to live to Him,

to find it our life; as we speak of a work wherein men do most, and with most delight employ themselves. That such a lust be crucified, is it thy will, Lord? Then, no more advising, no more delay. How dear soever that was when I lived to it, it is now as hateful, seeing I live to Thee who hatest it. Wilt thou have me forget an injury, though a great one, and love the person that hath wronged me? While I lived to myself and my passions, this had been hard. But now, how sweet is it! seeing I live to Thee, and am glad to be put upon things most opposite to my corrupt heart; glad to trample upon my own will, to follow Thine. And this I daily aspire to and aim at, to have no will of my own, but that Thine be in me, that I may live to Thee, as one with Thee, and Thou my rule and delight; yea, not to use the very natural comforts of my life, but for Thee; to eat, and drink, and sleep for Thee; and not to please myself, but to be enabled to serve and please Thee; to make one offering of myself and all my actions to Thee, my Lord.

Oh! it is the only sweet life, to be living thus, and daily learning to live more fully thus! It is heaven this, a little scantling of it here, and a pledge of whole heaven. This is, indeed, the life of Christ, not only like His, but one with His; it is His Spirit, His life derived into the soul, and, therefore, both the most excellent, and, certainly, the most permanent life, for *He dieth no more*, and therefore this His life cannot be extinguished. Hence is the perseverance of the saints; because they have one life with Christ, and so are alive unto God, once for all, for ever.

It is true, the former custom of sin would plead with grace old possession; and this the Apostle implies here, that because *formerly we lived* to our lusts, they will urge that; but he teaches us to beat it directly back on them, and turn the edge of it as a most strong reason against them: True, you had so long time of us, the more is our sorrow and shame, and the more reason that it be no longer so.

The rest of his time in the flesh, (that is, in this body,) is not to be spent as the foregoing, *in living to the flesh,* that is, the corrupt lusts of it, and the common ways of the world; but, as often as the Christian looks back on that, he is to find it as a spur in his side, to be the more earnest, and more wholly busied in living much to God, having lived so long contrary to Him, in living to the :flesh. *The past may suffice.* There is a rhetorical figure (*a lyptote*) in that expression, meaning much more than the words express: It is *enough*—oh! *too much,* to have lived so long so miserable a life.

Now says the Christian, O corrupt lusts and deluding world, look for no more; I have served you too long. The rest, whatsoever it is, must be to the Lord, to live to Him by whom I live; and ashamed and grieved I am, I was so long in beginning; so much past, it may be the most of my short race past, before I took notice of God, or looked [towards Him. Oh! how have I lost, and worse than lost, all my by-past days! Now, had I the advantage and abilities of many men, and were I to live many ages, all should be to live to my God, and honour Him. And what strength I have, and what time I have, through His grace, shall be wholly His. And when any Christian hath thus resolved, his intended life being so imperfect, and the time so short, the poorness of the offer would break his heart, were there not an eternity before him, wherein he shall live to his God, and in Him, without blemish and without end.

Spiritual things being once discerned by a spiritual light, the whole soul is carried after them; and the ways of holiness are never truly sweet till they be thoroughly embraced, and till ·there oe a full renunciation of all that is contrary to them. All his former ways of wandering from God, are very hateful to a Christian who is indeed returned and brought home ; and those are most of all hateful, wherein he hath most wandered and most delighted. A sight of Christ gains the heart, makes it break from all entanglements both of its own lusts, and of the profane world about it. And these are the two things the Apostle here aims at: exhorting Christians to the study of newness of life, and shewing the necessity of it, that they cannot be Christians without it. He opposes their new estate and engagement, to the old customs of their former condition, and to the continuing custom and conceit of the ungodly world, that against both, they may maintain that rank and dignity to which now they are called, and, in a holy disdain of both, walk as the redeemed of the Lord. Their own former custom he speaks to in these verses, and to the custom and opinion of the world, in those which follow. Both of these will set strong upon a man, especially while he is yet weak, and newly entered into that new estate.

Now, as to the first, his old acquaintance, his wonted lusts, will not fail to bestir themselves to accost him in their most obliging, familiar way, and represent their long-continued friendship. But the Christian, following the principles of his new being, will not entertain any long discourse with them, but cut them short, tell them that the change he hath made he avows, and finds it so happy, that these former delights may put off hopes of regaining him. No, they dress themselves in their best array, and put on all their ornaments, and say, as that known word of the courtesan, *I am the same I was,* the Christian will answer, as he did, *I am not the same I was.* And not only thus will he turn off the plea of former acquaintance that sin makes, but turn it back upon it, as, in his present thoughts, making much against it. The longer I was so deluded, the more reason now that I be wiser; the more time so misspent, the more pressing necessity of redeeming it. Oh! I have too long lived in that vile slavery. All was but husks I fed on. *I was laying out my money for that which was no bread, and my labour for that which satisfied not.* (Isa. lv. 2.) Now, I am on the pursuit of a good that I am sure will satisfy, will fill the largest desires of my soul; and shall I be sparing and slack, or shall any thing call me off from it? Let it not be. I who took so much pains, early and late, to serve and sacrifice to so base a god, shall I not now live more to my new Lord, the living God, and sacrifice my time and strength, and my whole self to Him?

And this is still the regret of the sensible Christian, that he cannot attain to that unwearied diligence and that strong bent of affection, in seeking communion with God, and living to Him, which once he had for the service of sin: he wonders that it should be thus with him, not to equal that which it were so reasonable that he should so far exceed.

It is, beyond expression, a thing to be lamented, that so small a number of men regard God, the author of their being, that so few live to Him in whom they live, returning that being and life they have, and all their enjoyments, as is due, to Him from whom they all flow. And then, how pitiful is it, that the small number who are thus minded, mind it so remissly and coldly, and are so far outstripped by the *children of this world,* who follow painted follies and lies with more eagerness and industry, than the *children of wisdom* do that certain and solid blessedness which they seek after! *Plus illi ad vanitatem, quam nos ad veritatem:* They are more intent upon vanity, than we upon verity. Strange! that men should do so much violency one to another, and to themselves in body and mind, for trifles and chaff; and that there is so little to be found of that allowed and commanded *violence,* for *a kingdom,* and *such a kingdom, that cannot be moved* (Heb. xii. 28); a word too high for all the monarchies under the sun.

And should not our diligence and violence in this so worthy a design, be so much the greater, the later we begin to pursue it? They tell it of Cæsar, that when he passed into Spain, meeting there with Alexander's statue, it occasioned him to weep, considering that he was up so much more early, having performed so many conquests in those years, wherein he thought he himself had done nothing, and was yet but beginning. Truly, it will be a sad thought to a really renewed mind, to look back on the flower of youth and strength as lost in vanity; if not in gross profaneness, yet, in self-serving and self-pleasing, and in ignorance and neglect of God. And perceiving their few years so far spent ere they set out, they will account days precious, and make the more haste, and desire, with holy David,

enlarged hearts to run the way of God's commandments.
(Psal. cxix. 32.) They will study to live much in a little time;
and, having lived all the past time to no purpose, will be sensible they have none now to spare upon the lusts and ways of the
flesh, and vain societies and visits. Yea, they will be redeeming all they can even from their necessary affairs, for that which
is more necessary than all other necessities, *that one thing
needful,* to learn the will of our God, and to live to it; this is
our business, our *high calling,* the main and most excellent of
all our employments.

Not that we are to cast off our particular callings, or omit
due diligence in them; for that will prove a snare, and involve
a person in things more opposite to godliness. But certainly,
this *living to God* requires, 1. A fit measuring of thy own
ability for affairs, and, as far as thou canst choose, fitting thy
load to thy shoulders, not surcharging thyself with it. An
excessive burden of business, either by the greatness or the
multitude of them, will not fail to entangle thee and depress
thy mind, and will hold it so down, that thou shalt not find it
possible to walk upright and look upwards, with that freedom
and frequency that becomes heirs of Heaven.

2. The measure of thy affairs being adapted, look to thy
affection in them, that it be regulated too. Thy heart may be
engaged in thy little business as much, if thou watch it not, as
in many and great affairs. A man may drown in a little brook
or pool, as well as in a great river, if he be down and plunge
himself into it, and put his head under water. Some care thou
must have, that thou mayest not care. Those things that are
thorns indeed, thou must make a hedge of them, to keep out
those temptations that accompany sloth, and extreme want that
waits on it; but let them be the hedge: suffer them not to
grow within the garden. *If riches increase, set not thy heart
on them,* nor set them in thy heart. That place is due to
Another, is made to be the garden of thy beloved Lord, made
for the best plants and flowers, and there they ought to grow,
the love of God, and faith, and meekness, and the other

fragrant graces of the Spirit. And know, that this is no common nor easy matter, to keep the heart disengaged in the midst of affairs, that still it be reserved for Him whose right it is.

3. Not only labour to keep thy mind spiritual in itself, but by it put a spiritual stamp even upon thy temporal employments ; and so thou shalt live to God, not only without prejudice of thy calling, but even in it, and shalt converse with Him in thy shop, or in the field, or in thy journey, doing all in obedience to Him, and offering all, and thyself withal, as a sacrifice to Him ; thou still with Him, and He still with thee, in all. This is to live to the will of God indeed, to follow His direction, and intend his glory in all. Thus the wife, in the very oversight of her house, and the husband, in his affairs abroad, may be living to God, raising their low employments to a high quality this way : Lord, even this mean work I do for Thee, complying with Thy will, who hast put me in this station, and given me this task. *Thy will be done.* Lord, I offer up even this work to Thee. Accept of me, and of my desire to obey Thee in all. And as in their work, so, in their refreshments and rest, Christians do all for Him. *Whether ye eat or drink,* says the Apostle, 1 Cor. x. 31, *or whatsoever ye do, do all to the glory of God :* doing all for this reason, because it is His will, and for this end, that He may have glory ; bending the use of all our strength and all His mercies that way : setting this mark on all our designs and ways, this for the glory of my God, and, this further for His glory, and so from one thing to another throughout our whole life. This is the art of keeping the heart spiritual in all affairs, yea, of spiritualizing the affairs themselves in their use, that in themselves are earthly. This is the *elixir* that turns lower metal into gold, the mean actions of this life, in a Christian's hands, into obedience and holy offerings unto God.

And were we acquainted with the way of intermixing holy thoughts, ejaculatory eyeings of God, in our ordinary ways, it would keep the heart in a sweet temper all the day long, and have an excellent influence into all our ordinary actions and holy performances, at those times when we apply ourselves solemnly to them. Our hearts would be near them, not so far off to seek and call in, as usually they are through the neglect of this. This were to *walk with God* indeed; to go all the day long as in our Father's hand; whereas, without this, our praying morning and evening looks but as a formal visit, not delighting in that constant converse which yet is our happiness and honour, and makes all estates sweet. This would refresh us in the hardest labour; as they that carry the spices from Arabia are refreshed with the smell of them in their journey, and some observe that it keeps their strength, and frees them from fainting.

If you will then live to God indeed, be not satisfied without the constant regard of Him; and whosoever hath attained most of it, study it yet more, *to set the Lord always before you*, as David professeth, and then shall you have that comfort that he adds,—He shall be still *at your right hand, that you shall not be moved.* (Psal. xvi. 8.)

And you that are yet to begin this, think what His patience is, that after you have slighted so many calls, you may yet begin to seek Him, and live to Him. And then, consider, if you still despise all this goodness, how soon it may be otherwise; you may be past the reach of this call, and may not begin, but be cut off for ever from the hopes of it. Oh, how sad an estate! and the more so, by the remembrance of these slighted offers and invitations! Will you then yet return? You that would share in Christ, let go those lusts to which you have hitherto lived, and embrace Him, and in Him there is spirit and life for you. He shall enable you to live this heavenly life to the will of God, *His God and your God, and His Father and your Father.* (John xx. 17.) Oh! delay no longer this happy change. How soon may that puff of breath that is in thy nostrils, who hearest this, be extinguished! And art thou willing to die in thy sins, rather than that they should die before thee? Thinkest thou it a pain to live to the will of

God? Surely it will be more pain to lie under His eternal
wrath. Oh! thou knowest not how sweet they find it who
have tried it. Or thinkest thou, I will afterwards? Who can
make thee sure either of that afterwards, or of that will? If
but afterwards, why not now presently, without further debate? Hast thou not served sin long enough? May not the
time passed in that service suffice? Yea, is it not too much?
Wouldst thou only live unto God as little time as may be,
and think the dregs of thy life good enough for Him? What
ingratitude and gross folly is this! Yea, though thou wert
sure of coming unto Him and being accepted, yet, if thou
knewest Him in any measure, thou wouldst not think it a privilege to defer it, but willingly choose to be free from the
world and thy lusts, to be immediately His, and wouldst, with
David, *make haste, and not delay to keep His righteous judgments.* All the time thou livest without Him, what a filthy
wretched life is it, if that can be called life that is without
Him! To live to sin, is to live still in a dungeon; but to live
to the will of God, is to walk in liberty and light, to walk by
light unto light, by the beginnings of it to the fulness of it,
which is in His presence.

Ver. 4. Wherein they think it strange that you run not with them to the
same excess of riot, speaking evil of you;
Ver. 5. Who shall give account to Him that is ready to judge the quick
and the dead.

GRACE, until it reach its home and end in glory, is still in
conflict; there is a restless party within and without, yea, the
whole world against it. It is a stranger here, and is accounted and used as such. *They think it strange that you
run not with them, and they speak evil of you:* these wondering thoughts they vent in reproaching words.

In these two verses we have these three things: 1. The
Christian's opposite course to that of the World; 2. The
World's opposite thoughts and speeches of this course; 3. The
supreme and final judgment of both.

1. The opposite course, in that *They run to excesses of riot —You run not with them.* They run to excesses (ἀσωτίας) *of riot* or *luxury.* Though all natural men are not, in the grossest kind, guilty of this, yet they are all of them in some way truly riotous or luxurious, lavishing away themselves, and their days, upon the poor perishing delights of sin, each according to his own palate and humour. As all persons that are riotous, in the common sense of it, gluttons or drunkards, do not love the same kind of meats or drink, but have several relishes or appetites, yet they agree in the nature of the sin; so, the notion enlarged after that same manner, to the different custom of corrupt nature, takes in all the ways of sin: some are glutting in, and continually drunk with pleasures and carnal enjoyments; others, with the cares of this life, which our Saviour reckons with surfeiting and drunkenness, as being a kind of it, and surcharging the heart as they do: as there he expresses it, (Luke xxi. 34,) *Take heed to yourselves, lest at any time your hearts be overcharged with surfeiting and drunkenness, and cares of this life.* Whatsoever it is that draws away the heart from God, that, how plausible soever, doth debauch and destroy us: we spend and undo ourselves upon it, as the word signifies, ἀσωτία, a making havock of all. And the other word, ἀνάχυσις, signifies profusion and dissolute lavishing, a pouring out of the affections upon vanity; they are scattered and defiled as water spilt upon the ground, that cannot be cleansed nor gathered up again. And, indeed, it passes all our skill and strength, to recover and recollect our hearts for God; He only can do it for Himself. He who made it can gather it, and cleanse it, and make it anew, and unite it to Himself. O! what a scattered, broken, unstable thing is the carnal heart, till it be changed, falling in love with every gay folly it meets withal, and running out to rest profusely upon things like its vain self, which suit and agree with it, and serve its lusts! It can dream and muse upon these long enough, upon any thing that feeds the earthliness or pride of it; it can be prodigal of hours, and let out floods of thoughts, where a little is too much, but is bounded and straitened where all are too little; hath not one fixed thought in a whole day to spare for God.

And truly, this *running out* of the heart is a continual drunkenness and madness: it is not capable of reason, and will not be stopped in its current by any persuasion; it is *mad upon its idols*, as the Prophet speaks, Jer. l. 38. You may as well speak to a river in its course, and bid it stay, as speak to an impenitent sinner in the course of his iniquity! And all the other means you can use, is but as the putting of your finger to a rapid stream, to stay it. But there is a Hand can both stop and turn the most impetuous torrent of the heart, be it even *the heart of a King*, which will least endure any other controlment. (Prov. xxi. 1.)

Now, as the ungodly world naturally moves to this profusion with a strong and swift motion, *runs* to it, so, it *runs together* to it, and that makes the current both the stronger and the swifter; as a number of brooks, falling into one main channel, make a mighty stream. And every man naturally is, in his birth, and in the course of his life, just as a brook, that of itself is carried to that stream of sin which is in the world, and then falling into it, is carried rapidly along with it. And if every sinner, taken apart, be so incontrovertible by all created power, how much more hard a task is a public reformation, the turning of a land from its course of wickedness! All that is set to dam up their way, doth at the best but stay them a little, and they swell, and rise, and run over with more noise and violence than if they had not been stopped. Thus we find outward restraints prove, and thus the very public judgments of God on us. They may have made a little interruption, but, upon the abatement of them, the course of sin, in all kinds, seems to be now more fierce, as it were, to regain the time lost in that constrained forbearance. So that we see the need of much prayer to entreat His powerful hand, that can turn the course of Jordan, that He would work, not a temporary, but an abiding change of the course of this land, and cause many souls to look upon Jesus Christ, and flow into Him, as the word is in Psal. xxxiv. 5.

This is their course, *but you run not with them.* The godly are a small and weak company, and yet run counter to the grand torrent of the world, just against them. And there is a Spirit within them, whence that their contrary motion flows; a Spirit strong enough to maintain it in them, against all the crowd and combined course of the ungodly. *Greater is He that is in you, than he that is in the world.* (1 John iv. 4.) As Lot in Sodom, his righteous soul was not carried with them, but was *vexed with their ungodly doings.* There is to a believer, the example of Christ, to set against the example of the world, and the Spirit of Christ against the spirit of the world; and these are by far the more excellent and the stronger. Faith looking to Him, and drawing virtue from Him, makes the soul surmount all discouragements and oppositions. So Heb. xii. 2, *Looking to Jesus:* and that not only as an example worthy to oppose to all the world's examples; the saints were so, yet He more than they all; but further, He is *the Author and Finisher of our faith;* and so we eye Him, as having *endured the cross, and despised the shame,* and as having *sat down at the right hand of the throne of God,* not only that, in doing so, we may follow Him in that way, unto that end, as our Pattern, but as our Head, from whom we borrow our strength so to follow *the Author and Finisher of our Faith.* And so 1 John. v. 4, *This is our victory, whereby we overcome the world, even our faith.*

The Spirit of God shews the Believer clearly both the baseness of the ways of sin, and the wretched measure of their end. That Divine light discovers the fading and false blush of the pleasures of sin, that there is nothing under them but true deformity and rottenness, which the deluded, gross world does not see, but takes the first appearance of it for true and solid beauty, and so is enamoured with a painted strumpet. And as he sees the vileness of that love of sin, he sees the final unhappiness of it, that *her ways lead down to the chambers of death.* Methinks a believer is as one standing upon a high tower, who sees the way wherein the world runs, in a valley, as an unavoidable precipice, a steep edge hanging over the bottomless pit, where all that are not reclaimed fall over before they be aware ; this they, in their low way, perceive not, and therefore walk and run on in the smooth pleasures and ease of it towards their perdition ; but he that sees the end, will not *run with them.*

And as he hath, by that light of the Spirit, this clear reason for thinking on and taking another course, so, by that Spirit, he hath a very natural bent to a contrary motion, so that he cannot be one with them. That Spirit moves him upwards whence it came, and makes that, in so far as he is renewed, his natural motion. Though he hath a clog of flesh that cleaves to him, and so breeds him some difficulty, yet, in the strength of that new nature, he overcomes it, and goes on till he attain his end, where all the difficulty in the way presently is over-rewarded and forgotten. This makes amends for every weary step, that every one of those who walk in that way shall *appear in Zion before God.* (Psal. lxxxiv. 6.)

2. We have their opposite thoughts and speeches of each other. *They think it strange, speaking evil of you.* The Christian and the carnal man are most wonderful to each other. The one wonders to see the other walk so strictly, and deny himself to those carnal liberties which the most take, and take for so necessary, that they think they could not live without them. And the Christian thinks it strange that men should be so bewitched, and still remain children in the vanity of their turmoil, wearying and humouring themselves from morning to night, running after stories and fancies, ever busy doing nothing ; wonders that the delights of earth and sin can so long entertain and please men, and persuade them to give Jesus Christ so many refusals, to turn from their life and happiness, and choose to be miserable, yea, and take much pains to make themselves miserable. He knows the depravedness and blindness of nature in this ; knows it by himself, that once

he was so, and therefore wonders not so much at them as they do at him; yet, the unreasonableness and frenzy of that course now appears to him in so strong a light, that he cannot but wonder at these woful mistakes. But the ungodly wonder far more at him, not knowing the inward cause of his different choice and way. The believer, as we said, is upon the hill; he is going up, and looking back on them in the valley, sees their way tending to, and ending in death, and calls them to retire from it as loud as he can; he tells them the danger, but either they hear not, nor understand his language, or will not believe him: finding present ease and delight in their way, they will not consider and suspect the end of it, but they judge him the fool who will not share with them, and take that way where such multitudes go, and with such ease, and some of them with their train, and horses, and coaches, and all their pomp, while he, and a few straggling poor creatures like him, are climbing up a craggy steep hill, and will by no means come off from that way, and partake of theirs; not knowing, or not believing that at the top of that hill he climbs is that happy, glorious city, *the new Jerusalem*, whereof he is a citizen, and whither he is tending; not believing that he knows the end both of their way and of his own, and therefore would reclaim them if he could, but will by no means *return unto them:* as the Lord commanded the Prophet, *Let them return unto thee, but return not thou unto them:* Jer. xv. 19.

The world thinks it strange that a Christian can spend so much time in secret prayer, not knowing, nor being able to conceive of the sweetness of the communion with God which he attains in that way. Yea, while he feels it not, how sweet it is beyond the world's enjoyments, to be but seeking after it, and waiting for it! Oh! the delight that there is in the bitterest exercise of repentance, in the very tears, much more in the succeeding harvest of joy! *Incontinentes veræ voluptatis ignari*, says Aristotle: The intemperate are strangers to true pleasure. It is strange unto a carnal man, to see the child of God disdain the pleasures of sin; he knows not the higher and purer delights and pleasures that the Christian is called to, and of which he hath, it may be, some part at present, but, however, the fulness of them in assured hope.

The strangeness of the world's way to the Christian, and of his to it, though that is somewhat unnatural, yet affects them very differently. He looks on the deluded sinners with pity, they on him with hate. Their part, which is here expressed, of wondering, breaks out in reviling: *they speak evil of you;* and what is their voice? What mean these precise fools? will they readily say. What course is this they take, contrary to all the world? Will they make a new religion, and condemn all their honest, civil neighbours that are not like them? Ay, forsooth, do all go to hell, think you, except you, and those that follow your way? We are for no more than good fellowship and liberty; and as for so much reading and praying, those are but brain-sick, melancholy conceits: a man may go to heaven like his neighbour, without all this ado. Thus they let fly at their pleasure. But this troubles not the composed Christian's mind at all: while curs snarl and bark about him, the sober traveller goes on his way, and regards them not. He that is acquainted with the way of holiness, can more than endure the counter-blasts and airs of scoffs and revilings; he accounts them his glory and his riches. So, Moses *esteemed the reproach of Christ, greater riches than the treasures in Egypt.* (Heb. xi. 26.) And besides many other things to animate, we have this, which is here expressed,

3dly, The supreme and final judgment. Oh, how full is it! *They shall give account to Him that is ready to judge the quick and the dead*—hath this *in readiness,* τῷ ἑτοίμως ἔχοντι, hath the day set; and it shall surely come, though you think it far off.

Though the wicked themselves forget their scoffs against the godly, and though the Christian slights them, and lets them pass, they pass not so; they are all registered, and the great Court-day shall call them to account for all these riots and excesses, and withal, for all their reproaches of the godly, who would not run with them in these ways. Tremble, then, ye despisers and mockers of holiness, though you come not near it. What will you do when those you reviled shall appear glorious in your sight, and their King, the King of saints here, much more glorious, and His glory their joy, and all terror to you? Oh! then, all faces that could look out disdainfully upon religion and the professors of it, shall *gather blackness*, and be bathed with shame, and the despised saints of God shall shout so much the more for joy.

You that would rejoice, then, in the appearing of that holy Lord and Judge of the world, let your way be now in holiness. Avoid and hate the common ways of the wicked world; they live in their foolish opinion, and that shall quickly end, but the sentence of that day shall stand for ever.

Ver. 6. But for this cause was the gospel preached also to them that are dead, that they might be judged according to men in the flesh, but live according to God in the Spirit.

It is a thing of prime concernment for a Christian, to be rightly informed, and frequently put in mind, what is the true estate and nature of a Christian; for this, the multitude of those that bear that name, either know not, or commonly forget, and so are carried away with the vain fancies and mistakes of the world. The Apostle hath characterized Christianity very clearly to us in this place, by that which is the very nature of it, *conformity with Christ*, and that which is necessarily consequent upon that, *disconformity with the world.* And as the nature and natural properties of things hold universally, those who in all ages are effectually called by the Gospel, are thus moulded and framed by it. Thus it was, says the Apostle, with your brethren who are now at rest, as many as received the Gospel; and for this end was it preached to them, *that they might be judged according to men in the flesh, but live according to God in the Spirit.*

- We have here, 1. The Preaching of the Gospel as the suitable means to a certain end; 2. The express nature of that end.

1. *For for this cause was the Gospel preached.* There is a
particular end, and that very important, for which the preaching
of the Gospel is intended: this end many consider not, hearing
it as if it were to no end, or not propounding a fixed, determined end in their hearing. This, therefore, is to be considered
by those who preach this Gospel, that they aim aright in it at
this end, and at no other,—no self-end. The legal priests
were not to be squint-eyed, (Lev. xxi. 20,) nor must evangelical ministers be thus squinting to base gain, or vain applause.
They should also make it their study, to find in themselves
this work, this *living to God;* otherwise, they cannot
skilfully or faithfully apply their gifts to work this effect on
their hearers: and therefore acquaintance with God is most
necessary.

How sounds it, to many of us at least, but as a well-contrived
story, whose use is to amuse us, and possibly delight us a little,
and there is an end,—and indeed no end, for this turns the
most serious and most glorious of all messages into an empty
sound. If we awake, and give it a hearing, it is much; but for
any thing further, how few deeply beforehand consider: I have
a dead heart; therefore will I go unto the word of life, that it
may be quickened. It is frozen; I will go and lay it before
the warm beams of that Sun which shines in the Gospel. My
corruptions are mighty and strong, and grace, if there be any
in my heart, is exceeding weak; but there is in the Gospel a
power to weaken and kill sin, and to strengthen grace, and this
being the intent of my wise God in appointing it, it shall be my
desire and purpose in resorting to it, to find it to me according
to His gracious design; to have faith in my Christ, the fountain of my life, more strengthened, and made more active in
drawing from him; to have my heart more refined and spiri-
tualized, and to have the sluice of repentance opened, and my
affections to Divine things enlarged, more hatred of sin, and
more love of God and communion with Him.

Ask yourselves concerning former times; and, to take yourselves even now, inquire within, Why came I hither this day?

What had I in mine eye and desires this morning ere I came forth, and in my way as I was coming? Did I seriously propound an end or not; and what was my end? Nor doth the mere custom of mentioning this in prayer, satisfy the question; for this, as other such things usually do in our hand, may turn to a lifeless form, and have no heat of spiritual affection, none of David's panting and breathing after God in his ordinances; such desires as will not be stilled without a measure of attainment, as the child's desire of the breast, as our Apostle resembles it, chap. ii. ver. 1.

And then again, being returned home, reflect on your hearts: Much hath been heard, but is there any thing done by it? Have I gained my point? It was not simply to pass a little time that I went, or to pass it with delight in hearing, *rejoicing in that light*, as they did in St. John Baptist's *for a season,* [πρὸς ὥραν,] as long as the hour lasts. It was not to have my ear pleased, but my heart changed; not to learn some new notions, and carry them cold in my head, but to be quickened, and purified, and *renewed in the spirit of my mind*. Is this done? Think I now with greater esteem of Christ, and the life of faith, and the happiness of a Christian? And are such thoughts solid and abiding with me? What sin have I left behind? What grace of the Spirit have I brought home? Or what new degree, or, at least, new desire of it, a living desire, that will follow its point? Oh! this were good repetition.

It is a strange folly in multitudes of us, to set ourselves no mark, to propound no end in the hearing of the Gospel. The merchant sails not merely that he may sail, but for traffic, and traffics that he may be rich. The husbandman plows not merely to keep himself busy with no further end, but plows that he may sow, and sows that he may reap with advantage. And shall we do the most excellent and fruitful work fruitlessly, hear only to hear, and look no further? This is indeed a great vanity, and a great misery, to lose that labour, and gain nothing by it, which, duly used, would be of all others most advantageous and gainful: and yet all meetings are full of this!

Now, when you come, it is not simply to hear a discourse, and relish or dislike it in hearing, but a matter of life and death, of eternal death and eternal life ; and the spiritual life, begotten and nourished by the word, is the beginning of that eternal life. It follows,

To them that are dead.] By which, I conceive, he intends such as had heard and believed the Gospel, when it came to them, and now were dead. And this, I think, he doth to strengthen those brethren to whom he writes : he commends the Gospel, to the intent that they might not think the condition and end of it hard; as our Saviour mollifies the matter of outward sufferings thus : *So persecuted they the Prophets that were before you.* Matt. v. 12. And the Apostle afterwards in this chapter, uses the same reason in that same subject. So here, that they might not judge the point of mortification he presses, so grievous, as naturally men will do, he tells them, it is the constant end of the Gospel, and that they who have been saved by it, went that same way he points out to them. They that are dead before you, died in this way that I press on you, before they died ; and the Gospel was preached to them for that very end.

Men pass away, and others succeed, but the Gospel is still the same, hath the same tenor and substance, and the same ends. So Solomon speaks of the heavens and earth, that they remain the same, while *one generation passes, and another cometh.* (Eccl. i. 4.) The Gospel surpasses both in its stability, as our Saviour testifies : *They shall pass away, but not one jot of this word.* (Matt. v. 18.) And indeed they wear and wax old, as the Apostle teaches us ; but the Gospel is from one age to another, of most unalterable integrity, hath still the same vigour and powerful influence as at the first.

They who formerly received the Gospel, received it upon these terms; therefore, think it not hard. And they *are* now *dead ;* all the difficulty of that work of dying to sin, is now over with them. If they had not died *to* their sins by the Gospel, they had died *in* them, after a while, and so died eternally.

It is therefore a wise prevention, to have sin judged and put to death in us before we die. If we will not part with sin, if we die in it, and with it, we and our sin perish together; but if it die first before us, then we live for ever.

And what thinkest thou of thy carnal will and all the delights of sin? What is the longest term of its life? Uncertain it is, but most certainly very short: thou and these pleasures must be severed and parted within a little time; however, thou must die, and then they die, and you never meet again. Now, were it not the wisest course to part a little sooner with them, and let them die before thee, that thou mayest inherit eternal life, and eternal delights in it, *pleasures for evermore?* It is the only wise bargain; let us therefore delay it no longer.

This is our season of enjoying the sweetness of the Gospel. Others heard it before us in the places which now we fill; and now they are removed, and we must remove shortly, and leave our places to others, to speak and hear in. It is high time we were considering what we do here, to what end we speak and hear; high time to lay hold on that salvation which is held forth unto us, and that we may lay hold on it, to let go our hold of sin and those perishing things that we hold so firm, and cleave so fast to. Do they that are dead, who heard and obeyed the Gospel, now repent of their repentance and mortifying of the flesh? Or rather, do they not think ten thousand times more pains, were it for many ages, all too little for a moment of that which now they enjoy, and shall enjoy to eternity? And they that are dead, who heard the Gospel and slighted it, if such a thing might be, what would they give for one of those opportunities which now we daily have, and daily lose, and have no fruit or esteem of them! You have lately seen, at least many of you, and you that shifted the sight, have heard of numbers cut off in a little time, whole families swept away by the late stroke of God's hand*, many of which did think no other but that they might have still been with you here in

* 1665.

X 2

this place and exercise, at this time, and many years after this. And yet, who hath laid to heart the lengthening out of his day, and considered it more as an opportunity of securing that higher and happier life, than as a little protracting of this wretched life, which is hastening to an end? Oh! therefore be entreated *to-day, while it is called To-day, not to harden your hearts.* Though the pestilence doth not now affright you so, yet that standing mortality, and the decay of these earthen lodges, tell us that shortly we shall cease to preach and hear this Gospel. Did we consider, it would excite us to a more earnest search after our evidences of that eternal life that is set before us in the Gospel; and we should seek them in the characters of that spiritual life which is the beginning of eternal life within us, and is wrought by the Gospel in all the heirs of salvation.

Think therefore wisely of these two things, of what is the proper end of the Gospel, and of the approaching end of thy days; and let thy certainty of this latter, drive thee to seek more certainty of the former, that thou mayest partake of it: and then this again will make the thoughts of the other sweet to thee. That visage of death that is so terrible to unchanged sinners, shall be amiable to thine eye. Having found a life in the Gospel as happy and lasting as this is miserable and vanishing, and seeing the perfection of that life on the other side of death, thou wilt long for the passage.

Be more serious in this matter of daily hearing the Gospel. Consider why it is sent to thee, and what it brings, and think— It is too long I have slighted its message, and many who have done so are cut off, and shall hear it no more; I have it once more inviting me, and to me this may be the last invitation. And in these thoughts, ere you come, bow your knee to the Father of spirits, that this one thing may be granted you, that your souls may find at length the lively and mighty power of his Spirit upon yours, in the hearing of this Gospel, that *you may be judged according to men in the flesh, but live according to God in the spirit.*

2. Thus is the particular nature of that end expressed. And not to perplex you with various senses, the Apostle intends, I conceive, no other than the dying to the world and sin, and living unto God, which is his main subject and scope in the foregoing discourse. That death was before called a *suffering in the flesh*, which is in effect the same; and therefore, though the words may be drawn another way, yet it is strange that interpreters have been so far wide of this their genuine and agreeable sense, and that they have been by almost all of them taken in some other import.

To be judged in the flesh, in the present sense, is to die to sin, or that sin die in us: and [1.] It is thus expressed suitably to the nature of it; it is to the flesh a violent death, and it is according to a sentence judicially pronounced against it. That guilty and miserable life of sin, is in the Gospel adjudged to death: there that arrest and sentence is clear and full. See Rom. vi. 6, &c., viii. 13. That sin must die in order that the soul may live: it must be crucified in us, and we to it, that we may partake of the life of Christ and of happiness in him. And this is called *to be judged in the flesh*, to have this sentence executed. [2.] The thing is the rather spoken of here under the term of being judged, in counter-balance of that judgment mentioned immediately before, ver. 5, the Last Judgment of quick and dead, wherein they who would not be thus judged, but mocked and despised those that were, shall fall under a far more terrible judgment, and the sentence of a heavy death indeed, even everlasting death; though they think they shall escape and enjoy liberty in living in sin. And that *To be judged according to men*, is, I conceive, added, to signify the connaturalness of the life of sin to a man's now corrupt nature; that men do judge it a death indeed, to be severed and pulled from their sins, and that a cruel death; and the sentence of it in the Gospel is a heavy sentence, *a hard saying* to a carnal heart, that he must give up all his sinful delights, must die indeed in self-denial, must be separated from himself, which is to die, if he will be joined with Christ, and live in him. Thus men judge that they are adjudged to a painful death by the sentence of the Gospel. Although it is that they may truly and happily live, yet they understand it not so. They see the death, the parting with sin and all its pleasures; but the life they see not, nor can any know it till they partake of it: it is known to him in whom it exists: it is *hid with Christ in God*. (Col. iii. 3.) And therefore the opposition here is very fitly thus represented, that the death is *according to men in the flesh,* but the life is *according to God in the Spirit.*

As the Christian is adjudged to this *death in the flesh* by the Gospel, so he is looked on and accounted, by carnal men, as dead, for that he enjoys not with them what they esteem their life, and think they could not live without. One that cannot carouse and swear with profane men, is a silly dead creature, good for nothing; and he that can bear wrongs, and love him that injured him, is a poor spiritless fool, hath no mettle or life in him, in the world's account. Thus is he *judged according to men in the flesh,*—he is as a dead man,—*but lives according to God in the Spirit;* dead to men, and alive to God, as *ver. 2.*

Now, if this life be in thee, it will act. All life is in motion, and is called *an act,* but most active of all is this most excellent, and, as I may call it, most lively life. It will be moving towards God, often seeking to Him, making still towards Him as its principle and fountain, exerting itself in holy and affectionate thoughts of Him; sometimes on one of His sweet attributes, sometimes on another, as the bee amongst the flowers. And as it will thus act within, so it will be outwardly laying hold on all occasions, yea, seeking out ways and opportunities to be serviceable to thy Lord; employing all for Him, commending and extolling His goodness, doing and suffering cheerfully for Him, laying out the strength of desires, and parts, and means, in thy station, to gain Him glory. If thou be alone, then not esteeming thyself alone, but with Him, seeking to know more of Him, and to be made more like Him. If in company, then casting about how to bring His name into esteem, and to draw others to a love of religion and holiness by speeches, as it may be fit, and most by the true behaviour of thy carriage;—tender over the souls of others, to do them good to thy utmost; thinking, each day, an hour lost when thou art not busy for the honour and advantage of Him to whom thou now livest;—thinking in the morning, Now, what may I do this day for my God? How may I most please and glorify Him, and use my strength, and wit, and my whole self, as not mine, but His? And then, in the evening, reflecting, O Lord, have I seconded these thoughts in reality? What glory hast thou had by me this day? Whither went my thoughts and endeavours? What busied them most? Have I been much with God? Have I adorned the Gospel in my converse with others?—And if thou findest any thing done this way, this life will engage thee to bless and acknowledge Him, the spring and worker of it. If thou hast stepped aside, were it but to *an appearance of evil,* or if any fit season of good hath escaped thee unprofitably, it will lead thee to check thyself, and to be grieved for thy sloth and coldness, and to see if more love would not beget more diligence.

Try it by sympathy and antipathy, which follow the nature of things : as we see in some plants and creatures that cannot grow, cannot agree together, and others that do favour and benefit mutually. If thy soul hath an aversion and reluctancy against whatever is contrary to holiness, it is an evidence of this new nature and life ; thy heart rises against wicked ways and speeches, oaths and cursings, and rotten communication; yea, thou canst not endure unworthy discourses wherein most spend their time ; thou findest no relish in the unsavoury societies of such as know not God, canst not *sit with vain persons,* but findest a delight in those who have the image of God upon them, such as partake of that Divine life, and carry the evidences of it in their carriage. David did not disdain the fellowship of the saints, and that it was no disparagement to him, is implied in the name he gives them, Psal. xvi. 2, *the excellent ones,* the magnific or noble, *adiri:* that word is taken from one that signifies a robe or noble garment, *adereth, toga magnifica ;* so he thought them nobles and kings as well as he ; they had *robes royal,* and therefore were fit companions of kings.   A spiritual eye looks upon spiritual dignity, and esteems and loves them who are *born of God,* how low, soever be their natural birth and breeding.   The sons of God have of His Spirit in them, and are born to the same inheritance, where all shall have enough, and they are tending homewards by the conduct of the same Spirit that is in them ; so that there must be amongst them a real complacency and delight in one another.

And then, consider the temper of thy heart towards spiritual things, the word and ordinances of God, whether thou dost esteem highly of them, and delight in them ; whether there be compliance of the heart with Divine truths, something in thee that suits and sides with them against thy corruptions ; whether in thy affliction thou seekest not to the puddles of earthly comforts, but hast thy recourse to the sweet crystal streams of the Divine promises, and findest refreshment in them.   It may be, at some times, in a spiritual distemper, holy exercises and ordinances will not have that present sensible sweetness to a Christian, that he desires ; and some will for a long time lie under dryness and deadness this way ; yèt, there is here an evidence of this spiritual life, that thou stayest by thy Lord, and reliest on Him, and wilt not leave these holy means, how sapless soever to thy sense for the present.   Thou findest for a long time little sweetness in prayer, yet, thou prayest still, and, when thou canst say nothing, yet offerest at it, and lookest towards Christ thy life.   Thou dost not turn away from these things to seek consolation elsewhere, but as thou knowest that life is in Christ, thou wilt stay till He refresh thee with new and lively influence.   It is not any where but in Him ; as St. Peter said, *Lord, whither should we go ?   Thou hast the words of eternal life.* (John vi 68.)

Consider with thyself, whether thou hast any knowledge of the growth or deficiencies of this spiritual life ; for it is here but begun, and breathes in an air contrary to it, and lodges in a house that often smokes and darkens it. Canst thou go on in formal performances, from one year to another, and make no advancement in the inward exercises of grace, and restest thou content with that? It is no good sign. But art thou either gaining victories over sin, and further strength of faith and love, and other graces, or, at least, art thou earnestly seeking these, and bewailing thy wants and disappointments of this kind? Then, thou livest. At the worst, wouldst thou rather grow this way, be further off from sin, and nearer to God, than grow in thy estate, or credit, or honours? Esteemest thou more highly of grace than of the whole world? There is life at the root; although thou findest not that flourishing thou desirest; yet the desire of it is life in thee. And, if growing this way, art thou content, whatsoever is thy outward estate? Canst thou solace thyself in the love and goodness of thy God, though the world frown on thee? Art thou unable to take comfort in the smiles of the world, when His face is hid? This tells thee thou livest, and that He is thy life.

Although many Christians have not so much sensible joy, yet they account spiritual joy and the light of God's countenance, the only true joy, and all other without it, madness; and they cry, and sigh, and wait for it. Meanwhile, not only duty and the hopes of attaining a better state in religion, but even love to God, makes them to do so, to serve, and please, and glorify Him to their utmost. And this is not a dead resting without God, but it is a stable compliance with His will in the highest point; waiting for Him, and living by faith, which is most acceptable to Him. In a word, whether in sensible comfort or without it, still this is the fixed thought of a believing soul, *It is good for me to draw nigh to God* (Psal. lxxiii. 28);—only good; and it will not live in a willing estrangedness from Him, what way soever He be pleased to deal with it.

Now, for the entertaining and strengthening of this life, which is the great business and care of all that have it,

1st, Beware of omitting and interrupting those spiritual means, which do provide it and nourish it. Little neglects of that kind will draw on greater, and great neglects will make great abatements of vigour and liveliness. Take heed of using holy things coldly and lazily, without affection : that will make. them fruitless, and our life will not be advantaged by them, unless they be used in a lively way. Be active in all good within thy reach : as this is a sign of the spiritual life, so it is a helper and a friend to it. A slothful, unstirring life will make a sickly, unhealthful life. Motion purifies and sharpens the spirits, and makes men robust and vigorous.

2dly, Beware of admitting a correspondence with any sin; yea, do not so much as discourse familiarly with it, or look kindly toward it; for that will undoubtedly cast a damp upon thy spirit, and diminish thy graces at least, and will obstruct thy communion with God. Thou knowest (thou who hast any knowledge of this life) that thou canst not go to Him with that sweet freedom thou wert wont, after thou hast been but tempering or parleying with any of thy old loves. Oh! do not make so foolish a bargain, as to prejudice the least of thy spiritual comforts, for the greatest and longest-continued enjoyments of sin, which are base, and but for a season.

But wouldst thou grow upwards in this life? 3dly, Have much recourse to Jesus Christ thy head, the spring from whom flow the animal spirits that quicken thy soul. Wouldst thou know more of God ? He it is who *reveals the Father*, and reveals Him as *His Father*, and, in Him, *thy Father ;* and that is the sweet notion of God. Wouldst thou overcome thy lusts further ? Our victory is in Him. Apply His conquest; *We are more than conquerors, through Him that loved us :* (Rom. viii. 37.) Wouldst thou be more replenished with graces and spiritual affections? His fulness is, for that use, open to us; there is life, and more life, in Him, and for us. This was His business here. He came, *that we might have life, and might have it more abundantly.* (John x. 10.)

Ver. 7. But the end of all things is at hand: be ye therefore sober, and
watch unto prayer.

THE heart of a real Christian is really taken off from the
world, and set heavenwards; yet there is still in this flesh so
much of the flesh hanging to it, as will readily poise all downwards, unless it be often wound up and put in remembrance of
those things that will raise it still to further spirituality. This
the Apostle doth in this Epistle, and particularly in these words,
in which three things are to be considered: I. A threefold duty
recommended; II. The mutual relation that binds these duties
to one another; III. The reason here used to bind them upon
a Christian.

I. A threefold duty recommended, Sobriety, Watchfulness,
and Prayer; and of the three, the last is evidently the chief,
and is here so meant, and others being recommended, as suitable and subservient to it; therefore I shall speak first of
Prayer.

And truly, to speak and to hear of this duty often, were our
hearts truly and entirely acquainted with it, would have still
new sweetness and usefulness in it. Oh, how great were the
advantage of that lively knowledge of it, beyond the exactest
skill in defining it, and in discoursing on the heads of doctrine
concerning it.

Prayer is not a smooth expression, or a well-contrived form
of words: not the product of a ready memory, or of a rich
invention exerting itself in the performance. These may draw
a neat picture of it, but still, the life is wanting. The motion
of the heart God-wards, holy and divine affection, makes prayer
real, and lively, and acceptable to the Living God, to whom it
is presented; the pouring out of thy heart to Him who made
it, and therefore hears it, and understands what it speaks, and
how it is moved and affected in calling on Him. It is not the
gilded paper and good writing of a petition, that prevails with
a king, but the moving sense of it. And to that King who
discerns the heart, heart-sense is the sense of all, and that which

only He regards: He listens to hear what that speaks, and takes all as nothing where that is silent.   All other excellence in Prayer, is but the outside and fashion of it; this is the life of it.

Though Prayer, precisely taken, is only petition, yet, in its fuller and usual sense, it comprehends the venting of our humble sense of vileness and sin, in sincere confession, and the extolling and praising of the holy name of our God, His excellency and goodness, with thankful acknowledgment of received mercies. Of these sweet ingredient perfumes is the incense of Prayer composed, and by the Divine fire of love it ascends unto God, the heart and all with it; and when the hearts of the saints unite in joint prayer, the pillar of sweet smoke goes up the greater and the fuller.   Thus says that song of the Spouse: *Going up from the wilderness, as pillars of smoke perfumed with myrrh and frankincense, and all the powders of the merchant.* (Cant. iii. 6.)   The word there (*Timeroth,* from *Temer,* a palm-tree) signifies *straight pillars,* like the tallest, straightest kind of trees.   And, indeed, the sincerity and unfeignedness of prayer makes it go up as a straight pillar, no crookedness in it, tending straight towards Heaven, and bowing to no side by the way. Oh! the single and fixed viewing of God, as it, in other ways, is the thing which makes all holy and sweet, so particularly does it in this Divine work of prayer.

It is true we have to deal with a God who of Himself needs not this our pains, either to inform or to excite Him: He fully knows our thoughts before we express them, and our wants before we feel them or think of them.   Nor doth this affection and gracious bent to do His children good, wax remiss, or admit of the least abatement and forgetfulness of them.

But, instead of necessity on the part of God, which cannot be imagined, we shall find that equity, and that singular dignity and utility of it, on our part, which cannot be denied.

1. *Equity.* That thus the creature signify his homage to, and dependence on his Creator, for his being and well-being; that he take all the good he enjoys, or expects, from that

Sovereign Good, declaring himself unworthy, waiting for all upon the terms of free goodness, and acknowledging all to flow from that spring.

2. *Dignity.* Man was made for communion with God his Maker; it is the excellency of his nature to be capable of this end, the happiness of it to be raised to enjoy it. Now, in nothing more, in this life, is this communion actually and highly enjoyed, than in the exercise of prayer; in that he may freely impart his affairs, and estate, and wants, to God, as the most faithful and powerful friend, the richest and most loving father; may use the liberty of a child, telling his Father what he stands in need of and desires, and communing with him with humble confidence, being admitted so frequently into the presence of so great a King.

3. The *Utility* of it. [1.] Prayer eases the soul in times of distress, when it is oppressed with griefs and fears, by giving them vent, and that in so advantageous a way, emptying them into the bosom of God. The very vent, were it but into the air, gives ease; or speak your grief to a statue rather than smother it; much more ease does it give to pour it forth into the lap of a confidential and sympathising friend, even though unable to help us; yet still more, of one who can help; and, of all friends, our God is, beyond all comparison, the surest, and most affectionate, and most powerful. So, Isa. lxiii. 9, both compassion and effectual salvation are expressed : *In all their affliction He was afflicted, and the angel of His presence saved them : in His love and in His pity He redeemed them ; and He bare them, and carried them all the days of old.* And so, resting on His love, power, and gracious promises, the soul quiets itself in God upon this assurance, that it is not in vain to seek Him, and that He *despiseth not the sighing of the poor.* (Psal. xii. 5.)

[2.] The soul is more spiritually affected with its own condition, by laying it open before the Lord; becomes more deeply sensible of sin, and ashamed in His sight, in confessing it before Him; more dilated and enlarged to receive the mercies sued for, as the *opening wide of the mouth* of the soul, that it *may be filled;* more disposed to observe the Lord in answering, and to bless Him, and trust on Him, upon the renewed experiences of His regard to its distresses and desires.

[3.] All the graces of the Spirit are, in Prayer, stirred and exercised, and, by exercise, strengthened and increased ; Faith, in applying the Divine promises, which are the very ground that the soul goes upon to God, Hope looking out to their performance, and Love particularly expressing itself in that sweet converse, and delighting in it, as love doth in the company of the person beloved, thinking all hours too short in speaking with Him. Oh, how the soul is refreshed with freedom of speech with its beloved Lord ! And as it delights in that, so it is continually advanced and grows by each meeting and conference, beholding the excellency of God, and relishing the pure and sublime pleasures that are to be found in near communion with Him. Looking upon the Father in the face of Christ, and using him as a mediator in prayer, as still it must, it is drawn to further admiration of that bottomless love, which found out that way of agreement, that *new and living way* of our access, when all was shut up, and we must otherwise have been shut out for ever. And then, the affectionate expressions of that reflex love, seeking to find that vent in prayer, do kindle higher, and being as it were fanned and blown up, rise to a greater, and higher, and purer flame, and so tend upwards the more strongly. David, as he doth profess his love to God in prayer, in his Psalms, so, no doubt, it grew in the expressing ; *I will love thee, O Lord, my strength,* Psal. xviii. 1. And in Psal. cxvi. 1, he doth raise an incentive of love out of this very consideration of the correspondence of prayer,—*I love the Lord because he hath heard;* and he resolves thereafter upon persistance in that course,—*therefore will I call upon him as long as I live.* And as the graces of the Spirit are advanced in prayer by their actings, so, for this further reason, because prayer sets the soul particularly near unto God in Jesus Christ. It is then in His presence, and being much with God in this way, it is powerfully assimilated to Him by converse with Him ; as we readily contract their habits with whom we have much intercourse, especially if they be such as we singularly love and respect. Thus the soul is moulded further to the likeness of God, is stamped with clearer characters of Him, by being much with Him, becomes more like God, more holy and spiritual, and, like Moses, brings back a bright shining from the mount.

[4.] And not only thus, by a natural influence, doth Prayer work this advantage, but even by a federal efficacy, suing for, and upon suit obtaining, supplies of grace as the chief good, and besides, all other needful mercies. It is a real means of receiving. *Whatsoever you shall ask, that will I do*, says our Saviour. (John xiv. 13.) God having established this intercourse, has engaged his truth and goodness in it, that if they call on Him, they shall be heard and answered. If they prepare the heart to call, He will incline His ear to hear. Our Saviour hath assured us, that we may build upon his goodness, upon the affection of a father in Him ; *He will give good things to them that ask*, says one Evangelist, Matt. vii. 11 ; *give the Holy Spirit to them that ask Him*, says another, Luke xi. 13, as being *the good* indeed, the highest of gifts, and the sum of all good things, and that for which His children are most earnest supplicants. Prayer for grace doth, as it were, set the mouth of the soul to the spring, draws from Jesus Christ, and is replenished out of his fulness, thirsting after it, and drawing from it that way.

And for this reason it is that our Saviour, and from him, and according to his example, the Apostles, recommend prayer so much. *Watch and pray*, says our Saviour ; (Matt. xxvi. 41 ;) and St. Paul, *Pray continually*, (1 Thes. v. 17.) And our Apostle here particularly specifies this, as the grand means of attaining that conformity with Christ which he presses : this is the highway to it, *Be sober and watch unto prayer*. He that is much in prayer, shall grow rich in grace. He shall thrive and increase most, who is busiest in this, which

is our very traffic with heaven, and fetches the most precious
commodities thence. He who sends oftenest out these ships of
desire, who makes the most voyages to that land of spices and
pearls, shall be sure to improve his stock most, and have most
of heaven upon earth.

But the true art of this trading is very rare. Every trade
hath something wherein the skill of it lies ; but this is deep and
supernatural, is not reached by human industry. Industry is
to be used in it, but we must know the faculty of it comes from
above, that spirit of prayer, without which, learning and wit,
and religious breeding, can do nothing. Therefore, this is to
be our prayer often, our great suit, for the spirit of prayer, that
we may speak the language of the sons of God by the Spirit
of God, which alone teaches the heart to pronounce aright those
things that the tongue of many hypocrites can articulate well to
man's ear. Only the children, in that right strain that takes Him,
call God their *Father*, and cry unto Him as their Father ; and
therefore, many a poor unlettered Christian far outstrips your
school-rabbies in this faculty, because it is not effectually taught
in those lower academies. They must be in God's own school,
children of His house, who speak this language. Men may give
spiritual rules and directions in this, and such as may be useful,
drawn from the word that furnishes us with all needful precepts ;
but you have still to bring these into the seat of this faculty of
prayer, the heart, and stamp them upon it, and so to teach it to
pray, without which there is no prayer. This is the prerogative
royal of Him who framed the heart of man within him.

But for advancing in this, and growing more skilful in it,
Prayer is, with continual dependence on the spirit, to be much
used. Praying much, thou shalt be blest with much faculty
for it. So then, askest thou, What shall I do that I may learn
to pray ? There be things here to be considered, which are
expressed as serving this end ; but, for the present, take this,
and chiefly this, By praying, thou shalt learn to pray.—Thou
shalt both obtain more of the Spirit, and find more of the
cheerful working of it in prayer, when thou puttest it often to

that work for which it is received, and wherein it takes delight. And, as both advantaging all other graces and promoting the grace of prayer itself, this frequency and abounding in prayer is here very clearly intended, in that the Apostle makes it as the main of the work we have to do, and would have us keep our hearts in a constant aptness for it: *Be sober and watch—* to what end ?—*unto prayer.*

Be sober.] They that have no better, must make the best they can of carnal delights. It is no wonder they take as large a share of them as they can bear, and sometimes more. But the Christian is called to a more excellent state and higher pleasures; so that he may behold men glutting themselves with these base things, and be as little moved to share with them, as men are taken with the pleasure a swine hath in wallowing in the mire.

It becomes the heirs of heaven to be far above the love of the earth, and in the necessary use of any earthly things, still to keep within the due measure of their use, and to keep their hearts wholly disengaged from an excessive affection to them. This is the Sobriety to which we are here exhorted.

It is true that, in the most common sense of the word, it is very commendable, and it is fit to be so considered by a Christian, that he flee gross intemperance, as a thing most contrary to his condition and holy calling, and wholly inconsistent with the spiritual temper of a renewed mind, with those exercises to which it is called, and with its progress in its way homewards. It is a most unseemly sight to behold one simply by outward profession a Christian, overtaken with surfeiting and drunkenness, much more, given to the vile custom of it. All sensual delights, even the filthy lust of uncleanness, go under the common name of insobriety, intemperance, ἀκολασία; and they all degrade and destroy the noble soul, being unworthy of a man, much more of a Christian; and the contempt of them preserves the soul, and elevates it.

But the Sobriety here recommended, though it takes in that too, yet reaches farther than temperance in meat and drink. It is the spiritual temperance of a Christian mind in all earthly things, as our Saviour joins these together, Luke xxi. 34, *sur-*

feiting, and drunkenness, and cares of this life: and under the
cares are comprehended all the excessive desires and delights
of this life, which cannot be followed and attended without
distempered carefulness.

Many who are sober men and of temperate diet, yet are
spiritually intemperate, drunk with pride, or covetousness, or
passions; drunk with self-love and love of their pleasures and
ease, with love of the world and the things of it, which cannot
consist with the love of God, as St. John tells us, I John
ii. 15; drunk with the inordinate, unlawful love even of their
lawful calling and the lawful gain they pursue by it. Their
hearts are still going after it, and so, reeling to and fro, never
fixed on God and heavenly things, but either hurried up and
down with incessant business, or, if sometimes at ease, it is as
the ease of a drunken man, not composed to better and wiser
thoughts, but falling into a dead sleep, contrary to the watching here joined with sobriety.

Watch.] There is a Christian rule to be observed in the
very moderating of bodily sleep, and that particularly for the
interest of prayer; but watching, as well as sobriety, here,
implies chiefly the spiritual circumspectness and vigilancy of
the mind, in a wary, waking posture, that it be not surprised
by the assaults or sleights of Satan, by the World, nor by its
nearest and most deceiving enemy, the corruption that dwells
within, which being so near, doth most readily watch unper-
ceived advantages, and easily circumvent us. (Heb. xii. 1.)
The soul of a Christian being surrounded with enemies, both
of so great power and wrath, and so watchful to undo it,
should it not be watchful for its own safety, and live in a
military vigilancy continually, keeping constant watch and
sentinel, and suffering nothing to pass that may carry the
least suspicion of danger? Should he not be distrustful and
jealous of all the motions of his own heart, and the smilings
of the world? And in relation to these it will be a wise
course to take that word as a good caveat, Νῆφε καὶ μέμνησο
ἀπιστεῖν. *Be watchful, and remember to mistrust.* Under the
garment of some harmless pleasure, or some lawful liberties,

may be conveyed into thy soul some thief or traitor, that will either betray thee to the enemy, or at least pilfer and steal of the most precious things thou hast. Do we not by experience find how easily our foolish hearts are seduced and deceived, and therefore apt to deceive themselves? And by things that seem to have no evil in them, they are yet drawn from the height of affection to their Supreme Good, and from communion with God, and study to please Him; which should not be intermitted, for then it will abate, whereas it ought still to be growing.

Now, II. The *mutual relation* of these duties is clear: they are each of them assistant and helpful to the other, and are in their nature inseparably linked together, as they are here in the words of the Apostle; *Sobriety*, the friend of *watchfulness*, and *prayer*, of both. Intemperance doth of necessity draw on sleep: excessive eating and drinking, by sending up too many, and so, gross vapours, surcharge the brain; and when the body is thus deadened, how unfit is it for any active employment! Thus the mind, by a surcharge of delights, or desires, or cares of earth, is made so heavy and dull that it cannot awake; hath not the spiritual activity and clearness that spiritual exercises, particularly prayer, do require. Yea, as bodily insobriety, full feeding and drinking, not only for the time indisposes to action, but, by the custom of it, brings the body to so gross and heavy a temper, that the very natural spirits cannot stir to and fro in it with freedom, but are clogged, and stick as the wheels of a coach in a deep miry way; thus is it with the soul glutted with earthly things: the affections bemired with them, make it sluggish and inactive in spiritual things, and render the motions of the spirit heavy; and, obstructed thus, the soul grows carnally secure and sleepy, and prayer comes heavily off. But when the affections are soberly exercised, and even in lawful things have not full liberty, with the reins laid on their necks, to follow the world and carnal projects and delights; when the unavoidable affairs of this life are done with a spiritual mind, a heart kept free and disengaged; then is the soul more nimble for spiritual things, for Divine meditation and prayer: it can watch and continue in these things, and spend itself in that excellent way with more alacrity.

Again, as this Sobriety, and the watchful temper attending it, enable for prayer, so prayer preserves these. Prayer winds up the soul from the earth, raises it above those things which intemperance feeds on, acquaints it with the transcending sweetness of Divine comforts, the love and loveliness of Jesus Christ; and these most powerfully wean the soul from the low creeping pleasures that the world gapes after and swallows with such greediness. He that is admitted to nearest intimacy with the king, and is called daily to his presence, not only in the view and company of others, but likewise in secret, will he be so mad as to sit down and drink with the kitchen-boys, or the common guards, so far below what he may enjoy? Surely not.

Prayer, being our near communion with the great God, certainly sublimates the soul, and makes it look down upon the base ways of the world with disdain, and despise the truly besotting pleasures of it. Yea, the Lord doth sometimes fill those souls that converse much with Him, with such beatific delights, such inebriating sweetness, as I may call it, that it is, in a happy manner, drunk with these; and the more there is of this, the more is the soul above base intemperance in the use of the delights of the world. Whereas common drunkenness makes a man less than a man, this makes him more than a man; that sinks him below himself, makes him a beast; this raises him above himself, and makes him an angel.

Would you, as surely you ought, have much faculty for prayer, and be frequent in it, and experience much of the pure sweetness of it? Then, deny yourselves more the muddy pleasures and sweetness of the world. If you would pray much, and with much advantage, then, *be sober, and watch unto prayer.* Suffer not your hearts to long so after ease, and wealth, and esteem in the world: these will make your hearts, if they mix with them, become like them, and take their quality; will make them gross and earthly, and unable to mount up;

will clog the wings of prayer, and you shall find the loss, when your soul is heavy and drowsy, and falls off from delighting in God and your communion with Him. Will such things as those you follow be able to countervail your damage? Can they speak you peace, and uphold you in a day of darkness and distress? Or may it not be such now, as will make them all a burden and vexation to you? But, on the other hand, the more you abate and let go of these, and come empty and hungry to God in prayer, the more room shall you have for His consolations; and therefore, the more plentifully will He pour in of them, and enrich your soul with them the more, the less you take in of the other.

Again, would you have yourselves raised to, and continued and advanced in, a spiritual heavenly temper, free from the surfeits of earth, and awake and active for heaven? Be incessant in prayer.

But thou wilt say, I find nothing but heavy indisposedness in it, nothing but roving and vanity of heart, and so, though I have used it some time, it is still unprofitable and uncomfortable to me.—Although it be so, yet, hold on, give it not over. Or need I say this to thee? Though it were referred to thyself, wouldst thou forsake it and leave off? Then, what wouldst thou do next? For if there be no comfort in it, far less is there any for thee in any other way. If temptation should so far prevail with thee as to lead thee to try intermission, either thou wouldst be forced to return to it presently, or certainly wouldst fall into a more grievous condition, and, after horrors and lashings, must at length come back to it again, or perish for ever. Therefore, however it go, continue praying. Strive to believe that love thou canst not see; for where sight is abridged, there it is proper for faith to work. If thou canst do no more, lie before thy Lord, and look to Him, and say, Lord, here I am; Thou mayest quicken and revive me if thou wilt, and I trust Thou wilt; but if I must do it, I will die at Thy feet. My life is in Thy hand, and Thou art goodness and mercy; while I have breath I will cry, or if I cannot cry, yet I will wait on, and look to Thee.

One thing forget not, that the ready way to rise out of this sad, yet safe state, is, to be much in viewing the Mediator, and interposing Him betwixt the Father's view and thy soul. Some who do orthodoxly believe this to be right, yet, (as often befals us in other things of this kind,) do not so consider and use it in their necessity, as becomes them, and therefore fall short of comfort. He hath declared it, *No man cometh to the Father but by me.* How vile soever thou art, put thyself under His robe, and into His hand, and He will lead thee unto the Father, and present thee acceptable and blameless ; and the Father shall receive thee, and declare Himself well pleased with thee in His well-beloved Son, who hath covered thee with His righteousness, and brought thee so clothed, and set thee before Him.

III. The third thing we have to consider, is, the reason which binds on us these duties : *The end of all things is at hand.*

We need often to be reminded of this, for even believers too readily forget it ; and it is very suitable to the Apostle's fore-going discourse of judgment, and to his present exhortation to sobriety and watchfulness unto prayer. Even the general end of all is *at hand;* though, since the Apostle wrote this, many ages are past. For, [1.] The Apostles usually speak of the whole time after the coming of Jesus Christ in the flesh, as *the last time,* for that two double chiliads of years passed before it, the one before, the other under the Law, and in this third, it is conceived, shall be the end of all things. And the Apostles seem, by divers expressions, to have apprehended it in their days to be not far off. So, St. Paul, I Thess. iv. 17, *We which are alive, and remain, shall be caught up together with them in the clouds,*—speaking as if it were not impossible that it might come in their time ; which put him upon some explication of that correction of their mistakes, in his next epistle to them, wherein, notwithstanding, he seems not to assert any great tract of time to intervene, but only that in that time great things were first to come. [2.] However, this might always have been said: in respect of succeeding eternity, the whole duration of the world is not considerable; and to the Eternal Lord who made it, and hath appointed its period, *a thousand years are but as one day*. We think a thousand years a great matter, in respect of our short life, and more so through our short-sightedness, who look not through this to eternal life; but what is the utmost length of time, were it millions of years, to a thought of eternity? We find much room in this earth, but to the vast heavens, it is but as a point. Thus, that which is but small to us, a field or little enclosure, a fly, had it skill, would divide into provinces in proportion to itself. [3.] To each man, the *end of all things* is, even after our measure, *at hand;* for when he dies, the world ends for him. Now this consideration fits the subject, and presses it strongly. Seeing all things shall be quickly at an end, even the frame of heaven and earth, why should we, knowing this, and having higher hopes, lay out so much of our desires and endeavours upon those things that are posting to ruin? It is no hard notion, to be sober and watchful to prayer, to be trading that way, and seeking higher things, and to be very moderate in these, which are of so short a date. As in themselves and their utmost term, they are of short duration, so, more evidently to each of us in particular, who are so *soon cut off, and flee away*. Why should our hearts cleave to those things from which we shall so quickly part, and from which, if we will not freely part and let them go, we shall be pulled away, and pulled with the more pain, the closer we cleave, and the faster we are glued to them?

This the Apostle St. Paul casts in seasonably, (though many think it not seasonable at such times,) when he is discoursing of a great point of our life, marriage, to work Christian minds to a holy freedom both ways, whether they use it or not; not to view it, nor any thing here, with the world's spectacles, which make it look so big and so fixed, but to see it in the stream of time as passing by, and as no such great matter. (I Cor. vii. 31.) *The fashion of this world passeth away*, παράγει, as a pageant or show in a street, going through and quickly out of sight. What became of all the marriage so-lemnities of kings and princes of former ages, which they were so taken up with in their time? When we read of them de-scribed in history, they are as a night-dream, or a day-fancy, which passes through the mind and vanishes.

Oh! foolish man, that hunteth such poor things, and will not be called off till death benight him, and he finds his great work not done, yea, not begun, nor even seriously thought of. Your buildings, your trading, your lands, your matches, and friendships and projects, when they take with you, and your hearts are after them, say, But for how long are all these? *Their end is at hand; therefore be sober, and watch unto prayer.* Learn to divide better ; more hours for prayer, and fewer for them ; your whole heart for it, and none of it for them. Seeing they will fail you so quickly, prevent them ; become free ; lean not on them till they break, and you fall into the pit.

It is reported of one, that, hearing the fifth chapter of Genesis read, so long lives, and yet, the burden still, *they died*—Seth lived nine hundred and twelve years, *and he died;* Enos lived nine hundred and five years, *and he died;* Methuselah, nine hundred and sixty-nine years, *and he died;*—he took so deeply the thought of death and eternity, that it changed his whole frame, and turned him from a voluptuous, to a most strict and pious course of life. How small a word will do much, when God sets it into the heart! But surely, this one thing would make the soul more calm and sober in the pursuit of present things, if their term were truly computed and considered. How soon shall youth, and health, and carnal delights, be at an end. How soon shall state-craft and king-craft, and all the great pro-jects of the highest wits and spirits, be lain in the dust! This casts a damp upon all those fine things. But to a soul ac-quainted with God, and in affection removed hence already, no thought so sweet as this. It helps much to carry it cheerfully through wrestlings and difficulties, through better and worse; they see land near, and shall quickly be at home: that is the way. *The end of all things is at hand;* an end of a few poor delights and the many vexations of this wretched life ; an end of temptations and sins, the worst of all evils ; yea, an end of the imperfect fashion of our best things here, an end of prayer itself, to which succeeds that new song of endless praises.

Ver. 8.   And, above all things, have fervent charity among yourselves: for charity shall cover the multitude of sins.

THE graces of the Spirit are an entire frame, making up the new creature, and none of them can be wanting ; therefore the doctrine and exhortation of the Apostles speak of them usually, not only as inseparable, but as one. But there is amongst them all none more comprehensive than this of *Love,* insomuch that St. Paul calls it *the fulfilling of the Law.* (Rom. xiii. 10.)   Love to God is the sum of all relative to Him, and so likewise is it towards our brethren. Love to God is that which makes us live to Him, and be wholly His ; that which most powerfully weans us from this world, and causeth us delight in communion with Him in holy meditation and prayer. Now, the Apostle adding here the duty of Christians to one another, gives this as the prime, yea, the sum of all; *Above all, have fervent love.*

Concerning this, consider, I. The Nature of it.   II. The eminent Degree of it.   And, III. The excellent Fruit of it.

I. The Nature of this love.   1. It is a union, therefore called a *bond* or *chain*, that links things together.   2. It is not a mere external union, that holds in customs, or words, or outward carriage, but a union of hearts.   3. It is here not a natural, but a spiritual, supernatural union : it is the mutual love of Christians *as brethren.*   There is a common benevolence and good-will due to all ; but a more particular uniting affection amongst Christians, which makes them interchangeably one.

The Devil being an apostate spirit, revolted and separated from God, doth naturally project and work division. This was his first exploit, and it is still his grand design and business in the world. He first divided Man from God; put them at an enmity by the first sin of our first parents; and the next we read of in their first child, was enmity against his brother. So, Satan is called by our Saviour, justly, *a liar and a murderer from the beginning*: (John viii. 44:) he murdered man by lying, and made him a murderer.

And as the Devil's work is division, Christ's work is union. He came to *dissolve the works of the devil*, ἵνα λύσῃ, by a contrary work. (1 John iii. 8.) He came to make all friends; to re-collect and re-unite all men to God, and man to man. And both those unions hold in Him by virtue of that marvellous union of natures in His person, and that mysterious union of the persons of believers with Him as their head. So the word, ἀνακεφαλαιώσασθαι, signifies, Eph. i. 10, *To unite all in one head.*

This was His great project in all; this He died and suffered for, and this he prayed for; (John xvii.;) and this is strong above all ties, natural or civil, Union in Christ. This they have who are indeed Christians; this they would pretend to have, if they understood it, who profess themselves Christians. If natural friendship be capable of that expression, *one spirit in two bodies,* Christian union hath it much more really and properly; for there is, indeed, one spirit more extensive in all the faithful, yea, so one a spirit, that it makes them up into *one body* more extensive. They are not so much as divers bodies, only divers *members of one body.*

Now, this love of our brethren is not another from the love of God; it is but the streaming forth of it, or the reflection of it. Jesus Christ sending His Spirit into the heart, unites it to God in Himself by love, which is indeed all, that *loving of God* supremely and entirely, with *all the mind and soul, all the* combined *strength of the heart!* And then, that same love, first wholly carried to Him, is not divided or impaired by the love of our brethren, but is dilated, as derived from the other. God allows, yea, commands, yea, causes, that it stream forth, and act itself toward them, remaining still in Him, as in its source and centre; beginning at Him, and returning to Him, as the beams that diffuse themselves from the sun, and the light and heat, yet are not divided or cut off from it, but remain in it, and, by emanation, issue from it. In loving our brethren in God, and for Him, not only because He commands us to love them, and so the law of love to Him ties us to it, as His will; but because that love of God doth naturally extend itself thus, and act thus; in loving our brethren after a spiritual Christian manner, we do, even in that, love our God.

Loving of God makes us one with God, and so gives us an impression of His Divine bounty in His Spirit. And His love, the proper work of His Spirit, dwelling in the heart, enlarges and dilates it, as self-love contracts and straitens it : so that as self-love is the perfect opposite to the love of God, it is likewise so to brotherly love; it shuts out and undoes both; and where the love of God is rekindled and enters the heart, it destroys and burns up self-love, and so carries the affection up to Himself, and in Him forth to our brethren.

This is that bitter root of all enmity in man against God, and, amongst men, against one another, *Self*, man's heart turned from God towards himself; and the very work of renewing grace is, to annul and destroy self, to replace God in His right, that the heart, and all its affections and motions, may be at His disposal; so that, instead of self-will and self-love, which ruled before, now, the will of God, and the love of God, command all.

And where it is thus, there this φιλαδελφία, this love of our brethren, will be sincere. Whence is it that wars, and contests, and mutual disgracings and despisings, do so much abound, but that men love themselves, and nothing but themselves, or in relation to themselves, as it pleases, or is advantageous to them? That is the standard and rule. All is carried by interest; so thence are strifes, and defamings, and bitterness against one another. But the Spirit of Christ coming in, undoes all selfishness. And now, what is according to God, what He wills and loves, that is law, and a powerful law, so written on the heart, this law of love, that it obeys, not unpleasantly, but with delight, and knows no constraint but the sweet constraint of love. To forgive a wrong, to love even thine enemy for Him, is not only feasible now, but delectable, although a little while ago thou thoughtest it was quite impossible.

That Spirit of Christ, which is all sweetness and love, so calms and composes the heart, that peace with God, and that unspeakably blessed correspondence of love with Him, do so fill the soul with lovingness and sweetness, that it can breathe nothing else. It hates nothing but sin, it pities the sinner, and carries towards the worst that love of good-will, desiring their return and salvation. But as for those in whom appears the image of their Father, their heart cleaves to them as brethren indeed. No natural advantages of birth, of beauty, or of wit, draw a Christian's love so much, as the resemblance of Christ; wherever that is found, it is comely and lovely to a soul that loves Him.

Much communion with God sweetens and calms the mind, cures the distempers of passion and pride, which are the avowed enemies of Love. Particularly, Prayer and Love suit well.

(1.) Prayer disposes to this love. *He that loveth not, knoweth not God*, saith the beloved Apostle, *for God is love*. (1 John iv. 3.) He that is most conversant with love in the Spring of it, where it is purest and fullest, cannot but have the fullest measure of it, flowing in from thence into his heart, and flowing forth from thence unto his brethren. If they who use the society of mild and good men, are insensibly assimilated to them, grow like them, and contract somewhat of their temper; much more doth familiar walking with God powerfully transform the soul into His likeness, making it merciful, and loving, and ready to forgive, as He is.

(2.) This Love disposes to Prayer. To pray together, hearts must be consorted and tuned together; otherwise, how can they sound the same suits harmoniously? How unpleasant, in the exquisite ear of God, who made the ear, are the jarring, disunited hearts that often seem to join in the same prayer, and yet are not set together in love! And when thou prayest alone, while thy heart is imbittered and disaffected to thy brother, although upon an offence done to thee, it is as a mistuned instrument; the strings are not accorded, are not in tune amongst themselves, and so the sound is harsh and offensive. Try it well thyself, and thou wilt perceive it; how much more He to whom thou prayest! When thou art stirred and in passion against thy brother, or not, on the contrary, lovingly affected towards him, what broken, disordered, unfastened stuff are thy requests! Therefore the Lord will have this done first, the heart tuned: *Go thy way*, says He, *leave thy gift, and be reconciled to thy brother: then come and offer thy gift.* (Matt. v. 23.)

Why is this which is so much recommended by Christ, so little regarded by Christians? It is given by Him as the characteristic and badge of His followers; yet, of those who pretend to be so, how few wear it! Oh! a little real Christianity were more worth than all that empty profession and discourse, that we think so much of. Hearts receiving the mould and stamp of this rule, these were living copies of the Gospel. *Ye are our epistle*, says the Apostle, 2 Cor. iii. 2. We come together, and hear, and speak, sometimes of one grace, and sometimes of another, while yet the most never seek to have their hearts enriched with the possession of any one of them. We search not to the bottom the perverseness of our nature, and the guiltiness that is upon us in these things; or we shift off the conviction, and find a way to forget it when the hour is done.

That accursed root, self-love, which makes man an enemy to God, and men enemies and devourers one of another, who sets

to the discovery and the displanting of it? Who bends the
force of holy endeavours and prayer, supplicating the hand of
God for the plucking of it up? Some natures are quieter and
make less noise, but till the heart be possessed with the love of
God, it shall never truly love either men in the way due to all,
or the children of God in their peculiar relation.

Among yourselves, &c.] That is here the point: the peculiar love of the saints as thy brethren, glorying and rejoicing
in the same Father, the sons of God, *begotten again* to that
lively hope of glory. Now, these, as they owe a bountiful disposition to all, are mutually to love one another as brethren.

Thou that hatest and reproachest the godly, and the more
they study to walk as the children of their holy Father, hatest
them the more, and art glad to find a spot on them to point at,
or wilt dash mire on them where thou findest none, know that
thou art in this the enemy of God; know that the indignity
done to them, Jesus Christ will take as done to Himself.
Truly, *we know that we have passed from death unto life,*
because we love the brethren: He that loveth not his brother,
abideth in death. (1 John iii. 4.) So then, renounce this word
or else believe that thou art yet far from the life of Christ,
who so hatest it in others. Oh! but they are but a number of
hypocrites wilt thou say. If they be so, this declares so much
the more thy extreme hatred of holiness, that thou canst not
endure so much as the picture of it; canst not see any thing
like it, but thou must let fly at it. And this argues thy deep
hatred of God. Holiness in a Christian is the image of God,
and the hypocrite, in the resemblance of it, is the image of a
Christian; so that thou hatest the very image of the image of
God. For, deceive not thyself, it is not the latent evil in
hypocrisy, but the apparent good in it that thou hatest. The
profane man thinks himself a great zealot against hypocrisy;
he is still exclaiming against it; but it is only this he is
angry at, that all should not be ungodly, the wicked enemies'
of religion, as he is, either dissolute, or merely decent. And

the decent man is frequently the bitterest enemy of all strictness beyond his own size, as condemning him, and therefore he
cries it down, as all of it false and counterfeit wares.

Let me entreat you, if you would not be found *fighters
against God*, let no revilings be heard amongst you, against
any who are, or seem to be, followers of holiness. If you will
not reverence it yourselves, yet reverence it in others ; at least,
do not reproach it. It should be your ambition, else, why are
you willing to be called Christians? but if you will not *pursue
holiness*, yet persecute it not. If you will not *have fervent
love to the saints*, yet burn not with infernal heat of fervent
hatred against them ; for truly, that is one of the most likely
pledges of those flames, and of society with damned spirits, as
love to the children of God is, of that inheritance and society
with them in glory.

You that are brethren, and united by that purest and
strongest tie, as you are one in your Head, in your life derived
from Him, in your hopes of glory with Him, seek to be more
one in heart, in fervent love one to another in Him. Consider
the combinations and concurrences of the wicked against Him
and His *little flock*, and let this provoke you to more united
affection. Shall the scales of Leviathan (as one alludes)
stick so close together, and shall not the members of Christ be
more one and undivided? You that can feel it, stir up yourselves to bewail the present divisions, and the fears of more.
Sue earnestly for that *one Spirit*, to act and work more powerfully in the hearts of His people.

II. Consider the eminent Degree of this Love. 1. Its emi-
nency amongst the graces, *Above all*. 2. The high measure
of it required, *Fervent love* [εκτενη], a high bent, or strain of
it, that which acts strongly and carries far.

1. It is eminent, that which indeed among Christians preserves all, and knits all together, and therefore called, (Colos.
iii. 14,) *the bond of perfection:* all is bound up by it. How
can they pray together, how advance the name of their God,
or keep in and stir up all grace in one another, unless they be

united in love ? How can they have access to God or fellow-ship with Him *who is love*, as St. John speaks, if, instead of this sweet temper, there be rancour and bitterness among them ? So then, uncharitableness and divisions amongst Christians, do not only hinder their civil good, but their spiritual much more ; and that not only *lucro cessante*, (as they speak,) interrupting the ways of mutual profiting, but *damno emergente*, it doth really damage them, and brings them to losses ; preys upon their graces, as hot withering winds on herbs and plants. Where the heart entertains either bitter malice, or but uncharitable prejudices, there will be a certain decay of spirituality in the whole soul.

2. Again, for the *degree* of this love required, it is not a cold indifferency, a negative love, as I may call it, or a not willing of evil, nor is it a lukewarm wishing of good, but fer-vent and active love ; for, if fervent, it will be active, a fire that will not be smothered, but will find a way to extend itself.

III. The Fruits of this Love follow. 1. *Covering of evil*, in this verse. 2. *Doing of good*, ver. 9, &c.

Charity shall cover the multitude of sins.] This expres-sion is taken from Solomon, Prov. x. 12 ; and as covering sins is represented as a main act of love, so, love is commended by it, this being a most useful and laudable act of it, that it *covers sins*, and *a multitude of sins*. Solomon saith, (and the opposition clears the sense,) *Hatred stirreth up strife*, aggra-vates and makes the worst of all, *but love covereth all sins :* it delights not in the undue disclosing of brethren's failings, doth not eye them rigidly, nor expose them willingly to the eyes of others.

Now this recommends Charity, in regard of its continual usefulness and necessity this way, considering human frailty, and that *in many things*, as St. James speaks, *we all offend ;* (James iii. 2 ;) so that this is still needful on all hands. What do they think who are still picking at every appearing infir-mity of their brethren ? Know they not that the frailties that cleave to the saints of God while they are here, do stand in need of, and call for, this mutual office of love, to cover and pass them by ? Who is there that stands not in need of this ? If none, why are there any who deny it to others ? There can be no society nor entertaining of Christian converse without it, without giving (as we speak) allowance ; reckoning to meet with defects and weaknesses on all hands, and covering the failings of one another, seeing it is mutually needful.

Again, as the necessity of this commends it, and the love whence it flows, so there is that laudable ingenuousness in it, that should draw us to the liking of it. It is the bent of the basest and most worthless spirits, to be busy in the search and discovery of others' failings, passing by all that is commendable and imitable, as base flies readily sitting on any little sore they can find, rather than upon the sound parts. But the more excellent mind of a real Christian loves not unnecessarily to touch, no, nor to look upon them, but rather turns away. Such never uncover their brother's sores, but to cure them ; and no more than is necessary for that end : they would willingly have them hid, that neither they nor others might see them.

This bars not the judicial trial of scandalous offences, nor the giving information of them, and bringing them under due censure. The forbearing of this is not charity, but both iniquity and cruelty ; and this cleaves too much to many of us. They that cannot pass over the least touch of a wrong done to themselves, can digest twenty high injuries done to God by profane persons about them, and resent it not. Such may be assured, that they are as yet destitute of love to God, and of Christian love to their brethren, which springs from it.

The uncovering of sin, necessary to the curing of it, is not only no breach of charity, but is indeed a main point of it, and the neglect of it, the highest kind of cruelty. But further than that goes, certainly this rule teaches the veiling of our brethren's infirmities from the eyes of others, and even from our own, that we look not on them with rigour ; no, nor without compassion.

1. Love is skilful in finding out the fairest construction of

things doubtful; and this is a great point. Take me the best action that can be named, pride and malice shall find a way to disgrace it, and put a hard visage upon it. Again, what is not undeniably evil, Love will turn it in all the ways of viewing it, till it find the best and most favourable.

2. Where the thing is so plainly a sin, that this way of covering it can have no place, yet then will Love consider what may lessen it most; whether a surprise, or strength of temptation, or ignorance, (as our Saviour, *Father, forgive them, for they know not what they do,*) or natural complexion, or at least, will still take in human frailty, to turn all the bitterness of passion into sweet compassion.

3. All private reproofs, and where conscience requires public accusation and censure, even these will be sweetened in that compassion that flows from Love. If it be such a sore as must not lie covered up, lest it prove deadly, so that it must be uncovered, to be lanced and cut, that it may be cured, still this is to be done as loving the soul of the brother. Where the rule of conscience urges it not, then thou must bury it, and be so far from delighting to divulge such things, that, as far as without partaking in it, thou mayest, thou must veil it from all eyes, and try the way of private admonition; and if the party appear to be humble and willing to be reclaimed, then forget it, cast it quite out of thy thoughts, that, as much as may be, thou mayest learn to forget it more. But this, I say, is to be done with the tenderest bowels of pity, feeling the cuts thou art forced to give in that necessary incision, and using mildness and patience. Thus the Apostle instructs his Timothy, *Reprove, rebuke, exhort,* but do it with *long-suffering, with all long-suffering.* (2 Tim. iv. 2.) And even *them that oppose, instruct,* says he, *with meekness, if God peradventure will give them repentance to the acknowledging of the truth.* (2 Tim. ii. 25.)

4. If thou be interested in the offence, even by unfeigned free forgiveness, so far as thy concern goes, let it be as if it had not been. And though thou meet with many of these, Charity will gain and grow by such occasions, and the more it hath covered,

the more it can cover: *cover a multitude*, says our Apostle, *covers all sins*, says Solomon. Yea, though thou be often put to it by the same party, what made thee forgive once, well improved, will stretch our Saviour's rule to *seventy times seven times in one day*. (Matt. xviii. 21.)

And truly, in this, men mistake grossly, who think it is greatness of spirit to resent wrongs, and baseness to forgive them: on the contrary, it is the only excellent spirit scarcely to feel a wrong, or feeling, straightly to forgive it. It is the Greatest and Best of Spirits that enables to this, the Spirit of God, that dove-like Spirit which rested on our Lord Jesus, and which from Him is derived to all that are in Him. I pray you, think, is it not a token of a tender sickly body, to be altered with every touch from every blast it meets with? And thus is it a sign of a poor, weak, sickly spirit, to endure nothing, to be distempered at the least air of an injury, yea, with the very fancy of it, where there is really none.

Inf. 1. Learn then to beware of those evils that are contrary to this Charity. Do not dispute with yourselves in rigid remarks and censures, when the mattter will bear any better sense.

2. Do not delight in tearing a wound wider, and stretching a real failing to the utmost.

3. In handling of it, study gentleness, pity, and meekness. These will advance the cure, whereas the flying out into passion against thy fallen brother, will prove nothing but as the putting of thy nail into the sore, that will readily rankle it and make it worse. Even sin may be sinfully reproved; and how thinkest thou that sin shall redress sin, and restore the sinner?

There is a great deal of spiritual art and skill in dealing with another's sin: it requires much spirituality of mind, and much prudence and much love, a mind clear from passion; for that blinds the eye, and makes the hand rough, so that a man neither rightly sees, nor rightly handles the sore he goes about to cure; and many are lost through the ignorance and neglect of that due temper which is to be brought to this work. Men think otherwise, that their rigours are much spirituality; but

Z 2

they mistake it. *Brethren, if a man be overtaken in a fault,
ye which are spiritual restore such an one in the spirit of
meekness, considering thyself, lest thou also be tempted.*
(Gal. vi. 1.)

4. For thyself, as an offence touches thee, learn to delight as much in that Divine way of forgiveness, as carnal
minds do in that base, inhuman way of revenge.- It is not, as
they judge, a glory to bluster and swagger for every thing, but
the *glory of a man to pass by a transgression.* (Prov. xix. 11.)
This makes him God-like. And consider thou often that Love
which covers all thine, that Blood which was shed to wash off
thy guilt. Needs any more be said to gain all in this that can
be required of thee?

Now, the other fruit of love, *doing good,* is first expressed
in one particular, ver. 9, and then dilated to a general rule, at
ver. 20.

Ver. 9. Use hospitality one to another without grudging.

HOSPITALITY, or kindness to strangers, is mentioned here as
an important fruit of love, it being, in those times and places,
in much use in travel, and particularly needful often among
Christians one to another then, by reason of hot and general
persecutions. But under this name, I conceive all other supply
of the wants of our brethren in outward things to be here comprehended.

Now, for this, the way and measure, indeed, must receive
its proportion from the estate and ability of persons. But certainly, the great straitening of hands in these things, is more
from the straitness of hearts than of means. A large heart,
with a little estate, will do much with cheerfulness and little
noise, while hearts glued to the poor riches they possess, or
rather are possessed by, can scarcely part with any thing, till
they be pulled from all.

Now, for the supplying of our brethren's necessities, one
good help is, the retrenching of our own superfluities. Turn
the stream into that channel were it will refresh thy brethren

and enrich thyself, and let it not run into the dead sea. Thy vain excessive entertainments, the gaudy variety of dresses, these thou dost not challenge, thinking it is of thine own; but know, (as it follows ver. 10,) thou art but *steward* of it, and this is not faithfully laying out; thou canst not answer for it. Yea, it is robbery; thou robbest thy poor brethren who want necessaries, whilst thou lavishest thus on unnecessaries. Such a feast, such a suit of apparel, is direct robbery in the Lord's eye; and the poor may cry, That is mine that you cast away so vainly, by which both I and you might be profited. *Withhold not good from them to whom it is due, when it is in the power of thine hand to do it.* (Prov. iii. 27, 28.)

Without grudging.] Some look to the actions, but few to the intention and posture of mind in them; and yet that is the main: it is all indeed, even with men, so far as they can perceive it, much more with thy Lord, who always perceives it to the full. He delights in the good He does His creatures, and would have them be so affected to one another; especially He would have His children bear this trait of His likeness. See then, when thou givest alms, or entertainest a stranger, that there be nothing either of under-grumbling, or crooked self-seeking in it. Let the *left hand* have no hand in it, nor so much as *know* of it, as our Saviour directs. (Matt. vi. 3.) Let it not be to please men or to please thyself, or simply out of a natural pity, or from the consideration of thy own possible in-cidency into the like case, which many think very well, if they be so moved; but here is a higher principle moving thee, love to God, and to thy brother in and for Him. This will make it cheerful and pleasant to thyself, and well-pleasing to Him for whom thou dost it. We lose much in actions, in themselves good, both of piety and charity, through disregard of our hearts in them; and nothing will prevail with us, to be more intent this way, to look more on our hearts, but this, to look more on Him who looks on them, and judges, and accepts all according to them.

Though all the sins of former ages gather and fall into the

latter times, this is pointed out as the grand evil, *Uncharitableness*. The Apostle St. Paul tells us, (2 Tim. iii. 2,) that *in the last days, men shall be covetous, slanderers, lovers of pleasure more than lovers of God*—but how? From whence all this confluence of evils? The spring of all is put first, and that is the direct opposite of Christian love : *men shall be* [φίλαυτοι] *lovers of themselves.* This is what kills the love of God, and the love of our brethren, and kindles that infernal fire of love to please themselves : riches make men voluptuous and covetous, *&c.* Truly, whatsoever become of men's curious computations of times, this wretched selfishness and decay of love may save us the labour of much *chronological* debate in this, and lead us, from this certain character of them, to conclude these to be the *latter times*, in a very strict sense. All other sins are come down along, and run combined now with this; but truly, uncharitableness is the main one. As old age is a rendezvous or meeting-place of maladies, but is especially subject to cold diseases, thus is it in the old age of the world : many sins abound, but especially coldness of love, as our Saviour foretells it, that in *the last days the love of many shall wax cold.* (Matt. xxiv. 12.) As the disease of the youth of the world was, the *abounding of lust*, (Gen. vi.,) so that of its age is, *decay of love.* And as that heat called for a total deluge of waters, so this coldness calls for fire, the kindling of an universal fire, that shall make an end of it and the world together. *Aqua propter ardorem libidinis, ignis propter teporem charitatis :* Water, because of the heat of lust, fire, because of the coldness of charity.

But they alone are the happy men, and have the advantage of all the world, in whom the world is burnt up beforehand, by another fire, that Divine fire of the love of God, kindled in their hearts, by which they ascend up to Him, and are reflected from Him upon their brethren, with a benign heat and influence for their good. Oh! be unsatisfied with yourselves, and restless till you find it thus, till you find your hearts possessed of this excellent grace of love, that you may have it, and use it, and it may grow by using and acting. I could, methinks, heartily study on this, and weary you with the reiterated pressing of this one thing, if there were hopes, in so wearying you, to weary you out of those evils that are contrary to it, and in pressing this grace, to make any real impression of it upon your hearts. Besides all the further good that follows it, there is in this love itself so much peace and sweetness, as abundantly pays itself, and all the labour of it ; whereas pride and malice do fill the heart with continual vexations and disquiet, and eat out the very bowels wherein they breed. Aspire to this, to be wholly bent, not only to procure or desire hurt to none, but to wish and seek the good of all : and as for those that are in Christ, surely, that will unite thy heart to them, and stir thee up, according to thy opportunities and power, to do them good, as parts of Christ, and of the same body with thyself.

Ver. 10. As every man hath received the gift, even so minister the same one to another, as good stewards of the manifold grace of God.

THIS is the rule concerning the gifts and graces bestowed on men. And we have here, 1. Their difference in their kind and measure. 2. Their concordance in their source and use.

1. Their difference in their kind and measure, is expressed in the first clause, *As every one hath received ;* then, again, in the last clause, [ποικίλη χάρις] *various* or *manifold grace ;* where χάρις, *grace,* is all one with the former, χάρισμα, *gift,* and is taken at large for all kind of endowments and furniture by which men are enabled for mutual good. One man hath riches; another, authority and command ; another, wit, or eloquence, or learning ; and some, though eminent in some one, yet have a fuller conjuncture of divers of these. We find not more difference in visages and statures of body, than in qualifications and abilities of mind, which are the visage and stature of it ; yea, the odds is far greater betwixt man and man in this than it can be in the other.

2. Now, this difference accords well, with the accordance here expressed in their common spring and common use. For

the variety of these many gifts suits well with the singular riches and wisdom of their one Giver, and with the common advantage and benefit of the many receivers. And in the usefulness of that variety to the receivers shine forth the bounty and wisdom of the Giver, in so ordering all that diversity to one excellent end. So, this ποικίλη χάρις, *manifold grace,* here commends that πολυποίκιλος σοφία, *manifold wisdom,* that the Apostle speaks of, Eph. iii. 10.

There is such an admirable beauty in this variety, such a symmetry and contemperature of different, yea, of contrary qualities, as speaks his riches, that so diverse gifts are from the same Spirit; a kind of *embroidering* *, of many colours happily mixed, as the word ποικίλλειν signifies : as it is in the frame of the natural body of man, that lesser world, and in the composition of the greater world, thus it is in the Church of God, the mystical body of Jesus Christ, exceeding both in excellency and beauty.

And as there is such art in this contrivance, and such comeliness in the resulting frame, so it is no less useful. And this chiefly commends the thing itself, and the supreme wisdom ordering it, that, as in the body, each part hath not only its place for proportion and order, but its several use; and as in the world, each part is beneficial to another, so here, every man's gift relates, and is fitted to some use for the good of others.

Infer. 1. The first thing which meets us here, it is very useful to know, that all is *received,* and received of *gift,* of most *free gift :* so the words do carry. Now, this should most reasonably check all murmuring in those who receive least, and all insulting in those that receive most. Whatever it is, do not repine ; but praise, how little soever it is, for it is a free gift. Again, how much soever it is, *be not high-minded, but fear :* boast not thyself, but humbly bless thy Lord. *For if thou didst receive it, why dost thou boast, as if thou hadst not received it ?* (I Cor. iv. 7.)

* The Psalmist's word applied to the body, Psal. cxxxix. 12.

Inf. 2. Every man hath received some gift, no man all gifts ; and this, rightly considered, would keep all in a more even temper. As, in nature, nothing is altogether useless, so nothing is self-sufficient. This should keep the meanest from repining and discontent : he that hath the lowest rank in most respects, yet something he hath received, that is not only a good to himself, but, rightly improved, may be so to others likewise. And this will curb the loftiness of the most highly privileged, and teach them, not only to see some deficiencies in themselves, and some gifts in far meaner persons, which they want, but, besides the simple discovery of this, it will put them upon the use of what is in lower persons ; not only to stoop to the acknowledgment, but even, withal, to the participation and benefit of it ; not to trample upon all that is below them, but to take up and use things useful, though lying at their feet. Some flowers and herbs, that grow very low, are of a very fragrant smell and healthful use.

Thou that carriest it so high, losest much by it. Many poor Christians whom thou despisest to make use of, may have that in them which might be very useful for thee ; but thou overlookest it, and treadest on it. St. Paul acknowledgeth he was *comforted by the coming of Titus,* though far inferior to him. Sometimes, a very mean, unlettered Christian may speak more profitably and comfortably, even to a knowing, learned man, than multitudes of his own best thoughts can do, especially in a time of weakness and darkness.

Inf. 3. As all is received, and with that difference, so the third thing is, that all is received, *to minister to each other,* and mutual benefit is the true use of all, suiting the mind of Him who dispenses all, and the way of His dispensation. Thou art not proprietary lord of any thing thou hast, but οἰκονόμος, *a steward ;* and therefore oughtest gladly to be a good steward, that is, both faithful and prudent in thy intrusted gifts, using all thou hast to the good of the Household, and so to the advantage of thy Lord and Master. Hast thou abilities of estate, or body, or mind ? Let all be thus employed.

Thinkest thou that thy wealth, or power, or wit, is thine, to do with as thou wilt, to engross to thyself, either to retain use-less, or to use ; to hoard and wrap up, or to lavish out, accord-ing as thy humour leads thee ? No, all is given as to a steward, wisely and faithfully to lay up and lay out. Not only thy outward and common gifts of mind, but even saving grace, which seems most intrusted and appropriated for thy private good, yet is not wholly for that : even thy graces are for the good of thy brethren.

Oh, that we would consider this in all, and look back and mourn on the fruitlessness of all that hath been in our hand all our life hitherto ! If it has not been wholly fruitless, yet how far short of that fruit we might have brought forth ! Any little thing done by us looks big in our eye ; we view it through a magnifying glass ; but who may not complain that their means, and health, and opportunities of several kinds, of doing for God and for our brethren, have lain dead upon their hands in a great part ? As Christians are defective in other duties of love, so most in that most important duty, of advancing the spiritual good of each other. Even they who have grace, do not duly use it to mutual edification. I desire none to leap over the bounds of their calling, or the rules of Christian prudence in their converse ; yea, this were much to be blamed ; but I fear lest unwary hands, throwing on water to quench that evil, have let some of it fall aside upon those sparks that should rather have been stirred and blown up.

Neither should the disproportion of gifts and graces hinder Christians to *minister one to another :* it should neither move the weaker to envy the stronger, nor the stronger to despise the weaker ; but each, in his place, is to be serviceable to the others, as the Apostle excellently presses, by that most fit re-semblance of the parts of the body : *As the foot says not, Why am I not the eye or the head, the head cannot say of the foot, I have no need of thee.* (1 Cor. xii. 15, 21.) There is no envy, no despising, in the natural body. Oh, the pity there should be so much in the mystical ! Were we more spiritual, less of this would be found. In the mean time, Oh, that we were more agreeable to that happy estate we look for, in our present aspect and carriage one towards another! Though all the graces of the Spirit exist, in some measure, where there is one, yet not all in a like measure. One Christian is more eminent in meekness, another in humility, a third in zeal, &c. Now, by their spiritual converse one with another, each may be a gainer; and in many ways may a private Christian promote the good of others with whom he lives, by seasonable admonitions, and advice, and reproof, sweetened with meekness, but most by holy example, which is the most lively and most effectual speech.

Thou that hast greater gifts hast more intrusted in thy hand, and therefore the greater thy obligation to fidelity and diligence. Men in great place and public services, ought to stir themselves up by this thought, to singular watchfulness and zeal. And in private converse one with another, we ought to be doing and receiving spiritual good. Are we not strangers here? Is it not strange that we so often meet and part, without a word of our home, or the way to it, or our advance towards it? Christians should be trading one with another in spiritual things; and he, surely, who faithfully uses most, receives most. This is comprehended under that word: *To him that hath,* (*i. e.,* possesses actively and usefully,) *shall be given; and from him that hath not,* (*i. e.,* uses not,) *shall be taken away even that which he hath.* (Matt. xxv. 29.) Merchants can feel in their trading a dead time, and complain seriously of it; but Christians, in theirs, either can suffer it and not see it, or see it and not complain, or, possibly, complain, and yet not be deeply sensible of it.

Certainly, it cannot be sufficiently regretted, that we are so fruitless in the Lord's work in this kind, that when we are alone we study it not more, nor seek it more by prayer, to know the true use of all we receive, and that we do not in society endeavour it accordingly; but we trifle out our time, and instead of the commerce of grace to our mutual enriching, we trade in vanity, and are, as it were, children exchanging shells and toys together.

This surely will lie heavy upon the conscience when we reflect on it, and shall come near the utter brink of time, looking forwards on eternity, and then looking back to our days, so vainly wasted, and worn out to so little purpose. Oh ! let us awake, awake ourselves and one another, to more fruitfulness and faithfulness, whatsoever be our received measure, less or more.

Be not discouraged: to have little in the account shall be no prejudice. The approbation runs not, *Thou hast much*, but, on the contrary, *Thou hast been faithful in little.* Great faithfulness in the use of small gifts hath great acceptance, and a great and sure reward. Great receipts engage to greater returns, and therefore require the greater diligence ; and that not only for the increase of grace within, but for the assistance of it in others. Retired contemplation may be more pleasing, but due activity for God and His Church is more profitable. Rachel was fair, but she was barren ; Leah blear-eyed, but fruitful.

Ver. 11. If any man speak, let him speak as the oracles of God ; if any
        man minister, let him do it as of the ability which God giveth ; that
        God in all things may be glorified through Jesus Christ ; to whom
      , be praise and dominion for ever and ever. Amen.

EVERY part of the Body of Christ, as it partakes of life with the rest, so it imparts service to the rest. But there be some more eminent, and, as I may say, *organic* parts of this Body, and these are more eminently useful to the whole. Therefore the Apostle, having enlarged into a general precept, adds a word in special preference to these special parts, the Preachers of the word, and (which here I conceive is meant by deacons or ministers) the other assistant officers of the Church of God.

These are co-ordained by Jesus Christ, as Lord of His own House, to be serviceable to Him in it. He fits and sanctifies for this great work, all who are called unto it by Himself. And they are directed for the acquitting of their great work, I. By a clear rule of the due manner; II. By the main end of its appointment.

I. Particular rules for the preaching of the word may be many, but this is a most comprehensive one which the Apostle gives: *If any man speak, let him speak as the oracles of God.* It is clear from the rule, what speaking is regulated, and for brevity it is once expressed. If any man speak the oracles of God, let him speak them like themselves, *as the oracles of God.*

It is a chief thing in all serious actions, to take the nature of them aright: for this mainly regulates them, and directs in their performance. And this especially should be regarded in those things that are of highest worth and greatest weight, in spiritual employments, wherein it is most dangerous, and yet with us most ordinary, to mistake and miscarry. Were prayer considered as presence and speech with the great God, the King of glory, Oh, how would this mould the mind! What a watchful, holy, and humble deportment would it teach! So that truly, all directions for prayer might be summed up, after this same model, in this one, If any man pray, let him speak *as speaking with God;* just as here for preaching, If any man speak in that way, let him do it as *speaking from God,* that is, *as the oracles of God.* Under this, all the due qualifications of this holy work are comprised. I shall name but these three, which are primary, and others may be easily reduced to these: 1. *Faithfully.* 2. *Holily.* 3. *Wisely.*

1. In the first, *Fidelity,* it is supposed that a man should have a competent insight and knowledge in these Divine oracles, that first he learn before he teach; which many of us do not, though we pass through the schools and classes, and through the books too, wherein these things are taught, and bring with us some provision, such as may be had there. He that would faithfully teach of God, must be *taught of God,* be θεοδίδακτός, *God-learned;* and this will help to all the rest; will help him to be faithful in delivering the message as he receives it not detracting, or adding, or altering; and as in setting forth that

n general truths, so, in the particular setting them home, declaring to His people their sins, and God's judgments following
sin, especially in His own people.

2. A minister must speak *holily*, with that high esteem and
reverence of the Great Majesty whose message he carries, that
becomes the divinity of the message itself, those deep mysteries
that no created spirits are able to fathom. Oh! this would make
us tremble in the dispensing of these oracles, considering our
impurities, and weaknesses, and unspeakable disproportion to
so high a task. He had reason who said, " I am seized with
amazement and horror as often as I begin to speak of God."
And with this humble reverence is to be joined, ardent love to
our Lord, to His truth, to His glory, and to His people's souls.
These holy affections stand opposite to our blind boldness in
rushing on this sublime exercise as a common work, and our
dead coldness in speaking of things which our hearts are not
warmed with ; and so, no wonder what we say seldom reaches
further than the ear, or, at furthest, than the understanding
and memory of our hearers. There is a correspondence ; it is
the heart speaks to the heart, and the understanding and memory the same, and the tongue speaks but to the ear. Further,
this holy temper shuts out all private passion in delivering
Divine truths. It is a high profaning of His name and holy
things, to make them speak our private pleas and quarrels ;
yea, to reprove sin after this manner is a heinous sin. To fly
out into invectives, which, though not expressed so, yet are
aimed as blows of self-revenge for injuries done to us, or fancied by us, this is to wind and draw the holy word of God to
serve our unholy distempers, and to make it speak, not His
meaning, but our own. Surely, this is not to speak *as the
oracles of God*, but basely to abuse the word, as impostors in
religion of old did their images, speaking behind them, and
through them, what might make for their advantage. It is
true, that the word is to be particularly applied to reprove most
the particular sins which most abound amongst a people ; but
this is to be done, not in anger, but in love.

3. The word is to be spoken *wisely*. By this I mean, in the way of delivering it, that it be done gravely and decently ; that light expressions, and affected flourishes, and unseemly gestures, be avoided ; and that there be a sweet contemperature of authority and mildness. But *who is sufficient for these things?*

Now, you that hear should certainly meet and agree in this too. If any hear, let him hear *as the oracles of God;* not as a well-tuned sound, to help you to sleep an hour; not as a human speech or oration, to displease or please you for an hour, according to the suiting of its strain and your palate ; not as a school lesson, to add somewhat to your stock of knowledge, to tell you somewhat you knew not before, or as a feast of new notions. Thus the most relish a preacher, while they try his gift, and it is new with them, but a little time disgusts them. But hear *as the oracles of God.* The discovery of sin and death lying on us, and the discovery of a Saviour that takes these off; the sweet word of reconciliation, God wooing man ; the Great King entreating for peace with a company of rebels,— not that they are too strong for him, Oh ! no, but, on the contrary, He could utterly destroy them in one moment ; these are the things brought you in this word. Therefore come to it with suitable reverence, with ardent desires, and hearts open to receive it *with meekness, as the ingrafted word that is able' to save your souls.* (James i. 21.) It were well worth one day's pains of speaking and hearing, that we could learn somewhat, at least, how to speak and hear henceforward; to speak, and to hear, *as the oracles of God.*

In the other rule, of *ministering as of the ability that God giveth,* we may observe : 1. Ability, and that received from God; for other ability there is none for any good word, and least of all, for the peculiar ministration of His spiritual affairs in His house. 2. The using of this ability received from Him for them.

And this, truly, is a chief thing for ministers, and for individual Christians, still to depend on the influence and strength of God; to do all his works in that strength. The humblest

Christian, how weak soever, is the strongest. There is a natural wretched independency in us, that we would be the authors of our own works, and do all without Him, without whom indeed we can do nothing. Let us learn to go more out of ourselves, and we shall find more strength for our duties, and against our temptations. Faith's great work is, to renounce self-power, and to bring in the power of God to be ours. Happy they that are weakest in themselves, sensibly so. That word of the Apostle is theirs; they know what it means, though a riddle to the world : *When I am weak, then am I strong.* 2 Cor. xii. 10. Now,

II. The *End* of all this appointment, is, *that in all God may be glorified through Jesus Christ.* All meet in this, if they move in their straight line : here concentre, not only these two sorts specified in this verse, but all sorts of persons that use aright any gift of God, as they are generally comprehended in the former verse. For this end relates to all, as it is expressed universally, *That in all,* in all persons and all things; the word bears both, and the thing itself extends to both.

Here we have, like that of the heavens, a circular motion of all sanctified good : it comes forth from God, through Christ, unto Christians, and moving in them to the mutual good of each other, returns through Christ unto God again, and takes them along with it, in whom it was, and had its motion.

All persons and all things shall pay this tribute, even they that most wickedly seek to withhold it; but this is the happiness of the saints, that they move willingly thus, are sweetly drawn, not forced or driven. They are gained to seek and desire this, to set in with God in the intention of the same end ; to have the same purpose with Him, His glory in all; and to prosecute His end by His direction, by the means and ways He appoints them.

This is His due, as God; and the declining from this, the squinting from this view to self-ends, especially in God's own peculiar work, is high treason. Yet, the base heart of man leads naturally this way, to intend himself in all, to raise his own esteem or advantage in some way. And in this the heart is so subtle, that it will deceive the most discerning, if they be not constant in suspecting and watching it. This is the great task, to overcome in this point; to have self under our feet, and God only in our eye and purpose in all.

It is most reasonable, His due, as God the author of all, not only of all supervenient good, but even of being itself, seeing all is from Him, that all be for Him: *For of Him, and through Him, and to Him, are all things: to Whom.be glory for ever. Amen.* (Rom. xi. *ult.*)

As it is most just, so it is also most sweet, to aim in all at this, *that God be glorified :* it is-the alone worthy and happy design, which fills the heart with heavenliness, and with a heavenly calmness; sets it above the clouds and storms of those passions which disquiet low, self-seeking minds. He is a miserable, unsettled wretch, who cleaves to himself and forgets God; is perplexed about his credit, and gain, and base ends, which are often broken, and which, when he attains, yet they and he must shortly perish together. When his estate, or designs, or any comforts, fail, how can he look to Him at whom he looked so little before? May not the Lord say, *Go to the gods whom thou hast served, and let them deliver and comfort thee;* seek comfort from thyself, as thou didst all for thyself? What an appalment will this be! But he that hath resigned himself, and is all for God, may say confidently, that *the Lord is his portion.* This is the Christian's aim, to have nothing in himself, nor in any thing, but on this tenure: all for the glory of my God,—my estate, family, abilities, my whole self, all I have and am. And as the love of God grows in the heart, this purpose grows: the higher the flame rises, the purer it is. The eye is daily more upon it; it is oftener in the mind in all actions than before. In common things, the very works of our callings, our very refreshments, to eat and drink, and sleep, are all for this end, and with a particular aim at it as much as may be; even the thought of it often renewed throughout the day, and at times, generally applied to all our ways and employments.

It is this elixir that turns thy ordinary works into gold, into sacrifices, by the touch of it.

Through Jesus Christ.] The Christian in covenant with God, receives all this way, and returns all this way. And Christ possesses, and hath equal right with the Father to this glory, as He is equally the spring of it with Him, as God. But it is conveyed through him as Mediator, who obtains all the grace we receive; and all the glory we return, and all our praise, as our spiritual sacrifice, is put into His hand as our High Priest, to offer up for us, that they may be accepted.

Now the holy ardour of the Apostle's affections, taken with the mention of this glory of God, carries him to a *doxology*, as we term it, a rendering of glory, in the middle of his discourse. Thus often we find in St. Paul likewise. Poor and short-lived is the glory and grandeur of men; like themselves, it is a shadow, and nothing; but this is solid and lasting, it is supreme, and abideth *for ever.* And the Apostles, full of divine affections, and admiring nothing but God, do delight in this, and cannot refrain from this at any time in their discourse: it is always sweet and seasonable, and they find it so. And thus are spiritual minds: a word of this nature falls on them as a spark on some matter that readily takes fire ; they are straight inflamed with it. But alas! to us how much is it otherwise! The mention of the praises and glory of our God is, to our hearts, as a spark falling either into a puddle of water, and foul water too, or at least, as upon green timber, that much fire will not kindle; there is so much moisture of our humours and corruptions, that all dies out with us, and we remain cold and dead.

But were not this a high and blessed condition, to be in all estates in some willing readiness to bear a part in this song, to acknowledge the greatness and goodness of our God, and to wish Him glory in all ? What are the angels doing ? This is their business, and that without end. And seeing we hope to partake with them, we should even here, though in a lower key, and not so tunably neither, yet, as we may, begin it ; and upon all occasions, our hearts should be often following in this sweet note, or offering at it, *To Him be glory and dominion for ever.*

Ver. 12. Beloved, think it not strange concerning the fiery trial 'which is to try you, as though some strange thing happened unto you.
Ver. 13. But rejoice, inasmuch as you are partakers of Christ's sufferings; that when his glory shall be revealed, ye may be glad also with exceeding joy.

THIS fighting life, surely, when we consider it aright, we need not be dissuaded from loving it, but have rather need to be strengthened with patience to go through, and to fight on with courage and assurance of victory; still combating in a higher strength than our own, against sin within and troubles without. This is the great scope of this Epistle, and the Apostle often interchanges his advices and comforts in reference to these two. *Against sin* he instructs us in the beginning of this chapter, urging us to be armed, *armed with the same mind* that was in Christ, and here again, *against suffering*, and both in a like way. In the mortifying of sin, we suffer with Him, as there he teaches, verse 1 of this chapter; and in the encountering of affliction, we suffer with Him, as here we have it; and so the same mind in the same sufferings, will bring us to the same issue. *Beloved, think it not strange concerning the fiery trial which is to try you, &c. But rejoice, inasmuch as ye are partakers of Christ's sufferings; that when his glory shall be revealed, ye likewise may be glad with exceeding joy.*

The words to the end of the chapter, contain grounds of encouragement and consolation for the children of God in sufferings, especially in suffering for God.

These two verses have these two things: I. The close conjunction of sufferings with the estate of a Christian; II. The due composure of a Christian towards suffering.

I. It is no new, and therefore no strange thing, that sufferings, hot sufferings, fiery ones, be the companions of religion. Besides the common miseries of human life, there is an accession of troubles and hatreds for that holiness of life to which the children of God are called.

It was the lot of the Church from her wicked neighbours, and in the Church, the lot of the most holy and peculiar servants of God, from the profane multitude. *Wo is me, my mother*, says Jeremiah, *that thou hast born me a man of strife, and a man of contention to the whole earth.* (Jer. xv. 10.) And of all the Prophets, says not our Saviour, handling this same argument in his sermon, *So persecuted they the Prophets that were before you?* (Matt. v. 12.) And afterwards, He tells them what they might look for : *Behold*, says He, *I send you forth as sheep in the midst of wolves.* (Matt. x. 16.) And, in general, there is no following of Christ, but with His badge and burden. Something is to be left, we ourselves are to be left— *Whosoever will be my disciple, let him deny himself;* and somewhat to take—*Take up his cross, and follow me.* (Matt. xvi. 24.) And doth not the Apostle give his scholars this universal lesson, as an infallible truth, *All that will live godly in Jesus Christ, shall suffer persecution?* Look in the close of that roll of believers conquering in suffering, what a cluster of sufferings and torture you have. (Heb. xi. 36, &c.) Thus in the primitive times, the trial, and fiery trial, even literally so, continued long. Those wicked emperors hated the very innocency of Christians; and the people, though they knew their blameless carriage, yet, when any evil came, would pick this quarrel, and still cry, *Christianos ad leones.*

Now this, if we look to inferior causes, is *not strange*, the malignant ungodly world hating holiness, *hating the light*, yea, the very shadow of it. And the more the children of God walk like their Father and their home, the more unlike must they, of necessity, become to the world about them, and therefore become the very mark of all their enmities and malice.

And thus indeed, the godly, though the *sons of peace*, are the improper causes, the occasion of much noise and disturbance in the world ; as their Lord, the Prince of Peace, avows it openly of Himself in that sense, *I came not to send peace, but a sword, to set a man at variance with his father, and the daughter against the mother,* &c. (Matt. x. 34) If a son in a family begin to inquire after God, and withdraw from their profane or dead way, Oh, what a clamour rises presently! " Oh, my son, or daughter, or wife, is become a plain fool," *&c.* And then is all done that may be, to quell and vex them, and make their life grievous to them.

The exact holy walking of a Christian really condemns the world about him ; shews the disorder and foulness of their profane ways. The life of religion, set by the side of dead formality, discovers it to be a carcass, a lifeless appearance ; and, for this, neither grossly wicked, nor decent, formal persons, can well digest it. There is in the life of a Christian a convincing light, that shews the deformity of the works of darkness, and a piercing heat, that scorches the ungodly, and stirs and troubles their consciences. This they cannot endure, and hence rises in them a contrary fire of wicked hatred, and hence the trials, the fiery trials of the godly. If they could get those precise persons removed out of their way, they think, they might then have more room, and live at more liberty : as it is, Rev. xi. 10, a *carousing* [χαρουσιν]. What a dance there was about the dead bodies of the Two Witnesses ! *The people and nations rejoiced and made merry, and sent gifts one to another, because these two Prophets tormented them that dwelt on the earth.* And from the same hearth, I mean the same wickedness of heart in the world, are the fires of persecution kindled against the saints in the world, and the bonfires of joy when they are rid of them.

And as this is an infernal fire of enmity against God, so it is blown by that Spirit whose element it is. Satan stirs up and blows the coal, and raises the hatred of the ungodly against Christians.

But while he, and they in whom he powerfully works, are thus working for their vile ends in the persecutions of the saints, HE who sovereignly orders all, is working in the same His wise and gracious ends, and attains them, and makes the malice of

His enemies serve His ends, and undo their own. It is true, that by the heat of persecution many are scared from embracing religion : such as love themselves and their present ease, and others that seemed to have embraced it, are driven to let it go and fall from it; but yet, when all is well computed, religion is still upon the gaining hand. Those who reject it or revolt from it, are such as have no true knowledge of it, or share in it, nor in that happiness in which it ends. But they that are indeed united to Jesus Christ, do cleave the closer to Him, and seek to have their hearts more fastened to Him, because of the trials that they are, or may probably be put to. And in their victorious patience appears the invincible power of religion where it hath once gained the heart, that it cannot be beaten or burnt out : itself is a fire more mighty than all the fires kindled against it. The love of Christ conquers and triumphs in the hardest sufferings of life, and in death itself.

And this hath been the means of kindling it in other hearts which were strangers to it, when they beheld the victorious patience of the saints, who conquered dying, as their Head did; who wearied their tormentors, and triumphed over their cruelty by a constancy far above it.

Thus, these fiery trials make the lustre of faith most appear, as gold shines brightest in the furnace; and if any dross be mixed with it, it is refined and purified from it by these trials, and so it remains, by means of the fire, purer than before. And both these are in the resemblance here intended; that the fire of sufferings is for the advantage of believers, both as trying the excellency of faith, giving evidence of it, what it is, and also purifying it from earth and drossy mixtures, and making it more excellently what it is, raising it to a higher pitch of refinedness and worth. In these fires, as faith is tried, so the word on which faith relies is tried, and is found *all gold*, most precious, no refuse in it. The truth and sweetness of the promises are much confirmed in the Christian's heart, upon his experiment of them in his sufferings. His God is found to be as good as His word, being with him when he goes through the fire, (Isa. xliii. 2,) preserving him, so that he loses nothing except dross, which is a gainful loss, leaves only of his corruption behind him.

Oh! how much worth is it, and how doth it endear the heart to God, to have found Him sensibly present in the times of trouble, refreshing the soul with dews of spiritual comfort, in the midst of the flames of fiery trial!

One special advantage of these fires, is, the purifying of a Christian's heart from the love of the world and of present things. It is true, the world at best is base and despicable, in respect of the high estate and hopes of a believer; yet still, there is somewhat within him that would bend him downwards, and draw him to too much complacency in outward things, if they were much to his mind. Too kind usage might sometimes make him forget himself and think himself at home, at least so much as not to entertain those longings after home, and that ardent progress homewards, that become him. It is good for us, certainly, to find hardship, and enmities, and contempts here, and to find them frequent, that we may not think them *strange*, but ourselves *strangers*, and may think it were strange for us to be otherwise entertained. This keeps the affections more clear and disengaged, sets them upward. Thus the Lord makes the world displeasing to His own, that they may turn in to Him, and seek all their consolations in Himself. Oh, unspeakable advantage!

II. The composure of a Christian in reference to sufferings, is prescribed in these two following, *resolving and rejoicing:* 1. Resolving to endure them, reckoning upon them, *Think it not strange*, μὴ ξενίζεσθε; 2. Rejoicing in them, χαίρετε, *Be glad inasmuch*, &c.

Be not strangers in it.] Which yet naturally we would be. We are willing to hear of peace and ease, and would gladly believe what we extremely desire. It is a thing of prime concern, to take at first a right notion of Christianity. This many do not, and so, either fall off quickly, or walk on slowly and heavily; they do not reckon right the charges, take not into the account the duties of doing and suffering, but think to perform some duties, if they may with ease, and have no other foresight; they do not consider that self-denial, that fighting against a man's self, and fighting vehemently with the world, those trials, fiery trials, which a Christian must encounter with. As they observe of other points, so Popery is in this very compliant with nature, which is a very bad sign in religion. We would be content it were true that the true Church of Christ hath rather prosperity and pomp for her badge, than the Cross; much ease and riches, and few or no crosses, except they were painted and gilded crosses, such as that Church hath chosen, instead of real ones.

Most men would give religion a fair countenance, if it gave them fair weather; and they that do indeed acknowledge Christ to be the Son of God, as St. Peter did, yet are naturally as unwilling as he was, to hear the hard news of suffering; and if their advice might have place, would readily be of his mind, *Be it far from thee, Lord.* (Matt. xvi. 22, 23.) His good confession was not, but this kind advice was, from *flesh and blood*, and from an evil Spirit, as the sharp answer tells, *Get thee behind me, Satan, thou art an offence unto me.*

You know what kind of Messiah the Jews generally dreamed of, and therefore took offence at the meanness and sufferings of Christ, expecting an earthly king, and an outwardly flourishing state. And the disciples themselves, after they had been long with Him, were still in that same dream, when they were contesting about imaginary places. Yea, they were scarcely well out of it, even after his suffering and death: all the noise and trouble of that had not well awaked them. *We trusted it had been He which should have restored Israel.* (Luke xxiv. 21.)

And, after all that we have read and heard of ancient times, and of Jesus Christ Himself, His sufferings in the flesh, and of His Apostles and His Saints, from one age to another, yet still we have our inclinations to this practice of driving troubles far off from our thoughts, till they come upon our backs, fancying nothing but rest and ease, till we be shaken rudely out of it.

How have we of late flattered ourselves, many of us one year after another, upon slight appearances, Oh, now it will be peace! And, behold, still trouble hath increased, and these thoughts have proved the lying visions of our own hearts, while *the Lord hath not spoken of it.* (Ezek. xiii. 7.) And thus, of late, have we thought it at hand, and taken ways of our own to hasten it, which, I fear, will prove fool's haste, as you say.

You that know the Lord, seek Him earnestly for the averting of further troubles and combustions, which, if you look aright, you will find threatening us as much as ever. And withal, seek hearts prepared and fixed for days of trial, *fiery trial.* Yea, though we did obtain some breathing of our outward peace, yet shall not the followers of Christ want their trials from the hatred of the ungodly world. *If it persecuted me,* says He, *it will also persecute you.* (John xv. 20.)

Acquaint, therefore, your thoughts and hearts with sufferings, that when they come, thou and they not being strangers, may agree and comply the better. Do not afflict yourselves with vain fears beforehand of troubles to come, and so make uncertain evils a certain vexation by advance; but thus forethink the hardest trial you are likely to be put to for the name and cause of Christ, and labour for a holy stability of mind for encountering it if it should come upon you. Things certainly fall the lighter on us, when they fall first upon our thoughts. In this way, indeed, of an imagined suffering, the conquest beforehand may be but imaginary, and thou mayest fail in the trial. Therefore, be still humble and dependent on the strength of Christ, and seek to be previously furnished with much distrust of thyself and much trust in Him, with much denial of thyself and much love to Him; and this preparing and training of the heart may prove useful, and make it more dexterous, when brought to a real conflict.   In all, both beforehand, and in the time of the trial, make thy Lord Jesus all thy strength.   That is our only way in all to be conquerors, *to be more than conquerors, through Him that loved us.* (Rom. viii. 37.)

Think it not strange, for it is not.   Suit your thoughts to the experience and verdict of all times, and to the warnings that the Spirit of God hath given us in the Scriptures, and our Saviour Himself from His own mouth, and in the example which He shewed in His own person.   But the point goes higher.

Rejoice.]   Though we think not the sufferings *strange,* yet may we not well think that rule somewhat strange, to *rejoice* in them?   No, it will be found as reasonable as the other, being duly considered.   And it rests upon the same ground, which will bear both.   *Inasmuch as you are partakers of the sufferings of Christ.*

If the children of God consider their trials, not in their natural bitterness, but in the sweet love from whence they spring, and the sweet fruits that spring from them, that we are our Lord's gold, and that he tries us in the furnace to purify us, (as in the former verse,) this may beget not only patience, but gladness even in the sufferings.   But add we this, and truly it completes the reason of this way of rejoicing in our saddest sufferings, that in them we are *partakers of the sufferings of Christ.*

So then, 1. Consider this twofold connected participation, of the sufferings of Christ and of the after-glory; 2. The present joy, even in sufferings, springing from that participation.

I need not tell you, that this communion in sufferings, is not in point of expiation, or satisfaction to Divine justice, which was the peculiar end of the sufferings of Christ *personal,* but not of the common sufferings of Christ *mystical.   He bare our sins in His own body on the tree,* and, in bearing them, took them away: we bear His sufferings, as His body united to Him by His Spirit.   Those sufferings which were His personal burden, we partake the sweet fruits of; they are accounted ours, and we are acquitted by them; but the endurance of them was His high and incommunicable task, in which none at all were with Him. Our communion in these, as fully completed by Himself in His natural body, is the ground of our comfort and joy in those sufferings that are completed in His mystical body, the Church.

This is indeed our joy, that we have so light a burden, so sweet an exchange; the weight of sin quite taken off our backs, and all bound on His cross only, and our crosses, the badges of our conformity to Him, laid indeed on our shoulders, but the great weight of them likewise held up by His hand, that they overpress us not. These fires of our trial may be corrective, and purgative of the remaining power of sin, and they are so intended; but Jesus Christ alone, in the sufferings of His own cross, was the burnt-offering, *the propitiation for our sins.*

Now, although He hath perfectly satisfied for us, and saved us by His sufferings, yet this conformity to Him in the way of suffering is most reasonable. Although our holiness doth not stand in point of law, nor come in at all in the matter of justifying us, yet we are called and appointed to holiness in Christ, as assimilating us to Him, our glorious Head; and we do really receive it from Him, that we may be like Him. So these our sufferings bear a very congruous likeness to Him, though in no way as an accession to His in expiation, yet as a part of His image; and therefore the Apostle says, even in this respect, that we are *predestinated to be conformed to the image of his Son:* Rom. viii. 29. Is it fit that we should not follow where our Captain led, and went first, but that he should lead through rugged, thorny ways, and we pass about to get away through flowery meadows? As His natural body shared with His head in His sufferings, so ought His body mystical to share with Him, as its Head,—the buffetings and spittings on His face, the thorny crowns on His head, a pierced side, nailed hands and feet: if we be parts of Him, can we think that a body finding nothing but ease, and bathing in delights, can agree to a Head so tormented? I remember what that pious Duke said at Jerusalem, when they offered to crown him king there, *Nolo auream, ubi Christus spineam :* No crown of gold, where Christ Jesus was crowned with thorns.

This is the way we must follow, or else resolve to leave Him; the way of the Cross is the royal way to the Crown. He said it, and reminded them of it again, that they might take the deep impression of it: *Remember what I said unto you, the servant is not greater than the Lord. If they have persecuted me, they will also persecute you: if they have kept my saying, they will keep yours also.* (John xv. 20.) And particularly in point of reproaches: *If they have called the master Beelzebub, how much more shall they call them of his household?* (Matt. x. 24.) A bitter scoff, an evil name, reproaches for Christ, why do these fret thee? They were a part of thy Lord's entertainment while be·was here. Thou art, even in this, *a partaker of His sufferings,* and in this way is He bringing thee forward to the partaking of His glory. That is the other thing.

When His glory shall be revealed.] Now that He is hidden, little of His glory is seen. It was hidden while He was on earth, and now it is hidden in heaven, where He is. And as for His body here, His Church, it hath no pompous dress, nor outward splendour; and the particular parts of it, the saints, are poor despised creatures, the very refuse of men in outward respects and common esteem. So He himself is not seen, and His followers, the more they are seen and looked on by the World's eye, the more meanness appears. True, as in the days of His humiliation some rays were breaking forth through the veil of His flesh and the cloud of His low despicable condition, thus it is sometimes with His followers: a glance of His image strikes the very eye of the World, and forces some acknowledgment and a kind of reverence in the ungodly; but, commonly, Christ and His followers are covered with all the disgraces and ignominies the World can put on them. But there is a day wherein He will appear, and it is at hand; and then *He shall be glorious,* even *in His* despised *saints,* and *admired in them that believe:* (2 Thess. i. 10 :) how much more in the matchless brightness of His own glorious person!

In the mean time, He is hidden, and they are hidden in Him: *Our life is hid with Christ in God.* (Col. iii. 3.) The World sees nothing of His glory and beauty, and even His own see not much; they have but a little glimmering of Him, and of their own happiness in Him; know little of their own high condition, and what they are born to. But in that bright day, He shall shine forth in His royal dignity, and *every eye shall see Him,* and be overcome with His splendour. Terrible shall it be to those that formerly despised Him and His saints, but to them it shall be the gladdest day that ever arose upon them, a day that shall never set or be benighted; the day they so much longed and looked out for, the full accomplishment of all their hopes and desires. Oh, how dark were all our days without the hope of this day!

Then, says the Apostle, *ye shall rejoice* with exceeding *joy;* and to the end you may not fall short of that joy in the participation of glory, fall not back from a cheerful progress in the communion of those sufferings that are so closely linked with it, and will so surely lead unto it, and end in it. For in this the Apostle's expression, this glory and joy is set before them, as the great matter of their desires and hopes, and the certain end of their present sufferings.

Now, upon these grounds, the admonition will appear reasonable, and not too great a demand, *to rejoice* even *in sufferings.*

It is true, that passage in the Epistle to the Hebrews, ch. xii. v. 11, opposes present affliction to joy. But, 1. If you mark, it is but in the appearance, or outward visage, *It seemeth not to be matter of joy, but of grief.* To look upon, it hath not a smiling countenance; yet joy may be under it. And, 2. Though to the flesh it is what it seems, grief, and not joy, yet there may be under it spiritual joy; yea, the affliction itself may help and advance that joy. 3. Through the natural sense of it, there will be some alloy or mixture of grief, so that the joy cannot be pure and complete, but yet there may be joy even in it. This the Apostle here clearly grants: *Rejoice* now *in* suffering, that you may *rejoice exceedingly after* it, ἀγαλλιώμενοι, *leaping for joy*. Doubtless, this joy, at present, is but a little parcel, a drop of that sea of joy. Now it is joy, but more is reserved. Then *they shall leap for joy*. Yet even at present, rejoice in *trial*, yea, in *fiery trial*. This may be done. The children of God are not called to so sad a life as the World imagines: besides what is laid up for them in heaven, they have even here their rejoicings and songs in their distresses, as those prisoners had their psalms even at midnight, after their stripes, and in their chains, before they knew of a sudden deliverance. (Acts xvi. 25.) True, there may be a darkness within, clouding all the matter of their joy, but even that darkness is the seed-time of after-joy: light is sown in that darkness, and shall spring up; and not only shall they have a rich crop at full harvest, but even some first-fruits of it here, in pledge of the harvest.

And this they ought to expect, and to seek after with minds humble and submissive as to the measure and time of it, that they may be partakers of spiritual joy, and may by it be enabled to go patiently, yea, cheerfully, through the tribulations and temptations that lie in their way homeward. And for this end they ought to endeavour after a more clear discerning of their interest in Christ, that they may know they partake of Him, and so that, in suffering, they are partakers of His sufferings, and shall be partakers of His glory.

Many afflictions will not cloud and obstruct this, so much as one sin; therefore, if ye would walk cheerfully, be most careful to walk holily. All the winds about the earth make not an earthquake, but only that within.

Now this Joy is grounded on this communion, [1.] in sufferings, then, [2.] in glory.

[1.] Even in sufferings themselves. It is a sweet, a joyful thing to be a sharer with Christ in any thing. All enjoyments wherein He is not, are bitter to a soul that loves Him, and all sufferings with Him are sweet. The worst things of Christ are more truly delightful than the best things of the world; His afflictions are sweeter than their pleasures, His *reproach* more glorious than their honours, and more rich than their treasures, as Moses accounted them. (Heb. xi. 26.) Love delights in likeness and communion, not only in things otherwise pleasant, but in the hardest and harshest things, which have not any thing in them desirable, but only that likeness. So that this thought is very sweet to a heart possessed with this love: What does the World by its hatred, and persecutions, and revilings for the sake of Christ, but make me more like Him, give me a greater share with Him, in that which He did so willingly undergo for me? *When he was sought for to be made a king,* as St. Bernard remarks, *He escaped; but when he was sought to be brought to the Cross, He freely yielded Himself.* And shall I shrink and creep back from what He calls me to suffer for His sake! Yea, even all my other troubles and sufferings, I will desire to have stamped thus, with this conformity to the sufferings of Christ, in the humble, obedient, cheerful endurance of them, and the giving up my will to my Father's.

The following of Christ makes any way pleasant. His faithful followers refuse no march after Him, be it through deserts, and mountains, and storms, and hazards, that will affright self-pleasing, easy spirits. Hearts kindled and actuated with the Spirit of Christ, will *follow Him wheresoever He goeth.*

As He speaks it for warning to his Disciples, *If they persecuted me, they will persecute you,* so He speaks it for comfort to them, and sufficient comfort it is, *If they hate you, they hated me before you.* (John xv. 18, 20.)

[2.] Then add the other: see whither it tends. *He shall be revealed in his glory,* and ye shall even overflow with joy in the partaking of that glory. Therefore, rejoice now in the midst of all your sufferings. Stand upon the advanced ground of the promises and the covenant of Grace, and by faith look beyond this moment, and all that is in it, to that day wherein *everlasting joy shall be upon your heads,* a crown of it, and *sorrow and mourning shall flee away.* (Isa. li. 11.) Believe in this day, and the victory is won.   Oh ! that blessed hope, well fixed and exercised, would give other manner of spirits.   What zeal for God would it not inspire !   What invincible courage against all encounters !   How soon will this pageant of the world vanish, that men are gazing on,   these   pictures and fancies of pleasures and honours, falsely so called, and give place to the real glory of the sons of God, when this blessed Son, who is God, shall be seen appearing in full majesty, and all His bre- thren in glory with Him, all clothed in their robes ! And if you ask, Who are they, Why, *these are they who came out of great tribulation, and have washed their robes in the blood of the Lamb.* (Rev. vii. 14.)

Ver. 14. If ye be reproached for the name of Christ, happy are ye ; for the Spirit of glory and of God resteth upon you ; on their part He is evil spoken of, but on your part He is glorified.

Ver. 15. But let none of you suffer as a murderer, or as a thief, or as an evil-doer, or as a busy-body in other men's matters.

Ver. 16. Yet, if any man suffer as a Christian, let him not be ashamed ; but let him glorify God on this behalf.

THE WORD is the Christian's magazine, both of instructions and of encouragements, whether for *doing* or for *suffering ;* and this Epistle is rich in both.   Here, what the Apostle had said concerning suffering in general, he specifies in the particular case of suffering *reproaches*.   But this seems not to come up to the height of that expression which he hath used before : he spoke of *fiery trial*, but this of *reproach* seems rather fit to be called an *airy trial*, the blast of vanishing words.   Yet, upon trial, it will be found to be (as here it is accounted) a very sharp, a *fiery trial.*

First, then, of this particular kind of suffering; and, *Secondly*, of the comfort and advice furnished against it.

If ye be reproached]   If we consider both the nature of the thing and the strain of the Scriptures, we shall find that re- proaches are amongst the sharpest sort of sufferings, and are indeed *fiery trials*.   *The tongue is a fire*, says St. James, and reproaches are the flashes of that fire ; they are a subtle kind of flame, like that lightning which, as naturalists say, crusheth the bones, and yet breaks not the flesh; they wound not the body, as do tortures and whips, but, through a whole skin, they reach the spirit of a man, and cut it. So, Psal. xlii. 10: *As with a sword in my bones, mine enemies reproach me.* The fire of reproaches preys upon, and dries up the *precious ointment of a good name,* to use Solomon's comparison. (Eccl. vii. 4.) A good name is in itself good, a prime outward good; and take us according to our natural temper and apprehensions, (according to which we feel things,) most men are, and some more excessively, too tender and delicate in it. Although, truly, I take it rather to be a weakness than true greatness of spirit, as many fancy it, to depend much on the opinion of others, and to feel it deeply, yet, I say, considering that it is commonly thus with men, and that there are the remains of this, as of other frailties, in the children of God, it cannot well be but reproaches will ordinarily much afflict men, and to some kind of spirits, possibly, be more grievous than great bodily pain or suffering.

And inasmuch as they are thus grievous, the Scripture accounts them so, and very usually reckons them amongst sufferings: it is apt to name them more than any other kind of suffering, and that with good reason, not only for their piercing nature, (as we have said,) but withal for their frequency and multitude; and some things we suffer do, as flies, more trouble by their number than by their weight.

Now, there is no one kind of suffering, of such constancy, and commonness, and abundance, as reproaches are. When other persecutions cease, yet these continue; when all other fires of martyrdom are put out, these burn still. In all times and places, the malignant World is ready to revile religion: not only avowed enemies of it, but the greatest part even of those that make a vulgar profession of it: they that outwardly receive the *form* of religion, are yet, many of them, inwardly haters of the *power* of it, and Christians who are such merely in name, will scorn and reproach those that are Christians indeed.

And this is done with such ease by every one, that these arrows fly thick : every one that hath a tongue can shoot them, even base *abjects;* (Psal. xxxv. 15 ;) and *the drunkards make songs,* as Jeremiah complains. The meanest sort can reach this point of persecution, and be active in it against the children of God. They who cannot, or dare not, offer them any other injury, will not fear, nor spare, to let fly a taunt or bitter word. So that, whereas other sufferings are rarer, these meet them daily :—*While they say daily unto me, where is thy God?* (Psal. xlii. 10.)

We see then, how justly reproaches are often mentioned amongst and beyond other trials, and accounted persecution. See Matt. v. 10, 11 : *Blessed are ye when men shall revile you and persecute you, and shall say all manner of evil against you falsely, for my sake.* In the history of the casting out of Hagar and her son, Gen. xxi. 9, all we find laid to Ishmael's charge is, *Sarah saw him mocking.* And as *he that was born after the flesh* did then, in this manner, *persecute him that was born after the Spirit,* (Gal. iv. 29,) even so it is now. And thus are reproaches mentioned amongst the sufferings of Christ in the gospel, and not as the least: the railings and mockings that were darted at Him, and fixed to the Cross, are mentioned more than the very nails that fixed Him. And so, Heb. xii. 2, *The shame* of the Cross: though He was above it, and despised it, yet that *shame* added much to the burden of it. So, ver. 3 : *Consider Him who endured the contradiction of sinners.*

Now the other thing is, that this is the lot of Christians, as it was of Christ. And why should they look for more kindness and better usage, and think to find acclamations and applauses from the World, which so vilified their Lord? Oh no! The vain heart must be weaned from these, to follow Christ. If we will indeed follow Him, it must be tamed to share with Him in this point of suffering, not only mistakes and misconstructions, but bitter scoffings and reproaches. Why should not our minds ply and fold to this upon that very reason which He so reasonably presses again and again on His Disciples?—*The servant is not greater than his master.* And, in reference to this very thing, He adds: *If they have called the master Beelzebub, how much more will they speak so of His servants.* (Matt. x. 24, 25.)

Infer. 1. Seeing it is thus, I shall first press upon the followers of Christ, the Apostle's rule here, to keep their suffering spotless, that it may not be comfortless. Resolve to endure it, but resolve likewise, that it shall be on your part innocent suffering. *Suffer not as evil-doers.* Besides that the ways of wickedness are most unsuitable to your holy calling, look to the enmity about you, and gain even out of that evil, this great good of more circumspect and holy walking. Recollect who you are, and where you are, your own weakness and the world's wickedness. This our Saviour represents, and upon it gives that suitable rule: *Behold, I send you forth as sheep in the midst of wolves: be ye therefore wise as serpents, and harmless as doves.—Prudens simplicitas.* Know you not what exact eyes of others are upon you? Will you not thence learn exactly to eye yourselves and all your ways, and seek of God, with David, *to be led in righteousness, because of your enemies, your observers.* (Psal. xxvii. 11.)

This is the rule here, ver. 16: *Suffer as Christians,* holily and blamelessly, that the Enemy may not know where to fasten his hold. As the wrestlers anointed their bodies, that the hands of their antagonists might not fasten upon them, thus, truly, they that walk and suffer as Christians anointed with the Spirit of Christ, their enemies cannot well fasten their hold upon them.

To you, therefore, who love the Lord Jesus, I recommend this especially, to be careful that all your reproaches may be indeed for Christ, and not for any thing in you unlike to Christ; that there be nothing save the matter of your rod. Keep the quarrel as clean and unmixed as you can, and this will advantage you much, both within and without, in the peace and firmness of your minds, and in the refutation of your enemies.   This will make you *as a brazen wall,* as the Lord speaks to the Prophet : *They shall fight against you, but shall not prevail :* Jer. xv. 20.

Keep far off from all impure, unholy ways.   *Suffer not as evil-doers,* no, nor as *busy-bodies.*   Be much at home, setting things at rights within your own breast, where there is so much work, and such daily need of diligence, and then you will find no leisure for unnecessary idle pryings into the ways and affairs of others ; and further than your calling and the rules of Christian charity engage you, you will not interpose in any matters without you, nor be found proud and censorious, as the World is ready to call you.

Shun the appearances of evil ; walk warily and prudently in all things.   Be not *heady, nor self-willed,* no, not in the best thing.   Walk not upon the utter brink and hedge of your liberty, for then you shall be in danger of overpassing it. Things that are lawful may be inexpedient, and in case there is fear of scandal, ought either to be wholly forborne, or used with much prudence and circumspection.   Oh, study in all things to adorn the Gospel, and under a sense of your own unskilfulness and folly, beg wisdom from above, that *Anointing that will teach you all things,* much of that *holy Spirit, that will lead you in the way of all truth ;* and then, in that way, whatsoever may befal you, *suffer* it, and however you may be vilified and reproached, *happy are ye, for the Spirit of glory and of God resteth upon you.*

Inf. 2.   But if to be thus reproached is to be happy, then, certainly, their reproachers are not less unhappy.   If on those resteth the *Spirit of glory and of God,* what spirit is in these, but the spirit of Satan, and of shame and vileness ?   Who is the basest, most contemptible kind of person in the world ? Truly, I think, an avowed contemner and mocker of holiness. Shall any such be found amongst us ?

I charge you all in this name of Christ, that you do not entertain godless prejudices against the people of God.   Let not your cars be open to, nor your hearts close with, the calumnies

and lies that may be flying abroad of them and their practices;
much less open your mouths against them, or let any disgrace-
ful word be heard from you.   And when you meet with undeniable real frailties, know the *law of love*, and to practise it.
Think, This is blameworthy, yet let me not turn it to the
reproach of those persons, who, notwithstanding, may be sincere, much less to the reproach of other persons professing
religion, and then cast it upon religion itself.

My brethren, beware of sharing with the ungodly in this
tongue-persecution of Christians.   There is a day at hand,
wherein the Lord will make inquiry after these things.   If we
shall be made accountable for *idle words*, (as we are warned,
Matt. xii. 36,) how much more for bitter malicious words
uttered against any, especially against the saints of God,
whom, however the World may reckon, He esteems His precious ones, His treasure!   You that now can look on them with
a scornful eye, which way shall you look when they shall be
beautiful and glorious, and all the ungodly clothed with
shame?   Oh, do not reproach them, but rather come in and
share with them in the way of holiness, and in all the sufferings and reproaches that follow it; for if you partake of their
disgraces, you shall share in glory with them, in the day of
their Lord's appearing.

The words contain two things, the *evil* of these reproaches
supposed, and the *good* expressed.   The *evil* supposed, that
they are trials, and hot trials, has been treated of already.
Now as to the good expressed.

Happy are ye.]   Ye are happy even at present, in the very
midst of them; they do not trouble your happy estate, yea,
they advance it.   Thus solid, indeed, is the happiness of the
saints, that in the lowest condition it remains the same: in disgraces, in caves, in prisons and chains, cast them where you
will, still they are happy.   A diamond in the mire, sullied and
trampled on, yet still retains its own worth.   But this is more,
that the very things that seem to make them miserable, do not
only not do that, but, on the contrary, do make them the more

happy: they are gainers by their losses, and attain more liberty by their thraldoms, and more honour by their disgraces, and more peace by their troubles. The World and all their enemies are exceedingly befooled in striving against them: not only can they not undo them, but by all their enmity and practices, they do them pleasure, and raise them higher. With what weapons shall they fight? How shall a Christian's enemies set upon him? Where shall they hit him, seeing that all the wrongs they do him, do indeed enrich and ennoble him, and that the more he is depressed, he flourishes the more. Certainly, the blessedness of a Christian is matchless and invincible.

But how holds this, that a Christian is *happy in reproaches and by them?* It is not through their nature and virtue, for they are evil; (so Matt. v. 11;) but first, by reason of the cause; secondly, by reason of the accompanying and consequent comfort.

[1.] By reason of the *cause* of these reproaches. This we have negatively at verse 15: *Not as an evil-doer:*—that stains thy holy profession, damps thy comfort, and clouds thy happiness, disprofits thee, and dishonours thy Lord. But the cause is stated positively, ver. 14, 16: *For the name of Christ.* And what is there so rough which that will not make pleasant, to suffer with Christ and for Christ, who suffered so much and so willingly for thee? Hath He not gone through all before thee, and made all easy and lovely? Hath He not sweetened poverty, and persecution, and hatred, and disgraces, and death itself, perfumed the grave, and turned it from a pit of horror into a sweet resting bed? And thus love of Christ judgeth: it thinks all lovely which is endured for Him, is glad to meet with difficulties, and is ambitious of suffering for Him. Scorn or contempt is a thing of hard digestion, but much inward heat of love digests it easily. Reproaches are bitter, but the reproaches of Christ are sweet. Take their true value (Heb. xi. 26): *The reproaches of Christ are greater riches than the treasures of Egypt,*—His very worst things, better than the best of the world. A touch of Christ turns all into gold: His reproaches are *riches*, as it is expressed there, and *honour*, as here. *Happy!* Not only afterwards shall ye be happy, but *happy are ye* at present; and that not only in apprehension of that after happiness, as sure, and as already present to Faith realizing it, but even [2.] in that they now possess the presence and comforts of the Spirit.

For the Spirit of glory.] This accompanies disgraces for Him; *His* Spirit, *the Spirit of glory and of God.* With your sufferings goes the name of Christ, and the Spirit of Christ: take them thus, when reproaches are cast upon you for His name, and you are enabled to bear them by his Spirit. And surely His Spirit is most fit to support you under them, yea, to raise you above them. They are ignominious and inglorious, He is the Spirit of glory; they are human reproaches, He, the Divine Spirit, *the Spirit of glory and of God*, that is, the glorious Spirit of God.

And this is the advantage: the less the Christian finds esteem and acceptance in the world, the more he turns his eye inward, to see what is there; and there he finds the world's contempt counterpoised by a weight of excellency and glory, even in this present condition, as the pledge of the glory before him. The reproaches be fiery, but the *Spirit of glory resteth upon you*, doth not give you a passing visit, but stays within you, and is indeed yours. And in this the Christian can take comfort, and let the foul weather blow over, let all the scoffs and contempts abroad pass as they come, having a glorious Spirit within, such a guest honouring him with His presence, abode, and sweet fellowship, being, indeed, one with Him. So that rich miser at Athens could say,—when they scorned him in the streets, he went home to his bags, and hugging himself there at the sight, let them say what they would:

——— Populus me sibilat; at mihi plaudo
Ipse domi, simul ac nummos contemplor in arca.

How much more reasonably may the Christian say, Let them revile and bark, I have riches and honour enough that they see not. And this is what makes the world, as they are a malicious party, so to be an incompetent judge of the Christian's estate. They see the rugged unpleasant outside only; the right inside their eye cannot reach. We were miserable indeed, were our comforts such as they could see.

And while this is the constant estate of a Christian, it is usually most manifested to him in the time of his greatest sufferings. Then (as we said) he naturally turns inward and sees it most, and accordingly finds it most. God making this happy supplement and compensation, that when His people have least of the world they have most of Himself; when they are most covered with the World's disfavour, His favour shines brightest to them. As Moses, when he was in the cloud, had nearest access and speech with God ; so, when the Christian is most clouded with distresses and disgraces, then doth the Lord often shew Himself most clearly to him.

If you be indeed Christians, you will not be so much thinking, at any time, how you may be free from all sufferings and despisings, but rather, how you may go strongly and cheerfully through them. Lo, here is the way: seek a real and firm interest in Christ, and a participation of Christ's Spirit, and then a look to Him will make all easy and delightful. Thou wilt be ashamed within thyself to start back, or yield one foot, at the encounter of a taunt or reproach for Him. Thou wilt think, For whom is it ? Is it not for Him who for my sake hid not His face from shame and spitting ? And further, He died : now, how should I meet death for Him, who shrink at the blast of a scornful word ?

If you would know whether this His Spirit is and resteth in you, it cannot be better known than, 1st, by that very love, ardent love to Him, and high esteem of Him, and, from thence, a willingness, yea, a gladness to suffer any thing for Him. 2dly, This *Spirit of glory* sets the heart on glory. True glory makes heavenly things excellent in our thoughts, and sets the world, the better and the worse, the honour and the dishonour of it, at a low rate.

The spirit of the world is a base, ignoble spirit, even the highest pitch of it. Theirs are but poor designs who are projecting for kingdoms, compared to those of the Christian, which ascend above all things under the sun, and above the sun itself, and therefore he is not shaken with the threats of the world, nor taken with its offers. Excellent is the answer which St. Basil gives, in the person of those martyrs, to that emperor who made them (as he thought) great proffers to draw them off, " Why," say they, " dost thou bid us so low as pieces of the world ? We have learned to despise it all." This is not stupidity, nor an affected stoutness of spirit, but a humble sublimity, which the natural spirit of a man cannot reach unto.

But wilt thou say still, This stops me, I do not find this Spirit in me : if I did, then I think I could be willing to suffer any thing. To this, for the present, I say not more than this : Dost thou desire that Christ may be glorified, and couldst thou be content it were by thy suffering in any kind thou mayest be called to undergo for him ? Art thou willing to give up thy own interest to study and follow Christ's, and to sacrifice thine own credit and name to advance His ? Art thou unwilling to do any thing that may dishonour Him, but not unwilling to suffer any thing that may honour Him ? Or wouldst thou be thus ? Then, be not disputing, but up and walk on in His strength.

Now, if any say, But His name is dishonoured by these reproaches—true, says the Apostle, *on their part it is so, but not on yours.* They that reproach you, do their best to make it reflect on Christ and his cause, but thus it is only *on their part.* You are sufferers for His name, and so you *glorify* it : your faith and patience, and your victory by these, do declare the power of Divine grace, and the efficacy of the Gospel. These have made torturers ashamed, and induced some beholders to share with those who were tortured. Thus, though the profane world intends, as far as it can reach, to fix dishonour upon the profession of Christ, yet it sticks not, but on the contrary, He is glorified by your constancy.

And as the ignominy fastens not, but the glory from the endurance does, so, Christians are obliged, and certainly are ready, according to the Apostle's zeal, ver. 16, *to glorify God on this behalf,* that as He is glorified in them, so they may glorify and bless Him who hath dignified them so; that whereas we might have been left to a sad sinking task, to have suffered for various guilts, our God hath changed the tenor and nature of our sufferings, and makes them to be *for the name of Christ.*

Thus, a spiritual mind doth not swell on a conceit of constancy and courage, which is the readiest way of self-undoing, but acknowledges all to be *gift,* even suffering: *To you it is given not only to believe, but to suffer,* and so, *to bless Him* on that behalf. Phil. i. 29. Oh! this love grows in suffering. See Acts v. 41: *They went away rejoicing that they were counted worthy to suffer shame for His name.*

Consider, it is but a short while, and the wicked and their scoffs shall vanish; *they shall not be.* This shame will presently be over, this disgrace is of short date, but the glory, and the *Spirit of glory,* are eternal. What though thou shouldst be poor, and defamed, and despised, and be the common mark of scorn and all injuries, yet the end of them all is at hand. This is now thy part, but the scene shall be changed. Kings here, real ones, are in the deepest reality but stage kings; but when thou comest to alter the person thou now hearest, here is the odds: thou wast a fool in appearance, and for a moment, but thou shalt be truly a king for ever.

Ver. 17. For the time is come, that judgment must begin at the house of God: and if it first begin at us, what shall the end be of them that obey not the Gospel of God?

THERE is not only perfect equity, but withal, a comely proportion and beauty in all the ways of God, had we eyes opened to discern them, particularly in this point of the sufferings and afflictions of the Church. The Apostle here sets it before his brethren, *For the time is come*, &c. In which words, there is, 1*st*, a parallel of the Lord's dealing with His own and with the wicked; 2*dly*, A persuasion to due compliance and confidence, on the part of His own, upon that consideration.

The parallel is in the *order* and the *measure* of punishing; and it is so that, for the *order*, it begins at the house of God, and ends upon the ungodly. And that carries in it this great difference in the *measure*, that it passes from the one on whom it begins, and rests on the other on whom it ends, and on whom the full weight of it lies for ever. It is so expressed: *What shall the end be*, &c., which imports, not only that judgment shall overtake them in the end, but that it shall be their end; they shall end in it, and it shall be endless upon them.

The time is.] Indeed, the whole time of this present life is so, is the time of suffering and purifying for the Church, compassed with enemies who will afflict her, and subject to those impurities which need affliction. The Children of God are in their under-age here: all their time they are children, and have their frailties and childish follies; and therefore, though they are not always under the stroke of the rod, for that they were not able to endure, yet they are under the discipline and use of the rod all their time. And whereas the wicked escape till their day of full payment, the children of God are in this life chastised with frequent afflictions. And so, *The time* [ὁ καιρός] may here be taken according as the Apostle St. Paul uses the same word, Rom. viii. 18, παθήματα τοῦ νῦν καίρου, *The sufferings of this present time.*

But withal, it is true, and appears to be here implied, that there are particular set times, which the Lord chooses for the correcting of His Church. He hath the days prefixed and written in His *Ephemerides*, hath his days of correcting, wherein He goes round from one church to another. We thought it would never come to us, but we have now found the smart of it.

And here the Apostle may probably mean the times of those hot persecutions that were then begun, and continued, though with some intervals, for two or three ages. Thus, in the sixth chapter of the Apocalypse, after the *white horse*, immediately follow at his heels, *the red*, and *the black*, and *the pale horse*. And as it was upon the first publishing of the Gospel, so, usually, upon the restoring of it, or upon remarkable reformations of the Church and revivings of religion, follow sharp and searching trials. As the lower cause of this is the rage and malice of Satan, and of the ungodly world acted and stirred by him, against the purity and prevalency of religion, so it is from a Higher hand for better ends. The Lord will discover the multitudes of hypocrites and empty professors, who will at such a time readily abound, when religion is upon an advancing way, and the stream of it runs strong. Now, by the counter-current of troubles, such fall back and are carried away. And the truth of grace in the hearts of believers, receives advantage from these hazards and sufferings; they are put to fasten their hold the better on Christ, to seek more experience of the real and sweet consolations of the Gospel, which may uphold them against the counter-blasts of suffering. Thus is religion made a more real and solid thing in the hearts of true believers: they are entered to that way of receiving Christ and His cross together, that they may see their bargain, and not think it a surprise.

Judgment.] Though all sufferings are not such, yet, commonly, there is that unsuitable and unwary walking among Christians, that even their sufferings for the cause of God, though unjust from men, are from God just punishments of their miscarriages towards Him, in their former ways; their self-pleasing and earthliness, having too high a relish for the delights of this world, forgetting their inheritance and home, and conforming themselves to the World, walking too much like it.

Must begin.] The Church of God is punished, while the wicked are free and flourish in the world, possibly all their days; or, if judgment reach them here, yet it is later; it *begins at the house of God.* [1.] This holds in those who profess His name, and are of the Visible Church, compared with them who are without the pale of it, and are its avowed enemies. [2.] In those who profess a desire of a more religious and holy course of life within the Church, compared with the profane multitude. [3.] In those who are indeed more spiritual and holy, and come nearer unto God, compared with others who fall short of that measure. In all these respects it holds, that the Lord doth more readily exercise them with afflictions, and correct their wanderings, than any others.

And this truly is most reasonable; and the reason lies in the very name given to the Church, *the House of God.* For,

1. There is *equity* in such a proceeding. The sins of the Church have their peculiar aggravations, which fall not upon others. That which is simply a sin in strangers to God, is, in His people, the breach of a known and received law, and a law daily unfolded and set before them: yea, it is against their oath of allegiance; it is perfidy and breach of covenant, committed both against the clearest light, and the strictest bonds, and the highest mercies. And still the more particular the profession of His name and the testimonies of His love, these make sin the more sinful, and the punishment of it the more reasonable. The sins of the Church are all twice dipped, *Dibapha, have a double dye:* Isa. i. 18. They are breaches of the Law, and they are, besides, ungrateful and disloyal breaches of promise.

2. As there is unquestionable *equity,* so there is an evident *congruity* in this. God is ruler of all the world, but particularly of His Church, here called *His House,* wherein He hath a special residence and presence; and therefore it is most suitable that there He be specially observed and obeyed, and if disobeyed, that He take notice of it and punish it; that He suffer not Himself to be dishonoured to His face by those of His own House. And therefore, whosoever escape, His own shall not. *You only have I known, of all the families of the*

earth: therefore will I punish you for all your iniquities:
Amos iii. 2. It is fit that He who righteously judges and rules
all nations should make His justice most evident and exemplary
in His own House, where it may best be remarked, and where
it will best appear how impartial He is in punishing sin. So a
king, (as the Psalmist, Psalm ci. 2,) that he may rule the land
well, makes his *own house* exemplary. It is, you know, one
special qualification of a bishop and pastor, to be *one that ruleth
well his own house, having his children in subjection; for if
a man know not how to rule his own house, how shall he take
care of the church of God?* (1 Tim. iii. 4.) Now this, therefore,
more eminently appears in the Supreme Lord of the Church:
He rules it as His own house, and therefore, when He finds
disobedience there, He will first punish that. So He clears
Himself, and the wicked world being afterwards punished,
their mouths are stopped with the preceding punishment of the
Church. Will he not spare his own? Yea, they shall be
first scourged. *What then shall be the end of them that obey
not the Gospel?*

And indeed, the purity of His nature, if it be every where
contrary to all sinful impurity, cannot but most appear in His
peculiar dwelling-house; that He will especially have neat and
clean. If He hate sin all the world over, where it is nearest to
Him He hates it most, and testifies His hatred of it most: He
will not endure it in His presence. As cleanly, neat persons
cannot well look upon any thing that is nasty, much less will
they suffer it to come near them, or touch them, or to continue
in their presence in the house where they dwell; so the Lord,
who is of purer eyes than to behold iniquity, will not abide it
within His own doors; and the nearer any come to Him, the
less can He endure any unholiness or sinful pollution in them.
He will be sanctified in all that come nigh Him, Lev. x. 3;
so, especially, in His ministers. Oh, how pure ought they to
be, and how provoking and hateful to Him are their impurities! Therefore, in that commission to the destroyers, Ezek.
ix. 6, to which place the Apostle here may have some reference,

Go, says He, *slay the old and the young, and begin at My sanctuary.* They were the persons who had polluted His worship, and there the first stroke lighted. And in a spiritual sense, because all His people are His own elect priesthood, and should be *holiness to the Lord;* when they are not really so, and do not sanctify Him in their walking, He sanctifies Himself, and declares His holiness in His judgments on them.

3. There is mercy in this dispensation too ; even under the habit of judgment, Love walks secretly and works. So loving and so wise a Father will not undo His children by sparing the rod, but *because He loves, He rebukes and chastens.* (See Heb. xii. 6, Prov. iii. 11, Apoc. iii. 19.) His Church is His house; therefore, that He may delight in it, and take pleasure to dwell in it, and make it happy with His presence, He will have it often washed and made clean, and the filth and rubbish scoured and purged out of it; this argues His gracious purpose of abiding in it.

And as He doth it, that He may delight in His people, so He doth it that they may delight in Him, and in Him alone. He embitters the breast of the World, to wean them ; makes the World hate them, that they may the more easily hate it ; suffers them not to settle upon it, and fall into a complacency with it, but makes it unpleasant to them by many and sharp afflictions, that they may with the more willingness come off and be untied from it, and that they may remember home the more, and seek their comforts above ; that finding so little below, they may turn unto Him, and delight themselves in communion with Him. That the sweet incense of their prayers may ascend the more thick, He kindles those fires of trials to them. For though it should not be so, yet so it is, that in times of ease they would easily grow remiss and formal in that duty.

He is gracious and wise, knows what He does with them, and *the thoughts He thinks toward them.* (Jer. xxix. 11.) All is for their advantage, for the purifying of their iniquities. (Isa. xxvii. 9.) He purges out their impatience, and earthliness, and self-will, and carnal security, and thus refines them for vessels of honour. We see in a jeweller's shop, that as there are pearls and diamonds, and other precious stones, so there are files, cutting instruments, and many sharp tools, for their polishing; and while they are in the work-house, they are continual neighbours to them, and often come under them. The Church is God's jewellery, His work-house, where His jewels are a-polishing for His palace and house; and those He especially esteems, and means to make most resplendent, He hath oftenest His tools upon.

Thus observe it, as it is in the Church compared to other societies, so is it in a congregation or family; if there be one more diligently seeking after God than the rest, he shall be liable to meet with more trials, and be oftener under afflictions than any of the company, either under contempt and scorn, or poverty and sickness, or some one pressure or other, outward or inward. And those inward trials are the nearest and sharpest which the World sees least, and yet the soul feels most. And yet all these, both outward and inward, have love, unspeakable love in them all, being designed to purge and polish them, and, by the increasing of grace, to fit them for glory.

Inf. 1. Let us not be so foolish as to promise ourselves impunity on account of our relation to God, as His Church in covenant with Him. If once we thought so, surely our experience hath undeceived us. And let not what we have suffered harden us, as if the worst were past. We may rather fear it is but a pledge and beginning of sharper judgment. Why do we not consider our unhumbled and unpurified condition, and tremble before the Lord? Would we save Him a labour, He would take it well. Let us purify our souls, that He may not be put to further purifying by new judgments. Were we busy reading our present condition, we should see very legible foresigns of further judgments; as for instance: [1.] The Lord taking away His eminent and worthy servants, who are as the very pillars of the public peace and welfare, and taking away counsel, and courage, and union, from the rest; forsaking us in our meetings, and leaving us in the dark to grope and rush one upon another.` [2.] The dissensions and jarrings in the State and Church, are likely, from imagination, to bring it to a reality. These unnatural burnings threaten new fires of public judgments to be kindled amongst us. [3.] That general de-spising of the Gospel and abounding of profaneness throughout the land, not yet purged, but as our great sin remaining in us, calls for more fire and more boiling. [4.] The general coldness and deadness of spirit; the want of zeal for God, and of the communion of saints, that mutual stirring up of one another to holiness; and, which is the source of all, the restraining of prayer, a frozen benumbedness in that so necessary work, that preventer of judgments, that binder of the hands of God from punishments, and opener of them for the pouring forth of mer-cies.—Oh! this is a sad condition in itself, though it portended no further judgment, the Lord hiding Himself, and the spirit of zeal and prayer withdrawn, and scarcely any lamenting it, or so much as perceiving it! Where are our days either of so-lemn prayer or praises, as if there were cause for neither! And yet, there is a clear cause for both. Truly, my brethren, we have need, if ever we had, to bestir ourselves. Are not these kingdoms, at this present, brought to the extreme point of their highest hazard? And yet, who lays it to heart?

Inf. 2. Learn to put a right construction on all God's dealings with His Church, and with thy soul. With regard to His Church, there may be a time wherein thou shalt see it not only tossed, but, to thy thinking, covered and swal-lowed up with tears: but wait a little, it shall arrive safe. This is a common stumbling stone, but walk by the light of the word, and the eye of Faith looking on it, and thou shalt pass by and not stumble at it. The Church mourns, and Babylon sings—*sits as a queen;* but for how long? She shall *come down and sit in the dust;* and Sion shall be glorious *and put on her beautiful garments,* while Babylon shall not look for another revolution to raise her again; no, she shall never rise. *And a mighty angel took up a stone like a great millstone, and cast it into the sea, saying, Thus, with violence, shall that great city Babylon be thrown down, and shall be found no more at all.* Rev. xviii. 21.

Be not hasty: take God's work together, and do not judge of it by parcels. It is indeed all wisdom and righteousness; but we shall best discern the beauty of it, when we look on it in the frame, when it shall be fully completed and finished, and our eyes enlightened to take a fuller and clearer view of it than we can have here. Oh, what wonder, what endless wondering will it then command!

We read of Joseph hated, and sold, and imprisoned, and all most unjustly, yet because, within a leaf or two, we find him freed and exalted, and his brethren coming as supplicants to him, we are satisfied. But when we look on things which are for the present cloudy and dark, our short-sighted, hasty spirits cannot learn to wait a little, till we see the other side, and what end the Lord makes. We see *judgment beginning at the house of God*, and this perplexes us while we consider not the rest, *What shall be the end of them that obey not the Gospel?* God begins the judgment on His Church for a little time, that it may end and rest upon His enemies for ever. And indeed, He leaves the wicked last in the punishment, that He may make use of them for the punishment of His Church. They are *His rod;* (Isa. x. 5;) but when He hath done that work with them, they are *broken and burnt*, and that, when they are at the height of their insolence and boasting, not knowing what Hand moves them, and smites His people with them for a while, *till the day of their consuming come. (Ver.* 16, 24, 25.) Let the vile enemy that hath shed our blood and insulted over us, rejoice in their present impunity, and in men's procuring of it, and pleading for it *; there is Another Hand whence we may look for justice. And though it may be, that the judgment begun

---

* I am ready to believe this refers to the escape of many who had deserved the severest punishments, for their part in the grand Irish rebellion, but were screened by the favour of some great men in the reign of King Charles II.—Dr. Doddridge.

at us, is not yet ended, and that we may yet further, and that justly, find them our scourge, yet, certainly, we may and ought to look beyond that, unto the end of the Lord's work, which shall be the ruin of His enemies, and the peace of His people, and the glory of His name.

Of them that obey not the Gospel.] The end of all the ungodly is terrible, but especially the end of such as heard the Gospel, and have not received and obeyed it.

The word ἀπειθούντων hath in it both unbelief and disobedience; and these are inseparable. Unbelief is the grand point of disobedience in itself, and the spring of all other disobedience; and the pity is, that men will not believe it to be thus.

They think it an easy and a common thing to believe. Who doth not believe? Oh, but rather, who does? *Who hath believed our report?* Were our own misery, and the happiness that is in Christ, believed, were the riches of Christ and the love of Christ believed, would not this persuade men to forsake their sins and the world, in order to embrace Him?

But men run away with an extraordinary fancy of believing, and do not deeply consider what news the Gospel brings, and how much it concerns them. Sometimes, it may be, they have a sudden thought of it, and they think, I will think on it better at some other time. But when comes that time? One business steps in atfer another, and shuffles it out. Men are not at leisure to be saved.

Observe the phrase, *The Gospel of God.* It is His embassy of peace to men, the riches of His mercy and free love opened and set forth, not simply to be looked upon, but laid hold on; the glorious holy God declaring His design of agreement with man, in His own Son, His blood streaming forth in it to wash away uncleanness. And yet, this Gospel is not obeyed! Surely, the conditions of it must be very hard, and the commands intolerably grievous, that are not hearkened to. Why, judge you if they be. The great command is, to receive that salvation; and the other is this, to love that Saviour; and there is no more. Perfect obedience is not now the thing; and the obedience which is required, that love makes sweet and easy to us, and acceptable to Him.   This is proclaimed to all who hear the Gospel, but the greatest part refuse it : they love themselves, and their lusts, and this present world, and will not change, and so they perish !

They perish—What is that?   What is their end?   I will answer that but as the Apostle doth, and that is even by asking the question over again, *What shall be their end?*

There is no speaking of it ; a curtain is drawn : silent wonder expresses it best, telling that it cannot be expressed. How then shall it be endured ? It is true, that there be resemblances used in Scripture, giving us some glance of it.   We hear of a *burning lake, a fire that is not quenched, and a worm that dies not.* (Isa. lxvi. 24, Mark ix. 44, Rev. xxi. 8.)   But these are but shadows to the real misery of them that obey not the Gospel.   Oh, to be filled with the wrath of God, the ever-living God, for ever!   What words or thoughts can reach it ?   Oh, eternity, eternity !   Oh, that we did believe it !

This same parallel of the Lord's dealing with the righteous and the wicked, is continued in the following verse in other terms, for the clearer expression, and deeper impression of it.

Ver. 18. And if the righteous scarcely be saved, where shall the ungodly
and the sinner appear ?

It is true, then, that they are *scarcely saved;* even they who endeavour to walk uprightly in the ways of God, that is, *the righteous,* they are *scarcely saved.*   This imports not any uncertainty or hazard in the thing itself as to the end, in respect of the purpose and performance of God, but only, the great difficulties and hard encounters in the way ; that they go through so many temptations and tribulations, so many *fightings without and fears within.*   The Christian is so simple and weak, and his enemies are so crafty and powerful, the oppositions of the wicked world, their hatreds, and scorns, and molestations, the sleights and violence of Satan, and, worst of all, the strength of his own corruptions ; and by reason of abounding corruption, there is such frequent, almost continual, need of purifying by afflictions and trials, that he has need to be still under physic, and is of necessity at some times drained and brought so low, that there is scarcely strength or life remaining in him.

And, truly, all outward difficulties would be but matter of ease, would be as nothing, were it not for the incumbrance of lusts, and corruptions within. Were a man to meet disgraces and sufferings for Christ, how easily would he go through them, yea, and rejoice in them, were he rid of the fretting impatience, the pride, and self-love, of his own carnal heart! These clog and trouble him worst, and he cannot shake them off, nor prevail against them without much pains, many prayers and tears; and many times, after much wrestling, he scarcely finds that he hath gained any ground: yea, sometimes he is foiled and cast down by them.

And so, in all other duties, such a fighting and continual combat, with a revolting, backsliding heart, the flesh still pulling and dragging downwards! When he would mount up, he finds himself as a bird with a stone tied to its foot; he hath wings that flutter to be upwards, but is pressed down with the weight fastened to him. What struggling with wanderings and deadness in hearing, and reading, and prayer! And what is most grievous is, that, by their unwary walking, and the prevailing of some corruption, they grieve the Spirit of God, and provoke Him to hide His face, and withdraw His comforts. How much pain to attain any thing, any particular grace of humility, or meekness, or self-denial; and if any thing be attained, how hard to keep and maintain it against the contrary party! How often are they driven back to their old point. If they do but cease from striving a little, they are carried back by the stream. And what returns of doubtings and misbelief, after they thought they were got somewhat above them, insomuch that sometimes they are at the point of giving over, and thinking it will never be for them. And yet through all these they are brought safe home. There is Another strength than theirs, which bears them up, and brings them through. But these things, and many more of this nature, argue the difficulty of their course, and that it is not so easy a thing to come to Heaven as most imagine it.

Inference. Thou that findest so little stop and conflict in it, who goest thy round of external duties, and all is well, art no more troubled; thou hast need to inquire, after a long time spent in this way, Am I right? Have I not yet to begin? Surely, this looks not like the way to Heaven, as it is described in the Scripture: it is too smooth and easy to be right?

And if the way of the righteous be so hard, then how hard shall be the end of the ungodly sinner that walks in sin with delight! It were strange if they should be at such pains, and with great difficulty attain their end, and he should come in amongst them in the end; they were fools indeed. True, if it were so. But what if it be not so? Then the wicked man is the fool, and shall find that he is, when he shall not be able to *stand in the judgment.* Where shall he appear, when to the end he might not appear, he would be glad to be smothered under the weight of the hills and mountains, if they could shelter Him from appearing?

And what is the aim of all this which we have spoken, or can speak on this subject, but that ye may be moved to take into deeper thoughts the concernment of your immortal souls? Oh, that you would be persuaded! Oh, that you would betake yourselves to Jesus Christ, and seek salvation in Him! Seek to be covered with His righteousness, and to be led by His Spirit in the ways of righteousness. That will seal to you the happy certainty of the End, and overcome for you all the difficulties of the Way. What is the Gospel of Christ preached for? What was the blood of Christ shed for? Was it not that, by receiving Him, we might escape condemnation? Nay, this drew Him from heaven: *He came that we might have life, and that we might have it more abundantly.* (John x. 10.)

Ver. 19. Wherefore let them that suffer according to the will of God, commit the keeping of their souls to Him in well-doing, as unto a faithful Creator.

Nothing doth so establish the mind amidst the rollings and turbulency of present things, as both a look above them, and a look beyond them ; above them to the steady and good Hand by which they are ruled, and beyond them, to the sweet and beautiful end to which, by that Hand, they shall be brought. This the Apostle lays here as the foundation of that patience and peace in troubles, wherewith he would have his brethren furnished. And thus he closes this chapter in these words:— *Wherefore, let them that suffer according to the will of God, commit the keeping of their souls to Him in well-doing, as unto a faithful Creator.*

The words contain the true principle of Christian patience and tranquillity of mind in the sufferings of this life, expressing both wherein it consists, and what are the grounds of it.

I. It lies in this, *committing the soul unto God.* The word εν ἀγαθοποιίᾳ, which is added, is a true qualification of this, that it be *in well-doing*, according to the preceding doctrine, which the Apostle gives clearly and largely. (*Ver.* 15, 16.) If men would have inward peace amidst outward trouble, they must walk by the rule of peace, and keep strictly to it. If you would commit your soul to the keeping of God, know that He is a holy God ; and an unholy soul that walks in any way of wickedness, whether known or secret, is no fit commodity to put into His pure hand to keep. Therefore, as you would have this confidence to give your holy God the keeping of your soul, and that He may accept of it, and take it off your hand, beware of wilful pollutions and unholy ways. Walk so as you may not discredit your Protector, and move Him to be ashamed of you, and disclaim you Shall it be said that you live under His shelter, and yet walk inordinately? As this cannot well be, you cannot well believe it to be. Loose ways will loosen your hold of Him, and confidence in Him. You will be driven to question your interest, and to think, Surely, I do but delude myself: can I be under His safeguard, and yet follow the course of the world and my corrupt heart? Certainly, let who will be so, HE will not be a guardian and patron of wickedness. No, *He is not a God that hath pleasure in wickedness, nor shall evil dwell with Him.* (Psal. v. 4.) If thou give thy soul to Him to keep, upon the terms of liberty to sin, He will turn it out of His doors, and remit it back to thee to look to as thou wilt thyself. Yea, in the ways of sin, thou dost indeed steal it back, and carriest it out from Him; thou puttest thyself out of the compass of His defence, goest without the trenches, and art, at thine own hazard, exposed to armies of mischiefs and miseries.

Inference. This, then, is primarily to be looked to: you that would have safety in God in evil times, beware of evil ways; for in these it cannot be. If you will be safe in Him, you must stay with Him, and in all your ways, keep within Him *as your fortress.* Now, in the ways of sin you run out from Him.

Hence it is we have so little established confidence in God in times of trial. We take ways of our own, and will be gadding, and so we are surprised and taken, as they that are often venturing out into the enemy's reach, and cannot stay within the walls. It is no idle repetition, Psal. xci. 1, *He that dwelleth in the secret places of the Most High, shall abide under the shadow of the Almighty.* He that wanders not, but stays there, shall find himself there hidden from danger. They that rove out from God in their ways, are disquieted and tossed with fears; this is the *fruit of their own ways;* but the soul that is indeed given to Him to keep, keeps near Him.

Study pure and holy walking, if you would have your confidence firm, and have boldness and joy in God. You will find that a little sin will shake your trust, and disturb your peace, more than the greatest sufferings: yea, in those sufferings, your assurance and joy in God will grow and abound most, if sin be kept out. That is the trouble-feast that disquiets the conscience, which, while it continues good, is a *continual feast.* So much sin as gets in, so much peace will go out. Afflictions cannot break in upon it to break it, but sin doth. All the winds which blow about the earth from all points, stir it not, only that within the bowels of it, makes the earthquake.

I do not mean that for infirmities a Christian ought to be discouraged. But take heed of walking in any way of sin, for that will unsettle thy confidence. Innocency and holy walking make the soul of a sound constitution, which the counterblasts of affliction wear not out, nor alter. Sin makes it so sickly and crazy, that it can endure nothing. Therefore, study to keep your consciences pure, and they shall be peaceable, yea, in the worst times commonly most peaceable and best furnished with spiritual confidence and comfort.

Commit the keeping of their souls.] The Lord is an entire protector. He keeps the bodies, yea, all that belongs to the Believer, and, as much as is good for him, makes all safe, *keeps all his bones, not one of them is broken;* (Psal. xxxiv. 18 ;) yea, says our Saviour, *The very hairs of your head are numbered.* (Matt. x. 30.) -But that which, as in the Believer's account, and in God's account, so, certainly in itself is most precious, is principally committed and received into His keeping, *their souls.* They would most gladly be secured in that here, and that shall be safe in the midst of all hazards. Their chief concern is, that, whatsoever be lost, this may not : this is the jewel, and therefore the prime care is of this. If the soul be safe, all is well ; it is riches enough. *What shall it profit a man, though he gain the whole world,* says our Saviour, *and lose his own soul?* (Mark viii. 36.) And so, what shall it disprofit a man, though he lose the whole world, if he gain his soul ? Nothing at all.

When times of trial come, Oh, what a bustle to hide this and that ; to flee, and carry away and make safe that which is but trash and rubbish to the precious soul ; but how few thoughts of that ! Were we in our wits, that would be all at all times, not only in trouble, but in days of peace. Oh, how shall I make sure about my soul? Let all go as it may, can I but be secured and persuaded in that point, I desire no more.

Now, the way is this, *commit them to God:* this many say, but few do. Give them into His hand, *lay them up* there, (so the word is,) and they are safe, and may be quiet and composed.

In patience possess your souls, says our Saviour. (Luke xxiv. 19.) Impatient, fretting souls are out of themselves; their owners do not possess them. Now, the way to possess them ourselves in patience, is, thus to commit them to him in confidence; for then only we possess them, when He keeps them. They are easily disquieted and shaken in pieces while they are in our own hands, but in His hand, they are above the reach of dangers and fears. '

Inference. Learn from hence, what is the proper act of Faith : it rolls the soul over on God, ventures it in His hand, and rests satisfied concerning it, being there. And there is no way but this, to be quiet within, to be impregnable and immovable in all assaults, and fixed in all changes, believing in His free love. Therefore, be persuaded to resolve on that ;— not doubting and disputing, Whether shall I believe or not? Shall I think He will suffer me to lay my soul upon Him to keep so unworthy, so guilty a soul? Were it not presumption! —Oh, what sayest thou? Why dost thou thus dishonour Him, and disquiet thyself? If thou hast a purpose to walk in any way of wickedness, indeed thou art not for Him; yea, thou comest not near Him to give Him thy soul. But wouldst thou have it delivered from sin, rather than from trouble, yea, rather than from hell ? Is that the chief safety thou seekest, to be kept from iniquity, from thine own iniquity, thy beloved sins? Dost thou desire to dwell in Him, and walk with Him? Then, whatsoever be thy guiltiness and unworthiness, come forward, and give Him thy soul to keep. If He should seem to refuse it, press it on Him. If He stretch not forth His hand, lay it down at His foot, and leave it there, and resolve not to take it back. Say, Lord, Thou hast made us these souls, Thou callest for them again to be committed to Thee; here is one. It is unworthy, but what soul is not so? It is most unworthy, but therein will the riches of Thy grace appear most in receiving it. And thus leave it with Him, and know, He will make thee a good account of it. Now, should you lose goods, or credit, or friends, or life itself, it imports not; the main concern is sure, if so be thy soul is out of hazard. *I suffer these things for the Gospel*, says the Apostle: *nevertheless, I am not ashamed—* Why?—*for I know whom I have trusted, and am persuaded that He is able to keep that which I have committed to Him against that day*. 2 Tim. i. 12.

II. The *Ground* of this Confidence is in these two things, the *ability* and the *fidelity* of Him in whom we trust. There is much in a persuasion of the power of God. Though few think they question that, there is in us secret, undiscovered unbelief, even in that point. Therefore the Lord so often makes mention of it in the Prophets. (See Isa. l. 3, &c.) And, in this point, the Apostle Paul is particularly express: *I am persuaded that He is able to keep*, &c. So this Apostle: *Kept by the power of God through faith unto salvation, ready to be revealed in the last time*. (Ch. i. v. 5.) This is very needful to be considered, in regard of the many and great oppositions, and dangers, and powerful enemies, that seek after our souls; *He is able to keep them, for He is stronger than all, and none can pluck them out of His hand*, says our Saviour. (John x. 29.) This the Apostle here implies, in that word, *Creator*: if He was able to give them being, surely, He is able to keep them from perishing. This relation of a Creator implies likewise a benign propension and good-will to the works of His hands; if He gave them us at first, when once they were not, forming them out of nothing, will He not give us them again, being put into His hand for safety?

And as He is powerful, He is no less faithful, *a faithful Creator*, Truth itself. Those who believe on Him, He never deceives or disappoints. Well might St. Paul say, *I know whom I have trusted.* Oh, the advantage of Faith! It engages the truth and the power of God: His royal word and honour lie upon it, to preserve the soul that Faith gives Him in keeping. If He remain able and faithful to perform His word, that soul shall not perish.

There be in the words, other two grounds of quietness of spirit in sufferings. [1.] It is according to the will of God. The believing soul, subjected and levelled to that will, complying with His good pleasure in all, cannot have a more powerful persuasive than this, that all is ordered by His will. This settled in the heart, would settle it much, and make it even in all things; not only to know, but wisely and deeply to consider, that it is thus, that all is measured in Heaven, every drachm of thy troubles weighed by That skilful Hand, which doth all things by weight, number, and measure.

And then, consider Him as thy God and Father, who hath taken special charge of thee, and of thy soul: thou hast given it to Him, and He hath received it. And, upon this consideration, study to follow His will in all, to have no will but His. This is thy duty, and thy wisdom. Nothing is gained by spurning and struggling, but to hurt and vex thyself; but by complying, all is gained—sweet peace. It is the very secret, the mystery of solid peace within, to resign all to His will, to be disposed of at His pleasure, without the least contrary thought. And thus, like two-faced pictures, those sufferings and troubles, and whatsoever else, while beheld on the one side as painful to the flesh, hath an unpleasant visage, yet go about a little, and look upon it as thy Father's will, and then it is smiling, beautiful, and lovely. This I would recommend to you, not only for temporals, as easier there, but in spiritual things, your comforts and sensible enlargements, to love all that He does. It is the sum of Christianity, to have thy will crucified, and the will of thy Lord thy only desire. Whether joy or sorrow, sickness or health, life or death, in all, in all, *Thy will be done.*

The other ground of quietness is contained in the first word which looks back on the foregoing discourse, *Wherefore*— what? Seeing that your reproaches and sufferings are not endless, yea, that they are short, they shall end, quickly end, and end in glory, be not troubled about them, overlook them. The eye of faith will do it. A moment gone, and what are they? This is the great cause of our disquietness in present troubles and griefs; we forget their end. We are affected by our condition in this present life, as if it were all, and it is nothing. Oh, how quickly shall all the enjoyments, and all the sufferings of this life pass away, and be as if they had not been!

CHAPTER V.

Ver. 1. The elders which are among you, I exhort, who am also an elder and a witness of the sufferings of Christ, and also a partaker of the glory that shall be revealed.

THE Church of Christ being one body, is interested in the condition and carriage of each particular Christian, as a part of it, but more especially in respect to those who are more eminent and organic parts of it. Therefore, the Apostle, after many excellent directions given to all his Christian brethren to whom he writes, doth most reasonably and fitly add this express exhortation to those who had the oversight and charge of the rest: *The Elders which are among you,* &c.

The words contain a particular definition of the persons exhorted and the persons exhorting.

1. The persons exhorted: *The Elders among you. Elders* here, as in other places, is a name not of age, but of office; yet the office is named by that age which is, or ought to be, most suitably qualified for it, importing, that men, though not aged, yet, if called to that office, should be noted for such wisdom and gravity of mind and carriage, as may give that authority, and command that respect, which is requisite for persons in their calling: not *novices,* as St. Paul speaks: not as a light

bladder, being easily blown up, as young unstable minds are ; but such as young Timothy was in humility and diligence, as the Apostle testifies of him, Phil. ii. 20, and as he further exhorts him to be, 1 Tim. iv. 12, *Let no man despise thy youth, but be an example of believers in word, in conversation, in charity, in faith, in purity.*

The name of *Elders* indifferently signifies either their age or their calling: and the name of *ruling elders* sometimes denotes civil rulers, sometimes pastors of the church ; as, amongst the Jews, both offices often met in the same person.   Here, it appears that pastors are meant, as the exhortation, of *feeding the flock*, evidences; which, though it sometimes signifies *ruling*, and here may comprise it, yet is chiefly by doctrine.   And then the title given to Christ, in the encouragement which is added, confirms this interpretation: *The Chief Shepherd.*

A due frame of spirit and carriage in the Elders, particularly the Apostles of the Church, is a thing of prime concern for the good of it.   It is one of the heaviest threatenings, when the Lord declares, that He will give a rebellious people such teachers and prophets as they deserved, and indeed desired : *If there be a man to prophesy of wine and strong drink, such a one shall be a prophet,* says He to that people, Mic. ii. 11.   And, on the other side, amongst the sweetest promises of mercy, this is not the least, to be furnished with plenty of faithful teachers. Though profane men make no reckoning of it, yet, were it in the hardest times, they who know the Lord will account of it as He doth, a sweet allay of all sufferings and hardship : *Though the Lord give you the bread of adversity and the water of affliction, yet shall not thy teachers be removed into a corner, but thine eyes shall see thy teachers.* (Isa. xxx. 20.) Oh ! how rich a promise is that, Jer. iii. 15 : *I will give you pastors according to My own heart.*

This promise is to be pressed and sued for by earnest prayer. Were people much in this duty, Pastors would find the benefit of it, and so the people themselves would receive back their prayers, with much gain, into their own bosom : they would have the returned benefit of it, as the vapours that go up from below, fall down upon the earth again in sweet showers, and make it fruitful. Thus, went there many prayers up for pastors, their doctrine would *drop as rain, and distil as dew,* (Deut. xxx. 2,) and the sweet influence of it would make fruitful the valleys, humble hearts receiving it. And, at this time, it is very needful that the Lord be much importuned for the continuance and increase of His favour in this His Church. As they who have power should be more careful of those due means which, in schools of learning, or otherwise, are needful for qualifying men for this service ; so all in general, both people and pastors, and such as are offering themselves to that service, should chiefly beg from the Higher Academy that teaching, abundance of that Spirit promised to those employed in that work, that might make them *able ministers of the New Testament.*

Oh ! it is an inestimable blessing, to have the saving light of the Gospel shining clear in the faithful and powerful ministry of it. They thought so who said of their worthy teacher, They had rather for them, that the sun should not shine, than that he should not teach. *Satius solem non luce*re, *quam Chrysostomum non docere.*

2. The person exhorting : *I, a co-presbyter,* or *fellow-elder,* with you. The duty of mutual exhortation lies on Christians at large, though it be little known amongst the greatest part; but truly, Pastors should be, as in other duties, so particularly in this, eminent and exemplary in their intercourses and converse, saying often one to another, Oh ! let us remember to what we are called ; to how high and heavy a charge ; to what holiness and diligence ; how great is the hazard of our miscarriage, and how great the reward of our fidelity. They should be often whetting and sharpening one another by these weighty and holy considerations.

And a witness of the sufferings of Christ.] He did indeed give witness to Christ, by suffering for Him the hatred and persecutions of the world in the publishing of the Gospel, and so was a witness and martyr before the time that he was put to

death : and this I exclude not.   But that which is more particularly here intended, is, his certain knowledge of the sufferings
of Christ, in his own person, as an eye-witness of them, and
upon that knowledge, a publisher of them.   (Luke xxiv. 48.)
And thus these two suit with the two motives urged, to bear
home the exhortation : the one couched in that expression, *the
flock of God,* (ver. 2,) His purchase with those His sufferings,
whereof I was an eye-witness ; the other motive, in the words,
a crown of glory, &c. (Ver. 4.) As if he had said, I may speak
the more confidently of that, for I am one of those who have a
real interest in it, and a firm belief of it, *a partaker of the glory
that shall be revealed.*   And these, indeed, are the things
which give weight to a man's words, make them powerful and
pressing.

   A witness of the sufferings of Christ.   The Apostles had a
singular advantage in this, who were αὐτόπται, *eye-witnesses ;*
and St. Paul, who wanted that, had it supplied by a vision of
Christ, in his conversion.   A spiritual view of Christ crucified,
is generally, I will not say absolutely, necessary to make a minister of Christ, but certainly very requisite for the due wit-
nessing of Him, and the displaying of the excellency and virtue
of His sufferings, and for so preaching the Gospel that there
shall need no other crucifix * ; after so clear and lively a way,
as that it may in some measure suit the Apostle's word, Gal. iii.
1: *Before whose eyes Jesus Christ hath been evidently set
forth crucified among you.*

   Men commonly read, and hear, and may possibly preach, of
the sufferings of Christ as a common story, and in that way it
may a little move a man, and wring tears from his eyes.   But
faith hath another kind of sight of them, and so works another
kind of affections ; and without that, the very eye-sight of them
had availed the Apostles nothing ; for how many saw him suffer as they did, who reviled, or at least despised Him !   But
by the eye of faith to see the only begotten Son of God, as

---

   * Alluding to the custom of many Popish preachers, to carry a little
crucifix into the pulpit with them.—Dr. Doddridge.

stricken and smitten of God, bearing our sorrows, and
wounded for our transgressions, Jesus Christ *the righteous,*
reckoned amongst the unrighteous and malefactors; to see Him
stripped naked, and scourged, and buffeted, and nailed, and
dying: and all for us; this is the thing that will bind upon us
most strongly all the duties of Christianity and of our particular
callings, and best enable us, according to our callings, to bind
them upon others. But our slender view of these things occasions a light sense of them, and that, cold incitements to
answerable duty. Certainly, deep impressions would cause
lively expressions.

Would we willingly stir up our own hearts and one another
to holy diligence in our station, study more thoroughly Christ
as suffering and dying: that is the very life of the Gospel and
of our souls; it is all we have to learn, and all we have to teach
and press on you. *I determined to know nothing among you,
save Jesus Christ and him crucified,* to make Christ's Cross
the sum of all my learning.

A partaker of the glory to be revealed.] As he was a witness of those sufferings, so, a partaker of the glory purchased
by those sufferings; and therefore, as one insighted and interested in what he speaks, the Apostle might fitly speak of that
peculiar duty to which those sufferings and that glory do peculiarly persuade. This is the only way of speaking of those
things, not as a discourser or contemplative student, but as
a partaker of them. There is another force in a pastor's exhortation either to his people or his brethren, who brings his
message written upon his own heart; who speaks of the guilt of
sin, and the sufferings of Christ for it, as particularly feeling
his own guilt, and looking on those sufferings as taking it away;
speaks of free grace, as one who either hath drunken of the
refreshing streams of it, or at least is earnestly thirsting after
it; speaks of the love of Christ, from a heart kindled with it,
and of the glory to come, as one who looks to be a sharer in it,
and longs earnestly for it, as one who hath all his joy and content laid up in the hopes of it.

And thus, with respect to Christians conversing with each other in their mutual exhortings and comfortings, all is cold and dead that flows not from some inward persuasion and experimental knowledge of Divine things. But that gives an edge and a sweetness to Christian conference:—to be speaking of Jesus Christ, not only as a King and as a Redeemer, but as *their* King and *their* Redeemer, in David's style, *My King and my God,* and of His sufferings as theirs, applied by faith, and acquitting them in St. Paul's style, *Who loved me and gave Himself for me;* to be speaking of the glory to come as *their* inheritance, that of which they are *partakers,* their home; as strangers meeting together abroad, in some foreign country, delight to speak of their own land, their parentage and friends, and the rich patrimony there abiding them. *Peregrinis in terris nulla est jucundior recordatio quam suæ civitatis.* Nothing is more delightful, says Augustine, to travellers in distant countries, than the remembrance of their native land. And this ought to be the entertainment of Christians when they meet. Away with trifling vain discourses; cause all to give place to these refreshing remembrances of our home. Were our hearts much on that rich inheritance above, it would be impossible to refrain our tongues, and to pass on so silent concerning it; to find matter of empty pratings, and be pleased with them, and to have no relish of this. Whither go your hearts? They are out of their way, and abase themselves, that turn so much downwards, and are not more above the sun, eyeing still that blessed land where our purchased inheritance lies.

Oh, seek after more clear knowledge of this glory, and of your interest in it, that your hearts may rejoice in the remembrance of it, that it be not to you as the description of a pleasant land, such as men read of in history, and have no portion in: they like it well, and are pleased with it while they read, be it but some imagined country or commonwealth finely fancied. But know this country of yours to be real, and no device: and seek to know yourselves to be partakers of it.

This confidence depends not upon a singular revelation, but

on the power of faith, and the light of the Spirit of God, which clears to His children the things that He hath freely given them; though some of them at times, some, it may be, all, or most of their time, do want it, God so disposing it, that they scarcely clearly see their right, till they be in possession; see not their heaven and home, till they arrive at it, or are hard upon it. Yet, truly, this we may and ought to seek after in humility and submission, that we may have the *pledge and earnest of our inheritance;* not so much for the comfort within us, (though that is allowed,) as that it may wean our hearts from things below, may raise us to higher and closer communion with God, and enable us more for His service, and excite us more to His praises, even here. What were a Christian without the hope of this glory? As one said, *Tolle religionem, et nullus eris: Take away religion, and you take away the man.* And, having this hope,—what are all things here to him? How poor and despicable the better and worse of this life, and this life itself! How glad is he that it will quickly end! And what were the length of it to him, but a long continuance of his banishment, a long detainment from his home, and how sweet is the message that is sent for him to come home!

The glory to be revealed! It is hidden for the present, wholly unknown to the children of this world, and even but little known to the children of God, who are heirs of it. Yea, they who know themselves *partakers of it,* yet, know not much what it is; only this, that it is above all they know or can imagine. They may see things which make a great shew here; they may hear of more than they see; they may think or imagine more than either they hear or see, or can distinctly conceive of; but still, they must think of this glory as beyond it all. If I see pompous shows, or read or hear of them, yet, this I say of them, These are not as my inheritance: Oh! it is far beyond them. Yea, does my mind imagine things far beyond them, golden mountains and marble palaces, yet those fall short of my inheritance, for it is such *as eye hath not seen, nor ear*

heard, nor hath it entered into the heart of man to conceive.
Oh, the brightness of that glory when it shall be revealed!
How shall they be astonished, who shall see it, and not partake
of it! How shall they be filled with everlasting joy, who are
heirs of it! Were the heart much upon the thoughts of that
glory, what thing is there in this perishing world, which could
either lift it up or cast it down?

Ver. 2. Feed the flock of God which is among you, taking the oversight
thereof, not by constraint, but willingly; not for filthy lucre, but of a
ready mind:

Ver. 3. Neither as being lords over God's heritage, but being ensamples to
the flock:

Ver. 4. And when the Chief Shepherd shall appear, ye shall receive a
crown of glory that fadeth not away.

In these words we have, I. The Duty enjoined: *Feed the flock
of God which is among you, taking the oversight of it;* II.
The due qualifications for this duty: *Not by constraint, not
for filthy lucre, not as lording it over God's heritage, but willingly, of a ready mind,* and as *being ensamples to the flock;*
III. The high Advantage to be expected: *An unfading crown
of glory, when the Chief Shepherd shall appear.*

I. The Duty enjoined. Every step of the way of our salvation hath on it the print of infinite majesty, wisdom, and
goodness, and this amongst the rest; that men, sinful, weak men,
are made subservient in that great work of bringing Christ and
souls to meet; that by the *foolishness of preaching,* (or what
appears so to carnal wisdom,) the chosen of God are called, and
come unto Jesus, and are made *wise unto salvation;* and that
the life which is conveyed to them by the *word of life* in the
hands of poor men, is by the same means preserved and advanced. This is the standing work of the ministry, and this
the thing here bound upon them that are employed in it, *to feed
the flock of God that is among them.* Jesus Christ descended
to purchase a Church, and ascended to provide and furnish it,
to send down his Spirit: *He ascended and gave gifts,* parti-

cularly *for the work of the ministry ;* and the great use of them this, *feed the flock of God.*

Not to say any more of this usual resemblance of a flock, as importing the weakness and tenderness of the Church, the continual need she stands in of inspection, and guidance, and defence, and the tender care of the Chief Shepherd for these things ; the phrase enforces the present duty of subordinate pastors, their care and diligence in feeding that flock. The due rule of discipline not excluded, the main part of this duty, is by doctrine, the leading them into the wholesome and *green pastures* of saving truths revealed in the Gospel, accommodating the way of teaching to their condition and capacity ; and with this they should be, as much as possible, particularly acquainted, and suit diligently and prudently their doctrine to it. They are to *feed the sheep*—those more advanced ; *to feed the lambs*—the younger and weaker ; to have special care of the infirm ; to learn of their Master, the great Shepherd, to *bind up that which is broken,* and *strengthen that which is sick,*—(Ezek. xxxiv. 16)—those that are broken in spirit, that are exercised with temptations ; and *gently to lead those that are with young*—(Isa. xl. 11)—those in whom the inward work of grace is as in the conception, and they heavy and weak with the weight of it, and the many difficulties and doubtings which are frequent companions and symptoms of that work. Oh, what dexterity and skilfulness, what diligence, and, above all, what affection and bowels of compassion, are needful for this task ! *Who is sufficient for these things ?* (2 Cor. ii. 16.) Who would not faint and give over in it, were not our Lord *the Chief Shepherd ;* were not all our sufficiency laid up in His rich fulness, and all our insufficiency covered in His gracious acceptance ?

Inf. 1. This is the thing we have to eye and study, to set Him before us, and to apply ourselves in His strength to this work :—not to seek to *please,* but to *feed ;* not to delight the ears, but to feed *the souls* of His people ; to see that the food be according to His appointment ; not empty or subtile notions, not light affected expressions, but wholesome truths, solid food, spiritual things spiritually conceived, and uttered with holy understanding and affection.

And we are to consider this, wherein lies a very pressing motive; it is *the flock of God:* not our own, to use as we please, but committed to our custody by Him, who loves highly and prizes His flock, and will require an account of us concerning it; His bought, His purchased flock, and at so dear a rate, as the Apostle St. Paul uses this same consideration, in the same argument, Acts xx. 28, *The flock of God that He hath bought with His own blood.* How reasonable is it that we bestow our strength and life on that flock for which our Lord laid down His life; that we be most ready to draw out our spirits for them for whom He let out His blood! *Had I,* says that holy man, Bernard, *some of that blood poured forth on the cross, how carefully would I carry it! And ought I not to be as careful of those souls that it was shed for?* (Advent Serm. 3.) Oh, that price which was paid for souls, which he, who was no foolish merchant, but wisdom itself, gave for them! Were that price more in our eyes, and more in yours, nothing would so much take either you or us, as the matter of our souls. In this would our desires and endeavours meet, we to use, and you to improve, the means of saving your precious souls.

Inf. 2. This mainly concerns us indeed, who have charge of many, especially finding the right cure of one soul within us so hard: but you are concerned in it, each for one. At least remember, this is the end of the ministry, that you may be brought unto Christ; that you may be led to the sweet pastures and pleasant streams of the Gospel: that you may be spiritually fed, and may grow in that heavenly life, which is here begun in all those in whom it shall hereafter be perfected.

And as we ought in preaching, so ought you in hearing, to propound this end to yourselves, that you may be spiritually refreshed, and walk in the strength of that Divine nourishment. Is this your purpose when you come hither? . Inquire of your

own hearts, and see what you seek, and what you find, in the
public ordinances of God's house. Certainly, the most do
not so much as think on the due design of them ; they aim
at no end, and therefore can attain none ; they seek nothing,
but sit out their hour, asleep or awake, as it may happen. Or,
possibly, some seek to be delighted for the time, as the Lord
tells the Prophet, to hear, *as it were, a pleasant song*, (Ezek.
xxxiii. 32,) if the gifts and strain of the speaker be any thing
pleasing. Or, it may be, they seek to gain some new notions,
to add somewhat to their stock of knowledge, either that they
may be enabled for discourse, or, simply, that they may know.
Some, it may be, go a little further ; they like to be stirred
and moved for the time, and to have some touch of good affection kindled in them : but this lasts but *for a while*, till their
other thoughts and affairs get in, and smother and quench it ;
they are not careful to blow it up and improve it. How many
when they have been a little affected with the word, go out
and fall into other discourses and thoughts : they either take
in their affairs secretly, as it were under their cloak, and their
hearts keep up a conference with them, or, if they forbear this,
yet, as soon as they go out, they plunge themselves over head
and ears in the world, and lose all which might have any way
advantaged their spiritual condition. It may be, one will say,
It was a good sermon. Is that to the purpose ? But what
think you it hath for your praise or dispraise ? Instead of saying, Oh, how well was that spoken ! you should say, Oh how
hard is repentance ! how sweet a thing is faith ! how excellent
the love of Jesus Christ ! That were your best and most real
commendation of the sermon, with true benefit to yourselves.

If some of you be careful of repeating, yet rest not on that :
if you be able to speak of it afterwards upon occasion, there is
somewhat requisite beside and beyond this, to evidence that
you are indeed fed by the word, as the flock of God. As
when sheep, you know, or other creatures, are nourished by
their pasture, the food they have eaten appears, not in the
same fashion upon them, not in grass, but in growth of flesh

and fleece; thus the word would truly appear to feed you, not by the bare discoursing of the word over again, but by the temper of your spirits and actions, if in them you really grow more spiritual, if humility, self-denial, charity, and holiness, are increased in you by it; otherwise, whatsoever literal knowledge you attain, it avails you nothing. Though you heard many sermons every day, and attained further light by them, and carried a plausible profession of religion, yet, unless by the Gospel you be transformed into the likeness of Christ, and grace be indeed growing in you, you are but, as one says of the cypress-trees, fair and tall, but fruitless *.

Are you not grieved and afraid, or may not many of you be so, who have lived many years under a fruitful ministry, and yet are as earthly and selfish, as unacquainted with God and His ways, as at the first? Consider this, that as the neglect of souls will lie heavy on unholy or negligent ministers, so, a great many souls are ruining themselves under some measure of fit means, and the slighting of those means will make their condition far heavier than that of many others. Remember our Saviour's word; *Woe to thee, Chorazin! Woe unto thee, Bethsaida! It shall be more tolerable for Tyre and Sidon in the day of judgment, than for you.* (Matt. xi. 21.)

II. The discharge of this high task we have here duly qualified: the Apostle expresses the upright way of it, both negatively and positively.

There be three evils the Apostle would remove from this work, *constrainedness, covetousness,* and *ambition,* as opposed to *willingness, a ready mind,* and an exemplary temper and behaviour.

1. We are cautioned against *constrainedness,* μὴ ἀναγκαστῶς; against being driven to the work by necessity, indigence, and want of other means of subsistence, as it is with too many; making a trade of it to live by, and setting to it as to any other calling for that end; yea, making it the refuge and forlorn resource of their insufficiency for other callings. And as men

Καλοὶ καὶ ὕψηλοι καὶ κάρπον οὐκ ἔχουσι.

are not to undertake the work, driven to it by that hard weapon of necessity, so, being engaged in it, they are not to discharge the duties of it merely upon necessity, because of fines
binding to it, or for fear of censure: this is a violent forced
motion, and cannot but be both very unpleasant and unprofitable, as to the proper end and profiting of this work. And as
the principle of the motion in this service should not be a com-
pelling necessity of any kind, but true *willingness of heart*, so,
this willingness should not arise from any thing but pure affection to the work.

2. Not *for filthy gain*, but purely from the inward bent of
the mind. As it should not be a compulsive or violent motion
by necessity from without, so, it should not be an artificial
motion by weights hung on within—avarice and love of gain.
The former were a wheel, driven or drawn, going by force;
the latter, little better, as a clock made to go by art, by weights
hung to it. But there should be a natural motion, like that of
the heavens in their course. A willing obedience to the Spirit
of God within, moving a man in every part of this holy work,
that is προθύμως, his mind carried to it as the thing he delights
in, and in which he loves to be exercised. So, Timothy *careth*
γνησίως, not artificially, but naturally. (Phil. ii. 20.) There may
be in a faithful pastor very great reluctance in engaging and
adhering to the work, upon a sense of the excellency of it and
his own unfitness, and the deep apprehension of those high
interests, the glory of God, and the salvation of souls; and
yet, he may enter into it, and continue in it, with this *readiness of mind* too; that is, with most single and earnest desires
of doing all he can for God, and *the flock of God;* only grieved
that there is in him so little suitableness of heart, so little holiness and acquaintance with God for enabling him to it. But
might he find that, he were satisfied; and, in expectation of
that, he goes on, and waits, and is doing according to his little
skill and strength, and cannot leave it. He is *constrained* indeed, but all the constraint is that of *love to Jesus*, and, for
His sake, to the souls he hath bought; (2 Cor. v. 14;) and

all the *gain* sought, is, to *gain* souls to Christ; which is far
different from the constraint and the gain here prohibited; yea,
this is indeed that very willingness and readiness of mind which
is opposed to that other constraint.   That is without; this is
within : that other gain, is base filthy gain, αἰχροκέρδος; this
noble and divine.

Inf. 1. Far be it from us, that necessity and constraint
should be the thing that moves us in so holy a work.   The
Lord whom we serve, sees into the heart, and if He find not
that primarily moving, accounts all our diligence nothing.   And
let not base earth within be the cause of our willingness, but
a mind touched with heaven.   It is true, the temptations of
earth with us, in the matter of gain, are not great; but yet,
the heart may cleave to them, as much as if they were much
greater, and if it do cleave to them, they shall ruin us; as well
a poor stipend and glebe, if the affection be upon them, as a
great deanery or bishopric.   If a man fall into it, he may drown
in a small brook, being under water, as well as in the great
ocean.   Oh, the little time that remains!   Let us join our desires and endeavours in this work, bend our united strength to
serve Him, that we may have joy in that day of reckoning.

And, indeed, there is nothing moves us aright, nor shall we
ever find comfort in this service, unless it be from a cheerful
inward *readiness of mind,* and that from the *love of Christ.*
Thus said He to His Apostle, *Lovest thou me?   Then, feed
my sheep, and feed my lambs.* (John xxi. 16.) Love to Christ
begets love to His people's souls, which are so precious to Him,
and a care of feeding them.   He devolves the working of love
towards Him, upon his flock, for their good, puts them in His
room, to receive the benefit of our services, which cannot reach
Him considered in Himself: He can receive no other profit
from it.   Love, much love, gives much unwearied care and
much skill in this charge.   How sweet is it to him that loves,
to bestow himself, *to spend and be spent,* upon his service
whom he loves!   Jacob, in the same kind of service, endured
all that was imposed on him, and found it light by reason of

love,—the cold of the nights, and heat of the days: seven years he served for his Rachel, *and they seemed to him but a few days because he loved her.* (Gen. xxix. 20.)

Love is the great endowment of a shepherd of Christ's flock. He says not to Peter, Art thou wise, or learned, or eloquent? but, *Lovest thou me? Then, feed my sheep.*

3. The third evil is ambition, and that is either in the affecting of undue authority, or the overstrained and tyrannical exercise of due authority, or to seek those dignities that suit not with this charge, which is not *dominium*, but *ministerium*. This temper, therefore, is forbidden, Luke xxii. 25, 26 : *The kings of the Gentiles exercise lordship over them, but ye shall not be so.* There is a ministerial authority to be used in discipline, and more sharpness with some than with others; but still, lowliness and moderation must be predominant, and not domineering with rigour; rather being examples to the flock in all holiness, and especially in humility and meekness, wherein our Lord Jesus particularly propounds His own example : *Learn of me, for I am meek and lowly of heart.*

But being ensamples.] Such a pattern as they may stamp and print their spirits and carriage by, and be *followers of you, as you are of Christ.* And without this, there is little or no fruitful teaching. Well says Nazianzen, *Either teach not, or teach by living.* So the Apostle exhorteth Timothy to be an *example in word,* but withal, *in conversation.* (1 Tim. iv. 12.) That is τύπος, the best printed copy.

But this pares off, will some think, all encouragements of learning; leaves no advantage, no respect, or authority. Oh, no: it removes poor worthless encouragements out of the way, to make place for one great one that is sufficient, which all the others together are not.

III. The high Advantage: *And when the Chief Shepherd shall appear, ye shall receive a crown of glory which fadeth not away.* Thou shalt lose nothing by all that restraint from base gain, and vain glory, and worldly power. No matter, let them all go for *a crown:* that weighs them all down; that shall abide for ever. Oh, how far more excellent! *A crown of glory,* pure, unmixed glory, without any ingrediency of pride or sinful vanity, or any danger of it. And a crown *that fadeth not,* ἀμαράντινον, of such a flower that withers not: not a temporary garland of fading flowers, such as all here are. *Wo to the crown of pride,* says the Prophet: Isa. xxviii. 1. Though it be made of flowers growing in a fat valley, yet their glorious beauty is a fading flower; but this will remain fresh and in perfect lustre to all eternity. May they not well trample on base gain and vain applause, who have this Crown to look to? They that will be content with those, let them be; but *they have their reward,* and it is done and gone, when faithful followers are to receive theirs. Joys of royal pomp, marriages and feasts, how soon do they vanish as a dream! That of Ahasuerus lasted about half a year, but then it ended! And how many since that are gone and forgotten! But this day begins a triumph and a feast, that shall never either end or weary, affording still fresh, ever new delights. All things here, the choicest pleasures, cloy, but satisfy not: those above shall always satisfy and never cloy. *When the Chief Shepherd shall appea*r. And that shall shortly be: this moment will shortly be out.

What is to be refused in the way to this Crown? All labour is sweet for it. And what is there here to be desired to detain our hearts, that we should not most willingly let go, to rest from our labours, and receive our crown! Was ever any king sad to think that the day of his coronation drew nigh? And then, there will be no envy, nor jealousies: all will be kings, each with his crown, each rejoicing in the glory of the others, and all in His, who that day shall be *All in all.*

Ver. 5. Likewise, ye younger, submit yourselves unto the elder ; yea, all of you be subject one to another, and be clothed with humility : for God resisteth the proud, and giveth grace to the humble.

Sin hath disordered all; so that nothing is to be found but distemper and crookedness in the condition and ways of men towards God, and towards one another, till a new Spirit come in and rectify all. And very much of that redress lies in this particular grace of *humility*, here recommended by the Apostle.

That grace regulates the carriage, 1. Of the *younger* towards the *elder*. 2. Of all men *one to another*. 3. Of all towards God.

1. The *Younger are to be subject to the Elder*. Which I take so to refer to difference of years, that it hath some aspect likewise to the relation of those that are under the discipline and government of the *elders,* πρεσβύτεροι, who, though not always such in years, ought, however, to suit that name in exemplary gravity and wisdom. It is no seigniory, but a ministry; yet there is a sacred authority in it, when rightly carried, which both duly challenges and effectually commands, that respect and obedience which is fit for the right order and government of *the House of God*.

The Spirit of Christ in his ministers, is the thing that makes them truly *Elders*, and truly *worthy of double honour ;* and without that, men may hunt after respect and credit by other parts, and the more they follow it, the faster it flies from them, or, if they catch any thing of it, they only grasp a shadow.

Infer. Learn you, my brethren, that obedience which is due to the discipline of God's House. This is all we plead for in this point. And know if you refuse it, and despise the ordinance of God, He will resent the indignity as done to Himself. And Oh, that all who have that charge of His house upon them, would mind his interest wholly, and not rise in conceit of their power, but wholly employ and improve it for their Lord and Master, and look on no respect paid to themselves, as for its own sake desirable, but only so far as is needful for the profitable discharge and advancement of His work in their hands! What are human differences and regards? How empty a vapour! And whatsoever it is, nothing is lost by single and entire love of our Lord's glory, and total aiming at that. *Them that honour Him, He will honour; and those that despise Him shall be despised.* (1 Sam. ii. 30.)

But though this [*likewise*] implies, I conceive, somewhat relative to the former subject, yet certainly, its full scope is more extensive, it directs us, touching the difference of years, to yield the *subjection,* that is, the respect and reverence which is due from younger to elder persons.

The presumption and unbridledness of youth require the pressing and binding on of this rule. And it is of undeniable equity, even written in nature, as due to aged persons. But, doubtless, those reap this due fruit in that season the most, who have ripened it most by the influence of their grave and holy carriage. *The hoary head* is indeed *a crown,*—but when?—*when found in the way of righteousness.* (Prov. xvi. 31.) There it shines, and hath a kind of royalty over youth; otherwise a graceless old age is a most despicable and lamentable sight. What gains an unholy old man or woman, by their scores of years, but the more scores of guiltiness and misery? And their white hairs speak nothing but ripeness for wrath. 'Oh! to be as *a tree planted in the house of the Lord, bringing forth fruit in old age.* (Psal. xcii. 12, 13.) Much experience in the ways of God, and much disdain of the world, and much desire of the love of God, a heavenly temper of mind and frame of life; this is the advantage of many years. But to have seen and felt the more misery, and *heaped up* the more sin, the greater bundle of it, *against the day of wrath,* a woful *treasure* of it, threescore, or threescore and ten years a gathering, and with so much increase every day; no vacation, no dead years, no, not a day wherein it was not growing; how deplorable a case!

A sad reflection, to look back and think, What have I done for God? and to find nothing but such a world of sin committed against Him! How much better he who gets home betimes in his youth, if once delivered from sin and death, at one with God, and someway serviceable to Him, or desiring to be so, and who hath a quick yoyage, having lived much in a little time !

2. *All of you be subject one to another.* This yet further dilates the duty, makes it universally mutual; *one subject to another.* This directly turns about the vain contest of men, that arises from the natural mischief of self-love. Every one would carry it, and be best and highest. The very company of Christ, and his exemplary lowliness, and the meanness of Himself and those His followers, all these did not bar out this frothy foolish question, *Who shall be greatest?* And so far it was disputed, that it occasioned heat about it, *a strife amongst them.* (Luke xxii. 24.) Now, this rule is just opposite: each is to strive to be lowest, *subject one to another.*

This doth not annul either civil or church government, nor those differences that are grounded upon the law of nature, or of civil society; for we see immediately before, that such differences are allowed, and the particular duties of them recommended; but it only requires that all due respect, according to their station, be given by each Christian to another. And though there cannot be such a subjection of masters or parents to their servants and children, as is due to them from these, yet a lowly, meek carrying of their authority, a tender respect of their youth, the receiving of an admonition from them duly qualified, is that which suits with the rule; and in general, not delighting in the trampling on, or abusing of any, but rather seeking the credit and good esteem of all as our own; taking notice of that good in them, wherein they are beyond us; (for all have some advantage, and none hath all;) and, in a word, (and it is the precept of St. Paul, like this of our Apostle here,) *In honour preferring one another,* (Rom. xii. 10,) *q. d.:* Let this be all the strife, who shall put most respect each on another, according to the capacity and station of every one: *in giving honour, go each one before another.*

Now that such carriage may be sincere, no empty compliment, or court holy water, (as they speak,) but a part of the solid holiness of a Christian, the Apostle requires the true principle of such deportment, the grace of *humility*, that a Christian *put on that;* not the appearance of it, to act in as a stage-garment, but the truth of it, as their constant habit. *Be ye clothed with humility.* It must appear in your outward carriage; so the resemblance of clothing imports. But let it appear as really it is; so the very name of it imports. It is not ταπεινοφανία, but ταπεινοφροσύνη; not a *shew of humility,* but heart-lowliness, *humility of mind.*

As it is the bent of humility to hide other graces, so far as piety to God and our brethren will permit, so it would willingly hide itself; it loves not to appear but as necessity urges. Appear it must, and it doth somewhat more appear than many other graces do, though it seeks not to appear. It is seen as a modest man or woman's apparel, which they wear not for the end that it may be seen; they do not gaudily flaunt and delight in dressing: though there is a decency as well as necessity, which they do and may have respect to, yet it is in so neat and unaffected a way, that they are a good example even in that point. Thus, humility in carriage and words, is as the decorum of this clothing, but the main is the real usefulness of it.

And therefore, a truly humble man desires not much to appear humble. Yea, were it not for disedifying his brethren, he would rather disguise and hide, not only other things by humility, but even humility itself, and would be content, upon the mistake of some words or gestures, to pass for proud and vain, being humble within, rather than to be big in his own eyes, under a semblance of outward lowliness. Yea, were it not that charity and piety do both forbid it, he would not care to do some things on purpose that might seem arrogant, to carry humility unseen, that doth so naturally delight in covering all graces, and is sorry that it cannot do so without being seen itself, as that garment that covers the rest, must of necessity be seen itself. But seeing it must be so, it is with the least show that may be, as a dark veil cast about rich attire, hides their show, and makes very little itself.

This, therefore, is mainly to be studied, that the seat of humility be *the heart*. Although it will be seen in the carriage, yet, as little as it can ; as few words as may be concerning itself; and those it doth speak, must be the real thoughts of the mind, and not an affected voice of it differing from the inward sense : otherwise, humble speech and carriage only put on without, and not fastened in the inside, is the most refined and subtle, and indeed the most dangerous kind of pride. And this I would recommend as a safe way : Ever let thy thoughts concerning thyself be below what thou utterest ; and what thou seest needful or fitting to say to thine own abasement, be not only content (which most are not) to be taken at thy word, and believed to be such by them that hear thee, but be desirous of it, and let that be the end of thy speech, to persuade them, and gain it of them, that they really take thee for as worthless and mean as thou dost express thyself.

Infer. But how little are we acquainted with the real frame of Christianity, the most living without a rule, not laying it to their words and ways at all, nor yielding so much as a seeming obedience to the Gospel ; while others take up a kind of profession, and think all consists in some religious performances, and do not study the inward reserve of their heart-evils, nor labour to have that temple purged : for the heart should be a temple, and it stands in much need of a sweeping out of the filthiness, and putting out of idols. Some there be, who are much busied about the matter of their assurance, still upon that point, which it is lawful indeed and laudable to enquire after, yet not so as to neglect other things more needful. It were certainly better for many, when they find no issue that way, to turn somewhat of their diligence to the study of Christian graces and duties in their station, and to task themselves for a time, were it to the more special seeking, first, of some one grace, and then, of another, as meekness, and patience, and this particularly of humility. To be truly heart-humble—many men despise it in others; but some that will commend it in the general, or in some of those in whom they behold it, yet seek not to *put it on* themselves. They love to be more gay, and to seem to be somebody, and not abase themselves. It is the way, say they, to be undone. This clothing is too poor a stuff, and of too sad a colour for them. Oh, my brethren, you know not the excellency of it. Ye look out at a distance, and judge according to your light vain minds. But will you see it by the light of the word, and then you shall perceive much hidden richness and comeliness in it. And do not only approve it, and call it comely on others, but put it on, and so it is most comely. And as it is with respect to all graces, so particularly, as to this clothing of humility, though it make least shew, yet come near, and you will see it both rich and comely; and though it hides other graces, yet when they do appear under it, as sometimes they will, a little glance of them so makes them much more esteemed. Rebecca's beauty and her jewels were covered with a veil, but when they did appear, the veil set them off, and commended them, though at a distance it hid them.

Again: As in all graces, so particularly in this grace; take heed of a disguise or counterfeit of it. Oh, for sincerity in all things, and particularly in this! To be low in thine own eyes, and willing to be so in the eyes of others, this is the very upright nature of heart-humility. 1st, Not to be deluded with a false conceit of advantages thou hast not. 2dly, Not to be swelled with a vain conceit of those thou really hast. 3dly, Not affecting to be esteemed by others, either upon their imagining thee to have some good that is not in thee, or discerning that which is. Is not the day at hand when men will be taken off the false heights they stand on, and set on their own feet; when all the esteem of others shall vanish and pass away like smoke, and thou shalt be just what God finds and accounts thee, and neither more nor less? Oh! the remembrance of that day when a true estimate will be made of all, this would make men hang less upon the unstable conceits and opinions of one another, knowing our judgment and day shall shortly end. Be it little or much that thou hast, the lower and closer thou carriest it under this cloak, the safer shall it and thou be, the more shall it increase, and thou shalt be the liker Him in whom *all fulness* dwells. In this He hath most expressly set Himself before us as our pattern; and one says well, " Surely, man might now be constrained to be proud, for whom God Himself became humble."

Now, to work the heart to an humble posture, 1. Look *into thyself* in earnest: and, truly, whosoever thou be that hast the highest conceit of thyself, and the highest causes for it, a real sight of thyself will lay thy crest. Men look on any good, or any fancy of it, in themselves, with both eyes, and skip over as unpleasant their real defects and deformities. Every man is naturally his own flatterer; otherwise, flatteries, and false cryings-up from others, would make little impression; but hence their success, they meet with the same conceit within. But let any man see his ignorance, and lay what he knows not over against what he knows; the disorders in his heart and affections, over against any right motion in them; his secret follies and sins, against his outwardly blameless carriage,—this man shall not readily love and embrace himself; yea, it shall be impossible for him not to abase and abhor himself.

2. Look on the good in others, and the evil in thyself: make that the parallel, and then thou wilt walk humbly. Most men do just the contrary, and that foolish and unjust comparison puffs them up.

3. Thou art not required to be ignorant of that good which really is so indeed; but beware of imagining *that* to be good which is not; yea, rather let something that is truly good pass thy view, and see it within, rather than beyond its true size. And then, whatsoever it be, see it not as thine own, but as God's, His free gift; and so the more thou hast, looking on it in that view, thou wilt certainly be the more humble, as having the more obligations: the weight of them will press

thee down, and lay thee still lower, as you see it in Abraham,
—the clear visions and promises he had, made him fall down
flat to the ground. (Gen. xv. 12.)

4. Pray much for the spirit of humility, the Spirit of Christ,
for that is it ; otherwise, all thy vileness will not humble thee.
When men hear of this or of other graces, and how reasonable
they are, they think presently to have them, and do not consider the natural enmity and rebellion of their own hearts, and
the necessity of receiving them from heaven. And therefore,
in the use of all other means, be most dependent on that influence, and most in the use of that means which opens the heart
most to that influence, and draws it down upon the heart, and
that is Prayer.

Of all the evils of our corrupt nature, there is none more
connatural and universal than pride, the grand wickedness,
self-exalting in our own and others' opinion. Though I will
not contest what was the first step in that complicated first sin,
yet certainly this of pride was one, and a main ingredient in it,
—that which the unbelief conceived going before, and the disobedience following after, were both servants to ; and ever
since, it sticks still dee in our nature. St. Augustine says
truly, *That which first overcame man, is the last thing he
overcomes.* Some sins, comparatively, may die before us, but
this hath life in it, sensibly, as long as we. It is as the heart of
all, the first living, and the last dying ; and it hath this advantage, that, whereas other sins are fomented by one another, this
feeds even on virtues and graces, as a moth that breeds in them,
and consumes them, even in the finest of them, if it be not
carefully looked to. This hydra, as one head of it is cut off,
another rises up. It will secretly cleave to the best actions,
and prey upon them. And therefore is there so much need
that we continually watch, and fight, and pray against it, and
be restless in the pursuit of real and deep humiliation, daily
seeking to advance further in it ; to be nothing, and to desire
to be nothing ; not only to bear, but to love our own abasement,
and the things that procure and help it, to take pleasure in

them, so far as may be without sin: yea, even in respect of our sinful failings, when they are discovered, to love the bringing low of ourselves by them, while we hate, and grieve for the sin of them.

And, above all, it is requisite to watch ourselves in our best things, that self get not in, or, if it break in, or steal in at any time, that it be presently found out and cast out again ; to have that established within us, to do all for God, to intend Him and His glory in all, and to be willing to advance His glory, were it by our own disgrace ; not to make raising or pleasing thyself the rule of exercising thy parts and graces, when thou art called to use and bring them forth, but the good of thy brethren, and in that, the glory of thy Lord. Now, this is indeed to be severed from self and united to Him, to have self-love turned into the love of God. And this is his own work : it is above all other hands : therefore, the main combat against pride, and the conquest of it, and the gaining of humility, is certainly by prayer. God bestows Himself upon them who are most abundant in prayer ; and they to whom He shews Himself most are certainly the most humble.

Now, to stir us up to diligence in the exercise of this grace, take briefly a consideration or two.

1. Look on that above pointed at, the high example of lowliness set before us ; Jesus Christ requiring our particular care to take this lesson from Him. And is it not most reasonable? He the most fair, the most excellent and complete of all men, and yet the most humble! He more than a man, who yet willingly became, in some sort, less than a man, as it is expressed, Psal. xxii. 6, *a worm and no man.* And when Majesty itself *emptied itself,* and descended so low, shall a worm swell and be high-conceited ?

Then, consider, it was for *us* he humbled Himself, to expiate our pride ; and therefore it is evidently the more just that we follow a pattern which is both so great in itself, and doth so nearly concern us. O humility, the virtue of Christ, (that which he so peculiarly espoused,) how dost thou confound the vanity of our pride !

2. Consider the safety of Grace under this clothing ; it is that which keeps it unexposed to a thousand hazards. Humility doth Grace no prejudice in covering it, but indeed shelters it from violence and wrong : therefore they do justly call it *conservatrix virtutum*, the preserver of graces ; and one says well, "That he who carries other graces without humility, carries a precious powder in the wind without a cover."

3. Consider the increase of grace by it, as here expressed ; the perfect enmity of God against pride, and His bounty towards humility : *He resisteth the proud, and giveth grace to the humble.*

God resisteth the proud, [ἀντιτάσσεται,] singles it out for His grand enemy, and sets Himself in battle array against it : so the word is. It breaks the ranks of men in which He hath set them, when they are not subject, ὑποτασσόμενοι, as the word is before ; yea, Pride not only breaks rank, but rises up in rebellion against God, and doth what it can to dethrone him and usurp His place : therefore, He orders His forces against it. And to be sure, if God be able to make His party good, Pride shall not escape ruin. He will break it, and bring it low : for He is set upon that purpose, and will not be diverted.

But he giveth grace,—pours it out plentifully upon humble hearts. His sweet dews and showers of grace, slide off the mountains of pride, and fall on the low valleys of humble hearts, and make them pleasant and fertile. The swelling heart, puffed up with a fancy of fulness, hath no room for grace. It is lifted up, is not hallowed and fitted to receive and contain the graces that descend from above. And again, as the humble heart is most capacious, and, as being emptied and hollowed, can hold most, so it is the most thankful, acknowledges all as received, while the proud cries out that all is his own. The return of glory that is due from Grace, comes most freely and plentifully from an humble heart : God delights to enrich it with grace, and it delights to return Him glory. The more He bestows on it, the more it desires to honour Him with all ; and the more it doth so, the more readily he bestows still more upon it ; and this is the sweet intercourse betwixt God and the humble soul. This is the noble ambition of humility, in respect whereof all the aspirings of pride are low and base. When all is reckoned, the lowliest mind is truly the highest ; and these two agree so well, that the more lowly it is, it is thus the higher; and the higher thus, it is still the more lowly.

Oh, my brethren, want of this is a great cause of all our wants. Why should our God bestow on us what we would bestow on our idol, self? Or, if not to idolize thyself, yet to idolize the thing, the gift that Grace bestowed, to fetch thy believing and comforts from that, which is to put it in His place who gave, and *to make Baal of it*, as some would render Hosea, ii. 8*. Now He will not furnish thee thus to His own prejudice therein. Seek, therefore, to have thy heart on a high design, seeking grace still, not to rest in any gift, nor to grow vain and regardless of Him upon it. If we had but this fixed with us—What gift or grace I seek, what comfort I seek, it shall be no sooner mine, but it shall be all Thine again, and myself with it ; I desire nothing from Thee, but that it may come back to Thee, and draw me with it unto thee ; this is all my end, and all my desire :—the request thus presented would not come back so often unanswered.

This is the only way to grow quickly rich : come still poor to Him who hath enough ever to enrich thee, and desire of His riches, not for thyself, but for him. Mind entirely His glory in all thou hast and seekest to have. What thou hast, use so, and what thou wantest, vow that thou wilt use it so : let it be His in thy purpose, even before it be thine in possession, as Hannah did in her suit for a son; (1 Sam. i. 11;) and thou shalt obtain as she did. And then, as she was, be thou faithful

---

* The words *Gnasu Lebagnol*, which we render *which they prepared for* Baal, may, as the margin notes, be translated *wherewith they made* Baal. Dr. Doddridge.

in the performance ; *Him whom I received* (says she) *by peti-tion, I have returned to the Lord.*

It is undoubtedly the secret pride and selfishness of our hearts, that obstruct much of the bounty of God's hand in the measure of our graces, and the sweet embraces of His love, which we should otherwise find. The more that we let go of ourselves, still the more should we receive of Himself. Oh, foolish we, who refuse so blessed an exchange !

To this humility, as in these words it is taken in the notion of our inward thoughts touching ourselves, and our carriage in relation to others, the Apostle joins the other humility, in rela-tion to God ; being indeed the different actings of one and the same grace, and inseparably connected each with the other.

Ver. 6. Humble yourselves, therefore, under the mighty hand of God, that He may exalt you in due time.

THIS is pressed by a reason both of equity and necessity, in that word, *The mighty hand of God.* He is Sovereign Lord of all, and all things do obeisance to Him ; therefore, it is *just*, that you His people, professing loyalty and obedience to Him, be most submissive and humble in your subjection to Him in all things. Again, mark *the necessity, His mighty hand :* there is no striving, it is a vain thing to flinch and struggle, for He doth what He will. And His hand is so mighty, that the greatest power of the creature is nothing to it. Yea, it is all indeed derived from Him, and therefore cannot do any whit against Him. If thou wilt not yield, thou must yield : if thou wilt not be led, thou shalt be pulled and drawn. Therefore, submission is your only course.

A third reason by which this duty is pressed, is that of uti-lity, or the certain advantage of it. As there is nothing to be gained, yea, rather, as you are certainly ruined by reluctance, so, this humble submission is the only way to gain your point. What would you have under any affliction, but be delivered, and raised up ? Thus alone can you attain that : *Humble your-selves, and he shall raise you up in due time.*

This is the end why He humbles you: He lays weights upon you, that you may be depressed. Now, when this end is gained, that you are willingly so, then the weights are taken off, and you are lifted up by His gracious hand. Otherwise, it is not enough, that he hath humbled you by His hand, unless you *humble yourselves* under His hand. Many have had great and many pressures, one affliction after another, and been humbled, and yet not made humble, as they commonly express the difference: humbled by force in regard of their outward condition, but not humbled in their inward temper; and therefore, as soon as the weight is off, like heaps of wool, they rise up again, and grow as big as they were.

If we would consider this in our particular trials, and aim at this deportment, it were our wisdom. Are they not mad, who, under any stroke, quarrel or struggle against God? What gain your children thus at your hands, but more blows? Nor is this only an unseemly and unhappy way, openly to resist and strive, but even secretly to fret and grumble; for He hears the least whispering of the heart, and looks most how that behaves itself under His hand. Oh, humble acceptance of His chastisement, is our duty and our peace; that which gains most on the heart of our Father, and makes the rod fall soonest out of His hand.

And not only should we learn this in our outward things, but in our spiritual condition, as the thing the Lord is much pleased with in His children. There is a stubbornness and fretting of heart concerning our souls, that arises from pride and the untamedness of our nature; and yet some take a pleasure in it, touching the matter of comfort and assurance, if it be withheld. Or, (which they take more liberty in,) if it be sanctification and victory over sin, they seek, and yet find little or no success, but the Lord holding them under in these, they then vex themselves, and wax more discontented, and nothing pleases them: as peevish children, upon the refusal of somewhat they would have, take displeasure, and make no account of the daily provision made for them, and all the other benefits they have by the care and love of their parents. This is a folly very unbeseeming the children that are the *children of wisdom,* and should walk as such; and till they learn more humble respect for their Father's will, they are still the further off from their purpose. Were they once brought to submit the matter, and give him heartily His will, He would readily give them theirs, as far as it were for their good: as you say to your children, of anything they are too stiff and earnest in, and make a noise for, " Cry not for it, and you shall have it."

And this is the thing we observe not, that the Lord often by His delays, is aiming at this ; and were this done, we cannot think how graciously He would deal with us. His gracious design is, to make much room for grace by much humbling : especially in some spirits which need much trying, or when He means much to enable for some singular service. And thus, the time is not lost, as we are apt to imagine, but it furthers our end, while we think the contrary. It is necessary time and pains that are given to the unballasting of a ship, the casting out of the earth and sand, when it is to be laden with spices. We must be emptied more, if we would have more of that fulness and riches which we are longing for.

So long as we fume and chafe against His way, though it be in our best supplications, we are not in a posture for a favourable answer. Would we wring things out of His hand by fretfulness? That is not the way: no; but present humble submissive suits: Lord, this is my desire, but thou art wise and gracious ; I refer the matter to thy will for the thing, and for the measure, and for the time, and all. Were we moulded to this composure, then were mercy near. When he hath gained this, broken our will and tamed our stoutness, then He relents and pities. See Jer. xxx. 17, 18. *Because they called thee an outcast, &c., thus saith the Lord, behold, I will bring again the captivity of Jacob's tents, &c.*

This I would recommend in any estate, the humble folding under the Lord's hand, kissing the rod, and falling low before Him ; and this is the way to be raised. But there may be some one who thinks he hath tried this awhile, and is still at the same point, hath gained nothing, and he may therefore be ready to fall back to his old repinings : let such a one know that his humbling and compliance were not upright ; it was a fit of false, constrained submission, and therefore lasts not ; it was but a tempting of God, instead of submitting to Him. " Oh, will He have a submission ? I will try it, but with this reserve, that if after such a time I gain not what I seek, I shall think it is lost, and that I .have reason to return to my discontent." Though the man .says not thus, yet this meaning is secretly under it. But wouldst thou have it right, it must be without condition, without reserve ; no time, nor any thing, prescribed : and then He will make his word good, *He will raise thee up*, and that

In due time.] Not thy fancied time, but his own wisely appointed time. Thou thinkest, Now I am sinking ; if He help not now, it will be too late. Yet he sees it otherwise : He can let thee sink still lower, and yet bring thee up again. He doth but stay till the most fit time. Thou canst not see it now, but thou shalt see it, that His chosen time is absolutely best. *God waiteth to be gracious.* (Isa. xxx. 18.) Doth He wait, and wilt not thou ? Oh, the firm belief of his wisdom, power, and goodness, what difficulty will it not surmount ? So then, be humble under His hand. Submit not only thy goods, thy health, thy life, but thy soul. Seek and wait for thy pardon as a condemned rebel, with thy rope about thy neck. Lay thyself low before him, stoop at His feet, and crave leave to look up, and speak, and say,—Lord, I am justly under the sentence of death : if I fall under it, Thou art righteous, and I do here acknowledge it ; but there is deliverance in Christ, thither I would have recourse : yet, if I be beaten back, and kept out, and faith withheld from me, and I perish, as it were, in view of salvation ; if I see the rock, and yet cannot come at it, but drown ; what have I to say ? In this, likewise, thou art righteous. Only, if it seem good unto thee to save the vilest, most wretched of sinners, and to shew great mercy in pardoning so great debts, the higher will be the glory of that mercy. However, here I am resolved to wait, till either Thou graciously receive me, or absolutely reject me. If Thou do this, I have not a word to say against it ; but because Thou art gracious, I hope, I hope, Thou wilt yet have mercy on me.—I dare say that the promise in the text belongs to such a soul, and *it shall be raised up in due time.*

And what though most, or all of our life, should pass without much sensible taste even of spiritual comforts, a poor all it is ! Let us not over-esteem this *moment,* and so think too much of our better or worse condition in it, either in temporals, or even in spirituals, so far as regards such things as are more arbitrary and accessory to the name of our spiritual life. Provided we can humbly wait for free grace, and depend on the word of promise, we are safe. If the Lord will clearly shine on us, and refresh us, this is much to be desired and prized ; but if He so think fit, what if we should be all our days held at a distance, and under a cloud of wrath ? It is but a *moment in his anger ;* (Psal. xxx. 5 ;) then follows a life-time in His favour, an endless life-time. It is *but weeping* (as it there follows) *for a night, and joy comes in the morning,* that clearer morning of Eternity, to which no evening succeeds.

Ver. 7. Casting all your care upon Him, for He careth for you.

AMONGST other spiritual secrets, this is one, and a prime one, the combination of lowliness and boldness, *humble confidence :* this is the true temper of a child of God towards his great and good Father ; nor can any have it, but they who are indeed His children, and have within them that *spirit of adoption* which he *sends into their hearts.* (Gal. iv. 6.)

And these two the Apostle here joins together : *Humble yourselves under the hand of God,* and yet, *Cast your care on Him :* upon that same Hand under which you ought to humble yourselves, must you withal cast over your care, all your care ; *for He careth for you.*

Consider, I. The Nature of this Confidence, *Casting all your care on Him;* II. The Ground or warrant of it, *For He careth for you.*

I. For the Nature of it. Every man hath some desires and purposes that are predominant with him, besides those that relate to the daily exigencies of life with which he is compassed ; and in both, according to their importance or his estimate of them, and the difficulties occurring in them, he is naturally carried to be proportionally thoughtful and careful in them. Now, the excess and distemper of this care, is one of the great diseases and miseries of man's life. Moral men, perceiving and feeling it, have been tampering at the cure, and prescribing after their fashion, but with little success. Some present abatement and allay of the paroxysm or extremity, their rules may reach ; but they never go near the bottom, the cause of the evil, and therefore cannot work a thorough sound cure of it. Something they have spoken, somewhat fitly, of the surpassing of nature's rule and size in the pursuit of superfluous, needless things ; but, for the unavoidable care of things needful, they know no redress, but refer men entirely to their own industry and diligence. They can tell how little will serve him who seeks no more than what will serve, but how to be provided with that little, or to be assured of it, and freed from troubling care, they cannot tell.

Now, truly it were a great point, to be well instructed in the former ; and it is necessary for the due practice of the rule here given, touching necessary cares, first, to cut off cares unnecessary, to retrench all extravagant, superfluous desires. For, certainly, a great part of the troublous cares of men, relate merely to such things as have no other necessity in them, than what our disordered desires create, nor truly any real good in them, but what our fancy puts upon them. Some are indeed forced to labour hard for their daily bread ; but, undoubtedly, a great deal of the sweat and toil of the greatest part of men is about unnecessaries : *ad supervacua sudatur.* Such an estate, so much by the year, such a place, so much honour, and esteem,

and rank in the world,—these are the things that make some
slaves to the humours of others, whom they court, and place
their dependence on, for these ends; and those, possibly, to
whom they are so enthralled, are themselves at as little liberty,
but captivated to the humours of some others, either above
them, or who, being below them, may give accession and fur-
therance to their ends of enrichment, advancement, or popula-
rity.   Men who are set on these things, forge necessities to
themselves, and make vain things as necessary as food and raiment, resolving that they will have them, or fall in the chase,
being wilfully and unavoidably bent on them.   *They that will
be rich,* says the Apostle, (1 Tim. vi. 9,) who are resolved on
it upon any terms, meet with terms hard enough,—*they fall
into temptation and a snare, and into many foolish and hurtful lusts, which drown men in destruction and perdition.*
Drown them : there is no recovering, but still they are plunged
deeper and deeper.   *Foolish lusts;* unreasonable childish desires; after one bargain, such another, and after one sin, another to make even, and somewhat then to keep that whole, and
so on without end.   If their hearts are set upon purchase and
land, still some house or neighbour-field, some *Naboth's vine-
yard* is in their eyes, and all the rest is nothing without that,
which discovers the madness of this humour, this dropsy-
thirst.

And this is the first thing, indeed, to be looked to, that our
desires and cares be brought to a due compass.   And what
would we have ? Think we that contentment lies in so much,
and no less ? When that is attained, it shall appear as far off
as before.   When children are at the foot of a high hill, they
think it reaches the heavens, and yet, if they were there, they
would find themselves as far off as before, or at least, not sensibly nearer.   Men think, Oh, had I this, I were well; and
when it is reached, it is but an advanced standing from which
to look higher, and spy out for some other thing.

We are indeed children in this, to think the good of our
estate lies in the greatness, and not in the fitness of it for us.

He were a fool that would have his clothes so, and think the bigger and longer they were, they would please him the better. And certainly, as in apparel, so in place and estate, and all outward things, their good lies not in their greatness, but in their fitness for us. Our Saviour tells us expressly, that *man's life consisteth not in the abundance of the things he possesseth.* (Luke xii. 13.) Think you that great and rich persons live more content? Believe it not. If they will deal freely, they can tell you the contrary; that there is nothing but a show in them, and that great estates and places have great grief and cares attending them, as shadows are proportioned to their bodies. And if they have no real crosses, luxury frames troubles to itself; like a variety of dishes corrupting the stomach, and causing variety of diseases. And instead of need, they have fantastic vain discontents that will trouble men as much as greater, be it but this hawk flies not well, or that dog runs not well, to men whose hearts are in those games.

So then, I say, this is first to be regulated: all childish, vain, needless cares are to be discharged, and, as being unfit to cast on thy God, are to be quite cast out of thy heart. Entertain no care at all but such as thou mayest put into God's hands, and make His on thy behalf; such as He will take off thy hand, and undertake for thee.

All needful, lawful care, and that only, will He receive. So then, rid thyself quite of all that thou canst not take this course with, and then, without scruple, take confidently this course with all the rest. Seek a well-regulated, sober spirit. In the things of this life, *be content with food and raiment;* not delicates, but *food;* not ornament, but *raiment,* τροφὴν ὀυ τρυφὴν, σκεπάσματα οὐ κοσμήματα; and conclude, that what thy Father carves to thee is best for thee, the fittest measure, for He knows it, and loves thee wisely. This course our Saviour would have thee take: (Matt. vi. 31 :) first, to cut off superfluous care, then, to turn over on thy God the care of what is necessary. He will look to that, thou hast Him engaged; and He can and will give thee beyond that, if He see it fit.

Only, this is required of thee, to refer the matter to His discretion entirely. Now, in thy thus well-regulated affairs and desires, there is a diligent care and study of thy duty ; this He lays on thee. There is a care of support in the work, and of the success of it ; this thou oughtest to lay on Him. And so, indeed, all the care is turned off from thee upon Him, even that of duty, which from Him lies on us. We offer our service, but for skill and strength to discharge it, that care we lay on Him, and He allows us to do so ; and then, for the event and success, with that we trust Him entirely. And this is the way to walk contentedly and cheerfully homewards, leaning and resting all the way on Him, who is both our *guide* and our *strength*, who hath us and all our good in His gracious hand. Much zeal for Him, and desire of His glory, minding our duty in relation to that, is the thing He requires, and while we are bending our whole care to that, He undertakes the care of us and our condition ; as that king said to his favourite, when persuading him to fidelity and diligence in his state trust, " Do my affairs, and I will do yours." Such a word directly hath St. Chrysostom : Σὺ μερίμνησον τὰ τοῦ Θεοῦ, καὶ αὐτὸς μεριμνήσει τὸ σόν: If thou have a concern for the things that are God's, He will also be careful of thee and thine.

The care of duty thus carried, is sweet and light, doth not cut and divide the mind ; it is united and gathered in God, and rests there, and walks in His hand all the way. He bears the weight of all our works, and *works them in us*, and for us ; and therein lies our peace, that *He ordains for us.* (Isa. xxvi. 12.) If thou wouldst shake off the yoke of obedience, thou art likewise to be shaken off thyself ; but if, in humble diligence in the ways of God, thou walk on in His strength, there is nothing tha concerns thee and thy work, but He will take the charge and care of thyself and all thine interests. Art thou troubled with fears, enemies, and snares? Untrouble thyself of that, for He is with thee. He hath promised to *lead thee in a straight and safe path*, (Psal. xxvii. 11 ;) and to rebuke all thine enemies, to *subdue thine iniquities for thee*, (Micah. vii.

19; and to *fight against those that fight against thee,* (Psal. xxxv. 1.) *No weapon formed against thee shall prosper,* (Isa. liv. 17;) *yea, when thou passest through the water, and through the fire,* He *will be with thee.* (Isa. xliii. 2.) Doth thine own weakness discourage thee? Hath he not engaged for that too? So lay over that care upon Him. Hath He not spoken of *strengthening the weak hands and feeble knees,* and said, *that the lame shall leap as an hart?* (Isa. xxxv. 3, 6.) And though there is nothing in thyself but unrighteousness and weakness, yet there is in Him for thee, *righteousness and strength,* (Isa. xlv. 24)—*righteousnesses,* to express the abundance of righteousness. When thou art ready to faint, a look to Him will revive thee; a believing look draws in of His strength to thy soul, and renews it. (Isa. xl. 29.) And know, the more tender and weak thou art, the more tender He is over thee, and the more strong will he be in thee. *He feeds his flock like a shepherd,* and the weakest he is the most careful of: *they are carried in His arms and His bosom,* (Isa. xl. 11,) and it is easy for the feeblest to go so.

And as for the issue and success of thy way, let not that trouble thee at all: that is the care He would have thee wholly disburden thyself of, and lay entirely upon Him. Do not vex thyself with thinking, how will this and that be, what if this and the other fall out. That is His part wholly, and if thou meddle with it, thou at once displeasest Him, and disquietest thyself. This sin carries the punishment of it close tied to it. If thou wilt be struggling with that which belongs not to thee, and poising at that burden that is not thine, what wonder, yea, I may say, what pity if thou fall under it? Art thou not well served? Is it not just, that if thou wilt do for thyself, and bear for thyself, what thy Lord calls for to bear for thee, thou shouldst feel the weight of it to thy cost?

But what is the way of this devolving of my burden? There is a faculty in it that all persons have not: though they would do thus with it, they cannot; it lies on them, and they are not able to cast it on God. The way is, doubtless, by praying and believing; these are the hands by which the soul can turn over to God what itself cannot bear : all cares, the whole bundle, is most dexterously transferred thus : *Be careful in nothing:* (Phil. iv. 6.) A great word! Oh, but how shall it be? Why thus, says he, *In all things make your requests known unto God*, and in a confident cheerful way, *supplication* mixed with *thanksgiving;* so shall it be the more lively and active to carry forth, and carry up thy cares, and discharge thee of them, and lay them on God. Whatsoever it is that presses thee, go tell thy Father ; put over the matter into His hand, and so thou shalt be freed from μεριμνα, that dividing, perplexing care, that the world is full of.

No more, but when thou art either to do or suffer any thing, when thou art about any purpose or business, go tell God of it, and acquaint Him with it ; yea burden Him with it, and thou hast done for matter of caring : no more care, but quiet, sweet diligence in thy duty, and dependence on Him for the carriage of thy matters. And in this prayer, Faith acts: it is a believing requesting. *Ask in faith, not doubting.* (Jam. i. 6.) So thou rollest over all on Him; that is the very proper working of faith, the carrying the soul, and all its desires, out of itself unto God, as expressed Psal. xxxvi. 5: *Roll over on God,—* make one bundle of all ; roll thy cares, and thyself with them, as one burden, all on thy God.

Now Faith, to do this, stays itself on the promise. It cannot move but on firm ground, and the promises are its ground; and for this end is this added, *He careth for thee.*

This must be established in the heart. 1. The firm belief of the Divine Providence, that all things are managed and ruled by it, and that in the highest power and wisdom; that there is no breaking of His purposes, nor resisting of His power. *The counsel of the Lord standeth for ever, and the thoughts of His heart to all generations.* (Psal. xxxiii. 11.) 2. The belief of His gracious Providence to His own people, that He orders all for their true advantage, and makes all different lines and ways concentre in their highest good; all to meet in that, how opposite soever in appearance. See Rom. viii. 28. 3. A particular confidence of His good-will towards thee, and undertaking for thee. Now, if this be the question, the promise resolves thee : trust Him, and He takes on the trust, and there is no other condition; cast on Him thy care, and He takes it on, He cares for thee. His royal word is engaged not to give thee the slip, if thou do really lay it upon Him. *Cast thy burden upon the Lord,* (Psal. lv. 22 ;)—hand it over, heave it upon Him,—*and He shall sustain thee ;* shall bear both, if thou trust Him with both, both thee and thy burden: *He shall never suffer the righteous to be moved.*

Inf. 1. The children of God have the only sweet life. The world thinks not so, rather looks on them as poor, discontented, lowering creatures; but it sees not what an uncaring, truly secure life they are called to. While others are turmoiling and wrestling, each with his projects and burdens for himself, and are at length crushed and sinking under them, (for that is the end of all that do for themselves,) the child of God goes free from the pressure of all that concerns him, it being laid over on his God. If he use his advantage, he is not racked with musings, Oh ! what will become of this and that ; but goes on in the strength of his God as he may, offers up poor, but sincere endeavours to God, and is sure of one thing, that all shall be well. He lays his affairs and Himself on God, and so hath no pressing care ; no care but the care of love, how to please, how to honour his Lord. And in this, too, he depends on Him, both for skill and strength ; and touching the success of things, he leaves that as none of his to be burdened with, casts it on God, and since he careth for it, they need not both care, His care alone is sufficient. Hence springs peace, inconceivable peace. *Be careful for nothing, but in every thing, by prayer and supplication, with thanksgiving, let your requests be made known unto God, and the peace of God, which passeth all understanding, shall keep your hearts and minds, through Jesus Christ.* (Phil. iv. 6, 7.)

Inf. 2. But truly, the godly are much wanting to themselves, by not improving this their privilege. They too often forget this their sweet way, and fret themselves to no purpose; they wrestle with their burdens themselves, and do not entirely and freely *roll them over on God*. They are surcharged with them, and He calls for them, and yet they will not give them Him. They think to spare Him, but indeed, in this, they disobey, and dishonour, and so grieve Him; and they find the grief return on themselves, and yet cannot learn to be wise.

Why deal we thus with our God and with our souls, grieving both at once? Let it never be, that for any outward thing thou perplex thyself, and ravel thy thoughts as in thickets, with the cares of this life. Oh, how unsuitable are these to a child of God, for whom a life so far more excellent is provided! Hath He prepared a kingdom for thee, and will He not bestow thy charges in the way to it? Think it not: *He knoweth you have need of these things.* (Matt. vi. 32.) Seek not vain things, nor great things; for these, it is likely, are not fit for thee; but seek what is needful and convenient in His judgment, and refer thyself to that.

Then, as for thy spiritual estate, lay over upon God the care of that too. Be not so much in thorny questionings, doubting and disputing at every step, Oh, is this accepted, and that accepted, and, So much deadness! &c.; but apply thyself more simply to thy duty. Lamely as it may be, halt on, and believe that He is gracious and pities thee, and lay the care of bringing thee through upon Him. Lie not complaining and arguing, but *up and be doing, and the Lord shall be with thee.* (1 Chron. xxii. 16.) I am persuaded that many a soul that hath some truth of grace, falls much behind in the progress, by this accustomed way of endless questionings. Men can scarcely be brought to examine and suspect their own condition, being carnally secure, and satisfied that all is well; but then, when once they awaken and set to this, they are ready to entangle themselves in it, and neglect their way, by pouring on their condition. They will not set cheerfully to any thing, because they want assurances and height of joy; and this course they

take is the way to want it still. Walking humbly and sincerely, and offering at thy duty, and waiting on the Lord, is
certainly the better way, and nearer that very purpose of thine ;
for *He meeteth him that rejoiceth and worketh righteousness,
those that remember Him in His ways.* (Isa. lxiv. 5.) One
thing the Christian should endeavour to obtain, firm belief for
the Church : all the care of that must be cast on God, that He
will beautify Zion, and perform all His word to her. And
then think, Do I trust Him for the whole Church, and the
great affairs concerning it, and shall I doubt Him for myself,
or any thing that concerns me ? Do I confide in Him for the
steering and guidance of the whole ship, and shall I be peevishly
doubting and distrusting about my pack in it ?

Again, when in addition to the present and the past, thou
callest in after evils by advance, and art still revolving the
dangers before, and thy weakness. It is good, indeed, to
entertain by these, holy fear and self-distrust ; but by that, be
driven in to trust on Him who undertakes for thee, on Him in
whom thy strength lies, and be as sure and confident in Him,
as thou art, and justly art, distrustful of thyself.

Further, learn to proscribe nothing. Study entire resignation, for that is thy great duty and thy peace ; that gives up all
into the hand of thy Lord, and can it be in a better hand ?
First, refer the carving of outward things to Him, heartily and
fully. Then, stay not there, but go higher. If we have renounced the comforts of this world for God, let us add this,
renounce even spiritual comforts for Him too. Put all in His
will : If I be in light, blessed be Thou ; and if in darkness,
even then, blessed be Thou too. As He saith of earthly
treasures, *Gold is mine, and silver is mine,*—(and this may
satisfy a Christian in those two, to desire no more of them than
his Father sees fit to give, knowing that He, having all the
mines and treasures of the world at His command, would not
pinch and hold short His children, if it were good for them to
have more ;) even thus it is in respect to the other, the true
riches : Is not the Spirit mine, may God say, and all comforts

mine? I have them to bestow, and enough of them. And ought not this to allay thy afflicting care, and to quiet thy repinings, and establish thy heart, in referring it to His disposal, as touching thy comforts and supplies? The whole golden mines of all spiritual comfort and good are His, and the Spirit itself. Then, will He not furnish what is fit for thee, if thou humbly attend on Him, and lay the care of providing for thee upon His wisdom and love? This were the sure way to honour Him with what we have, and to obtain much of what we have not; for certainly He deals best with those that do most absolutely refer all to Him.

Ver. 8. Be sober, be vigilant; because your adversary the devil, as a roaring lion, walketh about, seeking whom he may devour.
Ver. 9. Whom resist, steadfast in the faith, knowing that the same afflictions are accomplished in your brethren that are in the world.

THE children of God, if they rightly take their Father's mind, are always disburdened of perplexing carefulness, but never exempted from diligent watchfulness. Thus we find here, they are allowed, yea, enjoined, to cast all their care upon their wise and loving Father, and are secured by His care. He takes it well that they lay all over on Him, yea, He takes it not well when they forbear Him, and burden themselves. He hath provided a sweet quiet life for them, could they improve and use it; a calm and firm condition in all the storms and troubles that are about them; however things go, to find content, and *be careful for nothing.*

Now, upon this, a carnal heart would imagine straight, according to its sense and inclination,—as it desires to have it, so would it dream that it is,—that then, a man devolving his care on God, may give up all watch and ward, and needs not apply himself to any kind of duty. But this is the ignorant and perverse mistake, the reasonless reasoning of the flesh. You see these are here joined, not only as agreeable, but indeed inseparable: *Cast all your care on Him, for He careth for you,* and withal, *Be sober, be vigilant.*

And this is the Scripture logic. *It is He that worketh in you to will and to do.* (Phil. ii. 13.)—Then, would you possibly think, I need not work at all, or, if I do, it may be very easily and securely. No:—*therefore*, says the Apostle, because He worketh in you to will and to do, *work out your salvation,* yea, and do it *with fear and trembling ;* work you in humble obedience to His command, and in dependence on Him who *worketh all in you.*

Thus, here. *Cast your care on Him,* not that you may be the more free to take your own pleasure and slothful ease, but, on the contrary, that you may be the more active and apt to watch : being freed from the burden of vexing carefulness, which would press and incumber you, you are the more nimble, as one eased of a load, to walk, and work, and watch as becomes a Christian. And for this very purpose is that burden taken off from you, that you may be more able and disposed for every duty that is laid upon you.

Observe these two as connected, and thence gather, *First,* There is no right believing without diligence and watchfulness joined with it. That slothful reliance of most souls on blind thoughts of mercy will undo them : their faith is *a dead faith,* and a deadly faith; they are perishing, and will not con-sider it. Such persons do not duly cast their care on God for their souls, for indeed they have no such care. *Secondly,* There is no right diligence without believing.

There is, as in other affairs, so, even in spiritual things, an anxious perplexing care, which is a distemper and disturbance to the soul: it seems to have a heat of zeal and affection in it, but is, indeed, not the natural right heat that is healthful, and enables for action, but a diseased, feverish heat, that puts all out of frame, and unfits for duty. It seems to stir and further, but indeed it hinders, and does not hasten us, but so as to make us stumble: as if there was one behind a man, driving and thrusting him forward, and not suffering him to set and order his steps in his course, this were the ready way, instead of advancing him, to weary him, and possibly give him a fall.

Such is the distrustful care that many have in their spiritual course : they raise a hundred questions about the way of their performances, and their acceptance, and their estate, and the issue of their endeavours. Indeed, we should endeavour to do all by our rule, and to walk exactly, and examine our ways ; especially in holy things, to seek some insight and faculty in their performance, suiting their nature and end, and His greatness and purity whom we worship. This should be minded diligently, and yet calmly and composedly ; for diffident doubtings do retard and disorder all. But quiet stayedness of heart on God, dependence on Him, on His strength for performance, and His free love in Christ for acceptance, this makes the work go kindly and sweetly on, makes it pleasing to God, and refreshing to thy soul.

Inf. Certainly, thou art a vexation to thyself, and displeasest thy Lord, when thou art questioning whether thou shalt go on or not, from finding in thy service so much deadness and hardness ; thinking, therefore, that it were as good to do nothing, that thou dost but dishonour Him in all. Now, thou considerest not, that in these very thoughts thou dost more wrong and dishonour Him than in thy worst services, for thou callest in question His lenity and goodness, takest Him for a rigorous exacter, yea, representest Him to thyself as a hard master, who is the most gentle and gracious of all masters. Do not use Him so. Indeed, thou oughtest to *take heed to thy foot,* to see how thy heart is affected in His worship. Keep and watch it as thou canst, but in doing so, or in endeavouring to do, however thou find it, do not think He will use rigours with thee ; but the more thou observest thine own miscarriages towards Him, the less severely will He observe them. To think otherwise, to fret and repine that thy heart is not to His mind, nor indeed to thine own, to go on in a discontented impatience, this is certainly not the commanded watchfulness, but that forbidden carefulness.

Be sober.] This we have formerly spoken of, the Apostle having formerly exhorted to it once and again in this

Epistle. It were easy to entertain men's minds with new discourse, if our task were rather to please than to profit; for there be many things which, with little labour, might be brought forth as new and strange to ordinary hearers. But there be a few things which chiefly concern us to know and practise, and these are to be more frequently represented and pressed. This Apostle, and other inspired writers, drew from too full a spring to be ebb of matter; but they rather choose profitable iterations, than unprofitable variety; and so ought we.

This Sobriety is not only temperance in meat and drink, but in all things that concern the flesh. Even that of diet is, though not all, yet a very considerable part of it; and this not only hath implied in it, that one exceed not in the quantity or quality, but even requires a regulating of ourselves in the manner of using our repast; that as we are not to make careful and studious provision, or to take up our thoughts how to please our palate, so even in the use of sober, mean diet, we endeavour the mortifying of our flesh, not to eat and drink merely to please ourselves, or to satisfy our natural desire, but for God; even to propound this in our sitting down to it, in obedience to Him; to use these helps of life, and the life itself, to be spent in His obedience, and in endeavouring to advance His glory.

It is a most shameful idol, a dunghill-god indeed, to serve the belly, and to delight in feastings, or in our ordinary repast, laying the reins loose on our appetite to take its own career. And yet, in this, men most commonly offend, even persons that are not notably intemperate, neither gluttonous nor drunken, and yet, I say, have not that holy, retained, bridled way of using their repast, with an eye upon a higher end.

But this Sobriety, in its ample sense, binds not only that sense of lust, but all the rest in the use of their several delights, yea, and in the whole man, all the affections of the soul, in relation to this world, and the things of it: we are to be in it as weaned from it, and raised above it in the bent of our minds; *to use it as if we used it not.* (1 Cor. vii. 31.)

This we speak and hear of, but do not apply ourselves really to this rule. Each hath some trifle or earthly vanity, one or more, but especially some choice one, that he cannot be taken off from; as children readily have some toy that they set more by than the rest. We have childish hearts cleaving to vanity; one hankering after some preferment, another after some estate, lands, or houses, or money. And we are drunk in the pursuit of these, so that when our hearts should be fixed on Divine exercises, they cannot stand, but reel to and fro, or stumble down and fall asleep, roving after those thoughts of that which we affect, staggering ever and anon, or else, so plunged in them all the time, that we are as asleep in them.

Therefore, these two are here, and ordinarily, joined, *Be sober and watchful.* Glutting ourselves either with the delights, or with the desires and cares of earth, makes us sleepy: the fumes that arise from them surcharge us, and cast us into a deep sleep,—a secure unminding of God and of ourselves, the interest of our immortal souls.

The pleasures of sense are too gross for the Divine soul. Divine, I call it, for so by original it is; but we abase it, and make it flesh by those gross earthly things, and make it unfit to rise heavenwards. As insobriety, intemperance in diet, prejudices the very natural spirits, making them dull, clogs their passage, and makes them move as a coach in a miry way, thus doth all inordinate use and love of inferior things: it makes the soul of a low, heavy constitution, so that it cannot move freely in any thing that is spiritual. Yea, where there is some truth of grace, yet it is obstructed and dulled by taking in too much of the world, and feeding on it; which is no more proper for the finest part of the man, for the soul, than the coarse ploughman's diet is for delicate, tender bodies of higher breeding; yea, the disproportion is far greater.

If, then, you would have free spirits for spiritual things,

keep them at a spare diet in all things temporal. Let not out your hearts to any thing here below. Learn to delight in God, and seek to taste of his transcendent sweetness: that will perfectly disrelish all lower delights. So your sobriety in abstaining from them shall be still further recompensed with more enjoyment of God, and you shall not lose pleasure by denying yourself the pleasures of earth, but shall change them for those that are unspeakably better and purer in their stead. He shall communicate Himself unto you, the *light of whose countenance* feeds and satisfies the glorified spirits that are about His throne.

Be vigilant.] This watchfulness, joined with sobriety, extends to all the estate and ways of a Christian, being surrounded with hazards and snares. *He that despiseth his way shall die,* says Solomon. (Prov. xix. 16.) The most do thus walk at random *:* they give attendance on public worship, and have some customary way of private prayer, but do not further regard how they walk, what is their carriage all the day long, what they speak, how they are in company, and how alone, which way their hearts go early and late, what it is that steals away most of their affection from God.

Oh, my beloved, did we know our continual danger, it would shake us out of this miserable dead security that possesses us. We think not on it, but there are snares laid for us all the way, in every path we walk in, and every step of it; in our meat and drink; in our calling and labour; in our house at home; in our journeying abroad; yea, even in God's house, and in our spiritual exercises, both there and in private. Knew we, or, at least, considered we this, we should choose our steps more exactly, and look to our ways, to our words, to our thoughts, which truly, whatsoever noise we make, we really do not. *Ponder the path of thy feet,* says Solomon; and before that, *Let thine eyes look right on, and let thine eyelids look straight before thee.* And further, *Put away a froward mouth, and perverse lips put far from thee.* But, first of all, as the main reason, and spring of all, *Keep thy heart with all diligence,* or *above all keeping, for out of it are the issues of life.* (Prov. iv. 23—26.)

Because your adversary the devil.] An alarm to watchfulness is here given, from the watchfulness of our grand Adversary. There be other two usually ranked with him as the leading enemies of our souls, the World and our own flesh; but here, he is expressly named, who commands in chief, and orders and manages the war, using the service of the other two against us, as prime officers, under which most of the forces of particular temptations are ranked. Some others there be which he immediately commands and leads on himself, a regiment of his own, some spiritual temptations.

And we have need to be put in mind of the hostility and practices of Satan against us; for if the most were put to it, they would be forced to confess that they very seldom think on their spiritual danger from this hand. As we keep loose guard against the allurements of the world, and of our own corruption, so we watch not against the devices of Satan, but go on by guess, and suspect nothing, and so are easily a prey to all.ʹ

The least enemy being despised and neglected, as men observe, proves often too great. The smallest appearances of evil, the least things that may prejudice our spiritual good, while we make no reckoning of them, may do us great mischief. Our not considering them makes them become considerable, especially being under the command of a vigilant and skilful leader, who knows how to improve advantages. Therefore, in things which we many times account petty, and not worthy our notice as having any evil in them, we should learn to suspect the address of this Adversary, who usually hides himself, and couches under some covert, till he may appear irresistible, and seize on us; and then, indeed, he *roars*.

And this seeking the destruction of souls, is, you see, marked as all his work. The prey he hunts is souls, that they may be as miserable as himself. Therefore he is justly called *our adversary*, the enemy of holiness and our souls; first tempting to sin, and then accusing for sin, as his name here imports; appearing against us upon the advantages he hath gained. He studies our nature, and fits his temptations to it; knows tho prevalency of lust, or earthliness, or that great and most general evil of pride, so like himself, and that is his throne in the heart. Sometimes, *he boweth down,* as it is said of the lion, Psal. x. 9; he waits his opportunity craftily, and then assaults fiercely. And the children of God find sometimes so much violence in his temptations that they surprise them; such horrid thoughts cast in as poisoned arrows, or *fiery darts,* as the Apostle speaks, Eph. vi. 16. And this his enmity, though it is against man in general, yet is most enraged against the children of God. He goes about and spies where they are weakest, and amongst them, directs his attacks most against those who are most advanced in holiness, and nearest unto God. They were once under his power, and now being escaped from him he pursues them, as Pharaoh did the Israelites, with all his forces, raging and roaring after them, as a prey that was once in his den, and under his paw, and now is rescued.

The resemblance hath in it, his strength, his diligence, and his cruelty. His strength, *a lion;* his diligence, *going about and seeking;* his cruelty, *roaring* and *seeking to devou*r.

Inf. Is it not most reasonable hence to press watchfulness? to keep continual watch to see what comes in, and what goes out; to try what is under every offer of the world, every motion of our own natural hearts, whether there be not some treachery, some secret intelligence or not? Especially after a time of some special seasons of grace, and some special new supplies of grace received in such seasons, (as after the holy sacrament,) then will he set on most eagerly when he knows of the richest booty. The pirates that let the ships pass as they go by empty, watch them well when they return richly laden: so doth this great Pirate. Did he not assault our Saviour straight after His baptism? ὁ πειράζων. (Matt. iv. 3.)

And, that we may *watch*, it concerns us *to be sober*. The instruction is military; a drunken soldier is not fit to be on the watch. This most of us are, with our several fancies and vanities, and so exposed to this Adversary. And when we have gained some advantage in a conflict, or when the enemy seems to retire and be gone, yet, even then, are we to be watchful, yea, then especially. How many, presuming on false safeties that way, and sitting down to carouse, or lying down to sleep, have been re-assaulted and cut off! *Invadunt urbem somno vinoque sepultam.* Oh, beware when you think yourselves most safe! That very thought makes you least safe. Keep always your spirits free from surcharges, and lavish profusion upon the world ; keep from applying your hearts to any thing in it, sitting down to it. Oh! no. Be like Gideon's army, fit to follow God, and to be victorious in Him, not lying down to drink, but taking of it only, as for necessity, in passing. Take our Saviour's own word, *Take heed lest at any time your hearts be surcharged with surfeitings and drunkenness, and the cares of this life.* (Luke xxi. 34.) These will *overcharge* you, and make you drunk, and east you asleep.

Oh, mind your work and your warfare always, more than your ease and pleasure! Seek it not here ; your rest is not here. Oh, poor short rest, if it were ! But follow the Lord Jesus through conflicts and sufferings. A little while, and you shall have certain victory, and after it everlasting triumph, rest and pleasure, and a feast that shall not end, where there is no danger either of surfeiting or of wearying, but pure and perpetual delight. In this persuasion, you should be abstinent and watchful, and *endure hardship, as good soldiers of Jesus Christ,* as the Apostle speaks, 2 Tim xi. 4, *not entangling yourselves with the affairs of this life,* and thus be ready for encounters. Stand watching, and, if you be assaulted, *resist.*

Whom resist, steadfast in the faith.] To watchfulness, courage should be joined. He that watches and yields, seems rather to watch to receive, than to resist the enemy.

And this resistance should be continued even against multiplied assaults : for thou hast to deal with an enemy that will not easily give over, but will try several ways, and will redouble his onsets* ; sometimes very thick, to weary thee out, sometimes after a little forbearance interposed, to catch thee

---

* Οὐ δίδωσιν ἀνάπαυσιν, οὐδὲ νικῶν, οὐδὲ νικώμενος. Plutarch in vita Marcel.

unawares, when he is not expected. But in all, faint not, but be steadfast in thy resistance.

This is easily said, say you; but how may it be ? How shall I be able so to do ? Thus:

Steadfast in the faith.] The most of men are under the power of one of these two evils, security or distrust; and out of the one, we readily fall into the other. Therefore the Apostle frames his exhortations, and the arguments in support of it, in opposition to both these ; first, against security in the former verse, *Be sober and watch,* and presses that by the proper argument of great and continuing danger ; here, against distrust, *Whom resist, steadfast in the faith,* and he adds an encouraging consideration of the common condition of the children of God in the world. *Knowing that the same afflictions are accomplished in your brethren.*

Steadfast, or solid, *by faith.*] This is absolutely necessary for resistance. A man cannot fight upon a quagmire; there is no standing out without a standing, some firm ground to tread upon ; and this Faith alone furnishes. It lifts the soul up to the firm advanced ground of the promises, and fastens it there ; and there it is sure, even *as Mount Zion, that cannot be removed.* He says not, steadfast by your own resolutions and purposes, but, *steadfast by faith.* The power of God, by faith becomes ours ; for that is contained and engaged in the word of promise. Faith lays hold there, and there finds Almighty strength. *And this is our victory,* says the Apostle St. John, *whereby we overcome the world, even our Faith.* (1 John v. 4.) So Faith is our victory, whereby we overcome *the prince of this world. Whom resist, steadfast in the faith.* And, universally, all difficulties, and all enemies, are overcome by *faith.* Faith sets the stronger *Lion of the tribe of Judah,* against this *roaring lion* of the bottomless pit ; that delivering Lion, against this devouring lion.

When the soul is surrounded with enemies on all hands, so that there is no way of escape, Faith flies above them, and carries up the soul to take refuge in Christ, and is there safe.

That is the power of Faith; it sets a soul in Christ, and there it looks down upon all temptations, as at the bottom of the rock, breaking themselves into foam. When the floods of temptation rise and gather, so great and so many, that the soul is even ready to be swallowed up, then, by faith, it says, Lord Jesus, thou art my strength, I look to thee for deliverance; now appear for my help! And thus it overcomes. The guilt of sin is answered by His blood, the power of sin is conquered by His Spirit; and afflictions that arise are nothing to these: His love and gracious presence make them sweet and easy.

We mistake, if we think to do any thing, or to be any thing without Him; and we mistake again, if we think any thing too hard to be done or suffered with Him. *Without me you can do nothing,* says He, John xv. 5, and, *I am able to do all things,* says the Apostle, or *can all things,* πάντα ἰσχύω, (so the word is) *through Christ that strengthens me.* (Phil. iv. 13.) All things! Oh, that is a big word, yet, it is a true word; and thus made good—through Christ empowering me; that frees it both from falsehood and vanity. An humble confidence, for it is not in himself, but in Christ; and this boasting is good. *My soul shall make her boast in God,* says David. (Psal. xxxiv. 2.) Oh, they alone have warrant to boast and to triumph, even before the victory, who do it in this style! Such may give a challenge to all the world, to all adverse powers of Earth and Hell, as the Apostle doth in his own and every believer's name, Rom. viii. 35, 38, *Who shall separate us from the love of Christ?* &c. See the victory recorded in this same way, Apoc. xii. 11: *And they overcame him*—but how?—*by the blood of the Lamb, and by the word of their testimony.* That Blood, and the word of their testimony, believing that word concerning that Blood, these are the strength and victory of a Christian.

Inf. Although, then, thou seest thyself the most witless and weak, and findest thyself nothing but a prey to the powers of darkness, yet know, that by believing, the wisdom and strength of Christ are thine. Thou art, and oughtest to find thyself, all weakness; but He is all strength, Almightiness itself. Learn to apply His victory, and so it is thine. Be strong—how?— *in Him, and the power of His might.* But thou wilt say, I am often foiled, yea, I cannot find that I prevail at all against mine enemies, but they still against me. Yet rely on Him : He can turn the chase in an instant. Still cleave to Him. When the whole powers of thy soul are, as it were, scattered and routed, rally them by believing. Draw thou but in to the standard of Jesus Christ, and the day shall be thine ; for victory follows that standard, and cannot be severed from it. Yea, though thou find the smart of divers strokes, yet, think that often a wounded soldier hath won the day. Believe, and it shall be so with thee.

And remember that thy defeats, through the wisdom and love of thy God, may be ordered to advance the victory ; to put courage and holy anger into thee against thine enemies ; to humble thee, and drive thee from thine own imagined strength, to make use of his real strength. And be not hasty ; think not at the very first to conquer. Many a hard conflict must thou resolve upon, and often shalt thou be brought very low, almost to a desperate point, to thy sense past recovery ; then it is His time to step in, even in the midst of their prevailing. *Let God* but *arise, and His enemies shall be scattered.* (Psal. lxviii. 1.) Thus the Church hath found it in her greatest extremities, and thus likewise the believing soul.

Knowing that the same afflictions are accomplished in your brethren that are in the world.] There is one thing that much troubles the patience, and weakens the faith, of some Christians ; they are ready to think there is no one, yea, that there never was any one beloved of God, in such a condition as theirs. Thus sometimes they swell even their outward trials in imagination, but oftener their inward ones, which are most heavy and pressing to themselves, and the parallel of them in others least discernible by them. Therefore the Apostle St. Paul breaks this conceit, (1 Cor. x. 13,) *No temp-*

tation hath taken you, but such as is common to men. And here is the same truth, *The same afflictions are accomplished in your brethren.*

But we had rather hear of ease, and cannot, after all that is said, bring our hearts to comply with this, that temptations and troubles are the saints' portion here, and that this is the royal way to the Kingdom. Our King led in it, and all His followers go the same way ; and besides the happy end of it, is it not sweet, even for this simply, because He went in it? Yet, this is the truth, and taken altogether is a most comfortable truth : the whole brotherhood, *all our brethren,* go in it, and our Eldest Brother went first.

Ver. 10. But the God of all grace, who hath called us unto His eternal joy by Christ Jesus, after that ye have suffered a while, make you perfect, stablish, strengthen, settle you.

His divine doctrine and exhortations, the Apostle closes with prayer, as we follow this rule in public after the word preached. So St. Paul frequently did, and so Christ himself, John xvii, after that sermon in the preceding chapters. It were well if both ministers and people would follow the same way more in private, each for themselves, and each for the other. The want of this is mainly the thing that makes our preaching and hearing so barren and fruitless. The ministers of the Gospel should indeed be as the angels of God, going betwixt Him and His people ; not only bringing down useful instructions from God to them, but putting up earnest supplications to God for them. In the tenth chapter of St. Luke, the Disciples are sent forth and appointed to preach ; and in the eleventh, we have them desiring to be taught to pray ; *Lord, teach us to pray.* And without this, there can be little answer or success in the other ; little springing up of this seed, though ministers sow it plentifully in preaching, unless they secretly water it with their prayers and their tears.

And people, truly, should keep some correspondence in this duty, and that, if other obligation will not persuade, even for their own advantage; for it returns unto them with abundant interest. If much of the Spirit be poured forth on ministers, are they not the more able to unfold the spiritual mysteries of the Gospel, and to build up their people in the knowledge of them? Oh, that both of us were more abundant in this rich and sweet exercise!

But the God of all grace, who hath called us to eternal glory by Christ Jesus.] This prayer suits the Apostle St. Paul's word, in his direction to the Philippians (*ch.* iv. *v.* 6); it is *supplication with thanksgiving*, prayer with praise. In the prayer or petition, consider, 1st, the matter, and 2dly, the style.

The matter, or thing requested, is expressed in divers brief words, *Make you perfect, stablish, strengthen, settle you;* which, though they be much of the same sense, yet are not superfluously multiplied, for they carry both the great importance of the thing, and the earnest desire in asking it. And though it be a little light and unsolid, to frame a different sense to each of them, (nor are any of the ways that such interpreters have taken in it, very satisfactory to any discerning judgment,) yet, I conceive, they are not altogether without some profitable difference. The first [*Perfect*] implies more clearly than the rest, their advancement in victory over their remaining corruptions and infirmities, and their progress towards perfection. *Stablish,* hath more express reference to both the inward lightness and inconstancy that are natural to us, and the counterblasts of persecutions and temptations, outward oppositions; and it imports the curing of the one, and support against the other. *Strengthen,* has respect to the growth of their graces, especially the gaining of further measures of those graces wherein they are weakest and lowest. And *settle,* though it seems the same, and in substance is the same with the other word, *stablish,* yet it adds somewhat to it very worthy of consideration; for it signifies, to found or fix upon a sure foundation, and so, indeed, may have an aspect to Him who is the foundation and strength of believers, on whom they build by faith, even *Jesus Christ,* in whom we have all, both victory over sin, and increase of grace, and establishment of spirit, and power to persevere against all difficulties and assaults. He is that *corner foundation-stone laid in Zion, that they that build upon Him may not be ashamed;* (Isa. xxviii. 16;) that *Rock* that upholds the house founded on it, in the midst of all winds and storms. (Mat. vii. *ult.*)

Observe : 1*st,* These expressions have in them that which is primarily to be sought after by every Christian, *perseverance* and *progress* in grace. These two are here interwoven ; for there be two words importing the one, and two the other, and they are interchangeably placed. This is often urged on Christians as their duty, and accordingly ought they to apply themselves to it, and use their highest diligence in it ; not to take the beginning of Christianity for the end of it, to think it enough, if they are entered into the way of it, and to sit down upon the entry ; but to walk on, to *go from strength to strength,* and even through the greatest difficulties and discouragements, to pass forward with unmoved stability and fixedness of mind. They ought to be aiming at perfection. It is true, we shall still fall exceedingly short of it ; but the more we study it, the nearer shall we come to it ; the higher we aim, the higher shall we shoot, though we shoot not so high as we aim.

It is an excellent life, and it is the proper life of a Christian, to be daily outstripping himself, to be spiritually wiser, holier, more heavenly-minded to day than yesterday, and to-morrow (if it be added to his life) than to-day ; *Suavissima vita est indies sentire se fieri meliorem;* every day loving the world less, and Christ more, than on the former, and gaining every day some further victory over his secret corruptions ; having his passions more subdued and mortified, his desires in all temporal things more cool and indifferent, and in spiritual things more ardent ; that miserable lightness of spirit cured, and his heart rendered more solid and fixed upon God, aspiring to more near communion with Him, and labouring that particular graces may be made more lively and strong, by often exercising and stirring them up ; faith more confirmed and stayed, love more inflamed, composed meekness producing more deep humility. Oh, this were a worthy ambition indeed ! You would have your estates growing, and your credit growing; how much rather should you seek to have your graces growing, and not be content with any thing you have attained to !

Obs. 2ndly, But all our endeavours and diligence in this will be vain, unless we look for our perfecting and establishing from that *right hand,* without which we can do nothing. Thither the Apostle moves his desires for his brethren, and so teaches them the same address for themselves : *The God of all grace make you perfect.*

This prayer is grounded (as all prayer of faith must be) on the promise and covenant of God. He *is our rock, and His work is perfect.* (Deut. xxxii. 4.) He doth not begin a building, and then leave it off: none of His designs break in the middle, or fall short of their end. *He will perfect that good work which he hath begun, to the day of Jesus Christ.* (Phil. i. 6.) And how often is He called the *strength of those that trust in Him—their buckler, and His way, perfect.* (Psal. xviii. 30.)

Hence is the stability of grace, the perseverance of the saints ; it is founded upon His unchangeableness. Not that they are unchangeable, though truly sanctified, if they and their graces were left to their own management : no, it is He who not only gives that rich portion to those He adopts to be His children, but keeps it for them, and them in the possession of it. *He maintains the lot of our inheritance.* (Psal. xvi. 5.) And to build that persuasion of perseverance upon His truth and power engaged in it, is no presumption ; yea, it is high dishonour to Him, to question it.

But when nature is set to judge of Grace, it must speak according to itself, and therefore very unsuitably to that which it speaks of. Natural wits apprehend not the spiritual tenor of the Covenant of Grace, but model it to their own principles, and quite disguise it : they think of nothing but their resolves and moral purposes; or if they take up with some confused notion of grace, they imagine it put into their own hands, to keep or to lose it, and will not stoop to a continual dependence on the strength of Another, rather choosing that game of hazard, though it is certain loss and undoing, to do for themselves.

But the humble Believer is otherwise taught; he *hath not so learned Christ.* He sees himself beset with enemies without, and buckled to a treacherous heart within, that will betray him to them ; and he dares no more trust himself to himself, than to his most professed enemies. Thus it ought to be, and the more the heart is brought to this humble petitioning for that ability, and strengthening, and perfecting, from God, the more shall it find both stability, and peace from the assurance of that stability.

And certainly, the more the Christian is acquainted with himself, the more will he go out of himself for his perfecting and establishing. He finds that when he thinks to go forward, he is driven backward, and that sin gets hold of him, often-times when he thought to have smitten it. He finds that such is the miserable inconstancy of his heart in spiritual things, the vanishing of his purposes and breaking off of his thoughts, that they usually die ere they be brought forth : so that when he hath thought, I will pray more reverently, and set myself to behold God when I speak to Him, and watch more over my heart, that it fly not out and leave me,—possibly the first time he sets to it, thinking to be master of his intention, he finds himself more scattered, and disordered, and dead, than at any time before. When he hath conceived thoughts of humility and self-abasement, and thinks, Now I am down, and laid low, within myself, to rise and look big no more,—some vain fancy creeps in anon, and encourages him, and raises him up to his old estate ; so that in this plight, had he not higher strength to look at, he would sit down and give over all, as utterly hopeless of ever attaining to his journey's end.

` But when he considers whose work that is within him, even these small beginnings of desires, he is encouraged by the greatness of the work, not to despise and despair of the small appearance of it in its beginning, *not to despise the day of small things;* (Zech. iv. 10 ;) and knowing that it is *not by any power, nor by might, but by His Spirit,* that it shall be accomplished, he lays hold on that word, *Though thy beginning be small, yet thy latter end shall greatly increase.* (Job. viii. 7.)

The Believer *looks to Jesus,*—[ἀφορῶντες, Heb. xii. 2]—*looks off* from all oppositions and difficulties, *looks* above them *to Jesus, the author and finisher of our faith; author,* and therefore *finisher.* Thus, that royal dignity is interested in the maintenance and completion of what He hath wrought. Notwithstanding all thy imperfections, and the strength of sin, He can and will subdue it. Notwithstanding thy condition is so light and loose, that it were easy for any wind of temptation to blow thee away, yet he shall hold thee in His right hand, and there thou shalt be firm as the earth, that is so settled by His hand, that though it hangs on nothing, yet nothing can remove it. Though thou art weak, He is strong ; and it is *He that strengthens thee, and renews thy strength :* (Isa. xl. 28 :) when it seems to be gone and quite spent, He makes it fresh, and greater than ever before. The word here rendered *renew,* signifies *change :* they shall have for their own, His strength. A weak believer, and his strong Saviour, will be too hard for all that can rise against them. It is here fit, as in statues, *hominem cum basi metiri,* to measure the man with the basis on which he stands ; and there is no taking the right measure of a Christian but in that way.

Thou art now, indeed, exposed to great storms and tempests, but He builds thee on Himself, makes thee, by believing, to found on Him ; and so, though the winds blow and the rain fall, yet thou standest, being built on Him thy rock. And this, indeed, is our safety, the more we cleave to our Rock and fasten on Him. This is the only thing that *establishes* us, and *perfects,* and *strengthens* us; therefore, well is that word added, θεμελιωσαι, *found* you, or *settle* you, on your foundation. This is the firmness of the Church against the gates of hell; He is a strong foundation for its establishment, and a living Foundation, having influence into the Building, for perfecting it; for it is a living House, and the foundation is a root sending life into the stones, so that *they grow up*, as this Apostle speaks, *ch.* ii. *v.* 4.

It is the inactivity of faith on Jesus, that keeps us so imperfect, and wrestling still with our corruptions, without any advancement. We wrestle in our own strength too often, and so are justly, yea, necessarily, foiled; it cannot be otherwise, till we make Him our strength. This we are still forgetting, and had need to be put in mind of, and ought frequently to remind ourselves. We would be at doing for ourselves, and insensibly fall into this folly, even after much smarting for it, if we be not watchful against it. There is this wretched natural independency in us, that is so hard to beat out. All our projectings are but castles in the air, imaginary buildings without a foundation, till once laid on Christ. But never shall we find heart-peace, sweet peace, and progress in holiness, till we be driven from it, to make Him all our strength; till we be brought to do nothing, to attempt nothing, to hope or expect nothing, but in Him; and then shall we indeed find his fulness and all-sufficiency, and *be more than conquerors through Him who hath loved us.*

But the God of all grace.] By reason of our many wants and great weakness, we had need to have a very full hand and a very strong hand to go to, for our supplies and for support. And such we have indeed: our Father is the *God of all grace,* a spring that cannot be drawn dry, no, nor so much as any whit diminished.

The God of all grace: the God of imputed grace, of infused and increased grace, of furnished and assisting grace. The work of salvation is all Grace from beginning to end. Free Grace in the plot of it, laid in the counsel of God, and performed by His own hand all of it; His Son sent in the flesh, and His Spirit sent into the hearts of His chosen, to apply Christ. All grace is in Him, the living spring of it, and flows from him; all the various actings, and all the several degrees of grace. He is the God of pardoning grace, who *blotteth out the transgressions of* His own children *for His own name's sake,* (Isa. xliii. 25,) who takes up all quarrels, and makes one act of oblivion serve for all reckonings betwixt Him and them. And, as he is the God of pardoning grace, so withal, the God of sanctifying grace, who refines and purifies all those He means to make up into vessels of glory, and hath in His hand all the fit means and ways of doing this; purifies them by afflictions and outward trials, by the reproaches and hatreds of the world. The profane world little know how serviceable they are to the graces and comforts of a Christian, when they dishonour and persecute him; yea, little doth a Christian himself sometimes think how great his advantage is by those things, till he finds it, and wonders at his Father's wisdom and love. But most powerfully are the children of God sanctified by the Spirit within them, without which, indeed, no other thing could be of any advantage to them in this. That Divine fire kindled within them is daily refining and sublimating them, that Spirit of Christ conquering sin, and by the mighty flame of His love consuming the earth and dross that is in them; making their affections more spiritual and disengaged from all creature delights. And thus, as they receive the beginnings of grace freely, so all the advances and increases of it; life from their Lord still flowing and causing them to grow, abating the power of sin, strengthening a fainting faith, quickening a languishing love, teaching the soul the ways of wounding strong corruptions, and fortifying its weak graces; yea, in wonderful ways advancing the good of His children, by things not only harsh to them, as afflictions and temptations, but by that which is directly opposite in its nature, sin itself; raising them by their falls, and strengthening them by their very troubles; working them to humility and vigilance, and sending them to Christ for strength, by the experience of their weaknesses and failings.

And as He is the God of pardoning grace, and of sanctifying grace in the beginning and growth of it, so also, the God of supporting grace, of that supervenient influence without which the graces placed within us would lie dead, and fail us in the time of greatest need. This is the immediate assisting power that bears up the soul under the hardest services, and backs it in the sharpest conflicts, communicating fresh auxiliary strength, when we, with all the grace we have dwelling within us, are surcharged. Then He steps in, and opposes His strength to a prevailing and confident enemy, that it is at the point of insulting and triumph. When temptations have made a breach, and enter with full force and violence, He lets in so much present help on a sudden, as makes them give back, and beats them out. *When the enemy comes in as a flood, the Spirit of the Lord lifts up a standard against him.* (Isa. lix. 11.) And no siege can be so close as to keep out this aid, for it comes from above.

And by this, a Christian learns that his strength is in God; whereas, if his received grace were always party enough, and able to make itself good against all incursions, though we know we have received it, yet being within us, we should possibly sometimes forget the receipt of it, and look on it more as ours than as His; more as being within us, than as flowing from Him. But when all the forces we have, the standing garrison, are by far overmatched, and yet we find the assailants beaten back, then we must acknowledge Him who sends such seasonable relief, to be, as the Psalmist speaks, *a very present help in trouble.* (Psal. xlvi. 1.)

All St. Paul's constant strength of grace inherent in him, could not fence him so well, as to ward off the piercing point of that sharp temptation, whatsoever it was, which he records, 2 Cor. xii. 7. The redoubled buffetings that he felt, came so thick upon him, that he was driven to his knees by it, to cry for help to be sent down, without which he found he could not hold out; and he had an answer assuring him of help, a secret support that should maintain him: *My grace is sufficient for thee: q. d.,* though thine own be not, that is, the grace which I have already given thee, yet, *Mine* is, that is, the grace which is in Me, and which I will put forth for thy assistance.

And this is our great advantage and comfort, that we have a Protector who is Almighty, and who is always at hand, who can and will hear us whensoever we are beset and straitened. That captain had reason, who, on being required to keep Milan for the King of France, went up to the highest turret, and cried out three times, " King of France," and then refused the service, because the King heard him not, and nobody answered for him ; meaning to imply the great distance, and so the difficulty of sending aid, when need should require. But we may be confident of our supplies in the most sudden surprisals. Our King can, and will hear us when we call, and will send relief in due season. We may be in apparent hazards, but we shall not be wholly vanquished : it is but crying to Him in our greatest straits, and help appears. Possibly we see the host of enemies first, and that so great that there is no likelihood of escaping, but then, praying, we espy the fiery chariots and horsemen, and may say, *There are more with us than with them.* (2 Kings vi. 16.)

The Apostle St. Paul calls our God *the God of all consolation,* Rom. xv. 5, as here he is styled *the God of all grace.* And this is our rejoicing, that in His hand is all good, our sanctification and consolation, assistance and assurance, *grace and glory.* And this style suits most fitly with the present petition, that for our *perfecting, and stablishing, and strengthening in grace,* we have recourse to *the God of all Grace,* whose former gifts do not discourage us from seeking more, but indeed both encourage us, and engage Him for the perfecting of it. It is His will, that we have constant recourse to Him for all we want. He is so rich, and withal so liberal, that He delights in our seeking and drawing much from Him ; and it is by believing and praying, that we do draw from Him. Were these plied, we should soon grow richer. But remember, all this grace that we would receive from the God of all Grace, must be from *God in Christ.* There it flows for us, and thither we are directed. *It was the Father's good pleasure, that in Him should all fulness dwell,* (Col. i. 19,) and that *for us,* that we might know whither to go, and where to apply for it.

Now, for the further opening up of His riches, expressed in this title, *the God of all Grace,* there is added one great act of grace, which doth indeed include all the rest, for we have in it the beginning and the end of the work linked together; the first effect of grace upon us, in *effectual calling,* and the last accomplishment of it, in *eternal glory. Who hath called us to His eternal glory.*

This *calling,* I conceive, doth not simply mean the design of the Gospel in its general publication, wherein the outward call lies, that it holds forth, and sets before us, eternal glory as the result of Grace ; but refers to the real bringing of a Christian to Christ, and uniting him with Christ, and so giving him a real and firm title to glory,—such a call, as powerfully works grace in the soul, and secures glory to the soul ; gives it a right to that inheritance, and fits it for it ; and sometimes gives it even the evident and sweet assurance of it. This assurance, indeed, all the heirs of glory have not ordinarily within them, and scarcely any have at all times equally clear. Some travel on in a covert, cloudy day, and get home by it, having so much light as to know their way, and yet do not at all clearly see the bright and full sunshine of assurance ; others have it breaking forth at times, and anon under a cloud ; and some have it more constantly. But as all meet in the end, so all agree in this in the beginning, that is, in the reality of the thing; they are made unalterably sure heirs of it, in their effectual calling.

And by this the Apostle advances his petition for their support, and establishment, and advancement in the way of grace. The way of our calling to so high and happy an estate, did we apply our thoughts more to it, would work on us, and persuade us to a more suitable temper of mind, and course of life; would give us more noble and sublime thoughts, and ways above the world; and the stronger were our persuasion of it, the more strongly should we be thus persuaded by it. And as it would thus prevail with us, so might we use it to prevail with God for all needful grace.

All you who hear the Gospel, are, in the general, called to this Glory. It is told you where and how you may lay hold on it. You are told, that if you will let go your sins and embrace Jesus Christ, this glory shall be yours. It is His purchase, and the right of it lies in Him, and not elsewhere; and the way to obtain a right to Him is to receive Him for a Saviour, and at the same time for Lord and King; to become His subjects, and so to be made kings. This is our message to you, but you will not receive it. You give it a hearing, it may be, but do not indeed hearken to the motion; and this, of necessity, must proceed from unbelief. Were you indeed persuaded, that in coming unto Christ, you were immediately not only set free from a sentence of death, which is still standing over your head while you are out of Him, but withal entitled to a crown, made heirs of a kingdom, an eternal kingdom,—I say, if this were believed, were it possible to slight Him as the most do, and turn back the bargain, and bestow their money elsewhere upon trifles of no value, children's commodities, rattles, and painted toys? Such are your greatest projects, even for earthly kingdoms, in respect of Christ, and this glory provided in Him. How wonderful is it, that where this happiness is daily proclaimed, and you are not only informed of it, but entreated to receive it, not only is it offered you, but pressed and urged upon you, and you say, you believe the matter; yet, still, the false glory and other vanities of this world amuse and entangle you, so that you close not with this rich offer of *eternal glory!*

But where any do close with it, it is indeed by a Call that goes deeper than the ear, a word spoken home to within, a touch of the Spirit of God upon the heart, which hath a magnetic virtue to draw it, so that it cannot choose but follow, and yet chooses it most freely and sweetly; doth most gladly open to let in Jesus Christ and His sweet government upon His own terms, takes Him and all the reproaches and troubles that can come with Him.   And well it may, seeing, beyond a little passing trouble, abiding, eternal glory.

The state to which a Christian is called, is not a poor and sad estate, as the World judges; it is to no less than *eternal glory*.   The World think it strange to see the believer abridge himself in the delights of sin, their common pursuits and eager graspings after gains, or honours, or pleasures of sense; but they know not the infinite gain that he hath made, in that he hath exchanged this dross for down-weight of pure gold.   The World see what the Christian leaves, but they see not what he comes to, what his new purchase is, in another place; they see what he suffers, but not what he expects, and shall attain as the end of those sufferings, which shall shortly end.   But he, knowing well upon what conditions all these things run, may well say, *Non magna relinquo, Magna sequor*—How small is what I forsake, how great that which I follow after!

It is Glory, Eternal glory, *His eternal Glory*, true, real Glory.   All here that is so named, is no more than a name, a shadow of glory; it cannot endure the balance, but is found too light, as was said of a great monarch, Dan. v.; and even many principalities and provinces, put into the scale one after another, still add no weight: yea, possibly, as a late political writer wittily observes of a certain monarch, "The more kingdoms you cast in, the scale is still the lighter."   Men are naturally desirous of glory, and gape after it; but they are naturally ignorant of the true nature and place of it: they seek it where it is not, and, as Solomon says of riches, *set their hearts on that which is not*,—Prov. xxiii. 5—hath no subsistence or reality. But the glory above, is true, real glory, and bears weight, and so bears aright the name of glory, the term for which in the Hebrew [*Kebud*] signifies *weight*; and the Apostle's expression seems to allude to that sense: speaking of this same glory to come, he calls it *a far more excellent weight of glory*: 2 Cor. iv. 17.   It weighs down all labour and sufferings in the way so far, **as** that they are not once worth the speaking of in respect of it. It is the *hyperbole* καθ' ὑπερβολὴν εἰς ὑπερβολήν. Other glory is overspoken, but this Glory is overglorious to be duly spoken: it exceeds and rises above all that can be spoken of it.

Eternal.] Oh, that adds much! Men would have more reason so to affect and pursue the glory of the present world, such as it is, if it were lasting, if it stayed with them when they have caught it, and they stayed with it to enjoy it. But how soon do they part! They pass away, and the glory passes away, both as smoke. Our life itself is as a vapour. And as for all the pomp and magnificence of those that have the greatest outward glory, and make the fairest shew, it is but a shew, a *pageant* that goes through the street, and is seen no more. But this hath length of days with it—*Eternal Glory*. Oh, a thought of that swallows up all the grandeur of the world, and the noise of reckoning years and ages. Had one man continued, from the Creation to the end of the world, at the top of earthly dignity and glory, admired by all, yet, at the end, everlasting oblivion being the close, what a nothing were it to *eternal glory!* But, alas! we cannot be brought to believe, and deeply to take the impression of eternity; and this is our undoing.

By Jesus Christ.] Your portion, while out of Him, was eternal shame and misery, but *by* Him, it is even all glory. And this hath in it likewise an evidence of the greatness of this glory; it can be no small estate, which the blood of the Son of God was let out to purchase.

His glory.] It is that which He gives, and gives as His choicest of all, to His chosen, His children. And if there be any thing here that hath delight or worth, in the things which He gives in common even to His enemies; if there be such a world and such a variety of good things, for them that hate Him; Oh, how excellent must those things be which He hath reserved for His friends, for those He loves, and causes to love Him!

As it is His gift, so it is indeed Himself; the beholding and enjoying of Himself. This we cannot now conceive. But, Oh, that blessed day when the soul shall be full of God, shall be satisfied and ravished with full vision !   Should we not admire that such a condition is provided for man, wretched, sinful man ? *Lord, what is man, that Thou art mindful of him, and the son of man, that thou visitest him?* (Psal. viii. 3.)   And is it provided for me, as wretched as any who are left and fallen short of this glory, a base worm taken out of the mire, and washed in the blood of Christ, and within a while set to shine in glory without sin !   Oh, the wonder of this !   How should it excite us to praise, when we think of Such a One there, who will bring us up in the way to this crown !   How will this hope sweeten the short sufferings of this life !   And death itself, which is otherwise the bitterest in itself, is most of all sweetened by this, as being nearest it, and setting us into it. What though thou art poor, diseased, and despised here !   Oh consider what is there, how worthy the affection, worthy the earnest eye and fixed look of an heir of this glory !   What can he either desire or fear, whose heart is thus deeply fixed ? Who would refuse this other clause, *to suffer a while,* a little while, any thing outward or inward which He thinks fit ? How soon shall all this be overpast, and then overpaid in the very entry, at the beginning of this glory that shall never end !

Ver. 11. To Him be glory and dominion for ever and ever.   Amen.

THEY know little of their own wants and emptiness, who are not much in prayer ; and they know little of the greatness and goodness of God, who are not much in praises.   The humble Christian hath a heart in some measure framed to both.   He hath within him the best schoolmaster, who teaches him how to pray, and how to praise, and makes him delight in the exercise of them both.

The Apostle, having added prayer to his doctrine, adds here, you see, praise to his prayer.   *To him be glory and dominion for ever.*

The living praises of God spring from much holy affection,

and that affection springs from a Divine light in the understanding. So says the Psalmist, *Sing ye praises with understanding*, or, *you that have understanding*. (Psal. xlvii. 7.)
It is a spiritual-knowledge of God that sets the soul in tune
for His praises, and therefore the most can bear no part in this
song: they mistune it quite, through their ignorance of God,
and unacquaintance with Him. Praise is unseemly in the
mouth of fools: they spoil and mistune it.

Observe 1. The thing ascribed; 2. The term or endurance
of it. The former is expressed in two words; *glory*, and
power. *Glory*, that is, the shining forth of His dignity,
the knowledge and acknowledgment of it by His creatures;
that His excellency may be confessed and praised, His name
exalted; that service and homage may be done to Him.
Which all add nothing to Him, for how can that be? But
as it is the duty of such creatures as he hath fitted for it, to
render praise to Him, so it is their happiness. All created
things, indeed, declare and speak His glory: the heavens
sound it forth, and the earth and sea resound and echo it back.
But his reasonable creatures hath He peculiarly framed, both
to take notice of His glory in all the rest, and to return it from
and for all the rest; in a more express and lively way.

And in this lower world, it is man alone that is made capable
of observing the glory of God, and of offering Him praises.
He expresses it well, who calls man *the world's high-priest:*
all the creatures bring their oblations of praise to him, to offer
up for them and for himself, for whose use and comfort they
are made. The light and motion of the heavens, and all the
variety of creatures below them, speak this to man: He that
made us and you, and made us for you, is great, and wise, and
worthy to be praised. And you are better able to say this
than we; therefore praise Him on our behalf and on your own.
Oh! He is great and mighty, He is the Lord our Maker.

Power here expresses not only ability, but authority and
royal sovereignty; that, as He can do all things, He rules and
governs all things, is King of all the World, Lord paramount.

All hold their crowns of Him, and *the shields of the earth belong unto God ; He is greatly to be exalted.* (Psal. xlvii. 9.) He disposeth of states and kingdoms at His pleasure, establisheth or changeth, turns and overturns, as seems Him good ; and hath not only might, but right to do so. *He is the Most High, ruling in the kingdoms of the children of men, and giving them to whomsoever He will,* (Dan. iv. 32,) pouring contempt upon princes when they contemn His power.

The Term of this glory is *for ever.* Even in the short life of man, men who are raised very high in place and popular esteem may, and often do, outlive their own glory. But the glory of God lasteth as long as Himself, for He is unchangeable : His throne is *for ever,* and His wrath *for ever,* and His mercy *for ever ;* and therefore His glory *for ever.*

Reflection 1. Is it not to be lamented, that He is so little glorified and praised ? that the earth, being so full of His goodness, is so empty of His praise from them who enjoy and live upon it ?

How far are the greatest part from making this their great work, to exalt God, and ascribe power and glory to His name ! So far, that all their ways are His dishonour : they seek to advance and raise themselves, to serve their own lusts and pleasures, while they are altogether mindless of His glory. Yea, the Apostle's complaint holds good against us all ; we are *seeking our own things, and none the things of the Lord Jesus Christ:* (Phil. ii. 21.) It is true, some exceptions there are, but, as his meaning is, they are so few, that they are, as it were, drowned and smothered in the crowd of self-seekers, so that they appear not. After all the judgments of God upon us, how do luxury and excess, uncleanness, and all kinds of profaneness, still outdare the very light of the Gospel, and the rule of holiness shining in it ! Scarcely any thing is a matter of common shame and scorn, but the *power of godliness ;* turning indeed our true glory into shame, and glorying in that which is indeed our shame. Holiness is not only our truest glory, but that wherein the ever-glorious God doth especially glory.

He hath made known Himself particularly by that name, *The holy God ;* and the express style of His glorious praises uttered by *seraphims,* is, *Holy, holy, holy is the Lord of Hosts: the whole Earth is full of His glory.* (Isa. vi. 3.)

Instead of sanctifying and glorifying this holy Name, how doth the language of hell, oaths and curses, abound in our streets and houses! How is that blessed Name, which angels are blessing and praising, abused by base worms! Again, notwith- standing all the mercies multiplied upon us in this land, where are our praises, our songs of deliverance, our ascribing glory and power to our God, who hath prevented us with loving kindness and tender mercies; hath removed the strokes of His hand, and made cities and villages populous again, that were left desolate without inhabitants?

Oh, why do we not stir up our hearts, and one another, to extol the name of our God, and say, *Give unto the Lord glory and strength; give unto the Lord the glory due unto His name?* Have we not seen the pride and glory of all flesh stained and abased? Were there ever affairs and times that more discovered the folly and weakness of men, and the wisdom and power of God? Oh, that our hearts were set to magnify Him, according to that word so often repeated in Psal. cvii. *Oh! that men would praise the Lord for His goodness, for His wonderful works to the children of men!*

Reflection 2. But what wonder is it that the Lord loses the revenue of His praises at the hands of the common ungodly world, when even His own people fall so far behind it as usually they do? *The dead cannot praise Him ;* but that they whom He hath quickened by His Spirit, should yet be so surprised with dead- ness and dulness as to this exercise of exalting God, this is very strange. For help of this, take the three following directions.

Direct. I. We should seek after a fit temper, and labour to have our hearts brought to a due disposition for His praises. And in this view, [1.] See that they be spiritual. All spiritual services require that, but this service most, as being indeed the most spiritual of all. Affection to the things of this earth draws down the soul, and makes it so low set, that it cannot rise to the height of a song of praise ; and thus, if we observed ourselves, we should find, that when we let our hearts fall and entangle themselves in any inferior desires and delights, as they are unfitted generally for holy things, so especially, for the praises of our holy God. Creature-loves debase the soul, and turn it to earth, and praise is altogether heavenly.

[2.] Seek a heart purified from self-love, and possessed with the love of God. The heart which is ruled by its own interest is scarcely ever content, still subject to new disquiet. Self is a vexing thing, for all things do not readily suit our humours and wills, and the least touch that is wrong to a selfish mind distempers it, and disrelishes all the good things about it. A childish condition it is, if crossed but in a toy, to throw away all. Whence are our frequent frettings and grumblings, and why is it that we can drown a hundred high favours in one little displeasure, so that still our finger is upon that string, and there is more malcontent and repining for one little cross, than praises for all the mercies we have received ? Is not this evidently from the self-love that abounds in us ? Whereas, were the love of God predominant in us, we should love His doings and disposals, and bless His name in all. Whatsoever were His will, would, in that view, be amiable and sweet to us, however in itself harsh and unpleasant. Thus should we say in all : This is the will and the hand of my Father, who doth all things wisely and well; blessed be His name.

The soul thus framed, would praise in the deeps of troubles : not only in outward afflictions, but in the saddest inward condition, it would be still extolling God, and saying, However He deal with me, He is worthy to be loved and praised. He is great and holy, He is good and gracious; and whatsoever be His way and thoughts towards me, I wish Him glory. If He will be pleased to give me light and refreshment, blessed be He ; and if He will have me to be in darkness again, blessed be He, glory to His name ! Yea, what though He should utterly reject me, is He not for that to be accounted infinitely merciful in the saving of others? Must He cease to be praiseworthy for my sake? If He condemn, yet He is to be praised, being merciful to so many others; yea, even in so dealing with me, He is to be praised, for in that He is just.

Thus would pure love reason for Him, and render praise to Him. But our ordinary way is most untoward and unbeseeming His creatures, even the best of them, much more such worms as we are; that things must rather be to our mind than His, and we must either have all our will, or else, for our part, He shall have none of His praises.

[3.] Labour for that which on these two will follow, a *fixed heart*. If it be refined from creature-love and self-love, spirituality and love of God will fix it; and then shall it be fit to praise, which an unstable, uncomposed heart can never be, any more than an instrument can be harmonious and fit to play on, that hath loose pins, still slipping and letting down the strings, pins that never fasten. And thus are the most: they cannot fix to Divine thoughts, to consider God, to behold and admire His excellency and goodness, and His free love. Oh, that happy word of David, worthy to be twice repeated! When shall we say it? *O God, my heart is fixed:* well might he add, *I will sing and give praise.* (Psal. lvii. 7.) Oh, that we would pray much that He would fix our hearts, and then, He having fixed them, we should praise Him much.

Direct. II. If any due disposition be once attained for praises, then must the heart, so disposed, be set to study the matter of praises.

And 1. Study the infinite excellency of God in Himself; of which though we know little, yet this we know, and should consider it, that it is far beyond what all the creatures and all His works are able to testify of Him; that He transcends all we can speak, or hear, or know of Him. 2. Look on Him in His works. Can we behold the vast heavens above, or the firm earth beneath us, or all the variety of His works in both, without holy wonder excited in us, and that stirring us up to sing praises? Oh, His greatness, and might, and wisdom shining in these ! *Lord, how manifest are Thy works ! In wisdom hast Thou made them all.* (Psal. civ. 24.) But above all, that work, that marvel of His works, the sending of His Son forth of His bosom. This is the mystery which the Apostles do so much magnify in their writings, which is so much magnified in this Epistle, and which forms the chief incentive to the ascription of praise with which it closes. This praise looks particularly back to the style in the prayer. *The God of all grace, who hath called us to His eternal glory by Jesus Christ.* So many other mercies are not to be forgotten, but chiefly is He to be praised for that choicest of mercies. *To His glory, who hath called us to His glory.* Then, look through the work of saving His chosen, so redeemed by the blood of His Son. His maintaining His own work in them against all surrounding enemies and oppositions, the advancing of it in the midst of them, and even by means of those oppositions, and bringing them safe to glory; that *perfecting* and *establishment,* as in the foregoing words. It is this which so affects the Apostle in the very entry of this Epistle, that there he must break forth into praise: *Blessed be the God and Father of our Lord Jesus Christ, who, according to His abundant mercy, hath begotten us again unto a lively hope, by the resurrection of Jesus Christ from the dead,* ch. i. ver. 3. He begins there in praise, and here he ends in it, and so encloses all within that divine circle. And as we should consider these things in general, so should we also reflect on His particular dealing with us, His good providence both in spirituals and temporals. Would we search, Oh! what a surcharge of innumerable mercies should each of us find ! And were we better acquainted with the holy Scriptures, had we more our delight in them, they would acquaint us better with all these things, and give us light to see them, and warm our hearts, and excite them to His praises, who is the God of all our mercies.

Direct. III. The heart being somewhat disposed to praise, and then studying the matter of it, should be applied actually to render praise. And in order to this, we must be careful,

1. To aim at God in all, which is continued praise; to eye His glory in every thing, and chiefly to desire that, as our great end, that His name may be exalted. This is *the excellent way* indeed. Whereas most are either wholly for their self-ends, or often squinting out to them. That soul is most noble, which singly and fixedly aims at exalting God, and seeks to have this stamp on all it speaks, and does, and desires: All to the greater glory of my God. 2. To abound in the express and solemn return of praise this way, *To Him be glory*, not a customary dead saying of it over, as is usual with us, but the heart offering it up. What is so pure and high as this exercise, the praises of the ever-glorious Deity? What is heaven but these? And were it not best, as we can, to begin it here, and long to be there, where it shall never end? *To Him be glory and dominion for ever and ever.* Amen.

Ver. 12. By Silvanus, a faithful brother unto you, (as I suppose,) I have written briefly, exhorting, and testifying that this is the true grace of God wherein ye stand.

Ver. 13. The Church that is at Babylon, elected together with you, saluteth you; and so doth Marcus, my son.

Ver. 14. Greet ye one another with a kiss of charity. Peace be with you all that are in Christ Jesus. Amen.

THIS is a kind of postscript, and contains a testimony of the bearer, and the apostolic form of saluting. Withal, the Apostle expresses the measure of his writing, that it was *brief*, and the end of it, *that it was to testify the true grace of God.* And this is, indeed, the end of our preaching, and we ought each to seek it by the word, and by mutual exhortations; and sometimes a few words may avail much to this purpose, to our hearty establishment in the faith. And not only are we to believe, but to remember that we have the best of it; that there is truth in our hopes, and they shall not deceive us. They are no fancy, as the world thinks, *but the true grace of God;* yea, when all things else shall vanish, their truth shall most appear in their full accomplishment.

The entertainment and increase of Christian love, of due esteem one of another, and affection one to another, is no matter of empty compliment, but is the very stamp and badge of Jesus Christ upon His followers: it is, therefore, most carefully to be preserved entire, and unhappy are they that do by any means willingly break it. Oh, let us beware of doing so, and *follow peace*, even when it seems to fly from us!

This *peace* that is the portion of those in Christ, is indeed within them, and with God. But through Him, it is likewise *one with another*, and in that notion it is to be desired and wished jointly with the other.

They that are in Christ are the only children and heirs of true peace. Others may dream of it, and have a false peace for a time, and wicked men may wish it to themselves and one another; but it is a most vain hope, and will come to nought. But to wish it to them that are in Christ hath good ground; for all solid peace is founded on Him, and flows from Him. *Now, the peace of God, which passeth all understanding, keep your hearts and minds, through Jesus Christ.* Amen.

MEDITATIONS,

CRITICAL AND PRACTICAL,

ON

PSALMS IV., XXXII., AND CXXX.

TRANSLATED

FROM THE LATIN OF ARCHBISHOP LEIGHTON.

BY THE

Rev. Dr. PHILIP DODDRIDGE.

MEDITATIONS ON PSALM IV.

TITLE,

To the chief Musician on Neginoth, a Psalm of David.

MANY of the calamities of good men look like miseries, which yet, on the whole, appear to have conduced greatly to their happiness; witness the many prayers which they poured out in those calamities, the many seasonable and shining deliverances which succeeded them, and the many hymns of praise they sang to God their deliverer; so that they seem to have been cast into the fire on purpose that the odour of their graces might diffuse itself all abroad.

The Seventy Greek Interpreters seem to have read the word which we render *To the chief musician,* something different from the reading of our present Hebrew copy, i. e., *Lemenetz,* instead of *Lemenetzoth;* and therefore they render it, εἰς τέλος, as the Latin does, *in finem, to the end.* From whence the Greek and Latin Fathers imagined, that all the Psalms which bear this inscription refer to the *Messiah,* the great End and the accomplishment of all things; a sentiment which was rather pious than judicious, and led them often to wrest several passages in the Psalms by violent and unnatural glosses. Yet I would not morosely reject all interpretations of that kind, seeing the Apostles themselves apply to Christ many passages out of the Psalms and other books of the Old Testament, which, if we had not been assured of it by their authority, we should hardly have imagined to have had any reference to Him. Nor is it probable that they enumerated all the predictions of the Messiah which are to be found in the prophetic writings, but only a very small part of them, while they often assure us that all the sacred Writers principally centre in Him. And it is certain the passage out of this Psalm, which Austin, and some others, suppose to refer to Christ, may be applied to Him without any force upon the expression : *O ye sons of men, how long will ye turn my glory into shame**?   And what follows they explain with the same reference: *Know that the Lord has in a wonderful manner separated his Holy One unto Himself.* Others, however, render the title in a different manner, (*Victori,*) *To the conqueror.*   Moderns translate it *præcentori,* or *præfecto musicæ,* to the chief musician, or him who presided over the band of musicians, which after all seems the most natural interpretation.   The word *Neginoth,* which is sometimes rendered *stringed instruments,* did no doubt signify instruments of music which were struck to give their sound, as *Nehiloth,* in the title of Psalm v., seems, though not without some little irregularity in the etymology, to signify *instruments of wind music.*   The Psalm was written by David, as a summary of the prayer he had poured out before God, when some exceeding great affliction seemed to besiege him on every side, whether it was the persecution of Saul, or the conspiracy of Absalom his son.

Ver. 1. Hear me when I call, O God of my righteousness! Thou hast enlarged me when I was in distress, have mercy upon me and hear my prayer.

Hear me.] Behold the sanctuary to which this good man betook himself, in all the afflictions of his life; a sanctuary which therefore he sets off, by accumulating a variety of ex-

---

* They read it *gravi corde,* as expressive of the stupidity of heart which the rejecting of Christ and His gospel manifests.

pressive titles all to the same purpose: Psal. xviii. 1, *My rock, my fortress, my strength, my deliverer, my buckler,* &c. He is indeed a *place of refuge to His children ;* and therefore, as Solomon expresses it, (Prov. xiv. 26,) *In the fear of the Lord is a strong confidence.* There seems something of an enigma in that expression—confidence in fear, yet the thing itself is most true. And again, (Prov. xviii. 10,) *The name of the Lord is a strong tower ; the righteous runneth into it, and is safe.* And they who know not this Refuge are miserable ; and when any danger arises, they run hither and thither, as Antoninus beautifully expresses it, μυιᾶων ἐπ]ομένων διαδρομαῖς, " They fly and flutter they know not whither." The life of man upon earth is a warfare ; and it is much better, in the midst of enemies and dangers, to be acquainted with one fortress than with many inns. He that knows how to pray, may be pressed, but cannot be overwhelmed*.

Hear me, O Lord, hear my prayer.] He did not think it enough to have said this once, but he redoubled it. He who prays indeed, is seriously engaged in the matter ; and not only seriously, but vehemently too, and urges the address, because he himself is urged by his necessities and difficulties, and the ardent motion of his own desire and affection. And let it be observed, that these are the only prayers that mount on high, and offer a kind of grateful violence to Heaven. Nor does the Divine goodness grant any thing with greater readiness and delight, than the blessings which seem, if I may be allowed the expression, to be forced out and extorted by the most fervent prayer. So that Tertullian used to say, " That when we pray eagerly, we do as it were combine in a resolute band, and lay siege to God himself †." These are the perpetual sacrifices in the temple of God, (θυσίαι λογικαί,) rational victims ; prayers and intermingled vows, flowing from an upright and pure heart. But he who presents his petitions coldly seems to bespeak a denial : for is it to be wondered at, that we do not prevail on

---

* Premi potest, non potest opprimi.
† Precantes veluti stipato agmine Deum obsidere.

God to hear our prayers, when we hardly hear them ourselves while we offer them? How can we suppose that such devotions should penetrate heaven, or ascend up to it? How should they ascend, when they do not so much as go forth from our own bosoms, but like wretched abortives, die in the very birth? But why do I say that they do not go out from the inward recesses of our bosoms? Alas! they are only formed on the surface of our lips, and they expire there, quite different from what Homer ascribes to his wise and eloquent Ulysses, when he says,

Οπά τε μεγάλην εκ στήθεος ίει.
Forth from his breast he poured a mighty cry.

Thou God of my righteousness.] *q. d.*, O God, who art righteous Thyself, and art the patron of my righteousness, of my righteous cause, and of my righteous life. For it is necessary that both should concur, if we desire to address our prayers to God with any confidence; not that, depending upon this righteousness, we should seek the divine aid and favour as a matter of just debt: for then, as the Apostle argues, *it were no more of grace:* Rom. xi. 6. Our Prophet is certainly very far from boasting of his merits; for here he so mentions his righteousness, as at the same time to cast himself upon the Divine mercy; *Have mercy upon me,* exercise Thy propitious clemency towards me. And this is indeed the genuine temper of one who truly prays with sincerity and humility. *For polluted hands are an abomination to the Lord, and He hates the heart that is puffed up; He beholds the proud afar off,* as the celebrated parable of the Pharisee and Publican, (Luke xviii.,) is, you know, intended to teach us. *Thou art not a God that hast pleasure in wickedness. If I regard iniquity in my heart, the Lord will not hear me.* But *the righteous Lord loveth righteousness, and His countenance beholds the upright.* Whereas the words of the wicked, when he prays, are but as a fan, or as bellows, to blow up the Divine displeasure into a flame; for how can he appease God who does not at all please Him, or how can he please who is indeed himself displeased with God, and who utterly disregards his pure laws, and that holiness which is so dear to Him?

Thou hast enlarged me when I was in distress.] I have often experienced both the riches of Thy bounty, and the power of Thy hand; and I derive confidence from thence, because Thou art immutable, and canst never be wearied by rescuing thy servants from the dangers that surround them. The examples we have heard of Divine aid granted to others in their distress should animate us; as David recollected, (Psal. xxii. 4,) *Our fathers trusted in thee, they trusted in Thee, and Thou didst deliver them.* But our own personal experiences are later and nearer, and he who treasures them up in his memory, not only thereby expresses his gratitude to God, but wisely consults his own interest; for he enjoys all those benefits of the Divine favour twice, or rather as often has he needs and pleases to renew the enjoyment of them; and he not only supports his faith in new dangers, by surveying God's former interpositions, but by laying them open before God in humble, prayer he more earnestly implores, and more effectually obtains new ones. By a secret kind of magnetism, he draws one benefit by another; he calls out, and as it were, allures the Divine favour by itself.

Thou hast enlarged me.] The redeemed of the Lord may especially say so, in reference to that grand and principal deliverance by which they are snatched from the borders of Hell, from the jaws of eternal death. The remembrance of so great salvation may well excite songs of perpetual praise, to be ascribed *Deo liberatori*, to God the deliverer; and by this deliverance, so much more illustrious than any of the rest, they may be encouraged in the confidence of faith, to urge and hope for the aids of His saving arm in every other exigence.

One thing more may be observed here, but it is so very obvious that I shall only just mention it, as what needs not be much inculcated, That he who has not been accustomed to prayer when the pleasant gales of prosperity have been breathing upon him, will have little skill and confidence in applying himself to it when the storms of adversity arise; as Xenophon well observed in the person of Cyrus *.

Ver. 2. O ye sons of men, how long will ye turn my glory into shame? How long will ye love vanity, and seek after leasing? Selah.

JUSTLY may we admire the force and the speed with which Prayer flies up to Heaven, and brings down answers from thence, ἅμα ἔπος, ἅμα ἔργον, *no sooner said than done;* if not as to the accomplishment of the thing itself, which perhaps may be more opportune in some future hour, yet, at least, in clear, firm hope, and strong confidence, sent from above into a praying soul. Prayer soars above the violence and impiety of men, and with a swift wing commits itself to Heaven, with happy omen, if I may allude to what the learned tell us of the augury of the ancients, which I shall not minutely discuss. Fervent prayers stretch forth a strong, wide-extended wing, and while the birds of night hover beneath, they mount aloft, and point out, as it were, the proper seats to which we should aspire. For certainly there is nothing that cuts the air so swiftly, nothing that takes so sublime, so happy, and so auspicious a flight, as prayer, which bears the soul on its pinions, and leaves far behind all the dangers, and even the delights of this low world of ours. Behold this holy man, who just before was crying to God in the midst of distress, and with urgent importunity entreating that he might be heard, now, as if he were already possessed of all he had asked, taking upon him boldly to rebuke his enemies, how highly soever they were exalted, and how potent soever they might be even in the royal palace.

O ye sons of men.] The Hebrew phrase here used, *Bene Isch,* properly speaking, signifies noble men and great men, as persons of plebeian rank are called *Bene Adam* †: *q. d.,* Who-

* Παρὰ τῶν θιῶν πρακτικώτερος ἄν εἴη, ὥσπερ καὶ παρ' ἀνθρώπων, ὅςις μὴ, ὁπότε ἐν ἀπόροις εἴη, τότε κολακεύοι, ἀλλ' ὅτι πράττοι, τότε μάλιςα τῶν θιῶν μίμνηται.

† Accordingly, the Latin renders it, not *filii hominum,* but *filii virorum.*

ever you are, and however illustrious by birth, or inflated with pride, or perhaps formidable on both accounts, your greatness is false, and when it is most blown up, is most likely to burst. That is a sound and stable degree of honour to which God has destined His servants, whom you insult and deride. The height of your honour and vanishing glory, from the exaltation of which you look down upon me, will, if you desire I should speak the truth, only render your future fall more grievous and fatal, which he whose destruction you seek with such insatiable rage, sees indeed, but does not wish ; nay, he rather wishes that this misery may be averted from you, and that by a return to the exercise of your right mind, it may be totally prevented : and therefore he gives you this admonition, lest, while you are deriding him, unexpected destruction should come upon you, and your laughter should prove of the *Sardonic* kind, which nothing can quiet till it end in death. You have indeed great strength and deep counsel, but these things are only the blandishments of your ruin, and the splendid prelude to that misery which is hovering over you. You have spent time enough, and alas ! how much more than enough, in giving chase to such vanities; at last regard the man who, in the most disinterested manner, admonishes you of the most important truths.

How long will ye turn my glory into shame.] The *Septuagint* appear to have read these words something different from our copies, but the sense is nevertheless much the same * ; and though the Psalmist, in the affair which he had in view, speaks only of a few, the words themselves have such an expressive dignity, and are in truth so unhappily extensive, that without doing any the least violence to them, they may be considered as an admonition to all mankind. *O ye sons of men, how long will ye love vanity and lies?* For indeed, what are all those things which we foolish mortals pursue with

---

* They render it, ἕως ποτὶ βαρυκάρδιοι, " How long are ye slow of heart." And the Latins, *Usque quo gravi corde.* Instead of *Kebudi lekelesseh*, they read *Kebudi leklessi.*

such contention and ardour of spirit, but, as an ancient expresses it, " trifles that are but like the shadow of smoke * ?"
But we are to speak of this hereafter. In the mean time, let
us attend to the words before us, *How long will ye turn my
glory into shame?* The things which are the brightest ornaments of human nature, and which alone constitute its very
glory, are holiness, piety, and faith ; and these are treated as
if they were the most despicable and ignominious things in
the whole world. Among Christians, or those who are called
by that name, it is the greatest of all scandals to be a Christian indeed. We have long since lost the true names of
things: candid simplicity of manners is despised as rusticity ;
lively religion is called the delirious dream of superstitious
notions ; and gentleness, dulness and stupidity : while pride
has usurped the name of magnanimity ; and craft, that of wisdom. Thus we turn true glory into shame, and shame into
glory. And because few are able to discern what tends to
their eternal happiness, they squander away the whole day of
this short life in pursuing and catching at the false and ficti-
tious forms of it ; yea, they seek a lie, *lying vanity.* And
they who heap up riches seem to be wise both to themselves
and others ; but oh, how far from it, and with how base a lie
do they impose upon themselves ! For these riches are spent
upon gratifying their palate, and ministering in other respects
to their luxury. Into how foul a gulf do they throw what
they have laboured so eagerly to gain ! Or if they hoard up
their wealth, how soon do they pass over the property to their
heirs ! Men hunt after fame and vain-glory, and, when they
seem to have caught it, feed upon air, and become the slaves
of all, even the meanest, for a thing of nought. And as for
pleasure, who is so senseless as not to know how deceitful a lie
it proves at last ? It drives men into a weak frenzy, to run
after the most trifling objects of pursuit, which fly from them
like bees, who, if they are taken, yield but a drop of honey,
and repay the spoil of it with a painful sting ; a sting which

* Ψλίδονες ἅπαντα καί καπνοῦ σκιαί.

alas reaches the very heart.   Religion is a high, sublime thing,
royal, unconquerable, unwearied ; but pleasure is low, servile,
weak, and withering.   Religion is neither attended by sickly
disgust in the enjoyment, nor by bitter repentance in the reflection ; but what the world calls pleasure, is attended by
both.   Hear, my young friends, hear the Divine voice of celestial wisdom calling you with fervent affection and a loud
cry, from the trackless ways of error and precipices of misery.
How long, does she say, *how long will ye love vanity, and
seek after leasing ?* He that seeks me, shall not be wearied in
running hither and thither, but shall find me sitting at his door
and waiting admittance : and he who finds me, needs seek
nothing else, unless he be one whom a life of real happiness
cannot satisfy.   Oh, that the indefatigable labour and industry
with which men pursue flattering and uncertain enjoyments,
may stir up your minds to exert at least an equal diligence in
this sublime and most blessed pursuit !   For if, as St. Chrysostom speaks, it may seem indecent for me to press you further
to such an attachment to these objects as they require, it will
be a lovely thing to give it without further solicitation.   But
to proceed,

How long will you love vanity, and seek after leasing.]
Can any one deny that this is the character of almost every
thing that is to be found in human life ?   Should a man proclaim this in every company with a loud voice, he would soon
pass for a lunatic ; but certainly, he might reproach them with
the general madness which reigns among mankind, not only
among the vulgar that he meets with in the streets, but the
philosophers disputing in the school, the counsellors pleading
in our courts of judicature, yea, the senators and nobles that
sit in the most august assembly.   And Oh, how happy are
they, of whatever order, when the hand of God draws out of
the crowd, and turns their minds from these various lying and
transitory vanities, to the pursuit of true and lasting good !
Happy they whom He, by a wonderful interposition of grace

in their favour, *sets apart as dear to Himself.* Which leads
to the 3d verse.

Ver. 3. But know, that the Lord hath set apart him that is godly for
    Himself: the Lord will hear me when I call unto Him.

THE Prophet hath this great support both of his faith and of
his kingdom, the immutable and unshaken decree of the supreme and universal King, and it is the firm establishment of
David's infinitely greater Son in His throne and kingdom, I
will declare the decree. (Psal. ii. 7.)   In this verse, and there,
we may most properly understand it of both ; more immediately
of David as the type, but chiefly, and in its consummate sense,
as referring to Christ, the Lord, and having its full end and
accomplishment in His endless and eternal kingdom.   He is,
by way of eminence, *God's holy one, holy, and harmless,
undefiled, separate from sinners.*   And those, whoever they
are, who endeavour to oppose themselves to the Divine purposes, betray the most desperate madness, and on whatever
strength or counsel they depend in the enterprise, like waves
dashed against the solid rock, they shall be broken in pieces,
by what they vainly attempt to break.   And on this basis ,
does the whole safety of the whole Church rest, and that of all
God's saints, of all those *whom He sets apart for Himself,*
and (as the form of the original here has been thought to
imply) wonderfully separates, as His peculiar people and
treasure, the sacred charge of Christ the great shepherd and
bishop of souls, which all the powers of earth and the gates of
hell shall in vain attempt to wrest from Him.   And this is the
confidence on which Believers should repose themselves.   They
never trust to themselves or their own strength or virtues, but
they often redouble that cry, *Thou, Lord, art my rock, and
my fortress, and my deliverer.* (Psal. xviii. 2.)   And Psal.
xxxiv. 8, *Blessed, O Lord, is the man who trusteth in Thee,*
who must previously and necessarily despair first of himself, as

considered in himself alone, as the great Apostle says, *When I am weak, then am I strongest of all,* 2 Cor. xii. 10 ; according to that lively and just expression, " Faith, which is endangered in security, is secure in danger *."

The Psalmist adds, *The Lord will hear me when I call.* From the Divine decree and favour, he promises not to himself an entire freedom from all and every attempt of his enemies, but assures himself that God will be present in the midst of his calamities, present and propitious ; not to the indolent and drowsy soul, but to that which solicits His assistance by prayer. And this is the determination of every godly man, whom the Lord *has set apart for Himself,* that he will call upon God without ceasing, and that, if any unusual difficulty arise, he will call upon Him more fervently. Hence it appears how entirely all our safety depends upon prayer. Yet, all our prayers, and those of the whole church, are sustained by those prayers of our great King and Priest: as Augustine says in reference to that known story in the Evangelists, *Because the waves rise, the ship may be tossed, but because Christ prays, it cannot be sunk* †.

Ver. 4. Stand in awe and sin not: commune with your own heart on your bed, and be still. *Selah.*

Oh most friendly counsel which is here offered to enemies ! This is indeed overcoming hatred and injury with the very best of favours ; by far the most noble kind of victory. A sublime and heavenly mind, like the upper region of the world, is not only itself always calm and serene, as being inaccessible to every breath of injury and turbulent impression, but it also continually sheds down its benign influences without distinction on all below it, *on the evil and the good, the just and the unjust. Stand in awe :*—the Hebrew and Greek have it, *Be ye*

---

* Fides quæ in securitate periclitatur, in periculis secura est.

† Quia insurgunt fluctus, potest turbari navicula, sed quia Christus orat, non potest mergi.

moved; and as this emotion may arise either from anger, fear, or any other affection of the mind, the *Septuagint* renders it, *Be angry and sin not,* a maxim which St. Paul finding to his purpose, inserts in his epistle to the Ephesians, ch. iv. v. 26. Nevertheless, the Author of this psalm here seems apparently to demand their fear rather than their anger; and accordingly the *Targum* explains it, *Fear Him,* i. e., *God, and sin not:* Kimchi—*fear the Lord who has chosen me king,* and, Aben-Ezra—*fear God and despise not my glory, for that great King will require the derision at the hand of the deriders.*

The passions are the inmost wheels of this machine which we call man, whose motions all the rest of the life follows, and all the errors of this career of ours proceed from their irregularity. Of so great importance is it, that every one rightly determine what he should desire, and hope, and fear. And from the time that man lost the ingenuousness of his disposition, and became like a wild ass-colt, the use of fear is become very great. It is true that they who are born again, and who really are the sons of God, are especially led by the sweet and noble energy of this Divine principle, and therefore it is the saying of the beloved Apostle, that *perfect love,* or charity, *casteth out fear.* 1 John iv. 18. But as the generality of mankind are either entirely destitute of this Divine love, or possess it only in a very low and imperfect degree, so it is certain, that with regard to him whose heart is most entirely fired with this celestial flame, we may understand the words as signifying, that in such a one this great and fervent love does indeed cast out all despairings and diffident fears, but not that of a pious and reverential awe. Alas! most of us, under the pretence of avoiding a servile terror, perversely shake off the bonds of holy and ingenuous fear, and become obstinate and self-willed; whereas, when we look into the word of God, we shall find the holiest men there tremble in the Divine presence, and sometimes acknowledge even great horror of mind. *My flesh trembleth for fear of Thee, and I am afraid of Thy judgments.* Psal. cxix. 120. *Destruction from God was a terror to me, and because of His excellency I could not endure.* Job xxxi. 23. In this sense, as David declares, *The fear of the Lord is clean, and endureth for ever,* Psal. xix. 9, endures in the most happy agreement with perfect love. Nor is it to remain only in spirits that inhabit flesh, but in all the angelic choirs, pure and happy as they are. Nay, the profound reverence of that eternal and tremendous Majesty flourishes and reigns most of all there ; for in proportion to the degree in which the knowledge is clearer, and vision more distinct, are the veneration and the fear more deep and humble. How reasonable then must it be, that mortal men, beset with sore temptations and dangers, should, as Hezekiah expresseth it, *walk softly, and tremble* before that infinite Majesty, at *whose voice the earth is shaken,* and at whose *rebuke the pillars of heaven are moved.* With great propriety did one of the ancients say, " Fear is the first swaddling band of new-born wisdom*," or, as the Scripture expresses it, *The fear of the Lord is the beginning of wisdom.* It is observed that the original word there made use of, signifies both the *beginning* and the *top ;* and in both senses it is most true. The Author just mentioned admirably says, " Do they call such a one unlearned ? It is the only wisdom I know, to fear God ; it is the beginning of wisdom and the end of all discourse, as Solomon describes it : it is indeed the τὸ πᾶν, the whole matter, *the whole concern of man,* and it is *all in all—Fear God†.*" And elsewhere he adds, " This fear is most salutary to men, but at the same time most rare, superlatively so ‡." And once more, " It is (says he) the greatest of all good things, to fear God ; and the ungodly, in falling from it, shall not be permitted long to continue in the abuse of his own folly §." Well, therefore it is here added, *Sin not.* This fear, is the water of

---

* 'Ο φόβος πρῶτον τῆς σοφίας σπάργανον. GREG. NAZ.

† 'Απαίδευτον ὀνομάσουσι; μίαν σοφίαν οἶδα, τὸ φοβεῖσθαι Θεόν· ἀρχή τε γὰρ σοφίας, φόβος Κυρίου· καὶ τέλος λόγου, τὸ πᾶν ἄκους, ἔφη Σολομων, τὸν Θεὸν φοβοῦ. GREG. NAZ. OR. 28.

‡ Φόβος δὲ Θεοῦ, ἀνθρώπων σωτήριος, σπάνιος δὲ, σπανιώτατος.

§ ῎Αγαθόν γε μὴν μέγιστον εὐλαβεῖσθαι Θεόν, οὔπερ ἀσεβὴς ἐκπισὼν οὐ πολὺν χρόνον τᾶ ἑαυτοῦ μωρίᾳ καταχρήσεται.

the sanctuary, to quench all the flames of concupiscence. This, says Bernard, *is the arrow that strikes through all the desires of the flesh.* Hence arose Abraham's fear and apprehension among strangers : *Surely,* says he, *the fear of God is not in this pla*ce. Gen. xx. 11.

But in order to produce this fear, it is necessary that we should have right conceptions of God ; that nothing impure can please Him, because He is holiness itself; that nothing secret can be concealed from Him, because He is light ; nor can any sinner surely be mad enough to hope he shall escape the long hand of this righteous Judge and supreme King, whose power is immense, and who cannot be a *respecter of persons.* What evil then can escape with impunity ? *Thou, O Lord, Thou only art to be feared, and who can stand before Thee when once Thou art angry ?* Psal. lxxvi. 7.

Commune with your own heart.] Or, as some render it, *examine yourselves.* Oh, how few do this ! Men live abroad, and are indeed strangers at home : the great mark of human madness, to delight in speaking and hearing of what concerns others, " while no individual will attempt to descend into him-self *." Yet this faculty which we call reflection, is the peculiar privilege of human nature, and to be borne on wholly by external objects, is indeed brutal. And Oh, what heaps of disorder, what odious filthiness must there necessarily be in a breast which is never looked into and cleansed out! Dear youths, if amidst all your other studies, you do not learn to converse and commune with your own selves, whatever you know, or rather, whatever you imagine you know, I would not purchase it at the expense of a straw.

On your bed.] Or, as some would render it, *in your secret chambers,* when free from the noise of the world, and hurries of their daily business. An ancient said, " The reflections of the night are deepest †." And it has been observed, that David, in the nineteenth Psalm, ascribes speech to the day, and wisdom

---

* Ut nemo in sese tentat descendere, nemo !

† Βαθυτέραι γὰρ νυκτὸς φρένες.

to the silent night.   It is an excellent advice of Pythagoras, and the verses that contain it, do indeed deserve to be called *golden*, " That we should not allow ourselves to go to sleep, till we have seriously revolved the actions of the day, and asked ourselves, What have I done amiss ?   What good have I done, or neglected to do? that so we may reprove ourselves for what has been wrong, and take the comfort of what has been as it ought *."

And be still.]   This refers not so much to the tongue, as to the mind : for what does an external silence signify, if the inward affections be turbulent?   A sedate and composed mind is necessary in order to know ourselves and to know God ; as it is hinted in Psalm xlvi : *Be still, and know that I am God.* Such wisdom both deserves and demands a vacant soul : it will not, as it were, thrust itself into a corner, nor inhabit a polluted or unquiet breast.   God was *not in the whirlwind, nor in the fire, but in the still small voice.* (1 Kings xix. 12)   The

---

* The original, with Mr. Rowe's translation and paraphrase, is as follows :—

Μὴ δ' ὕπνον μαλακοῖσιν ἐπ' ὄμμασι προσδέξασθαι,
Πρὶν τῶν ἡμερινῶν ἔργων τρὶς ἕκαστον ἐπελθεῖν.
Πῆ παρέβην , τί δ' ἔρεξα , τί μοι δέον οὐκ ἐτελέσθη ;
Αρξάμενος δ' ἀπὸ πρωτοῦ ἐπίξιθί καὶ μετέπειτα,
Δεινὰ μὲν ἐκπρήξας, ἐπιπλήσσεό χρηστὰ δὲ, τέρπου.

Let not the stealing God of sleep surprise,
Nor creep in slumbers on thy weary eyes,
Ere every action of the former day
Strictly thou dost and righteously survey.
With reverence at thy own tribunal stand,
And answer justly to thy own demand,
Where have I been ?   In what have I transgressed ?
What good or ill has this day's life expressed ?
Where have I fail'd in what I ought to do ?
In what to God, to man, or to myself I owe ?
Inquire severe, whate'er from first to last,
From morning's dawn till ev'ning's gloom has past.
If evil were thy deeds, repenting mourn,
And let thy soul with strong remorse be torn.
If good, the good with peace of mind repay,
And to thy secret self with pleasure say,
Rejoice, my heart, for all went well to-day.

Holy Spirit is peaceful and pacific, but wicked men are turhulent and stormy, driven *like the sea,* whose waves are tossed about, and *throw up continually mire and dirt.* Impurity is the inseparable attendant of this inquietude: *but the wisdom that is from above, is first pure, then peaceable,* ἀγνὴ ἔπειτα εἰρηνικὴ *pacific,* (James iii. 17;) and in that blessed country to which it teaches us to aspire, there is the most perfect and everlasting cohabitation of purity and peace.

Ver. 5.   Offer the sacrifices of righteousness, and put your trust in the Lord.

THE mind of man is earthly, I say, οἷοι νῦν βροτοὶ εἶσι : *as mortals now are,* entangled in the folds of flesh and sense, it knows not how to rise to things celestial and divine; and when it is stimulated with some sense of the eternal Deity, and the worship due to Him, it generally slides into some lighter offices and external rites, how carelessly soever performed, and there it rests. *But God is a spirit,* and requires to be *worshipped in spirit and in truth.* And the solemn visible sacrifices, when instituted by the command of Him the great Invisible, are to be presented by every pious person with all humble and obedient regard; yet the chief labour is to be employed on the pure, sublime worship and obedience of the mind. The heathen philosophers objected to the primitive Christians, that they did not sacrifice; to which some of the early Apologists reply thus: " The Former and Parent of the whole universe has no need of incense and blood. The greatest sacrifice we can present to Him, is to know who has *stretched out the heavens,* who has *laid the foundations of the earth,* who has *gathered together the waters into the hollow of the sea,* and divided the light from the darkness, who has formed the whole animal world and the human species, and who governs them all by His nod; and, acknowledging Him, such an immense and omnipotent being, to *lift up pure and holy hands to Him* *." And the truth of

* Athenagoras.

this sentiment has generally prevailed throughout all ages :
even in the Jewish Church, while the obligation to sacrifice
did yet continue, with all the laborious institution of external
worship, holiness, and righteousness, and integrity of heart and
life, were acknowledged to be the most essential parts of religion, though, alas ! while all confessed it in words, there were
very few that set themselves seriously to perform it. Hence
arose the necessity of inculcating this lesson so frequently,
Psalm l., Isa. i., xxix., &c. And what is there taught at large,
is here hinted in this short clause. Since the Temple has been
demolished, and the priests with their sacrifices have ceased,
the Jews themselves have instituted, in the place of this, the
offering of the lip, with the commemoration only of ancient
sacrifice, persuaded that this would be equally effectual, and
have appointed three daily lessons, calling him who diligently
recites them, a son of eternal life.

Offer the sacrifices of righteousness.] It is no improbable
conjecture of some commentators, that David here refers to the
confidence and boast of some of Saul's courtiers in those sacrifices and that solemn worship from which their envy had perhaps banished him. It is certainly much easier to sacrifice a
ram or a bullock, than to slay anger or ambition ; easier,
indeed, to heap up whole hecatombs of animals, than to resign
one brutal affection or concupiscence ; yea, easier to present all
our goods, than ourselves as *living sacrifices,* though that is
undoubtedly our *reasonable service.* The Mosaic sacrifices,
though instituted by God, borrowed all their value from that
Evening Victim which was to be slain in the end of the world,
who was Himself the Sacrifice and the Altar, and the one only
High Priest, after the order of Melchizedec ; who yet instituted a perpetual succession of those who should *be a royal
priesthood,* the whole series of which priests, in their succeeding
generations, are daily offering to God, *the Father of spirits,* the
pure and spiritual sacrifice of righteousness, most acceptable to
Him, as passing through the hand of that great High Priest,
who incessantly ministers in that high and holy sanctuary. As

Bernard excellently speaks*, " Nothing, Lord, that is Thine can suffice me without Thyself, nor can any thing that is mine without myself be pleasing to Thee." And Augus‐ tine †, " Let Thy fire entirely consume me, so that nothing of me may remain to myself." And this one holocaust compre‐ hends all the sacrifices of righteousness; the understanding, the love, all the affections and faculties of the soul, and organs of our bodies ; all our words, actions, and thoughts, prayers and vows, hymns and thanksgivings, piety, modesty, charity, and the whole choir of virtues, exercised in a diligent and harmo‐ nious observance of all his precepts. These are victims and perfumes of incense worthy so pure a Deity, *who eats not the flesh of bulls, nor drinks the blood of goats ; who, if He were hungry, would not ask us, since all the beasts of the forest are His, and the cattle upon a thousand hills. Offer unto God thanksgivings, and pay thy vows unto the Most High. For he that offereth praise glorifies Him, and to him that orders his conversation aright, will He shew the salvation of God.*

Even the heathen philosophers and poets saw and taught, that these sacrifices of a pious mind were most fit for a rational worshipper, and must be most fit for God, to whom they are addressed. " Strange indeed would it be," says Socrates, " if the Gods should look to the gift and sacrifice, and not the soul." And passages of Horace ‡ and Persius § to this purpose are so well known that they need not be repeated. The lan‐ guage of the son of Sirach is also agreeable to it. Ecclus. xxxv. 1—3. *He that keepeth the law, bringeth offerings enough ; he that taketh heed to the commandment, offereth a peace*

* Nec mihi tua sufficiunt sine te, nec tibi placent mea sine me.
† Totum me consumat ignis tuus, nihil mei remaneat mihi.
‡ Immunis aram si tetigit manus :
    Non sumptuosa blandior hostia,
    Mollibit aversos Penates
    Farre pio, et saliente micâ.
§ Compositum jus fasque animi, sanctosque recessus
    Mentis, et incoctum generoso pectus honesto,
    Hæc cedo ut admoveam templis, et farre litabo.

offering. He that requiteth a good turn, offereth fine flour ; and he that gives alms, sacrificeth praise. To depart from wickedness is a thing pleasing to the Lord, and to forsake unrighteousness is a propitiation.

And put your trust in the Lord.] This very trust with which the mind reposes itself upon God, is both the great consolation of a good man, and the great sacrifice of piety and righteousness. The faith of Abraham was a sacrifice much dearer to God, not only than the ram which he actually offered, but even than his dearest Son whom he had brought to the altar. *He was strong in faith,* says the Apostle, *and so he gave glory to God.* And again, only they who offer the sacrifice of righteousness can rely upon Him with a true and solid confidence. Not that these sacrifices, though the choicest and best of all, can pretend to any merit, but because they are the most genuine signs and most certain seals of a soul in covenant with God. So that there is indeed a mutual signing ; God offering the dearest pledges of His favour to us, and we, in like manner, as is most fit, rendering all that we have, and all that we are, to Him, with the most humble and grateful heart. And certainly this union and perpetual undivided friendship, is the true ευθυμια of the holy soul ; that temperature which alone can give it solid tranquillity and felicity, as it follows presently after in this Psalm.

Ver. 6. There be many that say, Who will shew us any good ? Lord, lift Thou up the light of Thy countenance upon us.

THE Psalmist now returns to himself and his own affairs, and having sufficiently admonished his enemies concerning the true and only good, enforces his exhortation by his example, that if they thought fit, they might follow it ; (for this is the most efficacious manner of teaching ;) but if they would not, that he might at least enjoy the benefit of his own counsel, and wrapping himself up in his own happiness, might, from that eminence, look down upon all the vain and wretched pursuits of the mad

vulgar.   Like drunken men, they reel and stagger from place
to place ; they often fall down upon their face, and strike and
dash themselves against what they desired to embrace. Through
all their life, with an unstable pace, they catch at flying forms
of good ; and after all their falls and their bruises, they cry out
again and again, *Who will shew us any good?*   And when
they behold any new species or shadow of it, they immediately
run to it.   Nay, perhaps, so light and various are they in their
pursuit, they return again to that in which they had been frequently deceived, and which they had as often abandoned.
Rabbi Solomon paraphrases the words thus; " When Israel
saw the nations prosperous, he said, Who will shew us a like
prosperity ?   But David says, Envy them not ; we have a
sublimer prosperity in the light of thy Divine countenance."
" That is good," says the great philosopher of the schools,
" which all pursue." The various affections and desires of the
mind, are as the pulse and natural respiration ; but certain
internal principles, which, not inwrought by nature, are afterwards received and deeply engraved upon the heart, are the
springs of that motion : our different opinions of different
things do nevertheless all meet in this, *That we would see good.*
But they who select from the various objects that present
themselves, a suitable, complete, and substantial good, and
who, neglecting every thing else, bend all their pursuits to that,
are the only wise and happy men.

This the Psalmist professes he did, and freely invites all
that pleased, to join and take a part with him in these desires
and pursuits, well knowing that the happiness was abundantly
sufficient for many, for all that would apply themselves to it,
and such as could not at all be diminished by being imparted ;
for it was indeed the αὔταρκες καλόν, the Self-sufficient and
All-sufficient Good, which was one of the titles that some of
the wiser Heathens gave their *Jupiter*.   But He of whom we
speak is *The living and the True God ;* nor is there any other
good whatsoever adequate to the human mind.   And what we
say of His infinite sufficiency, is most aptly signified by this

adumbration which the Psalmist uses,—I say, *by the adumbration of light*, nor do I think fit to correct it as an incongruous expression, for *light* is indeed as it were the *shadow of God*, and that fulness of supreme good which is in Him, is in some degree shadowed out by light, which entirely illustrates, with the full stream of its rays, all who behold it, and is not broken into little fragments, to be sparingly distributed to each. Many seek *many things;* they pursue any good with uncertain and ignorant desires; but we have fixed upon the one petition we should insist upon, for in this one is all, *Lord, lift up the light of Thy countenance upon us.* Oh, rich, grand, and incomparable desire ! Without this, all the proudest palaces of monarchs are gloomy caverns, dark as hell, and all the riches of all the earth mere indigence. This is the proper light of the intellectual world, and it *puts gladness into the heart,* as it follows.

Ver. 7. Thou hast put gladness into my heart more than in the time that their corn and their wine increased.

Gladness into my heart.] To which the gross delights of earthly things cannot reach : they stick as it were before the threshold. *Corn and wine* are only the refreshment of these mean, frail, earthly bodies, and the support of this corporeal and terrene life, but have nothing συγγενές, congenial with and a-kin to the heaven-born spirit. It is said indeed that *bread strengtheneth man's heart,* and *wine makes it glad;* but the heart there spoken of, is that which is the spring of animal life and natural spirit : whereas, to that heart which holds the preference in human nature, which may therefore be called the ἡγεμονική, *the governing part,* there is nothing which gives light, and gladness, beneath the eternal *Father of lights and of spirits.* He cherishes the languishing soul with the rays of His love, and satisfies it with the consolations of His Spirit, as with a kind of heavenly *nectar* or *nepenthe,* that, while it confides in His safety, lays all its cares and fears asleep, and lulls it into deep peace, and calm, sweet repose : without which, if the mind be a little agitated, no gentle breeze of harmony, no melody of birds or harp, can bring on the pleasing slumber, during which, nevertheless, the heart awakes. Oh, happy man, who betakes his whole soul to God, and does not only choose Him above all, but in the place of all, waiting only on Him! Happy man, who, having been chosen by Him with preventing love, and unmerited benignity, embraces his ample, all-sufficient Creator for his inheritance and his wealth, often repeating with sacred transport, Deus meus et omnia! My God and my all! This is the man that has enough; and therefore, to allude to the words of the poet, " He is not disquieted by the raging of the sea, nor any severity of the seasons, whatever stars may rise and set *."

God fixes His gracious dwelling in the pure and holy soul which has learned to despise the vanity of riches, and makes it calm in the midst of hurries, and secure in the deepest solicitudes. And not merely to find, but even to seek after God, is better to such a soul, inexpressibly better, than to possess the richest treasure, the most extensive empire, or to have all the variety of sensual pleasures waiting upon its beck.

I remember to have read of some military officers, who crossing the Nile, in the same boat with the two *Macarii* of Egypt, said to them, in allusion to their name, " You are indeed happy, who laugh at the world." Yes, said they, it is evident that we are happy, not merely in name but in reality, but you are unhappy whom the world derides, as poor creatures whom it sees entangled in its snares.

St. Augustine also quotes, from Politian, a similar example of a Pretorian soldier, who walking out with his comrade, found in a cottage into which he accidentally came, a book containing the life of the hermit Anthony, and when he had read a little of it, looking upon his friend, said, " At what are we

———— Neque
Tumultuosum sollicitat mare,
Nec sævus Arcturi cadentis
Impetus, aut orientis hœdi.—Hor. lib. 2. Od. 1.

taking so much pains to arrive? What do we seek? For what do we go through the fatigues of a military life? The highest of our hopes at court, must be, to share some extraordinary degree of the Emperor's favour. And how frail and dangerous a situation is that! And through how many other previous dangers must we pass to it! And how soon will all the advantages we can hope from it be over! But I may this moment, if I please, become the friend and favourite of God." And he had no sooner uttered these words, than they both resolved upon quitting the world, that they might give up all the remainder of their days to religion.

Holy men, in former ages, did wonders in conquering the world and themselves; but we, unhappy, degenerate, and drowsy creatures as we are, blush to hear that they did what we cannot or will not do. We are indeed inclined to disbelieve the facts, and rather choose to deny their virtues, than to confess our own indolence and cowardice.

MEDITATIONS ON PSALM XXXII.

Ver. 1. Blessed is the man whose transgression is forgiven, whose sin is covered.

OH, the pure, the overflowing, the incomparably sweet fountain of Scripture !

"Hence light we draw, and fill the sacred cup*."

Whereas the springs of philosophy in human affairs, are not very clear, and in Divine, they are quite turbid and muddy ; which one of the greatest orators and philosophers among them all, freely confesses. "I think," says he, "we are not only blind to true wisdom, but are very dull and slow of apprehension even in those things which seem to be discerned and understood†." Nor is this to be wondered at ; for there would be little difference between things human and Divine, if the dim eye of our reason were sufficient to discover their secrets. One of the ancients excellently says, "If you examine things ever so accurately, you will never be able to discover them if God keeps them vailed‡."

It would be a vain and ridiculous labour, to light up a great number of lanterns and torches, and go out and look for the sun in the night; but when the appointed hour of morning comes, he arises, as if of his own accord, and freely manifests himself, by his own lustre, to every beholder. The wisest of the heathens undertook to find out the Supreme Being, and the Supreme Good ; but wandering through the devious ways of

---

* Illinc lucem haurire est, et pocula sacra.

† Mihi non modò ad sapientiam cæci videmur, sed ad ea ipsa, quæ aliquâ ex parte cerni videantur, hebetes et obtusi. SENECA.

‡ 'Αλλ' οὐ γὰρ ἂν τὰ Θεῖα κρύπτοντος Θεοῦ
Μάθοις ἄν, οὐδ' εἰ πάντ' ὑπεξέλθοις σκοπῶν. SOPHOCLES.

multiplied errors, they could attain to neither. Nor was it the least of their errors, that they sought them as two different things, when it is most certain that both are united in one ; for it is the only and ultimate happiness of man, to be united to that First and Supreme Being and Good, from which he drew his original. But since there has so sad a distance and disagreement arisen between God and Man, by our deplorable apostacy from Him, there could not be the least hope of attaining that union, did not infinite Goodness and Mercy propose the full and free pardon of our offences : so that the true determination of this grand question about happiness, is evidently that, *Blessed and happy is that man whose transgression is forgiven, and whose sin is covered.* Innocence was the first means of obtaining happiness, which being once violated, the only plank that can save us after our shipwreck, is remission and repentance ; which two things, the whole Scripture assures us that the Divine Wisdom has so connected, as with an adamantine band. And this Psalm now before us is a signal declaration of it, which, since it inculcates so grand a topic of religion, κυρίαν δόξαν, may well be styled as it is, *Maschil, a lesson of instruction.* For, as St. Augustine well observes, " That is instruction indeed, which teaches us that Man is not saved by the merits of his works, but by the grace of God*."

Blessed.] Or, O blessed man, or, Oh, the felicities of that Man, to denote the most supreme and perfect blessedness †. He only has attained to complete felicity, whose numerous debts are all remitted, though, far from being able to pay them, he could not so much as reckon them up. And blessed is he that knows it, as the proverb is, " No man is happy but he who thinks himself so ‡."

The man whose iniquity is forgiven.] As the word is *nesevi,*

---

* Quâ intelligitur non meritis operum, sed Dei gratiâ hominem liberari.

† As the Elephant, to denote its vast bulk, is spoken of in the plural number, *Behemoth.*

‡ Non est beatus qui se non putat.

it might be rendered, *Blessed is the man who is eased of the heavy burden of his sin*. A burden, indeed, too heavy for the strongest man upon earth; a burden so dreadfully great, that God's angels are not able to stand under it; for many of the chief of them were pressed down to hell by it, and can rise no more. But though no giant on earth or in heaven could bear it, A LAMB subjected himself to it. But it was *A Lamb without blemish and without spot*, burdened with no load of his own sin, nor stained with the least spot of pollution. *The Lamb of God, the Son of God*, who is Himself God, is he ὁ αἴρων τὴν ἁμαρτίαν τοῦ κόσμου, who takes away all the sins of the world, as one sin: taking the burden upon Himself, he bears it and carries it away.

Covered.] That sinners may more clearly apprehend, and more easily and firmly believe a thing that seems so difficult to admit, as the free and full remission of sin, it is pointed out by various beautiful expressions and figures in the sacred Scriptures; *washing, cleansing, blotting out, scattering like a cloud, entirely forgetting, casting into the bottom of the sea*, and here, by that of *taking away and covering*, and by that phrase, which explains both, of *not imputing* them. And this expression of *covering* them, is with great propriety added to the former phrase of lightening the sinner of the burden of them, that there may be no fear of their returning again, or coming into sight, since God has not only taken the heavy load from our shoulders, but for ever hidden it from His own eyes, and the vail of mercy has taken it away; that great covering of Divine love, which is large enough to overspread so many and so great offences. Thus it does, as it were, turn away the penetrating eye of His justice, which the most secret inquiry could not elude, did not He Himself in pity voluntarily avert it.

But you will know what is our *Propitiatory*, what the covering of the mercy-seat, even Jesus, who was typified by that *Caporeth* in the Temple, which the *Septuagint* render ἱλαστήριον ἐπίθεμα, a *propitiatory covering;* by which title our great

Redeemer is marked out, Rom. iii. 25, as the same Hebrew word, *Caphar*, signifies both *to cover* and *to expiate* *. But that the thing may be more evident and certain, the thought is repeated again in the second verse.

Ver. 2. Blessed is the man to whom the Lord imputeth not iniquity, and in whose spirit there is no guile.

ABEN-EZRA paraphrases it, *Of whose sins God does not think,* does not regard them, so as to bring them into judgment, reckoning them as if they were not ; οὐ μὴ λογίζεται, *does not count or calculate them, or charge them to account;* does not require for them the debt of punishment.   To us the remission is entirely free, our Sponsor having taken upon Him the whole business of paying the ransom.   His suffering is our impunity, His bond our freedom, and His chastisement our peace ; and therefore the Prophet says, *The chastisement of our peace was upon Him, and by His stripes we are healed.*   Distracted creatures that we are, to indulge in those sins which brought death upon our dear Redeemer, and to be so cold in our affections to that Redeemer who died for those sins !

This weighty sentence, of itself so admirable, Paul renders yet more illustrious, by inserting it into his reasonings on the topic of justification, Rom. iv. 6, as a celebrated testimony of that great article of our faith.   " David," says he, " thus describeth the blessedness of that man, saying, *Blessed is he whose iniquities are forgiven.*"   So that this is David's opinion concerning true happiness: he says not, Blessed are those who rule over kingdoms, blessed are those generals · who are renowed for their martial bravery and success, though he

---

* It is observed, the Hebrew word *Eschol haccopher,* which some render *a cluster of camphire,* Cant. i. 14, may, with a little variation in the reading, [i. e. reading it *Ish col haccapher,*] be rendered *a man of all kinds of redemption,* or *of all expiation.*   So the *Targum* interprets it by expiation.   And by the way, some assert that this Psalm used to be sung on the day of expiation.

himself had both these titles to boast of. It is not the enco-
miums of the greatest multitudes, nor the breath of popular
applause, nor any other degree of human honour, which en-
titles a man to this character. It is not said, Blessed is he who
ploughs many thousand acres of land, or who has heaped together mountains of gold and silver ; nor, Blessed is he who has
married a beautiful and rich woman, or, (which in his age, or
even now in those eastern countries, might be the case,) he who
was possessed of many such ; nor, Blessed is he who understands the secrets of nature, or even the mysteries of religion :
but *Oh, happy man whose sins are pardoned, and to whom
the Lord does not impute inquity, and in whose spirit there
is no guile*, whose breast is full, not of feigned repentance, but
of a fervent love of holiness, and hatred of sin. This makes
life happy, nay, absolutely blessed. But alas ! when we incul-
cate these things, we sing to the deaf. The ignorance and folly
of mankind will not cease to pronounce the proud and the covetous happy, and those who triumph in successful wickedness,
and who, in chase of these lying shadows of happiness, destroy
their days, and their years, and their souls.

" Alas," says the wise Roman, " how little do some who
thirst most impatiently after glory, know what it is, or where
it is to be sought * ! " Which is equally applicable to that
true calm and serenity of mind which indeed all pursue, but
yet few are able to attain. But as for us who enjoy the
celestial instruction of this sacred volume, if we are ignorant of
it, our ignorance is quite inexcusable, obstinate, and affected,
since we are wilfully blind in the clearest and most refulgent
light. This points out that good which can completely fill
all the most extended capacities of the human soul, and
which we generally seek for in vain on all sides, catching at
it where it is not to be found, but ever neglecting it where
alone it is. But is it then possible at once to be solidly and
completely happy ? You have not merely the ideas of it, but

* Quàm ignorant homines gloriæ cupidi quæ eâ sit, aut quemadmodum
petenda !—Seneca.

the thing itself, not only clearly pointed out, but most freely offered, with Divine munificence ; so that if you do not obstinately reject the offer, it must be your own. And this happiness consists in returning to the favour and friendship of God, who most mercifully grants us the free pardon of all our sins, if we do, with unfeigned repentance and a heart free of all guile, not only humbly confess and lament them, but entirely forsake, and with implacable hatred for ever renounce them. ὦ μάκαρ εὐδαίμων τε καὶ ὄλβιος. All the names, all the variety of felicities, bliss, and happiness, are accumulated on that man who has known this *change of the right hand of the Most High**, on whom this bright day of expiation and pardon has beamed. He easily looks down from on high on all the empty titles and false images of earthly happiness, and when he is bereaved of them all, yea, and beset on every side with what the world calls misfortunes and afflictions, ceases not to be happy. In sorrow he is joyful, in poverty rich, and in chains free : when he seems buried deep, so that not one ray of the sun can reach him, he is surrounded with radiant lustre ; when overwhelmed with ignominy he glories; and in death itself, he lives, he conquers, he triumphs. What can be heavy to that man who is eased of the intolerable burden of sin ? How animated was that saying of Luther, " Smite, Lord, smite, for thou hast absolved me from my sins †." Whose anger should he fear who knows that God is propitious to him,—that Supreme *King, whose wrath is indeed the messenger of death, but the light of His countenance is life ;* who gladdens all by the rays of His favour, and by one smile disperses the darkest cloud, and calms the most turbulent tempest ?

But we must now observe the complication of a twofold good, in constituting this felicity: for we have two things here connected, as conspiring to make the person spoken of blessed ;

* Alluding to Psalm lxxvii. 10, where the Vulgate renders *Seuih,* change, *mutatio dextræ Excelsi ;* and several other Versions nearly agree with it.

† Feri, Domine, feri ; nam à peccatis absolvisti me.

the free remission of sin, and the inward purification of the
heart. *In whose Spirit there is no guile.* This simplicity,
ἀφελότης, is a most excellent part of purity, opposed to all
wickedness and arts of deceit; and in common speech, that
which is simple, and has no foreign mixture, is called *pure.*
Pardon presents us as just and innocent before our Judge;
and that sanctity is not to be regarded as constituting any
part of our justifying righteousness before God, nor as only the
condition or sign of our felicity, but is truly and properly a
part of it.   Purity is the accomplishment of our felicity,
begun on earth, and to be consummated in Heaven: that
purity, I say, which is begun here, and shall there be consummated.   But if any one think he can divide these two things,
which the hand of God has joined by so inseparable a bond,
it is a vain dream.   Nay, by attempting to separate these
two parts of happiness, he will in fact only exclude himself
from the whole.   Jesus, our victorious Saviour, has snatched
us from the jaws of eternal death ; but, to be delivered from
the cruel tyranny and bonds of sin, and to be brought into
the blessed liberty of the sons of God, was another essential
part of our redemption, and if any one does not embrace
this with equal alacrity and delight as the other benefit, he
is a wretched slave of the most mean and ignoble spirit, and
being equally unworthy of both parts of this stupendous deliverance, he will justly forfeit and lose both.   And this is the
epidemical Antinomianism of the Christian world, because
they who labour under it have nothing but the name of
Christians ; they gladly hear of the pardon of their sins, and
the salvation of their souls, while they are averse to the doctrine of holiness and repentance.   It is a disagreeable message,
a hard saying, and who can bear it! But Oh! the incomparable charms of holiness!   It is to be desired, not only for
the sake of other benefits which come in its train, but especially for itself ; so that he who is not transported with a most
ardent love of it, is blind, and deserves to be thrust into the
mill to tread that uncomfortable round, and to grind there;

deserves to be a slave for ever, since he knows not how to use liberty when offered to him. Shall the Stoic say, " The servant of philosophy is truly free *," and shall we scruple to assert the same concerning pure religion, and evangelical holiness? Now, this freedom from guile, this fair simplicity of which the Psalmist speaks, is deservedly reckoned among the chief endowments of a pure soul, and is here named instead of all the rest, as nothing is more like to that God who inspects the very heart, in nothing do we so much resemble Him; and therefore it is most agreeable to Him, because most like unto Him. He is the most simple of all beings, and is indeed Truth itself, and therefore, He *desires truth in the inward parts*, and hates *a heart and a heart*, as the Hebrew phrase is to express those that are double-hearted. And how much our blessed Redeemer esteems this simplicity, we may learn from the earnestness with which He inculcates it upon His disciples, that they should be *simple as doves*. (Matt. x. 16.) We may learn it also from the honourable testimony he bears to this character in Nathanael, when he pronounces him, (John i. 47,) *an Israelite indeed, in whom there is no guile*. And especially from His own perfect example, as it is said of Him, (1 Pet. ii. 22,) *He did no sin, neither was guile found in His mouth*. Perhaps the Psalmist might the more willingly mention this virtue, as he reflected with penitential distress on his crafty and cruel attempt of covering that adultery which he had committed, with the vail of murder. But however that was, it is certain that this guileless sincerity of heart, holds the first rank in the graces that attend true repentance. It may be sometimes our duty to open our sins to men, by an ingenuous confession; but it is always our duty to do it to God, who promises to cover them only on this condition, that we do sincerely uncover them ourselves. But if we affect that which is His part, He will, to our unspeakable damage, do that which He had assigned to us. If we hide them, He will bring them into open light, and will dis-

* Qui philosophiæ inservit est verè liber.

cuss and examine each with the greater severity: "He," says Ambrose, " who burdens himself, makes his error so much the lighter *." " In proportion to the degree," says Tertullian †, " in which you are unwilling to spare yourself, God will spare you." But what madness is it to attempt to conceal any action from Him, from whom, as Thales wisely declares, " you cannot so much as conceal a thought ‡ !" But not now to in- sist upon the impossibility of a concealment, a wise man would not wish to cover his wounds and his disease from that physi- cian, from whose skilful hand he might otherwise receive heal- ing; and this is what the Psalmist presently after, for our in- struction, confesses.

Ver. 3.   When I kept silence, my bones waxed old, through my roaring
all the day long.

WHILE he suppressed the ingenuous voice of confession, the continually increasing weight of his calamity extorted from him a voice of roaring: " while I would not speak as it became a guilty man, I was compelled even to bellow like a beast §." Nevertheless, this wild roaring did not move the Divine com- passion, nor atone His displeasure.

Ver. 4. For day and night Thine hand was heavy upon me: my moisture
is turned into the drought of summer.

HITHERTO that voice was wanting, to which the bowels of the Father always echo back, the voice of a son full of reverence, and ready to confess his errors; without which, cries and lamentations in misery are no more regarded in the sight of God, than the howling of dogs, according to that expression of Hosea vii. 14, *They have not cried to me with their heart,*

* Allevat errores ille qui se onerat.

† Quantum tibi non peperceris, tantum tibi parcet Deus.

‡ Ὃν οὐ λανθάνεις οὐδὲ διανούμενος.

§ Dum nolui loqui ut hominem reum decet, mugire coactus sum ut brutum.

when they howled upon their beds. A dog howls when he is hungry, or when he is lashed: but from a son, when he is chastened, acknowledgments of his fault, and deprecations of his father's displeasure are expected; and when the son thus acknowledges his offence, and entreats for pardon, it is the part of a compassionate father to forgive, and to spare. Nor do we indeed confess our offences to our Father, as if He were not perfectly acquainted with them, but we fly to Him who requires we should repent, that He may not shew us by punishment, those things which we shun shewing to Him by confession. " I confessed unto the Lord," says Augustine, " to whom all the abyss of my sin and misery lay open; so that if I did not confess whatever was hidden in my heart, I should not hide myself from Him, but Him from me *."

Thy hand was heavy upon me.] That Hand, which when pressing, is so heavy, when raising, is so sweet and powerful, (Psalm xxxvii. 24,) and when scattering its blessings, so full and so ample. (Psalm civ. 28; cxlv. 16.) He would not at first be humbled by the confession of his iniquity, and therefore he is humbled by the weight of the hand of God. Oh, powerful hand! beyond all comparison more grievous than any other hand to press down, and more powerful to raise up! He who suppresses his sins without confessing them,

Vulnus alit venis, et cæco carpitur igne—
" Conceals an inward wound, and burns with secret fire."

Under the appearance of sparing, he is indeed cruel to himself; when he has drunk down iniquity, and keeps it within, and it is not covered by the Divine forgiveness, it is like a poison which consumes the marrow in the midst of his bones, and dries up the vital moisture. It may perhaps occasion more present pain, to draw out the point of the weapon which sticks in the flesh; but to neglect it, will occasion greater danger and more future torment. Nor will the dart fall out by his running

* Et tibi, Domine, cujus oculis nuda abyssus, quid occultum esset in me si non confiterer, non me tibi absconderem, sed te mihi.

hither and thither, but, on the contrary, as the poet expresses it with respect to the wounded deer, it fixes deeper and deeper *.

But the only healing herb that the sinner can find, is true repentance and humble confession: not that which acknow‑ ledges sin in a few slight words, when it has hardly looked upon it and known it, but that which proceeds from a previous true and vivid compunction of soul, and is inseparably attended by renovation and purity of heart and life; and so, as compre‑ hending this, it is sometimes put for the whole of repentance. 1 John i. 9. *If we confess our sins, He is faithful and just to forgive us our sins, and to cleanse us from all unrighteousness.* And so, in the Psalm before us.

> Ver. 5. I acknowledged my sin unto Thee, and my iniquity have I not hid. I said, I will confess my transgression unto the Lord, and Thou for‑ gavest the iniquity of my sin. *Selah.*

TRUE and genuine repentance hath eyes, as it were, on both sides, πρόσω καὶ ὀπίσω βλέπει: it looks back on sins already com‑ mitted, to lament them; it looks forward, and humbly resolves no more to commit what it has lamented. And each of these is expressed by each of the words by which repentance is signi‑ fied, μεταμελεία and μετανοία; which words are therefore used promiscuously, both by the sacred writers and by others, so that the received difference between them seems to me to have little foundation. For Phavorinus interprets the word μετανοία, an anguish of soul under a consciousness of having acted a fool‑ ish and absurd part; and the Latin has the same signification, if we will admit the judgment of Gellius, who seems to have been a very accurate critic in affairs of that nature. He ob‑ serves, " We are said to repent of things, whether our own actions, or those of others which have been performed by our advice or instigation, which do afterwards displease us, so that

* ——— Illa fugâ 'sylvas saltusque peragrat Dyctæos, hæret lateri lethalis arundo.

we change our judgment concerning them *." But we will waive all further concern about words; the thing itself demands our greatest attention. I entirely agree with him who said, " I had rather feel the inward working of repentance, than know the most accurate description and definition of it †." Yet how averse sinners are to this free though useful and salutary confession of sin, abundantly appears from this example of so great a man as the Psalmist, when taken in this unhappy snare; for he confesses that he lay long as senseless and stupid in that quagmire into which he was fallen, and that it was with difficulty that he was as it were racked into a confession, by such exquisite tortures both of body and mind. On the other hand, the gracious readiness of the Father of Mercies to grant pardon, is so much the more evident, as on the first word of confession that he uttered, or rather the first purpose that he formed in his mind, immediately the pardon, the full and free pardon, came down signed, as in the court of Heaven. *I said, I will confess, and Thou forgavest.* O admirable clemency! It requires nothing but that the offender should plead guilty, and this not that it may more freely punish, but more liberally forgive. He requires that we should condemn ourselves, that so he may absolve us.

Ver. 6. For this shall every one that is godly pray unto Thee, in a time when Thou mayest be found: surely, in the floods of great waters, they shall not come nigh unto him.

THIS is the joyful message, this is the great doctrine of the Gospel, which opens the first door of hope to sinners; that God is capable of being appeased, yea, that he is actually appeased; that he freely offers peace and favour to those who have deserted Him, when they return to His obedience; that He runs

---

* Pœnitere tum dicere solemus, cùm quæ ipsi fecimus, aut quæ de nostra voluntate nostroque consilio facta seunt, ea nobis post incipiunt displicere, sententiamque in iis nostram demutamus.

† Malo sentire compunctionem, quàm scire ejus definitionem. *Thom. à Kempis, l.* i. c. 1.

forth to meet them, and to receive them with a most affectionate embrace ; and having so importunately entreated our return, will not despise those who are treading back with prayers and tears the fatal path which their folly had chosen. This is what we so frequently read in Scripture, that *the Lord is gracious and very merciful, slow to anger, and ready to pardon.* If He were not such, who could dare approach Him ? But seeing He is such a God, who should refuse or delay his return! Surely, every rational and pious mind will, without delay, invoke so gentle and mild a Lord ; *will pray to Him while he is exorable,* or, as the Hebrew expresses it, *in a time of finding.* For He who promises pardon, does not promise to-morrow. There are the *tempora fandi,* certain times in which He may be spoken with, and a certain appointed day of pardon and of grace, which if a man by stupid perverseness despise, or by sloth neglect, surely he is justly overwhelmed with eternal night and misery, and must necessarily perish by the deluge of Divine wrath ; since he has contemned and derided that Ark of salvation which was prepared, and in which whoever enters into it shall be safe, while the world is perishing. Though all be one unbounded sea, a sea without shore, yet, as it is here said, the greatest inundation, *the floods of deep waters shall not come nigh unto him.* This, the Psalmist exhorts those that have experienced it, to teach, and determines himself so to retain it with deep attention and firm faith in his own mind, as in the following verse.

Ver. 7. *Thou art my hiding place.*] Thou hast been, and wilt ever be so. *Thou hast surrounded,* and Thou wilt surround *me, with songs of deliverance;* even me who was so surrounded with clamours of sin. Where he further intimates, that songs of praise are perpetually to be offered to God our deliverer. And that these faithful admonitions and counsels may meet with greater attention and regard, he offers himself to us as a most benevolent teacher and leader.

Ver. 8, 9, 10, 11, *I will instruct thee, and teach thee in the way in which thou shalt go,* &c.] See to it only, that thou be tractable, and dost not with a brutal obstinacy and fierceness repel this friendly and wise counsel, as capable of being governed only by violence, like a mule or unbroken horse, which must be held in by bit and bridle. Such indeed are the greatest part of men, whom the philosophers with great severity, but with too much justice, called βουγενῆ ἀνδρόπρωρα, "Wild bulls with human faces."

But it is added, as the sum of all admonition, and the great axiom most worthy of regard, that *Many sorrows shall be to the wicked* [the *Septuagint* render it, *many are the scourges of the sinners *,*] but *mercy shall embrace those that hope in the Lord.* And the Psalm concludes with this as the burden of it. *Rejoice in the Lord, ye righteous, and shout for joy, all ye that are upright in heart.*

Truly, my dear friends†, I have nothing further to wish for myself or you, than that we may heartily believe these things; for then it would be impossible that we should not with open arms embrace true religion, and clasp it to our hearts, since nature teaches every one to desire happiness, and to flee from misery. So that Epicurus himself would teach us to lay hold on joy and pleasure, as the τό πρῶτον οἰκεῖον, or first and proper good. This, therefore, let us lay down as a certain principle, and ever adhere to it, that we may not, like brute beasts, remain in subjection to the flesh; that safety, and joy, and all happiness are the property of him who is possessed of virtue, and that all virtue is comprehended in true piety. And let us remember what the prophet adds, (according to the Greek translators‡,) as the necessary consequence of this principle, that *to the wicked there can be no joy.*

* Πολλαὶ μάστιγες ἁμαρτωλοῦ.

† The word *Juvenes,* or *my dear youths,* occurs here and in several other places, as these Lectures were delivered to a society of young theological students; but it did not seem necessary to make the translation so exactly literal.

‡ Ὀυκ ἐστὶ χαίρειν τοῖς ἀσίβισι.

MEDITATIONS ON PSALM CXXX.

Ver. 1.   Out of the depths have I cried unto Thee, O Lord.

IT is undoubtedly both a useful and a pleasant employment,
to observe the emotions of great and heroic minds in great and
arduous affairs ; but that mind only is truly great, and supe-
rior to the whole world, which does in the most placid manner
subject itself to God, securely casting all its burdens and cares
upon Him, in all the uncertain alterations of human affairs,
looking at His hand, and fixing its regard upon that alone.
Such the royal prophet David declares himself every where to
have been, and no where more evidently than in this Psalm,
which seems to have been composed by him.   He lifts up his
head amidst surrounding waves, and directing his face and his
voice to Heaven, he says, *Out of the depths, O Lord, do I cry
unto Thee.*   For so I would render it, as he does not seem to
express a past fact, but as the Hebrew idiom imports, a prayer
which he was now actually presenting.

Out of the depths.]   Being as it were immersed and overwhelmed in an abyss of misery and calamities.   It is indeed
the native lot of man, to *be born to trouble, as* it is for *the
sparks* (the children of the coal, as the original expression signifies) *to fly upward.*   Life and grief are congenial * ; but
men who are born again, seem, as in a redoubled proportion, to
be *twice born to trouble ;* with so many and so great evils are
they as it were laden, beyond all other men, and that to such
a degree, that they may seem sometimes to be oppressed with
them.   And if any think this is strange, surely, as the Apostle
expresses it, *he cannot see afar off,* μυωπάζει ; at best, he only
looks at the surfaces of things, and cannot penetrate far into

* Ὡς ἄρα συγγενής ἐστι λύπη καὶ βίος.

those depths. For even the philosophers themselves, untaught by Divine revelation, investigated admirable reasons for such dispensations of Providence, and undertook in this respect boldly to plead the cause of God. " God," says the Roman sage, " loves His own people truly, but he loves them severely ! As the manner in which fathers express their love to their children, is generally very different from that of mothers ; they order them to be called up early in their studies, and suffer them not to be idle in those days, when their usual business is interrupted, but sometimes put them on labouring till the sweat flows down, and sometimes by their discipline excite their tears ; while the mother fondles them in her bosom, keeps them in the shade, and knows not how to consent that they should weep, or grieve, or labour. God bears the heart of a father to good men, and there is strength rather than tenderness in His love ; they are therefore exercised with labours, sorrows, and losses, that they may grow robust : whereas, were they to be fattened by luxurious fare, and indulged in indolence, they would not only sink under fatigues, but be burdened with their own unwieldy bulk *." Presently after, he quotes a remarkable saying of Demetrius, the Cynic †, to this purpose, " He seems to be the unhappiest of mankind, who has never been exercised with adversity, as he cannot have had an opportunity of trying the strength of his mind." To wish to pass life without it, is to be ignorant of one part of nature, so that I may pronounce thee to be miserable, if thou hast never

---

* Verè suos amat et severè Deus. Multo aliter patres, aliter matres indulgent: illi liberos ad studia obeunda maturè excitari jubent, feriatis quoque diebus non patiuntur otiosos, et sæpe sudorem illis, et interdum lachrymas excutiunt: at matres fovere in sinu, in umbra continere volunt ; nunquam flere, nunquam tristari, nunquam laborare. Patrium habet Deus adversus bonos viros animum, et illos fortiùs amat; et operibus, doloribus, ac damnis exagitantur, ut verum colligant robur. Languent per inertiam saginata : nec labore tantùm, sed et mole, et ipso sui onere deficiunt.—SENECA.

† Nihil mihi videtur infelicius eo, cui nihil unquam evenerit adversi ; non licuit illi se experiri.

been miserable.   If thou hast passed through life without ever struggling with an enemy, no one, not even thou thyself, can know whether thou art able to make any resistance : whereas in afflictions we experience, not so much what our own strength is, as what is the strength of God in us, and what the Aid of Divine grace is, which often bears us up under them to a surprising degree, and makes us joyful by a happy exit ; so that we shall be able to say, *My God, my strength, and my deliverer.* Thus the Church becomes conspicuous in the midst of the flames, like the burning bush, *through the good will of Him that dwelt in it.*   And when it seems to be overwhelmed with waters, God brings it out of them cleansed and beautified— *mergas profundo, pulchrior evenit;* He plunges it in the deep, and it rises fairer than before.

We will not here maintain that paradox of the Stoics, *That evils which happen to good men, are not to be called evils at all;* which, however, is capable of a very good sense, since religion teaches us that the greatest evils are changed, and *work together for good*, which comes almost to the same thing, and perhaps was the true meaning of the Stoics.   Banishment and poverty are indeed evils in one sense, *i. e.,* they have something hard and grievous in them ; but when they fall on a good and brave man, they seem to lay aside the malignity of their nature, and become tame and gentle.   The very sharpness of them excites and exercises virtue : by exciting they increase it, so that the root of faith shoots the stronger, and fixes the deeper, and thereby adds new strength to fortitude and patience. And as we see in this example before us, affliction does by a happy kind of necessity drive the soul to confess its sin, to flee as it were to seek its refuge under the wing of the Divine goodness, and to fix its hope upon God.   And this is certainly one great advantage which the pious soul gains by adversity, that it calls away the affections from earth and earthly things, or rather tears them away, when obstinately adhering to them. " It is necessary that they suffer such hardships as these," as one expresses it *, " lest they should love this inconvenient stable, in which they are now obliged to lodge, as if it were their own house." It is necessary that they should perceive that they are *strangers and foreigners upon earth,* that they may more frequently, and with more ardent desire, groan after that better country, and often repeat it, οἶκος φίλος, οἶκος ἄριστος, *Dear Home! Most desirable Home!* The children and heirs of the kingdom must be weaned by wormwood, lest they should be so enchanted by the allurements of the flesh, and the poisonous sweetness of secular enjoyments, as to barter away the true and pure joy of their blessed hope, for this false, polluted, and deadly joy; and lest, dissolved in pleasure, the Heaven-born soul should be broken under the yoke of this pernicious flesh, the root of so many passions †. Lastly, we see how much vigour and vehemence affliction adds to prayer; for the divine Psalmist, the deeper he sinks, cries to God in so much the louder accents—*Out of the deeps have I cried.*

This prayer contains those precious virtues, which, in a grateful temperature, render every prayer acceptable to God— faith, fervour, and humility. Faith, in that he prays *out of the deeps;* fervour, in that *he cries,* and both again expressed in the next word : faith, as in the midst of surrounding calamities he does not despair of redress; fervour, as he urges it with repeated importunity, and the same word uttered again and again. And to complete all, humility expresses itself in what follows, where he speaks as one that felt himself sinking, as one who was plunged in a sea of iniquities, as well as calamities; and acknowledges he was so overwhelmed with them, as to be unable to stand, unless supported by pure mercy and grace. *If Thou, Lord, shouldst mark iniquities, who shall stand?* Thus, here again, faith manifests itself more clearly, together with its kindred affections of hope and charity, which, like three graces, join their hands, and by an inseparable union

---

* Expedit omninò ut hîc dura experiantur, ne stabulum ament pro domo suâ.

† Σὰρξ ὁλόη, παθέων ρίζα πολυσχιδέων.

support each other.   You have faith in the 4th verse, *There is forgiveness with Thee :* hope in the 5th, *I wait for the Lord, my soul doth wait, and in his word do I hope ;* charity in the 7th and 8th, where he does in a most benevolent manner invite all Israel to a communion of the same faith and hope, and in order to confirm them more abundantly, does in a most animated manner proclaim the riches of the Divine benignity. Such is the composition of this excellent prayer, which thus compounded, like a pillar of aromatic smoke from myrrh, frankincense, and every other most fragrant perfume, ascends grateful to the throne of God.   And this you may take instead of the analysis of the remaining verses, which to handle by a more minute dissection of words, and to clothe in the trite phrases of the schools, to speak freely, would be as barren and useless as it is easy and puerile.   And, indeed, I cannot but form the same judgment of the common way of catching at a multitude of observations from any scripture, and of pressing it with violence, as if remarks were to be estimated by number rather than weight, propriety, and use.   But here let every one follow his own genius and taste ; for we are willing to give the liberty we take.   *Veniam damus petimusque vicissim.*

Out of the depths.]   Oh, the immortal power of Divine faith, which lives and breathes in the midst of the waves, in which it may be plunged, but cannot be sunk under any of the hugest billows ; but raises itself, and the soul in which it resides, and emerges and swims above all, φελλὸς ὡς ἀβάπτιστος, (like cork which will still be above water,) having this in common with that Divine love of which Solomon speaks in his *Song,* that *many waters cannot quench it.*   Whatever great things the Stoics may speak of their wise men, and whatever all philosophy may say of fortitude, it is Divine faith that truly and heartily performs all, by which the good man, though stripped of every help and comfort, wraps himself up as it were, not in his own virtue and strength, but in that of God ; and hence it is that he cannot be conquered by any tyranny, by any threatenings, by any calamities of life, by any fear of death, for he leans upon Omnipotence. *The Lord*, says he, *is my light and my salvation ; whom shall I fear ?   The Lord is the strength of my life, of whom shall I be afraid ?*   Let *war arise,* let the enemy measure out his tents against me, I, says Faith, am secure *under the shadow of the Most High,* and embracing Him, I will fear nothing.

You have here the Psalmist crying with confidence out of the deeps.   Behold also the prophet Jonah indeed, and, as we say, literally, *in the deeps,* and in circumstances which might have greater efficacy to shake his faith than the sea itself, than the bowels of the fish, or any other depth into which he might be cast, as he was not entirely free from blame, but had the intermingling guilt of his own perverseness ; yet, among all these discouragements, his faith is not swallowed up : *I have cried unto Thee in my distress, and from the very belly of hell.   Thou hast cast me into the deep, and all thy waves were going over me,* so that I might truly say, *I am cast out from Thy sight;* yet at the same time I said, *I will look again towards the temple of Thy holiness.*   I went down to the root and cavern of the mountains; the abyss surrounded me ; yet when my soul was thus *overwhelmed within me, I remembered the Lord.*   You have, among others, an excellent example of faith in David, 1 Sam. xxx., when the invading enemy had burnt Ziklag, and carried the women captive, and the people, in the madness of their rage and grief, speak of stoning David himself ; yet, besieged with all these miseries, he *strengthens himself in the Lord his God.*   Nor can any thing have greater depth and strength than that expression of Job, *Though He slay me, yet will I trust in Him :* not only when fainting and dying, but while expiring, as it were, of the wound which I had received from the- hand of God Himself, yet will I hope for life and salvation from that very hand which has given me death, and in the jaws of death would send out this last word with the last breath, and with my departing soul, Destroy not, O Lord, one that trusteth in Thee.

Nor is this confidence of a pious soul an opinion fluctuating

among the waves, or a light conjecture that it shall raise its
head above them, but a certain, firm, and infallible assurance.
That is a vulgar and weak word of comfort, "To-morrow may
be better than to-day*." But the language of Divine faith is
stronger and firmer, even when *deep calls unto deep*, and most
certainly determines that it will not be in vain; and therefore,
in the forty-second Psalm, not dubious and trembling, but with
a steady voice, he silences all the noisy tumults of an agitated
mind, and says, *Repose thyself on God, for I shall still praise
Him*, or, as it may be rendered, *I am going to praise Him:*
q. d. Amidst all those tempests which rage about me, I am
thinking of that hymn of praise which I shall pay to Him for
my deliverance, and for the happy exit out of all my sorrows.
Though at present we have nothing in sight but darkness, and
whirlwinds, and rocks, and the raging, foaming sea, let the
skill and power of the Great Pilot be opposed to all these.
And what the Psalmist says elsewhere of sailors, may evidently
be applied to those who go down into the sea : they gain this by
their dangers, that *they see the works* of this Great Pilot in the
abyss, and contemplate *His wonders in the deep.* And he who
gives himself up to His care, and fixes his eye and hope wholly
on Him, though he be, or rather seem to be, shipwrecked, and
lose all his goods, yet, if he does not *make shipwreck of faith*,
he loses nothing that is properly his own. Nay, when he is
swallowed up in the abyss of death, he does not perish, but
swims through it to the further shore of eternity, where he finds
a banquet, a palace prepared for him, and *a kingdom that cannot be moved*, but remains to endless ages.

I cried.] Prayer is the natural and genuine voice of the
children of God; and as the Latin word *Oratio* properly signifies articulate speech, as it distinguishes man from other
animals, so, in this other signification, it expresses that by which
the ungodly are distinguished from the rest of mankind: it is the
proper idiom of the citizens of Heaven. Others may recite
some words of prayer, but they do not pray : as parrots and

other birds, by the industry of their teacher, may learn to imitate human voices, yet they do not speak ; there is something wanting in all their most skilful chattering, which is the very thing that is also wanting in the language of most that are said to pray, and that is, *mind* and *meaning*, affections correspondent to the words, or rather, to which the words may conform as to their original cause, and of which they may be the true index and sign. The spirit of this world knows not how to pray, nor does a *spirit of adoption and liberty* know how to forbear praying,—the *spirit of adoption*, says the Apostle, *by which we cry, Abba, Father*. Nor can they who are new-born by that Spirit, live without frequent prayer. Prayer is to them, as the natural and necessary respiration of that new and Divine life, as Lam. iii. 56 : *Turn not away from my breathing :* the Hebrew word there made use of, *leruhethi,* properly signifies the *vital respiration* of animals. Yet, notwithstanding all this, what we said above is true, and evidently appears from the passage before us, that affliction often adds vigour to prayers, how lively and assiduous soever they may have been before. Let it be so, that Prayer is the natural language of believing souls, by which they daily address their heavenly Father, yet, when they are pressed with an uncommon pain or danger, it is no less natural that this voice should be louder than ordinary, and should be raised into a cry. It is indeed the breath of faith and heavenly affections, and when they are vehemently pressed by any burden, and almost expiring under it, they breathe quicker than before, and with greater effort. Thus they who have been used to the greatest heights of daily devotion, yet, in surrounding calamities, pray more fervently and more frequently than ordinary. And this is to be numbered among the chief benefits attending afflictions, and it would surely be well worth our while to experience all the hardest pressures of them, if we may gain this ; that the languor, and sloth, and stupidity, into which our minds and our souls are ready insensibly to sink while all is calm and serene about us, may be happily shaken off by something which the world may call an unhappy event; that some more violent gust of wind may fan the sacred flame that seems almost extinguished, and blow it up into greater ardour. It will be happy for us, that, with the Psalmist, we should sometimes *sink in deep waters*, that so we, who in prosperity do but whisper or mutter out our prayers, may from *the depths cry aloud unto God.* Oh, how frequently and how ardently did David pray in the deserts and the caves, and it is he who here cries out of the deep, and perhaps these deep recesses are those from which he was now crying; but when secure amidst the ease and delights of the court, and walking at leisure on his house-top, he was tempted by his own wandering eyes, and having intermitted the fervour of prayer, burned with impure fires. Our vows are cruel to ourselves, if they demand nothing but gentle zephyrs, and flowery fields, and calm repose, as the lot of our life; for these pleasant things often prove the most dangerous enemies to our nobler and dearer life.

Oh! how true is that saying, that " Faith is safe when in " danger, and in danger when secure ; and Prayer is fervent in " straits, but in joyful and prosperous circumstances, if not " quite cold and dead, at least lukewarm." Oh, happy straits, if they hinder the mind from flowing forth upon earthly objects, and mingling itself with the mire; if they favour our correspondence with Heaven, and quicken our love· to celestial objects, without which, what we call life, may more properly deserve the name of death !

Ver. 2. Lord, hear my voice ; let Thine ears be attentive to the voice of
my supplications.

WE see that he was not only in earnest, which comparatively few that pray are, but that his desires were vehement, and kindled into a flame, which is the case of yet fewer. The smoke of the incense will not rise to heaven, unless it be kindled on the altar; and hence it is that a great part of our prayers vanish like an empty sound, and are dissipated in the air. Nor is it wonderful, as we have elsewhere observed, that those petitions do not ascend, which hardly go out, which go not forth from the depth of the breast, and therefore they rise not on high, but are born and die upon the lips. How should they live, when they have no principle of life, neither the constancy of faith, nor the love of zeal? And if he who asks timorously, much more he that asks with cold indifference, may seem to bespeak a denial.

It is not the much speaking and the vain repetition condemned in the Gospel, to redouble the same words again and again, provided it be not from want of care and affection, but if, on the contrary, it proceeds from the vehemence and exuberance of it. The great Apostle tells us, that *he besought the Lord thrice;* and the Lord of the Apostle, and our Lord, prayed in the garden again and again, *speaking the same words.* He that pours out his words, inattentive to what he is about, seems to me to pray long, if he utters but two sentences; though his words be ever so few and well chosen, yet is he himself foolish and verbose. For what can be more foolish than the empty noise even of the best words, when they express nothing of the mind? But he who continues long in prayer, and urges the same petitions again and again, bursting out from the fervour of an influenced breast, he, truly, prays in a vivid and solid manner, and in a manner most acceptable to God; and what Fabius says of his orator, may with great propriety be applied to him, *Pectus est, quod disertum facit, et vis mentis:* It is the heart and the energy of the mind, that makes a man truly eloquent.

Hear me.] The great Author of nature and of all things does nothing in vain. He instituted not this law, and, if I may so express it, art of praying, as a vain and insignificant thing, but endows it with a wonderful efficacy for producing the greatest and happiest consequences. He would have it to be the key by which all the treasures of Heaven should be opened. He has constructed it as a powerful machine, by which we may, with easy and pleasant labour, remove from us the most dire and unhappy machinations of our enemy, and may with equal ease draw to ourselves what is most propitious and advantageous. Heaven and earth, and all the elements, obey and minister to the hands which are often lifted up to Heaven in earnest prayer. Yea, all works, and, which is yet more and greater, all the words of God obey it. Well known in the sacred Scriptures are the examples of Moses and Joshua, and that which James (*ch. v. v.* 17,) particularly mentions, of Elijah, whom he expressly calls ὁμοιοπαθής, *a man subject to like infirmities* with ourselves, that he might illustrate the admirable force of Prayer, by the common and human weakness of the person by whom it was offered. And that Christian legion under Antoninus is well known and justly celebrated, which, for the singular ardour and efficacy of its prayers, obtained the name of κεραυνοβόλος, *the thundering legion.*

It is true, indeed, that our desires and our hearts are open to God, when our tongues are entirely silent, and that He has paternal regard to all our concerns ; nor do we utter our petitions to Him, as if He were ignorant or negligent of our necessities and desires, for we well know that He sees and hears every thing, πάντ᾽ ἐφορᾷ καὶ πάντ᾽ ἐπακύει. It is also true, that His counsels are all fixed and immovable. But it can by no means be inferred from these premises, that the business of prayer is vain and needless. And if any one would represent these things as superseding prayer, surely he deceives himself, and by all his reasonings would make out nothing, unless it were to convict himself of a vast ingratitude to the Divine munificence, and a most shameful unworthiness of so excellent a gift.

Ought not this intercourse of Men with God by prayer, to be most reverently and gratefully received and cultivated by all, and numbered among the chief favours of the Divine nature, and the chief dignities of the human nature ? And truly this, as much as any thing that can be imagined, is a lamentable argument of the stupidity of man in this fallen state, that such an honour is so little regarded. Opportunities of conversing with nobles or princes of the earth are rare and short; and if a man of inferior station be admitted to such a favour, he glories in it, as if he were raised to Heaven; though they are but images made of the same clay with himself, and only set upon a basis a little higher than the rest. But the liberty of daily and free converse with the King of Heaven is neglected for every trifle, and indeed is counted as nothing, though His very aspect alone fills so many myriads of blessed spirits above with full and perpetual felicity.

Again, is it not most reasonable to acknowledge, by this spiritual sacrifice of prayer, His infinite power and goodness, and that most providential care by which He governs all human affairs? And when our very being and life depend upon Him, and all the comfort and happiness of life, how congruous is it to exhibit this sign and token of His holding us by the hand, and of our being borne up by Him! Again, what sweeter lenitive of all those miseries with which mortal life so continually abounds, can be invented, than this, to pour out all our care and trouble into His bosom, as that of a most faithful friend and affectionate father? Then does the good man lay himself down to sleep with sweet composure in the midst of waves and storms, when he has lulled all the cares and sorrows of his heart to sleep, by pouring out his prayer to God. And once more, how pleasant is it, that these benefits, which are of so great a value both on their own account and that of the Divine benignity from whence they come, should be delivered into our hands, marked, as it were, with this grateful inscription, *That they have been obtained by prayer!*

Hear, O Lord.] It is certain that the greater part of men, as they babble out vain, languid, and inefficacious prayers, most unworthy the ear of the blessed God, so they seem in some degree to set a just estimate upon them, neither hoping for any success from them, nor indeed seeming to be at all solicitous about it, but committing them to the wind, as vain words, which in truth they are. But far be it from a wise and pious man, that he should so foolishly and coldly trifle in so serious an affair : his prayer has a certain tendency and scope, at which he aims with assiduous and repeated desires, and doth not only pray that he may pray, but that he may obtain an answer ; and as he firmly believes that it may be obtained, so he firmly, and constantly, and eagerly urges his petition, that he may not flatter himself with an empty hope. For it cannot be that any pious and reasonable desire should be directed toward the throne of God in vain, since He has been pleased to assume it among His titles, that He is *a God hearing prayer*. And certainly, though the good man does not always obtain the very thing that he asks, yet pure and right petitions never ascend in vain ; but he who presents them, either obtains the thing he asks or receives, instead of what is pleasing, what is truly profitable, and instead of the things that he wishes for, those that are upon the whole the fittest and best, and that in the fittest and best time. Therefore, the vehemence of prayer is to be attempted with patience and long-suffering expectation. We often put ourselves, as it were, out of breath with the eagerness of speaking, and are presently weary, if we do not immediately obtain our request. Our prayers are often like those of the damsel who danced before Herod, *I will that thou presently give me* this or that. Whereas, he that prays fervently, urges this, that God would make haste to help him ; but in the mean time, as he believes, he will not make haste, nor will he suffer, if the delay be ever so long, that a speech like that of the impious king of Israel should escape him, *This evil is of the Lord, and why should I wait for the Lord any longer.* (2 Kings vi. 33.)

But Oh, how necessary is it, that souls worshipping so pure a God, should be purged from all the earthly dregs of impure affections ! Most true is that oracle of the Psalmist, *If I regard iniquity in my heart, the Lord will not hear my praye*r. The hands must be *washed in innocence,* before they can be lifted up to Him with acceptance. *Draw near to God,* says the Apostle James, *and he will draw near to you ;* but, in order to this, he subjoins, *Cleanse your hands, ye sinners, and* *purify your hearts, ye hypocrites,* or *ye double-minded,* who are the impurest of all. These things we only briefly suggest; but I beseech you, my dear charge, that ye embrace this Divine study, that you labour to obtain this sacred art, which is the best and only way of being enriched with all the most valuable blessings, even those of a celestial origin and tendency. O think, it is nothing unpleasant, nothing low and contemptible, to which you are now invited: on the contrary, there is nothing more delightful, nothing more sublime, than to meditate upon heavenly objects, to converse with God, and from thence to imbibe a contempt of this low and transitory world, to be raised above all perishing enjoyments, and to taste the prelibations of that celestial life itself.

But how accurately soever the precepts of this divine oratory may be delivered, none will effectually receive them, unless they are taught the skill by God himself. We must pray that we may be able to pray, and draw as it were from that supe-rior academy, that faculty of pure and pious speech which flies as with a swift, ready, and natural motion to Heaven from whence it came, and brings down with it the most precious gifts into the bosom of the person that utters it. And by the way, it is a most certain truth, that the greatest blessings are much more easily obtained from the great God who is so muni-ficent in his gifts, than others of a meaner nature; so that it were an argument of a low and abject mind, not to ask some-thing noble and excellent. *Covet earnestly the best gifts,* in this sense. If we ask only things of a low and trifling nature, unworthy such a Giver, He may answer as a prince did, " These are not royal gifts," οὐ βασίλικον τὸ δῶρον: but if we ask those things that are most precious and valuable, grace and glory, there will be no room to fear that denial, οὐκ ἀνθρώπινον τὸ λῆμμα, " It is not fit for a man to receive it." *If you who are evil know how to give good gifts to your children, how much more your heavenly Father!* Surely, He is goodness itself, and he gives only what is good; and the better those things are that we ask, the more freely and cheerfully does He bestow them. And you know Luke, repeating the same speech, expresses it by saying, *He shall give the Holy Spirit to them that ask it;* than which, nothing more noble can be either desired or bestowed.

Ver. 3. If Thou, Lord, shouldst mark iniquities, O Lord, who shall stand ?

AMONG all the virtues which are necessary to offer up our prayers with acceptance, none ascend with greater velocity, and rise higher, than that very humility which causes them, as it were, to descend the deepest of all; nor is there any more indubitable argument of humility, than a conscience which groans under the burden of its own sin and guilt amid all the abyss of calamities, crying especially from this depth. And thus we see the Psalmist, while he involves all other evils, how great soever they might be, under one common title, fixed upon this, to expatiate upon it at large, *If Thou, Lord, shouldst mark iniquities,* &c. Thus, if any one desires to mount more readily and more favourably from the depth of calamity, let him cry from this depth of profound humility, and plead a penitent sense of sin. For though of all imaginable depths, that of sin be the most remote from the most high and most holy God, yet, the depths of the humble soul, depressed under the weight of sin, is nearest of all to the deep bowels of Divine mercy; so that the words of the Psalmist may not improperly be accommodated to this, though in a sense something different from that which in their connexion they bear, *Deep calls unto deep,* and by an harmonious kind of *antiphony,* if I may be allowed the expression, they do most musically answer to each other.

One might have been ready, perhaps, to imagine from the vehemence with which he begins his address, and from his groanings as it were so thick and so short, that he was a somewhat bold petitioner, and that he had some confidence in himself, seeing that he presumed to knock so often and so loud at the door of Divine mercy. But what he here adds plainly shews that this was far from being the case: "*Hear me, O Lord, hear me;* and I urge the request because necessity presses urgently upon me. Not that I am, or judge myself to be one who can merit Thine assistance, but that I stand in such need of it, that if it be not granted me, I must perish. So far am I from being, or appearing to myself worthy of Thy help, that behold I am overwhelmed with sin more than with sorrows. It is free mercy that I invoke, and I beseech Thee, that in order to Thy hearing the voice of my prayer, Thou wouldst not hearken to the cry of my sins. Wash away the one, that Thou mayest graciously smile upon the other. For *if Thou, Lord, shouldst mark iniquity, who shall stand?*" Intimating that if he were drawn out of the other depths, yet if his sins continued unremitted, he could find no place on which to stand; yea, if it were possible for him in that case to flee away and hide himself, yet he would rather plunge himself into those depths again, and would rather be buried and lost in floods of the greatest calamities, than meet the more dreadful flame of the Divine anger and indignation.

But this humble acknowledgement of his own unworthiness and pollution, is so far from being inconsistent with the pious confidence of prayer, that it is not only congruous, but even congenial to it, and inseparable from it, so as to be most agreeable to that great King whom it addresses. Humility and contrition of heart are often thought by men to be the mark of a low and abject mind, and as such are often despised by them; but nothing is more honourable in the sight of God. "He," says Augustine *, "will bow down His ear, if thou dost not lift up thy neck." There is certainly no more efficacious method of supplicating and obtaining grace, than to do it, if I may so speak, *sub formâ pauperis*, confessing and pleading our poverty. He finds the most easy access in the court of Heaven, who meets the most frequent repulses on earth. Nay if I may so express myself, the Heavenly Court sits and resides in him.

---

* Inclinat aurem Deus, si tu non erigis cervicem.

The two chief temples and palaces of the great King, are that τρισάγιον, thrice holy place in the third heaven, and the humble and contrite heart upon earth. The best manner of praying, therefore, is that which is made up of faith, fear, and humility. By the equal libration of these wings, the soul mounts on high, while that of fear does not sink too low, nor that of confidence rise too high*. By these, we are daily and early to soar to God; and care must be taken that these wings of the soul be not dragged down by excess, nor scorched by lust, nor clogged and glued together, as it were, by covetousness, or any other terrene and viscid affection. But let us now a little more particularly see what this confession of the Prophet was.

If Thou, Lord, shouldst mark iniquity, O Lord, who shall stand? An uninstructed and incautious reader might, perhaps, imagine that the Psalmist was here seeking for refuge in a crowd, and desirous of sheltering himself under the common lot of human nature; at least, that he would endeavour to find some low excuse for himself, in the mention of its universal degeneracy. But the design of the Sacred Writer is far different from this. He confesses that whatever he, or any other person, on a transient and inattentive glance, may imagine of his innocence, yet when the eye of the mind is directed inward in a serious and fixed manner, then he sees the sum and bulk of his sins to be so immensely great, that he is even struck into astonishment by it; so that he finds himself beset, as it were, on every side with armed troops, which cut off all possibility of escape, otherwise than by flying to Divine mercy and to the freedom of pardoning grace. He perceives himself unable to bear the examination of an awakened conscience, exercising itself in impartial self-reflection; and arguing from thence, how much less he would be able to endure the penetrating eye and strict scrutiny of the Divine Justice, he cries out, in horror and trembling, under an apprehension of it, *If Thou, Lord, shouldst mark iniquities,* &c. He sees himself overwhelmed

---

* Oratio timida cœlum non attingit; temeraria resilit, et via suâ frangitur.—BERNARD.

with crimes, held at bay, as it were, by his sins on every side, which roar around him like so many savage creatures just ready to devour him.   And he that does not see this to be his own case, is either almost blind, or lives abroad, and never descends into his own breast.   Gross offences alone strike the eye of our fellow-creatures : but when we seriously consider that we have to do with an All-seeing Judge, who looks at once through every covering, and sees the most secret recesses of our hearts, who considers not only what may be concealed from men, but even what is concealed from ourselves, so as most clearly to discover every the least stain and speck of our inmost soul, and whose infinite holiness must also abhor it; is it possible that any one should be so infatuated as, in such a view, still to retain a false and foolish conceit of his own innocence? It cannot be doubted that they who daily and accurately survey themselves and their own hearts, though they may indeed escape many of those evils which the generality of mankind, who live as it were by chance, fall into, yet, in consequence of that very care and study, see so much the more clearly their own impurity, and contract a greater abhorrence of themselves, and a more reverential dread of the Divine judgments.   And it is certain that the holier any one is, the viler will he be in his own eyes; and I may also add, the viler he is in his own eyes, the more dear, precious, and honourable will he be in the sight of God.   But where is the heart, yea, I may say, where is the forehead of the generality of mankind, who boast of it as if it were some great matter to be free from the infamy of the most atrocious crimes ? Have they not continually the reward of this their egregious virtue ? " I have not committed murder and robbery—You are not gibbeted for the food of crows and ravens *." But they who bring the whole of their conduct, their deeds and their words, the glances of their eye and all the inward workings of their affections, and examine them by the pure and strait rule of the Divine Law, so as to perceive how many and how great errors attend every

* Furtum non feci—non pasces in cruce corvos.

most cautious day; and they who feel how wavering and weak
their faith is, how lukewarm at least, if not cold, their piety
and charity, how ardent their love of this world still continues,
how untamed the flesh, how unguarded the senses, how un-
bridled the affections, how attentive their hearts to trifles,
while in prayer so light and so wandering; they, I say, who
perceive and reflect on this, with what poignant grief, with what
overwhelming shame must they be seized, and how earnestly
and how justly will they cry out, *If Thou, Lord, shouldst
mark iniquity, who could stand?*

If Thou shouldst mark.] If Thou shouldst inquire and
scrutinize, and then shouldst retain and impute: (for the Hebrew word imports both :) if Thou shouldst inquire, Thou
wouldst find something of iniquity in the most righteous of
mankind; and when Thou hast found it, if Thou shouldst
retain it, and call him to an account for it, he could by no
means free himself of the charge, or expiate the crime. Inquiring, Thou wouldst easily find iniquity; but he by the
most diligent inquiry will be able to discover no ransom, and
therefore will be unable to stand, will have no place on which
to set his foot, but will fall by the irresistible judgments of
Thy law, and the sentence of Thy justice.

There have been great disputes one way and another, about
the merit of good works; but I truly think they who have
laboriously engaged in them, have been very idly, though very
eagerly employed about nothing, since the more sober of the
schoolmen themselves acknowledge there can be no such thing
as meriting from the blessed God, in the human, or to speak
more accurately, in any created nature whatsoever: nay, so
far from any possibility of merit, there can be no room for
reward any otherwise than of the sovereign pleasure and gracious kindness of God; and the more ancient writers, when
they use the word merit, mean nothing by it but a certain *cor-
relate* to that reward which God both promises and bestows of
mere grace and benignity. Otherwise, in order to constitute
what is properly called merit, many things must concur, which

no man in his senses will presume to attribute to human works, though ever so excellent; particularly that the thing done must not previously be matter of debt, and that it be entire, or our own act, unassisted by foreign aid; it must also be perfectly good, and it must bear an adequate proportion to the reward claimed in consequence of it. If all these things do not concur, the act cannot possibly amount to merit. Whereas I think no one will venture to assert that any one of these can take place in any human action whatever. But why should I enlarge here, when one single circumstance overthrows all those titles: the most righteous of mankind would not be able to stand, if his works were weighed in the balance of strict justice; how much less then could they deserve that immense glory which is now in question! Nor is this to be denied only concerning the unbeliever and the sinner, but concerning the righteous and pious believer, who is not only free from all the guilt of his former impenitence and rebellion, but endowed with the gift of the Spirit. The interrogation here expresses the most vehement negation, and signifies that no mortal, in whatever degree he is placed, if he be called to the strict examination of Divine Justice, without daily and repeated forgiveness, could be able to keep his standing, and much less could he arise to that glorious height. " That merit," says Bernard, " on which my hope relies, consists in these three things; the love of adoption, the truth of the promise, and the power of its performance *." This is the three-fold cord which cannot be broken.

Ver. 4. But there is forgiveness with Thee, that Thou mayst be feared.

THIS is the genuine method of Divine grace: it first demands a mind void of all confidence in itself, that so it may be filled with a pure and entire trust in God. For though that blind self-confidence which is so natural to us, be flatulent and empty,

* Meritum, cui innititur spes mea, tribus hisce constat, charitate adoptionis, veritate promissionis, et potestate redditionis.

yet while it possesses the mind, it is as it were blown up by it; and that swelling shakes off every thing more solid, and prevents its access even when it seems to surround us on every side. Yea, it seems that the riches and magnificence of Divine grace cannot with so much decency communicate itself, when it is, as it were, straitened by the receiver; for since it is so great as to be able to fill every thing, it requires a free and ample space in which to dilate itself. He who in the first original of the new-born world brought all things out of nothing, acts like Himself in the regeneration and restoration of mankind to holiness. The Holy Spirit finds nothing but *Tohu va Bohu*, nothing but what is *without form and void;* and whoever of mankind perceives and acknowledges this to be his case, may be assured that the Spirit of God already begins to move upon him to impregnate the face of the abyss; and then it is said concerning them, *Let there be light, and there is light,* even that light by which they see themselves unformed and dark, and destitute of every thing that is good. It is a great sign of a soul beginning to emerge from its misery, to give up every hope of emerging from it, except that one which arises from Free Mercy alone. And in this sense, it may truly be said, as it is by the Poet,

Una salus miseris nullam sperare salutem.
" The wretched find no safety but despair—"

i. e. in themselves, in their own righteousness or innocence, their own industry in fulfilling the Law, or any expiation they can make for the breach of it. And what the Apostle says of his own danger, may properly enough be applied to a confession of the soul, pressed under the burden of its own guilt. *We had received the sentence of death in ourselves, that we might not trust in ourselves, but in God who raises the dead.* (2 Cor. i. 9.) For the exclamation before us bears a remarkable resemblance to that expression, *If Thou, Lord, shouldst mark iniquity, O Lord, who could stand? But there is forgiveness with Thee, that Thou mayst be feared.* He who from justice found not any ground upon which he might stand, finds in mercy a place from which he may rise again. And this is the remedy of all our grief and distress, and in this sense we must be sick that we may recover, and must die that we may live. Grace exerts its power, where nature and art, and all the excellency and strength of human nature fail; nor does any soul celebrate the Divine benignity more signally than those who are snatched as it were out of the flames when they are beginning to seize them, and being rescued from the very jaws of hell, return to life again, and breathe in the land of the living.

That trite distinction of sin, into mortal and venial, which is so common among the schoolmen, is not only vain and destitute of all support from the word of God, but is indeed very faulty, and far from being itself venial, well deserves to be exploded as mortal, for that malignant influence which it has upon the morals of men. If the most open danger of the Divine displeasure, and of eternal death, cannot hinder the bold race of men from rushing on headlong to every crime *, and breaking all the barriers of duty which God has prescribed them, will it not add great licentiousness to all the crowd and tumult of headstrong desires, when some sins are said to be by their own nature, and in the whole kind of them, free from the condemning sentence of the Divine Law? But what I here oppose, is this; give me the holiest man upon earth, the man who above all others stands at the remotest distance, both in the affections of his mind and in the conduct of his life, from those sins which they acknowledge as mortal, will he not deeply feel his need of daily forgiveness, from the multiplied pollutions of his daily infirmities? He truly accounts no sin little, which is committed against the great and ever-blessed God, nor any pardon little, which he knows to proceed from His infinite grace. Nor will he promise himself the pardon of the least fault which he indulges: nor will he despair of obtaining a pardon of the greatest for which he is truly penitent. And this is the law of Grace. The poet said with a great

* Audax omnia perpeti,
Gens humana ruit per vetitum nefas.—HORACE.

deal of justice, " That no sinner is absolved by himself,"
because he is as it were turned informer against himself *.
Yet, in another sense, the sinner is absolved by that very self-
accusation, and sorrowing for his sins, is freed from the guilt
of them.   For it is not by any means to be conceived, that
any one can return into favour with God, unless he return to
God ; nor that any one can return to God, unless he renounce
every sin: which if he does, they are all entirely forgiven, and
those which he eagerly desires to cast behind his back, shall
never rise up to condemn him to his face, before the tribunal
of the Divine Justice.   This sentiment runs through all the
evangelical discourses of the Prophets, by which, as so many
heralds, they call a rebellious people to return to the allegiance
of God, their supreme King : *Return, ye backsliding children,
and I will heal your backslidings.*   Yea, the very Fountain
of Grace, the Lord of the Prophets, who is Himself the great
author and the sum of the Gospel doctrine, as soon as ever He
came forth to publish this grace, said, *Repent, for the kingdom of heaven is at hand.*   Nor can any mind that is not
fallen into utter madness and complete distraction, dream of a
pardon, how ample and glorious soever, to be imparted to a
sinner who will not repent or return.   Nor indeed can it be so
much as wished.   For how unworthy would it be of the Divine Majesty and Wisdom, to throw away such precious graces
on those who so obstinately despise them !   *But there is forgiveness with Thee,*—which is added with the utmost propriety ; with Him there is a treasure of mercy laid up, to be
imparted most freely and richly to every humble sinner that
applies to Him for it.   Nor is the dispensing of grace in this
way, at all inconsistent with the richness and freeness of it,
since the greatest sins, the most aggravated crimes, are absolutely forgiven, without any penalty or fine whatsoever imposed
upon the offender, yet on this most reasonable and happy condition, that they who are thus received into the Divine favour
should express their grateful acknowledgments for it, by love,

* Se judice nemo nocens absolvitur.

obedience, and sanctity of life. Neither is this forgiveness the less free and gracious, because Jesus Christ, as our surety and redeemer, has paid the price of it, having been appointed for and destined to this great and arduous work by the Father. For what does that great Father of mercies herein, but, in order to our complete discharge, by one certain and ever-to-be-admired way, satisfy Himself of His own, by fastening His only-begotten Son to the Cross? The repository of this treasure is opened, the whole price is poured out at once, that great price of redemption, more precious than all the treasures, than all the mines of gold in the world, or even the whole world itself. But they who anxiously debate the point, whether God could simply and absolutely pardon sin without any price, do but trifle; for whatever may be supposed concerning that, who is there that will deny that this way of the salvation of men which God has chosen, is so full of stupendous mystery, and so illustrious, if I may so speak, for that *trine*, and to us most benign *aspect* of Wisdom, Justice, and Mercy, that nothing can be thought of more worthy the Divine majesty, nothing sweeter, nothing more munificent with respect to unworthy man? So that, it will appear, Athanasius speaks very prudently when he says, " We ought not in this manner so much to consider the absolute power of God, as what is most advantageous to man, and what most worthy of the Divine Being *."

It was fit that our wise Creator should give us a law, and that law was both useful and pleasant to those who would carefully observe it; but when once violated, there would necessarily arise a fatal enmity between the law and the transgressors of it, an enmity which would continually become progressive, and gather new strength in the progress. But as for our obstinacy, what is it more than πρὸς κέντρα λακτίζειν, *to kick against the pricks?* The Law is inviolably safe in its own sanctity, dignity, and immortality; but we, by striving against it, what do we gain but iniquity, disgrace, and death?

---

* Οὐχ οὕτως; δεῖ ἐν τούτῳ πράγματι τὸ ἁπλῶς τοῦ θεοῦ δύνατον λογίζεσθαι, ὡς τὸ τοῖς ἀνθρώποις λυσιτελέστερον καὶ πάνυ γε ὁμῶς Θεοπρεπέστερον·

So that if there were no umpire to interpose, there would be no hope, but that the whole human kind should perish. But that blessed and efficacious Intercessor came from on high; and certainly He was Himself a Divine person, who could compose such a controversy, and who joining, by an indissoluble union, His infinitely better with our miserable and mortal nature, did so, by a most wonderful method, render to the Law all its accuracy of obedience, and to us, though guilty, impunity. And having thus made peace, that concord might afterwards continue and prevail, He animates all who partake of this blessed peace, by His own new, pure, and Divine Spirit, that they might not only be engaged sincerely to endeavour to observe diligently the sacred precepts of the Law, but might love them, and cordially embrace them. At the same time, He hath tempered the severity of the Law towards all those that are received into favour, that their diligent, pious, and affectionate observance of the Law, though not entirely complete, should by our indulgent Father be most graciously accepted, even as if it were perfect. And so, the honour of the Divine Legislator is secure among men, and his peace descends upon them; and this is what our text observes, *There is forgiveness with Thee, that Thou mayst be feared.*

It is well known, that *the fear of God* is commonly used in Scripture to signify, not only the whole of His worship, but all pious affections whatsoever, and consequently, the whole of true religion. And some translate the expression here, *That Thou mayst be reverently worshipped;* and it is thus used with the greatest propriety. I speak of that fear which is so far from denoting the servile, hostile dread and terror which some might think of, that, on the contrary, it entirely excludes it, being properly a reverence tempered with love. Yet I do not think that we are to exclude all dread of punishment and vindictive justice under the name of a servile and disingenuous fear; nay, I apprehend such a fear to be very necessary even to those who most ardently love, as long as they live in the flesh, in order to tame and rein in the petulancy of it; yea, love

itself places fear as a kind of bit and bridle to the flesh. Psal.
cxix. 128, *My flesh trembles for fear of Thee, and I am
afraid of Thy judgments.* Heb. xii. *ult., Let us serve God
with reverence and godly fear, for our God is a consuming
fire.* This is the fear which is called *the beginning of wisdom,* and which is marked with other very high titles of honour in the sacred Scriptures; without which, we can neither
conceive the beginning of Divine worship and true piety, nor
pursue the improvement of it.

As this holy and pure fear is the compendium and summary
of religion, so this pardon and free remission of sins is the
great foundation and support of that fear and religion. As the
whole human race is defiled with sin, the despair of pardon
would entirely drive us away from God, and, precluding all
ways of returning, would plunge the offender headlong into
eternal banishment and eternal hatred.

With Thee is forgiveness, that Thou mayst be feared;
that men may not dread Thee and flee Thee as an inexorable
judge and enemy, but may reverence, love, and serve Thee, as
a mild and gracious Lord, as a most merciful and loving Father. And this is that joyful message of the gospel, to which
sinners run, as soon as they hear and understand it, prostrat-
ing themselves with all humility at the feet of so mild a Lord
and so gracious a King. " For no one," as Ambrose says,
" will think of repenting, but he who hopes for indulgence *."
This merciful God calls back to his favour those who are as
it were flying from it, saying, *Return, ye apostates and rebels,
and I will pardon and heal your backslidings.* And they, as
if their bowels sounded to the unison note of Mercy with reci-
procal penitence and love, answer, *Behold we come unto Thee,
for Thou art Jehovah our God.* And this is what the great
Messenger and Author of our salvation preached and set
forth: *Repent,* says He, *for the kingdom of heaven is at
hand.* You are not now pursued by wrath and vengeance,
threatening utterly to extirpate you and cut you off, but *the*

* Nemo meditabitur pœnitentiam, nisi qui speraverit indulgentiam.

kingdom of heaven, the dispensation of love, mercy, and grace, opens its bosom to embrace you, and freely offers you the full pardon of all your former obstinacy and rebellion. Behold the compassionate Father meeting that prodigal son who had so basely run from him, while yet afar off on his return, and, instead of chiding and upbraiding him, burying not only all his sins, but even his very confession, as in a deluge of love, amidst the tenderest embraces, kisses, and tears. *Make me to hear*, says David, *the voice of joy and gladness, that the bones which Thou hast broken may rejoice.* By that lamentable fall, he had as it were dashed himself against the rock of Divine justice, so that all his bones were broken; but what a *voice of joy and gladness* is that which should restore full soundness and strength to bones which had thus been crushed and shattered to pieces! Surely, it is no other voice than that so often used by our Saviour in the gospel, *Son, be of good cheer; thy sins are forgiven thee.* That was the *grace*, softer than oil, sweeter than roses, *which flowed from His lips* into the sinner's wounds, and which being poured into the contrite heart, not only heals, but blesses it, yea, and marks it out for eternal blessedness. But alas! the greater part of sinners sleep in their misery, and though their distempers are mortal, feel them not. It is therefore no great wonder, that this grace, this precious, this invaluable remedy is despised by them. But Oh, how sweet is the voice of pardon to a soul groaning under the burden of sin!

—————— *Quale per æstum*
Dulcis aquæ saliente sitim restinguere rivo.
" Sweet as the living stream to summer thirst."

But, as one well expresses it, " He that has never known discomfort, knows not what consolation means. Men of this world, entangled in the cares of life and in its crimes, insensible of misery, attend not to mercy *." But if any who ima-

———————————————————————
* Quisquis autem desolationem non novit, nec consolationem agnoscere potest. Homines seculi negotiis et flagitiis implicati, dum miseriam non sentiunt, misericordiam non attendunt.—BERNARD.

gine themselves partakers of this forgiveness do not at the same time feel their hearts struck with a pious fear of the Divine Majesty, let them know, that their joys are all self-invented dreams, since it is for this very end that *there is forgiveness with God*, even *that He may be feared.*

In the remainder of this Psalm, the Author asserts his confidence in God, and labours to confirm and establish that of all true believers.

Ver. 5. I wait for the Lord, my soul doth wait, and in His word do I hope.

6. My soul waiteth for the Lord, more than they that watch for the morning; I say, more than they that watch for the morning.

7. Let Israel hope in the Lord, for with the Lord there is mercy, and with Him is plenteous redemption.

8. And He shall redeem Israel from all his iniquities.

I wait for the Lord.] With Thee is mercy. They who heartily believe this, are drawn by that sweet and amiable force of desire, to be partakers of it. And certainly, there is no true faith in the doctrine of salvation, unless it be attended with this magnetic force by which it draws the soul to God. One would think it were impossible, where this effect is not produced, that there should be so much as an historical faith; and surely it is contrary to, and inconsistent with the rational nature, to see so desirable and excellent a good laid down before us, and freely offered, without running most freely to embrace it with open arms, and an ardent impetuosity of soul.

The *faith*, therefore, of vulgar and merely nominal Christians, is quite *dead*, and deserves not the name of faith at all. I mean, that which is not sufficient to excite them earnestly to desire and expect that Divine grace in which they say they believe. True and lively faith is the eye of the inner man, which beholds an infinitely amiable God, the lucid and perpetual Fountain of grace, and is by the view immediately kindled into most fervent love. That Divine light which is sent from Heaven into the soul, is the vehicle of heat too, and, by its ardent rays, presently sets the heart on fire: the flame rises sublime, and bears all the affections of the mind with it, towards that consummate Beauty which it renders visible.

When a philosopher was asked, Why that which is fair attracts our love, he answered, " It is the question of a blind man," τύφλου ἐρώτημα. Well then might the Psalmist, when he had been contemplating the Divine goodness, represent himself as quite transported with its charms: *q. d.* It is nothing earthly, nothing mortal, that is the object of my wish ; my soul hangs on the Lord alone. *It thirsts for Thee,* and till it arrives at the enjoyment of Thee, it will still be waiting. Hasten, Lord, to support and comfort me, *for I am sick with love ; nor is there any thing in heaven or earth, beside Thee, O Lord,* which can satiate or delight this soul of mine, pierced through, as it were, with this sacred passion. And though I am, and feel myself to be, most unworthy of loving Thee, or of hoping ever to enjoy Thee, yet, my meanness and vileness, even when compared with Thine immense majesty and sublimity, do not so much deter me, as Thy boundless clemency and goodness, added to Thy truth ; while I have Thy word of promise before mine eyes for my support, sustain me and animate my courage. Therefore, while my love and desires are most ardent, I will nevertheless expect and wait with inward patience and perseverance ; and though a heart which loves like mine must find a delay grievous, yet unshaken hope shall alleviate that sickness of the soul. Just *as they that watch for the morning,* however they may be afflicted with the darkness and coldness of the night, are constantly supported with the assured hope that the dawn will come, and the day arise in all its glory.

Nor does the Psalmist envy others their share in those felicities which arise from love and hope ; on the contrary, with a cheerful and liberal mind, he invites all to this immense ocean of riches, which is not shut up, but free to all. *Let Israel hope in the Lord.* And lest the confluence of such vast numbers should suggest any fears of straitness and want, he confidently declares that there is wealth enough, and more than enough to supply all their necessities: *For with the Lord,* says he, *there is mercy, and with Him is plenteous redemption;* grace, rich and copious enough to support all sinners, and to forgive all sins; and all that apply to it shall infallibly find, that *He redeems Israel from all his iniquities.* The eye of faith is by no means evil, but bright and sparkling with unbounded charity: it wishes all good to all, and, above all, wishes them a beatific union with the Supreme and infinite Good. As in that kingdom of glory there is no malignity, no envy because there can be no straitness, but according to that emphatical saying of our blessed Saviour, *There are many mansions,*—there is boundless space, and the seats of pious souls are not marked out in any narrow boundaries, but in an ample court; so even in the previous kingdom and banquet of grace, our heavenly Father's house is magnificent, both on account of its amplitude, and the rich provision which it contains.

Let me beseech you, therefore, strictly to examine your own souls. Inquire what it is that they chiefly wish, hope, and desire; whether they give chase as it were to every painted fly; whether, *forsaking the Fountain of living waters,* they are digging for themselves *cisterns* of clay, and those leaky too, with great and unprofitable labour. O! wretched deceitfulness of every earthly hope, which mocks and deludes us so much the more in proportion to the extravagance of its promises! Blessed are they, and only they, who fix their eyes and their souls above, and say with the Psalmist, *Lord, I wait on Thee, my soul does wait, and in thy word do I trust;* and as elsewhere, *And now Lord what wait I for? My hope is in Thee.* Happy they who have quitted all those low desires and pursuits which are unworthy of a generous and immortal spirit, and have fixed their love on one; whose heart and hopes are set upon that One, in whom all things excellent meet and centre. A cheerful joy always shines on their face; nor do their cheeks glow with the shame of repulse and disappointment. While we are wandering hither and thither, in the

vicious and perplexed pursuit of flattering objects, what frequent lamentations, what fond complaints of delusive fortune,
and that tragical outcry, ἰὼ ἰὼ τραυμάτων ἐπωδύνων, of grievous
and painful wounds! What crowds of fears and cares divide
the mind and hurry it, now one way and now another! But
when we fix our hope and our heart on the only support, on
the only true and all-sufficient Good, all is safe, and the soul
treads firm while the whole globe trembles. Let external
things be borne this way or that, there is peace within; nor,
when all methods have been examined, can any other be found
for the establishment of the mind, than that it should lay all its
stress upon the one immovable and immutable Rock.

A FRAGMENT

ON PART OF

THE EIGHTH PSALM.

THAT which is needful and competent for us to know concerning God, He hath been pleased to reveal; and our most excellent and happy employment in this world, is, to learn it.

The third verse of this Psalm affords us clearly the doctrine of the creation. That part in the Psalmist's eye, *the heavens*, being the highest and largest of the visible world, surrounding and containing all the rest, is mentioned. *The work of Thy fingers,* importing the curious embellishments of them. *The moon and stars which Thou hast ordained,*—placed them in their orbits, and set them a going, and appointed them the periods and revolutions which they observe. So the same Hand hath fetched all other things out of the same nothing, as we have it in the beginning of this Book, *In the beginning God created,* &c. And it is therefore to be believed, because we find it there.

Can the Worker and His operation be discovered by strength of reason? Certainly they who have been of most confessed and famous ability in that way, have been partly of another mind; and we see it reduced to its truest principle, Heb. xi. 4: *By faith we understand that the worlds were framed by the word of God, so that things which are seen were not made of things which do appear.* Yet this we may boldly affirm, that there is not only nothing in sound reason crossing it, but that all the cavils alleged against it are most weak of themselves; and there be many things in nature that plead strongly for it, which we may, yea, ought to take notice of.

The continual turnings and changes of things, the passing of one thing to another, the destruction of some things, and the production of others, and the general decaying of all, the very heavens waxing old as a garment, declare that the whole frame is mutable and corruptible, and therefore not from eternity, but terminable in its beginning.

There is in this a very strong appearance of the beginning of the world and of time being according to the sacred history we have of it, and which faith receives; that there are not any records nor any memoirs or history of time, or things, produceable in the world that go higher up, no, nor any human histories that go near so high. Now, if there were thousands of ages before, whence is so deep a silence of what passed in them?

They who can conceive it, may take this reason into consideration, that if the world had been from eternity, then, certainly, the number of revolutions would be infinite: now, to that which is so, nothing can be added; so that it were impossible there could be any new days or years, &c. But, above all dispute, we believe it upon HIS word, who by His word gave all things a being. The whole Trinity, as, in all works without, They are together equally concerned, so in that first and great work of making all things.

As by the Father, so by the Word were all things made, and the Spirit moved upon the face of the deep: BARAH ELOHIM—Trinity in unity, *created*.

It is most vain to enquire why the world was not created sooner, *in tempore;* yea, it is nonsense, for the same question might equally be moved whensoever the world had been made, though it had lasted now millions of years; still there would have been an eternity preceding, wherein it *was not;* and Time itself was concreated. Nor was there any pre-existent unformed matter. It is a poor, shallow conceit, that any such thing was needful to the Almighty. It is even a monstrous, absurd conceit, that any such thing was possible, and destroys itself; for if this framed world could not have a being from eternity, much less frameless matter. So, of necessity, all things were made of nothing, received a being from the infinite Being, as the spring of all being. His hands stretched forth the Heavens, and laid the foundations of the earth. His fingers set them all in this sweet and admirable order, in a beautiful frame.

Now these expressions are suited to our reach, but the truth is, His finger and His whole hand are all one, and His hand is His word. (Psalm xxxiii. 6; Gen. i. 3.) And His word is His all-powerful and eternal will; that is the breath of His mouth, and His stretched-out arm. *He said*, i. e. He willed it, *and it was so.* When as yet there was no man nor angel, no heaven nor earth, no time nor being, but the alone blessed Trinity, eternally self-happy, upon the simple act of His absolute will came forth this whole frame, out of the womb of Omnipotence. And this is that certain truth which we believe under the name of *Creation.*

This supposed, it is very easy to conceive, yea, it is impossible to question it, that it had been as easy for THAT Power to have brought forth all in complete perfection at one instant, as to have divided the work into six days. And as we cannot think it easier, so we cannot but think it better, since He chose, yea because He chose it, as for that reason better. Well may His will be sufficient cause why that way of His production of all things was better, seeing that His will was purely the cause of the production and being of all.

But in part we may observe some advantage in that way, that He made so many days' work of it, and proceeded by degrees to bring it to perfection ; that we might the more clearly perceive, and more distinctly consider, the greatness and excelleney of the work, and the wise contrivance of it in its several parts and progress, which we could not so well comprehend altogether. Now, we consider Him as first framing one great mass, and then proceeding to beautify it, first with that which is indeed the first beautifier of all things, *light,* and then ordering the successive interchange of it with its opposite, darkness, that sets it off and makes its beauty appear the more, giving them their terms in *day* and *night;* then proportioning and dividing the rooms of the great house into upper and lower according to His model and design; then decorating them with rich furniture, and providing all kinds of store in great variety and abundance.   And thus, having first prepared all, having built, beautified, and replenished so stately a palace, then framed He the guest for whom He intended it, and whom He appointed to dwell in it.   *Then He said let* us *make man after Our image.*   Thus, the work of itself, and the order of it, and all the parts, carry on them HIS name who formed them.   How do His power, and wisdom, and goodness, appear in them! And yet how little do we see and observe it!   It shines bright in all His works, but we are blind; we look on *them,* and see *Him* not!   Oh, what a childish trifling thing is Man in all his ways, till he learns to remark God in all, and to have his soul upon all occasions musing and admiring, and sweetly losing itself in God, that immense sea of excellencies!   What a bottomless wonder is that Power, from which, by a simple act of will, issued forth all being!   This vast fabric, and all things in it, He willed they should be, and where never any thing was, *there* appeared, on a sudden, Heaven and Earth: the earth settled upon His word, so that it cannot be moved, and enriched with such a variety of plants, and flowers, and fruits growing forth, and springs and mines within the bowels of it; the seas fitted for navigation, together with the multitudes of creatures in it, small and great, and the impetuousness of it, yet confined and forced to roll in its channel, so that it cannot go forth; the small sands giving check to the great waters. Oh, how strong and large that Hand, which without help expands the heavens as a curtain!   Look up and see, consider their height and roundness, such a glorious canopy set with such sparkling diamonds; then think how swift their motion, and yet imperceivable to us, no motion here below comparable, and yet they seem not to stir at all.   And in all, their great Lord and ours so conspicuous!   And yet who looks on them with such an eye as to behold Him, as David here, *When I consider Thy heavens, the work,* &c.   He is admirable in all: the very lowest and smallest creatures have their wonders of Divine wisdom in their frame, more than we are able to think. *Magnus in minimis*—He is great in the least of His works. The smallest flies, how strange the fashioning of the organs of life and use in so little room!   The man who is still in search of wisdom will find a school and a lesson in all places, and see every where the greatness and goodness of his God.   If he walk forth in the evening, when this lower world is clothed with the dark mantle of night, yet still he can look upwards to the pavement of the throne of God, and think how glorious it is on the other side, when the moon and stars make this side, even in the night, so beautiful.   And this of David's, looks like a night meditation by the view of moon and stars.   *Thy heavens,* these Thy works so glorious, Thou, therefore, infinitely more glorious ; then can I not but increase in wonder, that, dwelling above these heavens, Thou regardest so poor a worm as man creeping on this earth.

What is man!   " Enosh," *weak, mortal man;* and " Ben-Adam," *the son of earth,* the earthly man.   David was taught so to look on his mean part and low condition, and on his better part, as follows, *ver.* **5,** as a sort of divinity being freely conferred upon him.

Thus men should learn to view themselves in this two-fold light.   *By the grace of God I am that I am,* saith St. Paul. Truly man is a wretched and proud creature, a bundle of vanity and vileness ; and yet he thinks himself some great matter while God is hid from him, and he is ignorant of HIS greatness.

No discourse or reasoning will humble the foolish heart of man : though he be even of the most worthless and basest sort of men, and hath in this condition nothing but what is despicable, yet he flatters himself with some fancy or other, some imagined advantage that swells him. He cannot be truly vile in his own eyes till they look up to the excellency of God, and return from that down upon himself. Then he is forced to bow, and fall low, and abhor himself in dust and ashes. Once he was wise and powerful, or some way deserving (as he thought) to be respected ; but now the glory and sublimity of God make him to be as nothing in his own eyes. *What is man !* David, a great and a good man, a king and a prophet, and yet a man, viewing and comparing himself with his own eyes, in respect of the great King of all the world, he cries out, *What is man, that Thou art mindful of him, and the son of man, that Thou visitest him ?* These words deserve to be considered. Thou mindest him in all these things, the works above him, even in the framing of these heavens, the moon and the stars, designing his good ; Thou makest all attend and serve him. It is not an empty *visiting* of him, but Thou seest all his necessities, and providest for them. He sets his heart on man, and all his delights are with the sons of men. (Prov. viii. 31.)

But, above all visits, that visit is to be remarked and admired, when the Eternal Word, by whom this world was made, came down, and was *made flesh ;* came from His glorious palace, from the bosom of the Father, to visit man in that deep and profound abyss of misery into which he was fallen, and to lift him out of it, and cleanse, and clothe, and dignify him ; came to make the slaves of Satan sons of God. And the Psalmist points at Christ, as the following words are applied, Heb. ii. 9. This is a descending indeed, which the angels are still prying into, looking into for the bottom, and cannot see it, for it hath none. Oh, that Christ should be disregarded, and His love slighted ! *He was in the world, and the world was made by Him, and the world knew him not.* (John i. 10.) He, the same who became like unto us, and united our flesh to His blessed deity, did give a being to all things, and *by Him all things consist.* (Colos. i. 17.)

Our Head and Saviour is no less than the Mighty Power, Creator of the world. He who is our flesh, He who had His arms wrapped up in swaddling clothes, and afterwards stretched upon the cross, He it was who stretched forth the heavens, and laid the foundation of the earth. The weight of the love of so great a King should press us low. And then, the persuasion of His almighty power assures us of complete redemption; for our salvation is in a sure and strong hand. We have a mighty Redeemer: *Thy Maker is thy husband, The Lord of Hosts is His name, and thy Redeemer, The Holy one of Israel, the God of the whole earth shall he be called.*

When I behold, says the Psalmist.

The carnal mind sees God in nothing, not even in spiritual things, His word and ordinances. The spiritual mind sees Him in every thing, even in natural things, in looking on the heavens and the earth, and all the creatures,—THY *heavens;* sees all in that notion, in their relation to God as His work, and in them His glory appearing; stands in awe, fearing to abuse His creatures and His favours to His dishonour. *The day is Thine, and the night also is Thine;* therefore ought not I to forget Thee through the day, nor in the night.

All that I use, and all that I have, is not mine, but Thine, and therefore all shall be *for* THEE; Thou art my aim and scope in all. Therefore God quarrels with His people, because they had forgotten this. Hos. ii. 8, &c. The most are strangers to these thoughts; they can eat, drink, and sleep, lie down and rise up, and pass one day after another, without one reverend or affectionate thought of God. They may give Him a formal good morrow, and then farewell for all the day long; they offer up their prayers, (as they speak,) and think they have done enough, and that afterwards their hearts may go whither they will, provided they escape grosser sins; they never check themselves in wandering from God all the day, if they fall not into some deep mire.

But even they who are somewhat more mindful of God, and see Him in His works, and consider them so as to observe Him in them, yet are very faulty in thinking of Him seldom, and in the slightness of such thoughts; they are not deep in them. We do not accustom ourselves to walk with God, to a continued and delightful converse with Him, to be still with Him. We can turn our eyes no way but He is visible and legible; and if He were our delight, and His name sweet to us, we should eye that more in every thing, than the things themselves.

The heart will readily espy and take hold of every small occasion of remembering that which it loves. That which carries any impression of the person on whom the affection is set is more looked upon on that side, and in that reference, than any other.

Certainly, were God the choice of our hearts, our natural use and enjoyment of things would not relish so much with us, nor take us up so much, as the viewing of Him in them all. In our affairs and our refreshments, in company and apart, in the beholding of heaven and earth, and all that is round about us, our eye would be most on HIM whom our soul loveth. What a pity, and what a shame is it, that we who profess ourselves to be His children, and even they who truly are so, should so little mind our Father and His greatness and glory, who is continually minding us and our good! It is indeed a double standing wonder in the world which he hath made, that God should take so much notice of Man, and Man should take so little notice of God.

Were this known truth of the creation wisely improved, we should find much in it that we commonly observe not, at least that we use not. This one thing, surely, it might gain upon us, to fear His displeasure who is so great, and so powerful, who hath the whole host of heaven, and the great army of all creatures, at His command.

What he commands they must obey; for He commanded and they were made: they have their being from His command. How quickly can He crush those who proudly rebel against Him! How easily can He shake them to pieces, the greatest and the strongest of them ! He poureth contempt upon princes. and, what are they ? Base potsherds of earth striving with their Maker, though somewhat bigger than others, yet as easily broken by His sceptre. O you that, after all warnings, dare walk on in your wicked ways, in drunkenness, or swearing, or any secret heart-wickedness, you know not who is your party ; the great God, the Former of all things. *Who would not fear Thee, O King of nations?* You who do not fear Him are in a fearful estate. Learn to know Him, and seek unto Him. *Seek the Lord, and ye shall live. Seek Him who hath the seven stars, and Orion; who turneth the shadow of death into the morning, and maketh the day dark with night.* Amos v. 8.

There is in this a strong ground of spiritual confidence, both for the Church's concernment and our own in every estate. This first work of God, rightly looked on, answers all the difficulties of the greatest works we can expect at His hands. Let Zion's enemies grow to their highest, they cannot rise so high as to be above this Almighty God, who framed the heavens. Let the Church be brought to the lowest depths of distress, yet cannot she fall so low, but His everlasting arm is long enough to reach her, and draw her out of it, which drew the whole world out of nothing. He doth therefore often represent, by His prophets, this very work as a certain evidence of His unbounded power. See Isa. xliii. 13 ; xliv. 24 ; and li. 12, 13. Jer. li. 19, 20. Zech. xii. 1. What task can be so great as to surcharge Him, who so easily brought forth a world ? What number can be too small, what instrument too weak in His hand, for the greatest work, who, without either working instrument or materials, built such a palace ?

Fear not, thou worm Jacob, and ye men of Israel—Why ? Wherefore have they no reason to fear, they being but as a worm ?—*I will help thee, saith the Lord. Behold, I will make thee a new sharp threshing instrument with teeth, and thou shalt thresh the mountains, and make the hills chaff.* (Isa. xli. 15.) A worm in thyself, but in My hand a threshing instrument. Weak Jacob and his strong God are too hard for all the world.

On the other side, what serve multitudes without Him ? All were originally nothing, and when HE wills, they prove as nothing. Severed from His concurrence, as ciphers, multiply them as you will, still they signify nothing. Ten thousand men, without God, are ten thousand *nothings*. We have had very late and very clear experiment of this, both to our grief and to our comfort. But both are forgotten, and indeed were never duly considered ; for if they had, they would not so soon, yea, they truly would never be forgotten by us. Well, however, it grieveth us, by reason of our own continuing hard in wickedness. Yet this I am sure of, that the strong arm of the Lord is engaged in this work : He hath already appeared in it, and therefore will not let it fall ; and though we were at a lower ebb than lately we were, yet should we rise again by His strength. Doubt it not, the enemies of our peace shall be ashamed, and God shall be yet more glorious in the world than ever, not only in our outward deliverance, but in that which is far richer and of higher beauty, the power and glory of His ordinances. He shall make things that *are not*, to *be*, by the mighty power of His mouth, and throughout the world Jesus Christ shall go on conquering. In His Name lies the reason of His prevailing. His name is called THE WORD OF GOD, that same Word by which all things were made ; there-fore, no opposite power is able to stand before Him. It is a great work to ruin great Babel, but His strength is enough for it. Mighty is the Lord God who judgeth. It is a great work to restore His Church, but here is power enough for it, and it is spoken of under the resemblance of the creation, Isa. li. 16.

For the estate of thy soul, thou that art thoughtful of that, what cause hast thou to suspect ? Is there any plea left for distrust in thy lowest condition ? Thou art about great things, and findest all, not only difficulties, but impossibilities to thee. Good is it that thou shouldst find it so, and be emptied of all fancy of self-strength. But then, look up above thyself, and all *created*, to a *creating* power. If thou canst not subdue thy lusts and iniquities, resolve to wrestle. Wrestle as thou wilt, still they are too hard for thee; but look to Him who came to destroy the works of Satan. Hath not thy Almighty Lord resolved to do it for thee? Thou findest nothing within but blindness and hardness, canst not repent, nor believe, nor think a right thought of God. It is so. But one word from Him can do all this, and make all those to subsist that now are not. Therefore, lay thyself before Him, as *dead*, yea, as very nothing. Say, Lord, I am nothing of all that which constitutes the being of a Christian in holiness, in faith, in love; but speak Thou the word, and I shall be a new creature, to Thy praise. There is nothing upon my soul but darkness; but art not Thou HE who said, "Let there be light, and there was light?" That word, again, Lord, say it to my soul, and it shall be so.—Think not to bring any thing with thee. Renovation is as absolute and free a work, as Creation. Could His creature oblige Him to make it, before it had a being? No more can it oblige Him to save it, or to give it a new being in Christ: all is free. The miracles of Christ, signs of power and goodness, are preludes to His greater work. It is most senseless to have a thought of preventing *Him*, from whom all good and all being flow. And this He does: *If any be in Christ, he is a new creature:* the word is, *all made new,* new delights and desires, and thoughts new—a new heaven and a new earth—a new soul and a new body; renewed in holiness, sanctified, and made conformable to Jesus Christ. And when thou findest some work of grace, which thou canst not wholly deny, and yet wantest that peace and joy which thou desirest, look to Him for that too. Thou findest it not from the word preached; yet, He can speak it, and even by that word wherein formerly thou didst not find it. It is *the fruit of the lips,* but it is so withal, that it is His creation: He only causes it to be. *I create the fruit of the lips, peace, peace.* (Isa. lvii. 19.) The Father wrought by the Son in the first creation, but in a new and special manner works by Him in this second creation. He is that *Word made flesh,* who is the life and the spring of all the grace and comfort thou desirest or readest of. Go to Him : He delights to let forth His mercies to thirsting souls; to revive them, to restore or turn them again, when they are in a swoon, as the word is, Psal. xxiii. The more thou puttest Him to it, the more shalt thou find His prevailing power, and the fulness of grace that dwells in Him, which is no more diminished by all He shews forth, than His Divine power was weakened by the framing of the world. There is no scarcity of spirit in Him; therefore, He proclaimed it as plural : *If any man thirst, let him come to me, and drink. He that believeth in me, out of his belly shall flow* RIVERS *of living water.*

How manifold are Thy works, O Lord! says the Psalmist, Psal. civ. 24; and then he adds that wherein all the variety of them agrees, the holding forth of His incomparable wisdom, from whose wisdom they are: *In wisdom Thou hast made them all.* As there are some of them more excellent than others, they certainly do, in a clearer and more eminent degree, glorify God. In the great fabric, that part which hath the place, the heavens, hath also this advantage; the greatness of the Great Architect appears somewhat more bright in them. Therefore are they singled out from the rest for that purpose, both here, *ver.* 3, and Psal. xix. *ver.* 1. But, beyond all the rest, and even beyond *them,* are the wisdom and goodness of God displayed in the framing of His reasonable creatures.

There are of them two stages; the one higher, the angels, the other lower, yet but *a little lower,* man; as here we have them together.

Thou hast made him a little lower than the angels,—of the nature of a spirit, a rational, intelligent spirit—

* * * * * * * * * * *

EXPOSITORY LECTURES

ON

PSALM XXXIX.*

LECTURE I.

Ver. 1. I said, I will take heed to my ways, that I sin not with my tongue; I will keep my mouth with a bridle, while the wicked is before me.

CERTAINLY it is a high dignity that is conferred upon man, that he may, as freely and frequently as he will, converse with Him who made him, the great King of Heaven and Earth. It is, indeed, a wonder, that God should honour poor creatures so much; but it is no less strange, that men having so great privileges, the most part of them do use them so little. Seldom do we come to Him in times of ease. And when we are spurred to it by afflictions and pains, commonly we try all other means rather than this, which is the alone true and unfailing comfort. But such as have learned this way of laying their pained head and heart in His bosom, they are truly happy, though in the world's language they be never so miserable.

This is the resource of this holy man in the time of his affliction, whatever it was,—prayer and tears, bemoaning himself before his God and Father, and that the more fervently, in that he finds his speaking to men so unprofitable; and therefore he refrains from it.

The Psalm consists of two parts, his silence to men, and his

---

* First published in the edition of the Expository Works, in two volumes, printed for David Wilson, Edinburgh, 1748.

speech to God; and both of them are set with such sweet notes of music, though they be sad, that they deserve well to be committed *To the Chief Musician.*

I said, I will take heed to my ways.] It was to himself that he said it; and it is impossible for any other to prove a good or a wise man, without much of this kind of speech to himself. It is one of the most excellent and distinguishing faculties of a reasonable creature; much beyond vocal speech, for in that some birds may imitate us; but neither bird nor beast have any thing of this kind of language, of reflecting or discoursing with itself. It is a wonderful brutality in the greatest part of men, who are so little conversant in this kind of speech, being framed and disposed for it, and which is not only of itself excellent, but of continual use and advantage; but it is a common evil among men, to go abroad, and out of themselves, which is a madness and a true distraction. It is true, a man hath need of a well set mind, when he speaks to himself; or otherwise, he may be worse company to himself than if he were with others. But he ought to endeavour to have a better with him, to call in God to his heart to dwell with him. If thus we did, we should find how sweet this were to speak to ourselves, by now and then intermixing our speech with discourses unto God. For want of this, the most part not only lose their time in vanity, in their converse abroad with others, but do carry in heaps of that vanity to the stock which is in their own hearts, and do converse with that in secret, which is the greatest and the deepest folly in the world.

Other solitary employments, as reading the disputes and controversies that are among men, are things not unuseful; yet all turns to waste, if we read not our own heart, and study that. This is the study of every holy man, and between this and the consideration of God, he spends his hours and endeavours. Some have recommended the reading of men more than books; but what is in the one, or in both of them, or all the world beside, without this? A man shall find himself out of his proper business, if he acquaint not himself with this, to speak much with God and with himself, concerning the ordering of his own ways.

It is true, it is necessary for some men, in some particular charges and stations, to regard the ways of others; and besides, something also there may be of a wise observing of others, to improve the good and the evil we see in them, to our own advantage, and the bettering of our own ways, looking on them to make the repercussion the stronger on ourselves; but except it be out of charity and wisdom, it flows either from uncharitable malice, or else a curious and vain spirit, to look much and narrowly into the ways of others, and to know the manner of living of persons about us, and so to know every thing but ourselves: like travellers, that are well seen in foreign and remote parts, but strangers in the affairs of their own country at home. The check that Christ gave to Peter is due to such, *What is that to thee? Follow thou me.* (John xxi. 22.) Look thou to thine own feet, that they be set in the right way. It is a strange thing, that men should lay out their diligence abroad to their loss, when their pains might be bestowed to their advantage nearer at hand, at home within themselves.

This that the Psalmist speaks here of, *taking heed to his ways,* as it imports his present diligence, so, also, it hath in it reflection on his ways past, and these two do mutually assist one another. He shall never regulate his ways before him, who has not wisely considered his ways past; for there is wisdom gathered from the observation of what is gone, to the choosing where to walk in time to come, to see where he is weakest, and lies exposed to the greatest hazard, and there to guard. Thus David expresses it in another Psalm, *I thought on my ways, and turned my feet unto Thy testimonies.* (Psal. cxix. 52.) And this should be done not only in the great change of one's first conversion from sin, but this double observance must be still continued every day: a man should be looking to his rule, and laying that rule to his way, and observing where the balk and nonconformity to the rule is, and renewing his repentance for that, and amending it the next day, that still the present day may be the better for yesterday's error.

And surely there is much need of this, if we consider how we are encompassed about with hazards, and snares, and a variety of temptations, and how little we have, either of strength to overcome, or of wisdom to avoid them, especially they being secretly set and unseen, (which makes them the more dangerous,) every where in the way in which we must walk, and even in those ways where we least think. Every where does the enemy of our souls lay traps and snares for us; in our table, in our bed, in our company, and alone. If the heart be earthly and carnal, there is the snare of riches and gains, or pleasures present, to think upon: and if it delight in spiritual things, that walk is not exempted neither; there are snares of doubtings, presumption, and pride. And in the converse of one Christian with another, where spiritual affection hath been stirred, it turns often to carnal passions; as the Apostle says of the Galatians, they *begin in the Spirit,* and *end in the flesh.* (Gal. iii. 3.)

This observing and watching, as it is needful, so it is a very delightful thing, though it will be hard and painful to the unexperienced. To have a man's actions and words continually curbed, so that he cannot speak or do what he would,— these are fetters and bonds; yet, to those that know it, it is a pleasure to gain experience, and to be more skilled in preventing the surprises of our enemies, and upon that to have something added to our own art, and to be more able to resist upon new occasions, and to find ourselves every day outstripping ourselves. That is the sweetest life in the world, for the soul to be dressing itself for the espousals of the Great King, putting on more of the ornaments and beauties of holiness. That is our glory, *to be made conformable to the image of God, and of Jesus Christ.* If an image had sense, it would desire nothing so much as to look on the original whence it received its name, and to become more and more like it; so it is the pleasure of renewed souls, to be looking on Him, and to be growing daily more like Him, whose living image they are, and to be fitting themselves for that day of glory wherein they shall be like him in the perfection they are capable of. And this makes death more pleasant than life to the Believer : that which seems so bitter to the most of men, is sweetened to them most wonderfully. The continual observance of a man's ways, the keeping a watch continually over them, this casts a light upon the dark passage of death, which is at the end of that walk, and conveys him through to the fulness of life. So that the man who observes himself and his ways through life, hath little to do in examining them when he comes to die. It is a piece of strange folly, that we defer the whole, or a great part of our day's work, to the twilight of the evening, and are so cruel to ourselves, as to keep the great load of our life for a few hours or days, and for a pained, sickly body. He who makes it his daily work to observe his ways, is not astonished when that day comes, which long before was familiar to him every day.

That I sin not with my tongue.] It is the Wise Man's advice, *Keep thy heart with all diligence,* or, *above all keeping ;* and he gives the satisfying reason of it, *For out of it are the issues of life.* (Prov. iv. 23.) Such as the spring is, so will the streams be. The heart is the spring whence all the natural life and vital spirits flow through the body ; and, in the Scripture sense, it is the spring of all our actions and conversation ; for it sends out emissaries through all, through the eye, the hand, and all the senses and organs of the body, but through none more constantly and abundantly than the tongue ; and therefore Solomon, after these words, immediately adds, *Put away from thee a froward mouth, and perverse lips put far from thee.* The current of the heart runs in that channel ; for it is the organ of societies, and is commonly employed in all the converse of men. And we can still, when all the other members are useless, use our tongues in regretting their unfitness for their offices ; as sick and old persons are wont to do. Thus David here, as it seems, under some bodily sickness, labours to refrain his tongue, and lest it should prove too strong for him, he puts a curb upon it: though it did not free him from inward frettings of his heart, yet he lays a restraint upon his tongue, to stay the progress of sin, that grows in vigour by going out, and produces and begets sin of the same kind in the hearts and mouths of others, when it passes from the heart to the tongue. The Apostle James does amply and excellently teach the great importance of ordering the tongue in all a Christian's life. But we are ever learning and never taught. We hear how excellent a guard this is to our lives, to keep a watch over our tongue; but I fear, few of us gain the real advantage of this rule. We are far from the serious thoughts that a religious person had of this scripture, who, when he heard it read, withdrew himself for many years to the study of this precept, and made very good proficiency in it.

In all the disorders of the world, the tongue hath a great share. To let pass those irruptions of infernal furies, blasphemies and cursing, lying and uncharitable speeches, how much have we to account for unprofitable talking! It is a lamentable thing, that there is nothing, for the most part, in common entertainments and societies of men together, but refuse and trash; as if their tongues were given them for no other end than to be their shame, by discovering their folly and weakness! So, likewise that of impatient speech in trouble and affliction, which certainly springs from an unmortified spirit, that hath learned nothing of that great lesson of submission to the will of God. But for all the disorders of the tongue, the remedy must begin at the heart. Purge the fountain, and then the streams will be clean. *Keep thy heart,* and then it will be easy to keep thy *tongue.* It is a great help in the quality of speech, to abate in the quantity; not to speak rashly, but to ponder what we are going to say. *Set a watch before the door of thy lips.* (Psal. cxli. 3.) He bids us not build it up like a stone wall, that nothing may go in or come out, but he speaks of a door, which may be sometimes open, oft-times shut, but withal to have a watch standing before it continually. A Christian must labour to have his speech as contracted as can be, in the things of this earth ; and even in Divine things, our words should be few and wary. In speaking of the greatest things, it is a great point of wisdom, not to speak much. That is David's resolution, to *keep silence*, especially *before the wicked*, who came to visit him, probably, when he was sick : while they were there, he *held a watch before his lips*, to speak nothing of God's hand on him, lest they should have mistaken him. And a man may have some thoughts of Divine things, that it were very impertinent to speak out indifferently to all sorts even of good persons. This is a talkative age, and people contract a faculty to speak much in matters of religion, though their words for the most part be only the productions of their own brain ; little of these things in their hearts. Surely, speeches of this kind are as bad as any, when holy things are spoken of with a notional freedom, where there is nothing but empty words. They who take themselves to solitude, choose the best and easiest part, if they have a warrant so to do ; for this world is a tempestuous sea, in which there are many rocks, and a great difficulty it is to steer this little helm aright amidst them. However, the Apostle James makes it a great character of a Christian's-perfection, *If any man offend not in word, the same is a perfect man.* (Jam. iii. 2.) But where is that man ? Seeing we find men generally, and most of all ourselves, so far from this, it cannot choose but work this, to stir up ardent desires in us to be removed to that blessed society where there shall be never a word amiss, nor a word too much.

LECTURE II.

Ver. 2. I was dumb with silence; I held my peace even from good;
and my sorrow was stirred.

Ver. 3. My heart was hot within me; while I was musing, the fire
burned: then spake I with my tongue.

IT is a very useful and profitable thing, to observe the motions
and deportments of the spirits of wise and holy men, in all the
various postures and conditions they are in. It is for that
purpose they are drawn out to us in the Scriptures. There
are some graces that are more proper, and come more in action,
in times of ease and prosperity, such as temperance, moderation of mind, humility, and compassion. Others are more
proper for times of distress, as faith, fortitude, patience, and
resignation. It is very expedient, if not necessary, that affliction have its turns, and frequently, in the lives of the children
of God; it is the tempest that gives evidence of the pilot's
skill. And as the Lord delighteth in all His works, looks on
the frame and conduct of all things with pleasure, so He is
delighted to look on this part, on this low sea of troubles, to
see His champions meet with hard and pressing trials, such as
sometimes do not only make them feel them, but do often
make the conflict dubious to them, so that they seem to be
almost foiled, yet do they acquit themselves, and come off
with honour. It is not the excellency of grace to be insensible
in trouble, (as some philosophers would have their wise men,)
but to overcome and be victorious.

Among the rest of this holy man's troubles, this was one,
that the wicked did reproach him. This is a sharp arrow, that
flies thick in the world. It is one of the sharpest stings of
poverty, that, as it is pinched with wants at home, so it is met
with scorn abroad. It is reckoned among the sharp sufferings
of holy men, Heb. xi. 36, that they suffered *bitter mockings*.
Now, men commonly return these in the same kind, that is, by
the tongue, whereof David is here aware. He refrains himself

even *from good;* not only from his just defence, but even from good and pious discourses. We do so easily exceed in our words, that it is better sometimes to be wholly silent, than to speak that which is good : for our good borders so near upon evil, and so easy is the transition from the one to the other, that though we begin to speak of God and good things with a good intention, yet, how quickly run we into another channel ! Passion and self having stolen in, turn us quite from the first design of our speech. And this chiefly in disputes and debates about religion, wherein, though we begin with zeal for God, yet, oft-times in the end, we testify nothing but our own passion ; and sometimes we do lie one against another in defence of what we call the truth.

It cannot be denied, that to a holy heart, it is a great violence to be shut up altogether from the speech of God. It burns within, especially in the time of affliction, as was the case of Jeremiah : *Then I said, I will not make mention of Him, nor speak any more in His name : but His word was in my heart as a burning fire shut up in my bones, and I was weary with forbearing, and could not stay.* (Jer. xx. 9.) So is it here with David ; therefore he breaks out : the fire burns upward, and he speaks to God.

Let this be our way, when we cannot find ease among men, to seek it in God. He knows the language of His children, and will not mistake it ; yea, where there may be somewhat of weakness and distemper, He will bear with it. In all your distresses, in all your moanings, go to Him, pour out your tears to Him. Not only fire, but even water, where it wants a vent, will break upward. These tears drop not in our own lap, but they fall on His, and He hath a bottle to put them in: if ye empty them there, they shall return in wine of strong consolation.

Ver. 4. Now David's request is, *Lord, make me to know mine end, and the measure of my days, what it is : that I may know how frail I am.* In which he does not desire a response from God about the day of his death, but instruction

concerning the frailty and shortness of his life. But did not
David know this? Yes, he knew it, and yet he desires to
know it. It is very fit we should ask of God that He would
make us to know the things that we do know; I mean, that what
we know emptily and barely, we may know spiritually and
fruitfully, and if there be any measure of this knowledge,
that it may increase and grow more. We know that we are
sinners, but that knowledge commonly produces nothing but
cold, dry, and senseless confusion: but the right knowledge
of sin would prick our hearts, and cause us to pour them
out before the Lord. We know that 'Jesus is the Saviour
of sinners; it were fit to pray that we might know more of
Him, so much of Him as might make us shape and fashion
our hearts to His likeness. We know we must die, and
that it is no long course to the utmost period of life; yet
our hearts are little instructed by this knowledge. How
great need have we to pray this prayer with David here,
or that with Moses, *Teach us to number our days, that we
may apply our hearts unto wisdom.* (Psal. xc. 12.) Did we
indeed know and consider how quickly we shall pass from
hence, it were not possible for us to cleave so fast to the
things of this life, and, as foolish children, to wade in ditches,
and fill our laps with mire and dirt; to prefer base earth and
flesh to immortality and glory.

That I may know how frail I am.] Most part of Men are
foolish, inconsiderate creatures, *like unto the very beasts that
perish,* (Psal. xlix. 12,) only they are capable of greater vanity
and misery; but, in as irrational a way, they toil on and hurry
themselves in a multitude of business, by multitudes of desires,
fears, and hopes, and know not whither all tends. But one well
advised thought of this one thing would temper them in their
hottest pursuits, if they would but think how frail they are,
now vain a passing thing, not only these their particular desires and projects are, but they themselves, and their whole
life. David prays that he may know *his end,* and his prayer
is answered; *Behold, Thou hast made my days as a hand-*

breadth. **If** we were more in requests of this kind, we should receive more speedy and certain answers. **If** this be our request, to know ourselves, our frailties and vanity, we shall know that our *days are few and evil,* know both the brevity and vanity of them.

Ver. 5. *Thou hast measured out my days as a hand-breadth.*] That is one of the shortest measures. We need not long lines to measure our lives by: each one carries a measure about with him, his own hand; that is the longest and fullest measure. It is not so much as a span: that might possibly have been the measure of old age in the infancy of the world, but now it is contracted to a hand-breadth, and that is the longest. But how many fall short of that! Many attain not to a finger-breadth: multitudes pass from the womb to the grave; and how many end their course within the compass of childhood!

Whether we take this hand-breadth for the fourscore years, that is ordinarily the utmost extent of man's life in our days, or for the four periods of our age, in which we use to distinguish it, childhood, youth, manhood, and old age, there are great numbers we see take up their lodging ere they come near the last of any of these, and few attain to the outmost border of them. All of us are but a hand-breadth from death, and not so much; for many of us have passed a great part of that hand-breadth already, and we know not how little of it is behind. We use commonly to divide our lives by years, months, weeks, and days, but it is all but one day; there is the morning, noon, afternoon, and evening. *Man is as the grass that springs in the morning.* (Psal. xc. 5.) As for all the days that are passed of our life, death hath them rather than we, and they are already in its possession. When we look back on them, they appear but as a shadow or dream; and if they be so to us, how much more short are they in the sight of God! So says David here: When I look on Thee and Thy eternity, *mine age is as nothing before Thee.* What is our life, being compared to God, before whom *a thousand years are but as one day!* And it is less,—*like yesterday when it is past,*

2 O 2

is but a thought! The whole duration of the world is but a
point in respect to eternity; and how small a point is the life
of man, even in comparison with that!

The brevity of our life is a very useful consideration. From
it we may learn patience under all our crosses and troubles;
they may be shorter than life, but they can be no longer.
There are few whom an affliction hath lain on all the days of
their life; but though that were the case, yet a little time, and
how quickly is it done! While thou art asleep there is a
cessation of thy trouble; and when awake, bemoaning and
weeping for it, and for sin that is the cause of it, in the mean
time it is sliding away. In all the bitter blasts that blow on
thy face, thou who art a Christian indeed, mayst comfort thyself in the thought of the good lodging that is before thee.
To others, it were the greatest comfort, that their afflictions in
this life were lengthened out to eternity.

Likewise, this may teach us temperance in those things that
are called *the good things of this world.* Though a man had
a lease of all the fine things the world can afford for his whole
life, (which yet never any man that I know of had,) what is
it? A feigned dream of an hour long. None of those things
that it now takes so much delight in, will accompany the cold
lump of clay to the grave. Within a little while, those that are
married and rejoice, shall be *as if they rejoiced not,* (1 Cor.
vii. 29,) as if they never had done it; and since they shall be
so quickly, a wise man makes little difference, in these things,
betwixt their presence and their absence.

This thought should also teach us diligence in our business.
We have a short day, and much to do; it were fit to be up
early; to *remember thy Creator in the days of thy youth.*
And ye that are come to riper years, he advised to lay hold on
what remains; ye know not how little it is.

The more you fill yourselves with the things of this life, the
less desire you will have after *those rivers of pleasure that are
at God's right hand.* These shall never run dry, but all those
other things shall be dried up within a little space; at the

furthest, when old age and death come, if not sooner. And on the other side, the more we deny ourselves the sensual enjoyments of the present world, we grow the liker to that Divine estate, and are made the surer of it. And I am sure, all will grant that this is a very gainful exchange.

Verily, every man at his best estate is altogether vanity.] It is no wonder that the generality of men are strangers to God, for they are strangers to themselves. The cure of both these evils is from the same Hand. He alone can teach us what He is, and what we are ourselves. All know and see that their life is short, and themselves vanity ; but this holy man thought it needful to ask the true notion of it from above, and he receives the measure of his life, *Even a hand-breadth.* There is a common imposture among people, to read their fortunes by their hands; but this is true palmistry indeed, to read the shortness of our life upon the palms of our hands.

Our days are not only few, but we ourselves are *vanity.* *Every man,* even a godly man, as he is a partaker of this life, is not exempted from vanity : nay, he knows it better than any other ; but this thought comforts him, that he hath begun that life which is above and beyond all vanity. The words are weighty and full. It is not a problem, or a doubtful thing, but, *surely every man is vanity.* I may call it a definition, and so it is proved, Psal. cxliv. 2, 3. *What is man? He is like to vanity, and his days are as a shadow that passes away.* His days do not only soon decline and pass away as a shadow, but also they are *like vanity.* While he appears to be something, he is nothing but the figure and picture of vanity. He is like it, not the copy of it, but rather the original and idea of it, for he hath derived vanity to the whole creation : he hath *subjected the creatures* to it, and hath thrown such a load of it upon them, that they groan under it ; and so, vanity agrees to him properly, constantly, and universally. *Every man,* and that *at his best estate,* or, as the word is, in his settled and fixed state. Set him as sure and as high as you will, yet he is not above that; he carries it about with him as he does his nature.

This is a very profitable truth to think on, though some kind of hearers, even of the better sort, would judge it more profitable to hear of cases of conscience. But this is a great case of conscience, to consider it well, and carry the impression of it home with you on your hearts,—the extreme vanity of ourselves, that we are nothing but vanity. And the note that is added here, *Selah*, if it import any thing to the sense and confirmation of what it is added to, it agrees well to this ; but if it be only a musical note, to direct, as some think, the elevation, or, according to others, the falling of the voice, it fits the sense very well. For you have man here lifted up and cast down again : lifted up—*Man at his best estate*, and from that thrown down to nothing—even in that estate, *Altogether vanity*. What is that ? It is, as the word signifies, *an earthly vapour*, and it is generally used to signify things of the least and meanest use, the most empty, airy things. So idols are often called by that name; they are nothing in respect of what is attributed to them by the children of men. And such a thing is man ; he seems to be something, and is, indeed, nothing : as it is Psal. lxii. 9. *Men of low degree are vanity*,—possibly that may be granted for a truth, and they pass for such, but he adds— *Men of high degree are a lie:* they promise something, and look bigger like, but they are nothing more, except this, *a lie ;* and the greater they are, the louder the lie.

This it is, then, that we should acquaint ourselves with ; that man in this present life, in all the high advantages of it, is an empty, feeble, fading thing. If we look to the frame of man's body, what is he but a muddy wall, *a house of clay, whose foundation is in the dust?* If we look within, there is nothing there but a sink and heap of filth. The body of man is not only subject to fevers, hectics, *&c.*, that make the wall to moulder down, but, take him in his health and strength, what is he but a bag of rottenness ? And why should he take delight in his beauty, which is but the appearance of a thing, which a fit of sickness will so easily deface, or the running of a few years spoil the fashion of? A great heat or a cold puts that frame into disorder; a few days' sickness lays him in the dust, or much blood gathered within, gathers fevers and pleurisies, and so destroys that life it should maintain; or a fly, or a crumb of bread, may stop his breath, and so end his days.

If we consider men in societies, in cities and towns, often hath the overflowing scourge of famine and pestilence laid them waste; and from these they cannot secure themselves in their greatest plenty and health, but they come on a sudden and unlooked for. If we could see all the parts and persons in a great city at once, how many woes and miseries should we behold there! How many either want bread, or scarcely have it by hard labour! Then to hear the groans of dying persons, and the sighs and weepings of those about them,—how many of these things are within the walls of great cities at all times! Great palaces cannot keep out death, but it breaks through and enters there, and thither, oft-times, the most painful and shameful diseases that are incident to the sons of men, resort. Death by vermin, hath seized on some of the greatest of kings that have ever been in the world. If we look on generals who have commanded the greatest armies, they carry about with them poor frail bodies, as well as others: they may be killed with one small wound, as well as the meanest soldier; and a few days' intemperance hath taken some of the most gallant and courageous of them away in the midst of their success. And, sure I am, he who believes and considers the life to come, and looks on this, and sees what it is, makes little account of those things that have so big a sound in the world: the revolutions of states, crowns, kingdoms, cities, towns, how poor inconsiderable things are they being compared with eternity! And he that looks not on them as such, is a *fool*.

LECTURE III.

Ver. 6.   Surely every man walketh in a vain shew; surely they are disquieted in vain: he heapeth up riches, and knoweth not who shall
gather them.

THERE is a part of our hand-breadth past since we last left
this place, and, as we are saying this, we are wearing out some
portion of the rest of it.   It were well if we considered this, so
as to make a better improvement of what remains, than, I
believe we shall find, upon examining of our ways, we have
made of what is past.   Let us see if we can gain the space of
an hour, that we may be excited to a better management of the
latter part of our time, than we have made of the former.

We are all, I think, convinced of the vanity of man, as to
his outside, that he is a feeble, weak, poor creature; but we may
have hope of somewhat better in that which is the man indeed,
his mind and intellectual part.   It is true, that that was originally excellent, and that there is somewhat of a radical excelleney still in the soul of man; yet, it is so desperately degenerate,
that, naturally, *Man*, even in that consideration, *is altogether
vanity*, in all the pieces of him: his mind is but a heap of
vanity, nothing there but ignorance, folly, and disorder.   And
if we think not so, we are the more foolish and ignorant.   That
which passes with great pomp, under the title of *learning* and
science, is commonly nothing else than a rhapsody of words and
empty terms, which have nothing in them to make known the
internal nature of things.

But even those persons who have the improvement of learning and education, who understand the model and government
of affairs, who see their defects, and entertain themselves with
various shapes of amending and reforming them, even in them,
we shall find nothing but a sadder and more serious vanity.   It
is a tormenting and vexing thing for men to promise to themselves great reformations and bettering of things.   That thought
usually deludes the wisest of men: they must at length come

to that conclusion of Solomon, after much labour to little purpose, that *crooked things cannot be made straight.* Eccles.
i. 15. Yea, many things grow worse by labouring to rectify
them; therefore he adds, ver. 18, *And he that increaseth
knowledge, increaseth sorrow.*

As for knowledge in religion, we see the greatest part of the
world lying in gross darkness; and even amongst Christians,
how much ignorance of these things: which appears in this,
that there are such swarms and productions of debates and
contentions, that they are grown past number. And each party
is confident that truth is on his side; and ordinarily the most
ignorant and erroneous are the most confident and most impe-
rious in their determinations. Surely it were a great part of
our wisdom to free our spirits from these empty, fruitless
janglings that abound in the Christian world.

It were an endless toil to go through all degrees, professions,
and employments of men in the world: we may go through
nations, countries, crafts, schools, colleges, courts, camps, councils of state, and parliaments, and find nothing in all these but
still more of this trouble and vexation in a finer dress and
fashion, *altogether vanity !*

Every man walketh in a vain shew.] His walk is nothing
but a going on in continual vanity, adding a new stock of vanity,
of his own coining, to what he has already within, and vexation
of spirit woven all along in with it. He walks in an image, as
the word is; converses with things of no reality, and which
have no solidity in them, and he himself has as little. He
himself is a walking image, in the midst of these images. They
who are taken with the conceit of images and pictures, that is
an emblem of their own life, and of all other men's also.
Every man's fancy is to himself a gallery of pictures, and there
he walks up and down, and considers not how vain these are,
and how vain a thing he himself is.

My brethren, they are happy persons, (but few are they in
number,) who are truly weaned from all those images and fan-

cies the world doats so much upon. If many of the children
of men would turn their own thoughts backwards in the evening but of one day, what would they find for the most part,
but that they have been walking among these pictures, and
passing from one vanity to another, and back again to and fro,
to as little purpose as the running up and down of children at
their play! He who runs after honour, pleasure, popular
esteem—what do you think? Does not that man walk in an
image, pursuing after that which hath no other being than
what the opinion and fancy of men give to it?—especially the
last, which is a thing so fluctuating, uncertain, and inconstant,
that while he hath it, he hath nothing? The other image that
man follows and worships, is that in the text, that wretched
madness of *heaping up riches*. This is the great foolishness
and disease especially of old age, that the less way a man has
to go, he makes the greater provision for it. When the hands
are stiff, and fit for no other labour, they are fitted and composed for scraping together. But for what end dost thou take
all this pains? If for thyself, a little sober care will do thy
turn, if thy desires be sober; and if not so, thy diligence were
better bestowed in impairing and diminishing of these; that is
the easier way a great deal. And if it be for others, why dost
thou take a certain unease to thyself, for the uncertain ease of
others? And who these are thou dost not know; may be,
such as thou didst never intend them for. It were good we
used more easy and undistracting diligence for the increasing
of those treasures which we cannot deny are far better, and
whosoever hath them may abound therein with increase; he
knows well for whom he gathers them; he himself shall possess
them through all eternity.

If there were not a hope beyond this life, there were reason
for that passionate word in Psal. lxxxix. 47; *Why hast Thou
made all men in vain?* To what purpose were it for poor
wretched man to have been all his days tossed upon the waves
of vanity, and then to lie down in the grave, and be no more

heard of? But it is not so: he is made capable of a noble and blessed life beyond this; and our forgetfulness of this is the cause of all our misery and vanity here.

It is a great folly to complain of the shortness of our life, and yet to lavish it out so prodigally on trifles and shadows. If it were well managed, it would be sufficient for all we have to do. The only way to live indeed, is to be doing service to God and good to men: this is to live much in a little time. But when we play the fool in mispending our time, it may be indeed a sad thought to us, when we find it gone, and we are benighted in the dark, so far from our home. But those that have their souls untied from this world and knit to God, they need not complain of the shortness of it, having laid hold on eternal life. For this life is flying away, there is no laying hold on it; and it is no matter how soon it go away; the sooner the better, for to such persons it seems rather to go too slow.

LECTURE IV.

Ver. 7. And now, Lord, what wait I for? My hope is in Thee.

To entertain the minds of men with thoughts of their own vanity, and discourses of their own misery, seems to be sad and unpleasant; but certainly it is not unprofitable, unless it be our own choice to make it so, and that were the greatest vanity and misery of all. Indeed, if there were no help for this *sore evil*, then the common shift were not to be blamed, yea it were to be chosen as the only help in such a desperate case, not to think on it, to forget our misery, and to divert our thoughts from it by all possible means, rather than to increase it, and torment ourselves, by insisting and poring on it; and in that case shallow minds would have the advantage, that could not converse with these sad thoughts, for to *increase this knowledge* were but *to increase sorrow*. But far be it from us thus to determine. There is a hope which is a help to this

evil, and this is what this holy man fixes on: *And now, Lord,*
my hope is in Thee.   Otherwise, it were strange that the most
excellent piece of the visible creation should be made subject
to the most incurable unhappiness; to feel misery which he
cannot shun, and to be tormented with desires that cannot be
satisfied.   But there is some better expectation for the souls of
men, and it is no other than HIMSELF who made them.

The wisest natural men have discoursed of man's vanity,
and passionately bemoaned it; but in this they have fallen
short, how to remedy it.   They have aimed at it, and come
near it, but have not been able to work it: they still laboured
to be satisfied in themselves.   They speak somewhat of reason,
but that will not do it; for man being fallen under the curse
of God, there is nothing but darkness and folly in himself.
The only way to blessedness is by going out of ourselves unto
God.

All our discourses of our own vanity will but further disquiet us, if they do not terminate here, if they do not fix on
His eternal happiness, goodness, and verity.

I am persuaded, if many would ask this question of themselves, *What wait I for?* they would puzzle themselves and
not find an answer.   There are a great many things that men
desire, and are gaping after, but few seek after one thing chiefly
and stayedly : they float up and down, and are carried about
without any certain motion, but by fancy and by guess; and
no wind can be fair for such persons, who aim at no certain
haven.

If we put this question to ourselves, What would I have?
it were easy for many to answer—I would have an easy, quiet,
peaceable life in this world.   So would an ox or a horse.   And
is that all?   May be you would have a greater height of pleasure and honour.   But think on this one thing: there is this
one crack and vanity that spoils all these things, that they will
not bear you up when you lean to them in times of distress ;
and besides, when you have them they may be pulled from
you, and if not, you must be plucked away from them within

a little while. There is much seeming content in the pursuit of these things, but they are lost with greater discontent. It is God's goodness to men, to blast all things in the world to them, and to break their fairest hopes, that they may be constrained to look above to Himself: He beats them from all shores, that he may *bring them to the Rock that is higher than they.* (Psal. lxi. 2.)

Oh, that God would once touch some of your hearts, who are under the *chains of darkness,* that ye might once bethink where to rest your heads in the midst of all our confusions. And here is the resting place; *hope in God. Now, Lord, what wait I for? My hope is in Thee.* Blessed soul that can say, "Lord, Thou seest I desire nothing but Thyself; (as Peter said, *Lord, thou knowest I love Thee;*) all the corners of my heart stand open in Thy sight; Thou seest if there be any other desire or expectation but to please Thee; and if there be any such thing in me, (for I see it not,) I pray Thee discover it to me, and through Thy grace it shall lodge no longer. My heart is Thine alone, it is consecrated to Thee; and if anything would profane thy temple, if it will not go forth by fair warning, let it be scourged out by Thy rod, yea by any rod whatsoever it pleaseth Thee to choose."

My hope is in Thee.] This holy man, seeing the vanity of all other expectations and pursuits of men, at length runs to this: *And now, Lord, what wait I for? My hope is in Thee.* He finds nothing but moving sand every where else; but he finds this Eternal Rock to be a strong foundation, as the Hebrew word by which He is styled doth signify. It is true, the union of the heart with God is made up by faith and love: but yet both these, in this our present condition of absence and distance from God, do act themselves much by the third grace which is joined with them, and that is *hope.* For faith is conversant about *things that are not seen,* and, in a great part, that *are not* as yet, but are to come; and the spirit of faith, choosing things that are to come, is called hope. It is true they are not so wholly deferred, as that they possess nothing; but yet the utmost they possess is but a pledge and earnest-penny, a small thing in respect of that eternal inheritance they look for.   What they have here is of the same kind with what they expect, but it is but a little portion of it; the smiles and glances of their Father's face foretastes of heaven, which their souls are refreshed with.   But these are but rare, and for a short time.

Hope is the great stock of believers : it is that which upholds them under all the faintings and sorrows of their mind in this life, and in their going *through the valley and shadow of death.* It is the *helmet of their salvation,* which, while they are looking over to eternity, beyond this present time, covers and keeps their head safe amidst all the darts that fly round about them. In the present discomfort and darkness of mind, and the saddest hours they meet with in this life, Hope is that which keeps up the soul; and it is that which David cheered up his soul with, Psal. xlii. 5. *Why art thou cast down, O my soul, and why art thou disquieted in me?   Hope thou in God, for I shall yet praise Him for the help of His countenance.*   And even in this point the *children of the world* have no great advantage of the *children of God,* as to the things of this life; for much of their satisfaction, such as it is, doth hang, for the most part, on their hope : the happiest and richest of them do still piece it out with some further expectation, something they look for beyond what they have, and the expectation of that pleases them more than all their present possessions.   But this great disadvantage they have, that all their hopes are but heaps of delusions and lies, and either they die and obtain them not, or if they do obtain them, yet they obtain them not ; they are so far short of what they fancied and imagined of them beforehand.   But the hope of the children of God, as it is without fail sure, so it is inconceivably full and satisfying, far beyond what the largest apprehension of any man is able to reach. *Hope in God!*   What is wanting there ?

This hope lodges only in the pure heart : it is a precious liquor that can be kept only in a clean vessel, and that which is not so cannot receive it, but what it seems to receive it corrupts and destroys. It is a confidence arising from peace, agreement, and friendship, which cannot subsist betwixt the God of purity and those who allow unholiness in themselves. It is a strange impudence for men to talk of their trust and hope in God, who are in perfect hostility against Ilim. Bold fellows go through dangers here, but it will not be so hereafter. (Jer. ii. 27.) *They turn to Me the back, and not the face; yet, in their trouble, they say, Arise and save us:* they do it as confidently as if they never had despised God, but they mistake the matter; it is not so. *Go and cry,* says He, *to the gods whom ye have chosen.* (Judg. x. 14.) When men come to die, then they catch hold of the mercy of God; but from that their filthy hands are beat off, there is no help for them there, and so they fall down to the pit. A holy fear of God, and a happy hope in Him, are commonly linked together. *Behold, the eye of the Lord is upon them that fear Him, upon them that hope in His mercy.* (Psal. xxxiii. 19.)

And even in those who are more purified from sin, yet too large draughts of lawful pleasures do clog the spirits, and make this hope grow exceedingly weak. Surely the more we fill ourselves with these things, we leave the less appetite for the consolations of this blessed hope. They cannot know the excellency of this hope, who labour not to keep it unmixed: it is best alone, as the richest wines and oils, which are the worst of mixtures. *Be sober and hope,* says the Apostle Peter (1 Ep. i. 13): keep your mind sober, and your hope shall be pure. If any thing or person leans on two supporters, whereof the one is whole and sound, and the other broken or crooked, that which is unsound will break, though the other remain whole, and that which was propped up by it will fall; whereas the one that was whole had been sufficient: thus it is when we divide our hopes betwixt God and this present world, or any other good. Those who place their whole hopes on God, they gather in all their desires to Him: the streams of their affections are not scattered and left in the muddy ditches of the world, they do not fall into stinking pools, but being gathered into one main torrent, they run on in that channel to the sea of His eternal goodness.

My hope is in Thee.] We cannot choose but all of us think that God is immensely good in Himself; but that which is nearer, whereon our hearts most rise, is a relative goodness, that He is good *to us*, and that He is so perfectly and completely good, that having made choice of Him, and obtained union with Him, we need no more. Were once the hearts of the children of men persuaded of this, all their deliberations were at an end: they would not only choose no other, but defer no longer to fix on Him. And what can trouble the soul that is thus established? No change or overturning of outward things. Though the frame of the world itself were shaken to pieces, yet still the bottom of this hope is upon Him who *changeth not*. And whatever thy pressures be, whether poverty, sickness, or disquiet of mind, thou mayest draw abundant consolation from Him in whom thou hast placed thy hope. There is only one thing that cruelly assaults it by the way, and that is the guilt of sin. All afflictions and troubles we meet with are not able to mar this hope or quench it, for where it is strong, it either breaks through them or flies above them: they cannot overcome it, for there is no affliction inconsistent with the love of God; yea the sharpest affliction may sometimes have the clearest characters of His love upon it. But it is sin that presents Him as angry to the view of the soul. When He looks through that cloud, He seems to be an enemy; and when we apprehend Him in that aspect we are affrighted, and presently apprehend a storm. But even in this case, this hope apprehends his mercy. And thus David here.

LECTURE V.

Ver. 8. Deliver me from all my transgressions: make me not the reproach
of the foolish.

THIS is indeed the basis and foundation of all our other hopes,
the free pardon of our sins. But none must entertain those
sins, if they desire to be pardoned. *Repentance* and *remission of sins* are still linked together in the Scriptures;
and he that would have sin pardoned, and yet live in it, or
retain the love of it, would have God and sin reconciled together, and that can never be. David finds his sins pressing
him down; he sees them as an army of men set in battle array
about him; and whither flies he for a deliverance? Even to
Him whom he had offended.

Ver. 9, 10. *I was dumb, I opened not my mouth, because
Thou didst it. Remove Thy stroke away from me: I am
consumed by the blow of Thine hand.* We are naturally very
partial judges of ourselves; and, as if we were not sufficiently
able by nature, we study and devise by art to deceive ourselves.
We are ready to reckon any good that is in us to the full, nay,
to multiply it beyond what it is; and further to help this, we
use commonly to look on those who have less goodness in them,
who are weaker, more foolish and worse than ourselves; and
so we magnify the sense of our own worth and goodness by that
comparison. And as in the goodness we have, or imagine we
have, so, likewise, in the evils we suffer, we use to extol them
very much in conceit. We account our lightest afflictions very
great; and to heighten our thoughts of them, we do readily
take a view of those who are more at ease and less afflicted than
ourselves; and by these devices we nourish in ourselves pride,
by the overweening conceit of our goodness, and impatience,
by the overfeeling sense of our evils. But if we would help ourselves by comparison, we should do well to view those persons
who are, or have been, eminent for holiness, recorded in holy
writ, or whom we know in our own times, or have heard of in

former times; and by this means, we should lessen the great
opinion we have of our own worth.   And so likewise should we
consider the many instances of great calamities and sorrows,
which would tend to quiet our minds, and enable us to *possess
our souls in patience*, under the little burden of trials that lies
upon us.   And, especially, we shall find those instances to fall
in together, that as persons have been very eminent in holiness,
they have also been eminent in suffering very sore strokes and
sharp scourges from the hand of God.   If we would think on
their consuming blows and broken bones, their *bones burnt as a
hearth*, and their *flesh withered as grass*, certainly, we should
entertain   our   thoughts   sometimes   with   wonder   at   God's
indulgence to us, that we are so little afflicted, when so
many of the children of men, and so many of the children
of God, suffer so many and so hard things; and this would
very much add to the stock of our praises.   We should
not think that we are more innocent in not deserving those
things that are inflicted on others, but rather, that He who thus
measures out to them and to us, knows our size, and sees how
weak we are in comparison of them; and that therefore He is
indulgent to us, not because we are better, but because we are
weaker, and are not able to bear so much as He lays on the
stronger shoulders.   Even in the sharpest of these rods, there
is mercy.   It is a privilege to the sheep that is ready to wander,
to be beaten into the right way.   When thou art corrected,
think that thereby thy sins are to be purged out, thy passions
and lusts to be crucified by these pains; and certainly, he that
finds any cure of the evils of his spirit by the hardest sufferings of his flesh, gets a very gainful bargain.   If thou account
sin thy greatest unhappiness and mischief, thou wilt be glad to
have it removed on any terms.   There is at least, in the time of
affliction, a cessation from some sins; the raging lust of ambition
and pride doth cease, when a man is laid upon his back; and
these very cessations are some advantages.   But there is one
great benefit of affliction, which follows in the text, that it
gives him the true measure of himself.

Ver. 11. *When with rebukes Thou dost correct man for iniquity. Thou makest his beauty to consume away like a moth: surely every man is vanity.* Selah.] *Man, at his best estate is altogether vanity ;* but at his lowest estate, it appears best unto him how much vanity he is, and how much vanity he was at his best estate, seeing he was then capable of such a change, to fall so low from such a height. As that great man who was seeking new conquests, when he fell upon the sand, and saw the print of his own body, " Why," says he, " so small a parcel of earth will serve me, who am seeking after new king-doms ;"—thus it is, when a man is brought down, then he hath the right measure of himself, when he sees how vain a thing he is.

Thus the Psalmist represents it here both as an argument to move God to compassion, and to instruct himself and other men. So Job xiii. 25. *Wilt thou break a leaf driven to and fro with the wind? and wilt thou pursue dry stubble?* And Psal. ciii. 14. *For He knoweth our frame: He remembereth that we are dust.* And his beauty, which seemed to be his perfection, yet, when the hand of God is on him, it is blasted as a moth-eaten garment. This should teach us humility, and to beware of sin, which provokes God to pour out His heavy judgments upon us. If any be proud of honour, let him remember Nebuchadnezzar and Herod; or if proud of riches, or of wit and endowments of minds, let him think how soon God can make all these to wither and melt away. *Surely, every man is vanity.*

Ver. 12. *Hear my prayer, O Lord, and give ear to my cry ; hold not Thy peace at my tears: for I am a stranger with Thee, and a sojourner, as all my fathers were.*] What is this life we cleave so fast to, and are so uneasy to hear of parting with, what is it but a trance, and a succession of sorrows, a weary tossing and tottering upon the waves of vanity and misery ? No estate or course of life is exempted from the causes of this complaint: the poorer and meaner sort are troubled with wants, and the richer with the care of what they have, and sometimes with the loss of it; and the middle sort betwixt the two, they partake, in common, of the vexations of both, for their life is spent in care for keeping what they have, and in turmoil for purchasing more; besides a world of miseries and evils that are incident equally to all sorts of men, such as sickness and pain of body, which is both a sharp affliction, and sits close to a man, and which he is least able, either by strength of mind, or by any art or rule, to bear; and this guest does as oft haunt palaces as poor cottages: there are as many groans of sick and diseased bodies within silken curtains, as in the meanest lodging. Neither does godliness exempt the best of men from the sufferings of this life. David, who was both a great man and a good man, did share deeply in these, so that his conclusion still holds true; no instance can be found to infringe it: *Surely every man is altogether vanity.*

It remains only to inquire, what manner of men they are who are furnished with the best helps, and with the most comfortable mitigations of their trouble, and with the strongest additions of support and strength to bear them up under it. And it will certainly be found, that godliness alone hath this advantage. And among the many consolations godly men have under their troubles, this is one, and the chief one, their recourse unto prayer. So here, and Psal. cxlii. 4, 5. So, Isa. xxxviii. 2, *Hezekiah turned his face towards the wall:* he turns his back on all worldly councils and vain helps, and betakes himself to prayer; and prayer brings ease, and support, and seasonable deliverance to the godly man. But *their sorrows shall be multiplied that hasten after other gods;* (Psal. xvi. 4;) and this all ungodly men do when they are afflicted: they run to other imaginary helps of their own, and those prove but the multipliers of sorrows, and add to their torment; they are *miserable* or troublesome *comforters,* like unskilful physicians, who add to the patient's pain, by nauseous, ill-chosen, and, it may be, pernicious drugs.

Now, in this prayer of David, we find three things, which are the chief qualifications of all acceptable prayers. The first is *humility*. He humbly confesses his sins, and his own weakness and worthlessness. We are not to put on a stoical, flinty kind of spirit under our afflictions, that so we may seem to shun womanish repinings and complaints, lest we run into the other evil, of *despising the hand of God,* but we are to humble our proud hearts, and break our unruly passions. There is something of this in the nature of affliction itself: as in the daytime men are abroad, but the night draws them home, so, in the day of prosperity, men run out after vanities and pleasures, and when the dark night of affliction comes, then men should come home, and wisely lay the matter to heart. It is meet we *humble ourselves under the mighty hand of God.* It is meet to say unto Him, as Job xxxiv. 31, *I have been chastised,* or *have borne chastisement, and I will not offend any more.* That is a kind of language that makes the rod fall out of His hand. That prayer ascends highest which comes from the lowest depth of an humbled heart. But God *resists the proud;* He proclaims himself an enemy to pride and stiffness of spirit ; but His grace seeks the humble heart, as water does the low ground.

If a holy heart be the *temple of God,* and therefore a *house of prayer*, certainly, when it is framed and builded for such, the foundation of that temple is laid in deep humility ; otherwise, no prayers that are offered up in it, have the smell of pleasing incense to Him.

The second qualification of this prayer is, *fervency* and *importunity*, which appears in the elegant gradation of the words : *Hear my prayer*, my words ; if not that, yet *Give hear to my cry*, which is louder ; and if that prevail not, yet *Hold not Thy peace at my tears*, which is the loudest of all ; so David elsewhere calls it *the voice of his weeping*. Though this gift of tears doth often flow from the natural temper, yet where that temper becomes spiritual and religious, it proves a singular instrument of repentance and prayer. But yet there may be a very great height of piety and godly affections where tears are wanting ; yea, this defect may proceed from a singular sublimity of religion in their souls, being acted more in the upper region of the intellectual mind, and so not communicating much with the lower affections, or these expressions of them. We are not to judge of our spiritual proficiency by the *gift of prayer*, for the heart may be very spiritually affected, where there is no readiness or volubility of words. The sure measure of our growth, is to be had from our holiness, which stands in this, to see how our hearts are crucified to the world, and how we are possessed with the love of God, and with ardent longings after union with Him, and dwelling in His presence hereafter, and in being conformed to His will here.

It is the greatest folly imaginable in some, to shed tears for their sins, and within a little while to return to them again: they think there is some kind of absolution in this way of easy venting themselves by tears in prayer, and when a new tempta-tion returns, they easily yield to it. This is lightness and foolishness, like the inconstancy of a woman who entertains new lovers in her mourning apparel, having expressed much sorrow and grief for her former husband.

Now, fervency in prayer hath in it, 1*st*. Attentiveness of mind. If the mind be not present, it is impossible that much of the heart and affections can be there. How shall we think that God will hear those prayers which we do not hear our-selves ? And shall we think them worthy of His acceptance, that are not worthy of our thoughts? Yet we should not leave off prayer because of the wanderings of our hearts in it, for that is the very design of the Devil, but still we must con-tinue in it, and amend this fault as much as we can ; by remem-bering, in the entry, with whom we have to do, by freeing our minds as much as may be from the entanglements and multi-plicity of business, and by labouring to have our thoughts often in Heaven. For where the heart is much, it will be ever and anon turning thitherward, without any difficulty.

2*dly*. Fervency of prayer hath in it an intense bent of the affections : to have our desires as ardent as can be for the par-don of sin, for the mortifying of our lusts and passions, for the

delivering us from the love of ourselves and this present world ;
and for such spiritual things to pray often, and to follow it
with importunity. That is to pray fervently, never to rest till
an answer come.

The third qualification is *faith.* *He who comes to God*
must believe that He is, and that He is a rewarder of all
that diligently seek Him. (Heb. xi. 6.) And certainly, as he
that comes to God must believe this, so he that believes this
cannot but come to God ; and if he be not presently answered,
he that believes makes no haste,—he resolves patiently to wait
for the Lord, and to go to no other.

: Surely, there is much to be had in prayer. All good may
be obtained, and all evil averted by it ; yea, it is a reward to
itself. It is the greatest dignity of the creature, to be admitted
to converse with God. And certainly, the soul that is much in
prayer, grows in purity, and is raised by prayer to the despising
of all those things that the world admires and is in love with,
and by a wonderful way is conformed to the likeness of God.

For I am a stranger with Thee, and a sojourner, as all my
fathers were.] In the Law, God recommends strangers to
the care and compassion of his people ; now David returns the
argument to Him, to persuade Him to deal kindly with him :
" *For I am a stranger with Thee,* that is, *before Thee,*—in
this world wherein Thou hast appointed me to sojourn a few
days. And I betake myself to Thy protection in this strange
country ; I seek shelter under the shadow of Thy wings ; therefore, have compassion upon me." He that looks on himself as
a stranger, and is sensible of the darkness both round about
him in this wilderness, and also within Him, will often put up
that request with David, Psal. cxix. 19, *I am a stranger on this*
earth ; hide not Thy commandments from me,—do not let me
lose my way. And as we should use this argument to persuade God to look down upon us, so, likewise, to persuade
ourselves to send up our hearts and desires to Him. What is
the joy of our life, but the thoughts of that other life, our
home, before us ? And, certainly, he that lives much in these

thoughts, set him where you will here, he is not much pleased or displeased; but if his Father call him home, that word gives him his heart's desire.

LECTURE VI.

Ver. 13.   O spare me, that I may recover strength, before I go hence, and be no more.

W HY is it that we do not extremely hate that which we so desperately love, sin? For the deformity of itself is unspeakable; and, besides, it is the cause of all our woes. Sin hath opened the sluices, and lets in all the deluge of sorrows which makes the life of poor man nothing else than vanity and misery, so that the meanest orator in the world may be eloquent enough on that subject. What is our life, but a continual succession of many deaths? Though we should say nothing of all the bitternesses and vexations that are hatched under the sweetest pleasures in the world, this one thing is enough, the multitude of diseases and pains, the variety of distempers, that those houses we are lodged in are exposed to. Poor creatures are oft-times tossed betwixt two, the fear of death, and the tediousness of life; and under these fears, they cannot tell which to choose. Holy men are not exempted from some apprehensions of God's displeasure because of their sins; and that may make them cry out with David, *O spare me, that I may recover strength, before I go hence, and be no more.* Or, perhaps, this may be a desire, not so much simply for the prolonging of life, as for the intermitting of his pain, to have ease from the present smart. The extreme torment of some sickness, may draw the most fixed and confident spirits to cry out very earnestly for a little breathing. Or rather, if the words imply the desire of a recovery, and the spinning out of the thread of his life a little longer, surely he intended to employ it for God and His service. But long life was suitable to the promises or that time : so Hezekiah, Isa. xxxviii. 5. There is no doubt those holy men under the Law, knew somewhat of the state of immortality ; their calling themselves *strangers on earth*, (Heb. xi. 13,) argued that they were no strangers to these thoughts. But it cannot be denied, that that doctrine was but darkly laid out in those times. It is Christ Jesus who *hath brought life and immortality to light*, who did illuminate life and immortality, which before stood in the dark.

Surely, the desire of life is, for the most part, sensual and base, when men desire that they may still enjoy their animal pleasures, and are loth to be parted from them. They are pleased to term it, a desire to live and repent ; and yet, few do it when they are spared : like evil debtors, who desire forbearance from one term to another ; but with no design at all to pay. But there is a natural desire of life, something of abhorrence in nature against the dissolution of these tabernacles. We are loth to go forth, like children who are afraid to walk in the dark, not knowing what may be there. In some, such a desire of life may be very reasonable ; being surprised by sickness, and apprehensions of death, and sin unpardoned, they may desire a little time before they enter into eternity. For that change is not a thing to be hazarded upon a few days' or hours' preparation. ' I will not say that death-bed repentance is altogether desperate, but certainly, it is very dangerous, and to be suspected ; and, therefore, the desire of a little time longer, in such a case, may be very allowable.

I will not deny but it is possible, even for a believer to be taken in such a posture, that it may be very uncomfortable to him to be carried off so, through the affrightments of death, and his darkness as to his after-state. On the other hand, it is an argument of a good measure of spirituality and height of the love of God, *to desire to depart, and be dissolved*, in the midst of health, and the affluence of worldly comforts. But for men to desire and wish to be dead, when they are troubled and vexed with any thing, is but a childish folly, flowing from a discontented mind, which being over, they desire nothing less than to die. . It is true there may be a natural desire of death, which at some times hath shined in the spirits of some natural men : and there is much reason for it, not only to be freed from the evils and troubles of this life, but even from those things which many of this foolish world account their happiness,—sensual pleasures, to eat and drink, and to be hungry again, and still to round that same course which, to souls that are raised above sensual things, is burdensome and grievous.

But there is a spiritual desire of death, which is very becoming a Christian. For Jesus Christ hath not only opened very clearly the doctrine of eternal life, but He Himself hath passed through death, and lain down in the grave ; He hath perfumed that passage, and warmed that bed for us ; so that it is sweet and amiable for a Christian to pass through and follow Him, and to be where He is. It is a strange thing, that. the souls of Christians have not a continual desire to go to that company which is above; (finding so much discord and disagreement among the best of men that are here ;) to go to *the spirits of just men made perfect,* where there is light and love, and nothing else ; to go to the *company of angels,* a higher rank of blessed spirits ; but, most of all, to go *to God, and to Jesus the Mediator of the New Testament.* And, to say nothing positively of that glory, (for the truth is, we can say nothing of it,) the very evils that death delivers the true Christian from, may make him long for it ; for such an one may say—I shall die, and go to a more excellent country, where I shall be happy for ever : that is, I shall die no more, I shall sorrow no more, I shall be sick no more, and, which is yet more considerable, I shall doubt no more, and shall be tempted no more ; and, which is the chiefest of all, I shall sin no more.

EXPOSITORY LECTURES

ON

ISAIAH VI.

LECTURE I.

Ver. 1—5.

THE division of this chapter (were that to any great purpose) may be stated thus :

1. The Prophet's vision, from ver. 1 to 3. *In the year that king Uzziah died, I saw also the Lord sitting upon a throne, high and lifted up, and His train filled the temple. 2. Above it stood the seraphims: each one had six wings; with twain he covered his face, and with twain he covered his feet, and with twain he did fly. 3. And one cried unto another, and said, Holy, holy, holy is the Lord of hosts; the whole earth is full of His glory.*

II. The effects of it upon him, relating to his calling, from ver. 4 to 13. *And the posts of the door moved at the voice of him that cried, and the house was filled with smoke,* &c.

In the Vision, besides the circumstances of time and place specied, ver. 1, we have a glorious representation of the majesty of God, ver. 2; a suitable acclamation, a voice of praise being joined with it, ver. 3, 4.

The Effects of it on the Prophet towards his calling are three, *viz.*, I. His Preparation. II. His Mission. III. His Message.

I. The Preparation, in these two particulars : 1. Humiliation;

2. Purification (ver. 6, 7); a deep conviction, and then, effectual removal of pollution.

II. In his Mission we have three things: 1. God's inquiry for a messenger, ver. 8, former part. 2. The Prophet's offer of Himself, the latter part of ver. 8. 3. God's acceptance, ver. 9, former part.

III. His Message—a heavy commination, from ver. 9 to 12, yet, allayed with a gracious mitigation, ver. 13; the judgment very lasting and wasting, yet, a remnant reserved.

Ver. 1. In the year that king Uzziah died, I saw also the Lord sitting upon a throne, high and lifted up, and His train filled the temple.

I saw.] Observe the freedom of God in His choice of men to be near Him, and know Him. And in the measuring out of the degrees of discovery unto those men differently, some had extraordinary revelations; and though prophetic visions now cease, yet there are certainly higher and clearer coruscations of God upon some souls, than upon many others, who yet are children of light, and partake of a measure of that light shining within them. Thus we are not carvers and choosers, and, therefore, are not peremptorily to desire any thing in kind or measure that is singular; that were pride and folly. But above all things we are to esteem, and submissively to desire, still more and more knowledge of God, and humbly to wait and keep open the passage of light; not to close the windows, not to be indulgent to any known sin or impure affection; that will soon obstruct it. Into a filthy soul, wisdom will not enter.

In the year that king Uzziah died, I saw the Lord on His throne.] There is another king named here, to denote the time by; but he was a diseased and a dying king, who lived some years a leper, and then died. Men may speak in a court style of vain wishes, *O king, live for ever;* but this King here on the throne is, indeed, THE KING IMMORTAL, the ever living God.

God measures and proportions all His means to their ends.

When He calls men to high services, He furnishes them with suitable preparations and enablements. Thus here with the Prophet: he was to denounce heavy things against his own nation, *a proud, stubborn people;* to deal boldly and freely with the highest, yea, with the king himself, ch. vii.; and he is prepared by a *vision of God.* What can a man fear after that? All regal majesty and pomp looks petty and poor after that sight. Two kings together on their thrones, in robes royal, (1 Kings xxii.) did no whit astonish him who had seen a greater: *I saw* (says Micaiah) *the Lord sitting on His throne, and all the hosts of heaven standing by.* Much like this is the vision of Isaiah here before us.

Eyes dazzled with the sun see not the glittering of drops of dew on the earth; and those are quickly gone, with all their faint and fading glory, to a soul taken with the contemplation of God. How meanly do they spend their days, who bestow them on counting money, or courting little earthen idols in ambition or love! From how high a stand doth he look down on those, who looks on God, and admires His greatness, wonders at what he sees, and still seeks after more! These two are therefore joined together, *beholding the beauty of the Lord,* and *inquiring in His temple.* Psal. xxvii. 4. *One thing have I desired of the Lord, that will I seek after; that I may dwell in the house of the Lord all the days of my life, to behold the beauty of the Lord, and to inquire in His temple.*

Ver. 2, 3. *Above it stood the seraphims; each one had six wings; with twain he covered his face, and with twain he covered his feet, and with twain he did fly. And one cried unto another, and said, Holy, holy, holy is the Lord of hosts: the whole earth is full of His glory.* These glorious courtiers, flaming spirits, are light and love, whose very feet are too bright for us, as His face is too bright for them; and they cry, *holy, holy, holy*—thrice holy, most holy THREE, one God —*Lord of hosts: the whole earth is full of His glory.* This they cry one to another, echoing it and returning it incessantly. They that praise Him most, come nearest their life. When we are to pray, or offer any worship to the great God in the sanctuary, especially in solemn worship there, let us think of Him as thus on His throne above, and the diffusion of His glory there, of His train filling the upper Temple, and so, stoop low and fall down before Him. *Holy, holy, holy*. This is the main thing wherein He is glorious, and we are to know and adore Him in this view, and abhor ourselves as in His sight.

The whole earth.] So many creatures and various works and affairs, fruits and plants, and rich commodities, and so many calamities and miseries that kingdoms and people are afflicted with as by turns, and so many disorders, and such wickedness of men in public and private matters ; and yet, in all these varieties and contrarieties of things, this one is the sum of all, and all is taken up in it, *The whole earth is full of His glory*. In framing and upholding, in ruling and ordering all, what a depth of power and wisdom.

Ver. 4.   The posts of the door moved at the voice of him that cried, and the house was filled with smoke.

How true must that be, that at His voice *the earth quakes* and *the mountains tremble*, when, at the voice of an angel crying or proclaiming His name, the very threshold of the Temple (the then holiest part of the earth) moves! This, in the vision, was intended to represent the dreadfulness of His great name, which vile men dare baffle in vain oaths, and can speak thereof without sense : but hearts that are indeed His *living temples* will find this emotion ; when His name is proclaimed, or when they mention or think of it, *the posts will be moved* with an awful trembling.

And the house was filled with smoke.] This was here a symbol of the presence and majesty of God. See Psal. xcvii. 2. *Clouds and darkness are round about Him, righteousness and judgment are the habitation of His throne ;* not a signal of displeasure, as some take it. *He dwells in light that is inac-*

cessible, and round about is *thick darkness,* shutting out the weak eyes of men, which were not able to abide the brightness of His glory. Much of our knowledge here lies in this, to know that we know Him not ; and much of our praise, to con. fess that we cannot praise Him,—*silentium tibi laus,* as they read Psal. lxv. 1.

Ver. 5.   Then said I, Wo is me ! for I am undone ; because I am a man of unclean lips, and I dwell in the midst of a people of unclean lips ; for mine eyes have seen the King, the LORD of Hosts.

Then said I, Wo is me.] He is not lifted up with the dignity, that he should be honoured with such a vision of God : but, on the contrary, is struck with humble, holy fear.   Oh, *I am undone !* , This constitutes much of the exercise of souls admitted nearest to God, even this astonishment and admiration, that such as they should be regarded and raised to that height, and holy fear in a sense of their unholiness.   When the blessed Virgin heard a voice very much to her own advantage, (Luke i. 28, 29) instead of rising in her own conceit upon it, *she was troubled, and marvelled what manner of salutation it should be,* and was struck with fear, so that the Angel found it needful to say, *Fear not.*

Illusions and deceits of spirit of this kind cannot be better distinguished from true manifestations of God, than by this, that they breed pride and presumption in the heart, make it vain and haughty ; while true senses, and joys, and discoveries of love, in what kind soever, do most powerfully humble.   *Is est, qui superbire non potest, cui Deus ostendit misericordiam suam.*   Augustine.

For mine eyes have seen the King, the LORD *of Hosts.*] The mother and nurse of pride is, ignorance of God.   A small glance of Him will make the best of men abhor themselves, and still the nearer sight of Him, the lower conceit will there be of self, and the deeper sense of impurity and vileness.   This tells us, though we hear and speak of God, alas ! we know Him not.

I am a man of polluted lips.] He mentions this the rather, because he heard that song which he would have joined with, but durst not, because of *polluted lips.* Thus we must confess we are polluted all over, but much of our pollution breaks out by the lips, yet, commonly, we think not on it.

I am undone.] We could not indeed bear much, could not see God and live; therefore He veils Himself. But surely, we might see much more than we do, and live the better for it, the more humbly and holily. Our pollutions hinder and unfit us, as he implies when he says, *A man of polluted lips.* But oh, that we saw so much of Him as to see this pollution, which makes us so unworthy and so unfit to see Him!

He first cries, *I am a man of unclean lips,* and then adds, *I dwell in the midst of a people of unclean lips.* This is the true method; there can be no right sense of pollutions about us, but that which begins with a sense of those within us. Few men reflect much on themselves; or if they do, they view themselves by a false light.

Polluted lips.] This he says in regard of the voice he heard. And with regard to the much irreverence with which we mention God, both ministers and people, as much of all our heart pollutions have their vent this way, so the promise of sanctifying His people runs much on this. Zeph. iii. 9. They of a *pure lip* shall offer. All are of the holy order, a *royal priesthood,* and through sanctified lips, as the censer, still they offer incense of prayer and praise. *He is a perfect man that offends not in word.* (Jam. iii. 2.) Commonly, by much speaking, there is much pollution: *In many words there wants not sin.* (Prov. x. 19.) Therefore, *let your speech be always seasoned with salt.* (Col. iv. 6.) Now, many speeches need much salt, otherwise some part will be rotten, at least unsavoury. Much of the sin of the land consists in this: there are few companies where God is not dishonoured and provoked by your communication; and till this be laid to heart, judgments will multiply and grow, instead of decreasing. Few, even of those who *fear the Lord, speak often one to another,* in strain that God delights, not only to hearken to, but to write down and register for their good.

And I dwell amidst a people of unclean lips.] We infect each other when we meet. There is little converse that a man returns the better by, yea, by the most he is the worse: he brings back often more pollution, more folly and vanity by most companies and discourses. But we see here, that impurity humbly acknowledged, is graciously removed.

LECTURE II.

Ver. 6—8.

Ver. 6. Then flew one of the Seraphims unto me, having a live coal in his hand, which he had taken with tongs off the altar.

IMPURITY well discovered to a man, is half cured. Whensoever God graciously shews a man his own unsanctifiedness, there He goes on to cleanse and sanctify him: the light that discovers, is followed by a *burning coal* that purges away.

The Holy Spirit is that purifying fire: a touch of it cleanseth the hearts, and lips, and all, and kindles that affection in the soul which cannot die out, which not many, which no *waters can quench again.* It doth this to all that are sanctified, but eminently it doth it (or, at least, they desire it may) to those who are to be the instruments of enlightening, purifying, and kindling others. So in the resemblance of *fiery tongues* came down this Spirit on the Apostles; and thence they themselves were as *burning coals* scattered through the nations, blessed incendiaries of the world, setting it on fire with the love of Christ: *tanquam ligna ardentia dispersa,* says Augustine.

Ver. 7. And he laid it upon my mouth, and said, Lo, this hath touched thy lips, and thine iniquity is taken away, and thy sin is purged.

Thine iniquity is taken away,—how impure soever before. This free grace is wonderful, to make some who have been notoriously unclean, by the change wrought by this fire, the touch of a coal, to become eminently gracious, and messengers of grace to others, carrying this and spreading it. They, though originally of dark clay, are by this fire made transparent glass, through which the light of the Gospel shines into the Church.

This *coal taken from the altar*, may denote the deriving of the Spirit from Jesus Christ, our Priest, Altar, Sacrifice, and all, by which we are purified and made fit for His service. He is the fountain of light, and life, and purity, and all grace to His messengers, and all His followers. His grace is indeed a *live coal*, where heavenly heat is mixed with earth, the fulness of the Godhead with our nature in human flesh. Thereby we draw near; and especially they who bear His name to men, under a sense of their own impurity, entreat His touch, as devout Bernard, who, in a holy hyperbole, exclaims, " Had the Prophet need of a coal ! Oh then, grant for me a whole globe of fire, to purge away my filthiness, and make me a fit messenger to this people !"

Thy sin is purged.] The children of God are a wonder to themselves, when that Spirit comes in, who conquers and purges so suddenly and easily what they before groan under and wrestle with, very long to little or no purpose. It is *a change of the right hand of the Most High,* as the Vulgate reads that word in Psal. lxxvii. 10. *I said, This is my infirmity, but I will remember the years of the right hand of the Most High—mutatio dextræ Excelsi.* A touch of that will cleanse and heal; the all-purifying virtue of His Spirit, whereof this baptism of the Prophet's lips was a symbol, takes away the dross which by other means than that *fire* cannot be purged. So in metals, much pains may be taken, and strength of hand used with little effect; that at most does but scratch the superficies, makes the outside a little bright and shining, but severs not the dross from within : that cannot be done without fire. Have we not found how vainly we attempt while God withholds His hand ? Yea, while a man fancies self-pureness, he is the more impure, as Job says, ch. ix. ver. 30, 31. *If I wash myself with snow-water, and make myself ever so clean, yet shalt Thou plunge me in the ditch, and mine own clothes shall abhor me.* Therefore, Prayer is the great resource of a soul under a sense of uncleanness, begging a new creation, for such it is indeed: *Create in me a clean heart, O God, and renew a right spirit within me;*—following God with this suit, and resolving to follow Him till he grant it: for we well know He is able, and may say, *Lord, if Thou wilt, Thou canst make me clean.*

This *fire* hath two effects: it works purity and activity; it takes away sin, and puts in spirit and life for obedience. And here, *Thy sin is purged*, and then says he, ver. 8, *Here am I: send me.* And the former is effectual towards the latter: the more the soul is cleansed, the more alive and able it is made for service. The purging out of those sickly humours makes it more vigorous and able; whereas they abounding, clog the spirits, and make the vital operations heavy and weak. A soul well cleansed from the love of sin, and the world, and self, is in a healthful temper, and goes nimbly to any work. Outward discouragements and difficulties are then nothing. A feverish distemper within hinders and makes one lazy and unwieldy, unwilling and unable to labour: but that well purged and cured, he cares less for the hot weather without; strength of nature endures that more easily. Oh, how sweet to be thus actuated by love, a pure intention and desire of doing God service, and of bringing Him in glory! Other motives, or the mixtures of them, are base; and though God may make use sometimes of such, yet he sees within, and knows what spring makes the wheels go, and he gives them their reward here,— somewhat possibly of that they seek, success, and credit, and a name; but the after-reward of faithful servants they need not look for in that work: for they receive their reward, and can they expect more? Many a *Here am I*, comes from other incentives than an *altar coal;* and so they may burn and shine a while, but they soon consume and die out in a snuff: the heavenly altar-fire alone keeps in, and returns to Heaven where it was kindled.

There is many a hot, furious march under the semblance and name of zeal for God, that loves to be seen; as Jehu, 2 Kings x. 16: *Come with me, and see my zeal for the Lord.* Such persons may flatter themselves into that conceit in the heat of action, to think it is for God, while he sees through it, and judges it as it is, zeal for self and their own interest; and He gives them, accordingly, some hireling journeyman's wages, and then turns them off. But, oh, where the heart is purely actuated by a desire of His glory, and seeks nothing else, for such remains that blessed word, *Well done, good and faithful servant, enter into thy Master's joy.*

This, then, is to be sought for by ministers and eminent servants in public affairs, yea, by all that offer any service to God, a readiness from love. Something of this there is in all who are truly His, though held down in many, and almost smothered with rubbish; and in these there is some mixture of flesh drawing back. *The spirit is ready, but the flesh is weak,* and a load to it, hindering its working; and this strife is often found as a horse to an unskilful rider, at once pricked with the spur and checked with the bridle. But where this spirit of love is, it doth prevail, and wastes that opposition daily, and groweth in strength, becomes more quick and ready, more freed from self, and more actuated by the will of God; attaining somewhat further in that conformity with Heaven, where shall be no will striving, but His alone; where those glorious bright spirits stand ready for all commands, *who excel in strength,* and employ it all *to do His commandments.* Psal. ciii. 20. And the more like them we be here, the more lively hope have we to be shortly with them, and to be wholly as they are.

Ver. 8. Also, I heard the voice of the Lord, saying, Whom shall I send, and who will go for us? Then said I, Here am I: send me.

THIS inquiry imports not a doubtful deliberation in God, but a purpose to send. He is represented as a king, advising with himself or his council. And this is by some conceived as an imitation of the mystery of the Trinity, as Gen. i. 26, *And God said, Let us make man in our own image—Whom shall I send, and who will go for us?* But were there not ready, millions of these winged. messengers? What need, then, of such a word? True; angels were ready, but a man was sought. God, vouchsafing to send an embassy to men, will send one that might speak their language to them, and might stay and treat with them in a familiar, friendly way, an ambassador in ordinary, to lie still and treat with them. And in this conde-scension much wisdom and love appear. He will take men, subject to the like infirmities and pollutions with the people, as the Prophet here acknowledges, but one purged from these pollutions, made holy; though not perfectly, yet eminently holy. This is very suitable, were not men invincibly obstinate, more suitable than that God should send by angels, that one of themselves should come and deal with men for God, and bear witness of His graciousness and readiness to forgive, so as to give himself for an instance of it, and say, " I have found Him so." And they being changed and sanctified, shew really that the thing may be done ; that it is feasible to sanctify a sinner ; and so, sinful men appear to be fitter for this service than embodied angels.

I said, Here am I: send me.] What a blessed change was wrought on Paul when cast to the ground! His own will was broken all to pieces, and now he is only for His service, whose name he so hated, and whose servants he persecuted. *Lord, what wilt thou have me to do?* (Acts ix. 6.) These are the very words and characters of a true convert. And thus, the soul turned to Christ may in some cases doubt what is His will, but that once resolved, there is no deliberation whether

to do it or not.   He says not, If the service be honourable or
profitable, that is, carrying worldly credit or profit in it, then
will I do it; no, but whatever it is, if it be Thine, and Thou
appoint me to it, *Here am I.*   And this makes the meanest
work of his station excellent.

Then said I, Here am I.]   A strange change in the Prophet;
even but now an *undone man*, and here presently a ready messenger, and so turned to an angel.   Something of this most
find who are truly called to this high work of delivering messages from God: sometimes a sense of pollution benumbs and
strikes them dead, and anon again they feel the flame of love
kindled by that coal, quickening them to such a readiness, and
such free offers of themselves to service, as, to those who
understand not the reason of it, would seem presumptuous
forwardness.   And there may be in some minds, at one and
the same time, a strange mixture and counterworking of these
two together; a sense of unfitness and unworthiness drawing
back, and yet, the strength of love driving forward, thinking
thus, How can I, who am so filthy, so vile, speak of God?
Yet hath he shewn me mercy?   How then can I be silent?

Send me.]   Moses's reluctance, this same Prophet would
have vented too, before the touch of the coal, while he said,
Wo is me, I am undone, or *struck down*, as the word may
signify; he cannot speak with such unholy lips of so holy a
God.   Isaiah cries out of *polluted lips*, as Moses complained
of *stammering lips.*   And this is fit to precede; first, a sense
of extreme inability and unworthiness, and then, upon a change
and call, ready obedience.   A man once undone and dead, and
then recovered, is the only fit messenger for God.   In such a
one, love overcomes all difficulties both without and within,
and in his work no constraint is he feeling but that of love;
and where that is, no other will be needed.   The sweet, all-
powerful constraint of love will send thee all-cheerful, though
it were through fire or water: no water can quench it, nor fire
out-burn it; it burns hotter than any other kindled against it.
After the touch of that *coal*, no forbearing.   So Jer. xx. 9.

But His word was in my heart as a burning fire shut up in my bones, and I was weary with forbearing, I could not stay. Feed the flock of God which is among you, says St. Peter, *taking the oversight thereof, not by constraint, but willingly ; not for filthy lucre, but of a ready mind.* (1 Pet. v. 2.) Yet the Prophet says, *Send me.* Though he had so ardent a desire and readiness to go, yet he will not go unsent, but humbly offers himself, and waits both for his commission and instructions: and how awful are they !

LECTURE III.

Ver. 9. And He said, Go and tell this people, Hear ye indeed, but understand not ; and see ye indeed, but perceive not.

10. Make the heart of this people fat, and make their ears heavy, and shut their eyes : lest they see with their eyes, and hear with their ears, and understand with their heart, and convert, and be healed.

His message, you see, is most sad, and so he is put to it, put to the trial of his obedience, as men usually are according to the degree of their fitness. Nothing is more sweet to a messenger than to have good news to carry. Oh, it is a blessed sweet thing to convert souls ! But how heavy to harden them by preaching ! Yet thus it is to many at some times, and almost generally to all. Certainly, before this, much had been heard and despised: they had been hardening their own hearts, and now they shall have enough of it ; their very sin shall be their plague, a plague of all others the most terrible, yet, as was said above, there are times of the height of this plague, as of others, and this was one of those times of its raging mortality. The Prophet did nothing but preach, and yet they were stupified by it. And indeed, wherever the word does not soften and quicken, it hardens and kills ; and the more lively the ministry of the word is where it works this effect, the more deeply doth it work it.

This was verified on the Jews : though then God's own

people, yet it was verified on them to the utmost. And this context is often cited against them in the New Testament; no place so often. So excellent a preacher as Isaiah, and so well reputed amongst his people, yet was sent to preach them blind, and deaf, and dead. And this same does the Gospel to most of many a congregation in Scotland ; and the more of Christ that is spoken, the more are unbelievers hardened. Isaiah, the most evangelical of all the prophets, was yet brought to that, *Who hath believed our report?* Yea, this was fulfilled in the preaching of Christ himself; as the hotter the sun, the more is the clay hardened.

Go tell this people.] Observe the mighty power of the word, to whatsoever it is sent. As it is wonderfully efficacious for softening, melting, reducing to God, so, if it be sent to harden, to seal to judgment, to bring in and hasten it ; and therefore it is spoken of as effecting the things it speaks : as in Jer. i. 10, *See, I have this day set thee over the nations, and over the kingdoms, to root out, and to pull down, and to destroy, and to throw down, to build and to plant.* So Ezek. xliii. 3, and Hos. vi. 5. Therefore, despise it not. Spiritual judgments are the heaviest of all : though least felt for a time, yet they stick closest and prove saddest in the end. The not feeling, is a great part of the plague : in this is the nature and malignity of the disease, that it takes away the sight and sense of other things, and of itself. The plague is a disease seizing on the spirits, and therefore is so dangerous ; but this seizes only on the spirit of the mind : and is any thing so dreadful ? Oh, any plague but that of the heart. People think it a good thing not to feel the word, not to be troubled. Well, as they love this, they are filled with it, and shall have enough of it. So, in self-love, *su i amator sibi dat.* God is righteous and pure in this. There are many cavils about his working on the heart to harden, which arise from an ignorant, low conceit of God, as of a dependent being, or tied to laws, or to give account. We ought rather to tremble before Him. *He doth no iniquity,* and we shall be forced to confess it. Many ways of His are obscure, but none are unjust. Find we not this people sit under the sound, and are many of them as if absent, as if they had never heard such things spoken of; so grossly ignorant of all these? *Hearing, they hear, but understand not.* Others are yet worse : they get a kind of knowledge, but it is dead, and works nothing. These *see*, and yet *perceive not*, and know not even what they know. Most are of this sort, and they are of all others the worst to convince. When they are told of Christ and forgiveness of sins, and are entreated to believe these mysteries, they cry out, Oh! we do, we know them, and can answer, if you ask us, what these doctrines are. But the heart is not changed, no sin is forsaken, no study of holiness, no flame of love. This *not perceiving*, is the great judgment of this land ; this is the great cause of lamentation, that Christ is so much known, and yet known so little. People do not think whither it tends, and what the importance of this message is. They hear it as *a passing tale*, or, at the best, as for the present, a pleasing sound, a *lovely song*, (Ezek. xxxiii. 32 ;) and if by an able minister, as sung by a good voice ; but no impression is made, it dies out in the air, it enters not into their hearts to quicken them, and so their evil is the more deadly. Oh! bemoan this, beg the removal of it, above all judgments, and the sending forth of that Spirit who causes *the mountains to flow down*, (Isa. lxiv. 1.) Many of you, my brethren, may be under somewhat of this, as there are divers degrees of it ere it comes to be incurable. Oh! pray to be delivered, lest it grow so far, that it be in vain to bid you do so. Better to be cast into extreme terrors for a time, than to continue thus : better to fall into a fever, than into this lethargy, which makes you sleep to death.

Convert and be healed.] These two go together : all miseries are healed, and grace and favour flow forth, when once the soul is stirred up to seek after God, and turn unto Him. Other courses of healing public or private evils are but mountebank cures, which vex and torment, as unapt physic does, and do no good : yea, make things worse than before. See Hosea v. 13, compared with chap. vi. verse 1. *When Ephraim saw his sickness and Judah his wound, then went Ephraim to the Assyrian, and sent to King Jareb; yet could he not heal you, nor cure you of your wound.—Come and let us return unto the Lord, for He hath torn, and He will heal us; He hath smitten, and He will bind us up.*

There is much in a custom of fruitless hearing, to stupify and make hard,—to make men sermon-proof. And the hearing of the most excellent hardens most, both against them, and against all others that are their inferiors; for being accustomed to hear the most moving strains, unmoved, makes them scorn and easily beat back that which is less pressing. A largely-endued and very spiritual minister, is either one of the highest blessings or heaviest curses that can come upon a people.

Hearing, hear not.] This, even the ministers themselves may fall under : speakers may have no ears, as the Italian proverb says of preachers, they do not hear their own voice. They may grow hard, by custom of speaking of Divine things without Divine affection; so that nothing themselves or others say can work on them. Hence it is that so few formal dead ministers are converted, that one said, *Raro vidi clericum pœnitentem ;* so hardened are they against the means of conviction, in which they have been so long conversant, and not converted by them. They have been speaking so often of Heaven and Hell, and of Jesus Christ, and feeling nothing of them, that the words have lost their power, and they are grown hard as the skin of leviathan, *esteeming iron as straw, and brass as rotten wood.* And this, by the way, besides that God's dispensation is so fixed, may be a reason why that sin mentioned in the sixth chapter of the Epistle to the Hebrews is unpardonable; it is in the nature of things, without such a miracle as God will not exert, *impossible,* that they who have stood out such things in vain, *should be renewed.* This should make us who are ministers, especially to tremble at an unholy life, or at the thought of declining from those ways of religion, of which we have known so much, and for which we have so many means of improvement.

Ver. 11. Then said I, Lord, how long ? And He answered, until the cities be wasted without inhabitant, and the houses without man, and the land be utterly desolate.

Ver. 12. And the Lord have removed men far away, and there be a great forsaking in the midst of the land.

Now this judgment fastening, was sure to draw on all other judgments. Therefore, the Prophet, touched with compassion, inquires, *How long?* and receives a very sad answer, *Until the cities be wasted.* God is sovereignly free in this; but usually He keeps that course, that long continued and spared sinning, makes long continued calamities when they come. Judgments, as the ancients thought comets to be, are as lasting as the matter is they are kindled with; and truly, upon this account, we may justly apprehend that *our* troubles are but just beginning, rather than near their end. Yet, repentance might prevail for the shortening of them : those sweet showers soonest lay the stormy winds.

And this consideration may have something hopeful in it, that in these latter times, things move something more speedily, as natural motions do towards their end ; for *a short work will God make upon the earth,* as the Apostle's word is ; and we see in our particular straits that were greatest, that the Lord hath made them short even beyond our expectation ; and what remains, is in His hand. I trust He will hasten the defeat of the plots and power of His enemies ; and doubt not all the late and present commotions of these poor kingdoms, are the birth-pangs of a happy deliverance and peace, and when they grow thickest, it is nearest the birth.

How long?] Observe the compassion of the messengers of God, not desiring the evil day, but mourning for it, pitying those they denounce judgment against, and melting for those they harden.

Till the cities be wasted.] This intimates there would be no relenting under all these judgments, but that these, as well as the word, and together with it, would harden them more, till they were almost quite consumed. And this is usual. Men think it would be otherwise, but it is found that times of great plagues and judgments are not times of great conversion : men are then more hardened both against the word and the rod ; their spirits grow stiff and obdurate in a kind of desperation. But mercy, coming as the spring sunshine, mollifies, and dissolves, and makes fruitful; therefore, such a day is to be longed for.   I suspect we shall not see much done by the Gospel till then ; and before that, we may suffer yet more dismal things, and be wasted with pestilence, sword, and famine. Yet, there is comfort in this, the Lord will not make a full end of us : *a tenth* shall be left ; and if not we, yet at least our posterity shall reap the sweet fruits of our bitter calamities, which are the just fruits of our iniquities.

Ver. 13. But yet in it shall be a tenth, and it shall return, and shall be eaten ; as a teil-tree, and as an oak, whose substance is in them when they cast their leaves, so the holy seed shall be the substance thereof.

THERE is still a remnant holy to God, the preservers of a land from utter ruin.   Profane persons despise the children of God, and know not that they are beholden to them for the subsistence of the land, and of the world : they are as those oaks, whose roots did bear up the earth of that highway that went between the king's house and the temple, as the resemblance is taken by some.

In judgments, the Lord remembers that. *Destroy it not, there is a blessing in it.* As for the personal condition of believers, there may be a great decay, a winter visage may be upon it ; but yet, the holy seed abideth in them, and is their stability, and still that word is true that is borrowed hence, *Semen sanctum, statumen terræ : The holy seed, the subsistence or establishment of the earth.* When their number is completed, time shall end, and this visible world shall be set on fire. And this day is hastening forward, though most of us think but little, if at all, of it.

EXPOSITORY LECTURE

ON

ROMANS XII. 3—12.

Ver. 3. For I say, through the grace given unto me, to every man that is among you, not to think of himself more highly than he ought to think; but to think soberly, according as God hath dealt to every man the measure of faith.

BESIDES the common word of *edification* implying it, we find often, in the Scriptures, *teaching* compared to *building* ; and, amongst other things, the resemblance holds in this, that in both, of necessity, there is a foundation first to be laid, and then the structure to be raised upon it. He that gives rules of life, without first fixing principles of faith, offers preposterously at building a house without laying a foundation: and he that instructs what to believe, and directs not withal a believer how to live, doth in vain lay a foundation without following out the building. But the Apostles were not so *foolish builders*, as to sever these two in their labours in the Church. In this Epistle, we find our Apostle excellently acquitting himself in both these. He first largely and firmly lays the groundwork, in the foregoing part of the Epistle: now, he adds exhortations and directions touching the particular duties of Christians.

The first thing, certainly, to be done with a soul, is, to convince it of sin and death, then to address and lead it unto Christ, our righteousness and life; this done, it should be taught to follow him. This is Christianity, *to live in Christ*, and *to live to Christ ;* to live in Him by faith, and to live to Him in holiness. These our Apostle joined in his doctrine,

Chap. viii. v. 1, *There is therefore now no condemnation to them which are in Christ Jesus, who walk not after the flesh, but after the Spirit.*

The exhortation that begins this chapter, hath in it the whole sum of Christian obedience, fitly expressed and strongly urged ; and in that, are all particular rules comprised.

But because of our ignorance and our sloth, we do not always readily draw forth particulars from those comprehensive general rules wherein they lie: we need, therefore, to be assisted in this; and to this the Scriptures descend, particularly the Apostles in their Epistles, and that usually in the latter part of them. And this is a main part of our duty in preaching the word, often to represent these rules to you, not so much that you may understand them better, though somewhat of this likewise may be needful, as that you may remember them, and eye them more, and walk according to them : and there is no more in these things truly known, than what is known after this manner. I have endeavoured, in the course of my teaching, to reach this end. My design, and I hope yours likewise, hath been, not to pass so much time, nor to pass it with empty delight, which in other things might be done at an easy rate, but that you be really built up heavenwards, and increase with the increase of God ; that the truth and power of Christianity may possess our hearts, and grow there, and may be evident in our lives, to the glory of our Lord Jesus.

We shall endeavour to lay before you the particular graces that are the ornaments of Christians ; and this, not that you may look on them simply, and commend them, but that you may pursue them, and be clothed with them, and then they will be much more comely and commendable: as a robe of rich apparel, if it seem fine while it hangs or lies by, it appears far better when it is put on.

The rule the Apostle is to give, he prefaces thus, *For I say, through the grace given to me*—I speak as the Messenger or Apostle of Christ, according to that knowledge and experience that He hath given to me of these things ; and so take it, as from one that hath some interest in, and share of, these graces I recommend to you. And this, indeed, makes recommendations carry home. Oh, that we could truly say this! Alas! it is an uncomfortable, and commonly an unprofitable thing, to speak of Christ and the graces of His Spirit, only as having heard of them, or read of them, as men that travel in their studies do of foreign countries.

Διὰ τῆς χάριτος. The Apostle represents this, to add the more authority, and gain the more acceptance, to what he had to say; and for this end, some care is to be had of the good opinion of people, so far as their interest is concerned, that the message we bring be not prejudged: otherwise, this truly set aside, it were little matter how we were mistaken or despised, yea, it were a thing some way desirable; only provided nothing be done on purpose, that may justly, yea, or that may probably, procure it, for that both piety and charity forbid.

To every man.] This is more pressing than if he had said simply, *to you,* or generally, *to you all;* for in men's talking of things, it proves often too true, *Quod omnibus, nemini,* What is said to all, is said to no one; but *To every one,* that each one may suppose it spoken to him, as an ingenious picture looking to each in the room. Thus we ought to speak, and thus ye ought to hear. We to speak, not as telling some unconcerning stories, but as having business with you; and you to hear, not each for another, as you often do—"Oh! such a passage touched such an one,"—but each for himself.

The first particular the Apostle recommends, is that gracing grace of humility, the ornament and the safety of all other graces, and which is so peculiarly Christian. Somewhat philosophers speak of temperance, justice, and other like virtues, but these tend rather to blow up and swell the mind with big conceit and confidence of itself, than to dwell together with self-abasement and humility. But in the school of Christ, the first lesson of all is, *self-denial and humility;* yea, it is written above the door, as the rule of entry or admission, *Learn of me, for I am meek and lowly of heart.* And out of all

question, that is truly the humblest heart which hath most of
Christ in it.

Not to think highly.]   Not aspiring and intending in things
too high.   And a great point of humility is subjection to God
in the point of knowledge; in this was our first climbing that
proved our fall; and yet still, amidst all our ignorance and
darkness, we are catching and gaping after the deadly fruit
of unhallowed knowledge.

This, withal, hath in it the attempering of our thoughts
and practices to our measure and station ; to know ourselves
truly and thoroughly : for that will certainly beget a very low
esteem of ourselves, to judge ourselves the unworthiest and
meanest of all.

And having truly this estimate of ourselves, we shall not
vainly attempt any thing above our reach, nor disdainfully
neglect any thing that is within the compass of our calling and
duty; which are the two evils so common among men, yea
even amongst Christians, and in the Church of God, and are
the cause of most of the enormities and disorders that fall out
in it.   It is a strange blindness, that they who do grossly miscarry in the duties of their own station, yet so readily fancy
themselves capable of somewhat higher, and think themselves
wronged if it be refused them.

The self-knowing Christian would rather descend, and finds
himself very disproportioned to his present station, be it never
so mean.   He can say with David, *Lord, my heart is not
haughty, nor mine eyes lofty ; neither do I exercise myself
in great matters, or in things too high for me.* (Psal. cxxxi. 1.)
But vain minds would still be tampering with the greatest
affairs, and dwell not with themselves.   Oh ! my brethren, be
entreated to study your own hearts better.   Be less abroad in
things that concern you not.   There is work enough within
you ; heaps of base lusts, and self-deceits, and follies, that you
see not yet; and many advantages of good things you seem to
see in yourselves, that indeed are not there.   Self-love is a
flattering glass, which represents us to ourselves much fairer

than we are ; therefore turn from it, if you desire a true account of yourselves, and look into the pure and faithful mirror
of God's Law.   Oh ! what deformities will that discover, which
you never saw nor thought of before ; it will make you the
lowest of all persons in your own eyes.

This low self-esteem doth not wholly take away the simple
knowledge of what gifts and graces God hath bestowed on a
man ; for that were to make him both unthankful and unuseful.
Qui se nescit, nescit se uti.   He who doth not know what God
hath freely given him, cannot return praise to God, nor make
use of himself for God in his station.   Yea, the Apostle's caution intimates a sober, humble reflection on the *measure* God
hath given a man, as what he not only allows but requires ;
and himself gives example of it in his own present expression,
declaring that he speaks these things *through the grace that is
given* to him.

But this knowledge of a man's own gifts and graces, that it
may not preclude his attaining more, but help him to more,
in the humble acknowledgment and use of what he hath, should
have these two qualifications: 1. That he beware of overweening ; that he take his *measure* much below, rather than
any whit beyond what he truly hath.   2. That whatsoever it
is, he always look on it not as his own, but as God's, having
His superscription on it, and all the glory of it being His peculiar tribute ; nothing of that to be interrupted or retained :
*Not unto us, O Lord, not unto us, but unto Thy name
give glory.*   Still, all the glory entirely sent up to Him.   Thus,
here, the Apostle sets all grace in that view, *As God hath dispensed the measure ;* and so speaks of his own, *Through the
grace given to me.*   Still, is it so to be looked on, not as what
we have, but as what He hath given.   That is the gospel style,
Grace, free gifts—χαρις, χαρίσματα.   Whereas philosophy
speaks of all as habits, or havings, or possessions.

Now, viewed in that relative dependent notion of *freely
given,* a man shall never be puffed up by any endowments,
though he see and know them : yea, the more he knows them

thus, he will be the more humble still, as being the more obliged. The more he hath received, the greater they are, the lower he bows, pressed down under the weight of his engagements to God: as Abraham *fell on his face* when *God talked with him,* and made so rich promises to him. (Gen. xvii. 3.) See David's strain, 1 Chron. xxix. 15. *But who am I, and what is my people, that we should be able to offer so willingly after this sort? For all things come of Thee, and of Thine own have we given Thee.* This the Apostle gives as the sovereign preservative against the swelling poison of self-conceit, *What hast thou that thou didst not receive?* (1 Cor. iv. 7.)

He who is thus regulated in his own esteem, will by this, certainly, be moderated in his desire of esteem from others, and cannot well meet with any thing that way, that will either puff him up, or cast him down: if overprized by others, he takes that as their mistake; if undervalued, he rejoices in that, having set himself so low in himself that others cannot well set him lower. So when men account meanly of him, they are really of his own opinion; and you know that offends none, but pleases them rather, to have others agree with their opinions, and be of their mind.

They who are busy after reputation, and would be esteemed, are but begging voices; they would have others think with them, and confirm the conclusion they have already resolved on, in favour of themselves; and this is a most foolish thing; for, disappointed in this, men are discontented, and so their peace hangs on others' fancies; and if satisfied with it, they surfeit and undo themselves with the delight of it. Bees sometimes kill themselves with their own honey; and there is such a word to this purpose. (Prov. xxv. 27.) *It is not good to eat much honey; so, for men to search their own glory, is not glory.*

Ver. 4, 5. For as we have many members in one body, and all members have not the same office; so we, being many, are one body in Christ, and every one members one of another.

IN this consideration we have God's wisdom manifested, and are instructed what is *our* wisdom. He, in the great world, made all by weight, number, and measure; so, in the lesser world, man, and in the new world, His Church, He proportions all to the use He hath designed them for. He could give to them who have least, more than the very greatest have, but He thought this unfit: it might be some advantage to them, yet to the whole body not so; and therefore not truly so to them neither, being parts of it, and having their good involved in the good of the body.

This resemblance is often used in Scripture, and holds excellently well, but is little learned. Our temper and carriage correspond not to it. Who is there almost that finds it, the Spirit of Christ in them, knitting them to Him as the common Head, and one to another, as one in Him; each busy to advance Him, and so seeking His glory, and to promote the good of one another? But álas! rather each is for self, accursed self, as of an independent divided substance; yea worse, hating and tearing one another, a monstrous sight, as if one limb of the same body should be pulling another to pieces. It signifies little to tell men what mutual tenderness there is in nature; that for a thorn in the foot, the back bows, the head stoops, the eyes look, the hands feel, and seek it, to pull it out *. Christians are still so rigid, so unchristian to each other, they drive one another with the thorn sticking in, foreing their brethren to ways against the persuasions of their consciences.

In the following verses, *viz.*, 6, 7, 8, we have a specification of divers offices, and the duties of them; the due observance of which is essential to the peace and growth of the Church, makes all go on sweetly and fruitfully. But men are either

* Spinam calcat pes, &c.—AUGUSTINE.

presumptuously or preposterously busy out of their own station, or slothfully negligent in it ; and both these, instead of edifying, are discomposing and destroying things.

Not to insist on the distinction of offices, it is evident, in all enumerations of this kind, that the same word sometimes means divers things, and divers words mean the same thing, as *ministry* may comprise all, though sometimes peculiar to deacons, sometimes taken for teachers or pastors.   Here it is general, and the particulars following distribute it : some are *to teach*, which is doctorial; some *to exhort*, which is more pastoral; some are *to give*, which is proper to deacons ; some have their whole charge *to rule,* as elders ; some are particularly for attendance on the sick.

But in all, fidelity and sedulity are requisite.   How high soever men are placed, if they are unfaithful, the higher judgment awaits them.   How low soever, if thou be sincere and studious of thy duty, thou shalt sustain no loss by thy low station, but rather thy faithfulness will be the more set off by it : *He that is faithful in little, shall be made ruler over much.* Oh, that *we* were more eaten up with zeal of our Lord's House and winning of souls, whom He deputes to that !   Oh, that they who rule would study more rule of their own houses, that should go before, and of their own hearts, that should be first of all !   Alas ! how shall men whose passions and lusts rule them, well rule the House of God ?   Be afraid and wise, ye who are called to that, and know at length, what is so generally either unknown or unconsidered, the exemplary holiness required in your persons, and the diligent watchfulness over the *flock of God.*   There are many debates, and troubles, and pains about these our liberties, but little diligence in the use of them.   Congregations are still as full of impiety and profaneness as ever.   Oh ! take heed lest we thus forfeit them after all they have cost, and provoke God to bereave us of them.   Men are busy, who, we know, are not friends to the Church of God.   But oh, that we were more careful to be on good terms with HIM !   *If HE be for us, who can be against us?* It is no matter who be; He is too wise and too strong for them all.

Ver. 9.   Let love be without dissimulation. Abhor that which is evil ;
cleave to that which is good.

THE whole sum of the Law is, Love ; love to God, and love to man : these two contain all, and the former of the two contains the latter.   Love to God is the only true principle and spring of all due love to man ; and all love that begins there, returns thither likewise, and ends there.

The engaging of the whole mind and soul to the love of God does not engross it so that there should be no kind of love communicable to man ; on the contrary, it is to refine it, that it may flow forth the purer and better. All love should be first called in to God, to be sublimated and purified there, and then set in its right channel and motion, so as man may be loved in Him and for Him ; not to impair our love to Him, but indeed to extend and act it as he allows.   And so to love man is to love God, that love taking its rise from Him, and terminating in Him ; and in this circle is the proper motion of celestial Divine love.

The duty, then, here meant and commanded, is this, *that we love one another*.   And our love must be thus qualified ; it must be unhypocritical and sincere, such as, though it may consist with, yet doth not wholly consist in civilities of expression and behaviour, but a real benevolence of soul, and good will to all ; a love disposing us readily to forgive evil, and to do-good upon all occasions.

Yet this is not such a tenderness of complacency as leads to partake with any in any evil ways : Oh ! no ; *abhorring that which is evil*, flying from it with indignation, with a kind of antipathy. And thus it will be from the new nature in a Christian, the holy Spirit of Christ, which cannot endure the unholiness or impurity of the world, but is chased away, as doves by noisome smells, or bees by smoke.   This delicacy of spirit profane men laugh at, as a weak, foolish meanness : but, fools as they are, they know not that it arises from that highest *wisdom which is from above,* which indeed is *peaceable,* but first is *pure,* and can admit of no peace nor agreement with any persons or things that are impure. This is to be like the all-wise God, with whom *wickedness cannot dwell:* His pure eyes cannot pleasantly behold any iniquity.

Oh ! much of the love of God would work more hatred of sin. But if thy hatred of evil be right, know it will begin at home ; as we feel aversions and abhorrences most when the things are nearest us. It is not the upright nature of holiness, to hate sin in others, and to hug it, or spare it in thyself, whether the same kind of sin, or any other ; for if this abhorrence be right, it is against all sin, the whole, as natural contrarieties are, and it is most against it, where nearest in thyself. It is the true Divine fire of zeal, kindled by the love of God, that burns up sin, but first that which is nearest it, as a fire in the hearth does, and so reaches what is further off. But if thy zeal fly most abroad upon others, it is an unruly, disordered wildfire, cracking and squibbing up and down, good for nothing but to set houses and towns on fire.

Cleave to that which is good.] This expresses a vehement and inseparable affection ; loving and rejoicing in all the good thou seest in others ; desiring and seeking after all the good thou canst attain unto-thyself; and being more pleased with the society of godly persons than any other, such as will put thee, and keep thee, most in mind of thy home and the way thither, and admonish and reduce thee from any declining steps. Their reproofs are more sweet to thee than the laughter and flattery of profane men : as one said to his master, " Thou shalt find no staff hard enough to beat me from Thee *." Though they seem harsh to thee, yet wilt thou say, *Let the righteous smite me, it shall be a kindness.* (Psal. cxli. 5.) And no opposition will drive thee from the truth of God and his ways, which are only good, if thy heart be once glued by love and fastened to them. Yea, thou wilt cleave the closer to

---

'Οὐ τὸ ξύλον εὑρήσεις, &c.

it, the more thou art persecuted for the truth; and the more thou sufferest for it, wilt love it the better. The word that is used in marriage, of the husband *cleaving to* the wife, holds true in the soul once married to that which is good : all violence will be too weak to sever thee. Learn to know what this is that is truly *good*, to know the excellency and sweetness of holiness, and it will be impossible to part thy affection from it. But this is the reason why men are so soon shaken, and the slender hold they have removed; the superficies of the soul, only, is tied to the outside of religion, by some external relations and engagements, and these are a running knot that easily slips. Few *receive the truth in the love of it*, and have their hearts united to Jesus Christ, who is indeed all that GOOD we have to seek after, and to cleave to.

Ver. 10.   Be kindly affectioned one to another with brotherly love; in honour preferring one another.

Now, in this way of holy, spiritual affection, seeking the true good of one another, be kind *in brotherly love;* not upon design of particular interest, but by a natural propension, such as is in creatures towards their young; such a tenderness as is amongst men of nearest relations, parents and children, and brethren; and know that you are indeed brethren of the highest birth and parentage, and so, beyond all brethren, Christians are obliged to love one another. Alas! that in them, likewise, it should prove so unhappily true, *Fratrum quoque gratia rara est*, that the love of brethren is rare; that they should be so hardly drawn to acts of love, and so easily stirred to fits of anger and bitterness, one towards another! My beloved, are we Christians? Oh, where is the spirit of Christ? Where that great law of His, that badge of His followers, *Love one another*, that by which the Christians of the first times astonished the Pagans about them? Yea, their very enemies and persecutors were amazed at it. It were well, and would be one considerable gain by our enemies, if their combinations and malice against the godly might drive them close together, and unite them more to one another in love.

In honour preferring one another.] Putting all possible respect on one another : this is not in ceremony or compliment, though those civilities that are due, and done without feignedness or affectation, are not disallowed, yea, are, I conceive, included ; but in matter of real esteem, each *preferring one another*. For, though a man may see the weakness of those he converses with, yet, passing, and, as far as he can, covering these, he ought to take notice of what is good. All have something commendable, and no one hath all ; so the meanest may in something be preferable to the highest. And Christian humility and charity will seek out for and espy that, and for it put all respect upon them, that their quality and station are able to bear : and in this, one should prevent another, and strive who shall do most in this kind, as a good and happy contention.

And the source of this is, *love to God*, which so mortifies the heart to all outward advantages, that, further than a man is tied by place and calling, he would not receive, much less desire, any kind of respect from any, but had rather be slighted and disregarded. What cares a soul enamoured with the glory to come, for the vain passing air of preference and honour here? That, it can easily bate ,to any, and, so far as a man has any power of it, would put it upon others, far rather than own it himself. Such a one can sweetly please himself in being the meanest in all companies where he comes, and passing for such, and he is glad of respect done to others ; still looking homeward, where there is no prejudging one another at all, but perfect unenvying and unenvied glory. Glory here, is to be shunned rather than pursued, and if it will follow, yet is less to be regarded than thy shadow. Oh, how light and vanishing is it, and even things more solid than it ! *The fashion of this world passeth away.*

Ver. 11. Not slothful in business, fervent in spirit, serving the Lord.

Not slothful in business.] These condensed rules have much in them; and this one is very needful, for often a listless, indisposed weariness overtakes even good men; seeing so little to be done to any purpose, they are almost ready to give over all; yet, they ought to bestir themselves, and apply to diligence in their place. Be not unduly stickling and busy in things improper, but enclosing thy diligence within thy sphere. Suffer it not to stand, but keep it there in motion. As to thy worldly affairs, be so diligent as to give them good despatch, when thou art about them, but have thy heart as little in them, as much disengaged as may be; yet, so acquitting them wisely, they shall trouble thee the less, when thou art in higher and better employments. As to thyself, be often examining thy heart and ways, striving constantly against sin; though little sensible advantage be gained, yet, if thou yield, it will be worse; if it prevail so much amidst all thy opposition, what would it do if thou should sit still! Use all holy means, how fruitless soever they seem for the present, and *wait on God. We have toiled all night,* said Simon, *and taken nothing,* Luke v. 5: and yet, at His command, essaying again, they took more at once, than if, after their ordinary way, they had been taking all night. So as to others, give not up because thou seest no present success, but, in thy place, *admonish, exhort,* and *rebuke,* with all meekness and patience. Doth God wait on sinners, and wilt not thou wait a little for others?

Fervent in spirit.] Beware of a fretful impatience; that is a sickly distempered heat, as that of a fever, which makes a man unfit for work, and men commonly in this break away from their business; but much healthful, natural heat makes a man strong and able to endure labour, and continue in it. This is the thing here recommended. To be so hot and *fervent in spirit* is a great advantage; it is the very strength of the soul in all employments. Much love to God, and desire of His glory, this is the heat that will not weary, will cheerfully go through all discouragements : *many waters will not quench it.* This fervour of spirit, wrought by the Spirit of God, doth clearly distinguish itself from that inordinate heat of our spirits, which may sometimes either act alone, or mingle itself with the other in the best causes and affairs. This holy fervour is composed and regular in working, runs not headily to unadvised or disorderly ways; it is a sweet delightful heat, not painful and vexing as the other ; it carries on to duty, and is not disturbed about events.

Serving the Lord.] Some copies have it, *serving the time ;* which may bear a fair construction, of taking present occasions of good, and being useful in our generation, and accommodating ourselves in all lawful things to times and persons, for their good, as our Apostle *became all things to all, to win some ;* yet, this kind of expression not being found elsewhere in Scripture, and the most copies having it as we read it, and some mistake of letters in transcribers seeming to have occasioned it, it is much rather to be taken as in our version.

But, out of all question, some do follow that mistaken reading in its worse sense : instead of *serving the Lord,* serving the times. And this some do even in evil ways; others, in ways that are good, yet, following upon trust, and complying, though unwillingly, because the times carry things so ; but when times change to the worse, these men are discovered, for still they serve their master, the times, and their own advantage in them : which way soever that goes, they follow : so that their following the better side in better times, is but accidental.

But this *serving the Lord,* is more even and lasting ; serving Him still in all times, doing all for Him, having no aim but His glory. Such a heart cannot be diverted from its course by any counter-blast of times.

Would you be steadfast in times of approaching trial, seek to have your hearts acquainted with God, and fixed on Him. For others will be shaken ; but such will follow Him through all hazards, and fear no ill while He is with them.

Ver. 12. Rejoicing in hope; patient in tribulation; continuing instant
in prayer.

Rejoicing in hope.] Oh, this we seldom do. When are our
hearts as if transported with the blessed *hope of our inheritance?* This would make us what follows,

Patient in tribulation.] People would hear much of this,
of preparing for suffering. There may be a distemper in
desiring to hear and speak so much of that. What though
trials be coming, as it is likely they are, we should account too
much of ourselves, and this present world, to dwell expressly
on that subject. We see the Apostles do not so, though they
lived and wrote in times of another sort of persecution than we
have yet seen; and they to whom the Apostle here writes
lived where it was most violent and potent, and yet they spend
not all on this: some brief words of it are interspersed with
the discourse, thrown as it were into a parenthesis; but still,
the main is, the doctrine of faith and rules of holiness. And
these are indeed the great furniture for all sufferings: I know
no other. To see much of the excellency and worth of Jesus
Christ, and the riches of our hope in Him; to have these in
our view, much in our hearts and in our mouths; these drown
all the little fears of present things. See how, in passing, our
Apostle speaks; as it were in a slighting way, of all sufferings
for Him: I have cast it up, says he, and *I reckon that the
sufferings of this present time (of this* now) *are not worthy
to be compared to the glory which shall be revealed in us.*

Again, the other thing is, the rules of holiness: these powerfully enable for suffering any thing rather than unholiness.
That sickness of the soul, those corrupt humours of sin make
it crazy, so that it can endure no blasts of air; but when it is
purged and free from these, and in communion with God in
His ways, then it is healthful and strong, and so is able to
endure any thing. The mortifying of our affections to the
world, that is what enables for suffering. Whither reaches the
cruelty of man, but to thy goods or thy body? And what

makes any faint, but an over esteem of these, by which they are filled with desires to preserve, and fears to lose them? Now, when the heart is disengaged from these, and hath taken up in God, is rich and content in Him, it stands not much to the courtesy of any : let them take the rest, *it suffers with joy the spoiling of goods, having in Heaven a more enduring substance.* (Heb. x. 34.) And for the utmost, killing them they look on it as the highest favour : it is to them but the making a hole for them in their prison-wall to get out at. Therefore, I say, there is nothing doth so fit for all encounters, as to be much instructed in that which is the substance of Christianity, hearts purified, and lives holily and spiritually regulated. In a word, much study of Christ, and much study of thyself, for aught I know, are the wisest and strongest preparatives for all possible sufferings.

How sweetly can the soul retire into Him, and repose in Him, in the greatest storms! I know nothing that can much dismay him who can believe and pray *. That, you see, is added,

Continuing instant in prayer.] If afraid of fainting, yea if at the point of fainting, this revives the soul, draws in no less than the strength of God to support it : and what then can surcharge it ?

Thy access to Him, all the enemies in the world cannot hinder. The closest prison shuts not out thy God; yea, rather it shuts out other things and companies, that thou mayest have the more leisure for Him, and the sweeter converse with Him. Oh! acquaint yourselves with this exercise of prayer, and by it with God, that if days of trouble come, you may know whither to go, and what way ; and if you know this way, whatever befalls you, you are not much to be bemoaned.

* Nempe tenens quod amo, nihil, illum amplexus, timebo.

END OF THE EXPOSITORY LECTURES.

LONDON.—Printed by W. CLOWES, Stamford-street.

CPSIA information can be obtained
at www.ICGtesting.com
Printed in the USA
BVHW061732051118
532204BV00010B/2647/P